MW00654292

Ethics and Values in Social Work

ETHICS AND VALUES IN SOCIAL WORK

An Integrated Approach for a Comprehensive Curriculum

ALLAN EDWARD BARSKY

OXFORD
UNIVERSITY PRESS
2010

OXFORD
UNIVERSITY PRESS

Oxford University Press, Inc., publishes works that further
Oxford University's objective of excellence
in research, scholarship, and education.

Oxford New York
Auckland Cape Town Dar es Salaam Hong Kong Karachi
Kuala Lumpur Madrid Melbourne Mexico City Nairobi
New Delhi Shanghai Taipei Toronto

With offices in
Argentina Austria Brazil Chile Czech Republic France Greece
Guatemala Hungary Italy Japan Poland Portugal Singapore
South Korea Switzerland Thailand Turkey Ukraine Vietnam

Published by Oxford University Press, Inc.
198 Madison Avenue, New York, New York 10016
www.oup.com

Library of Congress Cataloging-in-Publication Data

Barsky, Allan Edward.
Ethics and values in social work : an integrated approach for a
comprehensive curriculum / Allan Edward Barsky.
p. cm.
Includes bibliographical references and index.
ISBN 978-0-19-532095-4
1. Social service—Moral and ethical aspects.
2. Social workers—Professional ethics. I. Title.
HV10.5.B345 2010
174'.93613—dc22
2009002629

7 9 8 6
Printed in the United States of America
on acid-free paper

To Jocelyn Adelle:
May you be inspired by good values
and virtues throughout your life.

Preface

A MESSAGE FOR STUDENTS

Each year during student orientations at Florida Atlantic University, the director of our social work program asks professors to introduce the courses they teach and explain why students may be interested in this subject matter. I describe how I teach professional values and ethics, the study of "what is good" and "what is right" in how we practice social work. I suggest that students should be very interested in this subject matter because it can save them the emotional, social, and financial pain of being involved in malpractice lawsuits and professional disciplinary hearings. In truth, learning social work values and ethics can help social workers avoid legal and ethical problems with clients. More important, when social work practice is guided by the high ideals of social work values and ethics, we enhance the quality of services that we provide for our clients and communities. We also derive personal satisfaction from knowing that we are performing our service in a manner that promotes social justice, human growth, and respect for the dignity and worth of all individuals.

This textbook is designed to help you integrate social work values and ethics into all aspects of your social work curriculum and ultimately your practice in the field. Rote memorization of rules and laws is neither sufficient nor interesting. Instead, this textbook invites you to engage personally in a range of learning experiences: reflecting on your own values, analyzing case situations, role-playing social work-client interviews, and pondering over challenging ethical dilemmas. As you work through the exercises in this textbook, remember that learning can be amusing and imaginative. Push yourself to think through situations from other people's perspectives. Do not be afraid to play the devil's advocate, stating positions or asking questions that others might find politically incorrect. Be creative when you think of different ways to resolve ethical issues. Take risks during role-plays. Classroom exercises give you an opportunity to test different ideas, skills, and strategies without posing risks to real clients. The first time I counseled a suicidal client, I had no prior experience with the ethical and clinical issues that arose—not even in a role-play. I knew suicide intervention from a theoretical perspective, but I had little understanding of suicide intervention from an experiential one. Use the case scenarios in this textbook and raise your own questions to help bridge the gap between theory and practice.

If you are looking to this textbook for simple, definitive answers for how to handle difficult ethical issues, you may be disappointed, at least initially. Although social workers have a range of laws, agency policies, and ethical codes to guide them toward ethical practice, in many situations, the correct response to an ethical problem is not clear. In some cases, there may be conflicting ethical or legal obligations. In other cases, there may be no way to accurately predict which course of action will lead to the greater good—or avoid the greater harm. Being able to manage uncertainty, and the stress caused by uncertainty, is crucial. This textbook does not necessarily provide you with specific answers to your ethical problems, but it does provide you with a range of tools and strategies that can guide you toward solution.

Different programs may use this textbook in different manners, assigning different chapters or modules to different courses. By having a single ethics textbook, you will be able to refer back to earlier materials to review the basics, or refer forward to other materials to explore ethical issues at higher or more in-depth levels. Use the index to see how different ethical issues are applied in different contexts of practice (e.g., how confidentiality may be applied to work with individuals versus families, groups, or communities). Use the glossary to help you understand key concepts. Finally, use the websites and bibliography at the end of this textbook to locate further readings to assist with class assignments and issues that may arise in practice. There is a myriad of resources online and in scholarly journals, with practical information and thought-provoking debates of ethical issues. Your journey of professional development will continue long after you have completed your degree, so it is important to know where to find ethics and values resources to support you on this journey.

The image on the cover of this textbook, by Canadian artist Doris Cyrette, is entitled "Playmates." The notion of playmates suggests a group of people who have fun, fooling around, and building relationships as they engage in various games and activities. Although there are many serious aspects to social work values and ethics, we should not take ourselves too seriously. In order to manage ethical issues, we need to be able to play nicely. Even if we do not share the same values and beliefs, we share this world, and we need to learn how to proceed in a fair, just, and cooperative manner. Note how some playmates on the cover are bigger than others—yet none dominate the others. In fact, the more powerful birds may be looking out for the interests of the more vulnerable birds. Note also how the playmates are headed in different directions—yet out of apparent chaos, they are sharing space without colliding or blocking each other's course. They have found general rules of engagement and principles to guide their relationships. Enjoy the role-plays, readings, and exercises throughout this textbook, and have fun learning about values and ethics throughout your professional careers.

A NOTE FOR INSTRUCTORS

As we all learned in our introduction to social work courses, social work developed as a unique profession in the late nineteenth and early twentieth centuries. Social work pioneers such as Mary Richmond, Jane Addams, Helen Harris Perlman, Florence Kelly, Charles Levy, and Whitney Young each emphasized the importance of ethics and values in guiding all forms of practice. From its historical mandate of ameliorating social problems among the most vulnerable populations in society to its ongoing dedication toward facilitating social well-being and social justice, the profession of social work has been defined by its commitment to particular ethical ideals (NASW, 1999). Not surprisingly, ethics and values comprise a core component of social work education (Council on Social Work Education, 2008). Although modern schools of social work have access to a number of solid textbooks on social work values and ethics (Congress, 1999; Corey, Corey, & Callanan, 2007; Dolgoff, Loewenberg, & Harrington, 2009; Linzer, 1999; Reamer, 2006b), this textbook is the first that provides a comprehensive plan for teaching and learning ethics and values across the social work curriculum.

Given that values and ethics are already interspersed throughout social work courses and existing textbooks, one might ask why a comprehensive textbook on ethics and values is needed. Having taught at four different schools of social work, I have found that most programs provide students with a solid, general understanding of values and ethics from their theory and practice courses. Unfortunately, there are many gaps in traditional social work curricula. Course content on values and ethics is often repetitive. Students might be offered content on confidentiality in three different courses, for instance, but each time the content covers the same basics, never moving to the next levels of understanding, application, and analysis. Often, students do not have a chance to learn ethical analysis at an advanced level unless they take a stand-alone course on advanced ethics (Kaplan, 2006b). This textbook is designed to remedy these problems by providing a comprehensive set of educational materials that will take students from basic to advanced levels, using an explicit theory for teaching and learning ethics and values. Schools of social work that adopt this textbook will be able to fully integrate ethics and values into their existing courses in a comprehensive manner.

Part I of this textbook focuses on content for students in BSW and MSW foundation courses, consistent with the Educational Policies and Accreditation Standards of the Council on Social Work Education. To tailor course expectations to the different needs of BSW and MSW programs, professors should consult the Instructor's Manual, which offers specific suggestions for courses at both levels. Part II of this textbook focuses on content for students taking advanced or concentration courses in their MSW programs.

Social work educators often instruct their students to "start with the client." Likewise, I would suggest that social work educators "start with the student," ensuring that their educational activities fit with the students' current stage of knowledge and receptiveness to learning (Swindell & Watson, 2007). This textbook adopts a "developmental approach," meaning that students will experience certain types of learning in earlier courses and other types of learning in later courses, helping them work toward higher levels of understanding, application, analysis, and integration of ethics and values content. These stages of learning are informed by theories of moral, cognitive, affective, and behavioral development. Theories of moral development, for instance, suggest that infants are not born with a concept of right and wrong (Gibbs, 2003; Kohlberg, Levine, & Hewer, 1983). Eventually, they first learn about right and wrong by following particular authorities (parents, teachers, religious and cultural teachings, etc.). By analogy, when novice social workers begin their social work education, they are not familiar with the specific ethical standards governing social workers and the social work profession. They need to understand the authorities on social work ethics, including what types of consequences will ensue if they do not follow certain ethical guidelines. Initially, novice social workers may follow a social work code of ethics or agency policy simply because that is the ethical standard, agency rule, or law to be followed. As novices develop into more autonomous professionals, they will need to make more nuanced decisions about ethical behavior, based not only on following particular rules or standards but on their ability to analyze complex problems (Kaplan, 2006a). Developing social workers need to learn the rationale behind ethical standards and policies so they can make reasoned choices. Accordingly, this textbook initially provides novice social workers with relatively "black and white" ethical principles and standards that they should ordinarily follow. Once they have a basic understanding of these, this textbook will introduce them to more challenging issues that cannot be resolved by simply following one particular rule or standard. Thus, they will learn to assume full responsibility for decisions they make.

Theories of cognitive development suggest that knowledge acquisition occurs through different processes, each depending on the individual's stage of cognitive development (Piaget, 1999/orig.1932). Although theories of cognitive development often focus on stages extending from early childhood to adolescence, developmental theories have been used to enhance adult education curricula. Bloom's Taxonomy of Educational Objectives (Forehand, 2005), for instance, suggests that there are six levels of cognitive learning: remembering, understanding, applying, analyzing, evaluating, and creating. The first level, remembering, suggests that students must first learn how to retrieve, recognize, and recall information about ethics and values from their long-term memories. The second level, understanding, implies that students must be able to construct meaning from this information. Whereas reciting a definition of informed consent would constitute remembering, explaining informed consent in one's own words would demonstrate understanding. The third level, applying, requires the ability to link theory and practice. Thus, a student should be able to describe how to implement an informed consent process with a particular client. The fourth level, analyzing, indicates the ability to break material into constituent parts and assess how these parts relate to each other or to the overall purpose. In terms of informed consent, for instance, a student would need to be able to differentiate components of informed consent (i.e., providing information in user-friendly language, assessing the client's mental capacity and understanding, and ensuring that the client's consent is voluntary). The fifth level, evaluating, requires the ability to critique the theory or knowledge. Evaluating informed consent, for example, might include a critique of this ethical standard from a diversity perspective (e.g., although informed consent refers to obtaining permission from the individual, obtaining permission from a client's family or community might be more appropriate for clients who come from a collectivist culture). The sixth level, creating, refers to using the knowledge in a new or creative manner. A student might build on the diversity critique, for instance, by developing a new ethical standard for informed consent that takes diversity concerns into account. The readings and assignments in this textbook are designed to take students through each of these educational objectives. The materials in Part I focus primarily on recalling, understanding, and applying. Part II includes these three objectives but provides students more opportunities to analyze, evaluate, and create. Some ethics textbooks begin by presenting broad philosophical discussions, for instance, comparing deontological and teleological approaches to ethical analysis. Other textbooks begin by presenting students with a framework for determining tough ethical issues. Before students are able to understand and appreciate the importance of these higher level forms of moral reasoning and ethical analysis, students first need a solid grounding in the "black letter" standards and ethical guidelines. When instructors try to engage students in complex ethical decision making too early, they may hear student remarks such as, "But what is the answer?" even when there is no clear-cut answer. Accordingly, the initial chapters of this textbook have more focus on helping students make use of authorities (e.g., the NASW Code of Ethics, other codes of ethics, agency policies, and relevant laws) as well as how to find these authorities and what happens if a social worker breaches these authorities. Once students have a firmer grasp of these authorities and how to apply them, they will be better prepared for higher level ethical understanding and analysis presented in the later chapters.

Ethical decision making requires more than just formal, logical reasoning; it also requires attention to emotions such as anger, fear, delight, and caring, which exist in all social relationships (Gilligan, 1982). Theories of affective development suggest that a person's emotional capacities (called "emotional intelligence") can be cultivated through specific types of learning experiences: self-awareness, self-management, social awareness, and relationship management (Golman, 2004). Self-awareness requires raising one's consciousness of intuitions and emotional reactions to various situations. Consider a social worker who feels insulted by a client. If the social worker is not aware of feeling hurt, he might lash out at the client. If social workers are to follow the ethical standard about treating clients with respect, they must first have an awareness of their own affective responses. Self-management suggests that people can learn to manage their emotional reactions and motives in a deliberate manner. Thus, the social worker who feels insulted may turn to supervision or professional consultation for support but must continue to treat the client in a respectful manner. Social awareness refers to the ability to interpret what others are saying and feeling, and why they feel and act as they do. So the social worker who feels insulted must strive to understand why the client said what she said. Perhaps the client was anxious or was experiencing other forms of stress. By understanding the underlying motivations and issues of others, social workers can ensure that their own responses are consistent with ethical, competent practice. Relationship management refers to engaging others in a manner that promotes positive rapport or other desired results. Accordingly, the social worker engages the client by demonstrating empathy and unconditional positive regard, rather than acting defensively, with accusations or insults of his own. To foster emotional intelligence, this book provides a series of reflective and experiential exercises. Given that self-awareness, self-management, social awareness, and relationship management are ongoing processes, these exercises also provide students with skills and strategies they can use throughout their careers.

Theories of behavioral development suggest that behaviors can be learned, unlearned, and relearned through a variety of processes: associational learning, operant conditioning, modeling, self-awareness, provision of knowledge, and development of critical thinking skills. Hence, this textbook provides an array of learning experiences that will foster commitment to social work values and ethics, awareness of emotional responses that may inhibit behaving in an ethical manner, and skills for putting ethical decisions into practice.

The Transtheoretical Model is a model of behavioral development that focuses on one's readiness or motivation to change (Prochaska & Norcross, 2007). This model suggests that behavior change occurs through a sequence of steps—precontemplation, contemplation, decision, preparation, action, and maintenance. Initially, in the precontemplation stage, people are not aware that there is a problem in their behavior, so they are not motivated to change. Upon becoming aware of a problem, the person may experience ambivalence toward change and thus move into the contemplation stage. The person is unlikely to change behaviors until successful resolution of the contemplation stage, understanding that there are more benefits than costs to changing behaviors. Although the Transtheoretical Model was initially developed for people with alcoholism and other addictions, it is relevant to social work students in relation to development of ethical choices and behaviors (Brannen, Boling, & White, 2006). Initially, students may be unaware of potential problems in their usual ethical thinking and behaviors as these apply to social work practice situations. After all, students come into social work wanting to help people, so how could anyone find fault with their ethics and values? As students become more aware of situations where their personal values may conflict with the values of social work, their agencies, or their clients, they can then start to challenge their thinking and alter the ways that they interact with the people they serve. Consider, for instance, a student who values hugs, believing that outward demonstrations of physical affection have a positive impact on human growth and development. When the student first hears that hugging a client may be considered unprofessional, the student may initially resist this notion. Just being told not to hug a client is not sufficient to change the student's behavior. Rather, the process of change must allow the student to process the issues and eventually come to his own understanding of what is professional behavior in relation to hugging. Accordingly, this textbook offers a range of exercises, assisting students at various stages of change with experiential, affective, cognitive, and behavioral exercises.

Theories of acculturation suggest that when people move from one culture into another, a number of factors affect how effectively they adapt. The concept of maintenance refers to the degree to which people hold onto their original language, traditions, values, norms, and morals. Contact and participation refer to the degree to which people adopt the language, traditions, values, norms, and morals of the new culture. Effective acculturation requires a balance between maintaining original culture and adapting to the ways of the new culture. Although many people think of acculturation in terms of people who move from one part of the world to another and must learn how to adjust to a new culture, the concept of acculturation also applies to nonprofessionals who move into a new profession, such as social work. Ethical acculturation refers specifically to the manner in which people adapt to the values and ethics of the new profession (Bashe, Anderson, Handelsman, & Klevansky, 2007). Ideally, new social workers learn to integrate their original values and morals with the values and ethics of the social work profession. Integration does not require a complete shedding of personal values and morals but rather an ability to rely on social work values and ethics when acting in a professional manner and an awareness of any potential conflicts between professional and personal values. Three problematic responses to acculturation are separation, assimilation, and marginalization. Separation arises when workers maintain their original values and morals but reject social work values and ethics. By holding onto their original values and morals so strongly, they may feel alienated from the profession. Assimilation arises when social workers identify with social work values and ethics so strongly that they give up too much of their personal identity. The problem with assimilation in social workers is that it may dehumanize them, as workers may act without the individuality that makes each worker unique. Marginalization arises when workers give up their own values and morals but do not yet know or appreciate the values and ethics of social work. Often, marginalization occurs at an early stage of professional development, as students are making the transition from nonprofessional to professional (Bashe et al., 2007). The task for social work educators is to help students make a successful transition from maintenance of their original values and morals to a balanced integration with professional social work values and ethics.

Most social work ethics textbooks provide students with a strategic decision-making framework that guides them through the analysis of ethical issues so they can determine the "best" courses of action. These textbooks help students develop critical thinking skills for working through ethical dilemmas. They do not, however, provide students with guidance on the process of resolving ethical conflicts between social worker and client, client and client, social worker and supervisor, or between other parties that the worker may be helping. This textbook provides students with specific models of conflict resolution to help them work through ethical conflicts with clients, coworkers, and others. The interest-based model, for instance, shows students how to identify common ground and work toward win-win solutions, even when people initially seem to be at complete odds (Cohen, 2006; Fisher, Ury, & Patton, 1997). The transformative model shows students how to use respectful communication and develop positive ways of interacting with people, even when there is little or no room for consensus (Bush & Folger, 2005). Conflict resolution skills are particularly useful for social workers in the roles of supervisors, mediators, advocates, and facilitators (Barsky, 2007a).

Transforming knowledge into behavior is an important aspect of social work education. Learning about social work values and ethics does little good unless the social worker can translate these values and ethics into meaningful behaviors. The fact that social workers know how to determine an ethically correct response to an ethical problem does not ensure that they will behave in an ethically correct manner. Social workers may know, for example, that it is unethical to impose their cultural values on clients. Without sufficient clarification of their own values, however, they may impose values unintentionally. Similarly, social workers may know the right way to respond to an ethical problem but feel afraid to act ethically given the risks of losing their jobs or facing retribution from others who disagree. In order to act ethically, therefore, students must gain confidence to do what is right even when the challenge seems daunting. They must also learn how to manage risks deliberately and effectively. By engaging students at affective, cognitive, moral, and behavioral levels, this textbook is designed to help students not only understand values and ethics but also raise their capacity for integrating values and ethics in all aspects of their professional practice.

The study of values and ethics often involves analysis of complex laws, policies, values, and ethical standards. As I have written this book, I have tried to be careful with the information I provided and my choice of words to explain various concepts and situations. As you work through this text, you may question certain information or statements. I welcome your questions and feedback. I may be able to clarify information or provide support for what I have written. If I have provided misinformation, I will provide corrections online and in future editions. Feel free to email me at barsky@barsky.org.

ABOUT THE AUTHOR

Dr. Barsky has a background in social work, law, and mediation. He has taught at a university level since 1989 in four different schools of social work (University of Toronto, Ryerson University, University of Calgary, and Florida Atlantic University, where he is a full professor) as well as being a visiting professor at Bar Ilan University in Israel. He currently serves on the National Ethics Committee of the National Association of Social Workers. Dr. Barsky's prior books include *Conflict Resolution for the Helping Professions* (Brooks/Cole, 2007) *Counsellors as Witnesses* (Canada Law Book, 1997), *Interdisciplinary Practice with Diverse Populations* (Greenwood, 2000—co-edited), *Clinicians in Court* (Guilford, 2002); *Successful Social Work Education* (Brooks/Cole, 2006); and *Alcohol, Other Drugs, and Addictions* (Brooks/Cole, 2006). Dr. Barsky has taught professional ethics at the University of Calgary and Florida Atlantic University as well as social work and law courses at Ryerson. He is very familiar with accreditation standards in both Canada and the United States, having served on the accreditation committee of the Canadian Association of Schools of Social Work and having written the curriculum self-study for Florida Atlantic University School of Social Work (complying with the Council on Social Work Education's standards for re-accreditation of the School). Dr. Barsky's combined social work and law background provides him with important knowledge and insights into the development of professional knowledge and awareness of social work values and ethics in practice.

Acknowledgments

To paraphrase a popular cliché, no author is an island. From the moment I started developing ideas for this book through the processes of writing, reviewing, rewriting, reviewing, rewriting...through to publication, I have been surrounded with eight incredible waves of support. First, I thank all the bright and energetic students from my ethics classes for being my teachers, as they have helped me learn as much as I have taught. Second, I thank Dr. Michele Hawkins and the Florida Atlantic University School of Social Work for providing me with excellent teaching opportunities where I could develop and hone many of the educational materials that I have incorporated in this book. Third, I thank Maura Roessner, Mallory Jensen, Patterson Lamb, Lynda Crawford, and the other staff at Oxford University Press for their wonderful encouragement, ideas, feedback, editing, and support throughout the publication process. Fourth, I thank Deanne Bonnar (Boston University), Laura Kaplan (University of Northern Iowa), Pam Graham (Florida State University), José Torres (University of Wisconsin-Madison), and Katherine Van Wormer (University of Northern Iowa) who provided constructive criticism and insightful suggestions for improvement on earlier drafts. Fifth, I thank a former student, Holly Stewart, for helping me with the wording that social workers may use to explain confidentiality and informed consent to clients in a clear and comprehensive manner. Six, I thank various members of the Association of Social Work Boards and the National Ethics Committee of the National Association of Social Workers for their input concerning which ethical issues seem to be most challenging for social workers. Seventh, I thank my parents, Edith and Sam Barsky, for the values, virtues, and ethics that they instilled so lovingly throughout my upbringing. And finally, I thank my husband Greg and daughter Adelle for all their moral support and sacrifices, allowing me to spend far too much time in my office when I should have been out playing with them.

The cover image, *Playmates*, is courtesy of Canadian Ojibway artist Doris Cyrette. In it, the artist ponders the relationship of two- and three-year-olds who play separately together, enjoying the closeness of each other.

Contents

PART I

FOUNDATIONS OF VALUES AND ETHICS

Case 1: *Sandra is a social worker providing counseling to a client named Colby. Colby discloses that he has been having sex with professional sex trade workers (prostitutes). Although he claims he is using condoms, Sandra is concerned about the safety of Colby's wife. How should Sandra balance her ethical obligation to keep Colby's information confidential with possible ethical, moral, or legal obligations to protect Colby's wife from emotional or physical harm?*

Case 2: *Sofia is a Christian social worker providing community organization services for a neighborhood with a large Muslim population. When community leaders ask her to help them develop programs that instill Muslim morals and beliefs, Sofia feels a conflict with her own religious beliefs and her professional value for diversity. How should Sofia show respect for the community's beliefs and right to self-determination in light of the potential conflicts with own personal and professional belief systems?*

Case 3: *Stacey is a social worker who works for child protective services. During a child neglect investigation, she discovers that the parents leave Chauncey (their 8-year-old child) unattended after school because both need to work in order to pay the bills. They have recently immigrated to the United States, so they have no family or friends to help with child care. They have taken a number of precautions to ensure that the child is safe, but the law says that an 8-year-old cannot be left unattended. Stacey believes Chauncey is better off with the parents' plans rather than being placed in foster care. How should Stacey reconcile her legal, clinical, and ethical obligations toward the child and family?*

Case 4: *Sutcliffe is a social worker who provides counseling to people with learning disabilities. One of his clients, Calvin, starts to exhibit hallucinations and delusions that are more characteristic of schizophrenia than learning disability. Sutcliffe continues to provide counseling, even though he has never received* *training to help people with schizophrenia. Calvin hears voices that tell him to burn down a house. The owner of the burned house sues Sutcliffe for malpractice. What is the extent of Sutcliffe's legal or moral liability to the owner?*

Case 5: *Shelley is a social worker who provides support services to elder clients in a nursing home. Several clients inform Shelley that they have been mistreated by the nursing home staff. Upon hearing about this mistreatment, Shelley feels angry toward the nursing home staff. With the consent of the clients, Shelley refers them to an ombudsman responsible for investigating allegations of elder abuse. Although Shelley has helped her elder clients respond effectively to an abusive situation, what ethical and practical concerns arise in this case?*

These cases[1] portray five very different situations, yet all have one thing in common. They all involve a social worker who needs to make choices based on her[2] assessment of the values and ethics that apply to the particular situation. As you may hear throughout your professional social work education, values and ethics pervade all areas of practice. In many situations faced by social workers, the choices are easy and clear. In other situations, the choices are difficult and not so clear. This text is designed to help you integrate social work values and ethics in all aspects of your practice, whether you are faced with issues that are clear or unclear—easy or difficult.

Learning social work ethics does not mean simply memorizing specific rules and standards of practice for every situation that may arise. Ethical practice requires professional self-awareness, critical thinking, and the ability to manage complex information, values, and principles from a variety of sources. This textbook is designed to provide you with a practical understanding of the principles and standards that guide social work practice, as well as frameworks for raising awareness of your own values and biases, for thinking through difficult ethical issues, and for working with others to decide how to respond to such issues.

LEARNING OBJECTIVES

Upon successful completion of this introduction, you will be able to

- Recall the meanings of the key terms: ethics, values, laws, agency policies, morals, professional ethics, personal ethics, ethical problems, ethical breaches, ethical dilemmas, beliefs, feelings, convictions, rules, and principles.
- Define each key term in your own words.
- Identify the similarities and differences between the key terms.
- Provide an example of each key term.
- Make appropriate citations to sources of laws and ethics.

To begin your exploration of values and ethics, this introduction provides a definitional framework for the key terms used throughout this textbook. To help provide you with a practical understanding of each term, I will relate each term to the case scenarios at the top of this chapter.

As you work through later chapters in this text, refer back to the definitions in this section whenever you have questions regarding how certain terms are being used.

ETHICS VERSUS VALUES

In common parlance, some people use the terms *ethics* and *values* interchangeably. In professional discourse, these are two distinct but related

---

[1] The term *case* refers to a situation involving a social worker and people with whom the social worker is interacting (clients, coworkers, others in the community). I will use cases throughout the book to explore how values and ethics apply to various scenarios that a social worker may experience.

[2] In order to manage the issue of how to use male and female pronouns, I have rotated the use of "he/his" and "she/her" throughout the text. Case examples will include men and women in various roles, including social worker, client, supervisor, and other professionals.

terms. *Values refer to the ideals to which an individual, family, group, organization, or community*[3] *aspires.* Values identify what people believe are good or valuable. Values reflect a priority of preferences. All people have values, though different people may have a different selection or ordering of values. In Case 2, Sofia indicates she values diversity. This means that diversity is important to her. Values do not declare specific ways of behaving. Although Sofia values diversity, this information alone does not tell us what rules she lives by or how she will act in a particular situation. Diversity is not her only value. She may also value privacy, life, safety, authority, or an infinite number of other possible ideals or priorities. Assume Sofia's highest value is diversity, followed by peace, honesty, and humility, in that order. This set of interconnected values may be called Sofia's value system.

Ethics refer to the rules that define what types of behavior are appropriate and what types of behavior are inappropriate.[4] Different individuals, families, groups, organizations, or communities may declare or abide by different ethics. In Case 1, Sandra's ethics include a rule requiring her to maintain the confidentiality of information received from clients. If Colby discloses his affair to a friend rather than a social worker, the friend may not have an ethical rule regarding confidentiality. Ideally, ethical rules provide clear direction on how people should behave. In some situations, however, individuals may need to contend with two or more conflicting rules. Although Sandra has a rule stating she should maintain client confidentiality, she may also have a rule stating she should protect people from harm. In other situations, the person's ethical rules do not anticipate a particular set of circumstances. Consider an unemployed, single woman who asks a fertility doctor to implant six embryos, even though she already has six children. The doctor believes that patients should have the right to choose how many children they would like to have, but feels uncomfortable about the choice this particular patient is making. If the fertility clinic has never had to consider such a request before, its ethics policies may not provide the doctor with sufficient guidance on how to manage this issue.

Whereas values identify a person's sense of "what is good," ethics identify a person's sense of "what is right" (Dolgoff, Loewenberg, & Harrington, 2009). Thus, Sofia's value for diversity suggests that diversity is something good, an ideal worthy of pursuing. If Sofia wants, she can take this value and translate it into an ethical rule that describes what type of behavior is right and what type of behavior is wrong; for instance, as a social worker, she should not impose her values or beliefs on clients. If she persuades Muslim clients to accept Christian beliefs, for instance, her behavior would be inappropriate or unethical according to her own rule against imposing values. Remember, values are priorities or ideals, whereas ethics are rules of behavior that should be based on these priorities or ideals. In essence, ethics are "the application of values to human relationships and transactions" (Levy, 1993, p. 1).

ETHICS VERSUS LAWS, AGENCY POLICIES, OR MORALS

The existence of ethics tells us that there are rules establishing which types of behavior are appropriate or inappropriate. Whether these rules are

---

[3] For ease of reference, I will sometimes refer to "individuals, families, groups, organizations, or communities" collectively as "people." Given that social workers practice with all types of client systems, specific cases used throughout this textbook will demonstrate how values and ethics apply with each of them.

[4] Ethics may also be defined as the study of right and wrong behaviors, and how people should make such decisions (Ethics Resource Center, n.d.). The three branches of ethics are meta-ethics, normative ethics, and applied ethics. Meta-ethics refers to the study of the nature of morality and the sources of ethics. Normative ethics refers to the study of how people should live and behave. Applied ethics is a specific type of normative ethics. Applied ethics refers to the study of moral judgments in the context of specific life situations, for instance, particular practice issues faced by social workers or other professionals. In order to apply and analyze ethics at an advanced level, social workers should study all three branches of ethics.

enforceable, however, depends on whether and how specific ethical rules are formalized. In some situations, ethical rules may be implicit, with no formal mechanism for enforcement. In Case 1, Colby's personal ethics may tell him that it is OK to have extramarital sex, as long as he uses condoms. If he does not use condoms, he may feel guilt-ridden or blameworthy, but there is no law stating that he must use condoms.

Laws are rules enacted by the state and enforced by the state (e.g., by local, state, or national governments, courts, police, and public justice systems). Many laws are based on ethics (Knapp et al., 2007). For instance, criminal laws that prohibit murder, theft, rape, and other acts of violence are based on the ethical principle of preventing harm to others. Divorce laws that establish parental rights and responsibilities toward their children are based on the ethic of ensuring that children's needs and interests are satisfied. Mental health laws that allow the state to commit suicidal patients to psychiatric facilities are based on the ethic of preserving life. Thus, Calvin in Case 4 could have been committed due to his auditory hallucinations and risk of harming others. Likewise, in Case 3, Stacey is required to follow a law requiring children to have appropriate supervision. The law deems parents to be "neglectful" if they leave young children unattended for extended periods of time.

The consequences for violating laws vary depending on the specific law that has been broken. Such consequences range from imprisonment to fines, community service, probation, losing civil rights, terminating parental rights, or public censure. These consequences are intended to deter people from certain types of behavior, ideally promoting ethical behavior. Not all laws are ethical (Knapp et al., 2007). For instance, a law that discriminates against African Americans, Latinos, Jews, gays, or any other identifiable group may be viewed as unethical. In some situations, a particular law may be viewed as ethical by one segment of the population but unethical by another. Unethical laws, such as those authorizing slavery, may be challenged and changed over time. In fact, challenging unethical laws is a key aspect of a social worker's obligations to promote social justice (Furman, Langer, Sanchez, & Negi, 2007).

Agency policies are rules created by an agency and enforced by an agency. In some situations, agency policies can also be enforced through court proceedings.[5] Although many agency policies are not specifically intended to formalize ethical rules, other agency policies are specifically intended to do so. For instance, an agency policy may require employees to maintain the confidentiality or privacy of clients served by the agency. In Case 5, the nursing home may have policies on the appropriate treatment of its residents. Agency policies may also establish procedures for an ombudsman to investigate any complaints by the residents. Finally, agency policies may establish consequences for violating agency policies. Typical consequences for serious breaches of policy include suspension or termination of employment. For lesser breaches, agencies may simply require greater supervision or further training to ensure that the employee does not commit further violations. As with laws, agency policy may or may not reflect the ethics of particular individuals or groups. In Case 1, assume that agency policy tells Sandra to maintain client confidentiality, even though her client's extramarital sex could put his wife at risk. Although the agency may think maintaining confidentiality is ethical, Sandra's ethics may tell her otherwise.

Morals[6] *are first-order convictions about what types of behavior are right or wrong.* Similar to ethics, laws, and agency policies, morals are rules of conduct, or guidelines that distinguish between appropriate and inappropriate behavior. Unlike laws and agency policies, morals are

[5] Agency policies may establish the terms of the contractual relationship between the agency and its employees. If this contract is breached, the party hurt by the breach can go to court to sue for damages.

[6] Some people confuse the terms *morals* and *mores*. Mores are social customs or norms of behavior that are enforced by others in the same cultural group (e.g., through social approval or disapproval). Thus, morals are convictions whereas mores are behaviors.

not legislated by an external body and they are not limited to a specific professional role (such as social work). People adopt morals from their social context, including their family, religious or spiritual community, cultural community, neighbors, and close friends.[7] Universal morality refers to moral systems that are common to all people, religions, cultures, and social institutions (e.g., the notion that murder is wrong). Particular morality refers to moral systems that are specific to certain cultures or social groups (e.g., the belief among Christians that salvation is achieved by accepting Jesus Christ) (Beauchamp & Childress, 2009). Morals are considered "first-order convictions" because they are central to the person, guiding his or her understandings about good and evil without requiring the person to make conscious attempts to reflect upon why certain behaviors are right or wrong. In contrast, ethics are considered "second-order convictions" because they require the person to reflect on his or her values and morals in order to determine what types of behavior are considered right or wrong (Hinman, n.d.). We speak of "social work ethics" rather than "social work morals" because social workers must use second-order convictions, taking their professional role and context into account. Thus, in Case 3, we could consider how morals and ethics may have guided Chauncey's parents' belief that it was appropriate to leave Chauncey unattended while they were working. Perhaps the parents were operating on the moral principle that says people should be self-reliant. If so, they may not have thought about asking others for help with Chauncey. Self-reliance is something they learned from their upbringing, rather than something they follow because it is a law or official policy. Self-reliance is a way of life for them, not a choice that they deliberated over before coming to the conclusion that it was better to leave Chauncey unattended rather than ask for help.[8]

PROFESSIONAL ETHICS VERSUS PERSONAL ETHICS

Professional ethics are rules that guide social workers or other professionals in the choices that they make in their professional capacities. Personal ethics are rules that guide people in their private lives, in their roles as parents, family members, friends, neighbors, citizens, and so forth.[9] As a social worker, you will find that many of your personal ethics fit with your professional ethics. For instance, if you believe in your personal life that it is important to confront racism and oppression, your ethical obligation as a professional social worker to promote social justice will simply be an extension of your personal ethics. In many situations, however, you will find that your personal and professional obligations are different.[10] As a private person, for instance, you may provide friends with whatever advice you want, regardless of whether you have professional training to provide advice (e.g., "You should get married before you have a child"). As a social worker, however, you are not permitted to provide advice to clients unless that type of advice is within your specific training and area of competence. In Sofia's case, described earlier, the worker may be facing a conflict between her personal morals and professional ethics. In her personal life, she is an evangelical Christian and

---

[7] Some people equate morals with beliefs about right and wrong from a religious context. Although people may derive morals from their religions, one does not have to be religious to have morals. Further, religious people derive some of their morals from nonreligious sources.

[8] Some theorists use morals and ethics interchangeably, referring to both first- and second-order convictions. This also permits simplification of the discussion, avoiding the need to use both terms over and over again.

[9] Some theorists equate personal ethics with morals. Throughout this textbook, references to ethics will focus on professional ethics. Rather than referring to personal ethics, I will refer to morals.

[10] Case 1 at the top of this chapter provides another example of potential conflict between professional ethics and personal morals. Sandra has a professional duty to protect the confidentiality of her client, Charles, but her personal ethics may be telling her that his sexual activities with prostitutes are immoral and potentially harmful to Colby's wife.

she believes the teachings of Christ are good. In her private life, Sofia reaches out to friends and acquaintances to teach them the gospel of Christ, as per Matthew 28:19, "Go forth and make disciples of all nations." In her social work role, however, she is bound by a social work ethic, which prohibits evangelizing clients. According to the NASW Code of Ethics (1999, Ss.1.06[b] & [c]), for instance, social workers should avoid exploiting vulnerable clients for their own religious purposes and they should maintain appropriate boundaries with clients. Thus, what may be ethically appropriate in Sofia's private life is not ethically appropriate in her professional role (Sherwood, 2008b).

Professional ethics tend to be more formalized than personal ethics. Most individuals do not write out a list of ethical rules that they intend to follow. In contrast, professional ethics tend to be codified in agency policies, laws, or professional codes of conduct and standards of practice. Further, social work textbooks, including the present one, provide social work professionals with guidelines for making informed ethical decisions. Although the public education system provides students with some education on how to make ethical decisions in their personal lives, professional education helps developing social workers understand that they will be held to much higher standards when they are acting in a professional capacity.

ETHICAL PROBLEMS VERSUS ETHICAL DILEMMAS AND ETHICAL BREACHES

Ethical problems refer to any situations involving an ethical issue—a question of right or wrong behavior—to be decided. Each of the five cases at the top of this chapter reflects an ethical problem. *An ethical dilemma is a specific type of ethical problem in which the choice of how to respond to the issue is particularly difficult.* When someone is faced with an ethical dilemma, there is no clear, singular response that satisfies all the considerations that need to be taken into account. Case 1 involves an ethical dilemma because Sandra must choose between competing ethical obligations: Should she honor Colby's right to privacy and confidentiality concerning his extramarital sex activities, or should she promote health and safety by ensuring that Colby's wife knows that he may have a sexually transmitted disease? Case 2 involves an ethical dilemma because Sofia feels that she must choose between her personal Christian values and beliefs and her clients' Muslim values and beliefs. Ethical dilemmas are often marked by conflicts among ethics, values, morals, laws, rules, or agency policies. In some situations, ethical dilemmas are created because ethics, values, morals, laws, rules, and agency policies do not provide clear guidelines. With advances in biotechnology, for instance, professionals have had to figure out how to respond to ethical issues raised by the prospects of cloning, embryonic stem-cell research, and genetic engineering. In some situations, codes of ethics, agency policies, and laws are completely absent. In other situations, codes of ethics, agency policies, and laws are just developing, as professions, agencies, and lawmakers struggle with building consensus on what is right and wrong when responding to these issues. An ethical dilemma is defined from an objective perspective: Could reasonable people differ on what is the appropriate behavioral response to a particular situation? Consider the issue of same-sex marriage. One social worker might say that she believes the correct response is clear and unambiguous—same-sex marriage should be recognized as equal to marriage between a man and a woman. Although subjectively this worker does not view same-sex marriage as a dilemma, this issue is a dilemma if other people can reasonably disagree with her conclusion.

Whereas an ethical dilemma has no clear-cut or universally acceptable answer about right and wrong conduct, an ethical breach is a clear violation of a specific ethical rule. In Case 4, Sutcliffe provides services to a client with schizophrenia, even though Sutcliffe has no experience or training for work with this population. Sutcliffe has violated the social work ethic of practicing only within one's area of competence. In other words, choosing to practice outside his competence was an ethical breach, not an ethical dilemma. Reasonable social workers would generally agree that social workers should practice within their areas of competence. There is no conflicting ethical rule, value, law, or agency policy that would raise the prospect of a dilemma in this situation.

Although this text highlights situations requiring social workers to make challenging decisions on how to act ethically, remember that social workers also make many decisions that do not involve difficult ethical issues. When a client enters your office, for instance, do you initially say "Hello," "Pleased to meet you," or "Thank you for coming"? The choice among these three greetings does not involve a significant ethical question. The term *zone of moral indifference* describes choices that a professional can make without having to worry about moral or ethical issues; all of the choices would be considered appropriate. A greeting such as "Oh no, not you again," however, would go outside the zone of moral indifference because it violates the ethic of showing respect to all people.

VALUES VERSUS BELIEFS, CONVICTIONS, FEELINGS, OR ATTITUDES

A belief is an understanding of a particular phenomenon. Beliefs may be based on fact or fiction, accurate perception or misperception, and sound reasoning or faulty reasoning. Beliefs may also be based on faith, such as faith in a higher power, a trusted friend, or parents. In Case 3, Stacey believes Chauncey is better off with the parents' plans rather than being placed in foster care. Her belief is based upon her assessment of the situation, as she completed a home visit in which she spoke to family members and observed Chauncey directly. Her belief may be affected by her values. If she values the autonomy of the family, for instance, she may be more likely to favor solutions that respect the family's right to decide what is right for the child.

Convictions are beliefs that are strongly held. People may hold tightly onto convictions for various reasons. In some situations, convictions are based on religious faith. In other situations, convictions are based on information that has been indoctrinated into people by parents, teachers, media, or other important influences in their lives. In Case 2, Sofia's convictions may include a firm belief that Jesus Christ is the son of God and the Messiah. You could not easily sway her from this conviction by presenting evidence or well-reasoned arguments to the contrary. Her convictions about Jesus affect her values and ethics because she believes it is important to follow moral teachings of Jesus (for instance, do unto others as you would have them do unto you).

A feeling is an emotion or affective response such as fear, anger, excitement, eagerness, or hurt. In Case 5, Shelley feels angry toward the nursing staff for abusing clients. Sometimes, people use the word *feel* when they mean *think* or *believe*. Believing and thinking are primarily cognitive processes. If a social worker tells a client, "I *feel* you have made remarkable progress," the worker probably means "I *think* you have made remarkable progress." In this case, it would be more precise to say "think" rather than "feel." Feelings affect and are affected by values and beliefs. If a man believes that God will protect him from harm, he may feel calm or secure even in the face of danger. If a woman values privacy, she may feel particularly infuriated when someone invades her privacy.

An attitude is a complex mental state in which the interactions of a person's values, beliefs, and feelings predispose her to particular opinions or behaviors. In Case 4, Sutcliffe provided services to a client even though he was not competent to do so. If Sutcliffe valued his independence and believed that people with schizophrenia were not so different from his other clients, he may have been operating under the attitude of "I am a good social worker; I don't need anyone's help to serve Calvin." Unfortunately, this attitude may have led Sutcliffe to breach his ethical obligation to provide clients with competent services.

As discussed in Chapter 1, social workers should be keenly aware of their values, beliefs, convictions, feelings, and attitudes so they do not impose them on clients. Although Shelley is angry toward the nursing staff, her awareness of this anger permits her to act professionally and seek a positive response for her clients. If she were not aware of her anger, she might have responded defensively or aggressively.

RULES, STANDARDS, AND PRINCIPLES

Ethical rules, ethical standards, and ethical principles are all guides for professional behavior. Although some people use these terms interchangeably, there are significant differences.

Rules and standards tend to be more specific guides for professional conduct, whereas principles tend to be more general (Beauchamp & Childress, 2009). In Case 1, Sandra may consider two broad ethical principles: maintaining a client's confidentiality and protecting people from physical harm. Her decision on whether to inform Colby's wife about his extramarital sex could be aided by a more specific ethical standard, for instance, "Social workers should maintain client confidentiality, even if a client discloses having unprotected extramarital sex" or "Social workers should report all incidents of unprotected extramarital sex to the Department of Public Health." Most codes of ethics include both general principles and more specific standards of conduct. The advantage of general principles is that they can be applied across a broad range of situations. The advantage of specific rules or standards of conduct is that they provide more detailed directions about how to respond, provided that the rules or standards cover the specific situation under consideration. Similarly, laws and agency policies may utilize a combination of specific rules and standards, as well as broad principles in order to balance the needs for clear directions and coverage of a wide range of situations.

The primary difference between rules and standards is that rules prescribe mandatory and universal expectations about conduct, whereas standards merely state the customary or ordinarily accepted ways that professionals should conduct themselves. In other words, rules state specifically what social workers *must or must not do*, without leaving room for exceptions or professional discretion. In contrast, standards explain how social workers *should or should not* conduct themselves, based on general consensus of the profession. Social workers may deviate from the expected norms or standards of the profession, provided that they can provide appropriate ethical justification. Consider, for instance, a rule that prohibits social workers from having sex with clients. This rule is not a general expectation but a firm directive. As a rule, it does not leave social workers room to argue that sex with clients may be justified in certain circumstances. In contrast, a professional standard that says social workers should respect a client's right to self-determination suggests that self-determination is a general expectation, not a rule that applies steadfastly in all cases or social contexts. There are many exceptions to self-determination in practice, for instance, work with clients who are actively suicidal. In this situation, a social worker may be able to justify deviating from the general standard of self-determination because the value of protecting life supersedes the value of respecting client autonomy.[11] Standards suggest that social workers should ordinarily behave in a particular way, but there may be situations in which alternate forms of behavior could be ethically justified. Codes of ethics typically state their professional expectations in terms of standards rather than rules (NASW, 1999). Using standards balances the need to state the usual expectations for conduct while providing some room for deviation from the standards based on appropriate ethical justification. Federal and state statutes generally provide their expectations in terms of rules rather than standards. Because rules are stated in a mandatory manner, they are easier to enforce than general expectations or standards.

REFERENCING ETHICS AND LAWS

Have you ever heard that you are legally obliged to report suspicions of child abuse? You probably have. But do you know what specific law creates this obligation, and what this obligation specifically says? Do you know the legal consequences for failure to report? Whenever you are analyzing a situation with ethical and legal implications, the most persuasive sources are the original sources. This means going to the specific code of ethics,[12] agency policy, or statutory law that spells out the relevant ethical guidelines, agency

[11] I say that the worker "may be able to justify" rather than a definitive statement about being able to justify, because some people might argue that clients have a right to terminate their lives, in certain circumstances (e.g., withdrawing life supports from a person in a persistent vegetative state).

[12] See the bibliography for websites containing codes of ethics that may be relevant to social workers.

rules, or legal obligations. If you rely on a secondary source, such as a textbook or the Wikipedia website, you take your chances. Is the secondary source accurate? Is it up-to-date? Does the secondary source apply to your jurisdiction? Many laws affecting social workers vary from state to state. Your analysis and arguments will be much stronger if you rely on original sources.

In order to access primary sources of laws, you may need the assistance of a librarian with experience in legal research. Legal information gateways for particular areas of law make it relatively easy to find state and federal laws (e.g., for child welfare laws, see http://www.childwelfare.gov/systemwide/laws_policies/state/index.cfm). General legal search engines, such as LexisNexis and WestLaw, provide more comprehensive databases but may be more difficult to navigate. You may also find useful legal resources in the bibliography to this textbook. Still, remember that the laws cited in this textbook could be outdated tomorrow if new laws are passed or existing ones amended.

When you cite a code of ethics, make sure that code is applicable. The NASW Code of Ethics (1999) applies to social workers who are members of this association. Although nonmembers could be held to similar standards, they have not agreed to be bound by this code. If a situation involves psychologists, nurses, or other professionals, you should consider their codes of ethics. Do not assume that they have the same obligations as social workers.

Whenever you write or speak about ethical issues, consider providing specific citations to laws and ethical standards. Specific citations add credibility and weight to your ethical reasoning and arguments. Citations also permit others to critically analyze and respond to your assertions. Rather than stating that the NASW Code of Ethics endorses client self-determination, for instance, identify the specific standard (S.1.02) that describes self-determination. Rather than writing that state laws require social workers to report child abuse, indicate the specific section of the law (e.g., Florida Statutes, § 39.201).[13] I hope you will find that the use of legal and ethical references throughout this textbook provides a good model for how to identify and make use of specific citations in your own ethical analyses and advocacy.

TEXTBOOK OVERVIEW

Now that you have a better understanding of the key values and ethics concepts, this section provides an overview of the rest of the textbook. By having a clearer picture of the contents, you will be able to utilize these materials more effectively. I have written each chapter in a manner to complement the other educational materials used in your curriculum. Different schools and professors may use these chapters in different manners, for instance, as required readings or suggested readings, and for some or for all of your courses. Each chapter begins by identifying its learning objectives. Each chapter then presents theory and knowledge, explaining key concepts and demonstrating how they apply to case situations. Each chapter concludes with discussion questions and exercises designed to reinforce your learning—helping you remember, understand, apply, evaluate, and innovate from the core content of the chapter. Part I focuses on remembering, understanding, and applying the content. Part II goes into more depth for the other learning objectives.

To lay the foundation for your education on social work ethics and values, Chapter 1 begins with introspection: What are your own values? How can you identify them? How can you raise your awareness of what they mean? And how may they affect you as a professional social worker? Once you have a clearer sense of your own values, Chapter 1 provides a framework for attending to and appreciating the values of others. Finally, Chapter 1 introduces you to the values of social work from historic and current perspectives. The exercises in this chapter will help you compare and contrast your values with those of the profession and others, providing a basis that you will need for whatever ethical problems you may face in practice.

---

[13] The § symbol means "section. The 39 indicates the chapter of the legislation and the .201 indicates the specific section within that chapter.

Chapters 2 and 3 explore the values and ethics underlying social work theory. As you will learn in your social work theory courses,[14] knowledge has a political aspect; knowledge is not neutral. Thus, it is important to understand the worldviews and predilections that underlie theory and knowledge, including those of social work, psychology, sociology, medicine, law, and other disciplines that inform social work practice.

Chapter 4 focuses on values and ethics as they apply to the research process: What are the ethical issues to be considered when research involves human subjects? How can social work researchers ensure that clients have free and informed consent? How can researchers protect clients' privacy? What institutional safeguards can be used to ensure that researchers respect all client rights and minimize any risks?

Chapters 5 to 9 delve into values and ethics as they apply to social work with various types of clients: individuals, families, groups, organizations, and communities. To provide you with a solid foundation for ethical practice with various client systems, these chapters focus on the more "black and white" ethical rules defining what types of behavior are appropriate and what types of behavior are inappropriate. These chapters are meant to complement your practice courses, so they will have a very practical focus: How do you discuss confidentiality and informed consent with a client? How do you ensure that you do not impose values on a client? How do you tell if you are competent to work with a particular client and client concern? How do you operationalize values such as respect, empowerment, and the strengths perspective? As you work through these chapters, remember that ethics is not simply about complying with the minimum standards enunciated in codes of ethics or standards of conduct; ethics helps you aspire to the highest ideals of the social work profession (Corey, Corey, & Callanan, 2007).

Chapter 10 examines values and ethics in the context of social policy. Although only a minority of social workers specializes in policy work, all social workers have an ethical obligation to promote social justice and to advocate social change at a policy level. This chapter illustrates ways to incorporate values and ethics into the analysis of policies as well as the promotion of policy change.

Even though this book presents topics in a sequential manner, chapters may be read out of sequence. Chapter 1 is a seminal chapter and should be read first, even if you do not work through all the exercises. Otherwise, the rest of the chapters in Part I may be used in any order.

Part II requires foundational knowledge of values and ethics, including a practical understanding of the black-letter ethical rules that guide social worker practices. Part II begins with a framework for ethical analysis, decision making, and consensus building. This framework is designed to help social workers manage ethical dilemmas and problems involving more shades of gray—in other words, situations where there is no clear right answer or when the choice is between two or more problematic actions. Part II also goes into greater depth, breadth, and specificity regarding work with specific population groups (children, elders, etc.), contexts of practice (mental health, criminal justice, etc.), and advanced social work functions (administration, supervision, psychotherapy, etc.). Ideally, you will find that this textbook is not only a useful supplement to your coursework but also a valuable resource for values and ethical issues throughout your career.

DISCUSSION QUESTIONS AND EXERCISES

The following questions and exercises are designed to help you understand, distinguish, and apply key terms from this chapter.

1. *Understanding*: Describe each of the following terms in your own words: ethics, values, laws, morals, and beliefs
2. *Distinguishing*: Compare and contrast the terms within each of the following sets of terms:
   a. Ethics and values
   b. Ethics, laws, and agency policies

[14] E.g., courses with titles such as "Human Behavior in the Social Environment."

c. Ethical problems, ethical dilemmas, and ethical breaches
d. Ethics and morals
e. Professional ethics and personal ethics
f. Values, feelings, and beliefs

3. *Applying—Problem, Dilemma, and Breach*: Review Case 3 at the top of this chapter. Identify whether this case involves an ethical problem, an ethical dilemma, and/or an ethical breach. Explain why you believe this case involves a problem, dilemma, and/or a breach (that is, link your conclusion with the definitions of problem, dilemma, and breach presented in this chapter).
4. *Applying—Law, Rule, Feeling, and Belief*: Patty is a probation officer working with Theo. Theo was convicted for theft and ordered by the court to remain on probation for one year. Theo breached one of the conditions of his probation by entering the store where he was initially caught stealing. Patty thinks Theo is a good kid who has had a tough life. She feels sorry for him. She wants to give him a second chance. For Patty, respecting the individual is more important than respecting property. Unfortunately, Theo's court order says that he must go to jail if he breaches any conditions of his probation.

   Review this case and identify one example of each of the following: a law, an ethical rule, a value, a feeling, and a belief. Explain how each example relates to that specific concept. For instance, "Theo's probation order is an example of a *law* because it is a rule that was enacted by the court—an agency of the state—and enforced by the criminal justice system—also an agency of the state."
5. *Applying—Professional Ethic, Personal Ethic, Belief, and Conviction*: Felicity facilitates a group for people with early stages of dementia (memory problems). Felicity personally feels that society should take primary responsibility for taking care of people with dementia. Her parents always told her, "We are our brothers' and our sisters' keeper," and this is a credo that she has come to live by. As a social worker, Felicity understands that families often provide the primary support for individuals in need. She knows that one of her professional responsibilities is to help people take care of their own family members.

   Review Felicity's case and identify one example of each of the following: professional ethic, personal ethic, belief, and conviction. Explain how each example relates to that specific concept.

Chapter 1

Values—Mine, Theirs, and Ours

Samantha is a social work student who is working with Homer, a homeless man. Homer has no money, no job, no family, and no idea about where his next meal or bed will come from. When Samantha asks Homer about the dearth of his resources and support, Homer doesn't seem to think any of these items is important. In fact, Homer is quite content with his life. He is happy to have the freedom of living on the street. Samantha has trouble accepting this and offers to help him find a real job, a good home, and a chance to re-assimilate into productive society.

Values are deeply held preferences or ideals to which a person aspires.[1] Personal values are neither right nor wrong, so we should not expect people to defend the correctness their values. They are what they are, and social work ethics tell us to respect all people, irrespective of whether their values are similar to our own. As guides to how we conduct our lives, values are important. Ironically, many people are unaware or only vaguely aware of their values and how they affect important choices in their lives.

VALUES CLARIFICATION

Values clarification refers to a process of raising self-awareness by reflecting critically on deeply held preferences, giving names to them, and examining the meaning of each of these values or preferences and how they fit together as a system. Although you can reflect by thinking quietly to yourself, reflection can be enhanced through discussions with others or through journaling—writing down thoughts and experiences in order to examine them more fully (Swindell & Watson, 2006). Values clarification is an ongoing process, particularly for professional social workers who must continuously reappraise their values to ensure that they are using these values appropriately in their work with various clients. Values clarification, per se, does not tell people what their values should be, but rather, what their values are. As a developing social worker, you can use values clarification to gain a clearer and more specific understanding of your own predilections. Ethical social work requires the disciplined use of self. If and when you find that your values are inconsistent with those of your clients or the social work profession, you will be in a better position to make conscious and deliberate decisions about how to resolve these value conflicts.

---

[1] For a more detailed definition or comparison of values and ethics, see the introduction to Part I.

Piaget (1999/orig.1932), one of the leading researchers on cognitive and moral development, determined that children learn values and morals as a result of interactions with their environment. Children aged 3 to 10, for instance, tend to accept rules given to them by people in positions of authority, particularly teachers and parents. Young children determine what is good or fair in terms of whether a particular act or event fits into the simple rules that they know. For instance, they come to understand that "telling the truth" is good because persons in authority tell them it is good. Also, they know they may be punished for lying and rewarded for telling the truth. As their cognitive ability develops, they have greater capacity to consider rules critically and make up their own minds about what is good. Whether older children think critically about their values depends on the opportunities promoted by their families, schools, houses of worship, or other social milieus. Some parents and social systems encourage questioning, while others encourage acceptance of certain values and beliefs without critical thinking. As a social work student, thinking critically about your values is vital to your professional development. Consider, to what extent have your family members, schools, houses of worship, and others encouraged you to question the values and beliefs that they have tried to instill in you?

People tend to see their own values as the best values. If people doubted their values were the best, then they could change them. Values evolve, but because values are deeply held, value evolution is typically a gradual process. One of the biggest challenges for social work students is to truly re-assess their values as they apply to social work practice. For instance, a student who values her faith in Jesus might believe it is appropriate to encourage clients to accept Jesus into their lives. From the student's initial perspective, she is helping the client. Although social work ethics specifically prohibit workers from imposing specific forms of religion on clients, this student may originally question why this prohibition is necessary. She may experience this prohibition as contrary to everything she has learned through her own religious upbringing. Through values clarification, the student may come to understand that her faith in Jesus is not her only value, and further, there may be more than one way to express this value (e.g., incorporating some of Jesus' teachings that are consonant with ethical social work practice, such as showing respect for all people and not judging them).

LEARNING OBJECTIVES

The learning objectives for this chapter are

- To gain greater awareness and clarification of your own values.
- To appreciate the importance of understanding the differences between your values and those of others.
- To be able to attend the values of others, without imposing personal biases.
- To identify and understand the historical and current values of the social work profession.

To begin the process of values clarification, we will reflect on the items listed in Tables 1.1, 1.2, and 1.3. These lists identify values that may be held by different people, and with different levels of intensity. The lists are not meant to be exhaustive but simply to provide a sample of values to initiate the process of values clarification in different realms of life. Table 1.1 focuses on values relating to one's overall priorities in life. Rate each value in this table on a scale of −3 to +3, with +3 being something that you find highly desirable and −3 something you find very undesirable.[2] A rating of 0 would be something that you rate as unimportant or have no strong convictions about. The last three rows are blank so you can include three additional values that you want to rate (e.g., additional values that you would rate highly desirable or highly undesirable). Guard against any inclinations to mark all or most values as "highly desirable." In order to gain a sense of how each value truly rates in relation to others, you must begin to make distinctions in how strongly you rate each item.

[2] The values clarification charts in Tables 1.1, 1.3, and 1.4 build on the format developed for Bobek and Gore's (2004) Inventory of Worker Values, with additional values including those identified in the NASW Code of Ethics (1999).

TABLE 1.1 Values Clarification Chart—Overall Life Priorities

"*In terms of my overall values in life, I rate ______ as*"	Rating						
	highly undesirable			*neutral*			*highly desirable*
1. Physical safety	−3	−2	−1	0	+1	+2	+3
2. Emotional security	−3	−2	−1	0	+1	+2	+3
3. Personal happiness	−3	−2	−1	0	+1	+2	+3
4. Material wealth	−3	−2	−1	0	+1	+2	+3
5. Leading a meaningful life	−3	−2	−1	0	+1	+2	+3
6. Friends	−3	−2	−1	0	+1	+2	+3
7. Family	−3	−2	−1	0	+1	+2	+3
8. Intimate relationships	−3	−2	−1	0	+1	+2	+3
9. Community responsibility	−3	−2	−1	0	+1	+2	+3
10. Open communication	−3	−2	−1	0	+1	+2	+3
11. Privacy	−3	−2	−1	0	+1	+2	+3
12. Social justice	−3	−2	−1	0	+1	+2	+3
13. Competition	−3	−2	−1	0	+1	+2	+3
14. Integrity (honesty)	−3	−2	−1	0	+1	+2	+3
15. Sanctity of marriage	−3	−2	−1	0	+1	+2	+3
16. Sanctity of life	−3	−2	−1	0	+1	+2	+3
17. Individual choice and autonomy	−3	−2	−1	0	+1	+2	+3
18. Religion	−3	−2	−1	0	+1	+2	+3
19. Conservation (nature)	−3	−2	−1	0	+1	+2	+3
20. Beauty	−3	−2	−1	0	+1	+2	+3
21. Solitude	−3	−2	−1	0	+1	+2	+3
22.	−3	−2	−1	0	+1	+2	+3
23.	−3	−2	−1	0	+1	+2	+3
24.	−3	−2	−1	0	+1	+2	+3

To aid in making these distinctions, rate no more than four values as "+3" (highly desirable) and no more than four values as "+2" (very desirable). Remember, there are no "right" or "wrong" answers about your values. Also, remember that you can change your answers as you reflect further on these values, now as a student and later as a professional in practice.

Now that you have rated your values, consider what each of them means to you. For each value that you rated as +3 or −3, write two or three sentences explaining your understanding of these values. Each of the values listed could have different meanings to different people, so it is important to clarify your own understandings. Once again, there is no right or wrong answer about how you understand a particular value. Being as specific as possible, however, will help you gain a better appreciation of your values. If you are having difficulty defining a particular value, feel free to consult a dictionary or search for the meaning of the value in scholarly literature. Do not simply rely on someone else's definition. Describe the value in your own words, illustrating what it means to you. Give an example of how you have put this value into practice in your personal life.

Consider "family" as a value. When different people say they value family, they may or may not be talking about the same thing. For some, valuing family means getting married, having children, and taking care of one another. For others, valuing family means loving and caring for people who are considered family, even if they are not related by blood or by marriage. Getting married or having children may not be important to them. In some cultures, valuing family refers to extended family (e.g., aunts, uncles, and cousins). In other cultures, valuing family refers to the whole community.

"Social justice" is another value that evokes different images for different people. Some people view social justice as equality, having everybody treated exactly the same. Others view social justice as respecting differences, treating people differently because they have different needs, wants, or opportunities (Beauchamp & Childress, 2009). Consider, for instance, whether universities should offer affirmative action programs for student applicants from disadvantaged backgrounds. Your answer depends, in part, on how you define social justice and how important that value is, as compared to other values (e.g., diversity, universality, competition). Your understanding of social justice is also affected by your life experience. If you have experienced extensive discrimination as a member of a minority group, for instance, you may have a different understanding of social justice from that of someone from a socially privileged background who has not experienced discrimination.

Once you have defined your key values, consider where conflicts may exist between them. By comparing pairs of values, you can identify potential tensions and contradictions. Suppose you indicated that you valued both "open communication" and "privacy" very highly. Open communication could refer to the importance of sharing thoughts, feelings, and opinions with close friend and confidants. Privacy could refer to the importance of having your own space, without interference from others. There is nothing wrong with valuing open communication and privacy at the same time. Still, you should be aware of ways that these values may be at odds. Suppose you fail a test at school, leaving you feeling sad and embarrassed. As someone who values open communication, do you share this information with your partner or close friends? Or as someone who values privacy, do you keep this information to yourself? If you think you would share the information, this may indicate that you value open communication more than you value privacy. By considering other situations when open communication and privacy may conflict, you can further clarify your order of priorities in relation to these values.

Social workers often face circumstances in which values come into conflict. By gaining a better understanding of your own system of values, including how you prioritize them, you will be better prepared for making tough choices in a deliberate, strategic manner.

The values in Table 1.1 relates to overall life priorities. We can also look at values in relation to specific areas of life, for instance, work, medical care, religion, or friendships. The values in Table 1.2 relate specifically to priorities in relation to child rearing. In order to discern your values in relation to child rearing, rate each of the values in this table on the same scale as you used for Table 1.1. Add two additional child-rearing values to this chart and rate them.

To clarify your values further, you could write definitions for each of your highest priorities and identify potential conflicts, as you did for the values in Table 1.1. Another way to clarify values is to explore their sources, that is, how you learned

TABLE 1.2 Values Clarification Chart—Children

"In terms of my values in relation to child-rearing, I rate ______ as"	Rating *highly undesirable*			*neutral*			*highly desirable*
1. Children growing up to be independent	−3	−2	−1	0	+1	+2	+3
2. Children respecting elders	−3	−2	−1	0	+1	+2	+3
3. Children excelling in school	−3	−2	−1	0	+1	+2	+3
4. Spending quality time with children	−3	−2	−1	0	+1	+2	+3
5. Providing financially for children	−3	−2	−1	0	+1	+2	+3
6. Nurturing children emotionally	−3	−2	−1	0	+1	+2	+3
7.	−3	−2	−1	0	+1	+2	+3
8.	−3	−2	−1	0	+1	+2	+3

or acquired your values. For each of your highest values, identify the major source(s) from which you acquired your values: for example, did you acquire a particular value from your parents, grandparents, cultural community, primary education, secondary education, religious scripture, the legal system, or public media?

Consider "children growing up to be independent." If you rated this as highly desirable, reflect on your own upbringing. Perhaps your parents encouraged you to be independent, teaching you how to do things for yourself or offering praise when you reached each new milestone of independence. Perhaps your school prepared you with life skills (cooking, cleaning, budgeting, and earning a living) so you would not need to depend on others. Alternatively, consider whether your values developed as a reverse reaction to what your parents or others tried to instill. Perhaps you felt your parents smothered you with guidance and support, not allowing you to develop independence. Consciously or unconsciously you may have decided that independence was important for you or your children.

Consider also whether values promoted for boys and girls in your family were different. Some families encourage boys to be more independent, but encourage girls to be more dependent, or perhaps more relational. Whereas "dependence" sounds pejorative, "relational" has positive connotations, including involvement in caring relationships and showing concern for others, rather than just for oneself. Which values did you learn from your family? If your family instilled different values for boys than for girls, what was the nature of these differences?

By reflecting on the sources of your own values, you will gain a better understanding of how values can be transmitted. You will also gain a better appreciation of how values develop within a social context. What may seem like the best values to one person may seem questionable to another person, in part because of the different families, cultures, and communities in which each grew up and currently lives.

Table 1.3 lists values in relation to work (employment). Rate each of the values in this table from −3 to +3, and add two additional values to rate.

One reason for including an exercise on work is to help you identify your values as they relate to your impending career as a social worker. As you reflect on the values you rated as highly desirable, consider how well they fit with your career plans. If you indicated high ratings for "well-paying job" or "prestige," for instance, is this something you are likely to find within social work? If you rated "meaningful work" highly, then what type of meaning would you

TABLE 1.3 Values Clarification Chart—Work

"In terms of my values in relation to work, I rate ______ as"	Rating: *highly undesirable*			*neutral*			*highly desirable*
1. A well-paying job	−3	−2	−1	0	+1	+2	+3
2. Meaningful work	−3	−2	−1	0	+1	+2	+3
3. Creativity	−3	−2	−1	0	+1	+2	+3
4. Authority (someone with power to provide directions)	−3	−2	−1	0	+1	+2	+3
5. Intellectual stimulation	−3	−2	−1	0	+1	+2	+3
6. Prestige or high status	−3	−2	−1	0	+1	+2	+3
7. Equal status (between men, women, administrators, frontline workers, and all people in agency)	−3	−2	−1	0	+1	+2	+3
8. Autonomy (free of control from others)	−3	−2	−1	0	+1	+2	+3
9. Structure (guidelines concerning what to do or not to do)	−3	−2	−1	0	+1	+2	+3
10.	−3	−2	−1	0	+1	+2	+3
11.	−3	−2	−1	0	+1	+2	+3

expect from a career in social work? For each of the values that you rated highly, write a paragraph on the extent to which this value fits or conflicts with a social work career. Feel free to use an introduction to social work textbook to help you assess the goodness of fit between your values and your intended career.

Obviously, there is considerable variation between different social work jobs. If you are working in the criminal justice or child protection system, for instance, there may be a higher emphasis on authority and structure than, say, a position within a social outreach program for at-risk elders in the community. A career in social work administration tends to be higher paying than a career in frontline case management. A social work position in which you act as an advocate for social justice may be more meaningful than a social work position in which your primary task is to administer eligibility forms for food stamps. By reflecting on your values in relation to work, you can gain insight into whether social work is a good fit, as well as which types of social work practice may fit best with your highest values. Identify one type of social work practice that you are considering. Write a paragraph describing how well this type of work fits or conflicts with your highest values.

APPRECIATING THE VALUES OF OTHERS

Now that you are more aware of your own values, you are in a better position to enhance your appreciation for the values of others. *"Appreciating others' values" means striving to understand their ideals and deeply held preferences.* When others have values that are similar to our own, it is relatively easy to understand and demonstrate respect for their values. When others have values that conflict with our own, we must resist the temptation to judge or condemn their values. Attribution theory suggests that people have a tendency to assign positive thoughts and feelings toward people with whom they agree, but negative thoughts and feelings toward people with whom they disagree (Curtis, 1994). Consider a social worker who values collaboration and social well-being. This worker might think that business people have poor morals because they value competition and profits rather than collaboration and social well-being. The worker's thought patterns may lead the worker to feel distain and anger toward business people. By attributing negative thoughts and feelings toward business people, the worker has difficulty maintaining respect for their dignity and worth. Rather than attributing negative thoughts and feelings, the social worker should try to understand the values of business people from their perspectives.

The process of appreciating begins with attending to other people's values with an open mind and an open heart, neither assuming nor judging. Because values reflect what people view as *good* rather than what is *right,* remember: Appreciating does not mean analyzing whether the other's values are correct, desirable, or proper. Social workers respect all people, even when they have significantly different values (Reamer, 2006b; Strom-Gottfried, 2007).

Use your coursework, readings, and class activities to practice attending to others' values (Forehand, 2005). Every time you read a book chapter, article, or other assigned material in your social work program, pause to reflect on the values that underlie the author's writing. The author's values are typically reflected in the focus and perspectives represented in the writing. When comparing a chapter written by a psychologist to one written by a social worker, you may find that the psychologist focuses on individual mental illness whereas the social worker focuses on the stresses that occur in the relationships between people. By attending to their values, you can appreciate that the psychologist has a high value for the mental well-being of the individual whereas the social worker has a high value for positive social functioning.

During classroom discussions, attend to the values that may be motivating the thoughts and opinions of others. If your policy class is discussing the merits of a tax decrease, what values may be leading some people to support the idea and others to reject it? Those favoring a tax decrease may value *individual responsibility,* having people depend on themselves rather than depend on the government. Those opposing a tax decrease may value *distributive justice*, using the tax system to promote an equitable sharing of resources.

When attending to values of diverse populations, think in terms of relativity (more or less) rather than strict categories. A relative approach focuses on the degree to which a person or group values a particular ideal. One method of viewing values in relative terms is to place them along a continuum rather than in categories. *Consider the value of individualism. According to this value, the individual is important and each person should do what is best for himself or herself.* If one categorized people according to this value, one could say that a person was either individualistic or nonindividualistic. In reality, people have varying degrees of individualism. They may value individualism to a certain degree but balance individualism with another value, communitarianism. *According to communitarianism, the interests of the social unit are more important than those of the individual, and each person should suppress individual wishes in order to do what is best for the community (e.g., kinship group, neighborhood, society).* By looking at individualism and communitarianism as a continuum, you can view people's values in terms of where they fit along this line:

Highly Communitarian ←——————→ Highly Individualistic

If you compare mainstream American values with traditional Asian values, for instance, you will see that Asians tend to be more communitarian and Americans tend to be more individualistic (Appleby, Colon, & Hamilton, 2007). Consider a friend or colleague in your class who comes from a different ethnocultural background than you. Is this person more individualistic or less individualistic than you are? What differences in attitudes, opinions, or behaviors are you using to reach this conclusion? Remember, although research may demonstrate certain cultural tendencies, these tendencies do not apply to all people from a particular diversity group. To avoid the problems of overgeneralizing and stereotyping, we must consider within-group and individual differences.

When attending to values differences between people from different cultures, other important value pairings to consider are hierarchy-egalitarianism, mastery-harmony, masculinity-femininity, and uncertainty-certainty (Shiraev & Levy, 2004). Hierarchy-egalitarianism refers to preferences regarding the power distance between people. *People with higher value for hierarchy prefer greater power differentials between people in certain types of relationships, for instance, parents and children, elders and nonelders, husbands and wives, teachers and students, government leaders and the populace, clergy and parishioners, or helping professionals and clients. People with higher value for egalitarianism prefer lower power differentials between such pairings.* If you were raised in a family with rules such as "children should be seen but not heard" or "don't question your elders (or teachers, doctors, etc.)," this suggests that your family valued hierarchy. If your family encouraged children to speak their minds and express differences directly with parents, elders, and other adults as equals, this suggests your family valued egalitarianism. Mainstream Americans tend to have a higher value for egalitarianism, as compared to traditional Latinos or Asians (Shiraev & Levy, 2004).

The mastery-harmony continuum relates to how people view their relationships with society and natural resources. *People with higher value for mastery prefer to exercise control over their piece of the world. People with higher value for harmony prefer to fit in and conserve the world in its natural state* (Lum, 2004; Shiraev & Levy, 2004). Assume you inherited a tract of land that was rich in trees and wildlife. Would you see yourself as an owner with the rights or responsibility to determine the best use of the land and then implement changes to fulfill its best use? Alternatively, would you see yourself as the guardian of the land with responsibility to preserve the land, rather than violate or exploit it? Mainstream Americans tend to value mastery whereas Native Americans tend to value harmony (Appleby et al., 2007).

Masculinity and femininity refer to predilections that we typically associate with being male and female. *People with high value for masculinity tend to prefer decisiveness, responsibility, liveliness, and high ambitions. People with high value for femininity tend to prefer consensus building, caring for the vulnerable, gentleness, and modesty* (Shiraev & Levy, 2004). Although these predilections are affected by gender, different men and women possess varying degrees of masculine and feminine values. Different cultures also value masculinity and femininity to varying degrees. Consider your hopes for your children or grandchildren. Would you find it more gratifying if they grew up to be teachers, social workers, or nurturing parents (life paths associated with femininity), or more gratifying if they grew up to be successful athletes, stockbrokers, or inventors (life paths associated with masculinity)? Mainstream American culture tends to give higher value to masculinity; to illustrate, compare the salaries of teachers and stockbrokers. Can you think of a culture that gives higher value to feminine careers and attributes?

The uncertainty-certainty continuum relates to the degree to which people are comfortable with ambiguity. *People with higher value for certainty prefer social systems that provide clear beliefs, rules, order, and structure. People with higher value for uncertainty prefer nonconformity, unpredictability, creativity, and new forms of thinking and behavior* (Shiraev & Levy, 2004). People with fundamental or orthodox religious beliefs value the certainty provided by the clear rules, traditions, rituals, and norms that go along with strict adherence to their religious scriptures. Artists, explorers, and radical social workers value the uncertainty inherent in processes of creating, traveling to new places, and promoting fundamental social change. When you plan a vacation, do you prefer to stay at home or somewhere familiar, or do you prefer to head into uncharted territories, taking the chance of getting lost, not knowing the language and customs, or ending up somewhere other than where you intended?

How we respond to others depends on our knowledge, thoughts, emotions, and awareness. If we lack knowledge of others' values, how can we possibly attend to what they hold most important in their lives? By striving for greater knowledge and information about their values, at least we raise the possibility of responding in a manner that respects their values. When we gather information about others' values, we do so through the filters of our thoughts and emotions. While our cognitive and affective processes may help us understand others' values more clearly, they can also blur or confuse our perceptions and understandings. Consider an elderly client who yells at you when you explore the possibility of his moving into a nursing home. You asked about the nursing home because you were concerned about his ability to live on his own, but you were not trying to tell him what to do. His yelling could make you feel defensive. You might think he is angry, irrational, or obstinate. You may need to take a step back from your initial thoughts and feelings to explore his underlying values. Perhaps his response to the nursing home suggestion reflects his value for independence. Perhaps it also reflects his value for respect, which he defines as showing reverence for one's elders. Once you have tuned into possible values, you can check out whether your insights are accurate. "When you say that a nursing home is unacceptable, is this because independence is very important to you... or are there other reasons that a nursing home would be unacceptable?" By raising your awareness of emotional responses, you can gauge whether your feelings are biasing your appreciation of your client's values. If you feel attacked when the client yells, you might initially think the client values control or disrespect. In other words, feeling attacked has affected your understanding of the client's values. Further reflection might remind you that the client values independence. His yelling simply signaled his fear of losing something he values dearly.

At various stages of your social work education and career, you may think that you are attending well to others' values, only to be surprised that you have missed something or unintentionally imposed your own biases. None of us are perfect, so acknowledging mistakes and humbly moving ahead is part of being a professional social worker. This brings us to the next topic: understanding the values of social work.

HISTORIC AND CURRENT SOCIAL WORK VALUES

When social work applicants and incoming students are asked why they want to pursue a career in social work, the common refrain is that they want to help people. But what does "help" actually mean? Although helping people is a cornerstone of social work, many professions help people: Doctors and nurses help by providing medical care, lawyers help by providing legal advocacy, scientists help by inventing, journalists help by facilitating access to information, and waste management workers help by disposing of garbage. *What makes social work unique is its historic and ongoing mission to work with and on behalf of people with the greatest social needs and vulnerabilities.* The National Association of Social Workers expresses the mission of social work in the preamble to the Code of Ethics as follows:

> The primary mission of the social work profession is to enhance human well-being and help meet the basic human needs of all people, with particular attention to the needs and empowerment of people who are vulnerable, oppressed, and living in poverty. A historic and defining feature of social work is the profession's focus on individual well-being in a social context and the well-being of society. Fundamental to social work is attention to the environmental forces that create, contribute to, and address problems in living. (NASW, 1999)

In its definition of social work, the International Federation of Social Workers (IFSW)[3] describes social work values as follows:

> Social work grew out of humanitarian and democratic ideals, and its values are based on respect for the equality, worth, and dignity of all people. Since its beginnings...social work practice has focused on meeting human needs and developing human potential. Human rights and social justice serve as the motivation and justification for social work action. In solidarity with those who are disadvantaged, the profession strives to alleviate poverty and to liberate vulnerable and oppressed people in order to promote social inclusion. (IFSW, 2000)

Professional social work in the United States grew out of the charity organizations (Richmond, 1917) and the settlement movement, particularly the Jane Addams Hull House settlement association (Ehrenreich, 1985). Hull House was designed to serve an impoverished community in Chicago where a largely immigrant population suffered from disease, crime, and unemployment. Under the traditional model of helping, nonprofessional social workers and society matrons visited the poor during the workday but returned to their middle- or upper-class homes every evening. Unfortunately, many of these helpers imposed their values on those they helped, often assuming that differences in culture, ethnicity, and customs brought on the social problems experienced by the immigrants. Addams's model of helping required the helpers to live where they worked and to respect the dignity and worth of all people, including differences in their culture, ethnicity, and customs. *Addams's model not only reflected the value of helping those in greatest need but also helping through an equal partnership. Addams's model also emphasized community as a value.* Offering help to one person at a time was not sufficient, particularly for people experiencing a combination of poverty, poor education, discrimination, and lack of opportunity. By valuing community and equal partnership, Addams's model demonstrated that one of the most effective ways of helping people is to help them help themselves (Jane Addams Hull House Association, n.d.).

As you study the history of social work, you may hear about the tension between macro and micro practice (with macro practice focusing on community work and public policy development, and micro practice focusing on social work with individuals, families, and smaller systems).[4] Whereas Addams's macro model emphasized

---

[3] The IFSW is an international organization of professional social work associations representing over 80 countries (see http://www.ifsw.org for more information).

[4] Social work may also be divided into three categories—micro, mezzo, and macro—with mezzo practice including work with middle-sized systems, such as groups and organizations. Different people use different definitions of micro, mezzo, and macro practice, so it is helpful to define specifically which client systems are included when utilizing these terms.

the importance of working with communities, Richmond's micro (casework) model focused on helping individual clients, supporting their health, social functioning, growth, and adaptation to the stresses in their social environments (Richmond, 1917). Although some social workers still value one method of practice over the other, the generalist model of social work suggests that all methods of practice are equally valuable: Policy affects practice, practice affects policy, individuals are affected by families and larger systems, and families and larger systems are affected by individuals (Kirst-Ashman & Hull, 2006a, 2006b). A combination of methods is required to promote health, social well-being, growth, and social and economic justice. Thus, the generalist model combines the values derived from Addams's and Richmond's approaches in one value base for the whole social work profession.

Social work values define how the profession views people, its preferred goals for clients and society, and its preferred means of achieving those goals (Levy, 1993). The NASW Code of Ethics (1999) identifies six core values for the profession: *(1)* service; *(2)* social justice; *(3)* dignity and worth of the person; *(4)* importance of human relationships; *(5)* integrity; and *(6)* competence. This list represents a consensus among the NASW membership concerning social work's highest moral principles. Each ethical rule in the Code of Ethics is based on one or more of these values. Social work values and ethics are not just minimum standards to which practitioners are held accountable but ideals to which all social workers should strive. Other social work textbooks and codes of ethics may describe social work values in different terms. The reason that this textbook focuses on values as described in the NASW Code is that this code is the most commonly used and overarching one for social workers in the United States.[5] This textbook also includes two additional core values: human rights and scientific inquiry. These values were identified by the Council on Social Work Education (CSWE) in its 2008 revision to its Educational Policy and Accreditation. Although they are not specifically mentioned in the NASW Code as core values, they are implicit in many of the standards related to social justice, diversity, and competence.

The following sections define the core values. Understanding the scope of each value is just one step toward integrating these values into your professional persona. As you work through your courses and field education, strive to incorporate these values, not only in your behaviors at work but also in your professional identity, that is, who you are as a professional social worker. What do these values say about me as a professional and as a person? What do I do when my personal values seem to conflict with my professional values and obligations? It is easy to say that you believe in social work values. Still, true professional commitment comes through the passage of time and meeting everyday challenges that make applying certain values not so easy.

(1) Service

The value of service suggests that social workers give high priority to helping others. *By valuing service, social workers subjugate their personal desires in order to focus on the needs, interests, and wishes of the people they serve.* When a social worker says that she chose this profession because helping others is meaningful work, she is expressing service as a value. Indeed, if you have chosen social work primarily for the pay, you might find that you will have to become an advocate for better pay for this oft-undervalued profession.

Social work is an altruistic profession. In theory, what could be nobler than valuing service? In practice, applying this value can be quite challenging. Assume that a client discloses

[5] If you are operating under another code of ethics (such as one specifically for group workers, family mediators, parenting coordinators, or feminist social workers), you will need to understand the specific values enunciated in these codes. Websites for alternative codes of ethics are listed in the bibliography. In Part II, we will explore dilemmas that may arise when social workers have conflicting values from different codes of ethics or agency policies.

that he became wealthy defrauding widows with a phony investment scheme (e.g., Ponzi). He shows no remorse and even gloats about how devious he was. He now wants your help with a marital conflict. Although his current issue is unrelated to his past misconduct, you find his conduct and attitude reprehensible. Your first inclination is that you do not want to assist him. You understand that social workers believe all people deserve help, regardless of their ethnicity, culture, religion, socioeconomic status, or even history of criminal, immoral behavior. Still, you feel conflicted. Even if you agree to serve him, will you be able to serve him to your best ability?

Before you say that you can accept service as a core value, reflect on whether you possess any other values that may conflict with service:

- In Table 1.1, how did you rate "competition"? If you place a high value on competition, you may believe that the market should determine what services people should receive. If people can pay for services, then they are entitled to them. In other words, people have to fend for themselves. Competition may run contrary to service because service suggests that social workers are our brothers' and sisters' keepers. Social workers help clients in need, even if they cannot afford to pay market rates for such services.
- In Table 1.3, how did you rate "prestige or high status"? If you rated prestige highly, you may place your status and concerns higher than needs and wishes of your clients. In order to do what is best for clients, social workers often have to get their hands dirty, performing grunt work that receives little or no recognition. In my own practice, I have assisted clients by helping them to the toilet, making countless calls to secure a safe bed for the night, and allowing them to vent anger toward me until they calmed down and could be safe with others. Some incoming social work students envision themselves conducting exhilarating 50-minute psychotherapy sessions with highly motivated clients, in an office with gleaming furniture and awesome views. At the risk of understating the obvious, a lot of the most significant social work practice is not so glamorous.

Even if you feel ready to embrace service as a core value, be prepared for challenges. Social workers are human, with human needs and frailties. Although we aspire to be focused on the needs of others, we must take care of ourselves so that we can care for others. Caring for ourselves without putting our needs above those of our clients requires a fine balance.

(2) Social Justice

The *Social Work Dictionary* defines social justice as "An ideal condition in which all members of a society have the same basic rights, protection, opportunities, and social benefits" (Barker, 2003, pp. 404–405). In other words, *social justice refers to a world in which everyone is treated fairly*. By valuing social justice, social workers commit themselves to rectifying social injustices such as discrimination, poverty, unemployment, oppression, lack of opportunity, and social exclusion. Whereas some professions claim to be objective, neutral, or apolitical, social work takes firm positions on social justice issues and is necessarily political (Parrott, 2006). When a client is experiencing racism, for instance, some mental health professionals would focus on helping the client cope with the racism. Social workers not only help clients cope but also strive to remedy the racism (e.g., by offering advocacy, education, or community empowerment strategies) (Appleby et al., 2007). Although social workers do not impose their values on clients, this does not mean they are value free (Corey et al., 2007). They promote equality, respect, fairness, and inclusion throughout their practice.

Few if any incoming social work students would say that they value social injustice. Different students, however, may have different understandings of social justice and some of these definitions might conflict with social work's view of social justice. Consider the plight of undocumented noncitizen workers, sometimes disparagingly called "illegal aliens." Some might say that people working in this country illegally should be locked up or sent back, and at the very least, denied the privileges of citizens, such as medical care and schooling for their children. They do not want to encourage more "illegals" to come, and they want to protect America from being taken over by foreign criminals. Is their response socially just? Given social work's historic alliance with the most vulnerable members of society, social work would advocate finding solutions for the needs and interests of undocumented noncitizen workers and their families. Given your understanding of the issues, how easy or difficult would it be for you to advocate for vulnerable noncitizens?

(3) Dignity and Worth of the Person

Social workers value the dignity and worth of all individuals, meaning that everyone deserves respect. Racism, ethnocentrism, xenophobia, sexism, heterosexism, and other forms of bigotry have no place in social work. Social workers do not merely tolerate people from diverse backgrounds; they embrace diversity. Valuing the dignity and worth of all people translates into working with clients on the issues, concerns, and goals that they want to pursue. Whereas physicians and others using the traditional medical model diagnose patients and tell them what type of treatment they need (Kharicha, Illife, Levin, Davey, & Fleming, 2005), social workers work collaboratively with clients to assess what is going on in their lives and to help them make self-determined choices about how to proceed. Honoring client self-determination shows the utmost respect for the client's strengths, dignity, and autonomy.

As with other values, respecting the worth of an individual is often much easier to say than to carry out in practice. All of us are prone to biases such as racism, sexism, or religious chauvinism (the belief that one's own religion is superior and other religions have little value). We may have acquired biases and stereotypes from our families, peer groups, or media. We may treat others disrespectfully, not intentionally, but out of ignorance or haste. We may mean to do well by others, but our actions may have a negative impact. Take the Golden Rule, "Do unto others, as you would have them do unto you." This biblical lesson is meant to encourage people to treat others well. If you take the phrase literally, however, it says to treat others the way you want to be treated, not how they want to be treated. I am Jewish, so I appreciate hearing people say "Happy Chanukah" to me rather than "Merry Christmas." If I greet Christian clients with "Happy Chanukah," however, am I showing respect, taking their religious sensitivities into account? Though this example may sound trivial, it demonstrates how easy it is to demonstrate disrespect, even when you intend to treat others with benevolence.

One of the greatest risks to demonstrating respect to clients is imposing values or beliefs on clients. Consider a client who tells you that she is being abused by her husband. She does not want to leave him because she loves him and needs him. Would you advise her to leave her husband because he is abusive? If you do, you may be imposing your values and beliefs. How do you know whether leaving her husband is better for her? By trusting clients to make their own decisions, social workers are respecting their dignity and worth. For beginning social workers, this may sound counterintuitive. Shouldn't social workers tell clients what they believe? If a social worker can persuade a client to leave an abusive relationship, isn't this respecting the clients' dignity? Consider how you feel when someone tells you what to do, particularly if it is a professional who hardly knows you or your situation. Contrast this with your feelings when someone offers you moral support, showing confidence that you will make the right decisions for yourself.

(4) Importance of Human Relationships

Human relationships are integral to effective social work practice. *Social workers help clients by developing affirming relationships with them.* To engage clients in helping processes, social workers listen to clients, offering concern, support, empathic understanding, genuineness, and unconditional positive regard. Developing a positive therapeutic relationship with clients is a fundamental component of the helping process (Rogers, 1957). Clients who feel valued and respected will be more open, confident, and willing to take the risks that are involved in any change process. By demonstrating unconditional positive regard, social workers build trust with clients, who learn they can say anything and not be judged or embarrassed by the worker.

Social workers also demonstrate their value for "social relationships" through their ecological perspective. Social workers view clients in the context of their social environment, essentially their relationships with other individuals, family members, groups, and organizations. The ecological perspective directs social workers to consider problems as interactional rather than individual. Instead of looking at a client as having an individual problem called alcoholism, for instance, social workers look at alcoholism as a phenomenon that exists within the context of a family and community: What is going on in the family and community systems that encourages the person to drink, or prevents the person from dealing more effectively with the alcohol-related problems? Instead of blaming an individual for being unemployed, social workers look at what is going on in the individual's family, community, and former workplace that contributed to the employment issue. Social workers help individuals relate more effectively to their families, workplaces, and communities, but help does not stop there. Social workers also help families, workplaces, and communities provide a more supportive environment for the individual.

Once again, before you claim "human relationships" as a core value, reflect on the values you identified earlier in this chapter and how they might conflict with this value. In Table 1.2, for example, how did you rate "children growing up to be independent"? If you rated this item highly, you probably place high value on autonomy and personal responsibility. These values are common among mainstream Americans, particularly men. Having these values may offer a number of advantages: motivation to work hard rather than depend on others, willingness to accept responsibility for making changes, and confidence in one's abilities to make changes and achieve personal goals. A person with high value for autonomy, however, may feel too ashamed to ask for help. Asking for help may be tantamount to admitting weakness or inability to accept personal responsibility. When we teach children to be independent, we may be rejecting interdependence, which is inherent in valuing human relationships. Social workers believe that it is all right for people to rely on one another. In fact, for people to reach their highest potentials, relying on one another is vital. In essence, no man or woman is an island, and it takes a village to raise a child.[6]

Consider your own inclinations when you are facing a problem (e.g., difficulty at school, financial stress, conflict with your spouse or partner). Do you try to solve the problem on your own, or do you reach out for help from a family member, friend, or professional? On the continuum of "highly autonomous to highly relational," would you place yourself at either of the extremes, or closer to the middle?

(5) Integrity

Integrity refers to the importance of honesty, reliability, and responsibility. *Social workers demonstrate integrity by being open and honest, by following through on their professional obligations, and by being accountable for their actions.* Although it is morally correct for all people to act with integrity, professional social workers hold themselves to a higher standard than the general public because they are working with vulnerable people, including young children, frail elders, people with mental illness, and clients experiencing high levels of social stress. Different people have different views on what constitutes integrity, so it is important to understand as specifically as possible what the profession of social work means by integrity. Social workers must not exploit clients or be perceived to be exploiting them. Integrity is vital to building trust. When clients believe their workers are tainted by dishonesty, inconsistency, or irresponsibility, they may find it impossible to develop the confidence necessary for them to work together.

Various situations raise different challenges about what it means to act with integrity. In terms of honesty, for instance, is it all right to tell a "little white lie" in order to save a person from embarrassment? Would you tell a friend that his

[6] These well-known axioms reflect the value of human relationships.

new hairstyle looks great in order to boost his ego, even though you think the style looks ridiculous on him? Would you act differently if this were a client rather than a friend? In terms of responsibility, must social workers always follow agency policies—even if the policies are discriminatory? In terms of accountability, are social workers always responsible for what happens to their clients? Consider a client who commits suicide. At what points do clients, families, and communities have to accept responsibility rather than hold a social worker to account?

One might think that anyone who goes into professional social work must be doing so for the right reasons and must possess a relatively high value for integrity. One might be surprised at how often social workers act in a manner that conflicts with integrity—for instance, taking advantage of clients by having sex with them, breaching agency policy or ethical standards, and intentionally misguiding clients (Reamer, 2003). Sometimes these acts are based on poor judgment in a particular situation rather than faulty values. Sometimes these acts are committed while the worker is under extreme stress—for instance, putting inaccurate information in client records due to fatigue from working overtime, or exaggerating one's efforts in order to look good to a supervisor who has unreasonably high expectations. Acting under stress does not excuse a person from acting dishonestly, but the context does put the behavior into perspective. Social workers must not only want to act with integrity; they must commit themselves to developing working environments that promote integrity.

(6) Competence

Competence means having the knowledge, skills, and self-awareness required to perform social work tasks in an effective manner. The specific skills and knowledge required depend on the specific tasks to be undertaken. In the foundation courses of your social work program, you will learn basic knowledge (e.g., systems theory, developmental theory, and the generalist planned-change process) and basic skills (e.g., attending to a client's nonverbal behavior, reflecting feelings, paraphrasing thoughts, and asking open-ended questions). Your foundation courses are intended to provide you with the competence to practice as a generalist social work practitioner. Upon completion of these courses, you should be able to engage clients, conduct basic psychosocial assessments, guide clients through the planned-change process,[7] and evaluate their progress. While you will become competent to work with a range of clients with different presenting problems, be careful to stay within your competencies. If you are not competent to handle a particular situation, then the value of competence suggests that you should link clients with another worker who possesses the required skills and knowledge (e.g., your supervisor, a more experienced worker, or a professional with specialized training).

When people are experiencing social problems, many different kinds of people can provide help: family, friends, neighbors, charity workers, and professionals. What distinguishes professional help from the other types of help is the use of professional knowledge and skills. When a client asks for help, a social worker cannot simply give advice from personal experience or intuition. The social worker should apply professional knowledge and skills as appropriate to the situation.

For most social work students, embracing competence as a value is relatively easy. After all, they are taking courses in a professional degree program. The decision to pursue a degree in social work generally means that the person wants to improve his or her competence through education. Unfortunately, some students struggle with why professional knowledge and skills are important. They believe that they possess all the knowledge and skills they need, for instance, as natural-born social workers or as people who have developed social work skills through general education and life experience. They are only enrolled in a social work degree program because they need the credential to practice or to be eligible for promotion. The challenge for these students is to learn how additional knowledge and skills can enhance their ability to

[7] Sometimes called the "generalist problem-solving process."

practice effectively. In fact, competence is not something that we achieve through completion of a single social work program. Gaining competence is an ongoing process. All social workers may continue to gain competence, learning how to carry out certain functions more effectively, being open to the knowledge from new research findings, honing skills with different population groups, and so on. Thus, a commitment to competence is an ongoing endeavor.

Building competence is not just a duty but a potential source of happiness, pleasure, or fulfillment. Competence provides what Aristotle called *eudaimonia*, a sense of self-worth or well-being (Hursthouse, 2007). In other words, competence may offer social workers a sense of self-gratification or meaning from the ability to do their jobs in a skilled, proficient manner.

(7) Human Rights

Human rights refers to the system of privileges, civil liberties, and entitlements that every person should enjoy by virtue of his or her status as a human being. The value of human rights is related to the value of dignity and worth of the person, as treating people with respect includes respect for their human rights. The Council on Social Work Education suggests that human rights include the rights to freedom, safety, privacy, an adequate standard of living, health care, and education (Council on Social Work Education, 2008). Note that human rights are not the same as civil rights that a national government may grant to its citizens. Under the 14th Amendment of the U.S. Constitution (1868), U.S. citizens enjoy the rights to life, liberty, and property. However, the Constitution recognizes these rights for citizens only. Social workers value human rights for all people, regardless of their citizenship status. Similarly, various pieces of state and federal legislation grant rights to defined groups—patients, taxpayers, veterans, and so on. These are not human rights, as they are restricted to particular groups. At an international level, the United Nations has passed a variety of human rights codes, conventions, and charters that identify a broad range of human rights, including the rights to life, liberty, and security of the person, as well as the right to equality before the law (United Nations, 1948). Social workers believe in advancing the human rights for clients and society in general, regardless of whether current laws acknowledge or protect those rights. The value of human rights overlaps with social justice in the sense that social workers advocate and take action against forces that oppress people or deny them their rights.

(8) Scientific Inquiry

Scientific inquiry refers to learning about a particular phenomenon through sound processes of investigation. Social workers value a variety of scientific methods of inquiry, including quantitative and qualitative research, deductive and inductive reasoning, and experimentation and observation. There is no singular, correct way that social workers learn about individuals, families, groups, organizations, communities, and society. Regardless of which method of scientific inquiry is being used, social worker should incorporate the highest standards of rigor for that method (Grinnell 2007; Rubin & Babbie, 2008).

The social work value of scientific inquiry is related to the values of competence and respect for the dignity and worth of all people. In order to practice in a competent manner, social workers need to know and understand the most current theory and research. To respect the dignity and worth of clients, social workers need to understand which interventions are most effective for each client. Thus, social workers do not conclude their education when they graduate with a social work degree. Rather, social workers continue to learn throughout their careers, reading theory and research from academic literature, participating in research and evaluation in their agencies, and monitoring their work in a strategic manner to determine the effectiveness, ethicality, and efficiency of their work.

THE ONGOING CHALLENGES OF VALUES CLARIFICATION AND AWARENESS

This chapter has introduced you to the basics of understanding values. By reflecting on your own values, you have gained better insight into the ideals that motivate you and the way you interact with others. In order to gain an appreciation for others' values, you have learned how to view values from a relational context—for instance, how are a client's values similar to or different from your own, or how are the values of a minority group similar to or different from those of the majority population? Finally, by describing the core values from the NASW Code of Ethics and CSWE Accreditation Standards, this chapter has introduced you to some of the primary ideals to which the profession aspires.

The processes of clarifying your own values and appreciating the values of others do not end with this chapter. Continue to reflect on your core values, noting how they may be affecting your decisions and reactions when working with clients. Continue also to attend to the values of others, listening with an open mind and an open heart.

Although the NASW Code of Ethics is one of the primary sources on social work values, it is not the only source. Many, if not all, of your social work textbooks will refer to social work values. They may focus on the core values from the NASW Code, or they may promote additional values: for instance, preservation of life, privacy, equality and inequality, and benevolence (Dolgoff, Loewenberg, & Harrington, 2009). In addition, many social workers subscribe to different codes of ethics. They may belong to international, state, or local social work organizations that have their own codes of ethics or laws governing social work practice. They may belong to professional organizations in specific fields of practice, for instance, the Association for Specialists in Group Work, American Association for Marriage and Family Therapy, Clinical Social Work Association, Association for Conflict Resolution, National Organization of Forensic Social Work, School Social Work Association of America, or Association for Addiction Professionals. Social workers may also belong to professional associations for practitioners from particular diversity backgrounds or perspectives, such as the National Association of Black Social Workers, Feminist Therapy Institute, North American Association for Christians in Social Work, Clinical Social Work Association, or Latino Social Workers Association.[8] When social workers are sued for malpractice, however, courts often rely on the standards established the NASW Code, whether or not the worker subscribes to an additional code.[9] Finally, each agency has its own set of values. In many cases, these values are stated explicitly in agency mission statements and policies. In other cases, agency values are implicit in the type of work performed and the manner in which it is carried out.

Because of the introductory nature of this chapter, I do not intend to cover all social work values at this point. Remember that while the values enumerated in the NASW Code are broadly accepted, they are not the only values to consider throughout your professional education and practice.

DISCUSSION QUESTIONS AND EXERCISES

The following questions and exercises are designed to help you reflect on your values, gain greater appreciation for the values of others, and develop a deeper understanding of core social work values.

1. *Appreciating Values*: Refer to the case scenario at the top of this chapter. What values can you infer from Homer's statements? What values does Samantha demonstrate in her responses? Whose values are right?

[8] See Bibliography for website addresses containing the codes of ethics of these organizations. You can find additional professional codes of ethics on the webite of the Center for the Study of Ethics in the Professions at http://ethics.iit.edu/codes/coe.html.

[9] The NASW is recognized as the most authoritative association for social work, given its historical role in the development of social work as a profession, its broad membership, and its well-developed Code of Ethics. If a social worker's state requires that social workers abide by a state-authorized code of ethics, then that code may take precedence over the national code.

Should Samantha help Homer find a good home and a good job? Why or why not?

2. *Comparing Values*: Imagine that you are working with Cloey, who tells you that she exaggerated on her resume in order to get a job. Without exaggerating, she would not have met the minimum requirements that were advertised for the job. She claims she was unemployed for 3 months and was about to be evicted from her apartment. She needed money desperately for food and rent. What does this scenario tell you about how Cloey prioritizes values such as honesty, shelter, security, and survival? How are your value priorities similar to or different from Cloey's?
3. *Contrasting Values*: Assume you have an 18-year-old client, Cecilia, who tells you that she wants to marry Horace, a man she loves dearly. Her parents object to the proposed marriage because Horace comes from a different religious and racial background (e.g., Hindu and Asian). Cecilia says she would feel guilt ridden if she defied her parents' wishes. Describe the values that Cecilia and her parents may be expressing in this situation. How are your values similar to or different from theirs?
4. *Prioritizing Values*: Suppose you are working with Clyde who says that he values *having fun*, but also *taking work seriously*. These values seem to conflict. Is it possible for him to truly value both of these? Why or why not?
5. *Sources of Values*: Ask one of your parents, grandparents, or another elder from your family or community to speak with you about values. Engage him or her in a discussion about what personal values are most important. Also, ask about the sources of these values. Invite your family member to share stories of how he or she has put these values into practice, or to discuss occasions when these values have been challenged. Be prepared to define values in plain language and to help your interviewee identify values in different areas of his or her life. Take notes, so you can report back to the class.
6. *Values—From Words to Meanings*: When people say they value "family," "work," "education," or "democracy," we may think we understand what they are saying because we are familiar with these words. Still, different people could mean different things with the same words. For each of these values, write down your definition of what that value means to you and give examples of how this value is manifest within your family, if it is a value for your family. Compare your definitions and examples with those of another person in your class.
7. *Core Social Work Values*: For each of the following scenarios, identify which core social work values (if any) are reflected by the social worker's actions: *(1)* service, *(2)* social justice, *(3)* dignity and worth of the person, *(4)* importance of human relationships, *(5)* integrity, *(6)* competence, *(7)* human rights, *(8)* scientific inquiry, or *(9)* none of the above. If more than one value could apply, explain how.
   - Cloris asks her social worker if she can see what the worker wrote in her case records. Initially, the worker thought about removing a certain page because some notes on that page were not very flattering. The worker ultimately decided to show her the whole case file because she did not want to deceive the client.
   - Charlie asks his social worker to help him apply for Medicaid so he can access treatments that he could not otherwise afford. The worker personally believes that people should pay for their own medical bills. Still, the worker follows her professional duties and helps Charlie with his request.
   - Shainy wants to know if her work is being effective, so she decides to document her interventions and outcomes in order to evaluate them, incorporating what she has learned in her research class.
   - Sinbad advocates for a change in child welfare policy that would allow for greater involvement of extended family members when there are concerns about child abuse or neglect.

- Squiggy is concerned about discrimination against people with AIDS. He talks to his senator about passing legislation to protect them.
- Shevaun has a client who wants help with her fear of flying. Shevaun does not think she has enough experience and training in this area, so she refers the client to someone who specializes in this area.
- Chad calls his social worker an idiot because he is frustrated by lack of progress. The social worker tells Chad he is being childish and that he should find another worker.
- Sharna works with people with Down syndrome. One of the common complaints she hears is that others call them "tards" and other derogatory names. Sharna develops a media campaign to educate the public on how to treat people with Down syndrome more respectfully.
- Chana tells her social worker that she is a miserable person who has "lied on my taxes, cheated on my husband, and stolen drugs from a local pharmacy." Her worker says that he is not there to judge Chana, but to offer support and help her maximize her own potential.

8. *Alternative Social Work Values*: Select an ethics article or textbook by a key social work ethicist—for instance, Charles Levy, Frederic Reamer, Kimberly Stromm-Gottfried, Norman Linzer, Elaine Congress, Eileen Gambrill, Donald Dickson, or Ralph Dolgoff. What does this author say about the core values of social work, and how are these similar to or different from those identified in the NASW Code of Ethics?
9. *Emotional Reactions*: For each of the following scenarios, describe how you might feel. How might your emotional reactions either help or hinder your ability to assess the client's values and motivations?
   a. A charming client tells you that you have the most beautiful eyes. The client invites you to dinner to thank you for all the help you have provided.
   b. You are running a support group for marines who have returned home after experiencing trauma in a foreign war zone. Several group members suggest that it would have been better to just "nuke the whole country."
   c. You have been helping the Muslim community build a community center. The all-male organizing committee proposes a policy requiring all women who enter the center to wear veils to cover their faces.
   d. You are working with a 10-year-old client who discloses that his father calls him a "little sissy" because he likes to play with dolls.

Chapter 2

Theory, Values, and Ethics—Macro Perspectives

Broadly speaking, *a theory is an explanation of a particular phenomenon.* The word *theory* is derived from the Greek *theoria*, meaning contemplation or reflection. In other words, theories help people think and make sense of things around them (Harrington, 2004). Social work theories refer to explanations that are pertinent to understanding individuals, families, groups, organizations, and communities (Banks, 2006). In this chapter, we focus on the interplay between values, ethics, and macro theories of social work,[1] that is, theories related to larger social systems such as business organizations, professional associations, ethnocultural groups, neighborhoods, religious communities, political systems, and nations. In Chapter 3, we will focus on the interplay between values, ethics, and theories related to micro systems, particularly individuals and families.

This chapter explores the value-laden nature of theories and how social work values and ethics affect the choice of theories used by social workers. This chapter also explores the value base of other helping professions, including medicine, psychology, law, psychiatry, and nursing.

ASSESSING THEORIES FROM A VALUES PERSPECTIVE

Standard 1.04 of the NASW Code of Ethics requires social workers to practice within their areas of competence. Social workers acquire competence through a combination of classroom education, on-the-job training, supervision, and practice experience. One of the core elements of social work education is teaching students how to apply theory to practice. In fact, the ability to apply

[1] This chapter explores values and ethics as they relate to *theories* used to understand macro systems, including neighborhoods, communities, and nations. For exploration of values and ethics in relation to macro *practice* issues, see Chapters 9 and 10.

specific theories to practice is one of the key ways that professional social work differs from lay help (i.e., the help of families, friends, peers, and others without professional education). For students entering social work, the vast range of theories to choose from may seem overwhelming (Roberts, 2009). So how should social workers assess theories and determine which ones to apply?

Ideally, social workers should utilize theories based on logic and sound evidence, that is, information and knowledge that has been substantiated through scientifically accepted methods of research (Gibbs, 2003). In the social sciences, the complexity of the human condition is so great that it is difficult, if not impossible, to prove any theory with 100% certainty. In other words, most social theories are hypotheses or propositions that require further testing and research to determine their accuracy (Rubin & Babbie, 2008). A feminist theoretical perspective, for instance, strives to describe and explain the inequality that exists between men and women. Research to support the feminist theoretical perspective includes studies of income disparities, power disparities, and political disparities. Ongoing research is necessary to explore whether these types of disparities are improving or getting worse, and what factors may be contributing to the maintenance or amelioration of these disparities. Whether social workers decide to incorporate the feminist theoretical perspective in practice, however, depends not only on the veracity of the research evidence to support it but also on the values and ethics that underlie feminist theoretical perspectives. Feminists value social and economic justice, caring, understanding people from their own perspectives, caring for others, diversity, and plurality (Van Den Bergh, 1995). Although these values are consistent with social work values, nonfeminist social workers may hold a different system of priorities and therefore choose different theoretical perspectives to guide their practice.

Learning new theories does not mean you must accept them. Regardless of whether a particular theory fits with your value system, it may be worth learning. If you maintain an open mind, you may learn that the theory has some value. Alternatively, the more you learn about the theory, the better prepared you will be to describe what is problematic about the theory, including concerns about its moral and ethical underpinnings.

LEARNING OBJECTIVES

Upon successful completion of this chapter, students will be able to

- Assess the underlying values of theories that purport to explain the nature of organizations, neighborhoods, communities, societies, and other macro systems.
- Critique theories according to how well they fit or conflict with social work values.
- Compare and contrast the values of different helping professions, including how value differences may affect their theoretical perspectives.

Consider Marxist theory (Marx & Engels, 1848). Say "Marxist" aloud. When you hear yourself say this word, what thoughts and feelings does it arouse? For many Americans, the term *Marxism* is equated with the totalitarian regime of the former Soviet Union.[2] Thus, it elicits images of repression, government confiscation and control, conformity, and failed society. For Americans raised to value democracy, capitalism, and constitutional freedoms (such as freedom of speech, religion, and the press), the term *Marxism* may arouse feelings of repulsion, anger, contempt, or derision (e.g., the motto, "Better dead than red."). Given the images and feelings that Marxism evokes, why should social workers study Marxism and seriously consider how it might be relevant for practice in today's world? The answer lies in the values that underlie Marxism.[3]

In order to analyze the values upon which a theory is built, consider three questions:

1. What does the theory say about the nature of people?[4]

---

[2] Note, in the 2008 presidential election, how negative campaign advertisements against Barack Obama tried to paint him as a communist, alleging he was going to use the tax system to redistribute wealth.

[3] Marxism is related to other theories you may study, including conflict theory and structural theory.

[4] "People" may refer to individuals, families, groups, organizations, or communities.

2. What does the theory say about how people change?
3. What is the theory's preferred view of how people should be? (Levy, 1993; Lum, 2004)

In terms of the nature of people, Marxism suggests that all people have individual needs, capacities, pleasures, and productive forces. Marxism critiques capitalism for creating and maintaining gross inequalities between the owners of capital and the proletariat (i.e., the masses who provide labor but receive inadequate compensation and are unable to accumulate wealth). Marxism posits that the best way to create change is through revolution, raising the consciousness of the proletariat so they will demand change and overthrow the system of capitalism. The preferred view of people under a Marxist system is one of equality, in which each person receives an equal share of society's wealth and production, regardless of his or her job or other social status (Marx & Engels, 1848). Marxism replaces capitalistic competition with cooperation—one family of humanity in which everyone supports one another so that all people can reach their potentials (Dowd, 2002). Although this paragraph just begins to explain the essence of Marxist theory, it demonstrates three primary values of this theory: equality, collaboration, and maximizing human potential. One could question whether Marxism has ever fulfilled these values, or could fulfill them. In theory, however, Marxism does support certain values that are consonant with social work (Banks, 2006).

Once again, this analysis is not intended to suggest that you must adopt Marxist theory in your approach to social work; however, it might encourage you to reflect on your own biases and responses when you are studying different theories, and to analyze each theory according to its underlying values. This section has provided a framework for assessing which values form the basis of a particular theory. The following sections define social work values and demonstrate how to compare and contrast the values of a theory with core social work values.

DEFINING VALUES FOR THE PURPOSES OF CRITIQUE

Before we can critique theories in relation to social work values, we must define what we mean by social work values. Different social work practitioners, theorists, agencies, and associations may define them differently. The NASW Code of Ethics identifies the six core values of social work as *(1)* service, *(2)* social justice, *(3)* dignity and worth of the person, *(4)* importance of human relationships, *(5)* integrity, and *(6)* competence. The most relevant of these values for critiquing theories are social justice, dignity and worth of the person, and importance of human relationships, because these values relate to how social workers view people, change processes, and desired outcomes.[5] Additional social work values that can be used to critique theories are empowerment, strengths, beneficence, nonmaleficence, equality, and autonomy.[6] The NASW Code subsumes these principles under the values of social justice and dignity and worth of the person. For the purpose of critiquing theories, we will refer to both the NASW values and these additional principles.

For detailed explanations of social justice, dignity and worth of the person, and the importance of human relationships, refer to the definitions of these values in the introduction to Part I. Now, let us consider the definitions of the additional social work values: empowerment, strengths, beneficence, nonmaleficence, equality, and harmony.

---

[5] As the introduction to Part I indicates, service refers to the importance of helping others, integrity refers to the importance of acting honestly and reliably, and competence refers to acting within one's area of education, experience, and capability. Accordingly, these values are not directly relevant to critiquing social work theories.

[6] Some ethics literature refers to beneficence, nonmaleficence, and equality (or fairness) as principles rather than values. Some social work literature refers to strengths as a perspective rather than a value. Given the definitions used in this textook, these terms may be considered values.

Empowerment refers to enabling people to have greater control over their lives. Rather than telling clients what to do or doing things for clients, social workers prefer to facilitate conditions so clients can make their own choices and do things for themselves (Pinderhughes, 1983; Solomon, 1976). Consider Wilma, a woman who says her husband is abusive. She says he loves her and takes care of her, so she does not want to leave him. Telling Wilma to leave her husband or physically removing her from the home would be disempowering. A social worker could empower Wilma through a variety of techniques: using counseling to build her self-esteem and confidence, so she sees herself as someone who is capable of living on her own; exploring choices with Wilma that she may not have previously considered; helping her access resources so that she could live on her own; and educating her about legal processes that may be used to protect her from her husband. The social worker offers Wilma a range of helping possibilities but allows Wilma to make her own choices.

Valuing strengths refers to emphasizing the positive characteristics and capacities of the people and social systems we serve. Whereas some helping professions focus on problems, disease, mental illness, dysfunctions, and criminal wrongdoing, social workers focus on opportunities, health, mental health, positive social functioning, and the moral behaviors of clients.[7] Examples of an individual's strengths include creativity, flexibility, motivation, intelligence, spirituality, physical resources, and access to support systems, such as family and cultural community. Examples of a social system's strengths include its financial resources, sound structure, adaptability, leadership, clear avenues of communication, and positive relationships with other systems. Social workers help clients build on such strengths to overcome challenges and maximize their potentials (Dewees, 2005; Rapp & Goscha, 2006; Saleeby, 2009).

Beneficence refers to advancing good for others (Corey et al., 2007). Beneficence includes preventing evil or harm, and removing evil or harm (Beauchamp & Childress, 2009). For social workers, advancing good may be formulated as promoting biological and mental health, social functioning, social justice, and spiritual well-being. Social workers advance good by offering clients moral support, advocacy, education, access to resources, and a range of other services. Given that social work defines itself as an altruistic helping profession, the fact that social work values doing good seems obvious. The challenge of beneficence is how to define *good*. When determining good outcomes for clients, social workers must take the clients' personal and cultural perspectives into account. Assume Charmaine's parents are planning an arranged marriage for her. In your personal view, you may object to arranged marriages because you believe a person has a right to choose her own spouse. If you were Charmaine's social worker, would you encourage the family to allow Charmaine to choose whom she wants to marry? This may or may not be promoting good, depending on whose perspective one is taking. Charmaine may want her parents to arrange her marriage.

Nonmaleficence refers to the preference for doing no harm (Beauchamp & Childress, 2009). Nonmaleficence is related to beneficence, but speaks more specifically to avoiding behaviors that are known to cause harm. One of the primary challenges with nonmaleficence is that virtually any action carries some risk of doing harm. Consider a social worker who helps an elderly client obtain hot meals from Meals on Wheels (n.d.). What could be bad? Yes, the client will receive hot meals and a social visit from the Meals on Wheels volunteer. Consider, however, the risk that family, friends, or neighbors might visit and offer meals less often, assuming that Meals on Wheels is taking care of the person. Accordingly, when social workers make decisions on how to act with clients, they must consider both the risks (nonmaleficence) and the benefits (beneficence) of their various options.

[7] A social worker should not impose values, religious beliefs, or morals on clients. However, a social worker may help clients build on the strengths of their own morals (e.g., if a client discloses strong convictions about work or family, the worker may validate this as a strength).

Equality refers to the notion that all people should be afforded the same rights and opportunities, regardless of personal characteristics such as race, ethnicity, culture, gender, sexual orientation, gender identity, religion, disability, or socioeconomic status (Banks, 2006).[8] Equality is related to respect for the dignity and worth of all people, as well as social justice. Social work strives to rectify discrimination and inequities within society. Given social work's historic mandate to serve people from vulnerable backgrounds, promoting equality is a particularly important aspect of their work.

Autonomy refers to freedom from undue influence from the state or others. Autonomy is related to respect for the dignity and worth of the person, including the person's capacity to make voluntary choices. Sometimes, social workers may feel that clients are not making choices that are in their own best interests. The value of autonomy suggests that people should be able to make their own decisions, even if social workers or other professionals believe they are making poor choices (Guterman, 2006).

CRITIQUING THEORIES IN RELATION TO SOCIAL WORK VALUES

The previous sections demonstrate the first two steps required for critiquing a theory in relation to social work values: *(1)* identifying the values that underlie the chosen theory, and *(2)* identifying which social work values you are going to use in order to critique the theory. This section illustrates the third step, comparing the values underlying the theory with the identified values of social work. A critique answers the questions, "In what ways does the theory fit with and promote social work values?" and "In what ways does the theory conflict with and detract from social work values?"

In order to demonstrate how to critique theories, consider the criminal justice system. The typical American criminal justice system comprises police, judges, lawyers, probation officers, parole officers, prison staff, court and prison counselors, forensic social workers,[9] and so on. Two theoretical perspectives that can be used to inform and guide the criminal justice system are retributive justice and restorative justice (Hadley, 2001; Restorative Justice Online, n.d.; Umbreit, Coates, & Voss, 2005).[10] The following sections analyze these theories according to the social work values previously identified.

Retributive Justice

The basic premise of retributive justice is that people who commit wrongful acts must be punished. The roots of retributive justice lie in religious ideas such as people must atone for their sins, atonement requires suffering, and only an eye can compensate for an eye, or a tooth for a tooth. A retributive criminal justice system defines specific types of wrongful acts as crimes or violations against the state. The state establishes punishments intended to mete out justice for criminals. When someone has been accused of a crime, a court led by an independent judge hears evidence from the state prosecutors and from the accused. The court determines whether the accused has committed the alleged crimes and assigns blame accordingly. If the court finds the accused guilty, the judge determines an appropriate sentence, imposing pain or restricting freedom through orders of imprisonment, fines, corporal punishment, or capital punishment (Hadley, 2001).[11] As part of their punishment, convicts may also lose civil liberties, such as the right to vote, the right to privacy, and the freedom to associate with others of their choosing.

---

[8] See Chapter 10 for a more detailed description of equality and a related term, *egalitarianism*.

[9] "Forensic" refers to professional roles within a legal system, particularly with regard to gathering evidence. Forensic social workers may be used to assess people charged with crimes and provide evidence during a courtroom trial (Barsky & Gould, 2002).

[10] Other theories of criminal justice include restitution, rehabilitation, and utilitarian deterrence (Hadley, 2001).

[11] U.S. law does not permit corporal punishment, such as lashing. Also, some states prohibit capital punishment (e.g., death by lethal injection or electric chair).

When assessing retributive justice from a values perspective, the most obvious question is whether retributive justice fosters the social work value of social justice. Although many people believe that wrongful acts need to be punished, this concept of justice does not necessarily equate to social justice. Social justice requires treating people fairly, taking their social context and personal situation into account. Lady Justice, the personification of a retributive justice system, however, is a blindfolded woman who carries the scales of justice in one hand and a sword in the other. The blindfold suggests that a person's guilt or innocence should be judged blindly, without taking the person's status, sociocultural background, or other personal factors into account. The symbolic blindfold is intended to prevent courts from discriminating for or against the accused based on race, religion, ethnicity, or other diversity factors. In other words, courts are supposed to treat everyone equally. From a social justice perspective, however, this could mean ignoring important situational circumstances about the accused. When determining guilt or innocence, for instance, a court cannot consider whether the accused came from a troubled background. Likewise, the court cannot consider whether the alleged criminal acts were deemed moral by the accused's cultural or religious background. One only has to look at the disproportionate numbers of people from vulnerable minority groups who fill prisons or are destined for capital punishment (Siegel, 2010) to see that retributive justice has perpetuated social injustices rather than ameliorated them.

To assess whether retributive justice fosters good (beneficence) and avoids doing harm (maleficence), consider the impacts of punishment. Ideally, one of the core benefits of retributive justice is deterrence: When people know that they will be punished for committing crimes, they may be more likely to obey the law; when people are punished for committing crimes, they may be less likely to recommit these crimes. Society benefits by having order and by keeping people from causing harm to one another. Unfortunately, the deterrence effect of retribution is not universal. In addition, punishment—by definition—is causing harm; it restricts freedoms and imposes pain (financial, economic, emotional, social, and possibly physical). One could argue that imposition of pain is justifiable for the greater good, but social workers must also take their ethical duty to protect the most vulnerable people into account. This raises the question, "Do social workers owe a greater allegiance to victims or perpetrators of crime?" Perhaps it depends on the situation, for both groups may come from vulnerable backgrounds that could include discrimination, poverty, unemployment, or other social stresses. A complete analysis of the positive and negative effects of retributive justice goes beyond the scope of this analysis.[12] At the very least, retributive justice raises questions about whose good it supports, and at whose expense.

In terms of respect for all people, retributive justice divides people into those who are innocent and those who are guilty. Retributive justice imposes negative labels, such as criminal, juvenile delinquent, or felon. The stigma of being a felon or ex-convict stays with people throughout their lives, limiting their opportunities for jobs, loans, home ownership, and even friendships. Rather than focus on people's strengths, retributive justice focuses on their faults or moral failings. Rather than empowering people to take more control over their lives, retributive justice restricts freedoms and opportunities through state-imposed punishments.

Retributive justice does foster respect in terms of legal rights. It presumes people are innocent until proven guilty. It also offers the accused the rights to legal representation and a fair trial (at least in theory). Retributive justice limits the types of punishments that can be imposed, ensuring that the punishments are commensurate with the crimes committed.

[12] Incarceration, for instance, protects society while the criminals are in prison. Incarceration often fails to protect once ex-convicts are released, because they emerge from prison more alienated from society, more psychologically debilitated, and better educated about how to break the law without being caught (Hadley, 2001).

Arguably, retributive justice respects the rights of victims and their families, many of whom express a desire for the perpetrator of the crime to be punished.

Retributive justice views people as individuals who have free will, including the choice to do good or evil. If they commit evil acts, they should be held accountable. By focusing on the guilt or innocence of the individual, retributive justice ignores the value of social relationships. By valuing social relationships, social workers focus on the relationship between people and systems in their social environment. When a wrongful act has been committed, it has been committed within a social context. Accordingly, if blame is to be assigned, it should take social context into account. When a youth steals a car, for instance, is the youth solely to blame? Should the acts or omissions of the youth's parents, teachers, or peers, or broader community be considered? Even if the youth should be held to account, should the state be responsible for imposing punishment, or is there an important role for the parents, teachers, peers, victim, or others to play?

As this analysis indicates, retributive justice has many limitations in relation to its ability to foster social work values. The following section explores another theory, restorative justice, which offers a better fit with social work values.

Restorative Justice

Restorative justice views criminal acts as conflicts that arise within a community context and as such, they require community responses. Whereas retribution responds to criminal behavior by imposing punishment, *the focus of restorative justice is to restore or put people back into a position similar to the one they would have been in if the criminal act had not occurred* (Gumz, 2004). Although restorative justice encourages people who have harmed others to take responsibility for their actions, restorative justice also engages victims and the greater community in processes to rectify the harm done (Zehr & Toews, 2004). Restorative justice may be pursued through a range of interventions, including victim-offender mediation, family group conferencing, Native American healing circles, and faith-based healing processes (Barsky, 2007a).

In contrast to retributive processes (especially court hearings that determine blame and punishment), each of these restorative processes brings people together to engage in dialogue and work out their own solutions. In mediation, for instance, an impartial third party brings the victim and offender together to discuss what has happened and to determine how to respond. The outcomes of mediation may include apologies, agreements to compensate the victim, and creative plans on how to repair the parties' relationship and situation. Restorative justice helps build community by bringing people together for discussion and problem solving. Restorative justice may also include spiritual components, including rituals, prayers, enlightenment, and forgiveness (Lederach, 2005).

The values fostered by restorative justice generally fit well with social work values (Van Wormer, 2004). In terms of social justice and human relationships, for instance, restorative justice takes social context into account. Rather than focusing on an individual who commits murder, theft, rape, or any other crime, restorative justice understands that parents, peers, schools, media, and other social influences may have contributed to the commission of the crime and may be needed in order to restore people to their situations prior to commission of the crime. Rather than having an impartial judge determine an appropriate solution, restorative processes involve the victim, family members, and/or the entire community in deciding what justice requires. Restorative justice may include punishment in order to hold people accountable for their actions, but it allows for more creative responses, too. If poverty, unemployment, discrimination, inadequate education, homelessness, or other social injustices created conditions that led to the crime, then the response could include solutions aimed at remedying these social problems (e.g., providing job skills training to allow the offender to find a job or providing diversity education to counter racism in the community).

Restorative justice empowers victims, offenders, and communities by providing them with a constructive forum for dealing with crime and conflict. Whereas retributive processes take decision making away from victims, offenders, and communities (giving it to judges), restorative processes engage them in dialogue and make them responsible for deciding how to respond. Restorative justice also supports autonomy, reducing the need to take away people's rights and giving them more say in how they want to accept responsibility for their actions. Restorative justice also fits with the strengths perspective, trusting people—including perpetrators of crime—to have the knowledge, skills, and morals to engage in constructive dialogue and develop creative solutions (Van Wormer, 2004).

Although restorative justice builds on the strengths of the people involved in the conflict, some processes use language that perpetuates the use of stigmatizing labels. The term *victim-offender mediation*, for instance, separates people into categories and uses the term *offender*, as if the entire person's being is wrapped up in this identity. Some restorative justice processes avoid labeling people, simply referring to participants by their names. This approach fits better with the value of respect for individuals.

Another area where restorative justice has been criticized concerns its ability to safeguard the perpetrator's individual rights. Restorative justice does not guarantee a right to a lawyer, a right to a fair trial, or a right against self-incrimination, as would a traditional criminal court process. Arguably, these limitations go against the value of respecting the dignity and worth of all people. Restorative justice processes depend on the ability of whoever is facilitating the process (e.g., a mediator or an elder) to ensure that people are treated with dignity and respect. Rather than using legal rights, however, facilitators make use of ground rules and other structures for promoting respectful and constructive dialogue.

Insofar as supporting beneficence, restorative processes do good by helping people restore relationships, damaged property, or other casualties of crime. Whereas traditional forms of punishment do not help the victim or community recover from injuries, restorative justice is specifically designed to help. Methods of accountability may include punishment, but these can be individualized to maximize the good for the offender, victim, and community. If a person who vandalizes property agrees to repair the property, the person pays her debt in a manner that contributes to the victim and society. If we put the person in prison, the costs to society increase and the victim does not receive compensation. Some people question whether restorative justice actually causes harm (maleficence) because the punishments are not as strong as those under a retributive justice system. Research has shown, however, that restorative justice can lead to lower rates of recidivism or repeat offenses (Umbreit et al., 2005). People who meet those victimized by their crimes develop empathy for them. Also, solutions from restorative justice can deal with some of the underlying social issues that contributed to the original commission of the crime. Finally, the consequences developed under restorative justice processes can have strong deterrence components. Circle sentencing, for instance, has resulted in consequences such as long-term incarceration and even excommunication (banishment from the community).

Overall, restorative justice fits well with social work values. In part, the fit with social work values depends on which particular restorative processes are used and how they are implemented. Processes that do not use negative labels, for instance, foster greater respect for the individual. Processes that encourage family and community involvement foster greater support for human relationships. And processes that include protections for both individual rights and communal rights foster greater support for social justice.

This section illustrates how you can analyze theories according to how well they fit with social work values. As you study different theories, remember to consider what they say about the nature of people, how people change, and the desired objectives for such change processes. Then consider how well these perspectives fit with values such as social justice, dignity and worth of all people, human relationships, strengths, empowerment, and beneficence. This process will help you determine which theories to use to guide your practice, ensuring that how you assess and intervene with clients fits with the core values of social work.

Now that you have a better sense of the relationship between theory and social work values, we turn to other professions and the values they use to guide their practice.

VALUES OF OTHER HELPING PROFESSIONS

Social work views itself as a helping profession, but it is certainly not the only helping profession. Other helping professions include medicine, psychology, nursing, psychiatry,[13] law, and marriage and family therapy. Each profession comprises a macro system, which has its own theories, values, and code of ethics. Each profession also interacts closely with social work in a variety of contexts of practice. In order to work collaboratively and effectively with these professions, social workers need to understand how their values compare and contrast.

Social work textbooks and courses sometimes describe social work values as unique and even superior to those of other professions. Having pride in social work values helps social workers commit to their ideals and solidifies their professional identities. Still, social workers must be careful not to be chauvinistic about their professional values (e.g., "Our values are better than yours."). Other professionals may have similar values. Even when their values differ, their values may also be constructive, just different. The following sections describe the core values of medicine and psychology, demonstrating their similarities to and differences from social work values. In the assignments at the end of this chapter, you are invited to conduct similar comparisons between social work and psychiatry, nursing, law, and marriage and family therapy.

Medicine

Codification of medical ethics dates back to the fifth century B.C. in the Oath of Hippocrates (Beauchamp & Childress, 2009; Guterman, 2006). Two of the most important portions of this oath are the obligations to advance good and to avoid causing harm (Steinbock, Arras, & London, 2003). Social work draws its values of benevolence and nonmaleficence from the same sources, so it is not surprising that medicine and social work share these values.

Although both medicine and social work value doing good and not causing harm, they differ in how they define "good" and "harm." Traditionally, medicine focused primarily on physical health. From its beginnings, social work has held a broader view, promoting not just physical health but also psychological, social, and spiritual health. Thus, when social workers and physicians discuss how to proceed with a particular client, both can easily agree that they want to do what is best for the client. The challenge may be agreeing on which aspects of the client's life and well-being to focus upon. Value differences may also lead each profession to utilize different theoretical perspectives. Consider a client who is addicted to alcohol. A physician might focus on physiological theories of alcoholism whereas a social worker might focus on sociocultural theories. In some respects, medicine and social work are becoming more similar in values, as more and more medical practitioners recognize the linkages between physical, psychological, social, and spiritual health.

In part, the values of physicians depend upon their areas of specialization. A surgeon, for instance, is more likely to focus on physical well-being, whereas a psychiatrist is more likely to focus on psychological well-being. A family physician is similar to a generalist social worker in that both types of professionals need to take all aspects of the patient or client's life into account. Although medical research suggests a close link between physical health, mental health, social stress, and spiritual meaning, many physicians may still emphasize physical health as their primary value.

The Code of Ethics of the American Medical Association (2001) offers nine principles to guide medical practice:

- A physician shall be dedicated to providing competent medical care, with compassion and respect for human dignity and rights.
- A physician shall uphold the standards of professionalism, be honest in all professional interactions, and strive to report physicians deficient in character or competence, or

[13] A branch of medicine.

engaging in fraud or deception, to appropriate entities.

- A physician shall respect the law and also recognize a responsibility to seek changes in those requirements which are contrary to the best interests of the patient.
- A physician shall respect the rights of patients, colleagues, and other health professionals, and shall safeguard patient confidences and privacy within the constraints of the law.
- A physician shall continue to study, apply, and advance scientific knowledge, maintain a commitment to medical education, make relevant information available to patients, colleagues, and the public, obtain consultation, and use the talents of other health professionals when indicated.
- A physician shall, in the provision of appropriate patient care, except in emergencies, be free to choose whom to serve, with whom to associate, and the environment in which to provide medical care.
- A physician shall recognize a responsibility to participate in activities contributing to the improvement of the community and the betterment of public health.
- A physician shall, while caring for a patient, regard responsibility to the patient as paramount.
- A physician shall support access to medical care for all people.

This list illustrates the considerable overlap between the values of medicine and social work, including competence, compassion, integrity, respect for individual rights, privacy, and service. In terms of competence, both professions value specialized knowledge, clinical skills, and the ability to apply theory and research to practice. Medicine is ahead of social work in terms of using science to guide competent and effective practice. Various medical interventions—particularly surgery, diets, and pharmaceuticals—go through stringent testing and research before being approved for general use with patients. Until recently, social workers could experiment with new psychotherapies and psychosocial interventions with relatively little oversight as to their effectiveness and risks. Some social agencies simply assumed that well-meaning social workers could not cause much harm, and others assumed that given the complexities of the human condition, they could not really prove what type of intervention works best and with whom. Consider a medical problem such as appendicitis versus a social problem such as marital discord. To determine whether to use surgery, medication, or some other treatment for appendicitis, physicians must consult a vast system of evidence, ranging from clinical reference texts to case reports to control studies to evidence guidelines to meta-analyses of research. Although social workers should consult similar sources to determine what is effective for marital discord, how many social workers actually do? Evidence-based practice only started to take root in social work in the 1990s (Gibbs, 2003), with associations such as the Society for Social Work and Research (n.d.) promoting more strategic use of research evidence to guide practice.

Although social workers may argue that respect for the dignity and worth of the person is one of the defining values of social work, physicians also purport to value the dignity and worth of their patients. Both professions respect dignity and worth by offering confidentiality, informed consent, and access to services for their clients and patients. Confidentiality is essentially the same principle in medicine as in social work: professionals keep information private in order to provide people with a safe place to discuss potentially embarrassing issues. Informed consent, however, is somewhat different. Physicians view themselves as experts, whereas social workers view themselves as facilitators. Physicians use their expert knowledge to diagnose illnesses and to recommend treatments. Physicians are supposed to explain treatment options, including the benefits and risks of each so that patients can exercise informed consent. In practice, physicians often recommend one course of action with little discussion of other options, and patients often rely on their physicians' advice without fully understanding the nature of treatment, its benefits, and its risks (Agard, 2005). In contrast, social work training and ethics place greater emphasis on the importance of working collaboratively throughout the assessment process, helping clients identify problems and goals for change, and working toward a joint contract on how to proceed (Kirst-Ashman & Hull, 2007). Although some social workers do not fully explain their interventions and some clients are not fully informed about their choices, social work education teaches practitioners to encourage clients to make their own decisions rather than rely on the expertise of the social worker. The fact that physicians diagnose and recommend treatments based on their medical expertise does not make them ethically superior or inferior to social workers, just different. Depending on the context, some clients and patients may prefer to rely on a professional's expertise. For instance, if a patient is undergoing cardiac arrest, the patient will probably want the physician to provide a quick medical diagnosis and recommendation rather than engage the patient in an open-ended and time-consuming discussion of treatment options that requires a highly sophisticated understanding of medical research.

Perhaps the greatest difference between the values of social workers and physicians is reflected in their commitments to changing broader society. Physicians undertake a duty "to contribute to the improvement of the community and the betterment of public health" (American Medical Association, 2001, Statement of Principles). In contrast, social workers undertake a duty "to challenge social injustice" (National Association of Social Workers, 1999, Ethical Principles). In other words, both professions have a duty that extends beyond serving specific individuals and families, but the nature of this duty has a different focus. Physicians promote improvements to public health by promoting better use of health-care resources, prevention programs, good nutrition, exercise, medical research, and improved medical procedures (surgery, medication, and other treatments). Social workers promote social justice through advocacy, raising public consciousness of social issues, linking disadvantaged populations with better resources, and organizing communities to advocate on their own behalf. Both social workers and physicians could agree that access to health care is an important priority, and they could jointly advocate for more equitable access to health-care resources. Still, they may differ on how to prioritize their professional commitments to the other types of social change. Once again, this does not make medicine's values better or worse than social work values, just different.

Psychology

The "Ethical Principles of Psychologists and Code of Conduct" of the American Psychological Association (2002) identifies five principles to guide the practice of psychologies: beneficence and nonmaleficence, fidelity and responsibility, integrity, justice, and respect for people's rights and dignity. As with medicine's values, the first impression from this list of principles suggests that psychology's values are very similar to social work's. Both psychology and social work strive to do good for their clients, and at the very least, to cause no harm. Both professions recognize the obligations to be honest and to treat people with respect. Among the more apparent differences in how their values are stated, psychology speaks of an obligation to promote justice, whereas social work speaks of an obligation to promote social justice. Also, psychology speaks of fidelity and responsibility, whereas social work speaks of service and the importance of human relationships. So, to what extent do these similarities and differences in wording relate to actual similarities and differences in the orientations of these two professions to practice? The following analysis explores these similarities and differences in further detail.

Even though social workers and psychologists value beneficence and nonmaleficence, they differ in how they define doing good and causing harm for their clients. One difference relates to the type of work done by each profession. The majority of social workers are involved in direct practice, offering services to individuals, families, groups, organizations, and communities. Many social workers are also involved in administrative and social policy positions. Psychologists tend to be involved in clinical practice or research, but not organizational, administrative, or policy work. Although many social workers perform research and value the generation of knowledge through research, research careers are much more common for psychologists.

In terms of promoting good, clinical psychologists use assessment and intervention methods similar to those used by clinical social workers. Often, psychologists have specialized training on administering and interpreting psychological tests as part of their assessment processes. Although some social workers receive credentials to perform psychological testing, this is less frequent than among psychologists. Whereas social workers favor a generalist approach to practice (including work with micro, mezzo, and macro systems), psychologists tend to focus on micro systems. Psychologists use specialized therapies that help individual clients with problems related to emotions, cognitions, perceptions, memory, and other intrapsychic processes. Although social workers value human relationships and the person-in-environment perspective, these perspectives are not unique to social work (Corey et al., 2007). There are entire branches of psychology—including social psychology and environmental psychology—that emphasize the social context of clients (DeLamater & Myers, 2007).

Psychology's notion of "justice" differs significantly from social work's notion of "social justice." The APA's (2002) ethical code defines justice in terms of fair and equitable "access to and benefit from the contributions of psychology" (Principle D). It specifically prohibits discriminating against clients or violating their human rights. However, the current code of ethics does not specifically require psychologists to promote social justice or societal changes. In fact, the 2002 revision of the code removed "social responsibility," which was included in the 1992 version. Unlike social workers, psychologists do not typically receive education or training in advocacy or political processes. Many psychologists have recognized the limitations of treating individuals while ignoring the adverse societal conditions that cause these ills (Pettifor, 2004). Still, the profession as a whole has not assumed a professional obligation to promote changes at a community or societal level. In contrast, the principles of the NASW code expressly state that social workers have "a dual responsibility to clients and to the broader society." Social work students receive extensive education regarding community-based issues and interventions, and learn that promoting social justice is a central part of their mandate.

The American Psychological Association code of ethics includes two values that are not specifically mentioned in the NASW's statement of principles: fidelity and responsibility. Fidelity refers to the special relationship of trust that psychologists have with their clients. Because clients may be vulnerable to exploitation, psychologists recognize that they must hold themselves to high standards of loyalty, trust, and integrity. Responsibility refers to the professional obligation that psychologists have toward clients. These responsibilities include making services accessible to clients, upholding professional standards of conduct, explaining their roles to clients, and being accountable for their interventions with clients. Although the NASW statement of principles does not expressly mention fidelity and responsibility, these values seem to overlap with the NASW's value of service. Both psychologists and social workers view serving the interests of their clients as paramount, and both professions accept similar obligations to ensure that client interests are served (e.g., protections against exploitation, requirements to provide some free or low-cost services, and standards to ensure that the professionals act only within their areas of competence).

Professional Values and Choice of Theories

Most of the theories used by social work are not unique to social work. Social workers draw theories and knowledge from medicine, psychology, law, and many other disciplines. Still, there are differences in the way that social workers and these other professions choose and utilize theories. Given social work's values for human relations, for instance, social work cautions against too much emphasis on intrapsychic theories (e.g., cognitive, behavioral, and psychoanalytic). Rather, social work encourages a holistic perspective that takes physical, psychological, social, and spiritual perspectives into account. Given social work's value for the dignity and worth of people, social work cautions against theories that give too much emphasis on illness, pathology, dysfunction, or other negative attributes. Social work focuses on strengths and how to use strengths to overcome challenges (Saleebey, 2009).

When working with professionals with other value orientations, social workers must be careful to show respect, even when their values and preferred ways of helping clients conflict. Social workers may be able to use similarities in each profession's code of ethics to build bridges and come up with amicable solutions for how to serve clients. Consider, for instance, a multiprofessional team that is conducting a case conference to determine how to help a client who has recently attempted suicide. A psychiatrist might focus on the client's depression and offer antidepressant medications as the primary intervention. A psychoanalyst might focus on the client's subconscious processes and offer psychotherapy as the primary intervention. A social worker might focus on stresses in the client's environment (e.g., with work, family, and peers) and offer advocacy as the primary intervention. Although each professional's values lead the three to focus on different dimensions of the client, they can find common ground in their values. Each profession values beneficence and nonmaleficence. Doing good and avoiding harm requires the professionals to work together. By starting with these values, the professionals can begin to sort out an intervention plan that is truly in the client's best interests.

As this chapter illustrates, the theories that inform social work and related professions each have their own set of values. By looking at how each theory views the nature of people, how people change, and preferred outcomes for people, we can identify the values that underlie each theory. When social workers and others are trying to sort through their difference on how to work with clients, they need to consider both their commonalties and differences. Although there are important differences in the values and theories of different professions, there are also many similarities. Social work can act as a bridge between other professions, given its value for human relationships. Remember, human relationships include not only the relationships that clients have with others but also relationships that social workers have with others, including clients and other professionals.

DISCUSSION QUESTIONS AND EXERCISES

The following questions and exercises are designed to help you critique macro theories from a values perspective, and compare social work values with those of other professions.

1. *Assessing Values Underlying Theories*: The following paragraph describes a fictional theory of organizational behavior. Your tasks are *(a)* to identify the values represented by this theory and *(b)* to compare and contrast these values to social work values.

   The Moronian Theory of Organizational Behavior is based on the premise that employees are none too bright. In order to foster productive behavior, Moronian supervisors keep employees in the dark, providing them with as little information as possible. Any excess information just confuses employees and impedes their ability to perform menial tasks. In order to protect dim employees from stress, Moronian supervisors do not discuss any problems that the organization is experiencing. They simply provide the most basic information required in order for each employee to perform his or her task and play happy music to keep up morale.

2. *Critiquing Macro Theories*: Select a type of macro system, such as business organizations, cultural groups, religious institutions, health care, social assistance, or government. Identify a theory that explains the nature of your chosen macro system (e.g., bureaucracy theory, social identity theory, patriarchy, chaos theory, subculture theory, political power theory, or another theory from your social work textbooks). Read one or two articles on this theory so you will have a good, basic understanding of the theory. Analyze the values underpinning this theory by providing answers to the following questions:
   a. What thoughts did this theory evoke when you first read it (i.e., what were your first impressions)?
   b. What feelings did you experience when you first started to think about this theory?
   c. What does the theory say about the nature of people?
   d. What does the theory say about how people change?

e. What is the theory's preferred view of how people should be?
f. What values does this theory promote?
g. To what extent do the values promoted by this theory fit with or conflict with the core values of social work: *(i)* service, *(ii)* social justice, *(iii)* dignity and worth of the person, *(iv)* importance of human relationships, *(v)* integrity, and *(vi)* competence?

3. *Comparing Professions*: Earlier in this chapter we compared social work values with the values of medicine and psychology. To help you understand the similarities and differences between social work and other related helping professions, select one of the following professions and critically compare its values with those of social work: law (http://www.abanet.org), nursing (http://www.nursingworld.org/ethics/ecode.htm), psychiatry (http://www.psych.org/MainMenu/PsychiatricPractice/Ethics.aspx), or marriage and family therapy (http://www.aamft.org/index_nm.asp).[14] The following website contains links to codes of ethics for additional professions that you could study: http://ethics.iit.edu/codes/coe.html.

---

[14] The websites contain codes of ethics for the national associations for each of these professions. You may draw the values from these codes of ethics, or use codes of ethics specific to your state or locality. States are responsible for regulating professions, though many states adopt the national standards in order to support national consistency and consensus for the profession

Chapter 3

Theory, Moral Decision Making, and Ethics—Micro Perspectives

In Victor Hugo's book, Les Miserables (1987/orig.1862), protagonist Jean Valjean steals bread and is sentenced to 19 years in prison. Society generally considers theft to be wrong, a crime against the victim and the state. In Valjean's case, he stole the bread to save himself and his family from starvation. Does the threat of starvation justify his theft? We sometimes view moral decision making as a choice, but what choice did Valjean have? Valjean would not have considered stealing except for the urgency of the situation. If you had the opportunity to talk with Valjean before he decided to steal, what would you say in relation to his moral choices? Would you validate his plans to steal because necessity compelled him to steal? Would you encourage him to be more righteous by obeying the laws, regardless of the consequences? Would you explain that society should take some responsibility for the situation that gave rise to the theft, or must Valjean accept full responsibility for his situation and the consequences of his actions? Before we answer these questions, we need to understand the roots of his actions. Moral decision making and behavior are determined by a combination of biological, psychological, social, and spiritual factors. This chapter explores each of these factors, providing a conceptual understanding for how clients, social workers, and other individuals determine what constitutes morally correct behavior.

This chapter focuses on factors affecting *moral* decision making,[1] as opposed to factors that affect *ethical* decision making. To distinguish morals and ethics, remember that morals refer to general or societal conceptions of right and wrong behaviors whereas ethics refer to conceptions of right and wrong behaviors

---

This chapter explores values, morals, and ethics as they relate to *theories* used to understand micro systems, including individuals and families. For exploration of values and ethics in relation to micro *practice* issues, see Chapters 5 and 6.

[1] The terms *moral decision making, moral judgment,* and *moral choice* are used interchangeably in this chapter.

among a particular group with a specific role (e.g., professional social workers, nurses, or probation officers).[2] Moral decision making refers to the processes used by individuals to determine what is the right (or morally just) action to take in a particular situation. By understanding how individuals determine moral behavior, we gain insight into how to engage others in discussions of values, morals, and ethical issues. If I am concerned that a client is about to engage in morally questionable behavior, I can talk to her in a manner that corresponds to her biopsychosocial-spiritual situation. If I disagree with work colleagues about how to fulfill certain ethical requirements in our agency policy, I can assess their views and strategize the best way to influence their moral and ethical decision making. If I am advocating for a client who has been experiencing workplace discrimination, I can speak to the employers in language that fits with their patterns of moral decision making. Although this chapter focuses on moral decision making, it also demonstrates the link between moral decision making and ethical decision making. Understanding this link is vital to learning how to manage conflicts between morals and ethics and ensuring that social workers take proper account of morals when engaging in ethical decision making processes (including those presented later in this textbook).

This chapter takes a biopsychosocial-spiritual approach to understanding moral decision making, looking first at biological factors, then psychological, social, and spiritual ones. Although the following sections provide separate analysis of each of these factors, remember that these factors are interconnected, meaning that moral decision making is affected by a complex interaction of all these factors.

LEARNING OBJECTIVES

Upon successful completion of this chapter, students will be able to

- Identify biological, psychological, social, and spiritual factors that affect an individual's moral decision making, judgment, and behavior.
- Understand the validity of moral choices made by clients and coworkers, even when they do not conform to the students' conception of what is morally or ethically correct.
- Distinguish between influences that may affect their moral decision making and factors that should guide their ethical decision making.

BIOLOGICAL FACTORS

An individual's moral development is affected by psychological, social, and spiritual processes (Krebs & Denton, 2005; Zastrow & Kirst-Ashman, 2007), as described below. In other words, people are not predestined by biology to have specific values, morals, or propensities for deciding whether certain behaviors are right or wrong. Still, biology may have significant influence on the moral choices made by specific individuals (Casebeer, 2003). This section explores how biological needs and capacities may affect an individual's moral decision making. It concludes by considering the relevance of biological needs and capacities to a social worker's process of ethical decision making.

Needs, Capacities, and Moral Decision Making

Natural ethics refers to the natural (or intrinsic) valuing process of the human organism. According to this theory, the basis of moral decisions is determined, in part, because of what people need for proper growth and development (Casebeer, 2003). In terms of biological needs, Maslow's theory of needs posits that individuals have a number of innate physiological needs: sleep, food, water, breathing, homeostasis, physical security, and excretion (Maslow, Frager, & Fadiman, 1987). When a person is deprived of these basic needs, the person experiences

[2] See the introduction to Part I of this textbook for further explanation of the differences between morals and ethics.

anxiety and is motivated to do whatever is necessary to satisfy them. According to this theory, the person subjugates fulfillment of higher needs (e.g., love, self-esteem, and self-actualization) until the biological needs are satisfied. Thus, Valjean may be motivated by hunger (a basic need) when he steals food.[3] Although he would not contemplate stealing if his basic needs were met, his moral decision-making process is affected by his hunger. That is not to say that all people would steal when faced with Valjean's predicament. Biological needs are just one group of factors affecting a person's sense of right and wrong and ability to choose what is right, in a given situation. Consider, for instance, political activists who use hunger strikes to protest social injustices faced by others; the activists are subjugating basic biological needs to pursue a higher value. As the following sections on psychological, social, and spiritual factors will illustrate, many different factors may affect the moral choices made by Valjean, the activists, and others.

While needs theory is essentially a psychological theory, it demonstrates the importance of biology. People experiencing difficulty satisfying their physical needs will have difficulty pursuing high ideals. More generally, a functional approach to understanding the impact of biological factors on moral decision making suggests that one must look at both the biological needs and capacities of people (Casebeer, 2003). In terms of biological capacity, consider the major organ systems contained within the human body, for instance, the respiratory system, the digestive system, the reproductive system, and the urinary system. One reason that we engage in behaviors such as breathing, eating, reproducing, eliminating waste, and so on is because we can. When we lack certain capacities, we may not be able to perform certain functions regardless of their morality and motivation. Consider, for instance, a woman who values having children but is infertile. Given her infertility, she may consider adopting a child rather than giving birth to one. Her moral choices are affected by her biological capacities. Thus, when assessing why people make certain moral choices, we must consider biological abilities in addition to psychological motivations and values.

Consider the debate on whether it is moral for people to eat meat. Some argue that killing animals for food is unnecessary and inhumane, in part because people can survive on a vegetarian diet (Gandhi, 1959). Others argue, from an evolutionary perspective, that people would not have the capacity to eat and digest animal products if they were not meant to eat them (Cordain et al., 2005). Whether a particular person chooses to eat animal products partially depends on that person's biological capacity. If the person is unable to digest animal products, then that person's moral choices will be curtailed by this biological factor. Similarly, the person's moral choices could be affected by a biological need to consume certain animal products to survive.

Biological capacity is also important in terms of how it affects cognition and emotions. Although cognition and emotions are affected by environment and experience, they are also affected by the brain's physiological functioning, for instance, the neural networks of the brain that permit the processing of information. Through the use of brain imaging techniques, neuroethicists can explore how moral reasoning is controlled or affected by neurological processes and development, including aging and experience (Gazzaniga, 2005). Neurological research demonstrates that different parts of brain perform different functions: The ventromedial frontal cortex modulates emotions, the prefrontal cortex controls judgment, the amygdala plays a role in the experience of emotions such as fear, the hippocampus plays a key role in memory, and the hypothalamus manage the expression of emotions (Casebeer, 2003). Consider the following scenario:

> Cosette was recently in a car accident that injured her hippocampus and impaired her short-term memory. One day, her boss asks

[3] In the original facts, Valjean is stealing food to feed his family. For the purposes of this analysis of biological needs, assume that Valjean (as a member of this family) is hungry.

her to lock the office when she leaves. She forgets this request and leaves the office without locking the door. Someone enters the office that night and steals equipment.

Cosette's decision to leave without locking the door is obviously affected by her brain injury. She did not intend to put the office at risk of a theft. If a social worker wanted to help Cosette with future moral decision making, the worker would have to help Cosette develop strategies to deal with her memory issues (e.g., writing down important information).

Although the above example demonstrates how an injury can affect one's biological capacity, biological capacity is also determined by genetics and experience. Intelligence and the rate of a child's cognitive development, for instance, depend not only on the child's experience but also on genetic background (Forte, 2007). Moral decision making may also be influenced by biologically determined mental illnesses, for instance, certain forms of schizophrenia, depression, and addiction. Consider a person who has a biologically determined form of depression. Given his depression, that person might contemplate suicide as an appropriate moral choice. If the depression could be alleviated through medication or other interventions, the individual might make different moral choices regarding suicide. Similarly, people may genetically inherit personality traits such as narcissism or vindictiveness that are correlated with illegal and immoral behavior (Oakley, 2007). A person who is charming but lacks remorse for causing pain to others, for instance, may be more likely to use her charm to manipulate others to behave in ways that cause harm.[4]

The final biological factors to be considered in this section are physical pleasure and pain. According to the pleasure principle,[5] people seek pleasure and avoid pain (Mill, 1863). "If it feels good, do it." Of course, there are various forms of pain: physical (somatic), psychological, social, and spiritual. From a biological perspective, moral choices may be affected by the desire to experience many different forms of physical pleasure: touching, having sex, eating, drinking, and using drugs, to name a few. Moral choices are also affected by the desire to avoid physical pain, including injury, illness, fatigue, starvation, and thirst. Thus, a person's decision about whether to eat ice cream could involve the following thoughts, "If I eat the ice cream, I will enjoy the taste and satiate my hunger. On the other hand, I may raise my cholesterol, gain weight, and put myself at risk of heart disease. As a parent, do I want to put my immediate physical gratification ahead of my personal health and ability to take care of my children in the longer term?"[6] Thus, if you want to help this person make an effective moral choice, biological factors must be considered in conjunction with psychological and social ones.

Needs, Capacities, and Ethical Decision Making

As the prior section explains, a range of biological factors may affect a person's response to any given situation with a moral issue. Given that social workers are people, too, these same biological factors may affect social workers' responses. When social workers are acting in professional capacities, however, they must be aware of these influences and be careful about the extent to

[4] Given the strengths and ecological perspectives of social work, many social workers reject the view that people are born with immutable, negative personality traits. Rather than focusing on personality traits as the primary cause of behavior, social workers emphasize the importance of the interplay between biological, psychological, and social factors. According to the strengths perspective, social workers believe that people are not born "bad" or "evil," but that people are born good and have free will to choose either good or bad behavior. According to the ecological perspective, people are more likely to choose good if they grow up in supportive social environments.

[5] Concepts related to the pleasure principle include utilitarianism and hedonism.

[6] After reading this example, perhaps you are thinking that critical ethical analysis takes the fun out of enjoying even the most simple of life's pleasures.

which these factors actually affect their ethical decision-making processes. In other words, social workers acting in their professional capacities are held to different standards of behavior than individuals acting in their personal capacities. Thus, if Valjean were acting as a social worker, he would be expected to be aware of his hunger and how it might be affecting his ethical decision making. Consider, for instance, if Valjean were conducting a home visit with a client who offered Valjean some food. Valjean's decision about whether to accept this food should not be based on satisfying his hunger (a personal biological need) but upon the needs and interests of the client he is serving: For instance, if the worker accepted the food, would this help the client trust the worker and engage more effectively in the helping process, or would it lead the client to believe that food could be used to bribe the worker?

As Standard 1.01 of the NASW Code of Ethics suggests, a social worker's primary ethical responsibility extends to clients. This might mean that social workers should subjugate some their own needs (such as food, water, sleep, etc.) for the good of a client. If you are feeling tired, you might ordinarily decide to take a nap. If you have a client anxiously waiting to see you, however, it would be unethical to take a nap and make the client wait just because you felt a bit tired. On the other hand, Standard 1.01 does not require social workers to sacrifice their basic health. Social workers should not, for instance, deny themselves sufficient food or other basic needs if it would put their health at risk. After all, social workers cannot help their clients if they become ill or die.

When engaging in ethical decision making, social workers should guard against having personal biological factors impede their ability to think through ethical issues effectively. Ideally, social workers should ensure that they are not tired, thirsty, hungry, sick, or otherwise physically impaired when they are acting in their professional capacities. In practice, they are expected to behave ethically regardless of their personal biological state. If a social worker's ability to think is impaired by influenza and a high fever, the worker should stay home; still, the worker should call into work to ensure that the agency takes care of clients scheduled for appointments that day. Assume a worker is conducting a home visit and the client offers the worker a beverage. The worker's decision about whether to accept the client's offer should be decided primarily on the basis of the client's needs and expectations rather than the worker's. Within some cultures, refusing to accept coffee or another beverage could be perceived as a personal rejection. Acceptance may serve as an opportunity to engage the client in a more personal manner. Within other cultures, clients may expect more formal boundaries with their workers, so graciously declining an offer of a beverage would not be interpreted as a personal rejection. Workers can ensure that personal needs do not impede their decisions by taking care of these needs in advance (e.g., having a beverage to quench thirst before going to a client's home).

Most social work interventions are talk-based, rather than physical. Still, workers should be aware of their physical capacities, including strength and skills. Assume an agency is determining policies and procedures for how to respond to clients posing physical threats. Ethically, the question is how best to ensure the safety of clients, staff, and others, and whose safety takes precedence when it is not possible to ensure everyone's safety. Physically restraining a violent client should typically be considered as a last resort (Killick & Allen, 2005).[7] If the agency is contemplating physical restraint as an option, however, it should consider the physical abilities of the workers: Do they have sufficient strength and skill to safely restrain a client; would martial arts or other physical training provide them with the requisite skill? In other words, social workers should consider their own physical capacities insofar as they may have an impact on ethical decision making. In some situations, physical capacities are a given; in other situations, physical capacities may be enhanced through training, exercise, sleep, and even diet.

[7] Less intrusive and less risky responses might include crisis intervention, inviting the client to leave the premises, asking others to leave the premises, or calling the police.

This section has explored a variety of ways in which biological factors may affect moral and ethical decision making. We now turn to the relationship between psychological factors and moral and ethical decision making.

PSYCHOLOGICAL FACTORS

When most social work textbooks deal with morals, they focus on the moral development theories of Piaget (1999), Kohlberg (Kohlberg, Levine, & Hewer, 1983), and Gilligan (1982). This section begins with an exploration of the stages of moral development but also explores additional psychological factors that affect an individual's moral decision-making processes: attitudes, emotions, and psychological disorders. The final part of this section describes the relevance of psychological factors for moral decision making to the processes of ethical decision making by social workers.

Moral Development

According to Piaget (1999), Kohlberg, Levine, and Hewer (1983), and other developmental theorists, moral reasoning (the basis for moral behavior) develops through a series of stages from childhood to adulthood. Kohlberg's theory suggests that people progress through three levels of moral development, with each level divided into two stages:

Level I: Preconventional Reasoning
1. Obedience and punishment orientation ("What are the rules to follow?")
2. Self-interest orientation ("What's in it for me?")

Level II: Conventional Reasoning
3. Interpersonal accord and conformity ("What do I need to do to show I am a good boy/girl/friend/student/spouse/worker?")
4. Authority and social-order maintaining orientation ("What would a moral, law-abiding person do?")

Level III: Postconventional Reasoning
5. Social contract and individual rights orientation ("As a member of society, what rights, privileges, and laws should I promote?")
6. Universal ethical principles (Principled conscience)

Level I: Preconventional Reasoning

When children first become aware of moral issues, they apply preconventional (Level I) reasoning: What are the rules and what are the immediate consequences to me if I do not follow the rules? Young children are egocentric, meaning that they are only concerned with the implications of rules to themselves. They have not yet developed the cognitive and emotional capacities required to weigh concerns for others and social justice in their decision-making processes. If young children know their parents will give them a time-out for yelling in the house, the children will learn that yelling is wrong because there is a punishment for this type of behavior. In elementary school, children first learn to obey rules because they are the rules rather than learning the reasons for the rules

Stage 1 moral reasoning is authoritarian; that is, individuals respond to the authority of rules. Although preconventional reasoning is most common in young children, it may persist through adulthood or arise periodically throughout people's lives. Consider, for instance, to what extent do you follow rules simply because they are rules and there are punishments for breaking such rules?

- Assume you drive past a particular stop sign quite frequently. Do you always come to a full stop? Do you sometimes roll through the stop, provided you do not see any police monitoring the intersection?
- Assume you are driving a car in the middle of the night. You come to an intersection with a red light. You need to go to the toilet right away and waiting for the light to turn green will cause you to be too late. Do you go through the red light and get to the toilet on time, or do you follow the traffic laws but urinate in your clothes?

If you always stop at a stop sign, and you always obey red lights simply because you believe that it is important to follow the rules, then you are applying Stage 1 reasoning. If I wanted to convince you that running a red light to get to the toilet on time could be ethically justified, I would have a difficult task. If you are using Stage 1 reasoning, then you would not be open to analyzing whether traffic light rules are morally just, or whether there are times when rules should be broken in order to achieve a higher order goal. Because your approach to reasoning is based on the authority of rules, I could try to argue that there is a separate rule for people who need to go to the toilet.

Stage 2 reasoning is somewhat more complex than that in Stage 1. In Stage 2, individuals determine moral behavior by analyzing the consequences of an action for themselves. During this stage, individuals learn to act out of self-interest, making choices that help them avoid punishment or harm, or raise the likelihood of receiving positive treatment from others. "If I say that I love my parents, they will reward me with hugs and treats." A person's orientation during Stage 2 is toward individualism and instrumentalism. As an individualist, the person does not focus on the needs of others or act out of true compassion for them. The person simply thinks, "What's in it for me?" As an instrumentalist, the person looks at moral choices as means to particular ends. "What do I need to do in order to receive benefit X (e.g., a hug or a promotion)?" In a sense, the person's morality can be bought. Under Stage 2 thinking, a person could be bribed into acting a particular way by assuring the person that the benefits would outweigh the costs. In the driving examples, I could encourage the person to drive through stop signs and red lights if I could guarantee that the person would not be caught by police or if I could persuade the person that the benefits of breaking the law outweigh the risks. For instance, is "not urinating in your pants" worth the risk of "running the red light?"

To some extent, Stages 1 and 2 reflect the differences between two primary approaches to ethics, absolutism and relativism. *Moral absolutism (and its related ethical philosophy of deontology) suggests there are certain rules or laws that people must obey, always.*[8] For instance, we might teach children to always be honest, or never lie. Absolutists believe that such rules are inherently good and should be followed regardless of circumstances (Kant, 1979/orig.1779). In contrast, *relativism (and its related philosophies of consequentialism and teleology) suggests that there are no moral absolutes or universal imperatives: The morality of a decision must take the context and consequences into account.* Although telling the truth often leads to positive consequences, it could lead to negative ones. Consider the following scenario:

> A child accidentally breaks a vase while playing ball in the house. Her mother asks what happened. The child says the cat jumped on the table and broke the vase.

Here, the child decides to lie based on a somewhat simple analysis of the consequences: "If I tell the truth, I'll get in trouble. If I lie, I can avoid punishment." Rather than simply obeying rules, the child assesses the risks and benefits of different courses of action.

Although there are some similarities between Stage 1 reasoning and absolutism and Stage 2 reasoning and relativism, there are also differences. Remember that Stage 1 thinkers apply rules equally to all cases because they lack the cognitive ability to conduct a more mature analysis of the consequences of different actions. An absolutist may believe in universal application of rules out of deep convictions,[9] not necessarily because of a lack of cognitive abilities. Likewise, a Stage 2 thinker looks at consequences, similar to a relativist. However, a Stage 2 thinker is egocentric, looking only at the consequences of moral choices to himself or herself. A relativist may consider selfish interests but may also

---

[8] This section provides a brief introduction to the concepts of absolutism, relativism, deontology, and teleology. Chapter 10 and Part II of this textbook explore these concepts further

[9] For instance, an absolutist might believe in the universality of certain rules as natural laws or divinely inspired morals. See also the following section on spirituality, which includes religious and spiritual sources of moral beliefs and convictions.

consider the consequences of particular actions on others. "Is this in the interest of myself? My family? My community? The greater good?"

When you are working with clients or coworkers who are operating with preconventional thinking, remember that they are responding to moral issues with a focus on obedience to rules and self-interest. Although you may want to help them to apply higher levels of moral reasoning, they may not yet have developed the cognitive and emotional capacity to do so. When you engage preconventional thinkers in discussions of morality, consider how you might speak to them in terms they can appreciate: What are the rules, what are the consequences to them of following or not following the rules? If you want to take them to higher levels of moral reasoning, work slowly toward the next level, conventional reasoning. You may be able to help them see the reasonableness of the next highest stage of moral thinking. As developmental theory suggests, development occurs in a particular sequence of stages. People progress through the stages at different paces, but the overall sequencing is generally fixed.

Level II: Conventional Reasoning

According to Kohlberg, Levine, and Hewer (1983), most people move into conventional reasoning by adolescence, and most people continue to operate at this level throughout adulthood. During this level, people judge the morality of actions by comparing choices with the views and expectations of others, including family, peers, and general society. During Stage 3, individuals become aware of their social roles and tend to conform in order to fit in and be accepted. Within a family context, a child desires to be seen as a good boy or good girl. Within a peer context, an adolescent wants to be seen as cool, hip, popular, or whatever the peer group suggests as socially attractive. Within a work context, an employee seeks to be a good worker or company person. Stage 3 thinkers judge right or wrong according to the groups to which the individual most closely identifies. A youth belonging to a street gang might view solving conflict with knives and guns as morally acceptable because this is a norm or expectation within the peer group. Consider, what social groups do you identify with? To what extent do your moral choices reflect their expectations rather than your own individual assessment? As a developing social worker, are you more apt to follow professional standards because you are expected to do so by your professional peers or because you have personally evaluated whether each of these standards reflects your highest values? By conforming, Stage 3 thinkers avoid conflict and give the appearance of harmonious relations. Stage 3 thinkers are more relativist in their approach to moral decision making as they move from unquestioning obedience to certain rules to a search for good motives and how to fit in, depending on their roles and social circumstances.

Stage 3 thinking is somewhat related to virtue ethics. *According to the philosophy of virtue ethics, people should focus on what personal qualities makes them good people* (Knight, 2007). Whereas moral absolutism focuses on following rules and moral relativism focuses on taking actions that lead to the best consequences, virtue ethics suggest that people should simply focus on the qualities that make people good (e.g., patience, generosity, kindness, prudence, moderation). People who follow virtue ethics, however, do not necessarily adhere to certain virtues in order to fit in. Whereas Stage 3 thinkers make choices based on the expectations of others, virtue ethicists may determine which virtues are desirable, with or without the blessings of others.

During Stage 4, individuals focus on social conventions at a societal level. Whereas Stage 3 thinking is based on an assessment within a particular social relationship (e.g., among friends or family), Stage 4 thinking is more broadly focused on how to maintain societal order. At this stage, individuals obey laws, social norms, and other societal conventions, not simply because rules must be followed (as in Stage 1) but because people have a moral obligation to follow social conventions in order to ensure social order. If people did not obey traffic lights, the roads would be chaos; therefore, I should stop at red lights. I should even stop at red lights when there is no chance of getting caught by police for running a red light. If people stole other's property whenever they wanted, society would be dangerous and people could not trust one another; therefore, I should not steal. More generally, breaking laws or social conventions is morally wrong because society needs people to respect these laws and conventions in order to function effectively.

One of the major differences between Level I reasoning and Level II reasoning is that Level II reasoning takes the interests of others into account. In Stage 3, individuals consider the expectations of family members, friends, coworkers, or others into account, focusing on how to comply and fit in. In Stage 4, individuals move even further from self-interest, considering how their decisions and behaviors will impact society in general.

Level III: Postconventional Reasoning

As individuals move from conventional to postconventional moral reasoning, they focus once again on their own thinking and perspectives, but in a more mature manner than at the preconventional level. Individuals begin to take the interests of others and society into account but have developed the cognitive and emotional capacities to factor in their personal views, judgments, and perspectives. According to Kohlberg, most adults never attain Level III moral reasoning but remain at Level II (Kohlberg et al., 1983).

Both Stage 4 and Stage 5 thinkers desire a good, well-functioning society. Whereas Stage 4 thinkers accept existing laws and social conventions without critically analyzing their moral worth, Stage 5 thinkers determine what makes a good society by critically assessing what rights, values, and responsibilities that society *ought to uphold.* Stage 5 thinkers believe that social norms and laws reflect a social contract that people enter into through consensus and democratic processes. "I follow the law because laws are passed by democratically elected legislators. If I do not believe the current laws are just, I can vote for legislators who will promote better laws." Thus, Stage 5 thinkers will not acquiesce to discriminatory laws. They will critique these laws and decide whether or how to promote law reform. Stage 5 thinkers demonstrate a genuine concern for the interests of others but also understand that different people have different values and opinions. Stage 5 thinkers prefer to act within the law, even when they believe the law is unjust. Thus, if Valjean believed his family had a right to be protected from starvation, this right would not justify his stealing food for them. He would need to act within the rule of law to promote their welfare (e.g., starting a food bank or advocating for social policies that gave families a living wage).

Stage 6 represents the pinnacle of moral reasoning, though according to Kohlberg, Levine, and Hewer (1983), few people reach this stage or apply this reasoning to real-life decisions on a consistent basis. At Stage 6, individuals are more concerned about respect for universal ethical principles than adherence to existing laws, social conventions, or the will of the majority. Individuals should act out of personal conscience rather than out of obedience to the rule of law. Stage 6 thinkers are able to look at moral questions through the eyes of others in order to analyze moral questions. Ideally, individuals should act on principles that everyone can agree upon rather than simply apply principles that the particular decision maker thinks are appropriate. Stage 6 thinking does not dictate the application of a particular set of ethical principles but rather a process of searching for the appropriate principles to apply. The individual may ask, "By which ethical principles do good people act?" Thus, whether Valjean could ethically justify stealing a loaf of bread would depend on his assessment of relevant ethical principles. Valjean could reason that people should not be allowed to die of starvation. He could also reason that people should follow the law that prohibits stealing. In order to assess which principle to apply he would need to consider how others would assess the situation. He is personally involved, since the lives of his family members are at stake. How would a police officer, a social worker, or an independent third person assess which principles are paramount? If community consensus were possible, what would it be? Stage 6 thinkers determine how to act because the action is right rather than because the consequences are right. In other words, the ends do not justify the means. The individual should choose means that are ethical in and of themselves.

So how would a Stage 6 driver think critically about the traffic light issue? The driver would need to consider the views of others, not just his own views. Although his neighbors and family members may believe it is important to follow the law, they may be more interested in the law's underlying purpose, that is, safety.[10] If the driver slows down enough to ensure there is no ongoing traffic, he may be able to drive safely and proceed home in sufficient time to use the restroom. Such conduct could be considered morally correct even if it breaks a law. Safety is a universal law, a law by which good people act. Still, the driver may consider whether the police might stop him to issue a traffic ticket. The police may believe that laws should be enforced strictly, even when the violations are minor. The Stage 6 thinker might be willing to take this risk and fight a ticket in court, arguing that driving safely is the key issue.

Criticisms of Kohlberg's Theory

Although Kohlberg's theory of moral development is one of the most cited and researched, this theory is not without criticism. Some criticize his theory because it is based on moral judgment rather than on moral behavior (Krebs & Denton, 2005). Most of the research on Kohlberg's model is based on asking individuals how they would assess hypothetical ethical situations rather than studying how people actually behave when faced with real-life situations. As other sections in this chapter illustrate, moral development is just one factor that affects how people respond to specific ethical issues. People's choices are affected by a myriad of biological, psychological, social, and spiritual factors. A person who has reached Stage 5 thinking, for instance, may lapse into personal self-interest while experiencing extreme physical or psychological distress.

One of the primary criticisms of Kohlberg's model is that it suggests that all people progress through the same sequence of stages, and morality is not differentiated according to culture or other diversity factors. Gilligan (1982), for instance, suggests that Kohlberg's model is skewed toward male patterns of moral reasoning. She suggests that men tend to define moral problems in terms of rights and rules (the ethics of justice) whereas women tend to define them in terms of obligations to care for others and avoid hurting them (Taylor, Gilligan & Sullivan, 1995). Men tend to prefer a detached and objective analysis of ethical issues whereas women tend to believe that emotions and relationships play a key role in ethical analysis (Homer & Kelly, 2007). Accordingly, men and women experience different patterns of moral development. Whereas men tend to be socialized to value independence and autonomy, women tend to be socialized to value interpersonal sensitivity, connection, and nurturance of others (Vander Zanden, Crandell, & Crandell, 2003). The fact that men and women are socialized toward different values, however, does not translate into one gender being superior to the other in terms of moral or ethical judgments (Dobrin, 1989).

In spite of these critiques, Kohlberg's model does assist with understanding acquisition of moral perception and moral skill (Casebeer, 2003). An individual's cognitive ability and emotional intelligence do affect moral decision making. As an individual's cognitive and emotional capacities develop, so does his or her moral development. For social workers, this means that assessing a client's cognitive and emotional abilities will help them understand how a client is making moral decisions. It will also help them understand how to discuss moral decisions with clients. If a client is able to think in concrete terms, for instance, but has difficulty with abstract thinking, workers should engage the client in a manner appropriate to the client's cognitive ability. Discussing concrete examples may be more effective than abstract theoretical discussions (Amodio, Jost, Master, & Yee, 2007). Consider the following example of a worker explaining confidentiality to a client:

> I have an ethical obligation to maintain the confidentiality of information learned in

[10] This scenario alludes to the distinction between following the "letter of the law" versus the "spirit of the law" (its underlying intent), as discussed in Chapter 9.

> the client-worker relationship. In deciding whether to abridge this duty, I would need to balance the interests of maintaining confidentiality with some higher ethical principle, such as promoting safety or following the rule of law.

This abstract explanation would be completely inappropriate for work with a client who has limited ability for abstract thinking. To paraphrase this explanation in more appropriate, concrete terms, the worker could say:

> For the most part, what we talk about stays between you and me. If you tell me a funny joke or a sad story about yourself, I cannot tell my friends or family. If you tell me that somebody is planning to hurt you, I may need to tell others to help me make sure you are safe. If you tell me that you might hurt someone else, I may need to tell others to help me make sure they are safe.

Although a client may not understand the general concept of balancing the interests of privacy and safety, the client can understand specific examples of what types of information will stay between client and worker, and why some types of information may need to be shared.

Moral development is only one psychological factor that may affect moral decision making. The following sections delve into other psychological factors: attitudes, anxiety, and mental health disorders.

Attitudes

An attitude may be defined as the readiness of the mind to act or react in a particular way (Jung, 1921). In other words, attitudes are psychological predispositions to liking particular people, things, events, or ways of behaving. Accordingly, attitudes affect moral decision making and behavior. People develop attitudes from experience and may be affected by exposure to particular events, perceptions of and emotional responses to those events, and messages conveyed by others about those events.[11] Although psychologists suggest that attitudes endure over time, attitudes have varying degrees of strength (Skitka, Bauman, & Sargis, 2005). Stronger attitudes tend to be more durable, resisting change and having stronger impacts on the person's behavioral choices. Weaker attitudes are more susceptible to persuasion and to change.

The strength of an attitude may be defined in terms of extremity, certainty, and centrality (Skitka et al., 2005). Consider Warren, a person who holds negative attitudes toward affirmative action programs as a means of helpng minorities in schools or employment situations. Attitude extremity refers to how much an attitude deviates from a neutral position on a particular subject. If Warren holds an extremely negative view on affirmative action, for instance, he might equate affirmative action with evil and be strongly motivated to fight against affirmative action. If he holds a mildly negative view of affirmative action, he might be opposed to it but not attach extreme importance to this attitude or have strong motivation to take action to oppose it. A neutral position would mean that he did not care one way or the other about affirmative action. An extremely positive view might mean that Warren sees affirmative action as vitally important, perhaps making it his lifelong mission to support its adoption across the country.

Attitude certainty relates to the degree of confidence people feel about their position on an issue (Skitka et al., 2005). If Warren feels sure that affirmative action is wrong, then it will be difficult to persuade him otherwise. He may even reject objective factual information if it does not fit with his attitude. If he is not so certain about the morality of affirmative action, then he can

---

[11] Neurological research also indicates there is a biological component to attitudes. Amodio, Jost, Master, and Yee (2007), for instance, found differences in brain functioning between people with conservative attitudes and people with liberal attitudes. Conservatives tend to have more structured and persistent cognitive styles whereas liberals tend to be more responsive to complexity, novelty, and ambiguity. The researchers suggest that these differences are "hard-wired" in people's brains.

be more easily persuaded by facts and rational arguments.

Attitude centrality addresses the extent to which a particular attitude is rooted in the person's sense of identity (Skitka et al., 2005). If Warren is a Ku Klux Klan (KKK) member, his attitude toward affirmative action may be closely interconnected with his KKK identity: KKK members view themselves as members of a superior White Christian race that is being threatened by American social policies that promote integration and equality (http://www.kkk.bz). Because affirmative action goes against the core identity of KKK members, Warren may find it particularly difficult to even consider the possibility that affirmative action is morally correct. His entire sense of who he is as a person is wrapped up in beliefs, convictions, stereotypes, and other attitudes that oppose such a policy.

If a social worker wants to discuss moral decisions with a client or other individual, the worker should not only consider the nature of that person's attitudes but also the strengths of those attitudes. The stronger the person's attitudes, the more difficult it will be to persuade the person about moral choices that are inconsistent with those attitudes. A social worker may want to validate the person's attitudes and work within those attitudes, rather than against them. Consider the following scenario:

> Strom is a social worker who believes that all people have a right to health services. Strom approaches Claire, a congressperson, to advocate for universal health care. Strom has assessed that Claire has strong conservative attitudes.

If Strom argued the importance of government in ensuring access to health care, Claire would likely reject his views. Given her conservative attitudes, Claire supports the private sector, not government, in allocating resources. Strom might be more successful in his advocacy if he stressed points that fit with Claire's conservative attitudes: American car manufacturers and other industries would be more globally competitive if they had lower health-care costs, healthier Americans are more likely to be productive members of the workforce rather than relying on state-provided welfare, and universal health care may be more economically efficient than the current systems of Medicare for the elderly and Medicaid for the indigent. By working within Claire's attitudinal frame, Strom is more likely to affect Claire's decisions on the morality or virtue of universal health care.

Thus, attitudes affect moral judgment. Social workers should not dismiss attitudes as being "merely irrational." Although attitudes are affected by emotions and subjective perceptions, they must be taken seriously when one is engaging people in moral decision making.

Emotions

Emotions refer to feelings or moods such as joy, happiness, sadness, anxiety, sympathy, anger, resentment, or exhilaration. Emotions reflect a person's subjective experiences of an event or situation. Although some social scientists consider emotions to be intrinsically irrational and inferior to rational cognitive responses (logical thinking), social workers appreciate the value and worth of both emotions and cognitive processes (Forte, 2007). This section explores how emotions affect moral decision making.

Assume Corazon has a strong value for human life. Given this value, Corazon opposes capital punishment. One day, someone kills her child. Outraged, Corazon says the murderer deserves the death penalty. Why has her moral decision making changed? She still values human life. Her general attitude still opposes capital punishment. However, her emotional response to the loss of her child is outrage. She changes her moral position for this particular situation due to her feelings, not some rational decision-making process. If you were Corazon's social worker, would you point out the inconsistency between her stated values and her desire for capital punishment in this case? Generally, as social workers, we learn to start where the client is (Kirst-Ashman & Hull, 2006b). In this case, that could mean validating her feelings of outrage. More generally, social workers should understand that outrage or anger can affect an individual's moral decision-making process (Mullen & Skitka, 2006).

Fear is another emotion that often affects moral judgment. When people are fearful, for instance, they tend to favor safer options (Monin, Pizarro, & Beer, 2007). Consider Ethel, an employee at a financial institution. Ethel is aware that her bosses have been involved in fraudulent transactions. Her morals tell her to report her bosses to the police or other law enforcement authorities. Her fear of losing her job leads her to decide to do nothing. She thinks it is safer to remain silent rather than blow the whistle on her bosses. If she were not fearful of losing her job, she would be more willing to report them. Her fear affects her moral decision making, whether or not her fears are rationally justified. Even if objectively there were little chance that she would be fired, her subjective experience of fear motivates her to remain silent. If someone asked Ethel to explain her decision not to disclose, she might provide a very rational explanation. This explanation might cover the fact that her decision was primarily motivated by her emotions. In other words, people may provide rational explanations for their moral choices even when these decisions were primarily based on emotional factors (Monin et al., 2007).

Emotions such as fear, anger, hate, hurt, and frustration may lead individuals to feel anxious. When people experience higher levels of anxiety, they have greater difficulty making decisions on a rational basis. If Ethel were afraid of losing her job but knew that she could easily find another suitable job, the prospect of being fired might not cause her much anxiety. On the other hand, if she thought she could not get another job and she would quickly become destitute, she would experience much higher levels of anxiety. This higher level of anxiety would make it more difficult for her to think through her moral dilemma on a rational basis. Even if she were fired, for instance, she might be able to sue for wrongful dismissal.

Emotions can affect moral decision making even when they do not cause anxiety. Consider Larry, who loves his girlfriend dearly. His feelings of love do not cause him anxiety but rather calmness and fulfillment. Still, his love may affect (cloud?) his moral judgments. Ordinarily, Larry places high value on honesty. If his girlfriend asks him to lie for her, his feelings of love might lead him to do so.

The fact that emotions affect moral choices should not be surprising. Still, when reading theory and research on moral decision making, note that many scholars focus on moral decision making as a rational process (Mullen & Skitka, 2006). Although moral judgments may involve rational thought processes, social workers must consider emotions and other nonrational factors affecting moral decision making.

Mental Health Disorders

The previous sections focus on psychological processes—moral development, attitudes, emotions—that are pertinent to moral decision making among the general population. This section explores moral decision making among segments of the population with mental health disorders. Rather than try to cover the entire range of mental health disorders, the following analysis focuses on four exemplars: depression, schizophrenia, antisocial personality disorder, and narcissistic personality disorder. The first step in the analysis is to identify the manifestations of a particular disorder; the second step is to consider how these manifestations might affect moral decision making. Remember, just because a person has certain symptoms of a mental health disorder does not mean that the person cannot make appropriate moral decisions. The impact of a mental health disorder on moral decision making depends on the particular manifestations of the disorder and the person's ability to manage them.

A person with depression presents with a range of symptoms, typically including sadness, feelings of hopelessness, decreased energy, fatigue, and difficulty concentrating, remembering, and making decisions (American Psychiatric Association [APA], 2000). The potential impacts of these symptoms on moral decision making are obvious. A person who feels extreme sadness may contemplate committing suicide, even if suicide generally goes against the person's basic moral system. A person who feels hopeless and tired may give up rather than pursue a course of action that could lead to a better future. A person with difficulty concentrating and remembering will have difficulty processing complex information and conflicting interests that may arise in a moral decision-making process.

The signs and symptoms of schizophrenia include unusual thoughts or perceptions (e.g., hallucinations, delusions), paranoia, disorganized thinking, and other problems with memory and attention (APA, 2000). If a person is experiencing auditory hallucinations (e.g., hearing threatening voices), that person may be making moral decisions based on false information. Thus, a person with schizophrenia might kill another person in self-defense, believing that the threatening voices were real. Likewise, delusions of grandeur might lead a person to risk his own life, falsely believing he is an all-powerful god. Paranoia (irrational fear) may also lead the person to a faulty assessment of moral dilemmas: for instance, the person may believe that a crime should be reported to the police but erroneously fear that the police are out to get him. As with depression, schizophrenia is also marked by difficulties with memory and attention, making it difficult for the person to conduct a thorough, effective assessment of moral issues. The person may also be on medication to control symptoms such as hallucinations and delusions; unfortunately, this medication may also inhibit the person's capacity to make moral decisions because of side effects such as lethargy and problems in cognitive processing.

Criteria for diagnosing antisocial personality disorder include failure to conform to social norms, dishonesty, impulsivity, reckless disregard for the safety of self or others, and indifference to causing harm to others (APA, 2000). By definition, people with antisocial personality disorder have compromised moral decision-making abilities. People with this disorder lack empathy for other people. They also engage in risky activities without thinking through or caring about the consequences. Simply offering them a process for empathizing with others or a framework for moral decision making would not help. People with antisocial personality disorder are not just choosing to act in a manner that disregards risks and the feelings of others; their abilities to empathize and think are impaired.

Narcissistic personality disorder is marked by symptoms such as a grandiose sense of self-importance, the need for excessive admiration, a strong sense of entitlement, a lack of empathy, envy of others, and arrogant affect (APA, 2000). Because people with narcissistic personality disorder are so wrapped up in their own interests and situation, they tend to make moral decisions without giving due consideration to the interests of others. Consider a recently divorced man with narcissistic personality disorder. Given his narcissism, he may feel very envious that his former wife has custody of their children and may act in ways to hurt her, even though these actions may also hurt the children (e.g., encouraging his children to hate their mother by telling them lies about her). His moral judgment may be clouded by his distorted view of himself as perfect and his extreme sense of personal entitlement (i.e., that the children rightly belong to him and their mother does not deserve them) (Eddy, 2003).

By understanding how various mental health disorders may affect moral decision making, social workers are better able to demonstrate empathy concerning the choices made by clients (e.g., "I understand the voices are telling you to light these fires"). Empathizing with clients does not mean agreeing with their conclusions. In other classes, you will study interventions for people with different mental health disorders. As you learn these interventions, consider how you can use them to assist clients with moral decision making.

Psychological Factors and Ethical Decision Making

In order for social workers to engage effectively in ethical decision making, they should be aware of the psychological processes (discussed above) that may affect their judgment. When social workers act in their professional capacity, they should act deliberately, with the NASW Code of Ethics as their primary guide for ethical decision making. So how can social workers manage challenges related to their moral development, emotions, attitudes, or mental health disorders?

In terms of moral development, Kohlberg, Levine, and Hewer (1983) suggest that most adults operate at Level II conventional reasoning. In contrast, the NASW Code of Ethics asks social workers to act in ways more consistent with Level III postconventional reasoning. Standard 1.01, for instance, suggests that social workers' primary commitment is to each of their clients. Standard 6.01 suggests that social workers should promote the social welfare of society. Standard 6.04 suggests that social workers should respect cultural and social diversity. To put these principles into practice, social workers must be able to focus on the interests of others. They must also be able to critically assess what rights, values, and responsibilities society ought to uphold rather than simply applying given laws and rules. Given that social workers often work with disadvantaged, underrepresented minority groups in society, following conventional thinking may be detrimental to these clients (e.g., perpetuating a stereotype or discriminatory laws that exist in mainstream, conventional society). So, if a social worker has not attained Level III as regards moral development, does that mean the worker is unable to meet the professional demands of ethical decision making?

Remember that moral development does not equate to ethical decision making. Moral development relates to people acting privately whereas ethical decision making relates to people acting in a professional capacity. The fact that a person may act somewhat selfishly as a private person does not necessarily mean that the person is unable to act in an unselfish or altruistic manner as a professional. Thus, a person who primarily uses conventional thinking in private life may learn to use postconventional thinking as a social worker. The following processes can be used to promote higher levels of thinking:

- Learning to use a structured ethical decision-making framework (such as that presented in Part II) that provides specific guidance on perspective taking (the skill of considering the interests and values of others, from their points of view).
- Using reflective thinking and clinical supervision to ensure that the worker is acting in a deliberate, conscientious manner.

In my private life, there may be times when I act in a manner that is mean-spirited, unfriendly, or impatient. If another car cuts in front of me on my way to work, I might honk my horn out of anger rather than consider the interests of the other driver. When working with clients, however, I hold myself to a higher standard. I am able to control my self-interests, in part, because I am with my clients for finite periods of time. I can psych myself up for the one hour that I spend with each client, controlling dysfunctional impulses and focusing on the needs of my clients and others. If I am having difficulty focusing on client needs or social justice, I should consult my supervisor. If I am too sick or too self-involved, perhaps I should not be at work—and especially not meeting with clients.

Ideally, social workers self-select into the profession with postconventional moral decision-making capacities, including concern for others and the ability to think critically about social justice issues. In addition, schools of social work look for these qualities when they admit students (Barsky, 2006; Townsend, 2007). The capacities required for ethical decision making may also be enhanced through the educational process, including experiential role-plays, reflective written assignments (Swindell & Watson, 2006), and supervised field education (Handelsman, Gottleib, & Knapp, 2005).

With regard to attitudes, social workers should guard against making ethical decisions based on preconceived thoughts or stereotypes. If you believe that it is immoral for couples to cohabit unless they are married, you may use this attitude to guide your personal decisions. If you are involved in public policy development as a social worker, however, you should not let this attitude alone determine which policies to support. You should consider psychosocial research on the impacts of various policy choices as well as the perspectives of various cultural groups in your community. Being aware of your attitudes also includes being aware of the strength of your attitudes, as described earlier. The more extreme your attitude, for instance, the more difficult you may find it to view the issue from more moderate perspectives. If you are very certain about the truth of your attitude, you may not want to even consider any arguments against your view. And if your attitude is central to your personal identity, you may feel personally attacked and act defensively when others question your perspective. Each of these situations creates potential barriers to effective ethical decision making.

When you are trying to resolve an ethical issue in a particular case, your attitudes may hinder your ability to think critically and objectively. You may use the following strategies to ensure that you are aware of your attitudes and remain open to other perspectives based on a full analysis of facts and other points of view:[12]

- Identify attitudes that may be affecting your thought processes.
- Assess the strength of each attitude in relation to extremity, certainty, and centrality. Identify the source of each attitude (e.g., personal or professional experience, professional education, family role models, media, or religious upbringing).
- Remind yourself to be open to hearing facts, opinions, and perspectives that may conflict with their own attitudes and beliefs.
- Make use of supervision or consultation to help you assess how your attitudes might be impairing your ethical decision making and to help you strategize how to deal with these issues.

Emotions are similar to attitudes insofar as social workers should be aware of their potential impact on their ethical decision making. If you feel extremely anxious, scared, or angry, you may have difficulty engaging in rational thinking. The Greek concept of *akrasia* describes how people may know what is right but not necessarily do what is right (Casebeer, 2003). In such cases, the problem is not that the person lacks cognitive ability but that emotions overpower or temporarily sway one's moral judgment. Consider, for instance, the social worker who knows that Standard 1.09 of the NASW Code of Ethics prohibits sleeping with clients but still becomes sexually involved with a client. The social worker's ethical judgment may be overwhelmed by feelings of lust or affection. This does not exonerate the social worker; rather, it points to the need for all workers to be aware of their feelings toward their clients (Gutheil & Brodsky, 2008).

Although some models of ethical decision making promote purely logical thinking, emotions should be taken into account. Ignoring or suppressing emotions could actually hinder ethical decision making, as demonstrated below:

> Stefanie is providing vocational counseling to Cecil. Stefanie feels frustrated with Cecil because he never follows through on the job referrals that she provides. Stefanie tries to ignore her frustration, thinking that she is supposed to focus on helping Cecil rather than getting wrapped up in her own emotions.

In this scenario, Stefanie has good intentions, striving to help her client. Unfortunately, ignoring her frustration may actually cause her to make a risky ethical choice. She decides to continue to serve Cecil without assessing whether her frustration may be getting in the way of providing competent services. Had she taken time to assess the possible impact of her frustration on the helping process, she might have decided to transfer Cecil to another worker. Although she might have also decided that she could keep her frustration from hindering their work, the important point is that reflecting on feelings can be an important part of ethical decision making. To address how feelings may be affecting decision making, social workers must first identify their feelings and then consider how these feelings may be affecting the process. As with assessing attitudes, it may be helpful to reflect on feelings with the assistance of a supervisor or consultant.

Turning now to mental illness, we must first acknowledge that mental health disorders do exist among social workers. Although licensing bodies and certain agencies may screen out workers with mental health disorders, practicing social workers may have mental health disorders because they are working in a field of practice that does not screen out workers with mental health disorders, they developed mental health disorders after entering practice, their mental

---

[12] You may also use scales developed to assess attitudes in relation to issues such as sexuality (American Association for Sexuality Educators, Counselors, and Therapists, 2004; Worthington, Dillon, & Becker, 2005), aging (Cummings, Adler, & DeCoster, 2005), race (Green, Kiernan-Stern, & Baskind, 2005), and mental illness (Schwartz, 2003).

health disorder is not severe, or their mental health disorder is under control. As discussed earlier, various mental health disorders affect ethical decision making in a number of different ways—for instance, affecting their cognitive abilities, their motivation, or their capacity to focus on the interests of others. Whereas social workers should discuss attitudes and emotions with clinical supervisors or consultants, workers may also require the help of a therapist if their issues are related to mental health issues. Supervisors and consultants can help with ethical decision making, but they cannot provide therapy for the worker.

As this section illustrates, ethical decision making by social workers may be affected by the same types of psychological factors that affect moral decision making by the general population. As professionals, however, social workers have a special duty to be aware of these factors and take steps to ensure that they do not impair their ability to make effective ethical decisions. We now turn from psychological factors to social ones.

SOCIAL FACTORS

Social factors refer to interpersonal dynamics that affect moral decision making. As you will learn in other classes, there are numerous social factors that affect human behavior. Because it is impossible to cover all social factors in one chapter, this section highlights three factors that are particularly important to moral behavior: social learning, social identity, and social context.

Social Learning

Social learning theory suggests that people learn how to behave from modeling significant people in their lives, such as parents, teachers, or religious leaders (Bandura, 1977). Modeling may include observing and replicating moral decisions and behaviors. Young children tend to be more inclined to observational learning than adults because children are still developing their cognitive abilities to conceptualize and reason. In fact, early Greek philosophers (dating back to Aristotle over 2,300 years ago) recognized the importance of providing moral education by offering virtuous role models for young people to emulate (Kristjánsson, 2006).

When considering Valjean's moral choice, social learning would suggest that we consider whether he was emulating parents or other significant people in his life. Had others stolen food or engaged in similar criminal behaviors? Had they justified stealing because of poverty and hunger? As part of the French underclass, perhaps Valjean learned that petty theft was not only necessary to survive but was justified as a reaction against the oppression of the privileged classes. Thus, when trying to understand the derivation of any person's moral choices, we must consider *(a)* who the primary models are in the person's life, and *(b)* what moral messages these people modeled through their deeds and actions.

Social Identity

Social identity theory suggests that people develop a sense of who they are by identifying with particular social groups (e.g., African Americans, women, Muslims, or bisexuals) (Tajfel & Turner, 1986). Social identity affects moral behavior because people do not simply act as individuals but as members of one or more social groups. In other words, individuals tend to act in a manner that is consistent with the morals of their social identity groups (Reed & Aquino, 2003). People may take on different social identities, depending on the situation (Rapley, McCarthy, & McHoul, 2003). For example, a man may assume the identity of a husband and father at home but a business manager at work. Given his different social identity in each situation, he will make different types of moral decisions: at home, he may spend lavishly on his family; at work, he may be frugal with spending on his employees, seeing each as right for the particular social identity.

The impact of social identity on moral behavior can be very positive, particularly in relation to the high ideals of the particular identity group (Tajfel & Turner, 1986). For instance, when a social identity group aspires to values such as honesty, charity, fairness, and patience, group members will strive to behave in a manner consistent with these ideals. In fact, many cultural, religious, and other social groups consciously promote adherence to particular codes of conduct through their teachings and discourse.

In some instances, social identity may pose troublesome impacts on moral behavior, particular in terms of in-group versus out-group behaviors. People tend to have favorable views of people within their social identity group—for instance, seeing themselves as hardworking, caring, charitable, or possessing whatever other virtues they embrace. People often have less favorable views of people from outside their social identity groups—for instance, viewing them as lazy, immoral, or stupid (Reed & Aquino, 2003). These negative views tend to be exaggerated when there is long-standing conflict or fearfulness between the groups. In some cases, people use these negative views to justify denigration or violence against people from the out-group; examples are sexist jokes by men who devalue women, or suicide bombings by extremist Muslims who view Americans as infidels. Although you might personally view these actions as morally reprehensible and indefensible, they may be morally justified by the in-group. An individual's concept of what is moral is socially constructed in reference to her social identity group (Reed & Aquino, 2003). Of course, a social identity group's morals could embrace being kind and generous to other groups, in which case individuals from that group may act positively to people from an out-group.

In sum, to understand how social identity affects a particular individual's moral decisions, we must consider *(a)* the social context, *(b)* the social identities the person assumes in that particular social context, *(c)* what moral guides stem from the individual's situation-specific social identity, and *(d)* the ways in which in-group and out-group perceptions may affect how the individual treats others affected by the decision. The following section explores the importance of social context in further detail.

Social Context

As the ecological perspective of social work suggests, the behavior of individuals must be understood in the context of their social environment, including family, neighborhood, cultural community, school, workplace, health-care system, and criminal justice system (Kirst-Ashman & Hull, 2006b). Moral behavior is no different. Although morals may be defined as rules of conduct that determine how people behave, morals are implemented by individuals who take social context into account (Davydova & Sharrock, 2003). Behaviors that may be considered immoral for one situation may be considered moral in a different situation. As you read each of the following scenarios, visualize each situation and determine whether you think the behavior described is moral or not.

1. A man rubs his hands up and down the naked body of a 4-year-old girl. He grins with pleasure. Is his behavior moral? From the information provided, you might think this behavior is immoral because it seems to occur in the context of child sexual abuse. What if the behavior occurs in the context of a father giving his daughter a bath and he is not touching his daughter in a sexual manner; is it still immoral? Does the father's grin still bother you? What if he is grinning because his daughter said something funny?
2. Women are dressed from head to toe in black clothes. Only their eyes show. The weather his hot. Are you thinking that it is immoral to force women to dress this way? Would your assessment of morality change if you knew that the women voluntarily chose to wear these clothes in accordance with their religious and cultural beliefs?
3. A store owner gives the police $10,000 to protect his shop from vandalism. Is it moral for the police to accept this payment? Does your answer depend on whether the police work for a publicly paid police force versus a private police company?

As these examples illustrate, social context matters. If Valjean comes from an oppressed socioeconomic background, we might have a different moral assessment of his stealing than if he comes from a privileged socioeconomic background. We might not advise Valjean that it is appropriate to steal, but we might note that his community plays a role in his choices and should take at least part of the responsibility for ensuring that he is not put into a position of having to steal to survive.

Understanding that moral decisions take place within a social context does not mean that everyone will agree on what is moral. Consider female genital cutting, a practice considered morally appropriate within some African communities. To many Americans, this practice might seem patriarchic, backward, and brutally painful (Lyons, 2007). Even if they understood the cultural context, however, they might continue to believe that female genital cutting is immoral and should be eradicated (Burson, 2007). Thus, exploring the context in which moral decisions are made helps us understand the social basis for those decisions. In some situations, this will lead to an agreement on what is moral. In other situations, different people will assess morality differently.

Now that we have examined social factors that may affect moral decision making, we turn to the implications of these factors for ethical decision making.

Social Factors and Ethical Decision Making

When making moral decisions, social workers are influenced by the same factors as the general population, including social learning, social identify, and social context. Once again, social workers should be aware of these social factors and ensure that they do not inhibit their ability to make informed and unbiased ethical judgments. In terms of social learning, for instance, social workers should be aware of what they have learned from parents and significant others through modeling versus what they have learned through critical thinking (e.g., gathering and assessing information from a range of sources, reading scholarly research, or considering issues from a variety of perspectives). Consider a social worker who learned through modeling that adult children should make sacrifices to support their elderly parents; in fact, when her grandfather developed dementia, her mother quit her job to take care of him. When working with a client family faced with similar issues, the worker should avoid imposing her beliefs about making sacrifices on the client family. What was right for her family may not be right for her clients. The worker must consider the client family's perspective and what is right for them. If the family asks what options are available to them, the worker should not limit the options to ones that her own family promoted but explore the full range of options for taking care of an elder parent with dementia.

When assessing the impact of social identity on ethical decision making, social workers should reflect on groups to which they identify, including cultural, ethnic, religious, political, and professional groups. They should then consider how these social identities may be affecting their moral and ethical decision making (Bashe, Anderson, Handelsman, & Klevansky, 2007). By definition, professional social workers identify with the profession of social work. Their views on what is right or wrong in a particular situation are affected by their sense of who they are. For instance, social workers view themselves as allies and advocates for oppressed and vulnerable populations. When determining how to respond to a particular ethical issue, social workers might therefore be inclined to view issues from the most vulnerable person's perspective. Suppose a group of homeless people is refusing to go to a shelter even though the weather is extremely cold and they risk frostbite. Although police and community leaders may want social workers to counsel the homeless to go to the shelter, social workers might be inclined to advocate for the wishes of the homeless (e.g., giving them warm clothes and sleeping bags so they can continue to live on the streets). While it may be appropriate for social workers to advocate for the wishes of the homeless, they should not allow their social identities to block their abilities to view the situation from others' perspectives. When engaging police and community leaders in a discussion on the right course of action, for instance, social workers should be able to explore the ethics of different options from the positions of everyone represented at the table.

With respect to social context, the ecological perspective of social work teaches practitioners to understand and work with clients in the context of their social environment (Kirst-Ashman & Hull, 2006a). When engaging in ethical decision making, social workers must also factor in their own social environments, including their organizational context. Social workers practicing in school settings, for instance, will have a different set of ethical expectations from workers practicing psychotherapy in private practice. Whereas school social workers should generally abide by the policies established by the school board,[13] private practitioners can set their own policies. Regardless of organizational context, social workers should also reflect on sources of support and stress in relation to the ethical decisions to be made. If a frontline worker has a supportive supervisor, for instance, the worker may be more likely to consult the supervisor when ethical issues arise. If the supervisor is unsupportive, the worker may try to hide ethical issues. By assessing social context, social workers can build on supports and develop methods of coping with stress. Consider, for instance, a social worker who believes his agency is using funds for improper purposes (e.g., giving scholarships to the program director's children). Although the worker knows this activity is wrong and should be reported, he must consider the reactions of his supervisor and others within the organizational context. If the worker has developed positive relationships within the organization, he will be in a better position to report the wrongdoing. If he feels alienated within the agency, he may know that reporting is the right thing to do but still choose not to report, fearing negative repercussions, such as losing his job.

For social workers, social context includes both professional and personal social contexts. Professionally, social workers should make ethical decisions within the parameters of the policies, laws, and standards of practice established by their workplace. Still, social workers are not immune to influences from outside their professional context, including family, friends, and media. Consider a social worker from an agency that serves pedophiles. Under Standard 1.01 of the NASW Code of Ethics, the worker's primary duty is to her client; however, she may experience overt pressure from people in her community that might sway her thinking. When making ethical decisions about how to proceed with her clients, however, she must guard against having friends or family distort her analysis of the issues: for instance, community members might want to see a pedophile receive punishment, not understanding and support; still, the worker's professional mandate requires offering understanding and support.

Rather than try to enumerate all the ways that social factors can influence moral and ethical decision making, this section has provided a few important examples to illustrate the importance of social factors. The following section turns to the final category of factors, spirituality.

SPIRITUAL FACTORS

Spirituality and Moral Decision Making

Spirituality refers to human experiences that transcend the material world and mundane life. People may experience spirituality through connections with a higher power (e.g., God or Allah), morally significant relationships with other people, self-actualization (within-person integration), or other ways people strive for meaning in their lives (Heyman, Buchanan, Marlowe, & Sealy, 2006). People may express spirituality through participation in religious communities and activities, though spirituality does not require religious participation. For many people, spiritual factors play a very important role in moral decision making; for others, spirituality plays a much lesser role. In some situations spirituality has no impact on moral behavior. At its best, spirituality inspires people to do good and to strive for righteousness. Because different forms of spirituality define goodness and righteousness differently, however, people may have very different assessments of what is moral.

---

[13] Standard 3.09 of the NASW Code suggests that social workers should generally follow agency policy. If the policy is unethical, however, they should seek to change the policy and look for ways to act in an ethical manner. See Chapter 8 for further discussion.

The impact of spirituality on moral decision making may or may not be a conscious one. When faced with moral questions, for instance, some people specifically refer to the teachings of the Bible, the Qur'an, or other religious texts that act as moral guides (Hugen & Scales, 2008). Others may have internalized spiritually inspired morals in a manner that guides behavior without being conscious of the source of these morals. Individuals may also feel spiritual inspiration coming from an inner voice, a voice of a loved one, or the voice of a divine power.[14]

Although spiritually based morals can be strong influences on behavior (Gorsuch & Ortberg, 1983), spirituality may or may not be stronger than biological, psychological, or social factors. Let us reconsider Valjean. Assume that he is devoutly religious. A core commandment of his religion says, "Thou shalt not steal." If Valjean is a religious fundamentalist, he may take a literal reading of this commandment. Because the commandment does not provide for any exceptions, he may feel bound by it in spite of his personal hunger. On the other hand, his biological need for food may supersede his religious conviction. Alternatively, his family and social support system may tell him that it is permissible to steal food, in spite of what a strict reading of religious scripture says. Thus, spiritual factors should be assessed in relation to other factors that may affect moral decision making.

When assessing spiritually based morals, social workers should consider the source of the morals, the strength of the person's connection with his or her spirituality, and the degree to which the person balances spiritually based teachings with moral arguments from other sources. Assume you have a client, Cori, who says she is very spiritual. Cori has cancer and wants to terminate her life so she may die with dignity.[15] As a humanist, she believes that all individuals have the right to shape their own lives without undue influence from others. Her spirituality rejects religious beliefs or customs as determinants of moral decisions, in favor of human conscience and free thought based on science and rational thought (International Humanist and Ethical Union, n.d.). From a medical science perspective, Cori knows her cancer is terminal. Cori's husband opposes euthanasia and encourages Cori to live as long as she can, in hope of divine intervention. Although humanistic beliefs typically reject this form of moral thinking, Cori may be open to hearing her husband's arguments based on a hope or faith that goes beyond science. On the other hand, if her humanistic beliefs are very strong she may reject his arguments outright.

One of the greatest challenges to understanding the impact of religion on moral decision making is that religious scriptures may be interpreted in different ways. The Bible, for instance, has been used by some to justify African American slavery, Native American genocide, and other forms of violence and oppression (Haynes, 2002). Although the Bible teaches, "Love thy neighbor" (Leviticus 19: 17–18) and "Judge not that ye not be judged" (Matthew 7: 1), some people point to curses, expulsions, and other acts of discrimination in the Bible to rationalize the subjugation of certain groups. When it comes to moral judgments, one cannot say that all Christians, all Jews, or all of any other religious group believe in a particular interpretation of the Bible (e.g., "condom use is immoral because it interferes with the natural function of sex"). There are many different denominations within religions, each with different interpretations. Even within a particular branch of a religion, individuals may interpret religious scripture differently. Thus, although a person's moral decision making may be affected by religion, one must ask for that person's own interpretation of what the religion states as moral.

---

[14] Consider: If a client says he heard a voice tell him to act in a particular way, how would you distinguish whether this voice represents an auditory hallucination due to psychosis or substance use, or whether this is a voice of a true spirit that cannot be explained through science?

[15] See Chapter 16 for an in-depth discussion of end-of-life issues.

Spirituality and Ethical Decision Making

People from a particular religion may believe that their views on morality are the only correct views, suggesting that atheists and people from other religions lack morality. Social workers respect the dignity and worth of all people, meaning that they must respect people of all religions as well as atheists and others who do not subscribe to any particular religion. Social workers may be tempted to avoid discussions of spirituality and religion because they do not want to impose their morals (Hugen & Scales, 2008). Some may also believe that discussing religious and spiritual beliefs risks becoming divisive and destructive. Because religion and spirituality may have a significant impact on moral decision making, workers should not ignore these influences. Rather, they should find ways to discuss these factors in a manner that is integrative and constructive (Tjeltveit, 2004).

As discussed throughout this chapter, social workers need to be aware of their morals in order to ensure that they manage them appropriately. A social worker might personally believe in Jesus Christ as savior and son of God. In personal life, that worker might even encourage friends to accept Jesus into their hearts and souls. The worker's persuasion could be quite passionate, wanting to help friends go to heaven rather than suffer eternity in damnation. In professional work, however, the worker should not impose such religious beliefs on clients, no matter how strong the religious conviction and how well-meaning the worker's intentions (NASW Code of Ethics, 1999, Purpose). This does not mean there is no room in social work for spiritually based morals (Marson & MacLeod, 1996). Rather, social workers should determine appropriate boundaries for bringing spiritual content into practice.

When it comes to determining the appropriateness of bringing spiritually based morals into practice, social workers should pay heed to the ethical principles of client self-determination, informed consent, and respect for religious diversity (NASW Code, Ss. 1.02, 1.03, and 1.05).[16] The following points illustrate how these principles can be used to guide workers in determining whether and how to include spirituality in moral decision making:

- When clients are facing moral decisions in their lives, social workers may help them explore religious or spiritual convictions in order to help them make decisions (for instance, "Is it morally OK for me to have an abortion," or "Do I need to forgive a stepfather who abused me?"). As long as workers are not imposing spiritual convictions, they are merely facilitating client self-determination, helping clients make their own decisions (Hugen & Scales, 2008).[17]
- When working within a faith-based agency, the agency may have policies mandating inclusion of faith-based values and rituals within services. Workers at such agencies may involve clients in prayers or spiritual activities, provided the clients give voluntary, informed consent. In other words, workers should let clients know from the start that this is a faith-based program and that there will be certain types of religious content. If the clients agree, then the workers are not imposing values or religious practices on their clients. Ideally, workers should provide clients with alternatives; for instance, if a client does not want religious content, the worker could make a referral to a secular agency. By providing clients with alternatives, workers enhance client choice and self-determination. If Valjean approaches a faith-based agency for food and the worker says that you must pray first, this would amount to coercion rather than free and voluntary consent.

---

[16] These sections are discussed in more detail in Chapter 5.

[17] Logotherapy and various forms of existential therapy specifically include exploration of spirituality as part of the helping process (Frankl, 2006/ orig.1946).

- When workers have strong spiritual convictions that impede their ability to practice in an effective, nonjudgmental manner, they should link clients with other workers or agencies that do not have such impediments (NASW, S.2.06[a]). For instance, workers whose religious beliefs condemn homosexuality may need to refer gay or lesbian clients to other service providers to avoid imposing their morality on the clients.
- When workers are making their own ethical judgments, they may consider their own spiritual convictions but should also consider other sources of ethical direction, including their professional code of ethics, agency policy, and laws governing practice (Spano & Koenig, 2007). Consider the earlier discussion on euthanasia. If Cori asked you to assist with her suicide, you should contemplate your own convictions, including your spiritual ones. Whether or not you support euthanasia, you would also need to consider the laws, agency policies, and codes of ethics. In some cases, each source will give you different guidance and you may face negative consequences regardless of how you act (e.g., legal sanctions, agency sanctions, professional sanctions, or the sanctions of your higher power). When personal convictions conflict with professional ethics, agency policies, or laws, the worker faces an ethical dilemma. Part II of this textbook provides guidance on how to manage such dilemmas. At this point in your learning, it is important simply to recognize that a dilemma with your personal convictions is occurring.

Ethicists distinguish between autonomous and heteronymous ethics. *Autonomous ethics* refers to a system of behavioral rules or principles that are developed by people based on logic, science, and humanistic values. *Heteronymous (or religious) ethics* refers to a system of behavioral rules or principles that are inspired by a higher power, such as God or Allah (Dolgoff, Loewenberg, & Harrington, 2009). Members of a particular religion follow the word of their revealed authority out of faith, mystical experience, and spiritual emotionalism (Wood, 2006). *Naturalistic ethics* is a form of autonomous ethics. Naturalistic ethicists study ethics in the context of science. They consider what can be known through scientific research methods, including those of biology, psychology, and sociology. They discount deities or religious scriptures as the sources of moral or ethical guidance (Casebeer, 2003). A naturalistic ethicist might ask, "What rules of conduct are necessary to ensure the survival of humanity?" or "What moral rules would help a community of people live together in a more functional manner?" In contrast, a religious (heteronymous) ethicist might ask, "What rules of conduct has God prescribed for us?" or "How can we fulfill God's will for us as moral beings?"

Although some ethicists suggest that people following religious ethics are irrational, Kant and others suggest that having faith is rational. Kant justifies religion as a common devotion to the moral improvement of humanity (Wood, 2006). Religion itself is neither good nor bad, though specific religious beliefs or practices could be judged as moral or immoral depending on whether they contribute to the welfare of humanity and the world.

Given that the NASW is a secular organization, its code of ethics is based on autonomous ethics. Thus, social workers with strong religious beliefs may find occasion when their religious convictions conflict with their professional ethical obligations. Although ethics textbooks often highlight potential conflicts between religious morals and professional ethics, note that they coincide more often than not. Virtually every religion teaches respect for others (e.g., "Love thy neighbor"); the NASW Code advocates respect. Virtually every religion promotes acts of justice and charity; the NASW Code suggests that workers should promote social justice and ensure that people have access to resources they need. In fact, many social workers are inspired to practice social work because of their religious convictions (Heyman et al., 2006; Hugen & Scales, 2008). Spiritual convictions—whether religious or not—may motivate practitioners to work toward high ideals of ethical practice: to do what they ought to do, and to be what they ought to be.

CONCLUSION

Given the broad range of biopsychosocial-spiritual factors that may affect moral decision making, social workers should guard against reductionist thinking. In other words, rather than assuming that a client's moral judgments are determined by one factor (e.g., religious beliefs or parental modeling), social workers should assess how multiple factors may be affecting the decisions clients are making. By gaining a better understanding of the sources of a client's moral judgments, social workers are better able to validate clients' convictions and demonstrate empathy.

Social workers may also use the biopsychosocial-spiritual framework to help clients explore their own moral convictions. Through the process of exploration, clients may develop new insights and make different moral judgments in the future. When helping clients explore their morals, social workers must be careful to avoid imposing their own moral convictions. This means that social workers should continuously strive to maintain awareness of their own morals and how they may be affecting the helping process.

Finally, social workers should be aware of various factors that may be affecting their ethical decision making. Although the NASW Code of Ethics, agency policies, and public laws are the official guides for ethical and legal practice, social workers should not ignore the fact that their own system of morals may be affecting their ethical judgments and behavior. The first step in being able to manage conflicts between personal moral beliefs, professional ethics, agency policies, and legal obligations is to be aware of one's personal morals. Raising self-awareness is an ongoing process that can be facilitated by conducting periodic self-assessments of the biopsychosocial-spiritual influences on your moral decision making. As you work through the balance of this textbook, consider how your personal morals fit or conflict with professional standards, agency policies, and laws that may govern your practice. Also, reflect on what factors may be affecting your moral judgments.

DISCUSSION QUESTIONS AND EXERCISES

These questions and exercises are designed to help you understand and apply the following concepts: moral decision making, ethical decision making, and biopsychosocial-spiritual factors affecting moral decision making.

1. *Moral versus Ethical Decision Making*: What is the difference between "moral decision making" and "ethical decision making?" Why do social workers need to know about both types of decision making?
2. *Factors Affecting Moral Choices*: For each of the following scenarios, explain how biological, psychological, social, or spiritual factors may be affecting the client's moral decision-making process:
   a. You are working with Colin, a 10-year-old who has been picking on a Vietnamese American boy in his class, calling him names and taunting him into fights. Colin's father is currently unemployed. He blames his predicament on immigrants who come here and take all the good jobs. Colin's father has told him that America is for Americans and everyone else should stay home in their own countries.
   b. You are counseling Charlotte, a woman who suffers from kidney failure and urgently needs a kidney transplant. Over 70,000 people are on the waiting list for transplants. Charlotte feels desperate, so she has placed an advertisement on the Internet saying that she is willing to buy a kidney for $100,000. She knows that buying organs is illegal in the United States, so her advertisement uses an overseas address.
   c. You have been helping Clara deal with a loveless marriage. Her family and religious community pressured her into marrying a man who impregnated her. She says her religion prohibits divorce as marriage is a lifelong commitment. She feels sad and alone but believes trying

everything to make the marriage work is the right thing to do.

d. You are a case manager for Chris, a 24-year-old with Down syndrome. Cognitively, he functions at the level of a 6-year-old and lives in a supportive housing facility for other men and women with Down syndrome. Chris tells you that his parents want him to get a vasectomy. He thinks this is the right thing to do because his parents always know what is best for him.

3. *Assessing Attitudinal Factors*: Identify your attitudes in relation to each of the following issues. Assess the strength of your attitudes in relation to extremity, certainty, and centrality.
   a. Should the Veterans Administration (and government funds) be used to pay for transgender veterans to have sex-reassignment surgery?
   b. Should able-bodied people on welfare be required to work in order to collect their welfare benefits?
   c. Should the United States be responsible for giving asylum or safe haven to the majority of the refugees that are displaced due to a war that the United States has declared on another country?
4. *Moral-Ethical Conflicts*: For each of the following cases, identify the conflicts between the social worker's moral convictions and ethical obligations.
   a. Sripada likes her field instructor, Fritz, very much. In fact, she likes him so much that she wants to invite him to her mountain cottage for the weekend. She knows the Code of Ethics says something about dual relationships and maintaining professional boundaries. Still, she personally believes in free will and individuality, so what could it hurt to spend the weekend with Fritz?
   b. Sacha worked as a journalist before she became a social worker. She still writes articles for a human interest magazine. She finds that she gets good story material from the clients she works with. Her colleague says she is breaching client confidentiality, since she does not ask the clients for permission to tell their stories. Sacha thinks that people living in a democratic society have a right to know what is going on in their communities.
   c. Selwyn is working in a nursing home when he receives a phone call saying that he might be the winner of $1,000,000. All he has to do is fly to the Bahamas and participate in a televised talent contest. He has always wanted to be on television, so he informs his supervisor that he will be back in a couple of weeks, maybe. His supervisor says that he needs to take care of his clients first, but Selwyn says he has no time and this contest is more important. Besides, if he wins, he'll give a big donation to the home.
5. *Context of Moral Decisions*: An example earlier in this chapter described a man who rubbed his hands all over the naked body of a young girl. Although his behavior initially sounds immoral, assessing morality depends on the social context (e.g., a father giving his daughter a bath). For each of the following behaviors, describe a social context in which the behavior is immoral and a social context in which the behavior would be considered moral.
   a. Selling psychoactive (mind-altering) drugs.
   b. Lying.
   c. Voting in a presidential election.

Chapter 4

Research, Values, and Ethics

Research and evaluation textbooks typically include at least one chapter on research ethics (Bloom, Fischer, & Orme, 2005; Grinnell, 2007; Rossi, Lipsey, & Freeman, 2004; Rubin & Babbie, 2008). These chapters generally cover basic topics related to conducting ethical research with human subjects, including informed consent, confidentiality, protecting research participants from risks, deceiving research participants, conflicts of interests, and reporting findings honestly. In addition, many social work research courses ask students to take the free, online research ethics course provided by the National Institutes of Health (NIH) (http://ohsr.od.nih.gov/cbt/index.html). Successful completion of this web-based course is required for all researchers and research assistants involved in any research involving human subjects by an agency or program that receives federal funding for research.[1] Rather than repeat information that is readily available to you in your research textbook or on the NIH website, this chapter builds on the foundation provided by these materials by demonstrating how the general principles of research ethics can be put into practice.

This chapter uses two primary sources for standards and guidelines that regulate research: the NASW Code of Ethics (which governs social work practice, including research) and the Common Rule. The Common Rule is a set of federal research guidelines that govern research with human subjects in agencies that receive federal funding.[2] Because many social agencies receive federal funding, directly or indirectly,

[1] Even if your program does not require completion of the NIH training, this is a useful course to complete on your own. You will need it if you plan to conduct a thesis or other research project during your social work studies, and it may also enable you to participate as a researcher in projects carried out by your field agencies.

[2] See http://ohsr.od.nih.gov/guidelines/45cfr46.html for the complete set of Common Rule guidelines.

they must comply with these guidelines. Even when social workers do not work in an agency that is mandated to use the Common Rule, its guidelines provide generally accepted standards and protocols for researchers.

The following scenarios will be used to illustrate ethical issues that may arise in practice, as well as how these issues may be handled:

COPLA Case: A family service agency has developed a new support program for primary caregivers of people living with Alzheimer's (COPLA).[3] COPLA provides group education, skill building, and emotional support, as well as individual psychosocial assessments and referrals to additional services for family members and friends who are responsible for the care of loved ones with Alzheimer's disease. To assess the effectiveness of this program, the agency has developed an evaluation plan designed to measure the impact of COPLA on the primary caregivers and the people with Alzheimer's. The lead researcher for this project is a social worker named Risha. Risha also provides counseling services to the agency's clients.

Zaman Case: The Zaman El-Salaam[4] Community Center serves the Arab American community in a large metropolitan area. Zaman staff members are concerned about the impact of anti-Arab sentiment on the psychosocial well-being of the community, so they hire a social work researcher named Rahim to develop a study. The study will explore incidents of discrimination and the impact of such discrimination on the community. Rahim will gather information by interviewing members of the community and through participant observation (Grinnell, 2007). Rahim plans to publish an article based on this study so that other agencies in the community may also benefit from the research findings.[5]

LEARNING OBJECTIVES

Upon successful completion of this chapter, students will be able to

- Differentiate between a social worker's ethical obligations as a researcher and those as a direct service provider, including how to manage potentially conflicting obligations when a social worker is acting as both a researcher and a practitioner.
- Interact effectively with an institutional review board regarding informed consent, confidentiality, research risks, deception, and conflicts of interest.
- Engage research participants in constructive discussions related to informed consent, confidentiality and anonymity, benefits and risks, and voluntariness of participation.

The COPLA case will be used to illustrate ethical issues in relation to research on an intervention with individuals, families, and small groups. The Zaman case will be used to demonstrate ethical issues in relation to a community-based situation. The first part of this chapter explores how social workers may have different ethical obligations depending on their research and practice roles within an agency. The second part demonstrates how social work researchers can discuss ethics concerns with institutional review boards. The third part illustrates how to engage research participants[6] in conversations about informed consent, confidentiality, and risk management.

---

[3] For information on the nature of Alzheimer's and support for families affected by Alzheimer's see http://www.alz.org.

[4] Zaman El-Salaam is an Arabic name meaning, "Time for Peace."

[5] If this research was just a needs assessment for internal agency purposes, federal law would not require an ethics review. Because the findings will be published, the Common Rule does require ethics review.

[6] This chapter uses the term *research participants* rather than *research subjects* to reflect the idea that research is conducted with people who deserve to be treated with respect rather than on people who may be treated passively as objects.

ROLES: RESEARCHER VERSUS DIRECT PRACTITIONER

According to Standard 5.02 of the NASW Code of Ethics (1999), social workers have three specific ethical obligations regarding the promotion of research: to monitor and evaluate policies, the implementation of programs, and practice interventions (S.5.02[a]); to facilitate evaluation and research to contribute to development of knowledge (S.5.02[b]); and to keep current with emerging knowledge relevant to social work and to use research and evaluation evidence in professional practice (S.5.02[c]).[7] Further, the Education Policy and Accreditation Standards of the Council on Social Work Education (2008) states that scientific inquiry is one of the core values of social work. In fact, one of the primary elements of social work that distinguishes it as a profession (in contrast to lay helping) is that social workers value and make use of research-based knowledge to guide their practice. Research also helps workers in their ongoing pursuit of improving the quality of their services. The ethical principles of doing good (beneficence) and not causing harm (nonmaleficence) require that social workers facilitate and make use of research in all aspects of their work.

In some respects, the split between social work researchers and social work practitioners is a false dichotomy because all social workers have the same overarching ethical responsibilities: to promote the welfare of clients (S.1.01) and general welfare of society (S.6.02). Still, the nature of a social worker's specific duties depends on the role the worker is playing at a particular point in time. Standards 1.01 to 1.16 apply when a worker is practicing directly with clients (e.g., providing case management, counseling, therapy, support, advocacy, brokerage, mediation, or assessment services). Standards 5.02(a) to 5.02(p) apply when a social worker is acting as a researcher or working with research participants. Although ethical principles such as respect, beneficence, nonmaleficence, privacy, equity, and autonomy apply to work with both research participants and clients (Drewry, 2004), workers need to be aware of which roles they are engaged in and which specific standards may apply. The primary role of a practitioner is to serve the needs and wishes of each client. The primary role of a researcher is to gather information in accordance with scientific methods in order to generate new and better knowledge.

In the Zaman case, Rahim is a researcher who does not provide direct services to clients. Thus, he should abide by Standards 5.02(a) to 5.02(p) when working with research participants. In the COPLA case, Risha is both a researcher and a practitioner working directly with specific individuals and families. She should follow the NASW standards that apply to practitioners and researchers. If ethical standards conflict, the worker's primary duty is to serve the client, honoring the client's rights and needs (S.1.01). As a practitioner, for instance, Risha has access to confidential client information (S.1.07) that an independent researcher would not have. Thus, she must be careful about how she uses information gained in one role when she switches over to another role. In her practitioner role, clients may have provided information about the impact of Alzheimer's on their families. She should not use this information for research purposes unless she obtains specific consent from her clients.

When a social worker acts as both practitioner and researcher with the same client, the worker is engaging in a dual relationship, potentially violating two standards: Standard 1.06(c) which says workers should not engage in dual relationships with clients, and Standard 5.02(o) which says social workers should avoid dual relationships with research participants. To illustrate the potential exploitation of clients, consider Risha's request to her clients to participate in research. Her clients might feel compelled to agree to participate in the research in order to continue to receive services. Unwittingly, Risha might exert undue pressure on clients to participate in research in order to ensure a suitable sample size for the research. Given these concerns, how can a social worker ever act as both researcher and practitioner?

[7] This chapter focuses on two sets of research guidelines for social workers: Standard 5.02 of the NASW Code of Ethics, and the federal research guidelines known as the Common Rule (1991). For a code of ethics specifically related to evaluation research see American Evaluation Association (2004).

The NASW standards cited above do not place absolute prohibitions on dual relationships. In some instances, dual relationships are either unavoidable or desirable. Given the responsibility to evaluate practice, for instance, social work practitioners need to gather and assess client information in some manner.[8] Also, practitioners may be important members of research teams given their access to clients, as well as their skills at engaging them (Gantt & Levine, 1990). If COPLA wants to invite clients to participate in research, the agency respects client privacy by having practitioners (rather than strangers) solicit participation. If independent researchers were to contact clients directly, this could constitute a breach of their confidentiality. Because practitioners have a prior relationship with each client, they may also be in a better position to assess each client's capacity to consent to research. Clients with Alzheimer's, depression, uncontrolled addiction, or even high levels of stress may not be in a position to consent to research. Thus, practitioners can help determine whether such clients should be invited to participate in research, with or without the use of a proxy to provide consent. For clients who are capable of consenting, practitioners may be able to help them see how participation in research could be personally beneficial: for instance, clients may feel validated by telling their stories to researchers, knowing that their information may help others in similar situations. Practitioners may also help clients understand the potential risks of the research, knowing each client's specific strengths and vulnerabilities.

Whenever social workers engage in dual relationships, they should take all reasonable steps to minimize the risks inherent in such relationships. The following points suggest ways that workers can reduce the risks involved when they are acting dually as researchers and practitioners:

- Inform clients about the differences between a practitioner-client relationship and researcher-participant relationship, including how the worker's obligations to serve the best interests of the client take precedence over the needs of the researchers to gather information from research participants (S.1.01).
- Verbally reassure clients that they are not required to participate in research in order to receive services and that there will be no negative consequences from the agency should they decline participation.
- Assess clients for any questions, fears, confusion, or suspicion, validating their concerns and helping them make a voluntary informed decision about whether to participate in the research (Gantt & Levine, 1990).
- Help clients assess the risks and benefits of participating in research so clients can make better informed decisions about whether to participate in research.
- Provide clients with written consent forms that explain their rights as clients and potential research participants, and include the name of a supervisor, client advocate, or other official they may contact should they have any question or grievance about the voluntariness of their participation or any other ethical concerns (Melville, 2004).
- Periodically discuss the clients' participation in research to determine whether new concerns have arisen. Inform clients that they may voluntarily terminate participation in the research at any time and without fear of negative consequences (S.5.02[h]; Common Rule, 1991, §46.116[a]).
- Educate researchers and other agency staff on the importance of respecting client self-determination and access to resources even when honoring the dignity of clients in these ways may hinder the implementation of a specific research or evaluation project.
- In situations where issues of client mistrust and disempowerment are more likely to arise (e.g., with involuntary clients in criminal justice or child protection agencies), have an independent researcher solicit

[8] If evaluation is closely connected to the practitioner's role with a particular client, then the worker is not engaging in a dual relationship. If the practitioner is engaging in research for purposes that are not directly related to providing services to the particular client, then this would be considered a dual relationship.

participation, rather than the practitioner who is providing services.[9]

By taking these precautions, social workers enhance clients' right to self-determination and reduce the risks associated with asking clients to participate in research.

INTERACTING WITH AN INSTITUTIONAL REVIEW BOARD

An institutional review board (IRB) is an agency committee mandated to ensure ethics compliance for any research conducted by or at an agency that receives federal funding.[10] These boards review research proposals to ensure that proposed research complies with relevant laws, agency policies, and professional standards of practice (Common Rule, 1991). Ideally, researchers and IRB members see themselves not as adversaries but as members of the same team with similar goals: promoting ethics and excellence in research conducted by the agency. When IRBs reject research proposals or insist on changes to ensure ethical compliance, however, researchers may feel frustrated and angry (Bosk & De Vries, 2004). Social work and social science researchers, in particular, may feel misunderstood and devalued by ethics committees that are dominated by medical scientists or other disciplines (Melville, 2005). This section identifies potential areas of conflict between social work researchers and IRBs, suggesting ways that social workers can interact more effectively with IRBs.

Perhaps the best strategy for managing potential conflicts between researchers and IRBs is to pre-empt them. Conflicts often arise when researchers or IRB members have different understandings of the ethics review process and the ethics criteria that will be applied when assessing proposals. Even a relatively simple misunderstanding can cause significant grief and hurt feelings. Given the urgency of the concerns in the Zaman case, for instance, Rahim wants to begin his research immediately. He feels frustrated when the IRB tells him that he should have submitted the proposal at least one month in advance. If Rahim knew why it took so long to review a proposal (e.g., because meetings were scheduled only once a month) or the IRB had a mechanism to respond quickly to truly urgent requests, this frustration could be avoided. In the COPLA case, Risha submits an ethics proposal that complies with NASW standards as well as National Institutes of Health guidelines (Common Rule, 1991). The IRB responds that the proposal does not comply with agency policy, which uses its own standard forms and protocol. Once again, frustration could be avoided if everyone had better information and communication.

Serious complications arise when the IRB and researchers have different conceptions about what constitutes sound, ethical research. Some ethics review models, for example, are based on a framework designed to assess clinical trials of biomedical interventions (especially experimental designs comparing a group that receives an intervention with a control group that does not receive the intervention) (Drewry, 2004).[11] Although the review criteria are appropriate for this type of research, they may not be appropriate for assessing various types of social science research. Rahim proposes to study the impact of discrimination on Arab Americans

---

[9] To protect client confidentiality, the practitioner could ask the client for permission to have the researcher contact the client. The client does not provide permission to participate in the research until after the researcher has discussed all matters relating to informed consent.

[10] Even if you are working at an agency that does not receive federal funding, prudent practice suggests that all research projects should be reviewed and monitored by some type of research ethics committee.

[11] One reason that standards for ethical research developed with a bent toward biomedical research is that they were generated in response to atrocities that occurred in the field of biomedical research: the inhumane experiments conducted on Jews and others considered to be subhuman by scientists under the Nazi regime, and the Tuskeegee research on syphilis among African Americans in which participants were not informed of their condition and treatments available for it (Drewry, 2004).

by using an action research approach (Malone et al., 2006), including the use of qualitative, ethnographic methods (Rubin & Babbie, 2008). Whereas standard proposals for clinical trials include specific hypotheses, qualitative research is open-ended. Whereas there are relatively firm boundaries between the roles of researchers and research participants in standard quantitative research, the boundaries are more diffuse in action research (Eckhardt & Anastas, 2007). In fact, research participants are considered to be part of the research team. Whereas a clinical trial may have a fixed-item questionnaire, qualitative methods include open-ended interviews in which the specific questions cannot be determined in advance (Bosk & De Vries, 2004). If an IRB reviews Rahim's proposal using criteria to assess clinical trials, the proposal may appear deficient. The lack of hypotheses may look as if the research is shoddy because the researchers did not specifically identify what they sought to prove. The more diffuse researcher-participant boundaries may appear unduly risky because the researchers are handing decision-making power over to participants who will help determine how the research will be carried out. The open-ended nature of data gathering may appear to leave the agency open to untold risks because there is no control over who is asked what questions. Rahim faces many challenges in having the IRB understand and approve his proposal.

One way to make sure that IRBs understand the nature of social work research, and particular types of social work research, is to ensure that IRB membership includes people with social work backgrounds (Bosk & De Vries, 2004). Social work members can advocate for ethics review criteria that are appropriate for different types of research. They can also educate other IRB members about different types of research, including the legitimacy and value of them. If IRB membership does not include representation from social work, social workers could still offer consultation or education. To avoid suggesting that IRB members lack competence in research or ethics, such offers should be made in a sensitive manner:

> Most research conducted by this agency has used quantitative methods and experimental or quasi-experimental designs. Our social work department would like to propose a study using naturalistic inquiry. We were wondering if we could schedule a meeting with the IRB to discuss our proposal and make sure our proposal meets your expectations.

By asking the IRB for help, the social workers avoid putting IRB members on the defensive. During the meeting, they can identify any misunderstandings or problems, and determine the best way move forward in a collaborative manner (e.g., educating IRB members about social work research, proposing changes to ethics review criteria or forms, or drafting research proposals in a manner that meets the IRB's expectations).

The following sections highlight issues in which social workers and IRB members may come into conflict over the ethics of social work research: informed consent, confidentiality, research risks, deception, and conflicts of interests. The examples are not exclusive to social work research, although they do illustrate issues that are particularly relevant to social work. They also demonstrate how social workers can engage IRB members in constructive dialogues regarding potentially volatile ethical issues.

Informed Consent

As Standard 5.02(e) of the NASW Code of Ethics suggests, researchers should request written, voluntary, informed consent from potential participants before engaging them in research. Informed consent means that a person's decision about whether to participate in research should be made by the individual (or his or her legally authorized representative) without being pressured to hurry the decision, without coercion or undue influence from the researcher, and with relevant information provided in easily understood language (Citro, Ilgen, & Marrett, 2003; Common Rule, 1991, §46.116). Different states have different regulations regarding informed consent, so it is important to check local laws for possible restrictions on consent processes. For instance, some state regulations provide a one-year time limit on consent, meaning that a client's consent must be renewed if the research or intervention extends beyond one year. The informed consent process operationalizes a core value of social work, respecting the dignity and worth of all individuals, by letting them choose whether or not to participate in a particular study.

Because social workers often work with vulnerable populations, a key challenge to ensuring informed consent relates to the capacity of individuals to provide free and informed consent (Common Rule, 1991, §46.116). Potential research participants may lack mental capacity due to mental illness, cognitive disorders, uncontrolled substance abuse, or temporary conditions related to high levels of stress. In the COPLA case, people with Alzheimer's have diminished mental capacity meaning that researchers should take special precautions to assess for their ability to consent. For individuals without sufficient ability to understand the research, including its risks and benefits, the researchers should obtain consent from individuals who are authorized to provide consent on their behalf (proxies or legally recognized representatives). Risha decides to focus her evaluation on the family support systems rather than on the people with Alzheimer's. She believes that she only needs consent of the support people. Even though the research does not involve interventions with people with Alzheimer's, or gathering information from them, an IRB may still have questions about whether Risha should be required to obtain consent from proxies, as well as assent[12] from people with Alzheimer's who are unable to provide legal consent (Guinn, 2002). Risha could respond to such questions in a number of ways:

- Providing a detailed explanation of the focus of the research to illustrate how this is not a study on people with Alzheimer's but rather on family support systems.
- Altering the research to ensure that it does not directly affect the people with Alzheimer's.
- Agreeing to solicit consent from proxies and assent from people with Alzheimer's, depending on the capacity of each person with Alzheimer's.

In terms of process, Risha should validate the IRB's concerns that it is important to respect the rights of vulnerable populations (Citro et al., 2003). Once they have agreed to this general principle, Risha and the IRB can brainstorm different ways to put the principle into practice and resolve the issue. Sometimes, well-meaning researchers underestimate risks to research participants because the researchers are overly focused on achieving the goals of their studies. In this case, Risha does not look at the IRB's critique as a personal attack but rather as a reminder of the importance of protecting vulnerable research participants.

The Zaman case poses different types of concerns related to consent: How do you obtain consent when the research subject is a community rather than an individual? And how can you waive the requirement for signed consent when the research participants may be reluctant to sign forms? In terms of ascertaining consent from a community, soliciting permission from each person in the community would generally be too costly and impractical. Unfortunately, the NASW Code and most research ethics policies do not specifically address how to obtain consent from a community. Such polices seem geared for obtaining individual consents. Before submitting his research proposal to the IRB, Rahim could suggest development of a policy for obtaining consent from a community. In this way, he could ensure that his proposal will satisfy the standards of the new policy.

Rahim wants to engage the Arab American community in action research. At the time he is writing his proposal, he does not know exactly who will participate in the research and how. The nature of action research requires

[12] Although people without sufficient mental capacity cannot provide "legal consent" to participate in research, social work researchers can demonstrate respect for clients by asking for their assent. Assent refers to permission provided by a person without mental capacity, which supplements rather than replaces legal consent provided by the person's legal guardian or proxy. Chapter 14 provides further discussion on mental capacity, consent, and assent.

room for the research team and participants to evolve. Although Rahim has good intentions for his research, the community may have genuine concerns about being the target of a study: Could this study feed into anti-Arab stereotypes by painting a negative picture of this community; and could this study spur additional acts of discrimination against Arab Americans by publicizing different ways that the community could be tormented? Even if certain individuals within the community consent to the research, the community itself may have overriding concerns about the impact of the research on the community (Kaufman & Ramarao, 2005). To solicit informed consent from the community, Rahim could propose the research as a partnership. By building a research team that involves key constituencies of the Arab American community, Rahim is, in effect, obtaining its informed consent (Malone et al., 2006). For instance, his team may include representatives from Arab American community centers, houses of worship, cultural groups, social service providers, schools, and advocacy organizations. Rahim and the IRB would need to agree on how to document community consent, for instance, by having certain community representatives sign the research proposal or a separate form for community consent. Also, they would have to agree upon the extent of the community consent. For instance, the community consent might enable the researchers to passively observe community members at designated events. If Rahim wanted to interview particular individuals, he would need separate consent forms.

Assume Rahim wants the IRB to waive the general requirement of written consent (NASW Code, S.5.02[e]; Common Rule, 1991, §46.117). Within traditional Middle Eastern culture, being asked to sign a consent form after agreeing verbally might be considered an insult, demonstrating lack of trust by the researcher (Fontes, 2004). Rahim is also concerned that research participants will be reluctant to sign consents because this might give government officials a way to trace them and their answers. The IRB may initially insist on written consent, as signed consent forms provide clear evidence that participants were provided with specific information about the research and agreed to participate. Rahim may need to explain the cultural issues surrounding informed consent, particularly in the context of fear experienced by members of the target population. Once again, Rahim should not stress disagreement with the IRB, but rather agreement with the principle that there should be evidence that researchers abided by the informed consent process. Rahim and the IRB could brainstorm options: audiotape the oral consent processes, have two researchers conduct the consent process and both sign a statement confirming what occurred with each prospective participant, or ask participants who verbally agree to participate to complete an intake form that has informed consent information but does not expressly ask participants whether they agree to the terms of the consent (in other words, use an oral consent process to ensure that clients are properly informed about the research and use the intake form to document that this information has been explained).[13] By thinking outside the box (creatively), they may be able to develop solutions that meet ethical standards without compromising the effectiveness or efficiency of the research.

Confidentiality

Standards 5.02(l) and (m) direct social workers to safeguard the anonymity or confidentiality of participants and the data obtained from them (see also Common Rule, 1991, §46.116(a)[5]). Researchers ensure anonymity by collecting data from clients in a manner such that even the researcher cannot associate which participant provided which data (e.g., by asking participants to complete surveys without putting their names or other identifying information on the forms). Maintaining confidentiality means that the researchers know which data belong to which participants, but they do not release any identifying information when they disclose or publish

[13] The intake workers would need to be properly trained and supervised to ensure that they provide sufficient information about the research and obtain consent without coercion or misrepresentations.

the findings of the research. In other words, they protect the identities of the research participants (Citro et al., 2003).

Maintaining confidentiality may be particularly challenging when the research is based on a sample drawn from a relatively small, interconnected community (e.g., a small town, a cultural minority group within a larger city, or people with a relatively rare psychological disorder). In the COPLA case, Risha plans to draw her sample from the clients of a single agency. The IRB expresses concern regarding how the researchers will ensure that agency staff does not know which data come from which clients. To complicate matters, Risha is not only a researcher but also a staff member (Kaufman & Ramarao, 2005).

When preparing her proposal for IRB review, Risha should address such concerns in terms of how she intends to gather, analyze, and report her data (Ss.5.02[1] and [m]). In terms of gathering data, Risha could distribute questionnaires that participants may complete and return on an anonymous basis. Suppose, however, that Risha wanted data gathering to include interviewing participants. Risha could simply explain to participants that she is both a researcher and a practitioner with the agency, allowing participants to decide what information they wanted to disclose given her dual roles. Even if Risha promises not to share identifying information with other staff, participants may not completely trust her and may limit their responses accordingly. Alternatively, Risha could hire independent researchers to interview participants. Although the independent researchers would share the data they collected, they would remove identifying information before presenting it to Risha. Clients may not fully trust this approach either, but at least they are provided full information about the research process and can make informed decisions about what they want or do not want to disclose. If the IRB still has questions about confidentiality, Risha could admit that she shares such concerns and will take necessary precautions to minimize any threats to confidentiality.

In terms of managing data, Risha's proposal specifies how identifying information will be separated from other data. Only the two independent interviewers will have access to a key that identifies which interviews were conducted with which participants. Risha and others analyzing the data will therefore receive the data on an anonymous basis. Still, the IRB expresses concerns that information disclosed in the research report may include information attributable to particular clients (e.g., staff may recognize references to particular family structures, events, or dynamics). Initially, Risha feels defensive because the IRB seems to doubt her integrity and ability to maintain confidentiality. Rather than responding defensively, however, she validates their concern. She then explains how she will enhance confidentiality by reporting data in terms of themes rather than particular responses from each research participant. She provides an example:

> Suppose Mrs. X describes how frustrated she became when her mother walks around the nursing home without any clothes. A number of agency workers could identify Mrs. X from reading this information. Rather than reporting the incident as it happened, I would report on the theme of frustration.

Other precautions could include allowing research participants or IRB members to read the report before it is released to the public. If research participants or IRB members had any concerns about the way information was being reported, this information could be corrected before the actual release. Risha and the IRB would have to weigh the time and financial costs of taking these precautions in relation to the possible threats to confidentiality.

Standard 5.02(l) advises social workers to inform participants of any limitations of confidentiality (see also Common Rule, §46.116(a)[5]). In the Zaman case, Rahim drafts a consent form that explains the usual limitations on confidentiality, such as the duty to report concerns related to the abuse of children, elders, or people with disabilities. The form also includes the catch-all phrase that limits confidentiality, "and as otherwise permitted or required by law." The IRB asks Rahim what types of situations are covered by this phrase. Rahim responds that research records could be subpoenaed for use in a criminal trial or the Federal Bureau of Investigation (FBI) could search and seize records under section 215 of the Patriot Act (2001) for investigating terrorist threats. The IRB suggests that these exceptions should be stated explicitly, not generally implied. Although Rahim could add them, he prefers not to do so because of the impact on potential participants. Mention of the Patriot Act might elicit undue fears, resulting in a high rate of refusal from the research pool. Rahim suggests a compromise on the wording:

> All information will remain confidential, except as may be required by law in order to protect the lives or safety of others.[14]

This wording informs participants of the researcher's duty to release information to authorities without specifically mentioning terrorism or the Patriot Act. Rahim could also explain that his research is not likely to contain information related to terrorist threats and the FBI is unlikely to be interested in his data.[15] Further, the researchers and IRB must be careful in their research to avoid adding to stereotypes that Arab Americans are the only people involved in terrorism. Consider, should IRBs require consent forms to mention the Patriot Act for research on all populations, or was the suggestion about including it in this consent form due to the fact that the focus is on Arab Americans?

Research Risks

Social workers should protect research participants from unwarranted physical or mental distress, harm, danger, or deprivation (S.5.02[j]). When determining whether particular research risks are warranted, an IRB weighs the potential benefits of the research against the risks (Common Rule, 1991, §46.111(a)[2]). When research involves the evaluation of particular interventions, social workers should distinguish between the risks and benefits of the intervention versus the risks and benefits of the evaluation. In the COPLA case, the IRB questions the risks involved in COPLA's Anger Response Training Program. During this training, COPLA teaches family members how to respond when a person with Alzheimer's is angry and potentially violent. Initially, the IRB sees this research as risky because people could be hurt when they try to use what they have learned in the training. Risha explains that this is a risk of the services, not a risk of the proposed research. Clients will be engaging in the training program, whether or not they participate in the research. Clients will go through an informed consent process with their practitioners when they agree to services, including an explanation of the risks and benefits of participating in the COPLA program. Risha notes that consent to participate in the research is a separate process in which clients will be asked to complete a survey and participate in a focus group. The risks related to completing the survey and participating in a focus group are minimal, meaning that "the probability and magnitude of harm or discomfort anticipated in the research are not greater in and of themselves than those ordinarily encountered in daily life or during the performance of routine physical or psychological examinations or tests" (Common Rule, 1991, §46.102[i]).

The IRB may deem the intervention to be part of the research if the agency is conducting an experiment to test a new intervention, as opposed to evaluating an existing one. In this case, Risha would need to justify the risks of the intervention, in addition to the risks of the survey and focus group. The challenge in identifying risks of a novel psychosocial intervention is that there is no pre-existing research to document what the actual risks are. Risha could provide research evidence of the types, frequencies,

---

[14] Additional wording to cover other exceptions could follow this sentence.

[15] Another option would be for Rahim to apply for a confidentiality certificate from the National Institutes of Health or National Institute of Criminal Justice. If his research qualifies for such a certificate (based on the sensitive nature of his research topic), then he would not be compellable as a witness and his research could not be subpoenaed for court purposes (Citro et al., 2003). A confidentiality certificate would not necessarily protect the research from a Patriot Act investigation, but it could give some protection.

and magnitudes of risks experienced by families without the training. For instance, how do families normally manage wandering, disorientation, or episodes of anger? What types of harm do they experience in terms of property damage, physical abuse, social stress, emotional harm, or involvement in the criminal justice system (Citro et al., 2003)? Risha could then explain the nature of the intervention and the theory behind its use. For instance, teaching family members to respond to volatile situations by using distraction or redirection may be based on cognitive-behavioral theory. Pre-empting volatile situations by simplifying tasks for the person with Alzheimer's may be based on self-efficacy theory (e.g., creating simple routines for dressing and eating meals). The low-risk nature of some parts of the training may seem self-evident: For instance, the training suggests limiting access to sharp objects in the home; the training also suggests family members do not try to physically restrain a person with Alzheimer's who is verbally expressing anger (Alzheimer's Association of Los Angeles, n.d.). Still, without prior research evidence, Risha needs to inform prospective participants that the precise risks and benefits of the intervention are not known.

Risha may also explain how COPLA plans to minimize and respond to risks. In addition to providing group training, COPLA will assign social workers to work individually with families. These social workers can provide monitoring and support as well as referral to additional resources as needed. COPLA also plans to use weekly reports on the outcomes of the program rather than wait until the program has been completed. This will enable the program to manage any problems as they arise. By providing the IRB with a realistic assessment of the risks and how COPLA intends to manage them, Risha gains credibility and is more likely to have her research approved.

Research may pose risks not only to individuals and families but also to communities. In particular, social workers should consider risks that may arise when the research relates to topics that may be controversial within the community—for instance, questions about sex, experiments on fetal tissue, or biopsychosocial research exploring differences related to race or ethnicity. Although individuals may consent to such research, the community may have its own concerns. The research may violate certain norms or beliefs of the community, the research might pose risks of stigmatization to the community, and consumers of the research might misunderstand or misuse the results of the research. Demographic research, for instance, has been used by some life and health insurance companies to deny coverage to certain groups or to charge them higher premiums (Kaufman & Ramarao, 2005).[16] If those groups had been consulted about such risks before the research was conducted, they might have opposed the research. To demonstrate respect for the Arab American community, Rahim consults with community representatives about the potential risks of conducting his needs assessment. Overall, they support the purpose of his research, but they express concerns about some specific questions he intends to ask. The representatives help Rahim focus the research proposal on topics that maximize the benefits and minimize the risks of the research. They omit references to emotionally charged phrases, such as "Islamic fundamentalism" and "Muslim-Christian rift." They concentrate the research on the needs of the entire Arab American community and steer clear of topics that may be politically divisive or explosive.

The IRB asks Rahim about risks related to perpetuating stereotypes or misuse of the research findings by people with anti-Arab prejudices. Rahim assures the IRB that he has developed a plan for reporting the research findings designed to minimize these risks. First, the research report will be vetted by Arab American community representatives before it is released to the general public. They will ensure that the report includes an appropriate explanation of the research findings, including how they should be interpreted and used. The report will use language that discourages stereotyping and promotes a balanced picture of the strengths and

---

[16] E.g., if a study concludes that a particular ethnocultural group has a higher risk of cancer or heart disease, insurers may say this justifies imposing higher premiums on members of that group.

needs of the community. Further, the research team will provide community leaders with training on how to discuss the research findings with local media. The IRB feels reassured by the fact that Rahim has involved community representatives in a discussion of research risks, including plans for how to minimize them.

The IRB expresses one last concern about the participant observation aspect of the research. Rahim proposes to have researchers observe four town hall meetings in which people will be invited to discuss concerns about discrimination against Arab Americans. Some IRB members suggest that this is too risky because violence could erupt during the meetings. Rahim wonders whether this concern is based on stereotypes held by these IRB members ("Arabs are violent"). Would they have expressed the same concerns if the research involved participant observation of a town hall meeting in a European American community (Kaufman & Ramarao, 2005)? Rahim does not want to put IRB members on the defensive by accusing them of prejudice. Rather, he cites the history of peaceful meetings at the community center and invites IRB members to observe some meetings for themselves, as they are open to the public. In addition, Rahim suggests that the IRB could become more involved in ongoing monitoring of the research rather than relying on a one-time prospective review of the research (Bosk & De Vries, 2004). The IRB appreciates his invitation but suggests that members do not have enough time to monitor research on an ongoing basis. They work out a compromise in which Rahim will provide more frequent reports than the usual yearly reports that the IRB policy generally requires.

Deception

Under informed consent provisions in the NASW Code of Ethics (S.5.02[e]) and the Common Rule (§46.116), social workers should provide prospective participants with full and honest information about the research, its risks, and its benefits. Further, Standard 4.04 suggests that social workers should not participate in deceptive practices. These guidelines do not completely prohibit the use of deception in research. There may be certain degrees of deception that are necessary to facilitate particular types of research (Grinnell, 2007). Although some level of deception may be ethically justifiable, researchers and IRBs should be very cautious about its use given the negative effects that deception may entail: imposing risks on people without their consent, disrespecting the dignity and worth of particular individuals or groups, and creating mistrust and anger toward researchers among research participants and the general public. This section explores how researchers may try to justify a relatively small degree of deception to gain an IRB's approval. Remember, deception is not required for most social work research. As professionals who value protection of vulnerable populations, social workers should be particularly wary of misleading or manipulating people in order to further a particular research agenda.

To justify the use of deception, a researcher would need to demonstrate that *(a)* the type of deception does not pose significant risks to participants, and *(b)* there are no alternative methods of conducting the research in an effective manner. Suppose Risha wants to compare an experimental group and a control group in her study of families affected by Alzheimer's. Under Standard 5.02(i), she knows she should ensure that research participants have access to appropriate support services. She proposes to divide her research sample into two groups, one that receives the COPLA program immediately and one that goes onto a waiting list for two months. The only deception contemplated by this proposal is that the wait-listed participants will not be told that the primary purpose of putting them on a waiting list is to create a control group for comparison purposes. In other words, the researchers will compare the immediate-service group with the wait-list group to evaluate the effects of the program. Risha does not want to anger people who will be placed on the waiting list, as they may drop out of the research. Risha's proposal explains that the deception is minimal, as the wait-list group will receive services in just two months. Risha also suggests that the wait-list group may actually receive better services because social workers will improve the program based on the experiences of the initial group.

The IRB questions whether the research could be conducted in a manner that does not involve deception. Working together, Risha and the IRB develop a method that eliminates the need for deception. Risha will inform all research participants that they will be divided into two groups, one which will receive the full COPLA program and one which will initially receive supportive family counseling (but not the support group). After two months, the support group will be open to everyone. If some people assigned to the family counseling group want support group services, COPLA will refer them to similar services offered by another agency. This plan enables the researchers to be completely open and honest with research participants while also ensuring equitable access to services.

When reviewing the Zaman proposal, the IRB suggests that the participant observation aspect of the research involves deception. In particular, members of the research team will be posing as community members as they observe four town hall meetings. Rahim explains that even though the researchers are not identifying themselves as researchers, the deception is minimal. In fact, the researchers *are members* of the community, so they are presenting themselves in an honest fashion. IRB members contend that this is not full disclosure, which Rahim admits is correct. They jointly explore the risks and benefits of not exposing the researchers' identities as researchers. The primary benefit is that participants in the meeting will behave as they normally do; they will neither guard nor embellish their responses just because researchers are in the room. The researchers will be able to gather data in a natural community setting. Given the genuineness of the data, the researchers will be in a better position to identify real needs and recommend appropriate services for the Arab American community.

The primary risk is that some community members may feel duped or betrayed because their participation in a community meeting was being monitored and reported. Rahim explains that these risks are relatively low because the community meetings are open to the public, including the media. Participants will know that their input may be reported, though not specifically as part of Zaman's study. Further, community leaders will have already provided consent for the researchers to be present. Finally, the researchers will not gather or report information that identifies specific participants of the meetings.

The IRB asks whether the research could be implemented in a manner that does not include deception. Rahim advises the IRB of the benefits of participant observation and naturalistic inquiry, demonstrating why it is important for the researchers to basically blend into the environment (Rubin & Babbie, 2008). Given the minimal risks of the deception in this case, in conjunction with the safeguards proposed by Rahim, the IRB approves the use of participant observation without the researchers having to explicitly reveal their identities.

Conflicts of Interest

Standard 5.02(o) of the NASW Code states that social workers should avoid conflicts of interest with research participants. Workers should be particularly aware of conflicts that may arise when clients are participating in research. The primary obligation of a social worker is to serve clients as clients rather than as research participants or members of the research team (S.1.01). Thus, the needs of clients take precedence over the needs of the researcher. As explained earlier, social work researchers should ensure that clients have access to necessary services, even if this might pose challenges in obtaining a control group that does not receive services. Likewise, researchers should not exploit clients or impose risks, just to serve research purposes.

Risha proposes to use the last 15 minutes of each hour-long group session to have clients complete a questionnaire. The IRB considers this requirement to be contrary to client interests because the research is taking time away from services. The IRB asks Risha to consider other ways of collecting data that would not interfere with services—for instance, shortening the questionnaire, reducing the number of times data will be collected, offering the survey online so clients may complete it at their convenience, or giving clients a modest payment to stay after each session to complete the questionnaires. Risha agrees to review these options and resubmit her proposal.

In the Zaman case, Rahim's proposal entails dual relationships as an integral part of the research approach. Action research involves clients as members of the research team. In other words, Arab Americans who have been subjected to discrimination will be collecting data (as researchers) and also providing data (as members of the client community and research sample). The IRB has difficulty with the nature of action research because the board is more familiar with research methods that provide a clear separation of researcher and client-participant roles (Malone et al., 2006). In particular, the IRB expresses concerns that research team members will not be able to collect and analyze data in an objective manner because they are too closely involved with the research topic. Rahim takes an educative approach to explaining the nature of action research and how the multiple roles can be accommodated. Although research team members may have personal experience with discrimination, they will be trained in how to gather and analyze data without imposing their biases. The training includes self-appraisal of their own beliefs, biases, and experiences. By raising their self-awareness, they learn how to separate out their own beliefs, biases, and experiences from the beliefs and experiences of the research participants they will be interviewing. Although there are risks of involving clients as researchers, there are also benefits: members of the Arab American community may be more likely to trust and disclose information to people from their own community, Arab American researchers may be able to interview participants in Arabic, and Arab American researchers can help interpret participants' responses from a cultural perspective (Bein, 2003). As the IRB learns more about the nature of action research, it becomes more comfortable with involving members of the client community as part of the research team.

As this section suggests, the ethics review process is not simply a matter of filling out forms and asking for approval. At its best, ethics review is an interactive process between researchers and IRB members to ensure that proposed research will be carried out in an ethical, effective, and efficient manner. Unfortunately, some IRBs review ethics proposals in private and only provide researchers with formal written feedback, not allowing for face-to-face exchanges between researchers and IRB members (Citro et al., 2003). Still, when difficult questions or conflicts arise, researchers may ask for informal consultation with IRB representatives. By engaging IRBs in a direct, collaborative manner, researchers not only improve their chances of gaining timely ethics approval but also enhance their ongoing relationship with the IRBs.

ENGAGING CLIENTS

When submitting an ethics proposal for IRB approval, researchers generally need to include an informed consent form that they plan to use with prospective research participants (S.5.02[e]; Common Rule, 1991, §46.116 and §46.117).[17] IRBs typically focus on the content of the informed consent form rather than how the form will be explained to participants. Although consent forms are supposed to be written in easily understood language,[18] researchers should not simply hand out forms and ask clients to sign them. The mere signing of a form does not amount to giving informed consent (Kaufman & Ramarao, 2005) and does not guarantee that the true wishes of participants will be respected. Researchers should engage participants orally to ensure that they actually understand what they are being asked to sign. Documenting consent is actually of secondary importance in the consent process (Citro et al., 2003). The following sections describe how to engage participants in a discussion of informed consent, including topics related to informing participants about the

[17] The requirement of written consent may be waived under certain circumstances, such as when the research entails minimum risk and obtaining consent of participants is not feasible.

[18] Consider the education level(s) of the prospective research participants and ensure that the language is accessible to those at the lowest levels of education and literacy that you may expect. As a general guideline, consider writing consent forms in language suitable for people who read at a Grade 6 level.

research, confidentiality, risks and benefits, and voluntariness.

Information about the Research

The "informed" part of informed consent means that participants should be provided with sufficient information about the research to enable them to make educated decisions about whether or not to participate in the research (S.5.02[e]; Common Rule, §46.116). To inform participants about the basics of the research, ensure that you cover the "5 W's:" who, what, where, when, and why.

"Who" refers to both "Who is conducting the research?" and "Who is being asked to participate?" In the COPLA research, Risha might introduce herself to a prospective participant, Pete Peterson, as follows:

> Hello, Mr. Peterson. My name is Risha Richelieu. I am a counselor and researcher who works for COPLA, the caregivers' program for people living with Alzheimer's. We are inviting COPLA clients, like yourself, to provide feedback on their experiences with the program. Would you mind spending 5 to 10 minutes with me to discuss how you might be able to help out?

Risha explains who she is and who she is approaching in a succinct, matter-of-fact manner. She partializes the information into small chunks to avoid overwhelming Mr. Peterson and to allow him to respond throughout the informed consent process. For instance, Mr. Peterson could ask if Risha is going to be his counselor or whether all counselors are researchers. Risha should respond to his questions and concerns as they arise, meaning that she may be providing information in a different order than that provided below. Risha does not try to cover all the information in the consent form, focusing on what she believes is most important. For instance, the consent form identifies the government agency that is paying for the research. Since this source does not present any conflicts of interest, she decides not discuss who is paying unless Mr. Peterson asks. Her closing question shows respect for Mr. Peterson's time and choices by asking him whether he would mind talking further about the research.

"What" refers to "What is the nature of the research?" and "What is the participant being asked to do?" The researcher does not need to recite the whole research proposal. Providing detailed descriptions of research questions, hypotheses, and methodologies may only serve to confuse or frustrate participants. Risha simplifies her explanation as follows:

> Our agency is trying to assess how well the COPLA program is working and how we might be able to improve services. My job is to hand out a short questionnaire and ask clients to answer questions based on their own views. There are no right and wrong answers. The questionnaire includes 10 multiple-choice questions and 4 short-answer questions. You may answer as few or as many of the questions as you want, though we hope you feel comfortable answering all of them. Let me stop talking for a moment, so you can ask questions.

Risha's explanation informs Mr. Peterson about the type of research she is conducting, as well as what roles she and Mr. Peterson will play in this research. Explanations of the research will vary depending on the nature of the research and how complex it is. Most people have a basic understanding of what it is like to answer a questionnaire, so the explanation can be fairly brief. If the research involves focus groups, participant observation, or some type of psychosocial manipulation and testing, the explanation may require further detail. Note how Risha does not ask a closed-ended yes/no question, "Do you have any questions?" Instead, she openly invites Mr. Peterson to ask questions. Sometimes, people are too embarrassed to ask questions, for fear of showing ignorance or disrespect. By demonstrating that she expects questions, Risha tries to make Mr. Peterson feel more comfortable asking them.

"Where" refers to "Where does the research take place?" and *"When" refers to "When does the research participant carry out their obligations if they agree to participate?"* Typically, the when and where questions are straightforward and can be discussed together.

> We are conducting the research at the agency, in COPLA's board room. If you decide to take part in this study, I'll ask you to answer the questionnaire at the end of each group session. Since your group meets once a week for six weeks, you will be asked to complete the questionnaire six times. Each questionnaire takes 5 to 10 minutes to answer. [Risha pauses]

By explaining the duration of Mr. Peterson's participation, Risha ensures that he knows the extent of his obligations in the research. This not only respects his right to make informed decisions but also enhances the chances that he will follow through on his commitments. Risha pauses, giving Mr. Peterson a period of silence to think about Risha's information and formulate any questions he may have. He might ask about the confidentiality of the process, particularly whether the group facilitator will know who is completing the forms. He might also ask whether he could agree to the research but then drop out if he decides he does not want to fill out any more questionnaires. These issues (confidentiality and voluntariness) are explored below. However, if the participant raises these concerns at this point in the dialogue, the researcher should attend to them as they arise.

Why refers to "Why is this research being conducted?" In other words, the researcher should explain the purpose or rationale for the research. Risha partially answered this question earlier, when explaining that the agency is conducting an evaluation of its services. As this example illustrates, answers to the 5 W's are interconnected. Risha provides further explanation as follows:

> The reason we are conducting this evaluation is to improve services. We value your input. As a client of the COPLA program, you can tell us what parts of the program have been helpful to you and your family, and which parts could be improved. We will gather the feedback from all the research participants and make recommendations to the program staff regarding any changes that could enrich the program for future clients. I want to make sure I am explaining myself clearly. Perhaps you could summarize your understanding of the research.

Risha explains the purpose of the research in a manner that shows Mr. Peterson why his participation is important. If he does not know the rationale for the research, he may be less likely to agree to it. Risha concludes her explanation with an invitation for Mr. Peterson to summarize the research. She explains that she wants to make sure she was clear rather than suggesting that she is testing Mr. Peterson's understanding or memory. Asking participants to summarize what they have heard provides the researcher with an opportunity to clarify any misunderstandings. Further, it enhances the informed consent process by ensuring that the participants are truly informed—not just that the researcher has provided information but that the participants actually understand it.

Asking prospective research participants to explain their understandings of the research is particularly important when there are questions about the participant's mental capacity. For instance, if Risha was engaging a person with early stage dementia, she would need to be particularly careful to assess the person's ability to understand the nature of the research as well its risks and benefits (as described below). If the person is unable to convey a good general understanding of the research, then the researcher should terminate the informed consent process in a respectful manner.[19]

In some instances, researchers cannot fully explain the research or rationale for the research without compromising the research itself (Citro et al., 2003). Earlier, for instance, we discussed the possibility of an experimental design in which Risha would compare the effects of two different interventions: one a group intervention and one a family intervention. Assume the IRB approved this design, provided that the researchers

[19] The researcher could consider inviting a proxy to provide consent on the participant's behalf, as described in Chapter 13.

provide participants with sufficient information about the research. Risha is concerned that if she provides too much information about the two interventions, this will skew the results (e.g., creating a placebo effect or expectations among participants about what they should experience and report back to the researcher). Thus, Risha must find a way to ensure that clients have sufficient information about the research without having it bias the findings.

> The purpose of this research is to study how well our COPLA program works. We will randomly divide the clients into two groups. Half will have group counseling. Half will have family counseling. We will ask both groups for feedback on the program they receive in order to see what works well, and what can be improved. If you agree to participate in this research, you will not know which group you will be in until we assign you to one of the two groups.

Risha can provide further information about the nature of group versus family counseling, but her explanations may remain somewhat general, particularly with respect to the expected outcomes for each group. For instance, she might not disclose specific hypotheses about which group will have better results, so as not to plant expectations of certain outcomes in the minds of participants. Mr. Peterson may have questions about which option is better. Similar to a social worker-client relationship, the research-participant relationship is built on trust. Thus, it is important for the researcher to provide information in an honest and trustworthy manner. If this is the first time that an intervention is being tested, Risha can honestly say, "There is no research that says whether group or family counseling is better. We believe that both interventions can be helpful. The purpose of this research is to see what is most useful, and for whom." If Mr. Peterson expresses concern about random selection and wants to be assured of receiving group counseling, Risha could offer to refer him to services at another agency.

> To participate in services at this program, we are asking clients to agree to random selection into group or family counseling. If you are saying that you would only participate in group counseling, then I could refer you for group services at another program.

Many types of social work research are relatively clear and straightforward to explain. Often, clients do not have many questions about the nature of the research. Instead, they are more likely to raise questions and concerns about confidentiality, risks, benefits, and voluntariness, as discussed below.

Confidentiality

One of the most important ways that researchers can build trust with prospective research participants is to explain the nature of confidentiality—what confidentiality means, what is included in confidentiality, and what is not included in confidentiality. Confidentiality may be important to participants for various reasons: Some simply value their privacy for cultural or individual reasons; others may be concerned that sensitive information, if known by others, could hurt them in terms of employment, insurability, civil or criminal liability, family relationships, peer relationships, or other social connections (Citro et al., 2003). By providing clear explanations, participants learn what types of risks they are taking when they disclose personal information. Risha explains the general nature of confidentiality as follows:

> As a research participant, you have a right to confidentiality, meaning that we will respect your right to privacy. We will take all reasonable steps to make sure that nobody outside of the research team will know that you took part in this research. When we write our research report we will make sure that your name and other identifying information is excluded.

The informed consent form may explain specific steps being taken to ensure confidentiality—for instance, maintaining records in locked file cabinets or password-protected computer files. Orally, the researcher may omit the details of how data may be protected unless the participant expresses concerns. Mr. Peterson, for instance, may ask whether his counselor will have access to his responses. Risha may explain how the researchers will maintain client confidentiality, even within the agency:

> Only members of the research team will have access to the questionnaires. Other agency staff will only have access to our research reports. When we write our research reports, we will take out any information that identifies specific clients. Your counselor will not know how you responded to any of the questions. In fact, your counselor will not even know if you completed the questionnaire.

As noted earlier in the section on interacting with IRBs, confidentiality of research records is not absolute; there are numerous possible exceptions. When explaining exceptions to clients, the researcher needs to balance being open and honest with participants about possible threats to confidentiality, while not scaring away the participant. Rather than provide participants with a very long list of possible exceptions, the researcher should focus on the most likely exceptions given the particular circumstances of the research. In Risha's research, the participants are caregivers of people with Alzheimer's. Most of the caregivers are middle-aged or elder adults, and most of the people with Alzheimer's are elderly. Risha would not need to state explicitly that she has a duty to report child abuse for this research, because that type of abuse is less likely to be raised and would be covered by her general statement about disclosure of information required by state laws. She should specifically discuss her duty to report suspicion of abuse toward elders or people with disabilities, because these types of concerns are more likely to arise with the target population:

> As a social work researcher, I have an ethical and legal responsibility to ensure that vulnerable elders and people with disabilities are protected from mistreatment. If you provide me with information that raises concerns about the safety of an elder or person with a disability, then I may need to report it to appropriate authorities.

Notice how Risha states clearly that she has a duty to protect certain classes of people but leaves open whether she would be absolutely required to report particular information and to whom. If she wanted to be precise about what is reportable and to whom, she would need to provide a lot of detail. Her general information gives the client sufficient information to know that certain types of information *might* be reportable but leaves her with some discretion should actual abuse concerns arise. If the client asks what she means, she could offer concrete examples:

> My responses would depend on the seriousness of the situation. If you told me that you had a gun and you were going to go home and kill your father, then I would need to contact the police in order to protect your father. If you told me that you sometimes get angry at your father and yell at him, I would probably ask a few more questions to see if there are any serious risks. If the risks were not serious, then I might check to see if you have a social worker you can talk to about this, but I would not need to contact the police or your own counselor. I would respect your confidentiality.

Sometimes, the circumstances of the research do not allow for full confidentiality. Researchers should ensure that clients are aware of these circumstances. If Risha were to hold a focus group, for instance, the feedback from each individual would be heard by other individuals in the group. The researcher should explain how each member of the focus group will be asked to maintain the confidentiality of the rest of the members:

> During the focus group, we will ask everyone for his or her feedback on the COPLA program. We want everyone to feel comfortable sharing information in front of each other, so we will ask everyone to sign an informed consent form agreeing that information discussed during the focus group will not be shared with anyone outside the group. Although we ask everyone to agree, this is really an agreement based on trust. We cannot promise you that everyone in the group will respect the agreement.

Here Risha explains how she will encourage group members to respect confidentiality, but she is also honest about the difficulty of enforcing this agreement. This statement invites Mr. Peterson to discuss any concerns about sharing information in the focus group. If he is uncomfortable sharing certain information in the group, Risha may be able to offer him other ways of providing feedback (e.g., in written form or in an individual meeting).

Risks and Benefits

Explaining the risks and benefits of the research allows participants to assess the possible consequences, good and bad, of taking part in the research (Common Rule, §46.116). Social workers may use the biopsychosocial-spiritual perspective to consider the full range of possible consequences that may arise.

- Bio: Biological benefits include improvements to physical health and functioning. Biological risks include possible harm to physical health and functioning (e.g., side effects of medical interventions such as nausea, physical discomfort, constipation, heart attack, or sexual dysfunction). Physical harm may also arise due to accidents, for example, falling while engaged in physical activity.
- Psycho: Pyschological benefits include improvements to mental health, emotional well-being, cognitive functioning, or behavioral functioning. Psychological risks include possible harm to these same areas. Common risks for social work research include inducing anxiety or emotional distress.
- Social: Social benefits include improvements in family relationships, peer relationships, work relationships, financial well-being, or legal status. Social risks include harms in these same areas. Confidentiality is often related to such risks, as the possibility of improper disclosure of information could cause harm in various social relationships (e.g., an employer who fires an employee after discovering information that projects negative images of the employee).
- Spiritual: Spiritual benefits include doing something meaningful, such as contributing to a particular social cause, making sacrifices for the welfare of others, or fulfilling the expectations of one's religion or moral conscience. Often, participating in research does not provide participants with tangible benefits, but participants may feel good about helping others or enhancing knowledge so that better services can be provided in the future. Spiritual risks include placing participants in positions that are inconsistent with their religious beliefs or which place them in conflict with their core convictions.

When choosing which risks and benefits to discuss with participants, social workers should focus on those that are most significant, from the client's perspective. Risha knows that when she evaluates the COPLA program, participants will not receive direct benefits from the research. Their feedback will help enhance services for future clients, as Risha explains:

> If you choose to take part in this research, you will be helping us improve our program for the next clients that take part in it. Although this may not help you and your family directly, you may feel the sense of satisfaction that goes along with being able to help other families who are trying to cope with Alzheimer's.

Risha contemplates providing participants with gift cards from a local department store to compensate participants for their time. She has a very limited budget, so she decides instead to offer participants drinks and healthy snacks to eat while they are filling out the questionnaires. She hopes this will validate their contributions to the research project and make them feel comfortable as they provide their feedback.[20]

Risha's evaluation poses minimal risks to participants, which she explains concisely:

[20] Consider how offering snacks might skew or otherwise affect the research results.

> The risks of participating in this research are low. The main cost to you is your time, approximately 40 to 60 minutes spread over 6 weeks. If any questions or concerns arise when you are completing the questionnaire, feel free to ask me for assistance. If I am unable to provide you with the support you need, I will refer you to someone who can.

If the questionnaire dealt with sensitive topics (e.g., abuse, sexuality, trauma), the researcher could describe risks related to raising anxiety or distress more specifically. In general, the greater the research risks, the more time the researcher should spend engaging the client in a discussion of them. The questions in Risha's study deal with matters that are already being explored in the COPLA intervention, so participants will already have access to social work support for issues that may arise from the questionnaire.

To ensure that participants understand the potential consequences of participating in the research, the researcher could ask them to review its potential risks and benefits. Ensuring that participants understand the risks and benefits is particularly important when risks are significant or when there may be some question about the participant's mental capacity to provide consent. Consider how Risha could engage a client in a discussion of research risks if the research were not simply an evaluation of an existing service but a study comparing a new intervention with a more traditional one.

> Because we are testing a new approach to managing anger for people with Alzheimer's, we need to do whatever we can to minimize any risks. As the consent form explains, the COPLA program is designed to help family members respond when people with Alzheimer's become angry. Although this program is designed to decrease the risks of violence, we do not yet know how well the program will work and even if there is a possibility that violence could increase. If you have any concerns about the program or the research, feel free to discuss them with program or research staff. In addition, the consent form provides the name and phone number for a client advocate, who is an independent official who is available to hear any concerns and act on your behalf.

Risha informs Mr. Peterson about the availability of various support persons (S.5.02[i]), including an independent advocate, as a means of reducing risks and reassuring him. At this point, Risha should engage Mr. Peterson in a discussion of his questions or concerns about research risks and benefits. She should not ask him to consent until she is sure he has a solid understanding of the research, its confidentiality, and its risks and benefits.

The final part of the informed consent process is asking the client for consent. As the following section explains, researchers should ensure that prospective participants understand that they have a free choice about whether or not to consent.

Voluntariness

The voluntary nature of informed consent is so vital that it should be mentioned several times throughout the written and oral consent processes. Researchers must be sensitive to the fact that participants may feel pressured to consent to research, even when the researchers have not intended to pressure them. Voluntariness is presented here as the last element of informed consent because researchers should remind participants of the voluntariness of participating before finally asking clients whether they are willing to provide consent. Risha puts the principle of voluntariness into practice by explaining

> I want to assure you that participation in this research is completely voluntary. You should feel free to say either yes or no to our request. If you decide not to participate in the research, you will receive the same services and you will be treated the same by the agency. If you have felt pressured to agree to the research, by me or anyone else, this would be a good time to discuss it. I want to make sure you feel the decision about taking part in the research is completely up to you and I'd like to hear any concerns you may have.

Risha explains voluntariness in clear, concrete terms. She wants Mr. Peterson to understand that there will be no negative consequences if he rejects participation. She also lets him know that she wants to know if he feels any pressure to participate. Pressure to participate may come from the researcher, the social workers, other service providers, friends, or family members. Researchers should take particular precautions to ensure voluntariness when participants are in vulnerable situations. Consider involuntary clients, such as those involved in child protective services for abuse or neglect,[21] or clients who have been referred to services through the criminal justice system.[22] Such clients may feel pressure to participate in the research in order to receive favorable treatment from their child protection workers or corrections officers. In addition to explaining voluntariness to the participants, the researchers should also work with the program staff to ensure that they are not imposing any pressure on clients (e.g., asking protection workers or corrections officers to inform clients that they are free to choose whether to participate in the research, and to reassure clients that whether or not they participate will not affect their services or standing with the agency).

Voluntariness applies throughout the research process, not simply at the sample recruitment stage. Researchers should advise clients that they may end participation in research at any time, without incurring any negative consequences (S.502[h]). Risha explains

> If you agree to participate in research now, we hope you will complete all six questionnaires. You do not have to complete all of them. You may decide not to answer some questionnaires, or you may decide to skip certain questions. These are your choices. There are no penalties if you do not answer all the questions or if you change your mind and withdraw from the research altogether.

If, during the course of the research, a researcher observes that a participant is distressed or otherwise at risk, the researcher should remind the participant about the right to withdraw from the research at any time. The researcher should avoid any pressure to continue to participate, even though withdrawal means the researcher is losing valuable data.[23] If the participant loses mental capacity to provide informed consent, the researcher should request consent of a proxy about continuation or withdrawal from the research.

If and when a client provides verbal consent to research, the researcher may then ask the client to sign the consent form. The researcher should thank the participant for agreeing to participate, offering encouragement without putting pressure on the participant for continuing. When a prospective participant refuses to participate, the researcher should also thank the participant. Risha leaves the door open for future participation.

> Thank you for taking the time to hear about the research and thank you for sharing your concerns with me. I respect your decision not to participate at this time. If you have any questions or want to discuss participating at some point in the future, here is my business card with my phone number.

When having participants sign consent forms, researchers should help them complete any sections that need to be filled in, for instance, dates, names, and contact information. Sometimes, informed consent forms require the participant's initials on each page or initials next to specific provisions that the researchers want to highlight (e.g., acknowledgment of certain research risks and exceptions to confidentiality). Initialing provides the researcher and participant with another

---

[21] See Common Rule, 1991, §46.401 to §46.409 for special guidelines to protect the interests of children, including wards of the state.

[22] See Common Rule, 1991, §46.301 to §46.306 for special guidelines to protect the interests of prisoners and others involved in the criminal justice system (http://www.hhs.gov/ohrp/humansubjects/guidance/45cfr46.htm#46.301).

[23] Researchers may be feeling pressure from the agency or research sponsor to complete the research as quickly and efficiently as possible. They may require considerable moral fortitude to resist pressuring people into participating in their research.

opportunity to discuss any concerns about these aspects of the research. Once the participant has signed the consent form, the participant or another witness may sign the form to acknowledge witnessing the signature of the participant. The researcher should offer the participant a signed copy of the consent form so that both parties have a record of what was agreed. Although a consent form is a binding agreement, remember that it has an escape clause: The participant may terminate participation at any time (unless the consent form specifies other provisions regarding termination).

CONCLUSION

This chapter has highlighted how to apply ethical and regulatory guidelines during the first stages of the research process: obtaining an IRB's approval for the research and engaging clients in an informed consent process. The principles of informed consent, confidentiality, respect, honesty, avoiding conflicts of interest, and minimizing risks apply throughout the research process. Researchers should have methods for monitoring implementation of the IRB-approved research protocol to ensure that high ethical standards are maintained through all stages of the research process, including data collection, data storage, and reporting. Periodic reviews may be conducted by the IRB, by research supervisors, or by an independent research auditor (Reamer, 2001a). The reviewers may review documentation of informed consent processes, consult with members of the research team, and talk to a sample of research participants to obtain their feedback on the research process. Unfortunately, few agencies commit significant resources to monitoring the implementation of their research ethics protocols (Bosk & De Vries, 2004). In the absence of mechanisms for ongoing monitoring, problems may be brought to light only after serious breaches of ethical or legal standards and complaints raised by research participants hurt by such breaches. Ultimately, researchers must monitor themselves to ensure they are following ethical and legal standards, respecting participants' right to informed consent, treating them with honesty and respect, safeguarding confidentiality, avoiding conflicts of interest, and minimizing the risks of the research.

DISCUSSION QUESTIONS AND EXERCISES

The following questions and exercises are designed to help you apply ethical principles and standards to research situations involving institutional review boards and prospective research participants.

1. *Dual Roles*: Sunny runs a psychoeducational group for parents of children with developmental delays. She is also responsible for evaluating the effectiveness of this program. Sunny cooks supper for the group's final session, hoping that her efforts will make clients feel good when they are completing their evaluation forms. What are the potential benefits of having Sunny act as both a social work practitioner and a researcher? What are the risks of having Sunny act as both a practitioner and a researcher? Which standards from the NASW Code, if any, has Sunny violated?
2. *Managing Conflict With an IRB*: Review the section on "Interacting with IRBs" and identify examples in which the researcher used each of the following techniques to work through a conflict with the IRB:[24]
   a. Validating the IRB's concerns by agreeing to general ethics principles.
   b. Educating the IRB with information provided in a nonjudgmental manner.
   c. Requesting education or information from the IRB.
   d. Brainstorming options to develop a creative solution.
   e. Clarifying information to address a misunderstanding.
   f. Compromising to reach a somewhat satisfactory solution, even though neither side thinks it is a perfect solution.

[24] For further information on conflict resolution techniques, see Barsky, 2007a.

3. *Critiquing IRB Dialogue*: Rick and Jane have been hired by the department of corrections to evaluate the effectiveness of an "Anti-Violence Group" that is currently being offered to youths (aged 16–17) serving time for convictions related to gang violence. The following paragraph is an excerpt from their proposal for Human Participants Review to the IRB of the Department of Corrections:

   Selection of Participants: Participants for this evaluation will be drawn from the Anti-Violence Group offered at the Mahi-Mahi Detention Center. All participants of this group will be invited to participate by providing them with a flyer explaining the evaluation and the fact that their participation is purely voluntary. If they choose not to participate, there will be no negative consequences and they can continue to participate in the Anti-Violence Group. Anyone who agrees to participate will be provided with a $100 hardware store voucher that can be used upon release from jail.

   When Jane and Rick went before the IRB to defend their proposal, the following dialogue took place:

   IRB MEMBER: Your proposal says that participation is voluntary, but how can it be voluntary when these are people who are locked up in jail and have to do what they are told?

   RICK: That's stupid. We can't tell them anything. We're not jail guards or anything. We have no power over any of the potential participants. We won't even get to see them face-to-face unless they agree to see us.

   IRB MEMBER: I don't understand. They are in jail. They have to participate in this group and if they participate in the group, they have to participate in your research.

   JANE: Your first two points are exactly right. They are in jail and they do have to participate in the group. If you look at the sample flyer and consent form, though, you'll see that we explain that it's up to each person to decide whether or not to participate.

   IRB MEMBER: Won't they still feel pressure to participate? This is a vulnerable population, you know.

   RICK: Good point. One of the ways that we will reduce this risk is that we'll meet with the jail staff and the people running the group to let them know not to put pressure on anyone to participate. The cooperation of staff is important.

   IRB MEMBER: That would be helpful. My other concern is that these research participants are minors. Don't you need parental consent?

   JANE: There's no risk to the research itself, so parental consent really isn't a problem. All we'll be doing is giving participants a written survey when they complete their group program. At 16 or 17 years old, they should be old enough to give their own consent.

   Critique each of the responses of the principal investigators in terms of how well they covered ethical concerns such as voluntary participation, informed consent, anonymity, confidentiality, honesty, risks, and benefits. Also, critique the responses in terms of how well they implemented the following skills:

   - Provide clear, concise answers.
   - Respond assertively (rather than simply agreeing with everything the IRB suggests), without becoming aggressive or defensive.
   - Validate problems when IRB members raise significant issues, and describe possible ways to deal with these.
   - Thank the IRB for their time and suggestions.

   After you have critiqued the dialogue, draft "word-for-word" examples of how the researchers could have responded to the IRB more effectively.

4. Assume you are a member of an institutional review board (IRB) whose job is to review the following scenarios. Refer to

Standard 5.02 of the NASW Code of Ethics and §46.111 of the Common Rule to help you identify the potential ethical issues in relation to confidentiality, informed consent, risk, conflict of interest, or honesty. For each ethical issue, suggest a way that the social worker proposing the research could address the issue in a manner that satisfies ethical standards without hindering the researcher's ability to carry out the research in an effective and efficient manner (Sweet, 1999).

a. Randi proposes to study the acculturation process of women refugees. Her target population includes women from a culture in which it would be inappropriate to ask a woman to participate in research (or any activity in which family information could be made public) without the permission of her husband (if married) or father (if single). Randi develops a consent form designed to respect this cultural norm by requesting consent of the woman's husband or father.
b. Rhoda proposes to study the psychological motivations of people who write graffiti in public spaces. To solicit her research sample, Rhoda plans to have her researchers monitor places where graffiti often appears, inviting graffiti artists to participate in her research. To minimize risks to researchers, who will be doing most of their work at night in unlit locations, Rhoda plans to hire trained, plain-clothes security guards to accompany them. To protect the confidentiality of her research participants, Rhoda will advise participants that she will not tell police who drew the graffiti.
c. Robert proposes to study how people react to receiving HIV-positive test results. He plans to work with a communicable disease clinic that provides blood tests, as well as pretest and posttest counseling. Robert's informed consent forms suggest that the research is designed to assess the needs of people who receive HIV test results. Robert's questionnaire includes questions designed to identify the needs of this population but also some questions related to their psychological condition. He does not want to tell potential participants about the psychological questions because he thinks this may deter them from participating. Robert argues that there is no harm in simply describing his research as a needs assessment. He suggests that even the psychological questions are indirectly related to the needs of the population, because the answers may indicate the need for mental health counseling.

5. *Critiquing Informed Consent Dialogue*: Review the following dialogue between a researcher and client who is a potential research participant. Identify the strengths and areas of concern in relation to how well the researcher covers key elements of informed consent: nature of the research (5 Ws), confidentiality, risks and benefits, and voluntariness. Also, note whether the researcher uses plain (layperson's) language, demonstrates respect, and responds appropriately to client concerns.

RAQUEL (RESEARCHER): Good morning, Cody. I understand that you've recently separated from your wife and you're a client here in the Parenting After Separation Program.

CODY (CLIENT): Yes, how did you know that?

RAQUEL: I'm here to ask you to participate in a study of deadbeat dads, fathers who refuse to pay child support after divorce.

CODY: Who are you calling a deadbeat. I pay child support. In fact, I pay too much.

RAQUEL: Great. Then I really want you in this study because the purpose of the study is to conduct a factor analysis comparing the demographic backgrounds of deadbeat dads with those of upstanding fathers like yourself.

CODY: I don't think I'm interested.

RAQUEL: And I respect that. I don't want you to agree to anything that makes you feel uncomfortable. Before you give your final answer, though, I do want to inform you that we are providing $200 gift cards to anyone who completes our research. You can use the gift card at any store in the local mall.

CODY: Well, I could use the money. What would I have to do to get the $200?

RAQUEL: There are really no risks. All I'm asking for is 30 minutes of your time to answer some questions about yourself and your family. Some questions are about your job, income, ethnic background, and such. Other questions are about your relationship with your children and ex-wife.

CODY: Will my wife have access to my answers? Perhaps I should talk to my attorney, in case we end up fighting over stuff in divorce court.

RAQUEL: There's no need to speak with your attorney. All our research records are confidential. We would not share our information with your wife or the court unless you give us written consent to release confidential information. The only exception is that we have to call the police if you tell us that you have abused your children.

CODY: I'm no abuser, so I guess I have nothing to worry about.

RAQUEL: Yes, it's all pretty simple. All you have to do is sign this informed consent form and we can get started.

CODY: When do I get the gift card?

RAQUEL: Right after you correctly answer all my questions.

6. *Informed Consent Practice*: Review the informed consent dialogue between Risha and Mr. Peterson presented earlier in this chapter. Construct a similar informed consent dialogue between Rahim and a research participant based on the facts of the Zaman case. In this scenario, Rahim will invite Assiya (a 70-year-old woman from the Arab American community) to participate in a focus group to discuss experiences of discrimination. Be sure to cover the 5 W's, confidentiality, benefits and risks, and voluntariness. Pay particular attention to cultural issues and possible questions that Assiya may have about participating in such a group. You may write out this dialogue verbatim (word-for-word) or develop an outline of key points to use in a live role-play of this situation. Consider also, how would the informed process differ if Assiya were 17 years old?

Chapter 5

Practice, Values, and Ethics—Social Work with Individuals

The purpose of this chapter is to demonstrate how to put social work values and ethics into practice when working with individuals. This chapter focuses on the application of "black-letter"[1] ethical standards and principles, the relatively clear should's and should-not's of social work ethics. As you will surely experience in the field, ethical practice includes many gray areas—areas of uncertainty, controversy, and ambiguity. You may find that working through these gray areas is the most challenging and most interesting aspect of ethics. Still, it is important to develop a solid understanding of the black-letter standards and principles before moving onto the more complex problems explored later in this textbook. Well over 90% of the decisions that you make in practice will fit within the realm of how to follow the basic black-letter standards and principles.

When working with individuals, the primary ethical guidelines for practice derive from section 1 of the Code of Ethics, "Social Workers' Ethical Responsibilities." This section provides standards of practice related to self-determination, informed consent, competence, confidentiality, conflict of interest, and so on. Rather than go through these standards in the sequence presented in the Code, this chapter goes through the stages of the generalist intervention model—engagement, assessment, planning,

[1] This term originated in legal discourse dating back to the 18th century (*Naglee v. Ingersoll*, 1847). Black-letter laws refer to legal rules and principles that are clearly understood, well settled, and not likely to stir controversy between experts in the field. Similarly, black-letter standards refer to standards of professional conduct that are clearly understood, well settled, and not likely to stir controversy in their general application. Still, ethical controversies may arise when there are conflicting standards, or when it is not clear how standards apply to a particular situation. A "gray area" refers to a situation in which the applicable laws, ethical principles, or standards do not give clear guidance on the most appropriate course of action.

implementation, evaluation, termination, and follow-up (Kirst-Ashman & Hull, 2006b)—demonstrating ethical standards that are most relevant to each stage of the helping process. This chapter concludes with a discussion of standards that apply throughout all stages of the helping process and how to avoid some of the more common pitfalls experienced by social workers.

LEARNING OBJECTIVES

Upon successful completion of this chapter, students will be able to

- Understand and apply the clear ethical standards established by the NASW Code of Ethics for work with individuals.
- Explain the ethical principles of client self-determination, informed consent, confidentiality, privilege, maintaining professional boundaries, and safety, as they apply to various stages of the helping process.
- Identify behaviors that breach Standards 1.01 to 1.16 of the NASW Code of Ethics.
- Identify risk factors that may lead social workers to breach the NASW Code of Ethics.

ENGAGEMENT

During engagement, the first stage of the helping process, social workers strive to develop a positive working relationship with clients. Four ethical standards that are central to this stage are commitment to clients, conflicts of interest, privacy and confidentiality, and payment for services.

Commitment to Clients

Standard 1.01 of the Code of Ethics states, "Social workers' primary responsibility is to promote the well-being of clients." This Standard goes on to state social workers also have responsibilities to larger society and to obey the law. Beginning social workers need to know *(1)* what it means in practice to promote the client's best interests, and *(2)* under what circumstances a social worker should give societal interest or the law precedence over the client's interests.

One of the most important methods of building trust with clients is demonstrating that your primary mandate is to promote their well-being. Putting Standard 1.01 into practice requires both words and actions. You may explain the nature of your mandate

> My job is to help you. While I'm working with you, I am committed to doing whatever I can to advance your well-being.

Everything you say and do should focus on what is good for the client, putting the client's interests above the interests of all others. Assume you feel a bit tired and would like to cancel an appointment so you can go home early. Canceling the appointment would be unethical, as you need to put client interests above your own. Assume your client asks you to help her fill out a scholarship application but you think there are more deserving people than your client. Your duty still says you are to help your client complete the application. By demonstrating you are there for the client, you and the client develop trust and a solid working relationship.

The obligation to promote a client's best interests is not absolute, meaning that there are exceptions to this standard (Reamer, 2006a). In some situations, you should promote the interests of society (the greater good) over the interests of your client. In other situations, you should follow the law, even though it may not be in the client's best interests. Part II provides examples of how to make difficult decisions when client interests conflict with societal interests or legal obligations. Here are some examples demonstrating more clear-cut choices:

- Your client contracts a highly contagious and virulent form of bird flu. She refuses to be quarantined because of a phobia about being isolated. Personally, she might be better staying in her apartment. In order to protect her family and society, however, you should pursue a solution that involves some type of quarantine.
- Your client asks you to falsify a Medicaid application. He says he needs medical services but cannot afford them. Arguably, the client's interests are served by falsifying the Medicaid application. Falsifying

such documents constitutes fraud, a criminal offense. Ethically, you should help the client find other ways to access medical services.

Ideally, you should work toward solutions that accommodate both the client's well-being and societal interests. When the danger to society is very great, however, you may need to give priority to societal interests.[2]

Conflicts of Interest

Standard 1.06 of the Code of Ethics says, "Social Workers should be alert to and avoid conflicts of interest that interfere with the exercise of professional discretion and impartial judgment." A *conflict of interest refers to a situation in which a social worker has competing motivations, obligations, or concerns that may hamper the social worker's ability to act in the client's best interests.* Assume your client tells you that she wants an attorney to help her with her divorce. Coincidentally, your spouse is an attorney. It would be inappropriate to refer your client to your spouse because your relationship with your spouse does not allow you to make an unbiased decision about whom to refer your client to. Further, your client may perceive that you are exploiting her for personal gain.

Many conflicts of interest arise because of dual relationships, meaning that the social worker has a professional social work relationship with a client plus another personal or professional relationship with the same client. If a close friend comes to you for services, you would be wise to refer this friend to someone who does not have a prior personal relationship. Otherwise, your friendship could interfere with your ability to serve the client in a professional manner. Perhaps the client will expect you to act as a friend rather than a professional. Perhaps other clients will believe that you are favoring a particular client because of your prior friendship.

The social worker–client relationship is sometimes referred to as a "fiducial relationship," meaning a relationship built on trust. When clients make use of social work services, they are often in vulnerable situations. They may be mentally distraught, depressed, financially impoverished, or otherwise experiencing stress. They may feel embarrassed or exposed because they are revealing personal or family secrets. They may be relying on the social worker for advice, support, guidance, or access to resources (e.g., from a worker who decides whether a client is eligible for social assistance). Because social workers are in a position of trust with each client, they should act in a way that fosters and preserves this trust. They should not taint their relationships with anything that can be perceived as exploiting or taking advantage of a client. Legally and ethically, if social workers act in a manner that betrays this trust, they may be held accountable.[3] Accordingly, social workers are wise to avoid conflicts of interest.

Although Standard 1.06 cautions social workers against entering dual relationships or situations where conflicts of interest might arise, it does not completely prohibit them. In some situations, it may be impossible to avoid conflicts of interest (Kaplan, 2006). In others, the social worker might have some justification for the conflict of interest—for instance, the worker may be the only practitioner available to provide services, or it might cost less time and money if the client received services from one professional with dual roles rather than having to see two separate workers for related issues.[4] Whether or not

[2] For instance, when there is a significant terrorist threat or when the health of a community is put at risk.

[3] Methods of accountability for breach of trust and other forms of malpractice will be discussed later in this chapter.

[4] For instance, a social worker who provides couples counseling could offer to provide family mediation if counseling does not work and the couple decides to separate. If the couple went to a new professional to mediate, the mediator would have to spend time getting to know the couple. Switching from counseling to mediation, however, places the worker in a dual role, raising a number of ethical risks: the worker is referring clients to herself, which clients may view as self-serving; the information learned from counseling may not be privileged, but the information from mediation would be privileged; and the clients may experience confusion about the professional's role when switching from counseling to mediation (Barsky, 2007b).

a dual relationship is unavoidable or potentially beneficial, social workers must inform clients of any possible conflicts of interest. Further, if any harm befalls the client as a result of the conflict of interest, the social worker may be held responsible for compensating the client for the harm done.

To demonstrate the risks and realities of conflicts of interest, consider Cher, a child protection worker in a rural community. Cher is the only child protection worker within 100 miles. Cher receives a call alleging child abuse by Ned, one of her neighbors. If Cher accepts the case and starts an investigation against Ned, she risks a conflict of interest. They know each other and she might "go soft" on him, wanting to retain good relations with him as a neighbor. If anything goes wrong—for instance, she leaves the child in Ned's care and Ned abuses the child further—people may assume that Cher did not do her job properly because of this conflict of interest. On the other hand, if Cher turned down the case, who would conduct the investigation? For pragmatic reasons, Cher might need to take the case. However, she should take the following steps to minimize the risks:

- Check with her agency policy to see how conflicts of interest should be handled.
- Discuss the conflict of interest with her area supervisor for guidance on whether to accept the case, whether there are any other options, and how to ensure the child abuse investigation is conducted with as much objectivity as possible.
- If she accepts the case, discuss the possible conflicts of interest with the client and the steps necessary to minimize the risks (e.g., explaining how her role as social worker is different from her role as neighbor).

If other child protection workers were available, Cher could simply refer the case to that social worker. When a dual relationship is unavoidable, she should set clear and appropriate boundaries for her work with the client.

In some cases, a social worker may play two different roles with the same family. A social worker helping a couple work through marital problems, for instance, could be called to testify in a subsequent divorce case. The social worker's role as a couple's counselor is much different from the worker's role as a potential witness (Barsky & Gould, 2002). Accordingly, the worker should explain the nature of these two roles in advance. Clients can then make informed decisions about what they want to disclose to the worker as a counselor. To avoid a conflict of interest, the clients might decide to sign an agreement that they will not ask or subpoena their couple's counselor to testify in any family court proceedings.

In terms of practice, social workers should assess for possible conflicts of interest from the first stages of engagement. If they foresee potential problems, they should address them as soon as possible, pre-empting any further issues. Consider a stress management social worker who discovers that a potential client will be his daughter's teacher next year. The social worker could open a discussion of this issue as follows:

> I understand that you teach at Aristotle Elementary. That's where my daughter goes to school. Since you are going to be her teacher next year, perhaps we could discuss the possibility of referring you to another social worker. I want to make sure that you get the best help possible and to avoid any problems that could arise if you were to become both my client and my daughter's teacher.

By engaging the client in this discussion, the worker empowers the client to make her own decision. If the client does not want to be referred to another worker, the worker could discuss the risks of dual relationships and the benefits of a referral:

> I agree that we could probably work very well together. My code of ethics, however, says that I should avoid conflicting roles in order to make sure all clients have a social worker who can focus on the client's best interests. How do you think it might affect our stress management work if my daughter was disruptive in your class and you did not think I was handling it well as a parent?

By identifying and handling potential conflicts of interest early, you can reduce risks and promote higher levels of trust with clients.

Privacy and Confidentiality

Privacy refers to the right to keep personal information to oneself. Most social workers know that Standard 1.07 prohibits social workers from sharing a client's personal information with others. Unfortunately, some forget that this standard also prohibits social workers from "soliciting private information from clients unless it is essential to providing services or conducting social work evaluation or research." In other words, social workers should not ask questions or pry into personal issues with clients if the information is not directly relevant to the nature of the work they are doing. You may be surprised to learn that your own field agencies breach this standard. Many agencies ask workers to complete intake forms that include questions on topics irrelevant to the work being done.[5] Consider a question asking for a client's religion.[6] It may seem simple and innocuous. For some clients, the question may feel very intrusive. Consider clients who feel society fears or oppresses their religion. Many wiccans (or witches) keep their religion a secret, fearing persecution or intolerance. If you ask such a client about her religion, she may feel pressured to lie or to disclose information against her will. Although a client's religion may be significant for some social work purposes, it may not be important for others. Accordingly, it would be unethical to ask about a client's religion unless it serves a purpose for the work you are doing.

Once a social worker has gathered private information from a client, the worker has a professional obligation, called confidentiality, to safeguard this information. Offering confidentiality is vital to engaging clients. It encourages trust. Clients may be reluctant to share private information for a variety of reasons. Consider a client who has AIDS or who has been sexually abused by a relative. The client may feel embarrassed, perhaps because of social stigma attached to having AIDS or being forced into incest. The client may fear negative repercussions, such as losing family support, health insurance, or employment. The fear may or may not be based on an objective assessment of reality; regardless, fear makes it difficult for the person to share the information. Social workers provide clients with a safe place to talk by reassuring them that whatever they disclose will be kept confidential:

> As a social worker, I respect your rights to privacy and confidentiality. I hope you will be able to share whatever information is necessary to help us assess your concerns and work on your goals. I want to reassure you that, for the most part,[7] whatever we discuss stays between us. I will not share your personal information with your family, friends, employers, or others unless you provide me with clear instructions to do so. If you have any questions about privacy and confidentiality, this is a good time to discuss them.

Clients from diverse backgrounds may have different understandings and responses concerning confidentiality. Some clients may not believe a social worker will keep information confidential because they are used to having people in their communities share information. If one person knows he has AIDS, for instance, there is no way to control the rumors from spreading. Providing the client with a written confidentiality contract or policy may help reassure the client. In some cases, it may take days or weeks

[5] If agency policies and forms require you to ask inappropriate questions, you should discuss your ethical obligations with your supervisor to determine the best way to fulfill them. Chapter 8 explores how to ensure agency policies are consistent with social work ethics.

[6] Other information that some people may consider particularly private include sexual orientation, HIV status, political affiliation, mental health history, criminal history, and income. Some of these topics feel unsafe because of the stigma related to certain conditions or histories. If a sensitive topic is relevant to the purpose of the work, then the social worker may ask about it in spite of the sensitivity. If one of these topics is not relevant, the worker should respect the client's right to privacy and not inquire about it. The worker may show openness to hearing about sensitive topics, which allows the client to decide whether to disclose.

[7] Exceptions to confidentiality are described later.

to build clients' trust to the point that they will believe you will keep the information private.

Some of the more obvious breaches of confidentiality occur when a worker

- Discusses a client's situation with friends or family, out of amusement or to solicit their support.
- Discusses a client's situation with a supervisor or other agency coworkers in a venue where other clients or outsiders may hear the discussion.
- Discloses client information to professional colleagues from another agency, without the clients' permission.

Some social workers believe that they are free to discuss a client's situation with others, so long as they do not mention the client's name. This is a risky practice, because the worker may not know when others may be able to identify a client from the information provided. Consider a social work intern who tells his mother about a client who has a pierced upper lip. The next day, the intern and his mother are walking down the street and bump into the client, who says hello. The mother now knows who the client is and the private information shared by the intern.

Social workers are permitted to share client information with supervisors and other agency staff provided that it is for professional purposes. In other words, workers should not engage in idle gossip about clients. Workers may share client information during case conferences in order to obtain feedback on past efforts or how to proceed with the client in the future. Social workers should let their clients know, in advance, that certain information will be shared with others in the agency:

> I meet with my supervisor on a regular basis to discuss my work with clients. I will also write notes about our work, including your goals, plans for work, and progress toward those goals. My supervisor and the executive director go over my client files each month to ensure that I am following agency policies.

The specifics of what you tell your client about confidential and shared information depend on the particular situation, agency policy, and client interests. While you are a student, for instance, you should advise clients that you are a student and that you will be discussing your work in your practice classes, but on an anonymous basis. Anonymity means that you are describing some of your work but omitting identifying information. You might even change some identifying information (e.g., the client's name, age, ethnicity, or family structure) in order to disguise the client's identity further. If you are planning to write a paper or conduct a class presentation based on your work with a particular client, you could show respect for your client's right to privacy by asking the client for specific permission.

> I am taking a graduate course so I can learn advanced social work skills and practice. With your permission, I'd like to make a brief presentation to my class of 12 students, based on my work with you. I would not share your name or any other information that identifies you. If you prefer that I don't discuss your situation, I will respect your decision and it will not affect our work here. Before I ask for your permission, what questions do you have about this presentation?

Some social work programs do not require students to ask for such consent, provided the student does not share any identifying information. I have had occasion, however, when a student starts describing a client and students from another agency recognize the client because they are working with the same person. I now advise my classes, "If you think that you might recognize a client that another student is presenting, please excuse yourself from the class as soon as possible."

Exceptions to Confidentiality

So far, we have focused on maintaining a client's confidentiality. *Confidentiality is not an absolute right, meaning there are several exceptions to confidentiality.* To engage clients, you will want to reassure them that you respect their right to confidentiality, but you will also want to be honest about the limitations of confidentiality. By letting clients know the limitations as soon as possible, you allow them to make informed decisions about what to share or withhold from you. Clients are more likely to open up with you when you tell them that confidentiality is limited because they know you are being honest (Rogers, 1957).

The exceptions to confidentiality are many. In fact, there may be so many that listing all of them separately may take too much time and may confuse the client. Some agencies and workers opt to use a brief global statement on the exceptions:

> Generally, what we talk about stays within the agency. I will not share information with anyone outside the agency except as required by agency policy, the social work code of ethics, and the law.

This brief statement covers all possible exceptions and allows clients to ask about specific exceptions. Some clients will ask, while others may show no interest. *The more common exceptions include:*

- *Client consent to release information* (Ss.1.07[b] and [d])—If a client provides permission to release information to another agency or person, then you may share information with that agency or person. From a legal perspective, it is safest to have express written consent that states precisely what information is to be released, to whom, and on what date(s). Hospitals and certain other agencies have specific forms that must be used for any release of information. Some agency policies permit release of information without requiring written consent. You could document consent in your case notes, although this is not as strong evidence of consent as a form signed by the client (Polowy & Morgan, 2004).
- *Health-care information released to insurance providers*—A federal law, Health Insurance Portability and Accountability Act (HIPAA, 1996), permits health-care service providers to provide routine information to insurance providers for the purposes of requesting reimbursement (Legal Defense Fund, 2005).[8]
- *Subpoena*—A subpoena is a summons requiring a person to provide evidence to a court process (Polowy, Morgan, & Gilbertson, 2005). Accordingly, social workers might be required to submit their records and/or testify at court proceedings (Bernstein & Hartsell, 2004; Falvey, 2002). A social worker or client can challenge a court subpoena by filing a motion in court, but the court may decide to order the worker to testify.[9]
- *Suspicion of child abuse or neglect*—State laws require social workers (and related professionals) to report reasonable suspicions of child abuse or neglect to proper authorities. These authorities may be the state's child protective services, police, or other authorities designated by state laws. The purpose of this exception is to protect vulnerable children. The law requires workers to report child abuse and neglect even when they do not think the person will re-offend. States maintain a database of child abuse and neglect reports, which helps them monitor and enforce child protection concerns.

---

[8] Although HIPAA only requires service providers to provide clients with notice that they are releasing routine information to insurance providers, state laws or social work ethics may impose higher standards of practice (e.g., requiring that social workers request specific consent from clients to release such information).

[9] Courts have recognized the value of confidentiality in professional–client relationships and must balance this interest with the interest of having as much evidence as possible to make a correct determination about the facts of the court case. The legal concept of "privilege" permits the court to deem certain types of information as exempt or protected from disclosure in court processes (Falvey, 2002; *Jaffee v. Redmond* 1996). Whether and when information may be deemed privileged is a complex area, described further in Chapter 15, in relation to criminal justice. Laws governing specific areas of practice, including substance abuse treatment, provide the protection of privilege to clients. This enables clients who have used illicit drugs to come for treatment without fear that their practitioners will be called to testify against them (Substance Abuse and Mental Health Services Administration, 2004). State laws may also provide privilege to client communications for licensed clinical social workers and other mental health professionals (Polowy & Morgan, 2004).

- *Abuse, neglect, or exploitation of elders or persons with disabilities*—State laws require people to report various forms of maltreatment of elders and/or people with disabilities. The specific laws differ from state to state. See the National Center on Elder Abuse website at http://www.ncea.aoa.gov for state laws, contact information, and adult protective services in your area. For services and reporting requirements related to maltreatment of people with disabilities, search your state government's website, which can be found at http://www.usa.gov/Agencies/State_and_Territories.shtml.
- *Information required to prevent "serious, foreseeable, and imminent harm to a client or other identifiable person"* (S.1.07[c])—When a social worker discovers that some person is at risk of serious, foreseeable, and imminent harm, the social worker has an ethical obligation to take steps reasonable necessary to prevent that harm from happening. If a client says he is thinking about suicide, for instance, the worker should assess the actual risk of suicide. The worker should then decide what steps are appropriate, given the level of suicide risk: for instance, consult with a supervisor, refer the client for a second-level assessment by an appropriate mental health specialist, engage family members so they can monitor for risk of suicide, or initiate proceedings for involuntary committal to a psychiatric facility. Ideally, the worker takes these steps with permission of the client. If the client refuses permission, however, the worker may have to disclose some confidential information to others in order to safeguard the client. Similar standards apply for a client who threatens to kill or seriously injure another person. The worker must assess the risk, try to engage the client voluntarily, and determine what steps are necessary in order to safeguard the other person from harm. Some social workers assume that they must report any threats to the potential victim, citing the Tarasoff cases (1976). Tarasoff involved a university student (Poddar) who told his psychologist (Moore) that he intended to kill a woman (Tarasoff). Moore assessed Poddar as dangerous and called the campus police. The police took Poddar into custody but released him after questioning, believing he would keep his promise to stay away from Tarasoff. Shortly after, Poddar killed Tarasoff. Tarasoff's parents sued the university and its employees for failing to notify her. On an appeal of a lower court decision, the California Supreme Court ruled that the psychologist not only had a "duty to warn," but a "duty to protect" the intended victim. The court ordered the defendants to pay damages to the family.[10] Accordingly, social workers and other mental health professionals must take whatever steps are necessary to prevent harm. Warning the victim may or may not be required, depending on the circumstances. Because assessing risk and determining appropriate actions are complex and perilous processes, beginning social workers should always consult their supervisors about how to proceed whenever they sense a risk of serious harm to the client or others.[11] Other steps may include providing crisis intervention counseling and contracting, referring the client to services on a voluntary basis, escorting the client to another facility for a second-level assessment, initiating involuntary committal to a psychiatric facility, and calling the police or other authorities (e.g., child protective services or adult protective services). Social workers should clearly document their risk

---

[10] The Tarasoff case is a California case and is not binding on other states. Although most states have followed Tarasoff, others have said that mental health professionals are not liable for damages as a result of failing to protect a person from harm (*Boynton v. Burglass,* 1991; Gellerman & Suddath, 2005). The NASW Code of Ethics makes it clear that social workers have an ethical duty to protect clients from harm. Each state, however, may have different statutory or case law about the consequences of breaching this duty to report (e.g., whether the social worker is liable for damages or the worker's licensure could be suspended or revoked).

[11] Chapter 13, on psychopathology, provides further information on ethical issues related to suicidal and homicidal ideation.

assessments, consultations, and steps taken to prevent harm in order to provide evidence of how they discharged their ethical and legal duties.[12]

To explain some of these specific exceptions to confidentiality, a social worker might say:

> Under my agency policy and professional code of ethics, there are some important exceptions to confidentiality. For instance, if I become aware of a situation that puts a person at serious risk of harm, I must take appropriate actions to prevent that harm. It is also possible, though quite rare in my experience, to be called to court to testify. If there are any occasions that might require me to share your information with other people, I will try to discuss this information with you first, so I can ask you for your permission.

You do not need to go into all of the details of what may or may not be disclosed, provided you give the client clear information and allow the client to ask for further details. Tailor your explanation to the client's situation. If you know that child protection concerns might arise, you could specifically mention these. If you know the client feels too stressed to follow a long explanation during initial engagement, provide a shorter statement now and save the detail for a later session. You do not want to overwhelm clients with all the standards and ethics of practice, particularly since they are thinking of more pressing personal concerns as they walk into your office. You may discuss some ethical issues as they become relevant to the services being offered.[13]

Some agencies use written confidentiality contracts or handout material that explain the nature of confidentiality and its limitations in great detail. Before asking a client to sign such a form, be sure to review important points with the client, ensuring that the client is not overwhelmed with detail and technical language.

One distinction that often creates confusion is the difference between past harm and future harm. As described above, *social workers have an ethical obligation to protect people from serious, foreseeable and* ***imminent*** *harm. Social workers do not generally have an ethical obligation to report* ***past*** *harm, regardless of how serious it was* (Polowy & Gorenberg, 2004).[14] For instance, a client may disclose that she killed her mother. A social worker does not necessarily have a duty to report this to the police, as heinous as this crime may seem. If the worker believes that the client is going to kill her father, then the worker has a duty to protect the father, but this obligation arises out of future risk, not past harm. Remember, the social worker's primary role is to help clients by providing counseling and other services, not to act as police or police informants to enforce criminal laws. Offering confidentiality to clients permits them to discuss past crimes in a safe place and relationship. Through work with a social worker, clients might decide to speak with an attorney and decide to turn themselves in to authorities.

Specific types of social workers have duties to report or act on past crimes. For instance, probation officers must document past crimes and report these to the court. Probation officers and other court-affiliated officials have a duty to the criminal justice system, not just the client.

---

[12] The legal duty to warn potential victims varies from state to state. Some states impose a duty to warn when there is a general threat or a threat against the general public (e.g., Arizona, Delaware). Other states establish a duty to warn only when a threat is to a readily identifiable victim (e.g., North Dakota). Still other states have no legislation or case law clarifying whether social workers and other professionals have a legal duty to warn (e.g., unlicensed social workers in Florida) (Polowy & Gorenberg, 2004). Note that social workers may have an ethical duty to warn, from the NASW Code of Ethics, even if there is no legal duty to warn.

[13] The challenge is knowing what is relevant, and when. If you put off explaining the child abuse reporting obligation, for instance, clients may feel duped if you later state that you have to report them to child welfare authorities.

[14] Some states, such as Kansas, permit disclosure of criminal acts or violations of law. Remember, a law permitting disclosure is not the same as a law that requires disclosure.

They should explain this duty to clients, so clients can make informed decisions about what to disclose and what not to disclose to their probation officers. To find out if you have an obligation to report murder or other past crimes, check your agency's policies and laws that regulate the agency.

Another important distinction is the difference between a "duty to report" and a "justification to report." *If a law, policy, or code of ethics says that you **must** report certain information, then this constitutes a duty to report. If a law, policy, or code of ethics says that you may report certain information, then you **may** report this information if you have a reasonable ethical justification.* Some agencies permit workers to report past crimes. In other words, they are not required to do so but they are allowed to do so. The question of whether and when a worker is justified in reporting past crimes is a complex issue, discussed further in Chapter 15. For now, just note that the use of different terms such as *must* and *may* in laws, policies, and codes of ethics will have an impact on the nature of a worker's obligations. Further, if you have any questions about whether to report a past crime admitted by a client, consult with your supervisor, agency attorney, or other ethics consultants designated by your agency.

Context-Specific Confidentiality Laws and Policies

Different agencies and fields of practice may have confidentiality laws or policies that are specific to those agencies and fields of practice. Accordingly, when you start work at a new agency, check your agency's policy and procedure book to determine which additional laws and policies, if any, will govern your practice. Alcohol and drug treatment programs, for instance, must comply with laws that provide additional confidentiality protections for their clients (Substance Abuse and Mental Health Services Administration, 2004). Service providers must also abide by special confidentiality laws for clients with HIV and AIDS (Gostin, Lazzarini, & Flaherty, n.d.). Schools, hospitals, probation and parole departments, child protection agencies, and other services have specific laws and policies that affect how confidentiality is employed in each context (Polowy & Morgan, 2004).

Payment for Services

One question that should be covered in the engagement stage is, "How much will services cost?" Social workers value access to services. Some interpret this to mean that social work services should be free. In some agencies, services are free (though clients may pay indirectly through taxes or insurance premiums). The NASW Code of Ethics does not require that services be free but that "fees are fair, reasonable, and commensurate with services performed" (S.1.15[a]). When charging for services, social workers should consider the client's ability to pay. Assume a social worker advises a client that her regular fee is $150 per hour and the client says he cannot afford this amount. The social worker could respond by:

- Offering the client a reduced fee (sliding scale) or free (pro bono) services.
- Asking the client to share economic information, such as income or tax forms, to determine eligibility for reduced fees or scholarships at the agency.
- Offering to help the client apply for funding or reimbursement from other sources (e.g., insurance programs, scholarships, or advocacy and support groups).
- Referring the client to services at a program that can provide services at a fee the client can afford.

Because social workers value social justice, they should consider offering some services for free or on a sliding scale, depending on client income and wealth. Still, social workers are entitled to earn a living and agencies do have to make tough decisions on how to use their limited resources. Sometimes, social workers try to be creative by offering to provide services in exchange for something the client can provide (e.g., "Instead of paying cash, perhaps you can help paint our offices, or provide your culinary services in our kitchen…"). Standard 1.13(b) warns against such bartering but does not completely prohibit it. Bartering raises risks for clients, including conflicts of interest, exploitation, and inappropriate client–worker boundaries. If something goes wrong in a bartering relationship, the social worker and agency are held responsible, not the client.

Social workers should not accept direct, personal payment for their services when clients are entitled to such services from the agency. Some clients want to provide gifts, tips, or payment directly to the social worker who has helped them. In general, social workers should politely refuse such gifts or payments, letting clients know that the agency pays their salaries. Agencies may have specific policies on accepting gifts—for instance, allowing workers to accept them if they fall below a certain value and the worker discloses the gift to agency supervisors.

In the next section, we move from the engagement stage to assessment. As noted earlier, remember that ethical issues discussed during one stage of the social work process may arise again in later stages.

ASSESSMENT

The NASW Code of Ethics does not specifically refer to the assessment stage of the social work process, though a number of sections deal with matters that apply to social work roles and responsibilities at this stage. In particular, social workers should consider ethical standards related to confidentiality and competence, including cultural competence.

Confidentiality and Gathering Information

Often, when social workers conduct assessments, they need to gather information from other agencies or other collateral contacts (family members, teachers, physicians, etc.). Before contacting other agencies or collaterals, social workers should ask the client to sign a consent to release confidential information (Ss.1.07[b] and [d]). The consent form should specify which agency or collateral the worker may contact. If the agency or collateral also has an obligation to maintain confidentiality, the consent form should state that the client gives permission for the agency or collateral to release information to the social worker requesting it. Agency laws and policies may require use of specific consent forms, and in some cases, the client may need to sign separate forms for each contact: one for the worker to contact and share information with the agency or collateral, and one for the agency or collateral to share information with the social worker.

Remember that consent must be voluntary. This means that clients should be able to choose whether to give a social worker permission to contact others.[15] The worker should also discuss any questions that the client may have about signing such consent forms. Some clients may feel embarrassed for the worker to contact family members. Other clients may fear that contacting their employer may put their job in jeopardy. The worker should validate such concerns and explore ways to minimize the risks and maximize the benefits of contacting the other agency or collateral. If the client refuses permission, the client and worker will need to decide, jointly, whether they can conduct an adequate assessment without gathering information from other agencies or collaterals. In rare cases, the social worker may need to terminate services because of the inability to conduct an adequate assessment without contacting these agencies or collaterals. Typically, the worker and client are able to agree on what information will be gathered in order to conduct the assessment.

Competence and Cultural Competence

In terms of assessment, one of the most important standards of the Code is 1.04, which requires social workers to be competent in all the work they do. Accordingly, social workers should not embark on any client assessment unless they have sufficient education, training, license, certification, consultation, supervision, and/or other relevant professional experience (Falvey, 2002).

[15] Voluntary consent may not apply to certain involuntary clients, as discussed in the chapters on criminal justice, psychopathology, and child protection.

Beginning social workers, including students in field placements, may wonder what competence they have to conduct assessments. At a minimum, your social work practice courses and generalist education should provide you with the competence to conduct a generalist biopsychosocial assessment. Within this assessment, you may gather information about the client's strengths, needs, and challenges in a variety of areas. When gathering information about the client's biological health, for instance, you may ask about the client's physical well-being and related concerns. You would not be competent to conduct a physical examination in the manner of a medical doctor. In the psychological realm, you could gather information on the client's mood, thoughts, stresses, and behaviors. If you do not have specific training and expertise in diagnosis of mental illness or in psychological testing, then it would be inappropriate for you to diagnose a client or administer a psychological test. You must stay within your areas of competence, referring clients to professionals with other competencies, as needed.

Your level of competence is affected by your level of supervision. Assume that your supervisor is accredited to diagnose sexual disorders but you do not have such accreditation. Because your supervisor has competence to diagnose such disorders, you may be permitted to do so, provided you are receiving direct supervision from your supervisor.[16] The supervisor and you are jointly accountable for your services. Thus, your supervisor is responsible to ensure that your services are delivered in a competent manner, even though you are still developing your competence.

Standard 1.05 builds on Standard 1.04 by describing competencies related specifically to working with people from diverse backgrounds. Social workers have a professional obligation to develop knowledge, skills, and values for working with diverse populations. Social workers must be able to assess clients regarding culture, ethnicity, religion, sex, gender, sexual orientation, and other aspects of diversity. This includes assessing both the strengths and challenges that come from membership in various diversity groups. Students often wonder, "How can I be expected to know about every culture or every diversity group?" True, there are so many groups that this seems like an impossible expectation. Some students may think, "I can just refer clients to social workers from their own background." While this may be a solution on a case-by-case basis, it does not resolve the basic ethical imperative that social workers are supposed to be competent to work with people of diverse backgrounds. Rather than simply referring diverse clients to other social workers, all social workers should consider

- Enhancing their competence to work with specific diversity groups through further supervision, consultation, education, and training.
- Developing an approach to social work that permits the worker to learn from each client rather than depend only on knowledge from books, articles, and general education and training (Bein, 2003).
- Working collaboratively with other diversity experts when serving particular clients.

When conducting an assessment of a client from a different culture, for instance, social workers could bring in a cultural guide from the client's cultural community to assist with the assessment process (Geva, Barsky, & Westernoff, 2000). As the social workers gain assessment experience, their competence grows, permitting them to conduct types of assessments later in their careers that they might not be competent to conduct earlier.

PLANNING

During the planning stage of the social work process, social workers engage clients in a decision-making process about what to do and how to do it. They help clients reflect on their assessments and plan a course of action to address

[16] Legal authority to diagnose is provided in state laws. Some states permit MSW students to diagnose mental illness, provided they are doing so under the supervision of a licensed clinical social worker.

problems or challenges (Kirst-Ashman & Hull, 2006b). From an ethical perspective, this is a key stage in terms of promoting self-determination and informed consent. The following sections explore the rights to self-determination and informed consent, as well as the limitations on these rights.

Self-Determination and Informed Consent

Self-determination and informed consent are both ethical standards that put the value of respect for the dignity and worth of all people into practice (Dolgoff et al., 2009). If social workers want to show respect, what could be more important than allowing clients to make informed decisions about how to handle important biopsychosocial issues in their lives? If social workers want clients to trust them and follow through with their plans, what could be more important than respecting the clients' decisions on how to proceed?

Standard 1.02 of the NASW Code defines self-determination to include helping clients set goals and determine how to achieve them. This standard sounds simple: Just ask clients what they would like to achieve, and then ask how they would like to start working toward these goals. In practice, this standard is far more complicated. What if a client does not have clear goals? What if a client has diminished mental capacity because of a mental illness, addiction, or social stress? What if a client's goals are unwise, illegal, or irresponsible? What if a social worker thinks he knows what's better for a client? What if the client has no idea about how to achieve certain goals? What if the client has been ordered into services through the child protection system, criminal justice system, or mental health system?

Self-determination requires mutual work in the planning process. The social worker does not merely stand back and say, "You're the client, so you make all the decisions." The social worker may propose:

> Let's talk about all the concerns you raised in the assessment process and try to set some priorities. I will ask you some questions and I may have some suggestions about how to proceed. As the client, you will make the final decisions.

The worker lets the client know that although the client makes the ultimate decisions, the worker will also have input. Rather than telling the client what goals to pursue, the worker asks questions. These questions give the client insight about the possible issues and goals to pursue. The worker starts with the client, meaning that the worker validates the client's concerns and permits the client to discuss them further. The client may initially set one goal but with the guidance of the worker's questions may eventually decide to pursue others.

Consider a client who has recently immigrated to the United States. She says her goal is to get a job as a tax accountant, the same position she had in her country of origin. The worker acknowledges this desire but gently asks questions to help the client determine whether this goal is reasonable, at least in the short term. Upon questioning by the worker and further investigation by the client, the client discovers that U.S. tax laws are very different and it would take two years of study for the client to qualify for the same type of licensure she had in her country of origin. The client revises her short-term goals, agreeing to search for a different job to help pay her bills in the immediate future, and to enroll in a part-time course to begin work toward U.S. accreditation as a tax accountant.

Self-determination and informed consent are linked concepts. Both require client access to relevant information so clients can make the best decisions for themselves. Standard 1.03(a) states:

> Social workers should use clear and understandable language to inform clients of the purpose of the services, risks related to the services, limits to services because of the requirements of a third-party payer, relevant costs, reasonable alternatives, clients' right to refuse or withdraw consent, and the time frame covered by the consent.

When discussing possible interventions with a client, the social worker should provide information about possible interventions, how they work, their potential benefits, and their potential risks. The informed consent process may also include a discussion of the risks and benefits of doing no intervention. In some situations, workers give information in the form of advice, "This is what you should do." To provide clients with greater control over their decisions, social workers may provide information without specifically advising the client what to do or how to do it. Consider an alcohol-dependent client who says he wants to get his alcohol use under control. The worker could educate the client about the effectiveness of different interventions but allow the client to determine which intervention to pursue. Perhaps the literature shows that controlled use programs are not generally as effective as abstinence programs for people with chronic addictions (Fisher & Harrison, 2005). If the client still wants to try a controlled use program, the worker would accept this choice and help the client with his goal.

Clear violations of client self-determination and informed consent include:

- Imposing decisions on the client through the use of threats, coercion, or trickery,
- Failing to provide the client with sufficient facts and knowledge to allow the client to make an informed decision,
- Explaining interventions with language that the client cannot understand.
- Obtaining consent from a client who does not have the necessary mental capacity to provide consent.

Remember, informed consent also includes the right to *informed refusal*. Informed refusal refers to a clients' right to reject services without fear of negative consequences and with sufficient information to make an educated decision.

Limitations on Self-Determination and Informed Consent

Self-determination and informed consent are not absolute rights. The NASW Code and various laws provide a number of exceptions. Standard 1.03, for instance, states that social workers may limit a client's right to self-determination when they believe the client's actions or potential actions raise "a serious, foreseeable, and imminent risk to themselves or others." If a client wants to kill herself or another person, social workers would not be obliged to help the client fulfill this desire. Rather, the workers would be obliged to take necessary steps to prevent the killing (see Chapter 13 for further exploration of this issue). Likewise, if clients want to commit fraud, steal, or otherwise break the law, social workers are not required to support such self-determined acts. If they did, they could be criminally liable, as accomplices to the crimes.

Many social workers work with involuntary clients, clients who are mandated by the court to receive services. Requiring clients to see a social worker clearly infringes their right to self-determination. This infringement is ethically or legally justified, however, by a higher value. In child protection cases, for instance, protection of children from maltreatment is deemed a higher priority than noninterference with the autonomy rights of family and parents. In mental health cases involving involuntary commitment of a patient, preventing a client from committing suicide or homicide is deemed a higher priority than client autonomy. In criminal cases, protection of society from serious harm is deemed a higher priority than client autonomy. In each of these situations, social workers may face difficult questions in terms of where to draw the line between these conflicting priorities. At what point, for instance, does a child protection concern become serious enough to limit client self-determination? Consider a father who refuses to stop the car to let his children urinate, telling them to "hold it" until the end of a car trip. Does this warrant state intervention and limiting the father's right to decide how to raise his children? (For further exploration of child protection issues, see Chapter 14.)

When working with involuntary clients, social workers still have an obligation to respect client self-determination as much as possible. For instance, social workers should be honest about the consequences of a client's not cooperating with the social worker. The client may decide to accept these consequences (e.g., having children removed from the home; being incarcerated). Social workers should also offer to help clients work on their own goals:

> I understand that if it were up to you, you wouldn't be here today. Since you have to see a social worker, perhaps we can make the best of it.... Perhaps you could share some of your concerns, so we could spend some time on them.

Although the client comes into services as an involuntary client, the worker offers the client as much self-determination as possible. Ideally, the social worker connects with a client in a manner that turns the client into a voluntary one.

A final limitation on self-determination arises when the mental capacity of a client is in question. If a client does not have sufficient mental capacity to agree to services, including a particular form of intervention, the social worker must obtain the consent of a substitute decision maker (parent, guardian, or person legally authorized to represent the client).[17] Clients may not have sufficient mental capacity to provide informed consent for a variety of factors: age and mental maturity, mental illness, cognitive functioning, disorientation, communication impairment, memory impairment, or uncontrolled substance abuse. Mental capacity may be a complicated issue. In terms of age, for instance, there is no one age whereby a person automatically has full capacity to agree to services. Although 18 is the legal age of consent for many purposes, younger children may be able to provide consent for certain types of services (depending on agency policy, state regulations, and so on). In terms of mental illness, a client is not automatically deemed mentally incapacitated just because he has a diagnosable condition. Social workers should assess mental capacity in relation to the social context and decisions to be made. A client who has schizophrenia, for instance, may have adequate mental capacity while taking medication to control hallucinations, delusions, and other symptoms. A client with mild brain damage may not have capacity to consent to a complicated and risky intervention but may have capacity to consent to a simpler and safe intervention. Social workers are obliged to enhance clients' ability to provide consent. If a client is incapacitated due to high levels of stress, for instance, the workers could help the client deal with the stress first; once the client's stress has been reduced, the client may be able to provide consent. The main criterion for assessing a clients' capacity to consent to services is whether the client understands the nature of the services being offered, including their potential benefits and risks (American Bar Association Commission on Aging, 2005).

Although workers typically engage clients in planning and ask for agreement to services during the beginning phases of social work, client self-determination and informed consent are ongoing processes. Social workers should continuously pay attention to client wishes and desires. Social workers should allow clients to change their minds, renegotiate their contracts for work, and make new decisions on how to proceed. By respecting client rights to self-determination and informed consent on an ongoing basis, social workers ensure that they are working *with* their clients rather than *against* them.

IMPLEMENTATION

Once social workers and clients have agreed to a plan of action, the next stage is implementation: putting the plan to work. As with other stages, social workers should respect the ethical principles of confidentiality, self-determination, informed consent, and other client rights throughout the implementation stage. Rather than repeat these standards, this section explores the principle of competence in greater depth.

As noted above, social workers should restrict their practice to services for which they have sufficient competence. Different types of services require different types of skills, knowledge, education, experience, supervision, and certification. If you do not have sufficient training or certification to provide narrative therapy, for instance, you should not practice this therapy.

---

[17] The names of substitute decision makers varies from state to state and also depends on the types of decisions they are authorized to make (e.g., guardian ad litem for litigation-related decisions, power of attorney for property decisions, or health-care agent for medical decisions).

If you want to become competent at narrative therapy, you should take relevant courses and make use of appropriate supervision (S1.04[b]).

The ethical principle of competence not only requires that social workers possess competence; they must actually practice in a competent manner, that is, in a manner consistent with the most current theory and research. The purpose of this standard is to promote effective practice, including the maximization of benefits and minimization of harm to clients. Assume you are providing services to a victim of trauma, perhaps a marine who recently returned from active duty in a war zone. If you do not provide services in a competent manner, the client is less likely to recover from the trauma. Further, you might cause harm, such as retraumatizing the client and making it more difficulty for her to fulfill her responsibilities with family, work, and others in her life.

Failure to practice in a competent manner is called malpractice. Examples of malpractice during the implementation stage include:

- Using a particular technique, procedure, or intervention that would not have been used by a reasonable social worker (with similar training and background) in a similar situation.
- Implementing an appropriate intervention, but in a manner that was not up to the standard of practice in the worker's professional community (e.g., due to lack of knowledge or skill, or simple negligence of the worker).

When clients are harmed by malpractice, they may sue their practitioners and the practitioners' agencies for monetary compensation (Corey et al., 2007; see also Chapter 9).

With a trend toward evidence-based practice in schools of social work and in many agency settings, the standard expected of professional social workers includes the use of research and other evidence of best practices (Barsky, in press). Social workers need to keep attuned to the generally accepted standards for competent practice in whatever field they are practicing (Caudill, n.d.).

Social workers who do not use theory and research to guide their interventions may be putting themselves at higher risk of malpractice. In some fields of practice, research is limited or just emerging, and standards of competence may be unclear. In such instances, social workers must be particularly careful to protect clients from risks of harm (s.1.04[c]). As new research emerges, the standards for what constitutes competent, effective practice change. Accordingly, social workers must remain current on the latest research, including best practices and the risks and benefits of various interventions.

The definition of what constitutes competent practice depends on the situation, including the client's presenting problem, goals for work, agency context, and diversity background. Although you might find that a strategic family intervention works with most of your clients, it may be inappropriate for others, perhaps because of different cultures and family structures. Accordingly, social workers must gear their skills and strategies to the particular needs of each client, taking diversity into account (s.1.05). Consider the following scenario:

> Susi is working with Claudette, a client of Haitian descent recently diagnosed with AIDS. Claudette is initially reluctant to receive help from mainstream doctors. Susi helps Claudette develop and implement a plan that combines the use of traditional Haitian root medicine with mainstream American medicine and social work interventions.

Although Susi's usual standards of practice would not include the use of root medicine, she takes the client's ethnicity and belief system into account when deciding to help facilitate the use of root medicine with Claudette. Susi is not personally competent at providing traditional Haitian remedies, so she works jointly with a Haitian healer who has competence in this type of work. As this brief example illustrates, decisions about competent practice must take client diversity and cultural context into account.

The NASW Code of Ethics itself may be used to define competent practice. This code includes many standards to which social workers may be held accountable. For instance, competent practice includes following the Code of Ethics' standards with regard to maintaining confidentiality, providing clients with informed consent, and maintaining records. Likewise, agency policy and procedure books may also include standards of practice for social workers. Ideally, agency policies are consistent with professional standards. For situations in which agency conflicts with professional standards, the worker is faced with an ethical dilemma: Should the worker comply with agency policies or professional standards, and how does the worker decide? A framework for handling such dilemmas is provided in Part II of this textbook. For now, just be aware that standards defining competent practice may arise from more than one source.

TERMINATION, EVALUATION, AND FOLLOW-UP

During the final stages of the social work process, social workers are supposed to deal with any unfinished business with clients. Unfinished business may include helping clients deal with emotional reactions to termination of the social work relationship (e.g., anger, sadness, anxiety), evaluating client progress, determining whether further services are needed, and linking clients to necessary resources. The most pertinent standards of the NASW Code of Ethics to these stages are Standards 1.15 and 1.16.

Under Standard 1.15, social workers are obliged to make "reasonable efforts to ensure continuity of services in the event that services are interrupted by factors such as unavailability, relocation, illness, disability, or death." Thus, a social worker's duty to a client requires preventive actions. Social workers should have backup plans to cover potential situations in which they may be unable to provide services. When working in a social agency, a supervisor or colleague may serve as a backup. When working alone in private practice, the worker could provide clients with contact information for a professional colleague in the event of an emergency, to ensure continuity of services. When workers know that they will be leaving an agency or unable to continue work, they should advise clients and discuss plans for transferring the client to another worker in the agency or linking the client to other services. Breaches of Standard 1.15 include

- Going on holiday without advising clients how they may access help in case of emergency.
- Leaving a client in need of services without making appropriate referrals
- Refusing to answer telephone calls or emails from a client in need of help.

Standard 1.16 guides social workers on when to terminate services and when to continue services. If a client has reached her goals and no longer needs services, the worker should terminate the social work relationship. If services are no longer meeting the client's needs, the worker should also terminate services. If a client requires services, the worker should not abandon the client. The worker should either provide services or link the client to other more appropriate services. Social work believes that clients have a right to accessible services, so workers are obliged to link clients to the services they require.

Social workers should not terminate services in order to pursue a non–social work relationship with a client. For instance, it would be unethical for a social worker to terminate social work services so he could date or have sex with the client. Once a worker has established a social work relationship with a person, the worker should not engage in a social, financial, or other dual relationship with the person. Terminating social work services may not avoid the problems of dual relationships because a client may continue to be in a vulnerable situation even after termination. The safest way to view a client is, "Once a client, always a client." Although services may be discontinued following termination, some of the worker's ethical obligations toward the client continue. In particular, social workers must do no harm and avoid relationships that increase the risk of harm to former clients.

Social workers may terminate services with a client for failure to pay fees, provided the worker has given the client a reasonable chance to pay the fees and the client does not pose an imminent danger to self or others. Thus, if a client is homicidal or suicidal, a worker cannot turn her away simply because she cannot pay for services. Whenever clients have difficulty affording services, workers should consider reducing fees or referring them to services that are less expensive or free.

When referring clients to other services, social workers should pay attention to client needs and preferences. Social workers cannot simply discharge their duty to refer clients by giving them a list of names and telephone numbers. Workers should help clients assess their needs and wishes, consider a range of service options, and discuss the advantages and disadvantages of different options. Ideally, social workers should follow up with clients to ensure they connected well with the new service providers. One of the most common allegations in malpractice lawsuits is making an inappropriate referral (Reamer, 2003). The best safeguards against such lawsuits are properly evaluating the needs of the client, discussing referral options with the client to ensure the client is making an informed decision about the referrals, and following up to ensure the referral is appropriate.

ALL STAGES

The Code of Ethics is not divided into sections or standards of practice corresponding to the stages of the social work process. In fact, most sections and standards apply to more than one stage. The following discussion deals with two ethical issues that apply across all stages: record keeping and boundary violations.

Record Keeping

Social workers have an ethical obligation to maintain appropriate client records, accurately reflecting the services provided (S.3.04). If social workers provide false or inaccurate records, they may be held liable within their agencies or through their professional regulatory bodies, whether or not the inaccuracies were intentional. Each client record should include sufficient information to enable the worker to monitor progress from session to session, and to allow the agency to monitor the appropriateness and effectiveness of the services being provided. Good record keeping demonstrates that the worker is providing services in a competent and ethical manner (Polowy & Morgan, 2004). Whenever a client claims malpractice or inappropriate behavior by a social worker, case records provide a valuable source of information as to what issues arose, how the social worker handled them, and the reasons for key decisions made by the worker. Accordingly, case records may be vital to defend against a lawsuit or professional ethics complaint.

Each agency should have policies specifying what specific information should be kept in client records and for how long[18] (agency policies are discussed further in Chapter 8). Social workers should include only information relevant to work with the specific client—for instance, the client's presenting problem, the client's goals, and the information required for the worker and client to work toward fulfillment of these goals. To respect client confidentiality, workers should omit information that is not directly relevant to the services being provided (Polowy & Morgan, 2004). For instance, a client may disclose she is having an affair. If your role is to help find this client a job and the fact of her affair is irrelevant, then you should not include this information in her record, even if you think this information is interesting.

Standard 1.08 specifies that workers should provide clients with reasonable access to their records. Reasonable access typically includes allowing a client to see his or her client file, including the worker's psychosocial assessments and progress notes. Agencies may charge for photocopying records, but such fees should be used to cover the photocopying costs and should not be used simply to discourage clients from accessing their records. Beginning social workers sometimes assume that the worker or the agency owns the records and can decide whether to share them with clients. Agency policies and laws provide clients with specific rights to access to their own records (for example, the Health Insurance Portability and Accountability Act [HIPAA],

---

[18] Typically, state laws and agency policies specify that records be kept for a minimum of 2 to 6 years. This ensures that the agency has records should a client return for services or should a client sue the agency for malpractice.

which establishes client rights in health-care settings) (Legal Defense Fund, 2005; Polowy & Morgan, 2004). Social workers should withhold records only for exceptional reasons (e.g., when a client is currently homicidal and the case records identify where the potential victim may be found, or when protecting the confidentiality of a third person).[19] If you have any questions about whether or when to share records with your clients, consult your supervisor and/or the person in your agency designated to deal with records and confidentiality issues.

Boundary Violations

Social workers should maintain professional boundaries with clients. In order to maintain appropriate professional boundaries, social workers need to know what they mean generally, as well as how to determine what is appropriate in particular circumstances. *Boundaries refer to invisible demarcations between the client and social worker which determine appropriate roles and behaviors between them.* A social worker should respect the client's right to appropriate physical, psychological, and social space between them (Gutheil & Brodsky, 2008). When determining what is an appropriate physical boundary, workers should consider questions such as how close they sit to a client; whether it is appropriate to touch, kiss, or hug a client; and whether physical interventions such as massaging, bathing, or physically restraining a client are appropriate social work roles. When determining what is an appropriate psychological boundary, social workers should consider questions such as whether it is appropriate to ask a client to recount the details of past sexual abuse or other traumatic experiences; how to respond to a client who is falling in love with the worker; and whether to confront a client about an issue that may raise the client's level of anxiety. When determining what is an appropriate social boundary, social workers should consider questions such as whether it is appropriate to meet a client for lunch at a restaurant rather than at the office, how to respond to a client who invites the worker to a birthday party, and whether to attend a client's funeral.

Whether a particular response or behavior is appropriate depends on the particular context and circumstances (Gutheil & Brodsky, 2008). This makes it difficult for professional associations, agencies, and legislatures to dictate specifically what is appropriate and what is not appropriate. For instance, some agency policies suggest that workers should not accept gifts from clients. Accepting gifts might be viewed as accepting bribes or placing expectations on clients to remunerate workers, beyond their usual salaries. What if a 5-year-old client gives her worker a picture she has drawn? Would it be inappropriate for the worker to accept it? Arguably, accepting the gift is in the client's best interests because accepting the gift legitimizes the client's gesture of thanks. Arguably, accepting the gift is not a violation of professional boundaries because the gift was not costly to the client and there are no concerns that the gift is a bribe. If we change the circumstances slightly, however, and the worker asks the client to give her a picture, this may violate professional boundaries. As you can see, the standards demarcating appropriate and inappropriate boundaries are not as clear as black and white. There are many gray areas.

In order to determine the appropriateness of certain roles and behaviors, workers should consider what is generally accepted by their profession and agency, as well as the interpretations of clients. In other words, they should consider what is an appropriate boundary from multiple perspectives. A hospice for people with cancer, for instance, may permit some forms of hugging between staff and clients. Although hugging may be permitted, a worker should still assess how a particular client may interpret the hugging at a particular moment in time. If the worker thinks the client may perceive the hug as a sexual advance, then the worker should avoid hugging the client. If the worker thinks the client will interpret the hug as merely an expression

[19] Legislation that mandates reporting of child abuse, for instance, typically allows reporters to remain anonymous. In other words, the person who is the subject of an abuse allegation would not have a right to find out who submitted the allegation.

of professional caring, then a hug may be appropriate. In addition, workers should decide how to respond when a client initiates a hug. If a client invites a hug from the worker, verbally or nonverbally, this may indicate that the client is consenting to the hug. Still, the worker needs to be cautious about maintaining appropriate boundaries, not wanting to show disrespect by rejecting a hug but also not wanting to prompt further boundary crossings (including, perhaps, violating sexual boundaries). The worker could ask the client for permission to provide a hug. Asking for permission could show respect for client self-determination. Asking for permission, however, may not prevent a boundary violation from arising. The client may feel pressured into consenting or may not appreciate how a mere hug may impinge an appropriate professional relationship. To minimize risks of providing a hug, the worker could discuss the client's interpretation of the hug to assess whether any further issues arise (Abbott, 2003). The worker should document this interaction in the client's progress notes, including the client's permission and response to the hug.

Whenever workers interact with clients in a manner that is not characteristic of their usual roles and behaviors, they are crossing boundaries with clients. Boundary crossings are not necessarily ethical violations. Boundary crossings may be helpful to clients, though they are also risky. ***Boundary crossings** may become **boundary violations** if there are problems with the worker's intent or the effect of the crossing on the client* (Gutheil & Brodsky, 2008). In terms of intent, the behaviors of social workers should be guided by what is in the best interests of the client's well-being and growth. If a social worker acts in a manner to gratify himself—emotionally, financially, or otherwise—then the worker is not serving the client in a professional manner. Proper intent is important, but even with proper intent, a boundary crossing can turn into a violation. Suppose a worker offers to drive a client home, thinking the client would be better off than having to walk home in a snowstorm. If nothing bad happens, the client benefits from this boundary crossing. Although the worker means well, if something inopportune happens to the client during the car ride, the worker may be held responsible for a boundary violation. Typically, social workers do not drive clients home. Unless the agency specifically authorizes the worker to drive clients, the worker is taking a chance and may be held liable for any resulting harm.

The NASW Code of Ethics prohibits boundary violations in relation to sexual relationships (S.1.09), physical contact (S.1.10), sexual harassment (S.1.11), and derogatory language (S.1.12). The Code specifically prohibits social workers from engaging in sexual relationships or conduct with current or former clients. Although some practitioners believe that sex with clients is permitted if the relationship is based on "true love," the laws and ethical standards do not recognize such an exception (Caudill, n.d.). When clients make use of social work services, they are often placed in vulnerable situations. They may be emotionally distraught or confused. They may confuse the worker's professional help and caring with romantic love (Abbott, 2003). They may view the worker as an authority figure who can tell them what to do. They may feel they have to comply with the worker's suggestions, given the worker is the expert. By prohibiting sexual relationships with clients, the Code makes it clear that protection of clients from harm is one of the worker's highest priorities.[20] The NASW Code says social workers "should not engage in sexual activities or sexual contact with former clients" (S.1.09[c]), suggesting this restriction lasts forever. In contrast, the American Psychological Association's (2003) Code states that "psychologists do not engage in sexual relations with clients for at least two years following cessation of therapy" (S.10.08[a]). If psychologists do have sexual relations with clients after the 2-year period, they have the burden of proving that the relationship was not exploitative, taking the intensity of therapy, the client's situation, and other

[20] The NASW Code also advises social workers not to have sexual relations with people related to their clients, particularly if that might have a negative impact on a client. For instance, dating a client's former spouse may infuriate your client.

factors into account (S.10.09[b]). In other words, these provisions provide psychologists with some discretion about having sex with prior clients, whereas the NASW Code provides a lifelong ban on sex with prior clients.

Even when codes of ethics, agency policies, and even statutory laws clearly prohibit workers from having sexual relations with clients, some social workers still have sex with their clients. Typically, these workers know about the prohibitions. They are not ignorant or stupid. Although some workers knowingly exploit their vulnerable clients to have sex, many slip into having romantic relations with clients without intending to get into such situations and certainly without intending to hurt their clients. To help prevent yourself from violating sexual boundaries with clients, make sure you are aware of any romantic or sexual feelings that you have toward your clients—or that your clients have toward you. Make sure you deal with these feelings as soon as possible, through supervision, therapy, or other forms of support. When boundaries start to become unclear, take appropriate steps to make the boundaries more clear. If a client invites you to supper or a community event, discuss your professional role and why meeting socially would be inappropriate. If effective work becomes impossible because of a client's attraction to you, or vice versa, consider terminating your professional relationship and referring the client to another professional. If a client accuses you of having sex with him, it is no excuse to say that the client consented, or even that the client initiated the intimacy. As a professional, you are responsible for setting appropriate boundaries:

> Thank you for your invitation. I know that we have established a good working relationship and I do care for you, but in a professional manner.... If we were to meet socially, how might this affect our working relationship?

The Code of Ethics advises workers not to have physical contact with clients "when there is a possibility of psychological harm to the client" (S.1.10). The challenge is knowing when there is a possibility of psychological harm. Actually, there is always a possibility. Once, I gently touched a client's shoulder as I was guiding her into my office. She was very offended and told me so. If I wanted to avoid violating this standard altogether, I would never touch clients—not even for a polite handshake. Professors, field instructors, and agency supervisors often warn students and supervisees not to touch clients, and especially not to hug clients. In other words, they are trying to provide clear, black and white guidelines for what types of behavior are inappropriate. But is it okay to comfort a distraught client by holding hands or some other form of touch? Once again, it depends on the context. What does your agency policy say? What does the client's culture say? How might the client interpret your touch? Does the client have a history of sexual abuse? What does your theory of practice say? Suppose, for instance, that your agency subscribes to integrative mind–body therapy and this therapy requires you to touch a client in a particular manner. If the client has consented to the therapy, with full knowledge of its risks and benefits, you would be permitted to touch the client in accordance with your agreement with the client.[21] Still, you should be sensitive to the client's needs and refrain from touch that may be harmful. For beginning social workers, it may be safest to avoid any physical contact that could possibly be interpreted as sexual or unwanted. Even when deciding whether to shake hands, check the client's body language to see if hand-shaking is welcomed. Some cultures, for instance, prohibit men from having physical contact with any woman other than their spouse.

Although it should simply be common sense, the Code of Ethics specifically prohibits social workers from sexually harassing clients or using derogatory language with them. Prohibited forms of sexual harassment include sexual advances, requests for sexual favors, and making

---

[21] Given the potential risks of an intervention that involves touching, use risk management techniques such as documentation (e.g., ask the client to sign a consent form that includes the risks and benefits of the intervention, and document your reasons for using this particular intervention in the client's case records) (Caudill, n.d.). Another risk management strategy is to have a second staff member present to observe the intervention.

jokes of a sexual nature (S.1.11). Prohibited forms of derogatory language include labeling a client with terms based on sexual, racial, or cultural stereotypes, or using language that is obscene, vulgar, or insulting (S.1.12). What constitutes sexual harassment and derogatory language must be judged, in part, from the client's perspective. A worker who shows an R-rated movie to a group of clients may think that the movie is therapeutic. If some clients may be offended by the move, the worker should let them know the nature of the movie in advance, allowing them to decide whether or not to watch it. Likewise, a worker might write that a client is "promiscuous" in the client's records, thinking it is just an accurate description of the client's pattern of having sex with multiple partners. The client might view this as judgmental and derogatory. When considering what to say to a client or what to write in a client's file, consider how the client might interpret and view your message. If the client might take offense, find a different way to convey your message.

MANAGING RISKS

Often, when social workers breach ethical standards, they had no intention to breach the standards or to hurt their clients. This section explores risky situations that may lead to ethical violations. By detecting these risks early, social workers may be able to avoid ethical violations, or at least reduce the risk of running into ethical troubles in their dealings with clients. Risk factors include lack of knowledge of ethical and legal standards, high stress experienced by the worker, and inappropriate worker-client boundaries.

Lack of Knowledge

Consider the following situation: A man calls your agency asking for the time of his wife's next appointment so he can ensure that she can come to the appointment on time. You give him the time. Later, your supervisor censures you for breaching your client's right to confidentiality. You explain that you were just trying to help your client. You thought confidentiality did not apply between a husband and wife. You were mistaken, but your intent was good.

As the cliché goes, ignorance of the law is no excuse. Similarly, ignorance of agency policies or social work ethics is no excuse. All social workers are expected to know the legal rules and ethical standards that govern their practice. For beginning social workers, knowing all the laws and standards may seem to be a daunting task. It is vital, therefore, to be prepared before you see your first client and know where to access help should any questions quickly arise when you are seeing clients.

Your coursework should give you a solid understanding of general social work ethics. When you begin working at a new agency, however, you need to know the specific laws and policies that govern the agency and your work there. If you feel overwhelmed by the agency's huge policy book or by the legal jargon used in the laws that govern your agency, ask your supervisor for help: What do I need to know right away? What do I need to know in my next few months of work? When I have questions, whom should I consult (e.g., my supervisor, the program director, the ethics committee, the agency's attorney)? Do not be afraid to admit your ignorance by asking questions. It is better to risk embarrassment that you are lacking certain knowledge than to risk breaking laws, policies, or ethics because you were afraid to ask.

Worker Stress

When experiencing high stress, social workers may act in ways that they would never consider under ordinary situations. A worker with a high caseload may fall behind on writing progress notes, thereby breaching requirements to maintain proper client records. A worker with high financial debts might consider absconding with client funds, breaching ethical standards of integrity and criminal laws related to theft. A worker who becomes depressed might resort to drug abuse, making it difficult to provide services in a competent manner. A social worker who is going through a tough divorce may unintentionally impose personal feelings about marriage on an unsuspecting client. Social workers are human, with human vulnerabilities in response to stress.

Although high stress may help explain why a worker violated a law or ethical standard, this does not excuse the worker from accountability. As professionals, social workers are not supposed to let their own problems interfere with their work (Wharton, 2008). To prevent stress and personal problems from adversely affecting their practice, social workers should

- Strive for early awareness of stress and personal problems through self-reflection, journaling, or clinical supervision.
- Take steps to deal with the stress or personal problems as soon as possible (e.g., seeking help from a therapist or other professional from outside the agency; ask the agency to develop a less stressful, more supportive work environment).
- Develop strategies to ensure that work is not adversely affected by the stress or personal problems (e.g., take a leave of absence from work, ask your supervisor if you can focus on certain tasks or clients that you can manage effectively; use stress reduction techniques at home or prior to seeing clients).

In some situations, worker stress may affect the nature of the relationship that the worker has with clients. Problematic client–worker relationships are the topic of the next section.

Inappropriate Worker–Client Boundaries

Social workers often say that they go into social work because they want to help people. Although this motivation helps workers maintain passion about their work, wanting to help may also serve to put workers at risk of boundary violations. A worker might ponder:

> What type of help do clients need? Why can't I provide all the types of help that clients need?

Consider a client who is crying. Wouldn't it be helpful to put your arms around the client to comfort him? Consider an unemployed client who needs $50 to buy new clothes for upcoming job interviews. Wouldn't it be helpful to give the client the money to help her gain employment? Consider a client who says she has committed an adulterous sin. Wouldn't it be helpful to join the client in prayer for forgiveness?

Social workers are much more likely to get into ethical trouble when their relationships with clients start to look more like relationships between friends, family members, or neighbors. Workers can reduce ethical and legal risks by maintaining appropriate professional boundaries. To understand and maintain professional boundaries, consider the following strategies:

- Develop a clear explanation of your role as a social worker, including how that role is different from that of friend or family member.
- Provide this explanation to your clients at the beginning of your social work relationship; remind the client of the appropriate boundaries of your relationship should any boundaries issues arise.
- Check your own feelings toward the client—before, during, and after each session—to see if they may be getting in the way of effective, appropriate social work practice.
- Consider how you would feel if you were in the client's position (e.g., what type of boundaries would you expect, and how you would respond to the types of boundaries you plan to establish with the client?).
- Use supervision to help you distinguish behaviors and roles that fit within your professional boundaries, and those that do not.

By following the ethical standards explored in this chapter, you are more likely to serve your client well. You are also less likely to run into problems with your client, your employer, the social work profession, and the law. In your endeavor to practice ethically, you are not alone. Ask for help. Ask "stupid questions"[22] in class and with your agency supervisors, so you can make informed,

[22] As educators often say, "There is no such thing as a stupid question." Some students feel embarrassed about asking basic questions. Remember, it is better to risk embarrassment and learn the basics, rather than save face in class or with your supervisor but get into trouble with your clients because you lack basic information.

intelligent decisions when working with clients. Identify legal and ethical experts within your agency or community who can help you understand your legal and ethical obligations as a practitioner. If you are unsure of how to act or you feel something might be wrong, slow down the process. Access help before making important decisions or wading deeper into troubled waters. You and your clients will benefit.

DISCUSSION QUESTIONS AND EXERCISES

1. *Plain Language*: Write a definition for each of the following ethical principles using language that would be easily understood by a 10-year–old client: self-determination, informed consent, confidentiality, privilege, maintaining professional boundaries, and safety. When developing your definitions, you may refer to the Code of Ethics or materials in this chapter, but avoid jargon and use plain language.
2. *Identifying Breaches*: For each of the following scenarios, identify which Standard of section 1 of the NASW Code of Ethics has been violated by the social worker (whose names begin with "S"). Describe the specific behavior that violates this standard and how the social worker should have acted in order to follow the relevant ethical standard.

   Example: Shirlyn gets a new job. She tells her supervisor to say good-bye to all her clients because she has to start the new job tomorrow.

   Answer: Shirlyn violated Standards 1.15 and 1.16(b) by abandoning her clients without taking proper care to ensure continuity of services. Rather than leave right away for her new job, she should have stayed with her current agency long enough to be able to effect appropriate terminations and transfers of work with her clients.

   a. Selma comes home from work in tears. When Selma's husband asks her why she feels so sad, she confides that her client, Clarissa, committed suicide by hanging herself.
   b. Carly sees her worker Shaquile taking copious notes of their session. Carly asks if she can see what he is writing. Shaquile says, "No, I'm sorry, they're my personal notes to help me remember what we've discussed."
   c. The Condry family fails to show up for its second appointment in a row. Sammy writes in his case notes, "This family is irresponsible."
   d. Catarina says she cannot afford to pay Shorty for his social work services. Shorty says she can help paint his office in lieu of any cash payment. He warns her that if she does not do a good job painting, he will have to terminate services.
   e. Cristos tells Shona that he wants to help his son deal with a drug abuse problem. In order to encourage Cristos to try family therapy, Shona explains all the benefits of family therapy but does not discuss any risks.
   f. Salvador discovers that Colleen (78 years old) has been mistreated by her children. Salvador suggests that they call adult protective services for help. Colleen tells Salvador not to say anything to anyone because her children would probably become violent. Salvador respects her request.
   g. Sonja asks Cassidy to set goals. Cassidy says she wants to become a prostitute. Sonja agrees to help her with this self-determined goal.
   h. Calla meets her former social worker in a local bar and says, "Hey big guy. I've been bad. Want to come back to my place to spank me." Her social worker says, "Of course. My primary duty is to serve my clients."
   i. Chet is upset and turns to leave Sly's office. Sly quickly grabs Chet's hand to slow him down and says, "Stay for a moment. Perhaps you can tell me why you are upset."
   j. Sully assesses a client from El Salvador who is having trouble at school. Sully

assumes the problem is that the client had an inferior education in El Salvador. He never asks the client whether she has felt discrimination from her teachers, the main reason she has been acting out.

3. *Establishing Boundaries*: A client tells you, "You have beautiful eyes." When deciding how to respond, what type of boundary issues should you consider? How can you respond in a manner that is respectful but avoids problems related to maintaining appropriate boundaries?
4. *Accidental Disclosure*: A client signs a consent form asking you to forward her psychosocial assessment to her new social worker. You accidentally send an email of a client's psychosocial assessment to the wrong person, a social worker at a different hospital. What ethical standard have you breached? After you discover your breach, what should you do, and why?
5. *Risky Business*: A client with a fear of snakes wants to try a certain type of hypnotherapy that you think may be dangerous. What would you say to the client if you wanted to honor ethical standards related to protecting the client from harm but also respecting the client's right to self-determination?
6. *Preventing Breaches*: For each of the following scenarios, identify the ethical breach and what type of help the worker should have sought in order to prevent the breach from arising:
   a. Salma's first client was Conroy, a man with a chronic alcohol problem. During her initial session, she asked Conroy to sign the agency's informed consent contract. Conroy was obviously inebriated to the point of not understanding what he was signing, but Salma mistakenly thought that she had to have him sign the contract regardless of his current mental state.
   b. Shifra loves children and knows that children love peanut brittle. She tells her young clients that she loves them. She also gives them peanut brittle to reinforce their good behavior. One day, Clifford (aged 7) shows up at the front door of her house, telling her he has been good and asking for peanut brittle.
   c. Sharman has been having a lot of bad hair days this month. Perhaps it is the wet weather that has been frizzing up her hair, but she just feels frazzled. A client comes into her office and jokingly asks, "What's wrong with your hair? Another lightning strike?" Sharman tells the client where to go, using profanities that send the client off crying.
7. *Boundary Issues*: For each of the following scenarios, put yourself in the position of a client. Identify what you would think and how you would feel in response to the professional's boundary-crossing or violation.
   a. You go to your physician for an annual medical exam. The physician greets you with a hug and kiss on the cheek.
   b. You are seeing an attorney for help with a real estate transaction. The attorney asks you if you have any job openings at your agency because her son is looking for a job.
   c. Your bank teller says he has a great tip on an investment. His friend invented a new game and is looking for financial backers.
   d. A newspaper journalist wants to interview you to help with a story she is writing about your agency. She suggests meeting at her home, where the environment will be more friendly and comfortable.

Chapter 6

Practice, Values, and Ethics—Social Work with Families

Social workers value human relationships. Not surprisingly, the family system is one of the primary human relationships that social workers emphasize. This chapter delves into the values and ethical issues that arise when working with families. We begin by exploring the definition of a client and how social workers may have different ethical obligations depending on how they define their client. The following sections demonstrate how to put the principles of confidentiality, self-determination, and informed consent into practice when working with families. Whereas Chapter 5 introduced the basic standards of confidentiality, self-determination, and informed consent, this chapter pays greater attention to the words social workers can use to discuss these issues with clients. This chapter also explores complexities that may arise when different family members have different interests, needs, and motivation toward change.

WHO IS THE CLIENT?

Social workers have many ethical duties toward clients—confidentiality, self-determination, and informed consent, to name a few. Under Standard 1.01 of the NASW Code of Ethics, a social worker's primary ethical obligation is to promote each client's well-being. This begs the question, "Who is a client?" In some cases, the answer is obvious. If an individual seeks help, agrees to help, receives help, and pays for the help, then that individual is obviously the worker's client. But who is the client when a parent brings a child for services, or when an adult child pays for services for an elder parent? Similarly, what happens when a couple comes for services, but the services are paid by the wife's employer through an employee assistance plan? And who is the client when child protective services refer a family for services and the parents attend only because they fear their children will be taken away if they do not cooperate?[1]

To assist with determining who is a client, consider the following definitions of client and other related roles:

- *Client—an individual, family, group, organization, or community who agrees to receive the help of a social worker or is mandated by court or another authority to receive such help* (e.g., a family that voluntarily goes for family therapy, or a couple that is ordered by the court to try divorce mediation).[2]
- *Referral source—an individual or organization that suggests or requires a client to seek specific services* (e.g., a prospective parent who self-refers to an adoption agency, a teacher who helps a family set an appointment with a family counseling agency, or a mental health authority that involuntarily admits a suicidal client into a psychiatric facility).
- *Intervention focus*[3]*—the system(s) that the social worker works with as part of the planned change process* (e.g., if a child is having difficulties at school, one focus may be the child, another focus may be the parents, and another focus may be the school. Because social workers value human relationships and work from a generalist framework, the intervention focus is often the interaction between a number of individuals, families, groups, organizations, communities, or other social systems) (Dolgoff et al., 2009).
- *Beneficiary—the individuals, families, groups, organizations, or communities that derive positive results or advantages from the delivery of services* (e.g., a social worker who advocates for equality for a particular minority client may be doing work that benefits the entire minority community by setting a positive precedent) (Dolgoff et al., 2009).
- *Payer*[4]*—the individual, family, group, organization, or community that provides the fees or compensates the worker or social agency for its services* (e.g., a grandmother who pays for her grandson's psychotherapy, a support group for people with disabilities that pays a disabled person's fees, or a corrections department that contracts out substance abuse services for probation clients).

Consider a situation in which parents bring their 17-year-old son, Dan, for counseling services, to help him with depression. If the social worker sees Dan alone, then Dan would be the client. When parents bring their children for

LEARNING OBJECTIVES

Upon successful completion of this chapter, students will be able to

- Differentiate between a client, referral source, intervention focus, beneficiary, and payer.
- Understand how a social worker may have different types of ethical obligations to different family members.
- Engage family members in frank discussions regarding confidentiality, self-determination, and informed consent.

[1] Another interesting ethical question arises when a couple or family seeking services requires a diagnosis from the *Diagnostic and Statistical Manual* (*DSM*; APA, 2000) in order for their health insurance to cover the costs of treatment. *DSM* diagnoses are based on individual diagnoses rather than couples or family systems diagnoses. Therefore, the practitioner may need to designate one person in the family as the client for diagnostic and reimbursement purposes, even though the worker is providing services to more than one family member.

[2] In different settings, clients may be called by different names, for instance, *patients* in medical settings, *residents* in residential settings such as group homes, or *consumers* in social agencies that adopt a business model. A social worker's ethical obligations to clients apply whether or not the agency uses the specific term *client*.

[3] Some authors refer to the intervention focus as the *target*. This book avoids use of this term because target sounds like a passive system at which the social worker takes aim and hits, rather than active people with whom the social worker collaborates.

[4] Sometimes, called a sponsor.

services, often the worker tries to engage the whole family. If Dan and his parents agreed to see the social worker together, then the whole family would be the client. The determination of who is the client does not depend on whether the parents pay for services or whether the parents benefit from services.

Assume that a teacher reports Mr. Campbell to child protective services based on suspicions of child abuse. When a protective worker investigates the situation, the family becomes the client, not the teacher who reported the abuse and not the protective services agency which pays for the services. The protective services worker might refer the parents and child to separate workers, so that one worker has Mr. Campbell as the client and another worker has the child as a client.

As the above examples illustrate, there are times when a client is also a referral source, beneficiary, intervention focus, or payer, but there are also times when different people assume each of these roles. Many ethical obligations under the NASW Code of Ethics relate to the duties owed to clients. There are fewer explicit ethical obligations with regard to referral sources, beneficiaries, intervention foci, and payers. Some of the worker's obligations to these parties come from contractual or legal relations rather than from the NASW Code. For instance, if a child protection agency contracts your agency to provide parent training groups, the parents in these groups would be your clients, but the contract may state that you have particular obligations to the child protection agency (e.g., to provide them with information about who attends these trainings, which is a limitation on the clients' right to confidentiality). Similarly, if a parent is paying you to counsel her son, she may authorize you to provide some types of services (e.g., supportive counseling) but restrict you from providing others (e.g., no sex education). The following sections explore how ethical duties such as confidentiality, self-determination, and informed consent are affected by ethical standards, laws, and contractual obligations.

CONFIDENTIALITY—ETHICS, LAWS, AND CONTRACTS

From an ethics perspective, the general standard of confidentiality suggests that social workers should not share private client information with others (NASW, 1999, S.1.07). Laws regulating hospitals, substance abuse treatment services, and certain other types of agencies[5] also impose legal duties requiring maintenance of client confidentiality. But what happens when a referral source, intervention focus, beneficiary, or payer asks for or requires client information? Consider, for instance, a parent who pays for a child's counseling or an employer that wants information about employees who use the company's employee and family assistance program. There is no general right for a referral source, intervention focus, beneficiary, or payer to have access to such information. A worker must have specific authorization—by client consent or by law—in order to release information to any of these parties. Consider the following scenario:

> Tommy Teacher refers the Cowan family to a social worker because young Angel Cowan has been having attention difficulties in class. Tommy calls the social worker to see how Angel is doing in counseling. How should the social worker respond?

Tommy is a referral source but not a client. The social worker is not obliged to tell Tommy about the content of the counseling, or even whether the Cowans went for counseling. The worker could respond:

> As a social worker, I am required to maintain the confidentiality of all clients. I cannot even tell you whether this family ever contacted me. If you'd like me to answer your questions about this family, you would need to ask the parents to sign a confidentiality release form, which I can provide.

---

[5] Some states also have laws imposing duties of confidentiality on all licensed or accredited social workers, regardless of their agency context.

As this response indicates, clients may provide consent to share information with referral sources or others. A consent is essentially a contract in which the client and agency agree upon what information may be shared with specific others. The consent or agreement to release information should include the type of information that may be shared, with whom it may be shared, and over what time period. Some agencies use very general consent forms that give agency workers broad discretion in what to share, with whom, and over what period (e.g., open-ended permission to discuss anything about a client with no limit on when the permission ceases to operate). To protect a client's right to confidentiality, however, more specific consent forms are preferable.

A contract is an exchange of promises that can be enforced by a court. If one person breaks a contract, the other person can sue for damages (Madden, 2003). Consent forms are not the only form of contract that may be used to create an exception to confidentiality. A contract about confidentiality and its limits may be an oral agreement, a written agreement, or even an implied agreement. For instance, if a family walks into your office and you close the door, inviting the clients to trust you with personal information, you may have created an implied agreement to keep the information confidential. An explicit oral agreement about confidentiality is preferable to an implied agreement, as both the worker and the client are more likely to be clear about the nature and limits of confidentiality. By discussing confidentiality, for instance, the worker could explain her duty to report suspicions of child abuse or neglect. From a legal perspective, written agreements are generally preferable to implied or oral agreements. Although a court can enforce an implied or oral agreement, it may be difficult for one or both parties to prove that there was such an agreement or what the agreement contained. By having a written agreement signed by both parties, the court has concrete evidence of the terms of the contract (Barsky & Gould, 2002). Although it is not necessary to have a third party sign as a witness, a witness's signature can also help either or both parties prove that the parties signed the contract willingly and without coercion.

Assume you have been working for a family with concerns about religious discrimination. You advocate for policy changes that not only help this family but many others. Unless you are authorized by your primary client family, you cannot disclose personal information about this family to the others, even though they are also beneficiaries of the intervention.

Likewise, assume you are working for a client who is suffering from high degrees of stress. As part of your intervention, you want to speak with your client's boss (a focus of the intervention, since the boss may be able to facilitate a less stressful work environment). You would need your client's permission before you could speak with the boss about your client's situation. Even if the client provides consent, the worker should limit disclosures about the client to the minimum necessary to facilitate work with the boss.

Most referral sources, beneficiaries, and intervention foci can readily understand the need to protect a client's confidentiality and honor the client's right to withhold consent to release confidential information. Many payers, however, start from a different mind-set. "I'm the one paying for services, so I have a right to know what's happening during the sessions." The fact that a parent pays for services for a child (or even for an elder family member) does not mean that the parent has an automatic right to know everything that goes on between the worker and client. A payer may enter into a contractual relationship with the worker, the worker's agency, and the client that spells out what information will be shared and what information will not be shared. In the example of parents bringing 17-year-old Dan for services, for instance, they might agree to the following terms:

> The information shared by Dan with his social worker will remain confidential. The worker will not share Dan's information with his parents unless: *(a)* Dan provides explicit consent to share such information, or *(b)* Dan is at significant risk of seriously harming himself or others and disclosure of information is necessary to protect Dan or others from this harm.

This contract balances Dan's interest in having confidentiality with the parents' interest in knowing information. By giving Dan as much confidentiality as possible, the contract fosters a safer place for him to talk. He can share information to the worker that he might not be ready to share with his parents. Because Dan is an older adolescent (17), protecting his confidentiality may be particularly important. If Dan were only 4 or 5 years old, the social worker and agency would likely have a more expansive agreement concerning what types of information could be shared with the parents. The parents of younger children may have a greater need for information about the contents of the sessions, and younger children generally have more limited verbal skills to express themselves.

When criminal or child protection courts order services for individuals or families, state funds are often used to provide such services (for instance, through the department of corrections or department of children's services). Because these clients are mandated into services, they may not be free to contract about the confidentiality of their services. Right from the point of entry into services, however, the social worker should inform mandated clients about the nature of confidentiality, including what information will be shared with government officials, the court, or others. *By providing involuntary clients with notice of the limits of confidentiality, clients can then make informed decisions about what to share and what not to share.* Social workers and their agencies may advocate with the payers for as much confidentiality as possible so that clients will be more likely to trust and open up with the worker.

Anyone involved in providing health-care services needs to be aware of the impact of the Health Insurance Portability and Accountability Act (HIPAA, 1996) on client confidentiality. This law was established to facilitate transmission of information between health-care providers, managed care systems, and insurance providers. Health care is defined broadly to include physical-medical care and mental health services, so it does apply to many of the services provided by social workers. HIPAA purports to balance the need of protecting client confidentiality with the needs of health-care providers and insurance companies to share information (e.g., so health-care providers can submit patient information for insurance reimbursement and insurers can request information to monitor for fraudulent claims). You have probably noticed that whenever you initiate services with a doctor, dentist, or other health-care provider, you are asked to sign a document that tells you how information will be shared with your health insurance company and others. Often, health-care providers ask patients to sign such documents with little explanation or discussion. HIPAA legislates minimum standards for protection of client rights. The following paragraph describes these minimum standards. Note, however, that social workers can, and perhaps should, go beyond these minimum standards to respect client rights.

Under HIPAA, health-care providers do not actually need to solicit client consent to share basic patient information with insurance companies. *Providers are **required to give patients notice of their rights** and the practices of the entity, but providers are **not required to obtain a signed consent form** for release of information for "purposes of treatment, payment, and health care operations."* Providers must make good faith effort to obtain client's *written acknowledgment of receipt* of the notice of privacy rights and practices. Still, this written acknowledgment is not the same as consent and only requires that providers *try to obtain it.* HIPAA does require providers to obtain specific written authorization for sharing of "nonroutine information." For instance, routine information such as the patients' name, diagnosis, and course of treatment could be transmitted to an insurer without having to ask the client to sign a specific authorization or consent. If a third party wanted access to a client's progress notes or details of interviews, however, the provider would have to ask the client for written authorization. If you have any questions about what is routine or nonroutine information, your agency is supposed to have a privacy official who can answer HIPAA-related questions. You may also find useful HIPAA information on the NASW and American Psychological Association websites (http://www.socialworkers.org/hipaa/default.asp; http://www.apa.org/practice/pf/winter02/hipaa_affect.html). HIPAA also includes other specific provisions for how to ensure client confidentiality, including guidelines for training employees, writing agency policies, and record keeping.

Although HIPAA does not require health-care professionals to obtain consents to transfer client information for routine purposes, remember that these standards are just minimum standards. From an ethics perspective, you may go above and beyond these standards, for instance, explaining the client's right to confidentiality and what information will be shared, and asking the client for consent rather than just acknowledgment. Agency policies and practices may differ, with some agencies opting to do the minimum required, since obtaining acknowledgment is simpler and faster than obtaining consent.

The final aspect of confidentiality to be explored in this section is the extent of confidentiality between family members when the client is the whole family. Consider, for instance, a situation in which a worker has separate meetings with Dan and his parents. Suppose Dan's parents divulge their intention to divorce but ask the worker not to share this with Dan due to his current state of depression. What is the worker's obligation? Under Standard 1.07(f) of the NASW Code, social workers should seek agreement among family members regarding what should happen. Ideally, this agreement should be developed during the initial stages of work so clients know the parameters of the confidentiality before they make key disclosures. One approach to confidentiality among family members would entail maintaining confidentiality for information shared in individual meetings. The worker could explain:

> From time to time, I may need to speak with family members separately. One reason for separate meetings is to provide you with an opportunity to discuss matters that you might not be prepared to share with other family members. I will respect each family member's confidentiality, meaning that I will not share what anyone says in an individual meeting with other family members. At times, I may encourage the sharing of information. I may also need to share information if a serious risk of personal harm arises and I need to take steps to ensure someone's safety.

The advantage of this type of arrangement is that each family member will have a safe place to disclose concerns that he or she might not otherwise share. This allows workers to process each individual's concerns, perhaps empowering the individual to share the concerns with other family members. In some instances, the worker will need to maintain confidentiality in order to protect certain family members from harm. Consider a couples counselor who begins the helping process by meeting individually with Hank and Winnifred. Both agree the individual meetings will be confidential. The individual meetings provide the counselor with an opportunity to explore concerns about intimate partner abuse. In her individual meeting, Winnifred says she is fearful of couples counseling because Hank is abusive. After further assessment, the worker suggests terminating couples counseling before they even have their first joint meeting. The worker and Winnifred agree to a safety plan, including referral to an agency that provides support to survivors of spousal abuse. The worker does not want to set up Winnifred for further abuse. When the worker meets with Hank, they discuss Hank's concerns and the worker finds a reason to suggest individual counseling rather than couples counseling. Because the parties have agreed that the individual meetings are confidential, the worker is not obliged to disclose Winnifred's allegations of abuse.

The primary downside of offering confidentiality for individual meetings or disclosures is that workers may be placed in the position of maintaining family secrets. Consider a family receiving counseling for communication problems. The father calls the worker to discuss issues raised in the last session. The worker encourages the husband to share these concerns in the next session, but the husband refuses. The worker now has to respect the father's confidentiality. Unwittingly, the worker has become triangulated into the family's problems, including keeping secrets rather than communicating directly.

An alternate approach to confidentiality among family members is to say there is none. The worker could explain:

> My role is to be social worker for the whole family. To fulfill this role, I need to be able to share information from one person to another. If one of you wants to meet with me but says I cannot share what you say with

anyone else, then I would have to tell you that I cannot make such a promise. If you need to talk privately with a social worker, then I could refer you to another worker for individual counseling.

This approach puts family members on notice that information disclosed by one person may be shared with other family members. The worker may use discretion about what to share and what not to share, but this type of contract ensures that the worker is not stuck maintaining family secrets. On the downside, individuals may not share information that could be useful to the counseling process. As you can see, there is no perfect solution to the issue of confidentiality among family members. Regardless of which approach you use, make sure you inform your clients of your agency's policy and your own guidelines regarding whether and how confidential information will be shared among family members (NASW, 1999, S.1.07[g]).

SELF-DETERMINATION AND INFORMED CONSENT

Self-determination refers to the right of clients to decide what goals they want to pursue and how they want to pursue them (NASW, 1999, S.1.02). *Informed consent refers to a process of ensuring self-determination, whereby the worker explains the nature of an intervention, its risks, and its benefits, and asks clients for their voluntary permission to implement the intervention* (NASW, 1999, S.1.03). To enhance the informed consent process, social workers should also discuss alternative interventions, including their relative rates of success and the risks and benefits of no treatment at all. The principles of self-determination and informed consent are based on the value of respect for the individuality and self-worth of all people. Social workers also believe that clients are more likely to accomplish goals when clients set them rather than when the worker has imposed goals. When the client is a family, the family as a single system has the right to set goals. What does this mean in practice, however, when individual family members have different goals, when family members cannot agree on how to pursue common goals, or when only some members of the family have sufficient mental capacity to give consent? Do parents have the right to decide for the whole family? What is the worker's responsibility to young children, adolescents, elderly grandparents, or extended family members?

Ideally, when workers establish goals with families, they obtain consensus from all family members participating in the helping process as clients. Family members often come into the helping process with different understandings of the presenting problem and what they want to accomplish. By helping family members communicate, identify common concerns, and focus on mutual interests, social workers may be able to bring about consensus on goals for work.

Although children (and perhaps other family members) may lack the mental capacity to provide informed consent, this does not mean that the worker should ignore their thoughts or wishes. First, social workers must respect all members of the family, and second, children are more likely to cooperate if they are empowered to help set the goals for work. When children or other family members do not have the mental capacity to give *consent* from a legal perspective, you may obtain their *assent*, which is another form of permission or agreement to participate in certain types of services. If a child assents to services, the worker must still obtain parental consent. However, the assent process empowers the children by involving them in the family decision-making processes.

Parents may authorize services on behalf of a child even without the child's assent. The child essentially enters services as an involuntary client. The worker may try to engage the client on a voluntary basis, or at least on as voluntary a basis as possible. Consider the following scenario:

Maude is concerned that her 11-year-old daughter, Dierdre, has an eating disorder. Dierdre denies having a problem and feels coerced into seeing a social worker.

When trying to engage Maude and Dierdre, the worker acknowledges Dierdre's discontent and tries to identify goals that might interest Dierdre:

> I understand that you do not want to see me. You say you are not anorexic and you don't need any help.... Since you're already here, I wonder if there are some concerns that you might like to discuss.

By demonstrating empathy, the worker tries to build trust and open dialogue with Dierdre. The worker also invites Dierdre to help set the agenda. Although she might not agree to work on "anorexia," she might agree to work on her relationship with her mother. Dierdre is not a completely voluntary client, but the worker empowers Dierdre as much as possible to respect her right to self-determination.

While the above examples highlight conflicts between family members with and without mental capacity, conflicts over goals may also exist among family members who each have legal mental capacity. Consider a social worker who is meeting with Amy and her elderly mother, Ms. McPhee. Amy reports that her frail mother has fallen twice in the last month and can no longer live alone. Amy asks the social worker to help them find a good nursing home. Ms. McPhee says she does not want to go into a nursing home. She wants to continue to live independently, in her own house. At this point, the worker does not have a contract for work with the clients. If the worker accepts Amy's goal, then she is not respecting Ms. McPhee's wishes, and if she accepts Ms. McPhee's goal, then she is not respecting Amy's wishes. If Amy asks, "Why can't you just tell my mother that she's better off in a nursing home?" the worker could respond:

> My job is to help both of you. Both of you need to let me know what that help should look like. Both of you are competent to make decisions for yourselves[6] and both of you are in a much better position than I am to decide what is best.

The worker could then engage them in a discussion on possible goals that satisfy both their interests. Amy's suggestion about "finding a good nursing home," for instance, could be reframed into a goal of "determining the best living arrangements for Ms. McPhee." Amy and her mother agree that this is a good place to start. By finding a goal that both family members can agree upon, the worker respects their mutual right to self-determination. If, after searching for a mutual goal, family members still cannot agree on what they want to achieve from the social work process, the worker may have to terminate the social work process. Rather than impose a goal on certain family members, the worker could consider referring family members for individual work.

Remember, when working with families, the family as a social unit has a right to self-determination and informed consent. Although different family members have different views, wishes, and levels of mental capacity, strive to reach agreement on goals and methods of work with the whole family.

ENGAGING CLIENTS IN ETHICS-RELATED DISCUSSIONS

Social workers must understand ethical standards such as confidentiality, informed consent, and self-determination. Understanding the standards, however, is not sufficient. Workers must also be able to engage clients in effective discussions of ethics-related issues. This means using the communication and clinical skills that you have been learning in your practice courses: In particular, this means speaking clearly, using plain language, checking back for understanding, remaining open to disagreement, and respecting client choices.

In terms of clarity and use of plain language, make sure you can explain ethical standards, agency policies, and, or relevant laws in a manner that is easily understood by your clients. Pay

---

[6] In this situation, Ms. McPhee's mental capacity is not in question. If she were mentally incapacitated, then it would be possible for Amy or another legally authorized person to make decisions on Ms. McPhee's behalf.

particular attention to each client's age, cognitive ability, and cultural background. Typically, codes of ethics, agency policies, and laws are written for highly educated individuals who have the luxury of time to study these standards during their professional training. While a term like *confidentiality* might sound like a natural part of conversation for a social work student, many lay people are unfamiliar with this seven-syllable word. Try replacing confidentiality with a sentence composed of only one- and two-syllable words:

> I want to make this a safe place to talk. What you say will stay between you and me. I will not tell others what we discuss. The only time I may have to talk to others is if I have to talk to them to protect a person from being hurt.

Social workers must be careful to avoid the traps of too much detail and unnecessarily complicated descriptions. Consider the following explanation of informed consent:

> Prior to administering an intervention, I am ethically obliged to enumerate the nature, risks, and benefits of said process. Under the principles of informed consent, you are entitled to consent or dissent, on a purely voluntary basis.

Although this explanation is technically correct, many clients would have difficulty understanding what the worker is saying. Keep your explanations simple. Use short sentences. Avoid jargon. Mirror the client's language. If a client has used the term *voluntary*, then you could also use this term. If the client has used the term *choose*, then you could explain informed consent as, "You have the right to choose . . ." (giving examples of what choices are available).

"Checking back" is one of the best ways to ensure that clients understand our explanations. If you merely ask, "Do you understand confidentiality" or "Do you have any questions about self-determination?" clients are unlikely to admit their ignorance. They may feel too embarrassed to ask questions. Instead, check back with clients by asking them to summarize or paraphrase what you have explained about an ethical issue. If clients have difficulty providing a summary or paraphrase, then you may provide further information. You do not want to put clients on the defensive about what they know or don't know. Provide positive reinforcement for what they do know, clarifying misunderstandings and adding key information that they may have missed. Consider a client who believes that any mention of suicidal thoughts must be reported to the police or other authorities. The worker could respond:

> Yes, there could be times when I have to break confidentiality to protect you from harm. But just because you mention suicide doesn't mean that I have to report you to the police. First we'd talk things out and see if we can keep you safe, without having to break confidentiality.

When engaging clients in discussions of confidentiality, informed consent, and other ethical issues, social workers should convey openness to disagreement. Rather than telling clients what information is confidential or what type of consent they must provide, social workers should invite clients to engage in a frank and open discussion of these issues. Consider a social worker helping a couple that is coping with the fallout of the husband's recent affair. When discussing service options, the social worker might say:

> Both of you have expressed concern about trust. Perhaps we can talk about different alternatives for rebuilding trust.

Instead of telling the couple there is only one way to rebuild trust, the worker shows openness to discussing various alternatives. This permits the couple to express diverse views and make their own decisions. Even if the worker has a preferred intervention for trust building, the worker can simply present it as an option and invite the clients to discuss the possible benefits and risks of this intervention. An intervention that seems right to the worker may not be right for the clients.

Social workers should show respect for client choices, even when they run counter to the workers' professional opinions. Consider a social worker who asks a client family for consent to discuss confidential information with the child's teacher. The worker may believe that involving the teacher in the intervention plan will be helpful. If the family refuses consent, however, the worker should respect the decision of the family. The worker may engage the family in a discussion to consider the pros and cons of withholding their consent. Ultimately, however, the family should decide what is right for them. By showing respect for client choices, workers honor client rights to self-determination and build trust for future work together.

As the examples in this chapter demonstrate, working with families may raise a number of complicated ethical challenges. Social workers need to balance the needs, wishes, and interests of various family members. They may also need to take the needs, wishes, and interests of referral sources, payers, beneficiaries, and intervention foci into account. Although the NASW Code of Ethics and agency policies provide a general framework for managing issues related self-determination and client confidentiality, social workers may need to address these issues through individualized contracts with families, referral sources, payers, beneficiaries, and intervention foci. When contracting with these various systems, social workers should generally advocate for the needs, wishes, and interests of the client, as paramount considerations. By demonstrating respect for the dignity, worth, and autonomy of client families, social workers model ethical behavior and build trust needed to help work through difficult issues with clients.

DISCUSSION QUESTIONS AND EXERCISES

Exercise 1 is designed to help you distinguish between the roles of client, referral source, intervention focus, beneficiary, and payer. Remember, a social worker may have different ethical obligations toward different people, depending on their roles and relationships with the social worker. Exercises 2 and 3 provide case scenarios, so you can practice applying the ethical standards of confidentiality, self-determination, and informed consent in the context of family work.

1. *Identifying Clients and Others*: For each of the following scenarios, identify who is the client, referral source, intervention focus, beneficiary, and payer; provide a brief explanation for how you have categorized these people and systems.
   a. The Autism Foundation sponsors 5-year-old Chrissy Atwater to go to a therapeutic day camp. The Foundation picks up the costs of the day camp and the parents drop off Chrissy each day. The camp experience helps Chrissy communicate through animal-assisted (horse) therapy.
   b. Eighty-year-old Mrs. Chips is in the hospital after a fall that broke her hip. Her doctor refers Mr. and Mrs. Chips to the hospital social worker, Ms. Smyth, to help them with the psychosocial issues arising from the accident. The family's health maintenance organization covers the cost of Ms. Smyth's services.
   c. Mr. Cowan is concerned that his 13-year-old daughter, Donna, is homicidal. He takes her to the emergency ward at a general hospital. A psychiatric social worker determines that Donna poses a risk to others and has her committed to the psychiatric ward. The Cowans are on Medicaid, so Mr. Cowan does not have to pay for services, but he does agree to meet with the social worker to help Donna. Donna does not want to see the worker. The worker involves Donna's teacher in the intervention plan.

2. *Putting Ethics into Words*: Critique the strengths and limitations of the following dialogue in terms of the social worker's use of clear and plain language, checking back for understanding, remaining open to disagreement, and respecting client choices. Identify any violations of the NASW Code of Ethics in relation to confidentiality, self-determination, and informed consent. Rewrite the dialogue in a manner that corrects each of problems you identify.

Worker: Thank you for coming to meet with me today. I understand you were referred to me by Mrs. Kravitz, your neighbor. Mrs. Kravitz is a very nice lady. She's been coming to see me for her anxiety problems for several years now. Are you also coming for anxiety issues?

Festus: Actually, Mandy and I are here to discuss child-rearing issues. Our daughter Della just turned 6 and she is still wetting her bed.

Mandy: It's not really a problem. Festus is making too big a deal of it.

Worker: So, you're primary goal is to help Della with her bed-wetting?

Festus: No, it's really about child rearing. We disagree about everything.

Worker: OK. The best way for me to assess your coparenting skills is to observe both of you at home, interacting with Della.

Mandy: I really don't think that the issue is about how we're raising Della. Maybe she just has a small bladder.

Worker: In order for us to work together, we need to have an agreement on what the issue is and how we're going to deal with it. This is called your right to self-determination. Right now, each of you has a different understanding of the issues in the family. Perhaps we can explore these further before making any decisions.

Mandy: That's fine with me. But we don't have any coparenting issues.

Worker: Before we go on, perhaps I should explain confidentiality. Anything we discuss shall remain purely confidential. I must respect your confidentiality under all circumstances, save and except for suspicions of child maltreatment, suicidal ideation, or homicidal ideation.

Festus: What are you talking about? We don't mistreat Della. We love her and wouldn't do anything to hurt her.

Worker: Good, then there shouldn't be any problems, should there? Now, I will have to contact your pediatrician to find out if there are any medical problems that I should know about. We often find that it is important to work with doctors and teachers, because they have an important impact on the family.

Mandy: What about Della? I don't think she'll be too excited about seeing you. She'll probably clam up, not say a word. I don't think it's a good idea to force her to meet with you.

Worker: I won't meet with Della unless I have your permission. Perhaps we can talk about the best way for us to meet—for instance, at home, in my office, or at her school. What would be the best way for me to get to know Della, and to help her feel comfortable meeting with me?

3. *Shanessa's Supersized*[7] *Squabble*: Assume you are Shanessa's supervisor. Your job is to provide feedback on how she handled the situation described below. Help Shanessa identify the client, referral source, intervention focus, beneficiary, and payer. Then, help Shanessa identify her ethical obligations related to confidentiality, self-determination, and informed consent. For the purposes of this exercise, you do not need to help her resolve conflicting obligations but simply identify what these individual obligations are.

   Shanessa is a social worker who works in Soda Hills Public School. The kindergarten teacher, Ms. Tyson, refers one of her pupils, Paddy, to see Shanessa because he is morbidly obese, particularly for a 5-year-old. After receiving consent from Paddy's mother, Millicent, Shanessa conducts a thorough biopsychosocial assessment. Upon completing the assessment, Shanessa concludes:

- Paddy eats food items that tend to be high in sugars, cholesterol, and carbohydrates (chips, chocolate, pizza, and meals from fast-food restaurants); he eats very few fruits, vegetables, or whole grains.
- Paddy watches over 3 hours of television per day.

[7] Consider: I used the vernacular term *supersized* intending it to be funny. Is use of this term innocent and harmless, or disrespectful and harmful? What is the place of humor in professional communications, particularly when some people may take offense?

- Paddy's obesity puts him at risk physically (long-term risks for cancer, heart disease, and other medical conditions), psychologically (lower self-esteem because others may discriminate against him and he may have difficulty participating in physical games and activities with his peers), and socially (he may have difficulty with peer relationships as a child, adolescent, and adult).

Shanessa discusses these issues with Millicent, who says, "I don't think Paddy's weight is a problem. He is just naturally plump." Shanessa tries to persuade Millicent to accept the gravity of the situation. Throughout the discussion, Shanessa is respectful, supportive, and empathetic. Still, Millicent gets angry with Shanessa. Millicent argues, "I'm a good mother and a good mother feeds her child. I'm on a fixed income and I can't afford the fancy foods you're talking about. Just leave us alone. We're fine... not everyone has to look like a pixie stick like you." Ms. Tyson is relatively thin. Millicent is relatively chubby. Shanessa validates Millicent's suggestions that it is okay for people to have different body types and that some foods do cost more than others.

Shanessa offers several options—speaking with another social worker, going to their physician, getting a referral to a nutritionist, or a free after-school program with activities and life-skills training designed for children with weight problems. Millicent rejects each of these offers and says, "Just leave Paddy and me alone. We're fine." Shanessa says she may have to report Millicent to Child Protective Services (CPS) because Paddy is at risk. Millicent says, "You're kidding," and starts to walk out of the office. Shanessa picks up the phone and calls CPS to make the report. Millicent stops to listen to the call. CPS tells Shanessa that this is not a child protection issue, so they cannot help. Millicent boasts, "I told you it was none of your business." She slams the door as she leaves.

Chapter 7

Practice, Values, and Ethics—Social Work with Groups

Group work is a vital branch of social work, operationalizing the core value of "human relations" by engaging clients in a process in which people work together, building on their individual and shared strengths, and striving to resolve their individual and shared biopsycho-social-spiritual concerns. Although some social agencies promote group work as a method of providing services in a cost-efficient manner (one worker for many clients), group work ought to be justified primarily by its effectiveness for clients (Toseland & Rivas, 2009). This chapter begins with an exploration of ethical issues that may arise in the context of group work. The middle section of the chapter demonstrates the role of an ethics committee—as a form of task group—in helping social workers and other practitioners work through ethical issues. The final section presents five different methods of facilitated discussion that may be used to help social workers manage ethical conflicts with co-workers and clients.

ETHICAL ISSUES IN GROUP WORK

As described in Chapter 5, a social worker's primary obligations toward clients are defined by Standards 1.01 to 1.16 of the NASW Code of Ethics (1999). Although each of these standards applies to clients involved in group work, group work is mentioned specifically in just one standard, 1.07 on confidentiality (as described below). Some social workers are content that the NASW Code adequately covers ethical issues in group work; others suggest that the NASW Code should be amended to cover group work more specifically; still others suggest development of a separate code for group work (Gumpert & Black, 2006). Some social workers subscribe to the codes of ethics of associations that specialize in group work (e.g., American Group Psychotherapy Association [AGPA, 2002], Association for Specialists in Group Work [ASGW, 2007], and the Association for Advancement of Social Work with Groups [AASWG, 2006]). This chapter focuses on how the NASW Code applies to group work, with mention of ethical guidelines from other codes to fill gaps or enhance provisions in the NASW Code.

The following sections highlight ethical concerns related to informed consent, confidentiality, respect, maintaining appropriate boundaries, imposing values and beliefs, conflicting needs and interests, and groups with involuntary clients. As you work through these sections, consider the ethical issues that may arise in relation to an alcoholism group.

> Stedman is a social worker who runs an alcoholism recovery group, From Spirits to Spirituality (S2S). Three new clients have been referred to the group by various sources: Celeste (by her probation officer), Claudia (by her boss), and Cheryl (by a friend who is already in the group).

LEARNING OBJECTIVES

Upon successful completion of this chapter, students will be able to

- Apply the ethical principles of informed consent, confidentiality, respect, and maintaining appropriate boundaries in the context of social work with groups.
- Identify ethical issues pertaining to a facilitator's management of conflicts between group members (e.g., when members try to impose values or beliefs, when members have conflicting needs and wishes, or when involuntary clients are reluctant to participate fully).
- Describe the roles and functions of an ethics committee, including how committee facilitators should manage group process issues.
- Compare and contrast five methods of facilitating discussion of ethical issues among ethics committee members or other small groups: Socratic method of inquiry, debate, dialogue, interest-based mediation, and transformative mediation.

Informed Consent

Standard 1.02 of the NASW Code advises social workers to engage clients in an informed consent process at the outset of providing services. Social workers should explain the nature and purposes of the services, including risks and benefits, prior to asking clients whether they consent to services. Social workers should ensure that clients understand the information provided as well as their right to refuse consent or withdraw it at a later time. The Association for Specialists in Group Work suggests that group workers should disclose the following additional information during the informed consent process: the worker's professional credentials, address of the credentialing body,[1] the worker's theoretical orientation, the roles and responsibilities of the group members and the workers, policies for entering or leaving the group, policies related to substance abuse, policies related to involuntary clients, confidentiality, documentation requirements (client records), policies regarding out-of-group contact among group members, procedures for communication between group workers and members, time commitments, and fees (ASWG, 2007, Sections A6 and A7). If Stedman were to follow these guidelines, he might open the informed consent process with the following explanation:

> Thank you for coming to our group, From Spirits to Spirituality. Before I ask you to share information about yourselves, I'd like to tell you about the group and invite you to ask questions. The purpose of our group is to help people with alcohol-related problems. Our group is based on a theory called existentialism, which is just a fancy way of asking, "How can we put spirituality or meaning back into our lives?" Research shows that people have a better chance of overcoming problems with alcohol when they have a stronger sense of meaning or purpose in their lives. Our

[1] NASW, state licensing board, or other body that accredits the worker. This information provides clients with information needed should they have any questions or grievances about the worker's performance.

group will meet for 1 hour each week for the next 10 weeks. During each session, I will present information on different ways you can bring spirituality into your lives. We will then put spirituality into practice by trying different spirituality development exercises, such as meditation, breathing, and yoga. I am not a priest, minister, or religious leader. I am a social worker trained in spirituality through the Spirituality and Addictions Institute of America. This group is open to people of all religious and nonreligious backgrounds. I will not be promoting any particular religion, though you may discuss your own religious beliefs as they relate to how you put meaning into your life. Some of you have chosen to come to this group on your own. You are here voluntarily, which means that you are free to come or go as you please. If you agree to participate, I would ask that you commit to attending all 10 sessions. If you have any questions about leaving the program before it is over, I ask you to speak with me individually first so we can discuss your options. Some of you have been ordered by the court to attend. I am required to provide your probation officers with information about your attendance. If you need to miss any sessions, you should speak with both your probation officer and me to make appropriate arrangements. The primary benefit of this group is that it will help you develop a stronger sense of spirituality which will in turn help you gain greater control over your alcohol use. The risks of this group are minimal. Some group members may feel stress from having to speak up in groups. Others may feel anxious about having to explore spirituality issues. The yoga and breathing exercises are designed for beginners. If you have any heart, lung, back, or other health concerns, you should meet with your physician to discuss whether you can participate in these exercises. For the safety of all, you are expected to be sober when you come to this group. If you are noticeably impaired by drugs or alcohol when you arrive, I will ask you to set up an individual appointment before you are allowed back in the group. If you cannot attend a session because you have been drinking, you should call me in advance to let me know. Before we go on, let's open up the floor for questions about the program.

This paragraph covers many of the required components of informed consent (others, such as confidentiality, documentation, and boundaries issues are discussed later). Stedman could pause at various points to invite feedback and questions. Obviously, there are many questions that could be raised: What does meditation mean, what if I can't do yoga, or what if I don't want to talk about my religion or spirituality? The worker should attend to these questions as they arise. In addition to the oral discussion, the worker could provide written information about the group on a brochure or consent form. Asking clients to sign consent forms may be desirable when the risks of the group are high, or when the worker wants participants to be very clear about the group's expectations and members' specific commitments to the group.

When developing new groups, workers need to determine the best way to implement the informed consent process—individually, within the group, or some combination of both. From legal and practical risk-management perspectives, the safest way to discuss informed consent with clients is individually. As soon as you bring clients together, you are exposing them to risks that they may or may not have accepted if you had discussed the risks individually and in advance. Clients Cheryl and Claudia, for instance, may know each other as coworkers. Cheryl may not want anyone from work to know she has a problem with alcohol, so merely bringing them together for an information meeting could be troubling for Cheryl. Celeste has a history of violence. If Cheryl is not informed about the group prior to the first joint session she attends, she will be exposed to risk of violence without having the opportunity to decline this risk. Thus, pre-group individual meetings provide social workers with an opportunity to engage clients in a full discussion of the risks and benefits of participating in a group before they attend the first group session (Toseland & Rivas, 2009). Other advantages of individual pre-group meetings include

1. Clients may be able to discuss potentially embarrassing questions more easily on an

individual basis (e.g., as a mandated client, Celeste may have difficulty disclosing her criminal status to a group and how such status affects the voluntariness of her participation).
2. Social workers can examine a client's mental capacity and screen for potential violence more freely in an individual session without embarrassing the client before other group members.

Clients may feel freer to accept or reject services when asked individually; clients may feel pressure to participate in a group (and specific group activities) when surrounded by other group members (Corey et al., 2007).

Often, social workers do not engage clients in an informed consent process prior to the first joint session. From a pragmatic perspective, it takes less time to go through an informed consent process with the group as a whole rather than go through the same information with each member individually. Engaging a group jointly may also be advantageous because of the synergies that arise in group work (Corey & Corey, 2006). Cheryl may raise questions about the group process that the others had not considered (e.g., "What happens if I miss a group session? Can I be expelled from the group?"). Claudia may be too shy to ask questions but still benefit from the questions of the more assertive group members. In some cases, the group's goals and activities are not known prior to the first joint meeting. Accordingly, part of the informed consent process involves ascertaining the goals and wishes of group members, individually and as a whole. Thus, Stedman may initially advise clients that the general purpose of the group is to assist clients with recovery from alcoholism. During the first meeting or meetings, the group may discuss their personal goals (e.g., abstinence, controlled alcohol use, improved health) and plan group activities (e.g., education about the connection between spirituality and alcohol use, experiential exercises). The group's goals and activities may evolve over time, so the informed consent process could be conceptualized as an ongoing process rather than a one-time decision during the first session.

If Stedman's S2S group were an open group (in which new members could join and leave the group at various times), this would create added complications to the informed consent process. Because Celeste, Claudia, and Cheryl are joining a group that is already operating, they have had no say in developing the group's goals and activities. If they are given no say, then Stedman may not be respecting their right to self-determination (Standard 1.02). If Stedman renegotiates the group's contract each time a new member joins the group, then group members may become frustrated with the amount of time spent on contracting and informed consent, and having to negotiate a moving target for the group's goals. To balance the interests of new and existing members, Stedman could

- Inform prospective members about the group's current goals and activities (during pre-group screening and orientation meetings).
- Offer to refer prospective members to another group or agency if they are not satisfied with the goals and activities of his group (to facilitate choice and self-determination).
- Help each client develop personal goals to pursue within the general framework of the group's goals.
- Review the overall goals and activities with the group on a periodic basis (e.g., every 10th session) rather than when each new member joins the group.

When working with groups, social workers must attend to both the interests of the individuals and the interests of the group as a whole. In terms of facilitating informed consent, some combination of individual and group engagement may be best. At a minimum, social workers should provide group members with general information about the group prior to the first session (e.g., by providing them with brochures or online information). This ensures that they have sufficient information to determine whether they want to attend the first meeting. The social worker could engage the whole group in a more in-depth informed consent process during the first session. To protect individuals who may feel reluctant to voice their questions or opinions within the larger group, the worker could also offer to speak with clients individually, upon their request.

When the risks of a group intervention are high, prudent practice generally suggests engaging clients individually in the informed consent process, with a thorough discussion of the group's risks and benefits. Consider, for instance, a therapeutic group for survivors of sexual abuse. Participation in such a group may be emotionally risky because participants may be retraumatized by discussions of past abuse. They may not have sufficient coping skills to manage the stress they may experience. By engaging clients individually, the social worker can assess each particular client's level of risk and develop a risk-management plan. For some clients, a period of individual counseling prior to group involvement may help prepare the client for participation in the therapeutic group. Other clients may simply ask for reassurance that they will not be pushed to disclose issues that they are not ready to discuss.

Confidentiality

Section 1.07(f) of the NASW Code specifically advises group workers to seek agreement among clients regarding each individual's right to confidentiality and each individual's obligation to protect the confidentiality of others in the group. Whereas a professional social worker automatically has an obligation to safeguard the confidentiality of clients, clients do not have such an obligation unless they agree to it. By engaging clients in a discussion of confidentiality, social workers can educate clients about the nature of confidentiality within a group and surface any concerns that clients may have: Is it safe for me to talk about things that I consider private; what happens if other group members start to gossip about me; and what can I do if information from this group gets leaked to my family, friends, or employer? A social worker cannot guarantee that group members will respect each other's confidentiality,[2] so this should be discussed honestly with the group (Gumpert & Black, 2006). Consider the following exchange:

CLAUDIA: How do I know whether I can trust people that I don't even know? If my boss finds out some of the things I've done, I could lose my job.

STEDMAN: That's a valid question. What do others think about Claudia's concern?

CHERYL: We're all in the same boat. Why would I gossip about Claudia outside the group? I wouldn't want anyone to do the same to me.

STEDMAN: Good point. We all have the same interest in respecting everyone's privacy, but we can only do this if we have trust in each other. Claudia, what else could we do to make you feel more comfortable sharing personal information in the group?

The process of discussing confidentiality issues within the group helps build commitment and trust. Having a written consent form that formalizes the confidentiality agreement could further the commitment. Written consent also provides clients with legal recourse if a fellow group member happens to breach their confidentiality. In practice, group clients rarely sue one another for breach of confidentiality.[3] Still, a written consent form clarifies everyone's obligations and reinforces the seriousness of the commitments (Corey & Corey, 2006).

Group workers should advise clients of the limitations of confidentiality, including duties to report child and elder abuse, to respond to subpoenas issued by a court,[4] and to prevent serious personal injury from occurring (as discussed in Chapter 5). In addition, group workers should

---

[2] In an open group when new members may join at any time, the worker could meet individually with prospective clients prior to joining the group to ensure they understand that the group is confidential.

[3] In part, because it is difficult to prove that someone breached confidentiality and because it is difficult to show that such a breach caused specific damages to the client.

[4] Note that many counseling and support groups are not privileged, meaning that the worker and worker's records may be subpoenaed to court. As Chapter 5 explains, state laws may provide privilege to certain professionals and certain professional functions, including addictions treatment.

explain the limitations of confidentiality that arise out of the fact that information may be shared among group members (S.107[g]; AGPA, 2002, s.2.2; AASWG, 2006, s.III.a.1). Most groups operate under a guideline that each group member is responsible for deciding what personal information to share with other group members: Nobody (worker or client) should share another client's personal information with other group members without the client's consent. Thus, if a group worker receives a telephone call from a client explaining that she is too drunk to attend a session, the worker may not tell the group about this call unless the client specifically authorizes the worker to do so. Likewise, if two clients meet privately, neither one should share what the other says in this private meeting without the other's explicit consent.

Different groups may develop different agreements or ground rules around confidentiality. Support groups, counseling groups, and therapy groups tend to have strict confidentiality guidelines. In these contexts, confidentiality ensures a safe venue for people to open up and share private information. In contrast, many task groups operate on the principles of openness and freedom of information rather than confidentiality. For instance, a social action group may want its information to be shared with the public in order to persuade others to support their cause. Groups performing governmental functions may be required to be open to the public under state or federal freedom of information (or government in the sunshine) laws. Some task groups require confidentiality in terms of who says what during discussions, but issue a report or public document stating their conclusions or recommendations. Given the vast array of different approaches to confidentiality, group workers should clarify the extent of confidentiality for each group and ensure that group members are in agreement from the outset of the group.

Record keeping for groups may raise additional concerns about confidentiality. If the worker writes one progress note for each group session, then confidential information about each individual is included in the same document. If the worker writes individual progress notes for each individual, then the worker may not be able to document interactional issues that arose during the group session. Further, the worker will have to write some of the same information for each client, making documentation more time-consuming. One way to manage group work records is to write one group record that includes global group information (but excluding any information that identifies any particular group member), plus individual progress notes in each client's records that are pertinent to each particular client (Polowy & Morgan, 2004). When clients ask to see their records, they will be able to see information about the group and their own participation, without having access to personal information about others in the group. If one client's records are subpoenaed by the court, the social worker can easily provide the client's records without breaching the confidentiality of others.

Respect

Social workers have a professional obligation to respect the individuality and inherent worth of all individuals. Standard 4.20 says, "Social workers should not practice, condone, facilitate or collaborate with any form of discrimination." When working with individual clients, social workers need only to be concerned about how they are treating each client. When working with groups, however, social workers need to consider how to ensure that clients experience respect, and not discrimination, from other group members. As with confidentiality, group members are not bound by the NASW Code of Ethics. The best way to foster respect between group members is to develop and agree upon ground rules with the group.

Examples of ground rules that promote respect include: *(1) We are participating in this group in order to provide one another with support; (2) Everyone in the group has the right to speak or to choose not to speak to particular topics raised by the group; (3) When one person is speaking, we will give that person our undivided attention; and (4) From time to time, we may disagree or express different views, but we will do so in a way that shows respect for others in the group. We will remember that people come from diverse ethnic, cultural, religious, and personal backgrounds, and we will avoid making comments that may be experienced as discriminatory, hurtful, or insensitive.* Each group should develop guidelines that meet its specific needs regarding respect. In Stedman's group, Celeste asks for a rule to discourage raised voices. Cheryl suggests that respect means that everyone should arrive at the group on time—and finish on time. Claudia suggests that group members should respect each other by avoiding negative labels such as drunks, rubbies, and addicts. Different group members may have different sensitivities, so it is important for the worker to build consensus on what respect means and how it will be enforced within the group.

Each group has its own norms and values (Toseland & Rivas, 2009). Sometimes, a group's norms and values conflict with those of the worker, agency, or society (Gumpert & Black, 2006). Consider, for instance, how Stedman should respond if the group said it wanted to exclude Latinos from participating in the group. Although social workers should respect the values and goals of clients (S.1.02), they should not condone or participate in discrimination (S.4.02). Stedman could explore the reasons that the group wants to exclude Latinos to see if there is any possible justification or room for compromise (e.g., perhaps members are concerned about everyone speaking the same language so they can understand one another; they might resolve this concern by agreeing to use an interpreter). Stedman may need to educate the group about his professional ethics, agency policy, or state laws that prohibit discrimination against any group. Ideally, they work toward an agreement that everyone can live with. If they cannot reach agreement, Stedman may need to impose ground rules that reflect professional ethics, agency policy, and state laws.

Maintaining Appropriate Boundaries

Standards 1.06, 1.09, 1.10, and 1.11 define how social workers should maintain appropriate boundaries with their clients: They should not engage in dual relationships with clients, they should not have sex with clients, they should avoid physical contact when there is a possibility of psychological harm, and they should not sexually harass clients (as explored in Chapter 5). Although these standards apply to group workers, they only apply between the worker and each client; they do not establish boundaries among clients within a group. While the NASW Code does not give guidance on how workers should manage boundaries among group members, social workers should attend to the types of boundaries established among group members (Gumpert & Black, 2006).[5] In particular, group workers should consider developing ground rules for the following boundary issues:

- What types of touch, if any, are permitted between group members during group sessions?
- What types of interactions, if any, are group members permitted outside of group sessions—group-related support, social relationships, sexual relationships, or work relationships?
- To what extent are group members permitted to confront one another within the group?
- To what extent are group members allowed to ask each other about potentially sensitive topics, including politics, sexuality, religion, and criminal activity?

As with confidentiality, group workers cannot guarantee that members will respect whatever boundary guidelines are established. Accordingly, workers should discuss proposed guidelines and use consensus-building techniques to establish commitment from group members. Stedman proposes the following guidelines for his group:

- To ensure that everyone feels safe in group, group members will not hug, kiss, or touch other group members, other than to shake hands (which is permitted).
- Group members may socialize and support one another outside of group, provided they have the permission of one another.

[5] From an ethics perspective, the obligation to attend to boundaries between clients could arise out of Standard 4.01(c) on competence and the need to practice based on recognized social work knowledge.

- Group members may not engage in sexual relationships with one another.

Stedman engages the group in a discussion of the proposed rules. Cheryl asks why they can socialize but cannot engage in sex. The group talks about how people in group may be vulnerable and how such a rule provides safety during the early stages of recovery.[6] Claudia queries why they can socialize outside the group, since this could lead to sex or other vulnerable situations. Stedman acknowledges that the group could have a rule against socializing, but this might create a double standard of not allowing group members to socialize outside of groups, while encouraging them to develop relationships within the group (Gumpert & Black, 2006). By validating concerns and searching for common ground, Stedman helps the group reach consensus. The group agrees that socializing outside the group is permitted, but members should not be forced or even expected to socialize outside the group if they do not want to. Some workers and agencies prefer rules that prohibit contact between clients outside of group, in part to protect the agency from liability (e.g., is the worker or agency legally responsible if one client assaults or steals from another?). If the worker requires clients to get together outside of group, worker and agency liability may be more likely. If clients get together on their own accord, the risk of liability is lower. In either case, the worker could engage clients in a discussion of the risks and benefits of getting together outside of group.

Imposing Values and Beliefs

In order to respect the dignity and worth of the person (NASW, 1999, Ethical Principles), social workers should not impose their values or beliefs on clients. The Code of Ethics, however, does not specifically address the issue of a social worker's obligations when some members of a group try to impose values or beliefs on other group members. Assume, for instance, that Cheryl encourages another client, Carl, to come to her church. Going to church fits with the group's focus on encouraging clients to use spirituality to help them deal with their addictions issues. Still, is it ethical or appropriate for Cheryl to advise another client to attend her church? Does it violate ethical principles of equality and client autonomy (AASWG, s.I.a.2)? Clearly, it would be inappropriate for the social worker (Stedman) to encourage Carl to go to his church, but is this situation different because it is one client encouraging another?

Permitting clients to offer suggestions or advice to one another may have benefits. Specifically, group members may want to learn from each other's experiences, values, and beliefs, particularly when group members have common presenting problems and concerns (Corey & Corey, 2006). Whereas social workers have power over clients by virtue of their professional status, clients often have equal power and status within a group. Thus, allowing clients to provide suggestions or advice does not necessarily violate the principle of respecting the dignity and worth of the person. Friends, family members, and colleagues frequently provide others with suggestions or advice. Thus, a group facilitator could permit members to provide suggestions or advice, as long as other group members do not feel pressured into following the advice. When Cheryl encourages Carl to go to her church, Stedman would need to assess how Carl perceives this suggestion. If Cheryl uses a judgmental tone and Carl seems embarrassed into accepting her suggestion, then Stedman may need to intervene to protect Carl.

Social workers may address advice giving in their group rules. Some groups have strict rules against advice giving. The facilitator encourages group members to speak from their own experiences. Group members may accept or learn from each others' experiences, but members refrain from providing direct advice. Other groups permit advice giving, but have rules related to demonstrating respect (e.g., refraining from passing judgment or insulting others). The facilitator's choice of rules on advice giving may depend on

[6] Some AA members joke that the 13th step in recovery is having sex with another AA member.

the type of group. In certain therapeutic groups, members may feel particularly vulnerable, and strict rules against advice giving may be preferable. In task groups composed of members with equal power, having a rule that permits advice giving may be desirable.

Conflicting Needs and Interests

Standard 1.01 of the NASW Code says that a worker's primary commitment is to the client. In group work, conflicts may arise because the client is not only the group as a whole, but also each of the individuals within the group. What may be good for some group members may not be good for other members or the group as a whole. Stedman advises his group that a local personal trainer has offered to provide the group with a free session on physical exercise and spirituality at her gym. Nine group members believe this is a great idea and want to go during their next session. One group member (Cleveland) believes it is a waste of time and does not want to go. How should Stedman balance his obligations to the nine consenting members with his obligations to Cleveland? Assume that there are no easy answers that satisfy everyone's interests (e.g., persuading Cleveland to go, or using non–group time for the nine consenters to go). Should Stedman abide by the wishes of the majority or should Stedman abide by the concerns of the minority? Does it make any difference if Cleveland cannot go because he has a physical disability or because a court order prevents him from attending?

Ideally, the group has a mechanism for dealing with such conflicts. For instance, the group's rules may state how group decisions will be made (e.g., by a majority of participants, by consensus, or by the decision of the facilitator). Regardless of the group's rule for decision making, however, the facilitator still has to balance the needs of each individual and the group as a whole. Thus, the facilitator should work toward solutions that meet the wishes and needs of all clients. If the group is not meeting the needs of one or more group members, then the facilitator could meet with those members individually. This would give the facilitator another opportunity to explore whether the group can meet their needs and also to explore options outside the group (e.g., referrals to individual counseling or other groups).

Involuntary Clients

Although the ideal of client self-determination (S.1.02) suggests that clients should not be forced to receive social work services, clients may be required to participate in groups in a variety of circumstances: They may be mandated by the child protection system or criminal justice system to attend, they may be required as part of inpatient services (e.g., for addictions or mental health treatment) to participate in groups, and they may feel pressured into attending by employers, family members, or friends. Group facilitators should explore each group member's motivation and level of commitment to the group during intake or pre-group interviews. Facilitators should also ensure that group members understand their rights and responsibilities. For instance, the court may have mandated the client to participate in services, but not necessarily this particular group. Further, the client may be required to participate in some group activities, but may have the right to decline participation in other activities.

Group facilitators may be able to engage mandated clients on a more voluntary basis by offering services that fulfill the client's needs and wishes. Facilitators should not only help clients explore the consequences of refusing to attend the group, but also the consequences of participating in a minimal or reluctant manner (Corey et al., 2007). By helping clients understand the advantages of higher levels of participation, the facilitator can help them engage in a more personally beneficial manner. Assume that a drug court mandated Cicero into the S2S group. During intake, Stedman asks Cicero about his understanding of the court order. Cicero says he agreed to participate in S2S, but only because he did not want to go to jail. Stedman builds on Cicero's wish to avoid jail as a strength. Stedman encourages Cicero to try attending a couple of sessions before he decides whether to continue. By asking for a time-limited commitment, Stedman makes it easier for Cicero to provide consent. Stedman may ask for greater commitment once he has been able to engage Cicero and help him develop more meaningful goals for work.

When a group is composed of both voluntary and involuntary members, conflict may arise because of the disparate levels of commitment and motivation of the two groups. Voluntary members may resent the presence of involuntary members because they are not sharing personal information or participating as fully. Although no group member should feel pressured into divulging certain information or exploring certain issues, the facilitator should strive to build group consensus on the types of participation generally expected of the group. If the group is a therapeutic group, for instance, the expectation for sharing may be relatively high. If the group is a psychoeducational group, then the expectation for sharing may be lower. In matching clients to groups, facilitators should consider each potential member's level of commitment and the expectations for participation for the group as a whole.

Group workers abide by many of the same standards as other social workers with respect to ethical issues such as informed consent, confidentiality, respect, and boundaries. Still, group workers have to take into account ethical issues that are unique to working with groups, including how to manage relationships and interactions between group members. Professional codes of ethics and agency policies cannot be enforced with group members in the same ways they can be enforced with social workers. Accordingly, social workers should strive to gain commitment of group members to certain rules and standards through education and consensus building.

Now that we have explored how ethical issues may arise in groups, we turn to a new topic, the roles of an ethics committee as a form of task group.

ETHICS COMMITTEES

An ethics committee is a task group designed to help agencies deal with ethical issues (Hester, 2008).[7] Ethics committees typically perform four functions: formulating agency policies based on ethical standards and principles; educating practitioners and clients about ethical rules, principles and laws; consulting with practitioners and/or clients to help them manage specific ethical issues; and reviewing how practitioners handled cases[8] to see if further policies and education are needed[9] (Barker, 2003; Meyers, 2007; Reamer, 1987). Formal ethics committees are most common in health-care settings, including hospitals and hospices where they help professionals and patients make decisions pertaining to complex ethical issues such as end-of-life decision-making, providing treatment when efforts may be futile, ensuring patients have equitable access to limited treatment resources, and managing different belief systems (e.g., when professionals and family members come from different religions or cultures) (Csikai, 2002; Hester, 2007; McGee, Spanogle, Caplan, & Asch, 2001). Some agencies do not have formal ethics committees, but engage informal ethics committees on an as-needed basis. These informal committees may

[7] The reason that ethics committees are discussed in this chapter is not because ethics committees only deal with ethical issues raised in work with groups, but rather to remind students to apply what they are learning about group work when working with ethics committees.

[8] These are sometimes called *ex post facto* or "after the fact" reviews.

[9] In some agencies, all potential ethical violations must be reported to its ethics committee. The committee is responsible for monitoring and oversight, helping practitioners respond appropriately and avoid ethical violations. The committee also reviews actual ethical violations to see what can be learned from them: Upon reflection, how was the issue handled, and how might it be better handled? The ethics committee should assess what happened from an ecological perspective, considering factors from the social context that may have contributed to the ethical problem and its resolution. This assessment may help the committee recommend changes, such as revisions in agency policy and ways to provide better support or reduce stressors for practitioners and clients.

not even be called ethics committees (Barsky, 2007a). Various functions of an ethics committee may be performed through case conferences, interprofessional team meetings, task forces, agency trainings, or group supervision.

Membership

Formal ethics committees often include members representing a range of professions, including doctors, nurses, attorneys, social workers, ethicists,[10] clergy, laypeople,[11] administrators, and mental health professionals. Including members from a range of professional backgrounds ensures that the committee has a broad base of expertise and value systems (Geva, Barsky, & Westernoff, 2000). The composition of an ethics committee partially depends on the nature of the host agency, including what types of ethical issues may arise and what types of professionals are available within the agency (Reamer, 1987). An agency that provides only social work services might include only social workers on its committee. If the agency wants to add expertise from another profession, such as law, it may invite professionals from outside the agency. If an attorney is employed by the agency, the attorney's role is to advise and advocate on behalf of the agency.[12] The committee should clarify that the attorney does not act on behalf of specific practitioners or clients. If individual practitioners or clients want legal advice, they should hire independent attorneys to represent them.

The composition and size of an ethics committee depends on the nature of its work. An ethics committee mandated to develop agency policy should include representatives from across the range of the agency's professions. A committee of psychologists should not be determining standards of practice for social workers, or vice versa. A committee providing consultation on a particular case may not need broad representation. If a social worker was trying to determine whether to report a particular client for suspicions of child abuse, for instance, it may be sufficient for the worker to consult with a small group of social workers. In contrast, if a social worker was helping a family decide whether to remove life supports for an accident victim, it may be useful to consult with a range of social work, medical, and mental health professionals. When determining whom to involve on an ethics committee, the agency should consider who will be affected by the decisions, who will have to implement the decisions, and what types of expertise may be needed in resolving the ethics issues to be considered. If an ethics committee has multiple roles (e.g., case consultation, education, policy development), it may be divided into several subcommittees responsible for different parts of its mandate.

Facilitators, Consultants, Input Providers, and Decision Makers

Whenever people are brought together to discuss ethical issues, the facilitator should clarify the roles of everyone who is present: Who will be responsible for facilitating or leading the discussion, who will be acting as experts (providing ethics consultation and advice), who will be allowed to provide input, and who will be responsible for making the decisions. Additional group roles may include opinion seeker, energizer, procedure technician, recorder, time-keeper, and observer–evaluator (Toseland & Rivas, 2009). By ensuring that everyone knows his or her role

---

[10] E.g., a philosopher, a bioethics specialist, or someone trained in the field of ethics specifically related to the work of the agency.

[11] Laypeople are representatives of the community who do not have training or credentials as service providers. Sometimes, agencies choose former clients to serve on ethics committees because they will be able to bring a client's perspective to the table. Bringing former clients onto agency committees involves certain risks related to dual relationships and confidentiality. Former clients, and indeed all committee members, must be cautioned against allowing personal issues to interfere with their participation and must be careful to abide by the agency's policies on confidentiality.

[12] On some ethics committees, attorneys are the most influential members because of their ability to provide legal advice.

from the outset, each person can properly prepare for the meeting and avoid confusion concerning the types of contributions they can and cannot make. Consider the following scenario:

> Ceanna (17 years old) requests an abortion from a family planning clinic. She says she cannot tell her parents about her pregnancy for fear of how they will react. Shantal, the social worker who conducted the intake interview, refers the case to the agency ethics committee. Ordinarily, agency policy requires parental consent for clients under 18. Although state law in this jurisdiction permits waiver of parental notification and consent under some circumstances (Donohoe, 2007), agency policy requires consultation with the ethics committee whenever a minor requests an abortion.[13] The ethics committee consists of Sebastian (a social worker), Diane (a doctor), Nina (a nurse), and Preston (a psychologist).

Sebastian acts as committee chair. He facilitates the meeting, meaning that he helps guide the discussion but has no decision-making power and is not acting as an expert consultant. Because he has no say in how the agency should respond to Ceanna's case, he can remain independent and neutral. When facilitators are also decision makers or advisors, they risk losing their neutrality as facilitators and may not be trusted by other participants. Diane, Nina, and Preston act as consultants, using their clinical and ethical expertise to provide guidance to others in the agency. They receive input from Shantal about Ceanna's situation, and help Shantal decide the next steps. For instance, if Ceanna's fears indicate child abuse, should the agency notify child protective services? If Ceanna lacks mental capacity to make decisions, should the agency bring in an attorney, family members, or another type of advocate? If the situation indicates a medical emergency, should the agency help Ceanna to initiate court proceedings and seek the court's approval for the abortion? Initially, the committee meets with just Shantal. It may decide to bring in others, including Ceanna or an attorney, if they believe it would be beneficial. It is generally easier to start with a small group and bring new people into the consultation, as opposed to starting out with a larger group and having to ask some to leave.

Note that social workers may play a range of roles within ethics committees, including facilitators, consultants, input providers, and decision makers. Understanding group process and dynamics helps social workers in each of these roles (Meyers, 2007). Sebastian, for instance, is an effective facilitator because his social work education has taught him how to foster constructive dialogue and problem solving. Although none of the consultants in this case scenario are social workers, social workers can make effective consultants provided that they have sufficient ethics knowledge and training. Shantal can be effective as an input provider because she understands the nature of everyone's roles. If Shantal lacked such an understanding, she might feel defensive going to an ethics committee for guidance, thinking that she is competent to make decisions on her own. Rather, Shantal understands that ethical decision making may involve a complex process that benefits from dialogue among experts. She welcomes feedback from the committee and knows how to present her information and opinions in an assertive, nondefensive manner.

The above discussion skirts around the question of who is the decision maker. The answer depends on which decision we are talking about. If we are talking about whether to report suspicions of child abuse, this might be a decision to be made by Shantal and her supervisor. If we are talking about a decision on whether to

---

[13] The agency policy and state law in this case are listed for illustration purposes. Different agencies and different states may have different laws and policies (e.g., permitting clients to consent to counseling or medical services at younger ages). Municipal governments may also have laws regarding abortion services, for instance, prohibiting professionals from transporting minors outside the city for the purposes of procuring an abortion, unless the professionals have received parental consent.

involve other family members to help Ceanna, the ethics committee might make such a recommendation, but it would be up to Ceanna to decide (e.g., does she have grandparents, aunts, or uncles whom she could trust?). Because decision-making roles may shift depending on which decision is being discussed, facilitators should clarify who is playing which role(s) when discussion moves from one type of decision to another. For instance, a facilitator could suggest, "The discussion seems to be shifting from the question of reporting child abuse to the question of whether to initiate a court case. If the agency is going to intervene by initiating a court case, then we need to obtain approval from the executive director."

Group Process

Given that ethics committees are task groups, remember that what you are learning about group process applies to work with ethics committees. Because ethics committees are designed to deal with complex ethical issues, facilitators and members should be aware from the outset that diversity of opinions and conflict should not only be expected,, but encouraged. In order to reach informed decisions, conflict should not be squelched or avoided,, but managed in a constructive manner (Barsky, 2007a; Hester, 2007). Ethics committees should strive to build team chemistry and positive group norms on an ongoing basis, thus helping them build capacity to manage conflict when crises or other difficult situations arise (Nathoo, 2000). Ethics committees should also invoke procedures to guard against retaliation toward people who raise ethical concerns (Danis et al., 2008).

As ethics chair, Sebastian has fostered team chemistry by developing rules of engagement with his committee members:

- We welcome the information, opinions, and suggestions of all committee members and invited participants.
- In order to facilitate critical thinking, we will identify factual information as fact, opinions as opinions, and suggestions as suggestions (Shiraev & Levy, 2004).
- When differences of opinion arise, we will use active listening skills (paraphrase, summarization, etc.) to make sure we understand one another accurately, clarifying any misunderstandings, and validating others' points of view even when we disagree.
- When someone raises legal or ethical concerns about actions of a colleague, we will endeavor to protect the rights of both parties, guarding against retaliation toward the person raising concerns, as well as giving due process to the person alleged to have violated a law, policy, or ethical standard.

To build positive working relationships with clients, social workers and other helping professionals are taught to demonstrate empathic understanding, unconditional positive regard, and genuineness (Rogers, 1957). Similar strategies can be used to build positive rapport with groups dealing with ethical issues. Preston demonstrates these strategies in the following response:

> Diane, I understand that you believe Chantal is too young to make her own decision about having an abortion [empathic understanding]. As a physician, I know that you are concerned about Chantal's best interests [unconditional positive regard]. To be frank, however, I strongly believe that Chantal's best interests would not be served if we notified her parents at this time [genuineness].

Preston's paraphrase shows that he has heard what Diane has said. He demonstrates respect by acknowledging that Diane's motives are sincere. He concludes by sharing his beliefs in an honest manner, without attacking Diane personally or sugarcoating their differences on key points.

The primary job of an ethics committee facilitator is to help group members share their thoughts and deliberate together in a constructive manner (Nathoo, 2000). Ethics facilitators often use rational decision-making frameworks to guide the group's deliberations. Rational questions include: What are the facts of the case? What is the ethical issue that needs to be resolved? What do the law, agency policy, and professional codes of ethics say about how to resolve this issue? If law, agency policy, and codes of ethics provide clear and consistent guidance on how to resolve the issue, then follow these rules or guidelines. If there are conflicting obligations, then brainstorm options in order to find a creative solution that resolves the issues in the best way possible (Dolgoff et al., 2009). Rational decision-making models assume that given the proper developmental and intellectual capacities, people should be able to consider an ethical issue objectively, neutralizing extraneous factors that might interfere with a logical application of relevant laws, agency policies, and ethical standards. In practice, individuals are affected by emotions, cultural biases, and other nonrational factors (Prilleltensky, Valdes, Rossiter, & Walsh-Bowers, 2002). Thus, when facilitating an ethics committee (or any group that is discussing ethical issues), social workers should attend to both the rational and nonrational aspects of the decision-making process.

When discussing Ceanna's case, Nina becomes rigid and agitated. As facilitator, Sebastian provides Nina with feedback on her body language. This intervention provides Nina with the opportunity to admit that the discussion of a teenager having an abortion without parental notification has triggered certain emotions: fear and anguish. She notes that her own daughter is the same age as Ceanna. Unconsciously, she had started to construe and evaluate Ceanna's situation as if she were personally involved. Nina's disclosure helps her become more centered, remembering that this is a case involving Ceanna, not her own daughter.

Ethics committee chairs should also help members focus on the social context of the ethical issues, including culture, family background, religion, socioeconomic status, social supports, and social stressors (Prilleltensky et al., 2002). Laws, agency policies, and ethical standards have to be written so that they apply across a broad range of situations. When applying them to a particular case situation, deliberators should consider the social context of the case and how this could affect the application of relevant rules and principles.

Assume the law in Ceanna's case requires parental consent for a minor child who wants an abortion. The ethics committee might assume this means that Ceanna must obtain consent from her biological mother and father before she can have an abortion. Sebastian helps the committee explore Ceanna's context. Shantal reports that Ceanna has been living with her aunt for the past two years. Although Ceanna's parents know where she has been living, they have not had any role in her parenting during this time. Ceanna's aunt has been assuming the role of her parent, even though there is no contract or court order authorizing her role. When looking at the case in this context, the committee might decide that it would be ethical to make use of the aunt's consent in lieu of the parents' consent. The committee would then have to consider what legal processes could be used to authorize the aunt's consent. By helping committee members explore the social context of the case, Sebastian ensures that they consider not only the laws, policies, and ethical standards that apply globally but also the unique constellation of factors that define Ceanna's social situation.

Support

The work of ethics committees can be time-consuming and taxing—cognitively, emotionally, and socially. Agencies should ensure that committees have sufficient time and resources to deliberate and problem solve. Without such support, decisions and members may suffer. In Ceanna's case, the committee might feel pressure to resolve the issues quickly because the clock is ticking on her pregnancy. Delaying decisions may cause additional stress. Delays may also complicate the issue of whether she can have a safe and legal abortion. If the agency did not have an ongoing ethics committee and merely appointed ad hoc committees to deal with cases as they arise, the committees would face a number of disadvantages: lack of policies and procedures, working rapport, and collective resources. For instance, an ad hoc committee may need to research relevant laws each time a case arises, whereas an ongoing committee may have gathered relevant laws in advance, making them easier to access on short notice. Similarly, members of an ad hoc committee need to determine who plays which roles, whereas an ongoing committee already has established roles and experienced people in these roles. Thus, having an ongoing committee enhances its ability to respond to ethical issues in a more timely and effective manner (Bramstedt, Chalfant, & Wright, 2007).

Agencies can enhance the functioning of an ethics committee by providing the following types of support:

- Assigning specific people to serve on the committee and providing them with sufficient time in their work schedules to perform the tasks of the committee.
- Providing committee members with educational opportunities (e.g., participation in ethics conferences, in-service training, or web-based courses; membership in bioethics networks and associations).
- Ensuring access to relevant laws, agency policies, ethical standards and library resources (paper or web-based).
- Limiting the time that individuals may serve.

By limiting the time that individuals serve, the agency rotates different members on and off the committee (e.g., 3-year terms, staggered so the committee always has both new and experienced members). Rotation creates a sharing of responsibility and gives members respite after serving for a period of time. Rotation also fosters greater ethics expertise across the agency, as members take ethics knowledge and experience from their committee time into their general practice (Nathoo, 2000).

The emotional and social toll of ethics committee work should not be underestimated. Ideally, committee members and agency workers can work through ethical issues in a peaceful, respectful, and professional manner. In practice, discussion of ethical issues may invoke powerful emotions, defensive or aggressive responses, and other challenges to professionalism. Assume that the committee in Ceanna's case asks Shantal to meet with Ceanna to re-explore the issue of whether she could approach her parents for consent to the abortion. In spite of Shantal's best attempt at raising the issue in a positive manner, Ceanna responds with anger. Shantal, feeling as though the committee set her up, reports back to the committee in a defensive manner, accusing members of showing a complete lack of sensitivity to her client. Thus, arguments and attacks between two people can lead to further arguments and attacks between others. Sensitivities may be particularly high during ethical disputes when core values are at stake.[14]

Providing committee members with self-care techniques can help them manage the stress of their work more effectively. Committee members may need time to debrief among themselves or with supervisors in order to work through stressful incidents. Other self-care techniques include getting enough sleep, learning how to relax, meditating, and using positive self-talk (e.g., telling yourself that you may not be perfect but you are doing the best you can; asking yourself if the issue will still seem so important a year from now or 10 years from now; and letting go of something that you have no control over) (Barsky, 2006).

One of the best ways for ethics committees to prepare for difficult ethical issues is to practice with hypothetical situations. By working through case studies, members can develop norms for discussing ethical issues in a safe and constructive manner. They can observe how other members approach ethical analysis and deliberation, and determine which types of arguments and interactions tend to promote collaborative problem solving. By discussing hypothetical cases first, members may be less likely to become hijacked by their emotions. Members may learn what types of issues or arguments push their buttons. They can also learn how to keep their emotions in check (Lightman, 2007). In sum, committee members can use hypothetical cases to prepare for handling real issues, when urgent issues may suddenly arise and emotions are more likely to flare.

Managing Group Process Challenges

As most group work textbooks suggest, one of the primary roles of a group facilitator is to manage problems that may arise in group process (Toseland & Rivas, 2009). In other words,

[14] Consider, for instance, a person whose religious beliefs suggest that abortion is murder. Such a person may be so incensed at an abortion clinic that he or she might threaten violence against clinic staff.

group facilitators should assess and attend to potential barriers to effective communication between group members (e.g., silence, advice giving, intellectualizing, and blaming) (Corey & Corey, 2006). This section highlights potential process issues that may be particularly problematic for ethics committees or similar groups that are discussing ethics issues: domination, lack of diversity, group think, and grievances (Nathoo, 2000).

Domination

The value of empowerment suggests that the voices of all group members should be heard and validated. If one individual or a small subgroup dominates the discussion, then other members will feel disempowered. Ethics committee facilitators may empower members by assessing for domination and taking steps to equalize power (Prilleltensky et al., 2002). A number of different factors could lead to domination. First, some group members may naturally tend to be dominant participants. They may have strong voices, they may be very articulate, they may enjoy hearing their own voices, or they may feel very passionate about the issues being discussed. A person who acts in a dominant manner may or may not be doing so intentionally. Assume that Diane starts to take over the discussion of Ceanna's case. As group facilitator, Sebastian, should not assume that Diane is intentionally being controlling, mean, or subversive just because she is acting in a dominant manner. She may have good intentions and she may not realize that others are not having a fair chance to speak. Whatever her intentions, Sebastian should help Diane and the group have more equitable communication.

Domination may also be related to the professional roles and hierarchical organization of the agency. For instance, medical doctors are often given the highest level of authority in hospitals, and attorneys are often given the highest level of authority in child protection agencies. In the context of an ethics committee, the facilitator should ensure that all members of the committee are able to voice their concerns, even when they disagree with those in higher position of authority.

The worldview of particular individuals may also lead to issues of domination. When individuals have absolutist views on particular issues, they may try to impose their views on others, finding it difficult to back down or compromise. Consider a social worker who believes that marriage is a sacred bond. Given this religious belief, she is opposed to divorce under any circumstances. Because the worker's view on this issue is absolute, she may act in a particularly forceful way to defend her view. An ethics committee facilitator should validate the worker's perspective, but also ensure that other perspectives can be discussed in a safe and equitable manner.

A facilitator may foster equitable communication by establishing ground rules such as giving everyone an equal opportunity to speak and valuing the input of all group members. When Diane starts dominating the discussion, Sebastian could gently remind the group of the ground rules or redirect discussion so everyone gets a chance to speak. If Diane persists in dominating, Sebastian may need to deal with the issue more directly, either individually or with the group. As the only doctor in the group, for instance, Diane may assume that she has greater expertise, standing, or authority than other group members. In fact, agency policy or state law may even provide her with greater authority over certain types of decisions. Sebastian could engage the group in a discussion of who has decision-making responsibility and who has what type of expertise. By confronting these issues directly, the group can acknowledge any power differences, but also consider the value of hearing everyone's voice. Even if Diane has final say on whether to perform an abortion, the decision-making process can benefit from hearing from Nina, Preston, and Shantal. Each has different expertise and perspectives. They function as a team. Further, Shantal (as social worker) may be asked to discuss any agency decisions with the client. If she has not fully participated in the decision-making process, she may not fully understand the reasons for the decision and she may not be fully committed to it when she meets with Ceanna.

Sometimes, a dominant group member exerts undue pressure in a subtle manner. If Diane is officially the team leader, other members may fall into line with her opinions just to avoid conflict and the possibility of reprisals. If they speak out of line, she may give a certain look that tells others to stop crossing her (e.g., a raised eyebrow). Sebastian needs to be aware of both verbal and nonverbal cues in order to identify such subtle expressions of dominance. He may need to meet individually with group members to assess for dominance problems and to determine the best way to manage them. Sometimes, people behave in dominant manners not because they feel powerful but because they fear that they will look bad or lose face if they do not take charge. Facilitators and group members may be able to assuage such fears by validating the person's power and position. Facilitators may coach group members on ways to provide input in an assertive but respectful manner without putting the dominating person on the defensive.

Lack of Diversity

Diverse membership benefits ethics committees by ensuring that the committee considers a broad range of perspectives. Diverse membership also legitimizes the committee's decisions, as the clients, agency, and community affected by the decisions will see that the committee's composition reflects the composition of the agency and community. Ethics committees may lack diversity for a variety of reasons: Those selecting the committee may have discriminated against particular minorities, the pool of potential participants may lack people of certain backgrounds (e.g., an agency that has no Asian American social workers), or the committee may be too small to be able to reflect all the groups in a particular community. Ideally, group composition issues should be handled during the initial stages of group formation. Those responsible for selecting the group should consider a broad range of diversity factors, including age, sex, gender, sexual orientation, ethnocultural background, religion, political belief, and ability/disability (Code of Ethics, S.4.02). Different types of diversity may be more or less relevant depending on the types of issues to be decided. In Ceanna's case, because decisions about abortion have important religious connotations, it may be particularly helpful to have representation from different religious perspectives. If the primary ethics committee does not include religious diversity, the committee could seek input from outside representatives. If potential participants from minorities feel reluctant to participate on ethics committees, the agency should assess the reasons behind their hesitance. For instance, some people may decline invitations to participate if they feel that they are being treated as token representatives. Others may harbor ill feelings toward the agency for past experiences of discrimination. Thus, it is important for an agency to show that it values diversity in all aspects of its work and to invite critical feedback on how it can improve its record.

Group Think

Group think arises when one or two members express certain opinions and others in the group tend to agree without voicing or appraising alternate opinions (Toseland & Rivas, 2009). Group think may stifle constructive conflict and effective problem solving, as members do not sufficiently analyze all aspects of an ethical dispute and a broad spectrum of potential solutions. Group think may arise because members want to promote a high level of cohesion and avoid conflict. Individually, members may have a tendency to conform and agree (Janis, 1972). As a group, norms about cooperation and respect may be interpreted as "do not disagree or argue." Group members may fear that merely raising ethical questions or contradicting a supervisor's opinion could put positions within the agency at risk (Prilleltensky et al., 2002). Members may also be hesitant to voice unpopular views if they think their input will be shared outside the immediate committee.

To avoid group think, facilitators should institute ground rules and norms that encourage members to take risks and express a broad range of views. For example, before asking members for their opinions on how to handle Ceanna's case, Sebastian could ask each member to write down his or her thoughts. Each member has a chance to formulate his or her view individually, without being influenced by the others. Other ways to discourage group think include

- Instituting rules of confidentiality that prohibit disclosure of who says what during committee meetings, but allow final decisions and their rationale to be reported.
- Assigning all or some group members the role of "critical evaluator," whose function is to raise doubts, questions, or dissent (e.g., acting as devil's advocate).
- Inviting discussion from frontline workers before asking for feedback from supervisors or administrators.
- Inviting feedback from people outside the group who may bring fresh views or perspectives not influenced by within-group discussions (Janis, 1972).
- Democratizing discussion by ensuring that participants may express their opinions without fear of negative repercussions or threats to their personal interests (Prilleltensky et al., 2002).

Although group cohesion and consensus may be valuable assets, a well-functioning ethics committee needs to be a group that deals well with differences (Fisher & Brown, 1988).

Grievances

Because ethics committees deal with controversial issues, one should not be surprised that various practitioners and clients may be unhappy with the decisions or recommendations of the committee. Different people have different values, beliefs, and opinions. Further, there may be no solution that satisfies everyone affected by the decision. Ethics committees should have mechanisms for people to express concerns or grievances. First, the committee could institute periodic evaluations. Such evaluations provide people with the opportunity to provide feedback on the functioning of the committee, as well as feedback on particular decisions. An independent evaluator could conduct individual interviews, focus groups, or written survey evaluations. Interviews and focus groups provide the evaluator with an opportunity to explore concerns more deeply. Some practitioners and clients may be reluctant to provide oral feedback, fearing possible repercussions from agency administrators (even if they have been promised that no identifying information will be passed along). Some practitioners and clients may prefer completing and submitting surveys on an anonymous basis. The following types of feedback could be solicited, orally or in writing:

- Clarity of the ethics committee's roles and functions (facilitating, consulting, decision making, record keeping).
- Preparation of committee members for the meetings.
- Extent to which the committee listened to and validated the voices of different participants.
- Accurate application of relevant laws, policies, and professional ethics.
- Effectiveness of problem-solving skills.
- Absence of bias or partiality.
- Sufficient time and resources to support effective decision making.
- Transparency of decisions (e.g., providing reasons for decisions)
(Ascension Health, 2007).

In addition to evaluation procedures, ethics committees should institute formal appeals processes. Appeals processes permit practitioners or clients to question the decisions made by the initial group that heard the issue. Appeals processes recognize that nobody is infallible and it may be useful to solicit second opinions. Appeals processes act as a check on biases or potential abuses of power. The opportunity to review earlier decisions also provides constituents with a sense of fairness (Madden, Martin, Downey, & Singer, 2005).

Ethical issues frequently involve conflict among professionals, or between professionals and clients. Although social workers need to be able to assess and work through ethical issues on their own, they also need to be able to engage others in ethical decision-making processes (Dolgoff et al., 2009). This section has highlighted the roles of ethics committees in helping practitioners and clients deliberate jointly over ethical issues. The following section explores various methods of engaging people in discussions of ethical issues. These methods may be used by ethics committees or other groups faced with the task of how to resolve an ethical issue.

METHODS OF FACILITATED DISCUSSION

The manner in which we discuss ethical issues should reflect what we hope to achieve out of the discussion: For instance, do we want a better understanding of our own thoughts, beliefs, and emotional reactions; a better appreciation for the other's perspectives; a thorough examination of the issues; a quick decision; a resolution that satisfies all of the interested parties; or a more positive relationship among people with whom we may disagree? This section presents five different methods of facilitated discussion—the Socratic method of inquiry, debate, dialogue, interest-based mediation, and transformative mediation.[15] Each method has different strengths and limitations in relation to the aforementioned goals. The following case study will be used to compare and contrast how these methods of discussion may be applied in practice:

> Caleb has been seeing Sylvie, a social worker, for help with making friends. He describes himself as a bit of a loner because he feels awkward in social interactions. During the third session, Caleb mentions that he killed a woman 3 years ago. Following the session, Sylvie seeks help from her supervisor, Sanchay, wondering how she should respond to Caleb's disclosure.[16]

Socratic Method of Inquiry

The Socratic method of inquiry is a didactic process, based on the dialogical approach to teaching and learning first advanced by the Greek philosopher, Socrates. The facilitator asks one or more participants a series of questions in order to help them discuss and analyze a case scenario (Yassour-Borochowitz, 2004). The facilitator takes the role of "seeker of understanding," using questions to encourage participants to discuss issues that they may not have previously considered, and to explore issues from different perspectives (Maxwell, 2007). The facilitator shows interest in learning from the participants, perhaps even indicating ignorance about the issues in order to encourage participants to educate the facilitator. Traditionally, the Socratic method has been used most widely in law and philosophy courses, helping students develop knowledge through critical thinking and discourse. The Socratic method can be adapted for other groups, including social work students, social workers, other professionals, and clients who are faced with how to handle difficult ethical issues. In these contexts, the primary goal of Socratic inquiry would be for participants to gain a better understanding of the ethical issues and factors to be considered when trying to resolve them. Participants generate their own understanding, knowledge, or truths from engaging in a dialogue with the facilitator (Maxwell, 2007).

To facilitate Socratic inquiry, social workers may use the following skills and strategies in relation to the first two stages of the generalist problem-solving process:

- *Engagement stage*: introduces issue(s) to be discussed; explains nature of Socratic inquiry in plain language; invites questions about the issues and nature of process; demonstrates empathy regarding concerns raised; suggests ground rules to create safe environment for discussion and learning; and develops agreement regarding the issues, process, and ground rules.
- *Assessment and learning stage*: presents case situation; invites participants' to express initial views on issues; restates their views to demonstrate understanding or to invite clarification; poses questions to raise doubts or to look at issues from different angles; raises hypothetical questions to explore exceptions to previously

[15] This list of five methods is not exhaustive. Other methods of discussing and resolving ethical conflicts include negotiation, arbitration, litigation, narrative mediation, circle processes, and family group conferences (Barsky, 2007a).

[16] For a somewhat dated but still relevant video on this issue, see *Ethics in America: To Defend a Killer* (Annenberg Media, 1988).

stated views ("what if..."); raises doubts about deeply held beliefs or convictions; asks questions that take participants' views to the extreme (e.g., what would happen if their suggestions applied in every single case); demonstrates interest in learning from the participants, provides additional information to consider (e.g., different laws, ethical principles, or agency policies and procedures); asks participants how their views may change given this new information; demonstrates humility and patience toward participants when they are struggling with answers.

Socratic inquiry focuses primarily on the assessment and learning stage, as Socratic inquiry gives emphasis to understanding a situation rather than performing the planning, implementation, and follow-up stages of the problem-solving process. Still, once participants have completed the assessment and learning stage through Socratic inquiry, social workers may guide them through the rest of the problem-solving process.

Sanchay decides to use Socratic inquiry with Sylvie during a supervision meeting. The dialogue proceeds as follows:

SANCHAY: The question of whether we have a duty to report that someone has been killed is an important question...and one that I'd like to learn more about. Before we get into the specifics of Caleb's situation, perhaps we could talk about the issues more generally. I'd like to ask some questions to help us work through the ethical issues. My questions may sound direct or even pointed. I'm not trying to fool or attack you, though you may feel challenged by some difficult questions. In essence, I'd like you to act as my teacher, helping me learn by sharing your views on these issues. What are your questions and thoughts about having this type of discussion?

SYLVIE: I'm not sure I understand why we're not going to talk about Caleb right away. Don't we have to make a quick decision about what to do?

SANCHAY: Do you think it's more important to make a quick decision or an informed one?

SYLVIE: An informed one, but we may still have some time pressures...

SANCHAY: Good answer—The "time versus information" question does not necessarily require an either/or response. Sometimes the answers are more complex. I can see you're up to the task. One of the best ways to work though an ethical dilemma is to engage in a dialogue with someone. If it's okay with you, I'd like to pose a series of questions. I'm not grading or judging your answers, and you are allowed to change your answers at any time if your thinking starts to change. The purpose of this discussion is to help you gain a better understanding of the ethical issues at stake so you can make a more informed decision about the right way to handle situations such as the one you face with Caleb. Would you be willing to give this process a try?

SYLVIE: Sure. I'm not sure if I'll have all the right answers, but at least I'll be learning.

SANCHAY: Yes, this is a process of learning, for both of us. To start, please tell me how you explained confidentiality to Caleb during your first meeting.

SYLVIE: Well, I told him that what we talk about is confidential, meaning that I cannot share the information with others unless there is a serious possibility of harm to others. We didn't talk about what would happen if someone was killed, though.

SANCHAY: So, in general, should social workers be required to report when clients disclose they have killed someone?

SYLVIE: Yes, they've committed a serious crime. They need to be punished.

SANCHAY: So when people commit crimes they should be punished.

SYLVIE: Well, yes, when it's a serious crime like murder. If Caleb's crime was possession of marijuana, that's not so serious. But this is murder.

SANCHAY: Where does the Code of Ethics say that social workers should help police to make sure criminals are punished?

SYLVIE: Well, it doesn't say that directly, but we do have an obligation in Standard 1.01

to balance our commitment to clients with our responsibility to greater society. If a client murders once, he could murder again? Besides, killing someone is wrong. I don't know if I could live with myself if I let Caleb walk free.

SANCHAY: So your thoughts are affected not only by your professional obligations, but by your personal morals and feelings?

SYLVIE: Yes. Killing is wrong. I don't need a code of ethics to tell me that.

SANCHAY: So, killing is wrong and killers ought to be punished. Is this true in every situation?

SYLVIE: Yes, of course. It's in the law. It's even in the Bible... Thou shalt not kill.

SANCHAY: What if someone is being attacked. Does she have a right to defend herself, even if it means killing the other person?

SYLVIE: Sure, that's self-defense.... If the person had to kill the other to defend herself from being killed.

SANCHAY: So you wouldn't necessarily want to send this person to prison?

SYLVIE: I see what you're getting at. There are different reasons that people kill. There may be extenuating circumstances...

Sanchay continues to ask questions, helping Sylvie understand the differences between a killing that may be justified and a killing (or murder) that may require retribution or punishment. Sanchay also asks questions to help Sylvie understand the consequences—short-term and long-term—if social workers assumed the role of police informants on a regular basis. Sylvie may continue to feel uncomfortable about holding onto information that could result in a criminal prosecution against a murderer, but she also gains insight into the value of having professionals whom clients can trust, even when it means withholding information about heinous crimes. Sanchay also asks questions to help Sylvie understand that there may be creative options for resolving Caleb's situation. Initially, Sylvie thought that the question came down to whether she should report Caleb to the police. Through Socratic inquiry, she came up with a number of creative options, including the possibility of referring Caleb to an attorney so Caleb could ask questions and receive legal advice on his options (e.g., is there a good way to turn himself into authorities). Sylvie may be able to justify reporting Caleb to the police.[17] However, through her learning discussion with Sanchay, Sylvie understands that her primary role is not to act as a police informant.

Socratic inquiry facilitates critical thinking and stimulates learning. When engaging people in this process, creating a safe learning environment is vital. Participants may feel threatened by Socratic inquiry because it exposes errors in the ways that they are thinking. When facilitators establish a safe learning environment, however, participants can respond more effectively, particularly when the facilitator challenges their convictions and deeply held beliefs. If the facilitator does not establish safety, participants may feel too anxious or defensive to respond effectively. In the earlier dialogue, Sylvie was a willing participant with a professional background and education. When adapting Socratic inquiry for clients who may not be as motivated or educationally prepared to engage in such a process, the facilitator may have to be more cautious, for instance, extending the period of engagement, providing more positive feedback (validating participants and showing respect for their answers), and ensuring that questions are not too pointed or too blunt. Although the Socratic method is usually associated with teaching students, it fits with cognitive-based counseling with clients, helping them think through life's challenges from new perspectives. The facilitator uses thought-provoking questions to structure the discourse. The facilitator stating opinion conclusions, preferring that participants develop their own insights.

---

[17] For instance, because Caleb poses an immediate, foreseeable, and serious threat to another person (S.1.07[c]), or because it is in the interests of society or the bereaved family to resolve the crime (S.1.01).

Some critics of Socratic inquiry suggest that it promotes just one version of truth or knowledge (Yassour-Borochowitz, 2004).[18] When discussing ethical dilemmas, this concern is crucial because there may be no universal truth or answer to the dilemma. People may have valid differences of opinion based on having different values, beliefs, allegiances, and ways of thinking. To remedy this concern, the facilitator should ask questions in a manner that allows participants to come to their own conclusions, which may differ from one another, and particularly from the views of the facilitator. The facilitator should model openness to different points of view, validating different opinions and encouraging creative ways of thinking.

When implemented effectively, Socratic inquiry actually challenges the idea that there is one universal truth. Facilitators challenge participants' convictions, beliefs, and value systems, helping them deconstruct underlying assumptions (Maxwell, 2007). In the case example, Sylvie suggests that killing is wrong. By asking questions about self-defense, Sanchay surfaces an assumption—that is, that the person who killed did not have a valid reason for killing. Thus, Sylvie learns that simple maxims such as "killing is wrong" or "social workers should report crimes" have critical limitations when applied to complex, real-life situations. Even if Sylvie retains her belief that she should report Caleb to the police, she has gained some doubts, recognizing that there are different ways of looking at this dilemma.

When working with groups (e.g., during group supervision or training), facilitators encourage members to think of themselves as a community of learners. The object is not a competition to see who is the smartest or who gets the right answer, but rather to provide encouragement and support for one another so that all may learn from the dialogue. The dialogue stimulated though Socratic inquiry creates meaningful connections between participants (Yassour-Borochowitz, 2004). Different participants may play the role of questioner, or even Devil's advocate, to encourage the group to think critically about the issues at stake. More important, members validate one another's thoughts and opinions, demonstrating appreciation for the risks others are taking in order to facilitate learning for the whole group.

Socratic inquiry fits best when the goals for discussion are to promote dialogue, critical thinking, and a better cognitive understanding of the issues at stake. Socratic inquiry does not necessarily promote consensus or joint action. In fact, Socratic inquiry may be deemed successful when participants walk away having vastly different views and perspectives. Socratic inquiry may also leave participants with more questions than answers. Participants who initially express certainty about how an ethical issue should be resolved may leave the process with uncertainty and doubts.[19] Although uncertainty does not lend itself easily to direct action, it does encourage participants to deliberate further and may pre-empt premature action based on insufficient analysis.

Socratic inquiry may be used with either individuals or groups. When working with individuals, Socratic inquiry may prepare people for working together by helping them gain an appreciation for other views before bringing them together. In the work of a group, Socratic inquiry may lead participants to agreement (through common understanding), but this is not the primary goal.

Now that we have explored the nature of Socratic inquiry, we turn to a second form of facilitated discussion: debate. Socratic inquiry and debate share certain qualities. Both processes focus on logical analysis of ethical issues. Both also emphasize the understanding of issues rather than how to bring people to consensus. As you read through the following section, note also how Socratic inquiry and debate differ in terms of their process, goals, and methods of implementation.

---

[18] Feminist critics also suggest that Socratic inquiry has a male bias, focusing on male patterns of thinking (Yassour-Borochowitz, 2004), for instance, by focusing on the application of laws and rules, emphasizing logic over emotions or relationships, and removing gender or diversity from the analysis.

[19] The acquisition of knowledge includes the knowledge of what we do not know (Maxwell, 2007).

Debate

When people approach discussion of an ethical issue as a debate, participants assume different positions and act as advocates to defend their positions. Debates are adversarial. Each debater tries to put the best case forward, trying to convince others that his or her position is correct (Chasin et al., 1996; Maiese, 2003b).

Proponents of debates suggest that they are useful methods of handling controversial issues (including ethical dilemmas) because they bring out the strongest arguments from different sides of the case. The conflict and competition within debates promote intellectual curiosity, as each side wants to find the best evidence and best logical reasoning to win the debate. Proponents also argue that truth is more likely to emerge from debates, as compared to more collaborative processes in which conflicting perspectives may not be fully explored (Johnson, Johnson, & Smith, 1997).

Debates may be formal or informal. Formal debates are highly structured in terms of the roles of participants and the rules governing interaction. Typically, formal debates are structured around a single statement, for instance, "Social workers should report client disclosures of serious crimes to police." One or more debaters is assigned to argue in favor of this statement (the pro side), and an equal number of debaters is assigned to argue against this statement (the con side). Each side prepares its case by collecting the best evidence and formulating the strongest arguments to support its position. A neutral third person, called a moderator, facilitates the debate. The moderator states and enforces the ground rules, such as the order of speakers, the amount of time each person is allowed to speak, and the topics to which they should respond. A typical debate format includes the following stages:

1. The moderator introduces the topic of the debate, the debaters, and the ground rules for the debate.
2. The pro side summarizes its case.
3. The con side summarizes its case.
4. The pro side provides detailed arguments in support of its position.
5. The con side provides its rebuttal or counterarguments.
6. The con side provides detailed arguments in support of its position.
7. The pro side provides its rebuttal or counterarguments.
8. The moderator invites questions from a panel of decision makers or from the audience, and provides each side with an opportunity to respond.
9. The pro side states its conclusions.
10. The con side states its conclusions.

In some debates, a panel of judges makes a decision based on the arguments they have heard. Some debates conclude without a decision. Such debates serve to educate the audience about the issues rather than bring about any resolution or finding. Court cases and professional disciplinary hearings are essentially debates, though they use somewhat different structures (e.g., attorneys present evidence by calling witnesses to testify).

Informal debates are less structured dialogues. Participants assume different positions on their own, rather than being assigned. Participants do not necessarily prepare to defend their positions, as the debates may emerge naturally from a discussion of ethical issues. Facilitators encourage participants to contribute to the debate in a fluid fashion, without imposing fixed topics, time limitations, and orders of speakers. Facilitators develop ground rules to promote an open but safe discussion of the issues: For instance, participants may challenge other's views but should not attack them personally, participants may be passionate but should remain respectful, and participants may express views to defend a position even if they do not personally agree with it. Facilitators support the use of critical thinking and rational argumentation. They discourage the use of *ad hominem* arguments, attacks against the person rather than arguments dealing directly with the issues at stake. Ad hominem attacks violate the ethical principle of respecting the dignity and worth of the person (NASW Code, 1999). Facilitators also encourage participants to base their arguments on evidence, logic, and critical thinking rather than emotional pleas, stereotypes, misleading evidence, and faulty reasoning.

To illustrate an informal debate, consider the following excerpt,[20] in which Sanchay facilitates an informal debate between Sylvie and Patrick, a psychologist from the same agency:

SANCHAY: Sylvie, I understand that you believe our agency has a duty to report Caleb to the police [Sylvie nods in agreement]. Patrick, I hear that you have a different view. Tell us why you think we should not report Caleb.

PATRICK: I think that Sylvie is being naïve.

SANCHAY: Let's focus on what you think, without making personal remarks about Sylvie or anyone else.

PATRICK: I'm sorry. We have a duty to protect the right to confidentiality of our clients. This duty is clearly stated in Standard 1.07 of the NASW Code and Standard 4 of the APA Code. Clients would not trust us if they knew we were working with the police.

SANCHAY: Sylvie, what do you think about this duty?

SYLVIE: As professionals, we do have a duty to protect client confidentiality. Still, the sections cited by Patrick also state that there are exceptions to this duty. Standard 1.07(c) says we have to report information to prevent "serious, foreseeable, and imminent harm."

PATRICK: And in this case, there is no imminent harm. The killing has already happened. Caleb has not threatened to kill anyone else.

SYLVIE: If we can save just one life, isn't that more important than protecting confidentiality?

SANCHAY: I'm wondering how we would know if reporting Caleb to the police would actually save a life.

Sanchay asks Sylvie and Patrick to defend their positions. They respond, in part, by referencing ethical standards that support their cases. Notice how Sanchay intervenes, first to discourage Patrick from making an ad hominem attack against Sylvie, and then to ask Sylvie to back up her information with evidence. Sylvie's comment about saving a life appeals to human emotions, but is there any evidence to say that reporting Caleb will result in saving a life? How do we know? In fact, reporting Caleb could result in a further death, if Caleb is convicted of a capital murder and receives a death sentence. As facilitator, Sanchay encourages both sides to defend their positions strongly and passionately, but with sound reasoning and substantiating evidence.

Critics of the debate format for discussing controversial issues suggest that the adversarial nature of debates actually limits discussion and creative problem solving. Debaters tend to focus on the extremes, defending their *yes* or *no* positions on the topic of the debate. Often, ethical issues may be explored from a broader range of perspectives, including middle grounds and creative points of view. Although debates tend to bring out the strongest arguments for different positions, they fail to bring about consensus. Rarely would one side concede defeat and agree with the other. Each side becomes so entrenched in its position that it has difficulty seeing the other side. Further, debates may promote certain tactics that detract from effective decision making. Each side has incentive to hide information from the other side, not wanting to give the other side any advantages. Each side may try to use personal attacks, emotional pleas, or other nonrational arguments to win its case. Their arguments may promote polarization of issues rather than facilitate looking for common ground (Chaisin et al., 1996). Given these criticisms, debates may be inappropriate when the purpose of the discussion is to develop a consensus or bring people together on how to resolve an ethical issue.

In spite of the disadvantages of debates, they may be useful as educational tools, particularly for people who enjoy competition. Debates may stimulate interesting discussion and motivate participants to work diligently to find the best evidence and logical arguments to defend their cases (Johnson et al., 1997). A debate format

[20] The excerpts in this chapter are abbreviated examples used to demonstrate different methods of discussion. They illustrate specific skills and strategies that facilitators could use. Due to space limitations, however, they do not represent comprehensive or complete processes.

may be most appropriate when the actors must choose between two courses of action and it is more important to come up with a definite decision than to build consensus or develop creative solutions.

Dialogue

A dialogue is an open discussion designed to promote understanding and insight (Maiese, 2003b). In the context of managing ethical issues, dialogues help people express and learn about one another's worldviews, moral systems, emotional responses, religious beliefs, and other perspectives that may be affecting their thinking and actions (Spano & Koenig, 2003). When facilitators are used to guide dialogues, they may make use of flexible agendas and ground rules to promote fluid communication. Facilitators may foster consensus among participants, though consensus is not the primary goal of dialogue. The facilitator allows participants to agree or disagree, provided they treat one another with respect regardless of their differences. Whereas debaters often represent the polar views of an ethical issue, dialogue participants may represent the full spectrum of views, including extreme, moderate, and undecided. Facilitators encourage participants to speak with everyone, whether or not they have the same values or perspectives. Facilitators also encourage everyone to listen to one another, remaining open to new information and ideas (Chasin et al., 1996).

To prepare participants for effective dialogue, facilitators may meet with participants individually or in small groups before bringing them together for a joint meeting. During preparations, facilitators coach participants on how to ask open-ended questions, express opinions assertively without being aggressive, and listen actively. Facilitators may also encourage participants to share information with one another in advance, avoiding surprises or unfair advantages at the joint assembly.

Whereas the ground rules in a debate foster a competitive atmosphere, the ground rules in a dialogue promote collaboration and amicable relationships. Ground rules may include, "We will express information and opinions assertively, but we will also be open to hearing the thoughts and opinions of others," and "When we think we may have conflicting views, we will first clarify what the others are saying to avoid miscommunication or unwarranted assumptions." Facilitators promote a safe environment for participants to take risks, express doubts, and open themselves to persuasion and constructive feedback from one another. Whereas debaters typically express complete confidence to defend their positions, participants in a dialogue do not need to defend their views so unconditionally. They know that their role is to use communication to learn, rather than to convince others or win a contest.

The following excerpt illustrates a dialogue that Sanchay facilitates between Sylvie and Patrick. Note the contrasts between this dialogue and the earlier debate:

SANCHAY: Caleb's disclosure that he killed a woman raises a number of difficult ethical issues for Sylvie and the entire agency. I've called this meeting so we can engage in a dialogue. The main purpose of this meeting is not to reach consensus on what to do, but rather to gain a better understanding of each other's views on this matter. Sylvie, perhaps you can start by talking about the different concerns you've been thinking about.

SYLVIE: I'm really conflicted. On the one hand, I know that as a social worker I am supposed to protect the confidentiality of my clients. But on the other hand, my personal morals tell me that I cannot stand by and let a murderer go unpunished.

PATRICK: I can certainly understand your cautiousness about how to manage this situation. I wouldn't want to hold onto information that could be used to convict a murderer either. But, Sylvia, you're assuming that Caleb is a murderer.

SANCHAY: Rather than stating that Sylvia is assuming something, why don't we ask her. Sylvia, how would we know whether Caleb actually is a murderer?

SYLVIE: Murder isn't really a social work term, it's a legal one. I suppose we'd need to find out the legal definition.

PATRICK: I'm not an attorney, but I believe that the criminal justice system makes a distinction between killing and murdering. Caleb might have killed someone, but still be innocent of murder.

SYLVIE: How could there be a killing but no murder? It sounds strange.

PATRICK: Yes, it does sound a bit bizarre. But what if Caleb killed the woman by accident? If he didn't intend to kill her, then he might not be guilty of murder.

SYLVIE: I hadn't thought of that. Thanks. Caleb may be innocent. Actually, I still don't know whether we should report him to the police... but it does make me think that the issues are more complicated than I originally thought. Perhaps we could use some legal advice.

Sanchay initiates the dialogue by encouraging Sylvie to discuss various concerns, not simply to defend a particular position. Sylvie responds by explaining the conflicting professional and moral obligations she has been considering. This opens up the discussion, as Patrick and Sylvie feel free to explore various sides of the issue, admitting their doubts and asking questions. When Patrick suggests that Sylvie is making an assumption, Sanchay reframes his point into a question. Sylvie feels less defensive in response to the question, as opposed to how she responded to the initial accusation that she was making an assumption. As the dialogue progresses, Sylvie gains insight into the possible differences between killing and murdering. She is more open to hearing Patrick's perspectives than in the earlier debate because she views him as a colleague rather than a competitor.

Dialogue fits well when discussion involves the examination of complex ethical issues, when there may be no clear-cut answers, and when developing insight among participants is more important than coming up with a consensus or final decision. Whereas factual issues can be resolved relatively easily by gathering evidence and determining which evidence is strongest, conflict based on divergent morals or values may be intractable or irresolvable (Schultz, 2003). Because people hold morals and values so dearly, compromise is difficult (Maiese, 2003a). Dialogue provides participants with an opportunity to communicate respectfully with one another without asking them to forfeit their cherished morals or values. Sometimes, dialogue can be used as a first step in bringing disputing individuals or groups together. If dialogue is successful at promoting respectful relations and greater insight into the conflict, the participants may be better prepared for follow-up discussions aimed more specifically at resolution of the conflict. Interest-based mediation, described below, is one such example of a method designed to resolve conflict.

Interest-Based Mediation

Interest-based mediation (IBM) is a collaborative conflict resolution process in which an impartial third person facilitates communication between conflicting parties in order to help them reach a mutually acceptable resolution to their conflict (Barsky, 2007a). Mediators provide participants with a safe time and place to discuss their concerns and work together on a plan that addresses their primary needs and interests. Initially, participants tend to focus on their own positions, advocating certain opinions, wishes, conclusions, or solutions. Interest-based mediators help participants resolve conflict by guiding them away from adversarial debates and toward collaborative problem solving based on their underlying interests (Fisher, Ury, & Patton, 1997). Whereas dialogues are designed to enhance insight and understanding between participants, IBM is designed to help participants reach consensus. Because IBM facilitates collaborative problem solving, it may also lead to better relationships and improved communication between participants.

Interest-based mediators may draw from a range of skills and strategies to promote collaborative problem solving. Prior to bringing conflicting parties together, mediators may meet separately with the parties, assessing their readiness to mediate, coaching them on how to negotiate more effectively, and preparing them for the issues to be discussed (e.g., ensuring they bring information and documentation to help them make educated decisions). During the engagement stage, the mediator describes the mediation process and ascertains the parties' commitment to it. The mediator invites the parties to explain what has brought them to the mediation table, allowing them to share historical data and vent concerns in a structured manner. The mediator models positive communication skills, demonstrating empathy and validation by paraphrasing or reflecting back what each party says. The mediator then refocuses the parties from the past to the future, for instance, asking the parties how they might move forward in a more positive manner. The mediator helps the parties focus on their primary interests, searching for common ground and creative solutions that meet the interests of both parties (a win-win solution). The mediator may engage the parties in brainstorming to help them move away from their original positions and think about different options for resolving the issues at stake. The mediator then helps the parties assess the various options and select the best ones, using objective criteria and the parties' stated interests. If the parties are able to reach agreement, the mediator helps them finalize the agreement, either in oral or written form (Barsky, 2007a; Moore, 2003). If legal issues are involved, the mediator may ask the parties to have their lawyers draft a legally binding agreement or a consent order to be approved by a court (e.g., in a case involving child protection court or a mental health proceeding).

The following excerpt demonstrates IBM, building on Caleb's case.[21] In this scenario, assume Sylvie has advised Caleb that she is going to inform the police that he has admitted killing a woman. Caleb responds by voicing a complaint to Sylvie's supervisor, Sanchay. Sanchay calls a meeting between Sylvie and Caleb. She uses IBM skills to guide their discussion.[22]

SANCHAY: Thank you for agreeing to meet. As I mentioned in our individual meetings, the purpose of this session is to determine how to handle Caleb's disclosure that he shot a woman. We will try to work toward an agreement that satisfies everyone's interests. If we cannot reach an agreement, then we'll have to talk about the next steps. Caleb, perhaps you could start by briefly sharing your concerns.

CALEB: It's pretty simple. Sylvie told me that whatever we talked about stayed between us. She wouldn't tell anyone else. She needs to keep her promise.

SANCHAY: I can hear you're pretty upset with Sylvie, as if you feel she's betrayed your trust [Caleb nods in agreement].

SYLVIE: I did promise confidentiality, so I feel bad that I have to go back on what I said. I explained some exceptions to confidentiality, but I didn't talk about my duty to report serious violent crimes.

SANCHAY: So Sylvie, you believe you have a duty to report past crimes to the police, and Caleb, you think that Sylvie has an obligation to respect your privacy? [both nod, yes] Sylvie, when you say you have an obligation to report Caleb to the police, tell me why you think this is important. What interests might you satisfy by reporting Caleb?

SYLVIE: My main concern is public safety. If Caleb killed once, he could kill again. I couldn't live with myself if another person was killed and I could have prevented it.

SANCHAY: So your main concern is public safety. Caleb, I know this may sound like I'm asking the obvious, but could you please explain why you think that Sylvie should not report you to the police. What's your main concern?

21 As with previous excerpts in this chapter, this example portrays the use of certain skills and strategies, but not a complete process. If this were a real situation, Sanchay would need to engage the parties more slowly and work through the issues more cautiously.

22 In this scenario, Sanchay is not a purely impartial mediator. She is Sylvie's supervisor and she has certain obligations toward her agency (maintaining its standards and following its policies). A purely impartial mediator would need to come from outside the agency, but this would not be feasible under the circumstance of this case. Caleb and Sylvie would want to try to manage the issues within the agency first, because Caleb's main concern is that his disclosure remains confidential (using an external mediator may raise the risk that his disclosure will be reported to the police).

CALEB: Yes, it is obvious. I don't want to go to prison. If she reports me, that's it. I'm done. Nobody's going to listen to me. Not when it's her word against mine. I'll lose all my rights.

SANCHAY: Caleb, your main concerns have to do with your rights. You value your freedom, you value your privacy, and you want people to respect your rights, including the right to a fair trial, if it comes to that. Have I understood your main concerns accurately?

CALEB: That pretty much covers it.

SANCHAY: Sylvie, I know that you said your main interest was in public safety. Would you also agree that freedom, privacy, and a fair trial are also important interests?

SYLVIE: They're important, but maybe not as important as public safety.

SANCHAY: What I'd like everyone to consider is how we might be able to satisfy all these concerns, Caleb's and Sylvie's, without sacrificing one or the other.

CALEB: I'm not sure that's possible, but what could it hurt to try?

SANCHAY: Let's try brainstorming. Until now, we've been talking as if the decision is "to report or not report." What are some other things we could do? I'm not asking you to come up with ideas that you plan to actually carry out, just some brainstorm ideas or possibilities. They could be serious options or even not so serious ones. What could we do that might satisfy the interests of safety, freedom, privacy, and fair trial?

CALEB: Maybe I could go off to a deserted island somewhere, never to be seen again.

SANCHAY: Great. We have our first brainstorm option [Sanchay writes Caleb's suggestion on a flipchart]. Sylvie, any creative ideas?

SYLVIE: I'm not sure, but maybe if Caleb agreed to a risk assessment. If we knew he was not at high risk of re-offending, then the public safety issue isn't such a big deal.

CALEB: Or what if there was some way that I could make sure that I had a fair trial....I killed that woman, but it wasn't my fault. If I could just explain...

The parties continue to brainstorm ideas, some serious and some quite silly. Brainstorming helps them realize that there may be several ways to respond to the ethical and legal issues raised by this case. Caleb's question about whether there is a way he can get a fair trial leads them to consider whether Caleb should get legal advice. Sanchay explains that he can consult an attorney in full confidence. Under the principles of attorney–client privilege, the attorney cannot report him to police or be called to testify at a criminal court trial. They also explore the possibility of doing a risk assessment. Agency policy does not explicitly require practitioners to report past crimes, so Sylvie may be able to justify not reporting Caleb if he does not pose a risk to others. Everyone agrees that the next step is to refer Caleb for legal advice. They agree to meet again once Caleb has had a chance to meet with an attorney. If the attorney is able to help Caleb turn himself in and have a fair criminal justice process to clear his name, the issues will be resolved. Otherwise, the mediation process will continue.

As the above excerpt illustrates, IBM helps participants explore their underlying interests and focus on how to resolve potential conflicts between them. IBM is particularly useful in helping people resolve ethical conflicts when participants can identify common values or principles (safety, privacy, freedom, respect, etc.). When parties can agree on certain values or principles, problem solving can then focus on what needs to be done in order to implement these values or principles. When participants do not share core values or ethical principles, IBM may not be able to help them reach agreement (Barsky, 2008). The following section, Transformative Mediation, explores a conflict resolution approach that emphasizes improving the interaction between parties rather than focusing on securing an agreement. As such, it may fit well for conflicts in which participants have divergent values or ethical principles.

Transformative Mediation

Whereas interest-based mediation seeks to help people resolve conflicting interests, transformative mediation (TM) is designed to foster more constructive patterns of interaction between people (Institute for the Study of Conflict Transformation, n.d.). When conflict arises, people tend to become preoccupied with their own views and experiences, disregarding or discounting the views and experiences of others (Bush & Folger, 2005). Conflicts based on divergent values and ethics are particularly prone to breakdowns in relationships because people feel threatened when others disagree with their core values and convictions.

Transformative mediation strives to transform the way conflicting parties interact through two processes: recognition and empowerment. Recognition refers to the process of being open and responsive to the other person (Institute for the Study of Conflict Transformation, n.d.). Mediators facilitate recognition by helping parties listen and demonstrate empathy toward one another. When people are involved in ethical conflicts, they have different visions of what is right, depending on their own social location and subjectivity (Prilleltensky et al., 2002); for instance, clients who feel vulnerable may view confidentially differently from professional social workers who feel safe in their positions. Mediators help parties step out of their own shoes and view the conflict from the other's perspective. Mediators model how to demonstrate empathy and ask questions that help parties acknowledge the concerns, needs, values, morals, hopes, and dreams of the others.

Empowerment refers to restoring parties' strength and confidence, as well as their ability to take greater control of their own life situations (Bush & Folger, 2005). When people are engaged in high levels of conflict, they may respond defensively. They may lose sight of big picture issues and get sucked into petty fighting, retaliation, or other destructive patterns of behavior. Mediators help parties refocus their energies more positively and rebuild their self-confidence through a variety of techniques: validating their values and beliefs, demonstrating faith in their ability to move beyond the immediate conflict, helping parties resolve smaller issues first so they will build the trust and confidence required to resolve the bigger issues, and encouraging them to consider options that put destiny into their own hands rather than rely on others to make decisions for them (e.g., judges, police, supervisors, teachers, parents, or others in positions of authority) (Barsky, 2007a). Empowerment and recognition are interactive processes. Initially, each party experiences a downward spiral of conflict, "I feel attacked, so I must act defensively.... But this promotes further attacks, so I must act even more defensively." TM helps redirects parties to an upward spiral. When TM helps people feel confident and empowered, they feel freer to attend to the needs and interests of others. When TM helps people attend to the needs and interests of others, they gain self-confidence. By improving the interactions between conflicting parties, TM may lead them to agreement. Still, TM does not depend on the parties' ability to reach agreement. Parties may leave the process feeling empowered and recognized, whether or not their initial conflict is resolved.

The following excerpt illustrates TM using the same scenario that was used to demonstrate IBM. To raise the intensity of the conflict, however, assume the agency has an explicit policy requiring practitioners to report serious violent crimes to police.

SANCHAY: Caleb has advised me that he is concerned Sylvie is going to report him to the police. I wanted to bring you together to make sure each of you knows where the other is coming from, and to give each of you the opportunity to consider how you want to move forward. Caleb, perhaps you could start by discussing how you felt when Sylvie told you that agency policy required her to contact the police.

CALEB: At first, shocked. Then ticked. Major ticked off. Sylvie told me I could trust her. I told her something I never told anyone else. I thought she was there to help me, not rat on me.

SANCHAY: Sylvie, could you summarize what you hear Caleb saying?

SYLVIE: I didn't mean to set him up. I have to follow agency policy...

SANCHAY: Let's talk about your situation in a few moments. First, could you describe Caleb's concerns, from his perspective? You don't have to agree with him, just review what he said.

SYLVIE: OK. Caleb trusted me because I said our meetings were confidential. He wouldn't have told me about the killing if I had told him our agency policy. Caleb, I can see you're furious with me. I can understand how you felt betrayed.

SANCHAY: Anything you would like to add or clarify, Caleb?

CALEB: That covers it, sort of. But if you knew you had to report to the police, why didn't you tell me?

SYLVIE: Whenever we discuss confidentiality with clients, we have to decide how much detail to go into. There are so many exceptions to confidentiality that it would take an hour or more to explain them all. I never thought you might have killed someone, so I didn't think it was important to explain that exception. I'm sorry. Looking back, I should have...

SANCHAY: So Sylvie, it sounds like you wanted to be open and honest with Caleb. You weren't trying to set him up.

SYLVIE: Right. I like and respect Caleb as a person. I wish he had never said anything about the killing.

CALEB: Then let's just forget I said anything. Nobody will know.

SYLVIE: I can't do that. My code of ethics says that I have to be honest, and I also have to follow agency policy.

SANCHAY: It may be useful to discuss agency policy. Caleb, what do you understand about agency policy?

CALEB: It stinks. It says social workers have to rat on clients.

SYLVIE: That's certainly one way to look at it. The way I see it, we have to balance the interests of our clients and the interests of the public. Most of the time, when I do what is best for the client, it is also best for the public. In this case, it's a much tougher choice. I know that reporting you to the police feels like a betrayal, and I hate that.

CALEB: Not as much as I hate it! I'm the one that is going to get fried in court.

SYLVIE: And I also know that I might see things completely differently if I were in your shoes.

CALEB: Well, saying what you said doesn't save my hide from going to jail, but at least I see that you have some compassion...

SANCHAY: It doesn't sound like we're going to come to an agreement on whether or not Sylvie should make the report. Sylvie has a pretty clear obligation to do so. And Caleb, you've stated quite strongly that you don't want her to make the report. Perhaps we could talk about each of your options as we move forward...

In this scenario, Sanchay facilitates recognition by encouraging Sylvie to reflect Caleb's thoughts and feelings back to him. Given that Sylvie is a trained social worker with a high sense of self-awareness and conscious use of self, she is able to focus on Caleb's perspectives without too much trouble. Typically, a mediator would have to be more patient, building trust and working toward recognition more slowly. Still, this excerpt demonstrates the process of recognition, as Caleb's anger subsides when he hears Sylvie acknowledge the validity of his perspective. Sanchay acknowledges the parties are unlikely to agree on whether Sylvie should report Caleb. This acknowledgment is actually empowering to Caleb. Although Caleb cannot prevent Sylvie from making the report, they can talk about other issues within his control; for instance, should Caleb continue to see Sylvie for counseling; should he consult an attorney for legal advice; or is there anything that he can do to influence the timing and manner of Sylvie's report to the police?

Mediators democratize discussions by empowering people to speak clearly and assertively, and by ensuring that different voices are heard. TM permits people to discuss values and ethics without the pressure of having to reach a mutually agreeable solution. In some instances, people may not be able to reach agreement. Still, TM provides them with the opportunity to improve their relationship, take charge of issues within their power, and manage their differences in values and ethics in a respectful manner.

CONCLUSION

Ethical issues may arise in the course of group work, but they also may be resolved through group work. Social workers should be aware of ethical concerns that may arise in the unique context of working with groups. Ethical principles such as informed consent, confidentiality, respect, and maintaining appropriate boundaries require different types of considerations when working with groups versus working with individuals or other client systems. In particular, social workers need to distinguish between their obligations to clients and the types of relationships that they want to create between clients within a group. Group members are not subject to professional codes of ethics. Group facilitators may use informed consent processes, service agreements, and ground rules to foster within-group relationships that take social work ethics and values into account.

Ethics committees are essentially task groups that help agencies develop and maintain high ethical standards. Ethics committees serve a number of roles, including policy development, education, case consultation, and case review. Social workers can enhance the functioning of ethics committees by applying what they know about group process, whether they are acting as committee chairs or as group members.

Managing ethical issues often involves bringing people together. Social workers should be familiar with different structures for communication so they can select the appropriate method for the particular situation. Socratic inquiry is a didactic educational process in which the facilitator uses questions to help participants view ethical issues from different perspectives. Socratic inquiry is particularly useful when the goal of the process is to enhance individuals' understanding of the issues. Debates are adversarial processes in which participants act as advocates for particular positions. Debate formats motivate participants to identify and express the strongest logical arguments and best evidence to defend their positions. Debates may be most appropriate for ethical issues in which decision makers must decide between the rights or positions of two or more parties. Dialogues encourage participants to discuss issues in an open, supportive manner. Facilitators encourage participants to express themselves assertively without becoming aggressive. Facilitators also help participants listen to one another. Dialogues may fit best when the purpose of the discussion is to facilitate mutual understanding between participants. Interest-based mediation is a conflict resolution process that helps conflicting parties move from their original positions to their underlying interests. By focusing on interests, IBM helps parties develop solutions that satisfy everyone's primary concerns. IBM may be most appropriate when the purpose of the discussion is to bring parties to a mutual agreement on how to proceed. Transformative mediation strives to foster positive interactions between conflicting parties through the processes of empowerment and recognition. TM may suit ethical conflicts best when the goal is to improve the way parties relate to each other rather than to try to bring them to consensus. Each process has different strengths and limitations, and different people may feel more comfortable participating in different processes.

Some social workers may think it is easier to resolve ethical issues individually because they do not have to reconcile differences between people. Often, ethical issues involve a range of people, so some type of group process or interaction is unavoidable. Regardless of whether group interactions are chosen deliberately or simply become necessary, social workers may draw from the strengths of groups to manage ethical issues: the range of perspectives and expertise, the value of dialogue to spur thinking, and the energy that comes from working together in a group.

DISCUSSION QUESTIONS AND EXERCISES

Questions 1 to 10 focus on ethical issues that may arise in group process. Questions 11 and 12 relate to the work of ethics committees. Questions 13 to 15 correspond to methods of discussing ethical issues.

1. *Informed Consent*: Syran proposes to have a closed group in which members must

agree to attend all 10 sessions. How might this proposal violate Standard 1.03(a) and how could Syran rectify this potential violation?

2. *Involuntary Clients*: Serafina runs an anger management group for clients mandated by criminal court to participate. What are her obligations in terms of voluntariness and informed consent under Standard 1.03(h)?
3. *Group Risks*: Siobhan runs a healthy lifestyles support group through a web-based discussion group. Under Standard 1.03(e), what specific risks should she disclose to her clients during the informed consent process, particularly in relation to her use of the Internet to facilitate the discussion? What group ground rules should she suggest to limit the risks and to encourage safe discussion of personal issues?
4. *Suicide Confidential*: Shylock has to provide crisis intervention for a client who expresses suicidal thoughts during a group session. Which sections of Standard 1.07 should he consider when deciding whether to provide crisis assessment and counseling within the group, or individually with the client?
5. *Group Location*: Stu's support group for people with Parkinson's disease decides to hold its final session in a restaurant. Explain how this plan might violate confidentiality under Standard 1.07(i)? How could Stu support the group's decision to have the session in a restaurant, but modify the plan so it no longer violates this standard?
6. *Respect*: Sheila runs a support group for sport-accident survivors coping with long-term disabilities. Some clients suggest that they lobby government to provide publicly funded long-term care facilities for people like themselves. Privately, Cornelius tells Sheila that he believes in free enterprise and the group should not get involved in partisan politics. Further, Cornelius suggests that Sheila would be condoning discrimination against him on the basis of his political beliefs if she does not stop the group from pursuing their lobbying plans (S.4.02). How can Sheila show respect for Cornelius and the other group members, given their different values and beliefs?
7. *Boundaries*: Stratton facilitates a group for teens at risk of dropping out of school. At the end of a session, the clients ask Stratton if he would like to join them outside for a basketball game. At first, he thanks them for the invitation but says he cannot play with them because he has to maintain appropriate professional boundaries (S.1.06[c]). Group members remind him that one of the group ground rules is that they can socialize with each other after group. Analyze the pros and cons of Stratton playing basketball with the group. Based on your analysis, what should Stratton do?
8. *Dual Relationships*: Assume you are facilitating a counseling group for clients who have recently lost a spouse. One client, Mrs. Chambers, is also an attorney who specializes in estate planning. You have noticed that Mrs. Chambers has been distributing her business cards at several meetings, hoping to attract business from other group members. Although you realize her estate planning services may be useful to various members, you have concerns about the risks of dual relationships. What, if anything, does the NASW Code of Ethics say about such risks, and what factors should you consider to help you decide whether Mrs. Chambers should be allowed to solicit business at your meetings?
9. *Member Advice*: Assume you are facilitating a psychoeducational group for couples who want to improve their communication. One group member, Cathee, says she believes that a woman's place is in the home, taking care of her husband and children. Other women in the group respond passionately, telling Cathee she has a right to be her own person and should not be subservient to her husband. What are your ethical obligations, if any, in terms of remaining neutral, asserting a professional opinion, or trying to protect Cathee from feeling pressured or judged by other group members?

10. *Conflicting Commitments*: Assume you are facilitating a therapeutic group for people coping with obesity. Fourteen group members are Americans of European descent. Four group members are Native Americans. Your research suggests that the Americans of European descent would benefit most from a task-oriented cognitive-behavioral approach, but the Native Americans would benefit most from a process-oriented narrative approach. You do not have enough resources to hold two different groups. What guidance does the NASW Code of Ethics provide you in terms of how to weigh your ethical commitments to both subgroups? Also, consider whether the ethical standards of AASWG, APGA, or ASGW provide additional guidance.
11. *Ethics Committee Composition*: Paluka State Prison has 1,870 inmates, 15 administrators, 220 guards, 7 social workers, 3 psychologists, 1 medical doctor, 3 nurses, and 12 caseworkers who have no professional training. Most of the inmates and guards are men. Most of the social workers, psychologists, and caseworkers are women. Also, there are higher percentages of African Americans and Latinos among the inmate population than among the prison staff. Prison administrators want to create an ethics committee to develop and implement ethics policies governing all paid employees. Experience suggests that most ethical violations and questions have involved prison guards and case workers, rather than social workers or other professionally trained staff. How many people should be on the committee? What would be a desirable composition for this group in terms of professional and personal backgrounds? Provide reasons to support your recommendations.
12. *Spot the Process Problem*: Sabira runs a support group for recent retirees. Toward the end of one session, Sabira learns there is a tornado warning. She asks clients to stay for half an hour until the tornado warning clears. Some clients want to leave right away, so Sabira locks the doors and says she is responsible for their safety. Clients complain and the matter is referred to the agency's ethics committee for a review. For each of the following scenarios, identify the type of challenge to group process and suggest a strategy the facilitator could use to address it.
    a. Sabira expresses concern that the ethics committee is biased, because certain committee members do not like her.
    b. During the committee's hearing, Sabira's attorney provides a long, detailed summary. He refuses to answer questions until he has finished and he insists on presenting his whole case before he sits down. Committee members feel frustrated that he has taken over the hearing process.
    c. Sabira is a female social worker. Committee members include two male psychologists, one male vocational counselor, and one male representative from the community. Three of the four committee members are Asian Americans and only one is over 65 years old.
    d. The committee chair suggests that it is very important for group members to reach a unanimous decision on how to respond to Sabira's violation of client rights by her unlawful confinement or arrest. Committee members quickly agree that Sabira's detaining clients amounted to unlawful confinement. They do not explore possible justifications for her actions.
13. *Matching Issues with Methods of Discussion*: Identify which method of discussion fits best with each of the following ethical issues. Provide reasons, in terms of the purposes, strategies, strengths, and limitations of each method of discussion:
    a. A community that is split among socioeconomic lines (rich and poor) needs to determine whether to raise taxes to provide better services to people living in poverty. The community hires a social worker to design and facilitate a discussion exploring the ethical implications of raising taxes.
    b. Skylar conducts a screening interview with Colbert, a potential client for a

life skills training group. Colbert is 22 but functions cognitively at the level of a 12-year-old, due to prenatal alcohol exposure (his mother drank during pregnancy). During a group supervision session, Skylar asks his supervisor and work colleagues whether he needs to ask Colbert's parents for permission for him to participate in the group.

c. Dr. Strauss is a social work professor who wants to teach his group work class about the ethics of whether group facilitators should be allowed to hug their clients.

d. Sorrel is a social worker who recently messed up, badly. He was working with a client, Carys, on self-esteem issues. At the end of one meeting, Carys claimed her husband, Harvey, had been battering her. Sorrel asked her to come back next week to discuss the situation further. Carys agreed. Four days letter, Sorrel read in the newspaper that Harvey had been arrested for murdering Carys. Sorrel's notes indicated that he knew of the battering history. He pondered changing the notes so that he would not be called to testify at Sorrel's criminal trial. Since Harvey had already been arrested, what could it hurt? Sorrel contacts the agency's ethics committee for advice.

e. A group of social workers at a state-funded homeless shelter is split over whether they should provide services to undocumented aliens in spite of a new state law that restricts their services to U.S. citizens and documented aliens. Some say that providing access to services is their paramount interest. Others say that they must abide by the rule of law or they will all lose their jobs. Ultimately, the shelter's board of trustees, not the social workers, will decide whether the agency will comply with state law on this matter.

14. *Practising Methods of Discussion*: Select one of the scenarios from question 13. Identify a method of discussion that you want to practice. Write a script that illustrates the skills and strategies that a facilitator could use to apply this method of discussion to the ethical issues raised by the case scenario (add names of two or three other participants in the discussion). [Alternative group exercise: Assign the role of group facilitator to one person and the roles of group members to three or four others. Help the group facilitator prepare for a role-play by identifying strategies the facilitator could use in order to implement a Socratic inquiry, debate, dialogue, interest-based mediation, or transformative mediation. Engage in a role-play for 5 to 10 minutes and debrief, giving the facilitator feedback on which skills and strategies worked best.]

15. *Preferred Methods of Discussion*: Which method of discussion do you ordinarily prefer: Socratic inquiry, debate, dialogue, interest-based mediation, or transformative mediation? Explain how this method fits with your values, personality, educational background, family norms, cultural background, and communication skills.

Chapter 8

Practice, Values, and Ethics—Social Work with Organizations

Social organizations do not act by themselves. The people within them act. Accordingly, this chapter does not explore the ethics and values of organizations, per se, but rather the ethics and values of social workers acting within various organizational contexts.[1] Social workers perform a broad range of roles within organizations. In addition to providing clients with counseling, advocacy, and other direct services, social workers orient, train, supervise, manage, teach, and consult with many different people in organizations—volunteers, staff members, students, and other helping professionals (Levy, 1993). Thus, social workers are not simply responsible for ensuring that their own conduct is ethical. They are also responsible for promoting the ethical conduct of others. Social workers teach ethical conduct to others not only through their words, but also through their deeds. By modeling high standards of ethical conduct, social workers live by the motto, "Actions speak louder than words."

Social work with organizations comprises a range of roles and relationships. First, social workers act as helping agents for particular organizations. When social workers act as consultants, advocates, and mediators (or in other helping roles for an organization), the organization assumes the role of client and the social worker incurs ethical responsibilities toward that organization as a client. Second, social workers serve many functions within organizations. As staff members, they work with other staff as colleagues. Collegial relationships include interactions with other social workers, other professional staff, and support staff. Social workers also engage in supervisor–supervisee and educator–student relationships. Social workers incur different ethical obligations depending on whether they are acting as colleagues, supervisors, supervisees,

[1] For the purposes of this chapter, "organizations" refers to all types of organizations, including social agencies, governmental departments, for-profit and not-for-profit companies, and voluntary associations. For an analysis of the values underlying organizations and other macro systems, see Chapter 2.

educators, or students. Finally, social workers have ethical obligations toward their employing organization, as defined by their professional code of ethics and agency policies. This chapter explores the ethical standards and principles that apply to social workers within each of these relationships. This chapter concludes with a section on whistle-blowing, which explores how social workers should respond when serious ethical concerns arise in their organizations.

LEARNING OBJECTIVES

Upon successful completion of this chapter, students will be able to identify and apply the ethical obligations of social workers toward

- Client-organizations
- Colleagues
- Supervisees
- Students
- Employing organizations

RELATIONSHIPS WITH CLIENT-ORGANIZATIONS

In Chapters 5, 6, and 7, we explored social workers' ethical obligations toward clients, including informed consent, self-determination, competence, and maintaining appropriate boundaries (NASW Code of Ethics, 1999, Standards 1.01 to 1.16). In these chapters, the clients were humans (individuals, families, or groups of people). In the present section, the clients are organizations—entities that are made up of humans but have distinct cultures, rules, and structures. Although Standards 1.01 to 1.16 simply refer to clients, many of these standards were written as if clients were humans, not organizations. Consider, for instance, Standard 1.10 that says, "Social workers should not engage in physical contact with clients when there is a possibility of psychological harm to the client." What would it mean for a social worker to make physical contact with an organization? Does this section prohibit social workers from touching any person who works for the organization? Does it prohibit workers from touching the building where the organization is situated? Standard 1.07(o) refers to the death of a client. Organizations do not die, at least not in the same sense as humans. Clearly, some standards must be interpreted and applied differently when clients are organizations, as opposed to when clients are humans. The following scenario will be used to demonstrate the application of ethical standards in relation to client-organizations.

The Union of Farm Workers (UFW)[2] is an organization that promotes fair treatment of farm workers. The UFW hires Sinead, a social worker, as a consultant to assist with organizational development: setting priorities, improving organizational communication, and establishing stronger structures for its advocacy activities.

Standard 1.01 says social workers' primary responsibility is to promote the well-being of clients. Standard 1.02 suggests workers should promote client self-determination. In Sinead's case, she should promote the well-being and self-determination of the UFW as a whole. This commitment is relatively easy to follow when the various constituencies within the organization have the same interests and wishes. If everyone in UFW believes that Sinead should help them advocate for higher wages, for instance, Sinead should respect and promote this goal. In her personal life, Sinead is a consumer of farm products and may have a selfish interest in keeping farm wages and prices low. As a social worker, however, Sinead must put aside this interest and promote better wages for her client.

The situation becomes more complex when different constituencies within the client-organization have conflicting interests or wishes. Assume that some members of UFW want Sinead to advocate against a certain pesticide, iodomethane, believing that it is dangerous to farm workers. UFW's board of directors

[2] UFW is a fictional organization for illustration purposes.

disagrees, believing that iodomethane is not only safe but that it creates jobs and improves wages because this pesticide enhances farm productivity. When different constituencies have different interests or wishes, how should social workers determine whose interests or wishes are paramount? Ideally, the worker engages the organization in a dialogue to build consensus between the different constituencies (as described in Chapter 7). When consensus building is not possible, social workers typically take direction from the people who hire them, for instance, managers or administrators. If UFW's executive director hired Sinead, she would probably work with him or her to determine which interests and wishes to prioritize. The NASW Code does not give clear guidance on whose interests and wishes take precedence when there is conflict between the interests and needs of various constituencies within an organization. The answer may depend on the contract between the social worker and agency, as the contract should spell out the social worker's responsibilities. If the contract is not clear and the worker is not able to build consensus through dialogue, the worker may have to use the decision-making framework for managing difficult ethical dilemmas, presented in Part II of this textbook.

When contracting with an organization, social workers should inform the organization about the purpose, risks, benefits, and the timeframe of the services (S.1.03). Once again, the NASW Code does not specifically define who the worker must engage in order to satisfy this ethical requirement. Standard 1.03(c) does suggest that the worker requires informed consent from someone who has "capacity to provide consent." When the client is an organization, then capacity to consent may be defined according to who has legal authority within the organization to provide consent: typically, managers, officers, or directors. If UFW's executive director has authority to hire contractors, then Sinead should engage him or her in the informed consent process. When workers have questions about who has authority to hire contractors, they should check the organization's articles of incorporation, charter, bylaws, constitution, or policies. Different organizations have different documents explaining who is legally responsible for different functions.

Standard 1.04 defines social workers' obligations to provide services within their realms of competence. Social work with organizations requires different knowledge and skills than that required for work with other types of client systems. If Sinead is not competent to provide the types of organizational development that UFW is requesting, then she should refer them to a social worker or other professional who is competent to provide such services (S.2.06). Sinead should not solicit fees for referring UFW to another professional (S.2.06[c]). Clients may perceive such payments as kickbacks, questioning whether the referral is motivated by appropriate concerns for the clients or by the prospect of financial gain by making a referral to a friend. Giving or receiving payment for making referrals puts the integrity of both professionals in doubt.[3]

Standard 1.05 suggests that social workers should understand and respect the culture and social diversity of their clients. Although not explicitly stated, this includes understanding the culture of a particular organization. For instance, Sinead would need to understand how formal or informal the UFW is in its dealings with people, both inside and outside the UFW. What are its norms for communication? Further, what roles do power and politics play within the organization? Standard 1.05 does not specifically require social workers to be competent in the cultures of every employee or constituent of the organization. Although it may be desirable for social workers to be culturally knowledgeable about every person within an organization, it may not be feasible or necessary. The UFW has 120,000 members with representatives from 64 different nations of origin. Sinead should have general education and training in cultural competence, but it would be unrealistic to expect her to have

[3] Although payments for referrals may be unethical, social workers may charge for assessment and education services that may lead to a referral. For instance, Sinead could receive payment for conducting an assessment of UFW's needs and for providing information about the types of services available to address such needs. Sinead should not, however, charge a fee or commission for referring UFW to a specific service provider.

high-level education and training concerning each of the 64 nationalities. Further, the extent of cultural competence required depends on the nature of her functions. If she has been hired to advocate to the state legislature and has little interaction with the general membership of UFW, then she would need to understand the needs of the membership, but she would not need to possess high-level cross-cultural communication skills for each of the 64 nationalities. If, on the other hand, her job were to engage the membership in team-building dialogues, then she would need a higher level of cross-cultural communication skills. In all situations, social workers should possess competence in the culture of the organization as a whole. Whether they need cultural knowledge and skills related to the diverse backgrounds of the members of the organization depends on the nature of the work they are doing.

Standard 1.06 warns social workers to avoid situations that may put them into conflicts of interest. Conflicts of interest often arise when workers engage in dual or multiple relationships, for instance, if a person acts as a social worker for an organization that also provides services to the person. Standard 1.06 does not prohibit all conflicts of interest or multiple relationships, acknowledging that some multiple relationships may be desirable or even necessary. Assume that Sinead's husband is a farmworker and a member of the UFW. By virtue of her marriage, some people may perceive that Sinead has a conflict of interest. They may question, for instance, when she acts as UFW's advocate, is she advocating for the interests of UFW as a whole, or is she biased toward her husband's interests? Suppose that Sinead's husband had a strong, but rare, allergy to a certain pesticide. Will Sinead's concern for her husband overshadow the concerns of the majority who could easily tolerate exposure to the pesticide? Often, concerns about dual relationships with organizations can be resolved by making appropriate disclosures. Sinead should disclose her husband's membership in UFW during the informed consent process. The hiring officials may use this information to decide whether or not to hire her, and whether there are any special conditions that could be used to minimize risks of bias or exploitation. The hiring officials may also consider the advantages of Sinead's dual relationship. Because her husband works for UFW, she may be particularly motivated to work vigorously for UFW. She may also have a stronger sense of UFW and its members' needs than an outsider may have. Finally, the UFW may not be as vulnerable to exploitation as an individual (clinical) client might be. Individual clients may be experiencing depression, anxiety, low self-esteem, or other psychosocial concerns that put them at higher risk of exploitation. In the context of social work with organizations, multiple relationships may pose risks of financial exploitation. Risks of emotional, sexual, or other personal forms of exploitation are less likely, though still possible.

Multiple relationships are more likely to arise in the context of organizational work than in the context of individual or family work. Consider, for instance, working for a bank, insurance company, mortgage company, or other large institution. In a small town or rural setting, the institution may be the only one of its kind. When such an institution approaches a social worker to act for the company, the worker should disclose having a bank account, insurance policy, or mortgage with the company. Such disclosures would not necessarily bar the person from being hired to perform social work services for the organization, depending on the risks of exploitation by or against the worker. If the worker was receiving mental health counseling or social services from the organization, the risks of exploitation may be high.[4] The social worker may be in a vulnerable position because of his or her status as a client.

Standard 1.07 suggests that social workers should protect the privacy and confidentiality of their clients. Confidentiality is particularly important when social workers provide clinical counseling or therapeutic services. In such cases, workers are providing clients with a safe place to share private, potentially embarrassing

---

[4] For instance, if the institution is unhappy with the social worker's performance, it might be tempted to breach confidentiality and ask for the client records pertaining to the worker.

information. Organizations may have an interest in confidentiality, though their reasons are quite different. Some organizations may ask social workers to maintain confidentiality to ensure that competitor organizations do not gain access to trade secrets or other information that organizations use to gain competitive advantages (e.g., the secret recipe for its unique cookies). In the farmworkers' case, the UFW may want to ensure that its advocacy plans are kept confidential. They may ask Sinead not to disclose its plans to the public, including chemical producers or other potential adversaries, to maintain a tactical advantage in its social advocacy strategy. The UFW may also ask Sinead not to disclose the content of specific meetings. When working with individuals, families, and groups, social workers typically offer confidentiality for all meetings and communications with their clients. When working with organizations, social workers should clarify which types of meetings and communications are confidential, and which are not. There may be different rules regarding confidentiality depending on the nature and purpose of the interaction.

Organizations may have several reasons for wanting social workers to maintain openness, rather than confidentiality, for communications. First, the social worker may be responsible for facilitating communication between the organization and others. Sinead needs to share information about member needs and concerns in order to be able to advocate on their behalf. IFW may ask her not to disclose which individual member said what, but she will need to disclose their primary concerns. Second, some organizations act under laws or agency policies that require freedom of information. Government and publicly funded organizations, for instance, may operate under "open government," "freedom of information," or "sunshine laws." Such laws require meetings to be open to the public. They are intended to promote transparency, ensuring that the public can scrutinize how government decisions are made and how public funds are used (Tansey, 2006). The federal government and each state have their own rules, defining what types of meetings and information are open to the public, and which types can be kept private. Typical exceptions to public access to information include information related to national security, private information related to specific individuals, and deliberations of political committees. Each jurisdiction has its own rules concerning which types of information and meetings are open, and which are protected by privacy or confidentiality rules. For private organizations, agency policy spells out what types of information may be shared and what types of information should be kept confidential. Social workers need to be familiar with the laws and policies governing openness and privacy within their organizations.

Standard 1.09 prohibits social workers from engaging in sexual relationships with clients or former clients, though it does not specify whether and how this would apply to social work with organizations. The premise of this prohibition is to protect clients who may be particularly vulnerable to sexual exploitation by social workers. This same vulnerability may not apply to client-organizations. Thus, does this standard prohibit Sinead from having sexual relationships with anyone who works for UFW? Social workers should consider the potential risks related to having sexual relationships with members of the client-organization. Above, we considered the dual relationship issues that arise because Sinead is married to a UFW member. It seems unlikely that Sinead's having sex with her husband puts either the UFW or her husband at risk of exploitation simply because she is also providing social work services to the organization. Standard 1.09(d) suggests that social workers should not provide *clinical services* to individuals with whom they have had a prior sexual relationship. Although Standards 1.09(a), (b), and (c) do not specifically mention clinical services, it seems likely that the authors of the Code of Ethics intended these sections to apply to clinical services, not organizational social work. The social worker could also look to the organization's policies on sexual or romantic relationships. Some organizations prohibit such relationships, believing that they could detract from the work of the organization. Other organizations prohibit sexual harassment, but allow for consensual sexual or romantic relationships among employees.

As mentioned above, Standard 1.10 suggests that social workers should not engage in physical contact with clients when there is a possibility of psychological harm to the client. This standard may apply to contact between the social worker and members of a client-organization, though the Code's authors likely intended it to apply primarily to clinical services rather than organizational social work. Still, social workers should strive to maintain appropriate physical boundaries with anyone they are working with, whether the person is a client, colleague, or a member of a client-organization. Members of a client-organization may be less likely to be as vulnerable as clinical clients, but it is still prudent practice to set clear, appropriate, and culturally sensitive boundaries with all people.

This section has highlighted some of the main ethical standards for working with organizations as clients. In particular, it has explored how social workers need to adjust the way they interpret ethical standards when working with clients-organization as opposed to human clients. Still, social workers should remember that people are at the base of any organization. General ethical principles such as beneficence (do good), nonmaleficence (do no harm), and social justice apply regardless of the size and type of client system.

RELATIONSHIPS WITH COLLEAGUES

The preceding section explored the ethical obligations of social workers toward client-organizations. We now turn to the ethical obligations of social workers toward colleagues, as delineated by Standards 2.01 to 2.11 of the NASW Code. The NASW Code does not explicitly define colleagues, though these standards imply that colleagues are people with whom the social worker is working during the course of helping clients. Colleagues may include coworkers on an interdisciplinary team, professionals and nonprofessionals from other organizations, and professionals and support staff within the same agency. In some Standards, the NASW Code refers specifically to social work colleagues, but in others, the term *colleagues* could also include non–social work colleagues. Social workers' ethical obligations to colleagues fit into six categories: respect, confidentiality, collaboration and conflict, sexual boundaries, corrective action, and defending colleagues.

Respect

Standard 2.01 describes social workers' obligations regarding respect toward colleagues. These obligations include demonstrating respect, being honest, being cooperative, and avoiding unwarranted negative criticism, idle gossip, or discriminatory comments. One might question why social workers need a code of ethics to tell them to act respectfully. Isn't this just common sense? Even though social workers should know how to act respectfully, including respect in the code of ethics ensures that social workers can be held accountable to this standard. Ordinarily, adherence to this standard should be relatively easy. After all, social workers go into this profession to help people, not hurt them. Still, social workers should continuously monitor themselves through self-checks and attention to feedback from colleagues. If you are feeling overwhelmed by work, for instance, you might procrastinate on returning calls to colleagues. If you feel that you are being attacked by a colleague, you might respond defensively or out of anger. If you feel passionate about pursuing a cause for a particular client, you might attack a colleague who seems to be getting in your way. Social workers may experience stress from a range of sources. Although social workers should understand how stress may lead to nonprofessional behaviors, they should not use stress as an excuse for showing disrespect to colleagues. Rather, they should find more effective ways of dealing with the stress and take responsibility for their actions (Wharton, 2008).[5]

---

[5] Methods of managing stress include consulting with supervisors, going for therapy, and making use of self-care techniques (exercise, meditation, healthy eating, positive self-talk, and balancing work with social activities).

Confidentiality

Standard 2.02 advises social workers to "respect confidential information shared by colleagues in the course of their professional relationships." Remember (from Chapter 5) that confidentiality is owned by the client, not by the social worker or other professional. Clients decide what information may be shared, and with whom. Social workers should not provide confidential information to other professionals and should not receive confidential information from other professionals, unless the client has provided consent for such sharing (S.1.07).[6] Even when a client consents to disclosing information to others, social workers have an obligation to limit further disclosures based on what information is needed to serve the client, as well as what the client has specifically consented to. Consider the following scenario:

> Clarice is having marital problems. She might be suffering from depression as a result of these problems. She signs a consent form allowing Sergio (her social worker) to forward a psychosocial assessment to her psychiatrist, Dr. Portius. The consent also authorizes Sergio to discuss her situation with Dr. Portius for the purposes of developing a joint treatment plan. Clarice signs a reciprocal consent form, permitting Dr. Portius to share confidential information with Sergio.

Although Sergio and Dr. Portius belong to different professions, both have ethical obligations to respect client confidentiality. This duty applies to information that each professional gathers directly from the client or indirectly through other colleagues. To safeguard Clarice's confidentiality, Sergio should include a note on his assessment stating, "This assessment contains confidential information and should not be released to anyone else without the express written consent of the client." If Sergio has any doubt about whether Dr. Portius understands the nature of the client's confidentiality, including exceptions, he should discuss these matters before exchanging any confidential information. Assume, for instance, that Sergio is mandated to prepare a report for a criminal sentencing hearing. Sergio should inform Dr. Portius that he is gathering information for this purpose, and any information that Dr. Portius shares could be used in such a report. Thus, each professional should respect a client's right to confidentiality, which includes the obligation of making sure that colleagues also understand the nature of the client's confidentiality.

Collaboration and Conflict between Colleagues

Standards 2.03, 2.04, 2.05, and 3.06[7] provide social workers with guidance on how to collaborate with colleagues, including how to manage conflict when it arises. Ideally, social workers are proactive, considering potential conflicts with colleagues before they arise or become aggravated. Early identification of issues makes it easier for co-professionals to pre-empt conflicts or manage them in a professional manner.

Social workers often work with other professionals on interdisciplinary teams (Geva, Barsky, & Westernoff, 2000). Interdisciplinary work may entail many benefits for clients (especially the combined expertise of people with different training and experience). Interdisciplinary work may also pose ethical challenges. In particular, social workers and other professionals may have conflicting professional values and ethical standards. Standard 2.03 of the NASW Code reminds social workers to discuss their values and ethical standards with other professionals in order to clarify each other's obligations. If

[6] When social workers share information with colleagues within the same agency, they often do so with the client's oral consent (e.g., the worker lets the client know from the outset of work that some information will be shared with colleagues within the agency). If social workers want to share information with colleagues at other agencies, written forms should be used to document consent.

[7] Standard 2.06 provides guidance on referral for services. Although this standard is relevant to the topic of collaboration between colleagues, it has been discussed earlier in relation to obligations to clients.

disagreement about ethical issues arises, they should strive to work through the disagreement and find solutions that are consistent with client well-being. If they cannot reach agreement, they should seek assistance from others, such as supervisors, the agency's board of directors, the agency's attorneys, or their respective professional associations.

In Clarice's case, assume that Sergio and Dr. Portius have conflicting values concerning her treatment plan. As a social worker who values human relationships, Sergio may prioritize couples counseling to help Clarice deal with her marital problems. As a doctor who values medical treatment for psychiatric illness, Dr. Portius may prioritize medication for Clarice's depression. Sergio and Dr. Portius should explain how their professional values and ethics may be affecting their opinions. If they are unable to develop a joint treatment plan that complies with both sets of professional values and ethics, they may need to consider alternatives that focus on the client's best interests. Rather than triangulate a client in their dispute, for instance, one professional may agree to terminate services and allow the other to take full responsibility for treatment planning.

Standard 2.04(a) warns social workers not to take advantage of a dispute between a colleague and an employer to advance the social worker's position or interests. Assume Sergio is angry at Dr. Portius for putting Clarice on antidepressant medication before they had a chance to try family counseling. Sergio lodges a complaint with Dr. Portius's employer, making false allegations about his competence. Although Sergio justifies his false allegations in light of furthering client interests, his actions violate Standard 2.04(a).[8] Social workers should use professional approaches to further their positions or interests.[9]

Standard 2.04(b) advises social workers against exploiting clients in disputes with colleagues or engaging clients in inappropriate discussion of conflicts with colleagues. Thus, it would be unethical for Sergio tell Clarice rumors about Dr. Portius in order to get her riled and issue a complaint against him. If Sergio has issues with Dr. Portius, he should deal with Dr. Portius directly and professionally.

Standard 2.05 provides social workers with guidelines for consulting with colleagues. Social workers should consult colleagues whenever consultation is in the best interests of their clients (S.2.05[c]). When Sergio initially met Clarice, he identified symptoms that seemed to indicate clinical depression. Because Sergio does not have the required training for making psychiatric diagnoses, it was appropriate for him to consult with Dr. Portius about the possibility of Clarice being depressed. When social workers seek advice or counsel from colleagues, they should ensure that the colleagues have appropriate knowledge, expertise, and competence (S.2.05[b]). For Sergio, this meant ensuring that Dr. Portius had appropriate expertise on matters of depression. To respect client confidentiality, social workers should provide the least amount of information necessary to achieve the purposes of the consultation (S.2.05[c]). Assume that Sergio contacts Dr. Portius about the possibility of referring Clarice for services. During the initial telephone contact, Sergio describes Clarice's situation generally, without disclosing her name or other identifying information. If they concluded that Clarice did not need to be referred to Dr. Portius, then her identity would be protected. Social workers should also avoid spreading gossip about clients. They should only disclose information that is required for colleagues to work together on the client's goals and for the client's benefit.

Standard 3.06 provides social workers with ethical guidance on how to manage client transfers between different agencies or service providers. When a social worker meets a potential client who is already receiving services from another service provider, the worker should carefully review

---

[8] He also violates Standard 4.04, regarding honesty and integrity.

[9] Some might argue that the end justifies the means. In this situation, however, Sergio can pursue the same objective (end) through more appropriate means (e.g., asking his supervisor to contact Dr. Portius's supervisor to see if they can help resolve the dispute in the client's best interests).

the situation before agreeing to provide services. The worker should avoid possible confusion and conflict with the other service provider. For instance, the worker may need to clarify the roles of each provider and how to ensure collaboration, if appropriate. If the client is using insurance to pay for services, the worker may encourage the client to check whether the insurance will pay for both service providers. The worker should review the possible benefits and risks of engaging the new service provider. The worker may also discuss whether the worker should consult with the previous service provider. Because clients have a right to confidentiality, the worker should not contact the other provider without the client's informed consent. The worker should explain the purpose for the contact, for instance, to determine how the two providers will work together for the benefit of the client. If the client intends to terminate services with the first provider, they could discuss how to carry out the transfer of services most effectively. Communication between service providers may be useful to pre-empt problems that might otherwise arise.

The ecological model of social work reminds social workers that client well-being depends on the relationships that clients have with the many systems in their social environments. These systems include colleagues from social work and other helping professions. Accordingly, social workers often work with colleagues for the best interests of their clients. Interprofessional conflicts may arise with respect to different values, ethical obligations, goals for work, or methods of practice (Geva et al., 2000). When interprofessional conflicts arise, social workers should respond with respect and understanding, keeping client interests as the primary concern.

Sexual Boundaries between Colleagues

Standard 2.07(a) suggests that social workers acting as supervisors or educators should not engage in sexual activities with supervisees, students, trainees, or other colleagues over whom they exercise professional authority. This section is intended to protect employees who may be in vulnerable situations from sexual exploitation. It also protects employees against conflicts of interest. Suppose Sergio started dating and having sex with his supervisor. If the supervisor gave Sergio a pay raise, others might think that he was being rewarded for his sexual relationship. Standard 2.07(b) suggests that social workers should avoid engaging in sexual relationships with colleagues when there is risk of conflict of interest. Note how these standards do not provide the same type of absolute prohibition of sexual relationships as Standard 1.09 does with respect to worker–client relationships. Standard 1.09 suggests there are no circumstances that would justify allowing workers to have sex with clients. Consider whether Standard 2.07(b) would prohibit Sergio from having a sexual relationship with Dr. Portius. Although they both work for Clarice, they work at different agencies. Neither professional has supervisory responsibility over the other. Still, there may be risks of these professional colleagues having a sexual relationship. If Sergio refers Clarice to Dr. Portius for psychiatric services, Clarice might think Sergio is motivated by his romantic relationship with Dr. Portius rather than by Clarice's best interests. Further, Clarice may be concerned about Sergio and Dr. Portius sharing information about her, without her consent. She may think, "If they are sleeping together, maybe they are also talking about me." Some agencies prohibit sexual or romantic relationships between employees in order to avoid these risks. Other agencies allow such relationships, in spite of the risks. Before entering into a sexual or romantic relationship with professional colleagues, social workers should consider what types of risks may arise. In some cases, social workers may need to transfer professional duties in order to avoid a conflict of interest.[10]

Standard 2.08 informs social workers not to sexually harass supervisees, students, trainees, or colleagues. Once again, this should be common sense. Social workers should know that it is inappropriate to tease, pester, stalk, or bully colleagues in a sexual manner, particularly when

[10] If Sergio and his supervisor wanted to enter a romantic relationship, for instance, the agency could consider transferring Sergio to work with another supervisor.

they are acting as supervisors or in other positions of authority. Some forms of sexual harassment may seem more ambiguous than others. A social worker may intend to entertain by making sexual jokes, but still offend her colleagues. Likewise, a worker might intend to compliment coworkers on their looks, but be perceived as harassing. Or a worker might innocently request a date, but have it interpreted as a sexually exploitive demand. Social workers should consider whether their behaviors amount to sexual harassment according to how they may be interpreted by their colleagues rather than by their own intentions (U.S. Equal Employment Opportunity Commission, 2002). If the worker thinks a certain behavior might be interpreted as an unwanted sexual solicitation or other form of harassment, the worker should avoid the behavior.

Corrective Action

Standard 2.09 describes social workers' obligation to take corrective action when social work colleagues suffer from impairments that affect the performance of their duties. Examples of impairment include being under the influence of drugs or alcohol, having a mental illness, or experiencing other forms of psychosocial stress. If such personal problems are not affecting work performance, then a social worker could speak to the colleague out of personal compassion. Still, the Code of Ethics does not *require* the worker to take any action.

When a social worker has direct knowledge of a social work colleague's impairment, the social worker should initially consider consulting directly with the colleague as one of the first steps. Direct discussions could be used to help the colleague seek help and take responsibility for remedial action. Direct discussions also permit the colleague to share any pertinent information with the social worker before the worker contacts the colleague's supervisor, professional association, or licensing body. Standard 2.09 suggests that if the colleague does not take adequate steps to address the impairment, then the worker should "take action through appropriate channels established by employers, agencies, NASW, licensing and regulatory bodies, and other professional organizations." The most appropriate action will depend on the facts of the particular case—for instance, is the colleague self-employed or employed by an agency, is the colleague a member of NASW or licensed by a regulatory body, and what types of measures do each of these organizations have to help address impairment issues? Consider the following example.

> Clarice tells Sergio that Dr. Portius has a serious memory problem. She suggests that he does not remember what she says from one session to the next.

Clarice's disclosure to Sergio is secondhand (hearsay) information. Sergio does not know whether her information is accurate because he has not had similar experiences with Dr. Portius. Standard 2.09 speaks to a social worker's obligations when the worker has *direct* knowledge of the colleague's impairment. Sergio should not report Dr. Portius to his supervisor or other authorities simply based on Clarice's disclosure. Sergio could provide Clarice with information about possible avenues she could take to redress her concerns—for instance, talking to Dr. Portius or his supervisor, or checking the agency's policy on what clients should do if they have concerns about their service providers. Sergio must be careful about demonstrating respect to Dr. Portius, and not engaging in gossip or other inappropriate discussions with Clarice. Sergio does not want to become triangulated in a conflict that involves Clarice and her psychiatrist. At the same time, he cares about his client and wants to offer support. For the purposes of the following analysis, assume that Sergio speaks to Dr. Portius on another matter and discovers that Dr. Portius does seem to have a memory problem. Thus, Clarice's concern is confirmed by Sergio's direct experience.

Standard 2.09 applies to social work colleagues, but Dr. Portius is a psychiatrist. One of the main purposes of Standard 2.09 is to protect clients from harm.[11] Although the NASW Code does not enunciate obligations in relation

[11] The wording of this section also covers situations that do not directly involve clients (e.g., a support staff whose paperwork suffers because she cannot concentrate due to chaos in her personal life).

to impairments of non–social work helping professionals, social workers could use the underlying principle of Standard 2.09 to infer an ethical obligation to protect clients from risks that may arise when other helping professionals have impairments that are hindering their work. Sergio decides to speak to Dr. Portius, explaining his concern that Dr. Portius may have a memory problem that is interfering with his ability to practice. Sergio is careful to speak from his own experience with Dr. Portius, not mentioning Clarice's concerns because he does not want to set up a possible conflict between Dr. Portius and his client.

In spite of Sergio's attempts to be supportive, Dr. Portius responds defensively, denying any memory problem and refusing to speak with Sergio further. Sergio speaks with his own supervisor to discuss what further actions, if any, Sergio should take. They discuss various courses of action, including discussions with Dr. Portius's supervisor, filing a complaint with his state licensing body, and issuing a request for a professional review with the American Psychiatric Association. They decide to contact Dr. Portius's supervisor first. If the matter can be handled informally within the agency, then they will not need to initiate more formal complaint processes.

Standard 2.10 describes social workers' obligations that arise when they have direct knowledge of a social work colleague's incompetence. First, they should consider speaking with the colleague directly and assist with remedial action. Second, if the colleague does not take sufficient steps to address the incompetence, they should take actions through appropriate channels established by employers, agencies, the NASW, licensing and regulatory bodies, and other professional associations. Similar to Standard 2.09, this section is intended to protect clients from harm. Also similar to 2.09, this section requires direct knowledge of the colleague's incompetence and only applies to social work colleagues. Arguably, social workers should take remedial steps whenever they identify a helping professional who is performing incompetently, putting clients at risk of biological, psychological, social, or spiritual harm. One of the challenges in applying this standard is knowing when a colleague is acting incompetently. Different professionals may have different but equally legitimate ways of assessing and intervening with clients. Just because Sergio disagrees with Dr. Portius's decision to prescribe antidepressants to Clarice does not mean that Dr. Portius is incompetent. Incompetence means lacking the required knowledge and skills to perform in a manner that is expected of a particular type of professional in a particular field of practice. Thus, Sergio should consider whether Dr. Portius has the required knowledge and skills to perform a psychiatric diagnosis and prescribe treatment for a patient who may have depression.

Standard 2.11 articulates social workers' responsibilities with regard to the unethical conduct of colleagues. Unlike Standards 2.09 and 2.10, the wording of this section is not limited to social work colleagues. Social workers have a general obligation to discourage, prevent, expose, and correct the unethical conduct of colleagues. In order to carry out this obligation, social workers need to be knowledgeable about the ethical obligations of various professionals, as well as the policies and procedures for handling concerns about unethical misconduct. Different agencies, professional associations, and licensing bodies have different policies, so it is important to refer to the policies of the particular organization to which you are issuing an ethics complaint. Some organizations provide consultants or advocates who can assist with preparing a complaint.

When feasible, social workers should consult with the colleague first, before issuing complaints. Consultation is common courtesy. It also permits informal resolution of issues. For instance, colleagues may clarify information that justifies their actions. Alternatively, they may take responsibility and make corrective actions that alleviate the need for a formal complaint. In some situations, consulting a colleague first may be infeasible or unproductive:

- The colleague intentionally avoids telephone calls or other contact with the worker.
- The worker needs to report the colleague to his or her supervisor, regulatory body, police, or other authorities immediately in order to prevent serious, imminent harm to clients or others.

- The worker fears the colleague will respond violently to any direct discussions of unethical misconduct.

Defending Colleagues

Standard 2.11(e) recognizes that not all allegations of unethical conduct are justified. Thus, social workers should defend colleagues who are unjustly charged with unethical conduct. Carrying out this responsibility may be complicated when the social worker and colleague work in the same agency. If agency administrators are falsely accusing one social worker of ethical misconduct, other social workers may fear retribution if they stand up for this colleague. When faced with such situations, social workers should consult with others to determine whether there is a safe way to assist a colleague who has been unjustly charged. Given the volatility of the issues within the agency, the worker may need to seek consultation from someone outside the agency (e.g., an attorney, the ethics committee of the worker's professional association, or an ombudsman who is responsible for the agency). If a colleague has been wrongly accused of an ethical violation and you do nothing, your failure to act could be considered a violation of Standard 2.11(e).

RELATIONSHIPS WITH SUPERVISEES

The previous section explored ethical obligations of social workers toward colleagues. These obligations apply to supervisor-supervisee relationships, which constitute a special form of relationship between colleagues. In addition to the obligations cited above, supervisors[12] have special ethical obligations that arise because they are persons in positions of authority. Supervisory relationships are fiduciary relationships, relationships in which the supervisors have higher standards of care because they exercise power or control over supervisees: for instance, supervisors have the authority to review the performance of supervisees, providing feedback and direction on how to interact with clients (Falve, 2002). Some supervisors also have the power to hire, fire, reward, or sanction supervisees. Although supervisors have many sources of power over supervisees, they should use their powers fairly—avoiding bias, extortion, or undue manipulation. The following sections explore supervisors' ethical obligations in relation to competence, boundaries and dual relationships, and education, training, and evaluation.[13] To demonstrate how these obligations apply in practice, consider the following scenario.

> Sigrid supervises the social workers at an agency that provides advocacy for clients alleging housing discrimination.[14] One of her supervisees is Norman, a frontline social worker of Native American descent.

Competence

Social workers should provide supervision only within their areas of knowledge and competence (S.3.01[a]). The competence required to supervise includes knowledge and skills related to the work being performed by the supervisee, as well as the knowledge and skills related to being a supervisor. Accordingly, Sigrid should have competence in advocacy work as well as in supervising advocacy work. To have competence in advocacy, for instance, she would need to be knowledgeable about nondiscrimination laws and procedures for enforcing them. To have competence in supervising Norman, she would also need to be skilled at providing information, feedback, support, and guidance (Munson, 2002). Further, she would need to have cultural competence—in this case, being aware of Norman's Native American

---

[12] This section refers to the obligations of supervisors. Similar obligations apply for social workers in the role of professional consultant under Standards 3.01 to 3.03.

[13] See Chapter 12 for more in-depth analysis of ethical issues between supervisors and supervisees.

[14] For information on how to file complaints for housing discrimination, see http://www.hud.gov/complaints/housediscrim.cfm.

ethnicity and any implications this may have for how to engage him in the supervisory process.

Boundaries and Dual Relationships

Social work supervisors are responsible for establishing clear, appropriate, and culturally sensitive boundaries with their supervisees (S.3.01[b]). The NASW Code does not specify what constitutes "appropriate boundaries," so supervisors may look to standards established in agency policy, social work literature, and research for guidance. According to Kadushin & Harkness (2002), for instance, supervisors may provide supervisees education and support, but not therapy. The appropriateness of boundaries may depend on the context of work and the theoretical framework for practice. Larger institutions and agencies may have more hierarchical structures, with more rigid boundaries between supervisors and supervisees. Smaller institutions and agencies may have less hierarchy and more flexible boundaries. Supervisors who operate from a feminist perspective also tend to have more egalitarian relationships and more flexible boundaries with supervisees (Szymanski, 2003).

The boundaries that supervisors establish with supervisees may be used as models by the supervisees for their relationships with clients. Thus, supervisors should discuss how their boundaries are similar to and different from the boundaries that the supervisor believes the supervisee should establish with clients. Some supervisors establish collegial, almost friend-like, relationships with supervisees. Although supervisors retain some professional distance due to their status and functions within the organization, the supervisor–supervisee relationship often involves less of a power differential than the social worker–client relationship.[15] Both Sigrid and Norman have MSWs and both feel secure in their current life situations. In contrast, most of Norman's clients do not have professional degrees and they are experiencing stress and vulnerability because they have been subjected to housing discrimination. Thus, the boundaries that Sigrid sets with Norman may be different from those which Norman sets with his clients. Whereas it may be appropriate for Sigrid to take Norman out for a business lunch, the agency may prohibit Norman from taking clients to lunch. Once again, these are just examples. What constitutes an appropriate boundary depends on the context (Gutheil & Brodsky, 2008). If Norman had difficulty maintaining professional boundaries, for instance, Sigrid might model firmer boundaries and decide not to take him for lunch.

Standard 3.01 suggests that social workers should not engage in dual relationships with supervisees if there is a risk of exploitation or potential harm to the supervisee. If Sigrid asks Norman to baby-sit her children, she is proposing a dual relationship with him. Such a relationship may seem innocuous, even helpful to Norman since he is being paid extra for his services. Still, there is potential for exploitation. Norman might feel he is being pressured into baby-sitting or accepting insufficient fees for his services. Even if Sigrid intends to ask Norman to help on a voluntary basis, he may feel that his social work position is in jeopardy if he refuses to baby-sit. Consider, also, how she might react to him as a supervisee if her children complained that he was a mean baby-sitter. Although the Code of Ethics does not prohibit supervisors from entering dual relationships with supervisees, it does discourage them and puts supervisors on notice that they are responsible should anything untoward happen because of the dual relationship. If supervisors do enter dual relationships with supervisees, they should try to minimize the risks. Methods of minimizing risks depend on the circumstances, but may include

- Ensuring that the dual relationship is permitted by agency policy.
- Asking the supervisor's supervisor for permission to enter into the dual relationship.
- Discussing the potential risks and benefits of the dual relationship with the supervisee,

[15] Of course, there are many occasions when the power differential between supervisor and supervisees is very large (e.g., when supervisees are working on a probationary basis so the supervisor may determine whether or not they should be hired on a permanent basis).

and asking for informed, voluntary consent.
- Brainstorming what "could go wrong" to make sure the supervisor and supervisee have thought through all the contingencies in advance.

During brainstorming, Norman raises the possibility that he gets injured while working in Sigrid's home. Sigrid notes that she will be personally responsible, not the agency, and that her home insurance includes accident coverage for baby-sitters.

When social workers are promoted to supervisory positions, they may face special challenges in establishing new boundaries with their coworkers. As coworkers, social workers are not generally responsible for training, monitoring, or evaluating one another. The roles and power dynamics change when one worker becomes the supervisor of the others. The new supervisor may try to maintain friendly or peer-like relationships with coworkers ("Just because I'm supervisor doesn't mean that our close relationship will change"). Alternatively, the supervisor may try to establish a clear cut from the former ties in order to establish supervisory authority (Now that I'm supervisor, I can't go out to lunch or socialize with you"). In either case, supervisees may question the supervisor's actions and motivations. In order to avoid confusion or misunderstanding, the new supervisor should meet with the supervisees to have a frank discussion of how their relationships may change and how they may stay the same, given the supervisor's recent promotion and responsibilities.

Education, Training, and Evaluation

Social work administrators and supervisors are responsible for ensuring that their supervisees have appropriate training, education, and staff development (S.3.08). This responsibility includes ensuring that new staff members are properly prepared for their work. Administrators and supervisors are also responsible for continuing education—ensuring that practitioners are apprised of the most current knowledge and emerging developments in their fields of practice, including what constitutes ethical practice.

Supervisors evaluate the performance of supervisees, providing feedback and support. Supervisees may feel anxious, vulnerable, and defensive when receiving performance evaluations. Agencies use evaluations to make decisions regarding the supervisee's pay, sanctions, and future position in the agency. Because of the gravity of these implications, the supervisor's obligation to provide evaluations in a fair and respectful manner is particularly important (S.3.01[d]). Supervisors should inform supervisees about their evaluation criteria from the outset of their work together (S.3.03[d]). This provides supervisees with notice of the supervisor's expectations. Often, supervisors meet periodically with supervisees to identify specific objectives and to provide feedback on the extent to which these objectives are being met. Fairness dicates that supervisees should be provided with ongoing feedback so they know what they are doing well and where they may need improvement.

RELATIONSHIPS WITH STUDENTS

As with other social work relationships, educator–student relationships are governed not only by the NASW Code of Ethics but by agency policies and contracts. In the case of educators, the policies of the university and social work department identify a range of student rights and obligations (e.g., the right to know all the course assignments at the start of the term, and the obligations to attend and participate in class). Social work departments typically provide students with program manuals and field education manuals that explain these rights and obligations. Course syllabi also act as contracts between educators and students. Syllabi state course objectives, educational procedures, requirements, and criteria for evaluation. By registering for courses, students agree to abide by the terms established in the syllabi. Professors and other instructors should also abide by the terms of the syllabi. Ideally, the rights and obligations established by school policies and course syllabi are congruent with the values and standards established by the NASW Code of Ethics. In fact, social work programs incorporate the NASW Code of Ethics into their policies by asking students to join the NASW and having them to sign a pledge agreeing to abide by the NASW Code. In situations where policies of the educational institution conflict with the NASW Code, students and professors may be faced with ethical dilemmas,[16] specifically, which policies or standards take precedence when there is a conflict. Students and educators should use the ethical decision-making framework, explored in Part II, to determine how to respond to such dilemmas.

Standard 3.02 of the NASW Code provides guidelines for social workers who function as educators, trainers, and field instructors (i.e., supervisors for student social workers).[17] To serve competently in such educative capacities, social workers need to be familiar with the most current professional social work knowledge. For the purposes of this section, assume Norman is a student and Sigrid is his field instructor. To fulfill Standard 3.02, Sigrid should be familiar with current research on evidence-based advocacy practices. Educators may be held to higher standards of competence than frontline service providers because they are responsible for educating others (i.e., they are in a position of trust). If educators provide misinformation to students, how can the students perform competently?

Educators and field instructors are responsible for ensuring that clients are routinely informed when they are being served by student social workers (S.3.02[c]). Typically, field instructors ask students to inform clients that they are students during their first meeting. Thus, Sigrid might teach Norman to introduce himself to clients as follows:

> My name is Norman Chabot. I am a bachelor of social work student with State University. I am working here at Housing Advocacy Services under the supervision of Sigrid Sands, who is the director of Housing Advocacy.

Because clients are entitled to voluntary, informed consent (S.1.03), they should be allowed to reject services from student practitioners and access help from regularly employed practitioners. Students should discuss agency policy with their field instructors to determine how the agency handles requests for other practitioners.

As with supervisors, educators and field instructors should evaluate students' performance in a fair and respectful manner (S.3.02[b]). Students may feel particularly vulnerable during evaluation processes because their ability to graduate and practice depends on the evaluations they receive. The primary role of an educator is to facilitate students' learning. Thus, they should not expect students to have the same level of competence as a social worker who has graduated and is currently employed by the agency. They should provide specific, critical feedback, however, that lets students know where they stand in relation to the expectations of their BSW or MSW program. Unfortunately, some field instructors try to avoid conflict and withhold negative feedback, hoping performance will improve (Phelan, Barlow, Myrick, Rogers, & Sawa, 2003). If students do not receive ongoing feedback on their strengths and learning needs throughout their courses and field experiences, they are being deprived of the opportunity to take remedial steps required to develop professionally and pass their courses.

Social work educators and field instructors are responsible for setting clear, appropriate, and culturally sensitive boundaries. Further, they should not engage in dual relationships with students when there is a risk of exploitation or potential harm to the students (S.3.02[d]). The concerns about boundaries and dual relationships with students are similar to those expressed earlier for supervisor–supervisee relationships. Educators and field instructors are in special relationships of trust, given their power and authority over

[16] Consider the dilemma that arises, for instance, if a social work program's policy requires students to participate in a particular form of prayer. This requirement may conflict with the NASW Code's provisions regarding nondiscrimination on the basis of religion (S.4.02).

[17] Some agencies refer to field instructors as field educators or field supervisors. Professors, instructors, and faculty field liaisons who work in schools of social work are also covered by the provisions of S.3.02.

students. Once again, different social workers have different thoughts on what constitutes an appropriate boundary in a particular situation, or what types of dual relationships are too risky to enter. Some professors, for instance, hire students as research or teaching assistants. These positions offer students valuable experience and salaries. On the other hand, students could be exploited in these situations. What happens if a student's school work seems to suffer because she is spending too much time on her work for a professor? What happens if one student alleges that another is being treated with favoritism by the professor who hired him? The safest approach may be to avoid dual relationships; however, there may be times when the potential benefits of dual relationships outweigh the risks. When determining whether to enter into dual relationships with students, educators should consider agency (or university) policy. Agency approval does not negate all risks, but it does inform educators about which risks the agency is willing to accept, and which ones it will not.

In the past three sections, we have been exploring the relationship between social workers and various people: colleagues, supervisees, and students. In the following section we explore social workers' relationships with their employing organization.

RELATIONSHIPS WITH EMPLOYING ORGANIZATION

Social workers have a range of rights and responsibilities in relation to their employing organizations. This section begins with an exploration of the general commitments that workers have to their employers. The balance of this section explores ethical standards in relation to specific organizational activities: record keeping, billing, administration, and labor-management disputes.

Commitments to Employers

The primary standard in the NASW Code regulating the relationship between social workers and their employers is Standard 3.09. Subsection (a) of this standard suggests, "Social workers should generally adhere to commitments made to employers and employing organizations." Social workers incur commitments with employers through written, oral, and implied contracts. When social workers are hired, they may be asked to sign employment contracts specifying their rights and obligations as employees (e.g., the pay they will receive and the services they will provide). Some employers also ask social workers to sign additional forms, committing themselves to maintain client confidentiality, to follow agency policy, to adhere to state laws, to abide by the NASW Code of Ethics, or to avoid conflicts of interest with the employer (e.g., setting up a competing private practice). As noted in Chapter 5, contracts do not have to be written in order to be legally enforceable. Thus, when social workers orally agree to work overtime (for extra pay), their commitments are enforceable. Social workers may also incur commitments through implied contracts. During a job interview, a social worker says she is fluent in three languages. By implication, she is offering to provide services in these languages. Thus, social workers' commitments to employers may come from a variety of written and unwritten sources.

Note that social workers have a "general" obligation to adhere to commitments made to employers, not an absolute obligation. Although social workers should fulfill their commitments under most circumstances, there are many possible exceptions to this general standard. To illustrate, consider the following scenario.

> Simon is a social worker at Everfast Eating Disorder Services (EEDS). Due to funding cuts, EEDS decides to shorten the duration of counseling services for families affected by anorexia. In the past, families were offered four to six sessions. Under new policies, EEDS provides single-session family counseling. Simon speaks up at a staff meeting, urging EEDS to consider other options. After the meeting, the program director tells Simon to "keep his mouth shut" about this issue or he will lose his job.

Ordinarily, Simon should comply with the agency policies. The following analysis demonstrates how various exceptions under Standard 3.09 could apply to this scenario.

- "Social workers should work to improve employing agencies' policies and procedures and the efficiency and effectiveness of their services" (S.3.09[b]). Simon has concerns about the effectiveness of single-session family counseling for issues related to anorexia. Thus, he should gather information about the effectiveness of single-session counseling, inform EEDS about his concerns, and advocate for policies that support more effective services. Simon does not want to put his job at risk, so he strives to act respectfully, empathically, and collaboratively when he asserts his concerns. He acknowledges that funding concerns are legitimate and it is important to find ways to save time and resources. Although he is generally committed to following agency policies, his concerns about single-session counseling lead him to advocate for policy change.
- "Social workers should take reasonable steps to ensure that employers are aware of social workers' ethical obligations as set forth in the NASW Code of Ethics and of the implications of those obligations for social work practice" (S.3.09[c]). The agency rejects Simon's request to reconsider its single-session policy. Rather than simply accept the agency's decision, Simon should inform the agency that his primary commitment under the NASW Code is to promote the best interests of clients (S.1.01). In addition, Standard 6.04(a) directs him to advocate for access to necessary resources for all people, particularly vulnerable populations (including families affected by anorexia). This information may help the agency understand why Simon is advocating so strongly.
- "Social workers should not allow an employing organization's policies, procedures, regulations, or administrative orders to interfere with their ethical practice of social work. Social workers should take reasonable steps to ensure that their employing organizations' practices are consistent with the NASW Code of Ethics" (S.3.09[d]). This section suggests that a social worker's professional ethical obligations take precedence over an agency's policies and procedures. Social workers cannot excuse themselves from their ethical obligations by saying that they were simply following policies or orders from the agency.[18] Accordingly, Simon should not simply tell clients, "I am only providing single-session counseling because I have to follow agency policy." Simon does not believe single-session counseling is effective, so he should consider other options: for instance, referring clients to more effective services at other agencies, fund-raising so the agency can afford more effective services, or advocating for policy changes that permit other forms of counseling when indicated by client needs. In some situations, social workers need to place their jobs on the line in order to fulfill their ethical obligations. As a last resort, Simon considers resigning from EEDS rather than providing ineffective services.
- "Social workers should act to prevent and eliminate discrimination in the employing organization's work assignments and in its employment policies and practices" (S.3.09[e]). The EEDS fact situation does not raise concerns about discrimination. However, if EEDS' threat to fire Simon was based on discrimination, this standard would guide Simon to take a stand and challenge the discriminatory practices. Further, he should challenge any discriminatory practices within the agency, not just ones directed toward himself.
- "Social workers should accept employment or arrange student field placements only in organizations that exercise fair personnel practices" (S.3.09[f]). Simon is concerned

[18] As the introduction to Part I suggests, not all laws or policies are ethical. In the famous Nuremberg trials, various Nazis accused of war crimes suggested that they were not legally responsible because they were only following orders. The Nuremberg court found following orders is not a valid excuse, particularly for heinous war crimes such as genocide. Laws, policies, and orders from superiors should not be followed if they are unethical, particularly when the consequences of following the orders are grave (Lambek, 1987; Minow, 2007).

that EEDS' personnel practices are oppressive. His voice has been muzzled under threat of being fired. Given the unfair practices of the agency, this standard would suggest that he should not arrange field placements there.

- "Social workers should be diligent stewards of the resources of their employing organizations, wisely conserving funds where appropriate and never misappropriating funds or using them for unintended purposes" (S.3.09[g]). Simon believes that providing one session of family counseling is futile. The agency's resources could be put to better use. Rather than offering single-session family counseling, he might suggest referring families to services at other agencies, and using EEDS' resources to provide better individual counseling.

Social workers should be aware that agency policies and agency practices may differ. Sometimes, agencies exhibit double morality, preaching one way of doing things but doing another (Prilleltensky et al., 2002; Reamer, 2001a). In some cases, the policies may be ethical, but the practices not (e.g., an agency that says it supports equality, but discriminates on the basis of race). In other cases, the policies may be unethical, but the practices are ethical (e.g., agency policy seems to impose particular interventions on clients, but in practice, social workers engage clients in voluntary, informed consent processes). Social workers should advocate for changes, regardless of whether the ethical problems relate to policies, practices, or both.

Client Records

Social workers should maintain client records in a manner that is timely, accurate, and reflective of the services provided (S.304[a] & [b]). Proper maintenance of records facilitates delivery of services, as documentation permits workers to keep track of their work, follow up on commitments, and share information with other services providers within the agency, as necessary. Sloppy, inadequate, and tardy documentation are common factors in malpractice lawsuits and professional disciplinary hearings (Reamer, 2003). Supervisors, disciplinary boards, and judges may associate poor record keeping with poor practice. On the other hand, social workers can use clear and accurate records to defend against allegations of malpractice (Barsky & Gould, 2002). As some malpractice attorneys joke, "If it isn't in writing, it didn't happen" (Myers, 2002, p.1007). The courts will consider the worker's oral testimony, of course, but written evidence tends to be given greater credibility.

Various agencies have different requirements for documentation, depending on client needs and legal regulations. Some agencies require social workers to provide very detailed notes of all client contacts. Child protection workers, for instance, take copious notes of their interactions with families, knowing that their records may be used in future court proceedings (Kanani, Regehr, & Bernstein, 2002; Myers, 2002). Other agencies have minimal requirements for documenting services. In an agency that serves street youth, for instance, outreach workers may take minimal notes because they have only brief encounters with clients. Outreach workers offer help, but typically do not gather in-depth assessment information because their main focus is connecting with youth who are already distrustful of social services. Thus, when considering the type of information and level of detail to include in client records, social workers should consider the agency's regulations and the nature of the work.

To respect client privacy, social workers should limit documentation of information to that which is directly relevant to the services provided (S.3.04[c]). Consider a social worker whose job is to screen clients for social assistance eligibility. Eligibility is based on income, job status, marital status, disabilities, and number of dependents. The worker should document this information. The client may tell the worker how smart his daughter is, how hard he had to work to find his last job, and how nosy his neighbors can be. None of this information is relevant to the services provided, so the worker should not include it in her client notes.

Different agencies have different policies regarding how long to store client records.[19] Social workers should encourage their agencies to set their record storage practices to meet the particular needs of their workers and clients. Workers may need to refer back to records if clients return for follow-up services, if clients request copies to be sent to other service providers, and if records are needed as evidence in court cases, disciplinary hearings, or other legal processes (e.g., grievances against the worker, civil law suits, or criminal trials). Agencies often set the length of time for record storage according to requirements established by state statutes or relevant contracts (S.3.04[d]). Social workers may also consider the likelihood that clients will return for services over a certain period of time. A "statute of limitations" is legislation that restricts people from initiating civil lawsuits to a particular period of time, generally within 2 to 6 years of when the incident causing damages took place. Social workers need to consider laws related to their own areas of practice to determine what limitation periods apply to their work. Limitation periods may be extended to protect vulnerable populations; for instance, children who have been abused may be able to initiate lawsuits as adults even though the usual limitation period has expired. Thus, agencies that document child abuse may want to keep records longer than the usual 2 to 6 years used by most agencies.

Billing

Social workers should also keep accurate records of their services so they can substantiate their billing, for instance, the number of contact hours with clients or collaterals, the nature of services provided, and the hourly rate used for charges. In some cases, social workers bill clients directly. In other cases, they bill insurance companies, health maintenance organizations, governmental departments, or other contractors. Regardless of who pays for services, workers should ensure that the agency maintains transparent, accurate records (S.3.05).

Administration

When social workers act as administrators, they assume responsibility for functions such as fundraising, hiring, firing, purchasing, and allocation of resources. As administrators, they incur ethical obligations regarding the management of agency resources (S.3.07). In particular, social work administrators should advocate and work for

- Adequate resources[20] to meet client needs.
- Resources allocation procedures that are fair and open (e.g., nondiscriminatory and based on transparent, consistently applied principles).
- Adequate resources for appropriate supervision of staff.
- A work environment that is consistent with the NASW Code of Ethics.

Many social agencies operate under tight budgets. Administrators are often faced with difficult decisions about how to allocate limited resources. Faced with a budget cut, for instance, should an administrator reduce the number of frontline workers or supervisors? Fewer frontline workers may hurt service provision, as clients may be put on waitlists or denied services altogether. Fewer supervisors may hurt the quality of services, as frontline works may not have adequate supervision. Rather than simply accept budget cuts that harm services, administrators should advocate for additional resources. When they have to make difficult decisions, such as where to reduce staffing, they should do so in a fair and transparent manner.[21]

---

[19] Client records include progress notes, psychosocial assessments, audio or video recordings of client sessions, client contact logs, bills, and any other documentation of services provided to clients. Agencies storing records on computers or other digital formats should ensure proper safeguards to protect client confidentiality.

[20] Remember that in some respects, codes of ethics set minimum standards. Social workers can strive for even higher standards. Rather than advocating for "adequate resources," for instance, administrators could advocate for "first-rate resources" for clients.

[21] Chapter 10 offers more detailed analysis of the ethical issues pertaining to resource allocation.

The obligation to promote a work environment that is consistent with the NASW Code of Ethics is very broad and potentially very challenging. This obligation encompasses everything from ensuring that staff members respect client rights to confidentiality and informed consent, to challenging inequities and social justice, to avoiding conflicts of interest, and maintaining appropriate billing and record keeping practices. In some situations, social work administrators have the power to ensure such compliance. In other situations, administrators have little control (e.g., when an agency's board of directors passes a policy that discriminates against a certain class of clients). A social work administrator's responsibilities under Standard 3.07 are to "take reasonable steps" to eliminate conditions that violate or discourage compliance with the Code. The Code recognizes that social workers may face violations that are beyond their control. The notion of what is reasonable for an administrator to do depends on the circumstances. Options for confronting ethical issues in the work environment include

- Speaking privately with decision makers to make changes.
- Identifying and working with people within the agency who support the changes.
- Identifying and working with people outside the agency who support the changes.
- Making use of appropriate dispute resolution processes to promote change (e.g., negotiations, mediation, legislative advocacy, public investigations, or court challenges). (Barsky, 2007a; Kirst-Ashman & Hull, 2006a).

Labor-Management Disputes

Standard 3.10(a) permits social workers to "engage in organized action, including formation and participation in labor unions, to improve services to clients and working conditions." Note that this section does not require or suggest participation in unions; it only allows participation. Different social workers may hold different views on union participation, job actions, or labor strikes. Consider the following situation:

> A Speed of Their Own (ASTO) is an agency that provides social support services for schoolchildren with developmental delays. The workers have not had a pay raise in 5 years. Many are considering leaving the agency because they cannot support themselves under the existing pay scales. Some workers support a strike, arguing that they are not just advocating for themselves, they are advocating for a work environment that offers better services for clients. Others argue that a strike would go against their ethical commitment to serve clients.

The NASW Code does not specifically advise workers about how to resolve such a conflict. Standard 3.10(b) provides general guidance, saying workers should consider their values, ethical principles, ethical standards, and the impact of a strike on their clients. Thus, social workers should consider values such as service, social justice, and dignity and worth of the person. They should consider ethical principles such as beneficence, nonmaleficence (do no harm), and social justice. And they should also consider ethical standards such as 1.01 (commitment to clients), 3.09 (commitment to employers), and 6.04 (social and political action). This combination of values, principles, and standards can be argued in different ways, for different results. A social worker's decision may depend on specific circumstances. ASTO provides services for children with developmental delays. Although a strike could hurt their progress at school, the risk is not like a life or death situation that might arise if a suicide-prevention center were considering a strike. For now, be aware of the different types of values, principles, and standards that need to be considered. If you are faced with having to decide whether or not to support a strike, consult with your professors and field instructor.[22] Part II of this text offers a framework for making

[22] Three weeks into my first field placement, I received a call from my agency's secretary informing me that employees were initiating a strike and I should not cross the picket lines. As a student, I was not a union member. I did not like being threatened by the secretary, but I did not know how to balance my ethical duties to my clients, my agency, and my school. When I consulted my faculty field advisor, she informed me that school

difficult decisions when there are conflicting values, principles, and standards.

WHISTLE-BLOWING

Of all the ethical obligations described in this chapter, one of the most difficult challenges is how individual social workers should respond when they have serious ethical concerns about certain agency practices and the people in power support the status quo. *Whistle-blowing refers to any action by an employee or former employee that brings attention to illegal activities, misconduct, or serious problems within the organization* (e.g., mistreating clients, financial corruption, exploitation of staff, or mismanagement of resources) (Polowy, Williams, Pelas, & Pryor, 2005). Genuine whistle-blowers are motivated by the hope that notifying people with power will result in holding wrongdoers accountable and prevent harm to others (Greene & Latting, 2004; Mansbach & Bachner, 2008). Within many organizational cultures, whistle-blowing is frowned upon as traitorous "tattle-telling," as whistle-blowers are often portrayed as betraying friends and colleagues. Ethical standards for social workers suggest whistle-blowing is not only permissible, but desirable when an agency's practices are unethical or unlawful (Ss.2.11 and 3.09).[23] Too often, social workers and other professionals have turned a blind eye to serious concerns (including the abuse of children and elders) for fear of hurting the organization, their friendships, or their jobs. In some cases, social workers have been complicit in covering up unethical and unlawful practices (Greene & Latting, 2004).

Green and Latting (2004) suggest that social workers consider the following steps when confronted with a situation that may require whistle-blowing:

1. *Assess the situation, including your readiness to go forward.* Not every possible ethical violation requires whistle-blowing. Before acting on a potential violation, assess the severity of the possible violation, the degree of harm it poses, and the reliability of evidence that you are depending on. If the violation or damages are not severe, try to resolve the issues through inside channels, but avoid the riskier act of whistle-blowing. As the cliché goes, "Choose your battles wisely." Ensure that you have sufficient evidence before making accusations that could harm others. Also, examine your own motivations to ensure that you are acting out of genuine concern rather than anger, revenge, mistrust, or bias. Weigh the benefits of pursuing the cause versus the risks to yourself (e.g., alienation, harassment, or job loss), your clients (e.g., embarrassment, loss of services), and your agency (e.g., loss of face, funding, clients, or licensure).
2. *Begin first with the alleged offenders.* If you decide to pursue the concerns, discuss them first with the alleged offenders (S.2.11[c]). This puts them on notice and allows you to assess whether the problems can be worked out amicably, without resorting to more formal, costly, or adversarial actions (Barsky, 2007a).
3. *Establish a track record of credibility.* Develop credibility over time by practicing in a manner that demonstrates honesty, integrity, and professionalism. New workers and workers with spotty professional records may have a harder time convincing others that they are honest and properly motivated when they make allegations of impropriety against others. Make sure you have a positive track record before making claims against others (e.g., wait until

policy required me to refrain from going to work during a strike. The policy seemed to be aimed at protecting students from harm (physical harm, but also, social harm, as I could have been alienated by coworkers if I crossed the line). This decision put my education at risk, because I needed a certain number of field hours to complete my degree. Ultimately, the strike was over within a week and I was able to make up my field hours. The most difficult task was dealing with clients who felt betrayed by those who supported the strike.

[23] Some social workers believe the NASW Code of Ethics should address whistle-blowing more specifically (Van Wormer, 2004). Although the NASW Code has general provisions about promoting social justice, integrity, and compliance with professional ethics, the Code could also provide workers with more explicit guidance on what types of concerns social workers should act upon and how they can raise controversial issues in an ethical, effective manner.

after you receive a positive performance evaluation before taking steps that may disturb your supervisors).

4. *Develop allies within the organization.* If you assume everyone else is unaware or uncaring, these people will act as adversaries. Explore who might be supportive of your cause and try to work together. Try to gather allies discreetly. Validate concerns of potential but wary allies. Empathize with their discomfort about becoming a whistle-blower or advocating for a cause when there is a possibility of retribution.

5. *Gather corroborating evidence.* If you make an allegation and the only evidence is "the allegator's word"[24] versus the "alleged perpetrator's word," you will have difficulty proving the alleged perpetrator did something wrong. You can strengthen your case by gathering corroborating evidence, such as eye witnesses, documents, photographs, and other recordings of events (Barsky & Gould, 2002). Keep careful records (including a chronology of events) in case a grievance or court hearing is initiated against you as retribution for whistle-blowing.

6. *Follow the agency's policies and procedures for expressing complaints.* Unless the situation is dire and urgent, you should initially follow the agency's usual protocols for raising concerns. Generally, this means proceeding up the chain of command or organizational hierarchy (e.g., speak to the worker, then the supervisor, then the program director, then the board of directors, then the governmental body responsible for the agency, if any). Following agency procedures demonstrates professionalism.

7. *Consult for support and expertise.* Given the emotional, social, legal, and financial risks involved with whistle-blowing, consider consulting with others who can help with each of these risks—for instance, the NASW state or national ethics committees, state regulatory bodies, knowledgeable colleagues, or legal counsel. Different consultants may offer you different types of information and advice.[25] Some may also offer you a place to vent anger, grief, despair, and other emotions. Do not consult with family members, friends, or your own therapist if doing so would require a breach of client confidentiality. In some cases, the agency violations do not involve confidential client information, so accessing help from family, friends, and therapists may be appropriate. You are permitted to consult with attorneys, professional ethics committees, and state regulatory bodies even if the issues involve confidential client information. Limit your disclosures of client information to what is necessary, so as to respect client confidentiality as much as possible. The Government Accountability Project is a nonprofit group that offers information and support for whistle blowers (see http://www.whistleblower.org). IF YOU ARE CONCERNED ABOUT SERIOUS ETHICAL OR LEGAL VIOLATIONS WITHIN YOUR AGENCY BUT YOU ARE AFRAID TO ACT, CONSULT WITH OTHERS. Some of the most important social changes have occurred because someone took a risk. Still, you want to determine what risks to take based on the best information and advice available.

8. *Consider going outside your agency only as a last resort.* Before making a decision to voice your concern with the media, the government, the court, or some other forum outside your agency, make sure you have considered every other alternative. Once you go outside the organization, you must be prepared for the consequences, including the likelihood that you will have to leave the agency and find another job. Make use of your supporters and consultants to minimize risks and maximize your chances of successful resolution of the conflict. Make use of what you are learning about advocacy in your

---

[24] "Allegator" is not a real word, but rather an insulting name that alleged perpetrators give to the people who make allegations against them.

[25] E.g., attorneys can advise you on whether state or federal legislation provides whistle-blower protection, permitting greater freedom to report wrongdoing without fearing firing, harassment, or other forms of retaliation by the employer (e.g., the Whistleblower Protection Act, 1989; Whitaker, 2007). Some legislation also provides rewards for people who blow the whistle on abuses within government agencies.

social work courses, including those on policy development, community organization, and social change (Kirst-Ashman & Hull, 2006a).

Ideally, social workers practice in work environments that support the same values and ethical principles as the social work profession. In practice, social agencies may experience many of the same social problems that exist in general society (e.g., corruption, discrimination, and abuse of power). Thus, social workers should be prepared to manage ethical problems both within and outside their organizational contexts.

DISCUSSION QUESTIONS AND EXERCISES

The following questions and exercises are designed to provide you with practice applying standards from the NASW Code of Ethics to situations involving client-organizations, supervisor–supervisee relationships, educator–student relationships, and social worker–employer relationships. Applying ethical standards requires the use of four skills: identifying standards that are relevant to the practice situation, interpreting relevant standards for the context in which they are being applied, recognizing how certain behaviors breach specific standards, and identifying ethical obligations arising out of particular practice situations. The final exercise (whistleblowing) provides you with an opportunity to explore how you might respond in a situation when you know the right thing to do, but there may be physical, psychological, social, and spiritual risks that may dissuade you from doing the right thing.

1. *Identifying and Interpreting Standards for Client-Organizations:* Indigo Charitable Foundation has been having problems with fund-raising and staff morale. The media have raised allegations that Indigo has misused its funds to throw lavish parties rather than focus on its primary mission, to support aging musicians who are homeless and destitute. Indigo advertises a contract position for a social worker who can assist with organizational development and fund-raising. Shawndria wants to apply for this contract but wonders how Standards 1.01 to 1.16 of the NASW Code of Ethics might be interpreted if she were to work for Indigo. She seeks your counsel on the following questions:
   a. Shawndria is a big fan of country music, but dislikes pop, jazz, and hip-hop. Does she need to disclose this information, and would she be barred from acting for Indigo because she has a bias or conflict of interest?
   b. Shawndria knows that some of the major donors for Indigo dislike the current board of directors and executive director. When working for Indigo as her client, how should Shawndria determine whom she should engage to fulfill her obligations regarding informed consent?
   c. Shawndria has had sexual relations with a former board member of Indigo and her son is currently dating a successful hip-hop star. Which NASW standards should she consider, and how would they apply in her situation?
   d. If Shawndria discovered any illegalities in the management of Indigo's financial affairs, would she be bound by confidentiality to keep this information to herself?
2. *Breaches with Colleagues:* For each of the following conflicts between social work colleagues, identify the standard of the NASW Code of Ethics that has been violated and explain how the worker's actions amount to a violation.
   a. Sammi asks a client (Caitlyn) for consent to request her medical records from her primary care physician. Caitlyn agrees. When Sammi receives the records she makes a copy for Caitlyn's psychologist, who is also interested in her medical history.
   b. During a case conference, Stacia and Harold are arguing over whether to terminate work with a client who cannot

afford to pay. Stacia calls Harold a stupid toad for wanting to turn this client onto the street without any help.

c. Clint is going through a nasty divorce. He complains to his social worker, Shayla, that his divorce attorney is charging $750 per hour and doesn't have the courtesy to return his phone calls. Shayla tells Clint that his attorney's fees are outrageous and that he should report the attorney to the local bar association.

d. Silas conducts a child abuse screening interview with Charles, a 12-year-old living in foster care. Charles reports that his last social worker, Simone, did not know how to help children. He says that he sat silently in her office for 1 or 2 hours at a time, as she would just wait for him to speak. Silas calls Simone to discuss Charles's concerns. Simone tells him to mind his own business and refuses to talk with him. Silas calls Simone's licensing board to report her for incompetence.

e. Sybil provides home support services for elderly clients living in a small town. One of her clients requires exercises she can do in bed so that she can prevent bedsores. There is only one physical therapist within 200 miles, and Sybil does not like her. Sybil buys a book on exercise for elders and teaches her client how to perform these exercises.

f. Samira helps Cassidy with self-esteem issues. Cassidy stutters, so Samira googles "stuttering help" and gives Cassidy the name of a local speech-language pathologist that she finds on the Internet. She provides Cassidy with a letter of introduction that she can take to her first meeting. The speech-language pathologist sends Samira two movie tickets as thanks for the referral.

3. *Obligations to Supervisees:* For each of the following scenarios, identify which standard of the NASW Code of Ethics applies and describe how the social work supervisor should respond given the ethical obligation(s) stated in this standard.

a. Sheldon has just been promoted to supervisor at a family counseling agency. He wants to meet with all of the supervisees to discuss their goals and objectives. When a supervisee asks how her performance will be evaluated, Sheldon discovers that the agency policies do not provide any guidance on this matter.

b. Having worked in the agency for 12 years, Sheldon is good friends with many of the frontline social workers that he is now responsible for supervising. In the past, they have had supper at each other's homes, they have gone to movies and theater together, and they have given each other hugs upon greeting or parting. Sheldon wonders whether and how he should change his interactions with his supervisees.

c. Sheldon is working with a supervisee, Eugene, who seems to be falling in love with one of his clients. Sheldon is not sure how to help supervisees with this types of countertranference (strong personal feelings toward clients).

4. *Breaches With Students* For each of the following cases, identify the standard of the NASW Code of Ethics that has been violated and explain how the actions of the educator or field instructor amount to a violation:

a. Santos is a field instructor at a group home for adults with severe cognitive impairment. A friend asks if he can accept his daughter, Denise, as a field student, because he knows Santos will provide an excellent learning experience. Santos agrees.

b. Professor Stumps teaches ethics. A student asks whether or not a social worker can be convicted of treason if she does not warn the authorities that a client has threatened violence toward the president. Professor Stumps does not know the answer, but pretends he does so he will not look foolish.

c. Ronnie is a BSW student who gets into a car accident while driving a client home. The agency does not permit workers to drive clients, but Ronnie did not know this. Ronnie's field instructor, Suzette, writes the following note in her midterm evaluation: "Student completely lacks common sense and has no business practicing social work, ever."

5. *Obligations to Social Worker-Employers:* Identify the relevant ethical standards for each of the following scenarios and describe the worker's obligations to the employer:
   a. Samica works in a prison, where one of her clients complains that inmates have absolutely no privacy. They even have guards watching them when they shower or use the toilets. Samica believes these practices go beyond what is required for safety. Under the NASW Code of Ethics, all people should have a right to be treated with dignity and respect.
   b. Sally facilitates support groups for people trying to quit smoking. One day, she wins a photo contest. Her prize is a once-in-a-lifetime Caribbean cruise. She asks her supervisor for time off to enable her to go on the cruise. The supervisor denies her request because she has used all her vacation time. Sally thinks the agency policy is unfair.
   c. Sean works as a family support worker for the air force. His superiors order him to disclose whether any of his clients have told him that they are gay or lesbian. Sean believes that this order breaches client confidentiality and could be used to discriminate against his clients. Still, in the military, an order is an order (Minow, 2007).[26]
6. *Whistle-Blowing:* Assume you are working for a large psychiatric health facility. You notice that several clients seem to have more severe psychiatric diagnoses than their situations would indicate. Upon further investigation, you discover what seems to be a fraudulent scheme by the hospital to bilk health reimbursement dollars from Medicaid and private health insurance companies. When you approach your supervisor for guidance on how to handle this situation, she says, "If you want to keep your job here, it's better to pretend you haven't seen anything or heard anything. Besides, we're helping patients receive the services they need, which is our primary ethical commitment." To analyze how you might respond in this case, develop two lists—one that describes factors that might lead you to blow the whistle, and another that describes factors that might lead you to remain silent. Your analysis should include consideration of ethical factors (e.g., your obligations under the NASW Code) and personal factors (e.g., physical, psychological, social, and spiritual risks and benefits). Of all the factors you have considered, which ones do you think would raise the greatest challenges for you?[27]

---

[26] For the statute that enacts the military's "don't ask, don't tell" policy, see http://www.law.cornell.edu/uscode/html/uscode10/usc_sec_10_00000654——000-.html.

[27] For further discussion of ethical courage (the strength to do what is morally correct in the face of various challenges), see the introduction to Part II. For more detailed explorations of ethical decision making in mental health settings, see Chapter 13.

Chapter 9

Practice, Values, and Ethics—Social Work with Communities

One of the primary factors distinguishing social work from psychology, psychiatry, and the other mental health professions is its commitment to social justice. Although *some* social psychologists and other mental health professionals work with communities to promote social justice, the NASW Code of Ethics (1999) indicates that *all* social workers should participate in such work (Ss.6.01 to 6.04). In other words, the Code suggests that social workers should not work solely with individuals or families; they have an ethical obligation to ameliorate problems in the social environment such as oppression and discrimination (Miley & DuBois, 2007). This chapter begins with an exploration of values and ethics as they apply to work with communities, particularly in the context of advancing social justice. The following sections explore ethical responsibilities that cut across all areas of practice: social workers' responsibilities to the profession and their responsibilities as professionals. Finally, this chapter delves into the ways in which social workers may be held accountable by the individuals, families, groups, organizations, and communities they serve.

As you work through this chapter, note the difference between minimum and aspirational ethical standards. Minimum standards[1] refer to the most basic ethical expectations or obligations of social workers. In other words, what types of professional conduct should clients, agencies, and society be able to expect of social workers—at the very least? Aspirational (or maximal) standards refer to the highest ideals of professional practice that social workers should pursue (Gert, 2006). Minimum ethical standards are sometimes called

[1] Some authors refer to minimum standards as "mandatory ethics," suggesting that social workers are required to follow these rules. The NASW Code of Ethics, however, expresses most of its standards in terms of "should" rather than "must," suggesting that these standards are not mandatory, even though they are offered as general expectations of social workers.

the floor, the level of practice beneath which social workers should not fall. Aspirational ethics are sometimes called the ceiling, the level to which social workers should reach, even though the ceiling may always rise above their reach (Kirkland & Kirkland, 2006). Aspirational ethics do not dictate what types of behaviors are required, but rather what types of behaviors are broadly praised for their goodness (Beauchamp & Childress, 2009). Social workers should pay heed to both types of standards. In terms of minimum standards, for instance, social workers should practice in a manner that demonstrates basic competence (NASW, 1999, S.1.04), they should respect client confidentiality (S.1.07), and they should ask clients for consent rather than imposing interventions on clients (S.1.03). In terms of aspirational ethics, social workers should strive for practice excellence (rather than mere competence), they should strive to enhance client confidentiality (rather than merely respect it), and they should broaden clients' choices (rather than simply asking clients for consent to a single intervention). In terms of accountability, social workers may be held responsible for falling below the floor or minimum standards. For instance, they may become subject to discipline from their agencies, they may be sued by an injured client for malpractice, or they may be held to account by their professional association or regulatory body (e.g., the NASW or their state licensing board). Although social workers are expected to strive for the ceiling, there are typically no penalties or disciplinary actions for failing to reach the ceiling (Gert, 2006). Social workers may be motivated to avoid discipline for falling beneath the floor. Ideally, they should be motivated to aspire much higher, based on deeply held values rather than fear of punishment. From a practical perspective, social workers are less likely to be exposed to malpractice lawsuits and professional disciplinary complaints if they strive toward aspirational standards, rather than settling for mere observance of minimal standards (Kirkland & Kirkland, 2006).

ETHICAL RESPONSIBILITIES TO THE BROADER SOCIETY

The NASW Code breaks down social workers' responsibilities to broader society into four areas: social welfare, public participation, public emergencies, and social and political action. To illustrate the differences between these responsibilities, consider the following vignette.

> **LEARNING OBJECTIVES**
>
> Upon successful completion of this chapter, students will be able to
>
> - Appreciate their ethical responsibilities to broader society in terms of social welfare, public participation, public emergencies, and social and political action.
> - Describe their ethical responsibilities in relation to other social workers and the profession of social work.
> - Interpret ethical standards according to both the "letter" and "spirit" of the provision.
> - Compare and contrast different systems of professional accountability, including criminal law, civil (tort) law, licensing, certification, registration, professional associations, contract law, community norms, and personal conscience.

Serena provides social work services to individuals and families affected by post-traumatic stress disorder (PTSD). Most of her clients are soldiers returning from active duty. She is very concerned about the recent increase in the number of soldiers with PTSD (U.S. Army, 2007). Her job focuses on intervention, not prevention.

Social Welfare

Standard 6.01 defines social workers' responsibility to promote the general welfare of society, from local to global levels. This standard indicates that social workers should promote the development of people, their communities, and environments. In other words, workers should incorporate the ecological perspective into their practice. Although the primary focal points of Serena's practice are individuals and families, she should consider the broader contexts of her clients. For instance, how well does the community accommodate the special needs of people with PTSD? Are they supported and respected, or alienated and oppressed? What could be done to offer stronger support for people with PTSD and their families? When Serena assesses the broader context, she identifies a number of needs. At a local level, many community members do not understand PTSD and tend to disassociate with families affected by it. At an organizational level, the army could do more to prepare soldiers and their families for traumatic experiences in hopes of preventing PTSD. At a global level, violent conflicts have been increasing and more effective peace building approaches are needed.

You may be familiar with the Friends of the Earth motto, "Think globally, act locally." Thinking globally reminds us that we must think about our environment from a worldwide perspective. What happens in one part of our planet affects other parts of our planet. Acting locally reminds us that we may not be able to solve all the world's problems, but we can make significant impact if each of us takes care of our own back yard. For social workers, the motto could be, "Think and act globally and locally." Yes, social workers should support causes in their own localities. At the same time, social workers can also have an impact globally by working in the international sphere, for instance, with nongovernmental organizations (e.g., Oxfam; Doctors Without Borders, Red Cross) and government-operated civil society organizations in other countries. Obviously, no single social worker could be expected to educate and change the attitudes of an entire community, revolutionize the practices of a large bureaucratic organization, and bring about world peace. At the same time, every single social worker should participate in at least one type of activity that promotes social justice. If you are not part of the solution, you are part of the problem (Oxford Dictionary of Proverbs, 2004).

From a practical perspective, you might be wondering, "How am I supposed to decide which social justice issues to pursue when I have limited time and when my employer is not necessarily paying me to do this work?" The Code does not prescribe which social justice issues to prioritize or how much time and effort to put into each. You may use the following factors to help make your decisions:

- What are my special skills and expertise, and how could these be put to use in the best way to promote social justice?
- Which social causes and which types of advocacy excite me in a way that will act as a source of motivation, even on days when pursuit of a particular cause seems overwhelming?
- Am I looking to effect change in the short-term (days or months) or the long-term (years or generations)?
- What types of social justice efforts complement my other work, helping my clients or my social agency?

Serena acknowledges that her social welfare skills and interests lie in prevention. Although her job description does not include prevention, she decides to volunteer time to work with the army to develop an evidence-based PTSD-prevention program. She hopes that if she can show that this program is working, her agency will pay her (or other workers) to offer this program on an ongoing basis. In the long term, she hopes her program may serve as model for prevention for other agencies, locally and abroad.

The obligation to promote social welfare is an aspirational one. The achievement of full equality, social justice, and empowerment are dreams or ideals. Although social workers may make practical choices about which social welfare causes to pursue at a particular moment in time, they should also aspire and work toward what could be.

Public Participation

Standard 6.02 advises social workers to "facilitate informed participation by the public in shaping social policies and institutions." Whereas Standard 6.01 encourages social workers to *advocate on behalf of the public,* this standard encourages social workers to empower members of the public to *advocate on their own behalf.* A key challenge to implementing this charge is how to facilitate public participation in public policy processes without going against the interests of a particular client. Standard 1.01, for instance, states that social workers' primary commitments are to their clients. Suppose Serena provided a client with information on upcoming congressional hearings about the impact of war on soldiers. Although providing such information satisfies Standard 6.02, it may not be in the client's best interests to participate in the hearings. The client has PTSD. Having to recount events from the war in a public forum could actually exacerbate his problems. Thus, when Serena is considering whether to empower particular clients to participate in certain social policy processes, she should consider whether such involvement is in the client's interests, not just societal interests (Hinterlong & Williamson, 2006).

When social workers encourage clients to participate in social policy processes, they must take care to avoid imposing their values and beliefs on clients (Ss.1.02 and 1.03). Social workers can empower clients to participate in democratic processes, for instance, by helping register clients to vote and by ensuring that they have proper access to vote on election day. When social workers are acting in their professional capacities, however, they should not promote a specific political party. In other words, it would be unethical to register only Republicans, or only Democrats, or only members of any single party. A social worker acting privately (not during work hours) may become a member of a particular party and advocate for that party. Consider, however, potential conflicts that may arise when clients know a worker is a staunch supporter of a certain party. Serena knows that discussing politics is a sensitive issue for members of the armed forces. If she came out strongly for the peace movement or strongly for a party that opposed a particular war, she might distance herself from certain military clients. Given this risk, Serena decides not to become publicly involved in politics, even on her own time (Pipes, Holstein, & Aguire, 2005). She also decides that, given the culture and policies of the army, she will not try to foster public participation in elections or other social policy processes. She chooses to focus her efforts on preventive work in collaboration with the military infrastructure.[2] Although Standard 6.02 encourages workers to support public participation in social policy processes, this type of activity may not be appropriate for workers in certain fields of practice.

Public Emergencies

Standard 6.03 encourages social workers to provide professional services in response to public emergencies. Such services may include community organization, counseling, support, advocacy, and linkage to services. To be able to implement this standard effectively, social workers should anticipate and plan for potential emergencies. Serena has special expertise in working with trauma survivors. Her services could be in high demand after a range of traumatic events, so she identifies agencies in her community that could use her help. Consider your own community. Which of the following catastrophic events pose the greatest risks—earthquake, hurricane, tornado, flooding, forest fire, terrorist attack, communicable disease epidemic, or interethnic riots? How could you assist in the event of such emergencies? Also, consider your primary client populations and how you could assist them in times of emergency. National, state, and local organizations should already have plans for how to respond (e.g., national Homeland Security and local police; see http://www.fema.gov). You and your agencies could work with these organizations to determine how to collaborate. After Hurricane Katrina hit New Orleans in 2005, many professionals who offered their services were initially turned away because there was no properly organized response system in place. Although some types of professional support may be offered on a last-minute basis, many types of support require advance planning. The Red Cross (n.d.), for instance, offers training for professionals to participate in emergency rescue and response. In order to be available to serve in

[2] In the case as presented, Serena focuses on doing good work within the military. If Serena believed that the essential purposes or mandates of the military went against her core values and beliefs, she might decide to leave her position with the military rather than work within it. For instance, Serena may question working for the military because it trains people to kill and to follow orders even when they may question the ethicality of the orders (Minow, 2007).

an emergency, you may also need an emergency plan for your own family. For instance, who will take care of your children while you are doing emergency work? One of the greatest challenges to responding to emergencies is not *having the motivation to help*, but rather *being prepared to provide timely and appropriate help* when emergencies arise (Trotter, 2007).

Social and Political Action

Standard 6.04 essentially provides greater detail concerning Standard 6.01's obligation to promote social welfare. Promoting social welfare includes

- Ensuring that all people have equal access to the resources, employment, services, and opportunities they require to meet their basic needs and develop fully (S.6.04[a]).
- Expanding the choice and opportunity for all people, with particular regard to vulnerable and disadvantaged groups (S.6.04[b]).
- Promoting policies, practices, programs, and knowledge-building that respect cultural and social diversity (S.6.04[c]).
- Taking actions necessary to prevent and eliminate domination or discrimination against any person, group, or class on the basis of race, ethnicity, national origin, color, sex, sexual orientation, age, marital status, political belief, religion, or mental or physical disability (S.6.04[d]).

As noted earlier, social workers may promote social welfare in various ways. The NASW Code does not prescribe specifically what each social worker should do. Serena notes a number of social justice concerns among the population she serves. Gay and lesbian clients, for instance, feel oppressed by the military's "don't ask, don't tell" policy which prevents them from being open and honest about their sexuality. Clients with physical and mental disabilities often face discrimination when looking for new employment. Clients from minority ethnocultural groups report lack of culturally competent health service providers. Serena does not have the time or resources to solve all these concerns, so she should use her professional discretion to decide which social welfare issues to promote. Ethically, there is no right or wrong answer about which specific social causes to pursue. The bottom line is that every social worker should be doing *something* to promote social welfare.

SOCIAL WORKERS' ETHICAL RESPONSIBILITIES TO THE SOCIAL WORK PROFESSION

Social workers bear a myriad of ethical responsibilities—first and foremost to their clients (S.1.01), but also to their colleagues, supervisees, students, employing organizations, and communities (as described in Chapter 8 and earlier in this chapter). In this section, we explore social workers' responsibilities to the profession of social work under Standard 5.01.[3] One might ask, with all these other responsibilities, why should social workers owe an obligation to themselves? If social workers fulfill their obligations to all these other entities, what other ethical responsibilities are necessary? To some extent, Standard 5.01 reinforces social workers' obligations described elsewhere in the Code. Standard 5.01(b), for instance, advises social workers to "uphold and advance the values, ethics, knowledge, and mission of the profession." The fact that this provision is listed under the heading of "Responsibilities to the Profession" reminds social workers that any breach of social work ethics may have implications for the whole profession, not just the worker, client, or other people who are directly affected. The social work profession, in essence, is a community. As a community, social work has its own set of values, norms,

[3] In this chapter we focus on Standard 5.01's provisions regarding integrity of the profession. Standard 5.02, on evaluation and research, is listed in the Code under the heading of obligations to the profession. Arguably, this standard is misplaced in the Code, as many of its provisions apply to responsibilities toward research participants and partners, not responsibilities to the profession. The provisions of Standard 5.02 are explored in Chapter 4.

and expectations of one another. The manner in which each person acts can reflect, positively or negatively, on the whole community. Consider the following scenario:

> Shiloh performs custody evaluations for divorcing families. In one case, he submits an evaluation to the court stating that he based his opinions, in part, on information gathered from the children's teachers and pediatrician. The parties discover that he did not contact them.

Shiloh's dishonest evaluation report not only harms the clients; it harms other social workers. After learning of Shiloh's indiscretion, many potential clients, attorneys, and judges may question whether social workers can be trusted. In contrast, if Shiloh had acted with greater integrity, his performance would reflect positively on the profession and people would be more likely to trust social workers.

Social workers' obligations to the profession extend beyond compliance with minimum standards. Standard 5.01 promotes excellence, not just mediocre or satisfactory performance. Subsection (a), for instance, says that social workers should "work toward the maintenance and promotion of high standards of practice." This broad provision covers all areas of practice. When Shiloh conducts a custody evaluation, he should make use of the highest standards for custody evaluators (Association of Family and Conciliation Courts, 2006). He should make use of the most current and strongest research to guide his evaluation process and decision making. He should demonstrate the highest respect possible for his clients. He should ensure that he is in top physical, psychological, social, and spiritual condition so that he can offer his clients the best services possible. He should avoid any temptation to cut corners, for instance, because he is tired or has a high caseload. He may use the desire to do good (beneficence and moral courage) to motivate him to maintain high standards, even in the face of personal or professional challenges.

The fact that social work is a profession with a common set of social work values and ethics does not mean that all social workers should think alike, act alike, agree, and avoid conflict. Standard 5.01(b) specifically encourages active discussion and responsible criticism of the profession. This standard acknowledges the need for ongoing research and knowledge building. What social workers accept as best practices today may or may not be considered best practices 10 or 20 years from now. Social workers need to challenge themselves and what they think they know, helping the profession maintain an openness to advancements in knowledge and practice.

Assume that Shiloh is called to court to defend his custody evaluation. The father's attorney challenges his use of a certain instrument designed to measure the child's attachment to each parent. The attorney asks Sondra, a social worker who has a high level of evaluation expertise, to critique Shiloh's evaluation. While Sondra may critique Shiloh's use of this instrument, she should do so in a respectful and constructive manner. When Shiloh defends his use of this instrument in court, he should be apprised of the research pertaining to its validity and reliability. When Sondra testifies, she should also focus on the research, avoiding personal or demeaning attacks against Shiloh. Reasonable professionals may have reasonable disagreements about best practices. Personal attacks and insults not only hurt the targeted social worker, but also the profession as a whole.

Standard 5.01(c) encourages social workers to contribute time and professional expertise to activities that promote respect for the value, integrity, and competence of the social work profession. As with the responsibility to promote social welfare, this is a broad and open-ended ethical responsibility that can be operationalized through a variety of activities: teaching, research, consultation, service, legislative testimony, community presentations, and participation in professional organizations (e.g., the NASW or associations that pertain to particular fields of practice). As a custody evaluator, Shiloh works with a variety of other professionals, including attorneys, judges, and forensic mental health specialists. He promotes the value and integrity of social work by volunteering to work with an association of family court professionals. Shiloh educates his colleagues about the ecological perspective of social work and encourages them to consider systemic and social justice issues when establishing guidelines for custody evaluators. He also advocates for social workers to be given equal standing with psychologists and other mental health professionals when acting as expert witnesses in court (Barsky & Gould, 2002).

Standard 5.01(d) encourages social workers to contribute to the knowledge base of social work and share their knowledge with colleagues. Social workers may generate knowledge through ongoing reflection and evaluation of their practice, as well as through participation in formal research (as per Chapter 4). Social workers may share their knowledge by contributing articles to professional newsletters and journals, or by participating at professional meetings and conferences. For many social workers, the greatest challenges to complying with this standard are time and priorities. Social workers may feel they need to commit their limited time and resources to direct practice, helping clients, and performing the day-to-day essential tasks of their jobs. Ideally, social workers should view generating and sharing knowledge as essential; social workers can do more good, for more people, when they collectively generate and share practice wisdom and other forms of social work knowledge. Social workers may need to advocate within their agencies to value and support knowledge building and knowledge generating activities.

Standard 5.01(e) implores social workers to prevent unauthorized and unqualified practice of social work. Unauthorized practice refers to the performance of certain social work functions without having the required licensure or accreditation. Some social work functions do not require licensure or accreditation. For instance, state laws do not typically require any sort of professional credentials for someone to perform case management or supportive counseling services. In contrast, state laws do require licensing or accreditation for services such as psychiatric diagnoses and psychotherapy. Unqualified practice refers to the performance of certain social work functions without having the necessary skills or training to perform those functions in a competent manner. Shiloh was licensed as a clinical social worker, but he lacked training in how to perform child custody evaluations. In other words, Shiloh was authorized to practice social work, but he lacked proper qualifications to perform custody evaluations. Sondra could use a staged approach to preventing Shiloh from conducting further evaluations. First, she could speak with Shiloh directly, asking him to restrict his practice to functions for which he was qualified. She could also contact his agency supervisor and any professional associations to which he belongs (e.g., social work or evaluation associations). If his state has laws restricting who can conduct custody evaluations, Sondra may also have a duty to report Shiloh to the licensing or accrediting body (as described later in this chapter). Social workers should not only ensure that they maintain high standards of practice. They should also encourage others to do the same. When social work colleagues do not meet minimum standards, social workers have an obligation to take corrective action in a respectful, direct manner.

RESPONSIBILITIES AS PROFESSIONALS

Standards 4.01 to 4.08 fall under the heading of "Social Workers' Responsibilities as Professionals." Arguably, every standard in the NASW Code could be viewed as a responsibility as a professional. Further, several Part 4 standards overlap with provisions in other parts of the code, as they reference responsibilities to clients, colleagues, and employing organizations. In some respects, Part 4 is a catch-all portion of the Code, including ethical standards that do not fit neatly into other parts or cut across more than one component of practice. The following analysis describes Standards 4.01 to 4.08 and identifies how they relate to other standards in the Code.

Competence

Standard 4.01(a) states, "Social workers should accept responsibility or employment only on the basis of existing competence or the intention to acquire the necessary competence." This standard overlaps with Standard 1.04(a), which suggests that social workers should provide services only within their areas of competence. Standard

4.01(b), however, builds on these responsibilities by encouraging social workers to continue their professional development and knowledge building by reading relevant literature and participating in other forms of continuing education (e.g., attending conferences or trainings, engaging in web-based training, or consulting with professional colleagues). Social workers should not assume that once they achieve a certain level of competence through a BSW program, MSW program, or specialized training that their educational requirements are fulfilled for the rest of their careers. Continuing education offers workers new information, specialized knowledge and skills, and current research findings, as well as reminders of knowledge that may have lapsed from their memory. Social workers who are licensed or accredited may have specific continuing education requirements in order to maintain their licensure or accreditation (e.g., a certain number of hours of training in diversity, ethics, or domestic violence).

Standard 4.01(c) says, "Social workers should base practice on recognized knowledge, including empirically based knowledge." This means that social workers should not rely on personal intuition, superstition, or information that does not have a scientific basis. Consider the following vignette:

> Soledad facilitates a group for people with fears of public speaking. Her friend's daughter was able to overcome this problem by practicing speaking in front of a mirror while standing on one foot. She recommends this to her clients as a homework assignment.

Drawing conclusions about the effectiveness of an intervention based on a sample of one is fraught with risk. How does Soledad know whether standing on one foot actually helped her friend's daughter, and even so, whether it would help or hurt others? While asking clients to stand on one foot may seem innocuous, it may entail a number of dangers: people could fall and hurt themselves, people could be wasting their time, and people could be suffering from their fears longer than need be. If it were not for the one-leg exercise, clients might have engaged in more effective methods of overcoming their fears. Basing interventions on erroneous information also has an impact on social work as a profession. Clients and co-professionals will not take social workers seriously if they do not make use of an appropriate knowledge base to guide their practice.

Discrimination

Standard 4.02 states, "Social workers should not practice, condone, facilitate, or collaborate with any form of discrimination on the basis of race, ethnicity, national origin, color, sex, sexual orientation, age, marital status, political belief, religion, or mental or physical disability." Although this list is relatively inclusive, it leaves out a number of groups. For instance, this standard does not specifically prohibit discrimination against people who are transgender, people who are short, or people who have extremely high IQ's. Does this mean that social workers are permitted to discriminate against such people? Arguably, this is not what the authors of the NASW Code intended. Social workers should consider both the "letter" and the "spirit" of the provision. The letter of the law (or in this case, the letter of the standard) refers to the explicit message of the provision—what the words say, given a precise, literal interpretation. The spirit of the law refers to the intention or purpose of the provision. A social worker who believes transgenderism is immoral might argue that Standard 4.02 does not specifically prohibit discrimination against transgender people, so such discrimination is permitted. The spirit of this standard, however, is to prohibit discrimination against various classes of people. Thus, proponents of social justice would argue that social workers should interpret this standard according to its spirit, not according to a literal interpretation. A literalist might argue that the framers of the Code should have used more inclusive language (e.g., "discrimination against any group, including..."). Unfortunately, people who write codes of ethics, agency policies, or laws cannot anticipate every possible situation that may arise in practice. Thus, social workers should consider both the letter and the spirit of the law, policy, or ethical standard that they are trying to interpret.

One of the greatest challenges in meeting Standard 4.02 concerns how a social worker should respond when the entire system that the worker is operating within is discriminatory. Assume Shana works in an agency with policies favoring clients and workers who are legally married. Standard 4.02 prohibits practicing in a manner that facilitates discrimination on the basis of marital status. Shana decides to raise this issue with the agency's board of directors. The directors respond by saying its policies are justified because children raised in homes by single or cohabiting parents are more susceptible to child abuse, addiction, and poverty. Shana explains that, as a social worker, she cannot condone discrimination toward unmarried clients and that clients have a right to respect and self-determination, including the choice of whether to marry. If the agency continues to support policies that discriminate on the basis of marriage, what should Shana do? What would you do? Disobeying agency policy or confronting the directors more harshly may result in a social worker's being fired. Ethically, Standard 4.02 seems to suggest that you should leave the agency rather than participate in discrimination. Does the type of discrimination matter? Would you be more inclined to put your job on the line if the agency's discrimination were based on race or ethnicity?

Private Conduct

Standard 4.03 advises social workers "not to permit their private conduct to interfere with their ability to fulfill their professional responsibilities." Thus, social workers may incur professional responsibilities even when they are not working. The line between private conduct and professional conduct may be blurred in a range of circumstances. Consider "drinking alcohol." Standard 4.03 does not generally restrict social workers from drinking at home, on their own time. However, it would prohibit drinking at home if such drinking results in impaired functioning when the worker is trying to serve clients (e.g., being intoxicated or hung over).

Social workers should be aware that how they behave outside their professional capacities may affect their professional image and standing with clients and colleagues. At work, Sylvan is the model of political correctness. He demonstrates respect to all people and is careful not to offend anyone. After work, he likes to let loose. He tells friends jokes based on racial stereotypes, he says he would never date a Black woman, and he would never support a Hispanic candidate for election. Sylvan assumes his private remarks will not affect his practice, but how does he know? What if a current client overhears his racist jokes, either directly or through a friend? Further, how can Sylvan ensure that the attitudes beneath his racist comments do not affect his work? The boundary between professional and private life may not be as clear as Sylvan thinks (Pipes et al., 2005).

Some social workers believe they have the same right to self-determination as their clients, particularly on their own time and within the privacy of their own homes. When private conduct interferes with performance of professional duties, however, social workers cannot argue that this interferes with their right to self-determination. Social workers relinquish their autonomy when they agree to serve clients. Clients, not social workers, have a right to self-determination. Social workers have an ethical obligation to serve clients in a competent manner. This obligation extends to private behavior that may affect professional practice.

Dishonesty, Fraud, and Deception

Standard 4.04 provides, "Social workers should not participate in, condone, or be associated with dishonesty, fraud, or deception." Obvious violations of this standard include lying to clients about the effectiveness of an intervention, underreporting income to avoid paying taxes, and billing Medicaid or other health insurance providers for services that were not actually provided. In each of these instances, someone may be hurt by the social worker's dishonesty, fraud, or deception (e.g., a particular client, the general public, or anyone who buys insurance). But is it unethical to lie if nobody is hurt by the lie? Is it unethical to lie if the lie actually does more good than harm?

Lying refers to inviting others to trust and rely on what one says by warranting its truth, but, at the same time, betraying that trust by making false statements that one does not believe (Carson, 2006). Some people use the term "white lies" to describe false statements that, while straying from the truth, are harmless. In some cases, social workers stray from the truth with innocent or even benevolent intentions. A client with low self-esteem asks you if you like his tie. You think the tie is hideous, but want to say something positive to boost his self-esteem. Would it be unethical to say, "I think it looks wonderful! The fluorescent blue brings out the color of your eyes." The client appreciates the compliment and feels better. Nobody is hurt, perhaps...What if the client senses that you are being disingenuous? Or what if the client wears this tie to a job interview, based on your positive response, but the job interviewer questions his judgment given the garish tie he has chosen to wear.

The provisions in Standard 4.04 are not absolute.[4] As in most ethical provisions of the NASW Code, this standard says "should" rather than "must." This wording recognizes that there may be instances when it is ethical to stray from absolute truth and full disclosure. Although honesty is an important ethical principle, some social work ethicists argue that it is not as important as principles such as protection of life, equality, autonomy, least harm, quality of life, and privacy (Dolgoff et al., 2009). Accordingly, there may be situations in which social workers can justify certain infringements of honesty and full disclosure in order to advance a higher or more compelling value. The following examples illustrate situations in which some social workers might argue that compromising full honesty and disclosure is ethically justifiable.

- *Life*: A gun-wielding client who is threatening to kill your program director asks if you know where she is. You know where she is, but wanting to protect her life and de-escalate the situation, you say, "I don't know where she is."
- *Equality*: You are interviewing for a social work job and the clinical supervisor asks if you have any disabilities. You have a learning disability, but you also have good reason to believe that if you disclose this disability you will not be hired. You also believe that if you tell her the question violates antidiscrimination laws, the supervisor will surely reject your application. You decide to withhold the truth about your disability on the basis of promoting equality.
- *Autonomy*: A client wants an abortion but lives in a state that requires the biological father to be notified. The client fears that if the father is notified, he will put undue pressure on her to have the baby. You support her decision to tell the abortion clinic that she has no idea of the father's identity, believing that her autonomy (freedom from control of others) is more important than honesty and full disclosure.
- *Least Harm*: A client desperately needs eye surgery but cannot afford it. The client has no medical insurance. Her income is slightly too high for her to be eligible for Medicaid. You decide to list a lower income on her Medicaid application, believing that the misinformation is justified by the least harm principle (i.e., lying is less harmful than denying needed surgery).
- *Quality of Life*: The eye surgery example could also be argued from a quality of life perspective. Falsifying the Medicaid form enables the person to receive surgery that prevents her from becoming blind. Thus, one could argue that improving her quality of life justifies straying from honesty and full disclosure.
- *Privacy*: A client wants an anonymous HIV test but all the providers require clients to provide their names. You counsel the client to provide a fictitious name so he can receive the test and maintain his privacy.

If some or all of these justifications for dishonesty make you feel a bit queasy, that queasiness is a good sign. Different social workers may disagree on when bending or breaching the principle of full truth and disclosure is ethically justified. In part, it depends on how the worker

[4] See Chapter 5 for further discussion of absolute versus relative ethical standards.

assesses the circumstances of the case. In the *Life* example, would it be possible to counsel the homicidal client not to kill, without having to make any false statements? In the *Equality* example, would it be possible to confront the supervisor honestly about the inappropriateness of her question, without putting her on the defensive? Further, some social workers may hold honesty to be a higher principle than some of the competing ones. In the *Autonomy* example, some social workers might rank honesty higher than autonomy, believing that honestly disclosing the father's name is more important than protecting the client from the father's influence. Finally, social workers must consider the immediate and long-term risks of breaching honesty and full disclosure, even when they have benevolent motives. Social workers who make false statements may be caught and held liable. In the *Least Harm* and *Quality of Life* case, would you be willing to accept the risk of fines and losing your license to practice for participating in Medicaid fraud? In the *Privacy* case, consider the risk of becoming known in the community as a professional who encourages clients to act dishonestly. If you are ever in a situation in which you are tempted to bend the truth to promote equality, privacy, equality, or other worthy goals, make sure you consider all other options first and think through all the consequences for each potential course of action. Also, consult with supervisors, trusted colleagues, or attorneys for their expertise and to ensure that you have analyzed the situation objectively and comprehensively.

Misrepresentation

Standards 4.04 and 4.06 overlap in the sense that both deal with dishonesty and deception. Standard 4.06 deals with three specific types of representations made by social workers. First, social workers should clarify whether they are making statements as a private individual or as a representative of the social work profession, a social work organization, or the worker's employing agency (S.4.06[a]). If I were presenting my views on the ethics of stem-cell research at a professional conference, for instance, my employer (Florida Atlantic University) would not be pleased if I indicated that I was presenting the views of the university. I am entitled to present my views (under the principles of academic freedom), but I should claim them as my views. Second, social workers who speak on behalf of professional social work organizations should accurately represent the official and authorized positions of the organizations. Thus, if the National Ethics Committee of the NASW (of which I am a member) asks me to speak on its behalf about professional malpractice, I should ensure that I know the committee's policy and I convey this policy accurately. Third, social workers should report their credentials accurately (S.4.06[c]). Thus, I have a Juris Doctor (law) degree. This does not mean that I am a practicing or licensed attorney. I should not tell clients that I have a J.D. without explaining the difference between having a degree and being licensed to practice. Likewise, if my employer's website states that I am a lawyer, I should inform the employer to correct this information. I should not exaggerate my credentials or take advantage of any confusion about them. Likewise, social work students should identify themselves to clients as students (e.g., field practice students). Although some field educators encourage students to call themselves *interns*, this term could be misleading if clients equate this term to mean medical interns.[5]

Although social workers may run into problems with Standard 4.06 by making misrepresentations intentionally, social workers may also breach this standard unintentionally. Social workers should strive to represent themselves as accurately as possible, avoiding language that could be misleading or misinterpreted.

Acknowledging Credit

Like Standards 4.04 and 4.06, Standard 4.08 promotes honesty. Specifically, this standard says social workers should take responsibility and credit only for work they have actually

[5] Traditionally, medical students complete their primary medical school training before taking on an internship whereas social work students enter their field education work as part of their primary education.

performed or to which they have contributed. In addition, they should honestly acknowledge the contributions of others. Assume that you developed a community-based program designed to combat racism. If the program works well, you may be inclined to take full credit for the program. Even if you initiated or took a leadership role in developing the program, you should acknowledge the work of others. If you did not significantly contribute to the program, then you should not take credit for it. Conversely, if the program experiences problems, you should also take responsibility for your part in development of the program. In other words, be honest.

When professionals collaborate on creative works such as academic research or professional publications, they should consider how credit will be assigned for each of their contributions (Strom-Gottfried & D'Aprix, 2006). Universities and research institutions often place a high degree of significance on the order of authorship. Unless otherwise stated on a publication, many organizations assume that the first author contributed the most, with the other authors contributing in descending order of significance. To avoid conflicts over authorship, collaborators could negotiate a written or oral agreement at the outset of their project, specifying the expectations of each contributor and the order of authorship for any publications that arise out of their work.

Impairment

Standard 4.05(a) advises social workers not to allow their personal problems, psychosocial distress, legal problems, substance abuse, or mental health difficulties to interfere with their work. This standard complements Standard 1.01, which states that workers' primary obligation is toward their clients. To be able to fulfill Standard 4.05, social workers should maintain a high level of self-awareness. It may be easy for a social worker to rationalize that her financial problems are not having an impact on her work, even though she has started to become easily agitated by clients who question her fee structure. Social workers can raise self-awareness through ongoing self-reflection and participation in supervision. When social workers become aware that personal problems are affecting their professional judgment and performance they should take appropriate remedial action (S.4.05[b]). Examples of remedial action include seeking therapy, reducing their workload, and suspending or terminating practice.

Social workers experiencing personal problems affecting their work may be confronted by supervisors and professional colleagues who have a responsibility to protect clients from harm (S.2.09; cf. Chapter 8). Consider how you might react if a colleague initiated a discussion with you about how a mental health or other personal problem is affecting your work. Would you tend to react defensively, denying or minimizing problems to save face or protect your job? Would you try to listen with an open mind and demonstrate appreciation for this colleague's concern? Supervisors and close professional colleagues should not try to provide therapy, but they may be helpful in raising your awareness of how personal problems are affecting your work and what corrective actions might be available and in everyone's best interests.

In addition to problems arising from personal life, social workers need to be aware of work-related stress that may lead to compassion fatigue, vicarious trauma, and burnout. Social workers often enter social work because they feel a sense of gratification from helping others and promoting social justice. This sense of gratification acts as a protective factor, helping workers cope with stress because they are finding meaning in their work. Still, the stresses of a large workload, hearing traumatic stories from clients, and having limited support from agencies can overwhelm the social worker's coping capacities and impair the worker's ability to practice in a competent, professional manner (Wharton, 2008). Thus, social workers and their supervisors should incorporate training and support to prevent compassion fatigue, vicarious trauma, and burnout, and to respond in a timely manner when these problems begin to arise.

Solicitations

The purpose of Standard 4.07 is to ensure that social workers do not take advantage of clients or others who are vulnerable to undue influence, manipulation, or coercion. Standard 4.07(a) suggests that social workers should not solicit potential clients who are vulnerable and have not initiated requests for information. Examples of soliciting clients include handing out business cards or promotional materials, telephoning potential clients who have not initiated any request for services, or offering services through direct email advertising. Standard 4.07(b) suggests that social workers should not ask clients or others who are vulnerable for testimonial endorsements. Examples of testimonials include written quotations that could be used in print advertising, live presentations at conferences, or video-recorded testimonials for use on television or web-based advertising.

The Code does not specifically define who is vulnerable. Any person could be vulnerable to influence, manipulation, or coercion, so the safest approach might be to avoid direct solicitation of potential clients and solicitation of testimonials altogether. Unfortunately, this would impose severe restrictions on how social workers could advertise their services or share information with potential clients. Social workers should be able to promote their services, but they should be particularly careful to safeguard clients with higher levels of vulnerability. Clients with higher levels of vulnerability include people with cognitive impairments, involuntary clients, people experiencing high levels of stress, people with severe mental illnesses, and children. Some forms of solicitation may also present higher levels of risk than others. The following examples illustrate solicitations in which there are relatively high levels of risk.

- A social worker who is helping a suicidal client offers the client a lower fee if he signs a contract for 10 additional sessions.
- A prison-based worker invites clients to participate in a new intervention that involves deep probing into childhood traumas.
- A worker periodically attends Alcoholics Anonymous (self-help) meetings to recruit clients for stress reduction counseling.[6]
- A worker asks a former client with paranoid schizophrenia to appear with the worker at a professional conference to discuss how she benefited from group counseling.
- A worker advertises her services for safer sex education during a children's television program.[7]

When soliciting clients or asking for testimonials, social workers should consider ways in which they can reduce the risks of exploiting or manipulating clients. *Risk management refers to assessing levels of risk and determining the best way to manage that risk.* When advertising children's services, for instance, workers do not want to manipulate children who could be easily influenced. To reduce this risk, workers could direct their advertising to parents rather than children. When soliciting potential clients in a prison population, workers do not want potential clients to feel coerced into services, given that many fear negative repercussions from the prison if they do not acquiesce to the worker's solicitations. To manage this risk, workers could ensure that clients are offered more than one choice of services and are given permission to refuse services of any kind without fear of negative consequences. When inviting a vulnerable client to offer a testimonial, workers put clients at risk of personal embarrassment or negative reactions from the community. To reduce this risk, workers could consider offering the testimonial in a manner that protects the client's confidentiality (e.g., a written testimonial that does not include the client's name, or a video testimonial in which the client's face is not shown). Social workers are permitted to promote their services, but they must prioritize protection of the client's interests. When in doubt, workers should err on the side of protecting the client.

Now that we have reviewed social workers' responsibilities as professionals, we turn to ways in which professional social workers may be held accountable for their conduct.

---

[6] This conduct also breaches AA's policies.

[7] Interestingly, food producers may advertise sugary cereals to children, but social workers must be cautious about marketing services designed to promote biopsychosocial-spiritual well-being.

PROFESSIONAL ACCOUNTABILITY

Professional accountability refers to the responsibilities that social workers incur in relation to those they serve, including clients, agencies, communities, and the profession of social work itself (Walker, 2002). Social workers incur responsibilities from a variety of sources: criminal law, civil (tort) law, professional regulatory laws, professional codes of ethics, agency policies, legally enforceable contracts with clients, and community norms and expectations. Each of these sources provides rules or standards of conduct, delineating what types of behavior are appropriate and inappropriate. Some sources are mandatory, in the sense that they prescribe certain types of behavior or prohibit other types of behavior. Some sources are quasi-mandatory, meaning that they provide general standards of behavior but leave room for interpretation and applicability given the specific context of the behavior. When social workers breach a mandatory rule or quasi-mandatory standard, they may be held accountable for their actions. Consequences for breaching rules or standards range from punishments (imprisonment, fines) to compensation (paying for damages) to protecting the public (prohibiting further practice, rehabilitating the professional through education or counseling) to restoration (making right the wrong through healing processes or restitution). The following sections explain each source of accountability, including who may initiate an action against the worker, what types of rules or standards apply, and what types of consequences may result from a successful action.

Criminal Law—Accountability to the State

Criminal law refers to the system of laws enacted by state or federal governments to protect the public from specific types of harm, for instance, theft, assault, rape, and trespass.[8] Crimes are defined as wrongs against the state, even if there is a specific individual or group that is the target of the crime. Thus, the state is primarily responsible for enforcing criminal laws.[9] The criminal justice system includes police, courts, prosecuting attorneys, jails, and prisons. Traditionally, the primary focuses of the criminal justice system were punishment, retribution, and deterrence. The state imposes fines, incarceration, or other punishments as retribution (or payback) for committing a wrongful act and to deter people from recommitting similar offences. Thus, the criminal justice system seeks to prevent harm to individuals and maintain social order (Madden, 2003). Although punishment, retribution, and deterrence remain as primary goals of the criminal justice system, greater emphasis has been placed on rehabilitation and restorative justice since the 1970s. Thus, the criminal justice system has been expanded to include programs such as rehabilitative therapy, mediation, community services, family group conferences, healing circles, victim assistance, and other interventions that divert cases from court and prison (Restorative Justice Online, n.d.).

Social workers are subject to the same criminal laws as members of the general public. Thus, if they murder, steal, or assault, they are subject to the same criminal laws and consequences as non–social workers. Criminal offenses that relate specifically to acts that social workers may commit in their professional capacities include fraud and unlawful confinement of clients. Social workers may be convicted of fraud for intentionally overcharging clients, forging documents, stealing directly from clients, receiving kickbacks for referring clients to certain service providers, and billing clients, Medicare, Medicaid, or private insurance providers for services never rendered (Payne & Gray, 2001). Social workers may be convicted of unlawful confinement for restricting a person's movement without that person's consent. Thus, social workers should be cautious about preventing clients from leaving their facilities. Although a social worker may be justified in

---

[8] For federal crimes see Title 18 of the U.S. Code at http://www4.law.cornell.edu/uscode/18. To locate the criminal code of your state, see Legal Information Institute (n.d.) at http://www.law.cornell.edu/topics/state_statutes2.html#criminal_code.

[9] Although the vast majority of criminal cases are initiated by state officials, some types of cases may also be initiated by private persons.

restricting the movement of homicidal or suicidal clients,[10] social workers are not generally permitted to restrain other clients against their will.

In order to convict a person of a crime, the prosecution must prove all the elements of the crime *beyond a reasonable doubt.* This high standard of proof is required because the state does not want to infringe an alleged criminal's rights and freedoms unless there is a high degree of certainty that the allegations are true. The elements of a crime include the *actus reus* (guilty act) and *mens rea* (guilty state of mind). Thus, to convict a person of murder, the state must prove not only that the alleged criminal killed, but also intended to kill.[11]

Although social workers may be criminally charged for acts that infringe the NASW Code of Ethics, the basis for charging them would have to be a violation of a criminal law, not merely a violation of the Code. Thus, stealing from a client would not only be a violation of the Code (S.4.04), it would also be a criminal offense for which the worker could be charged. In contrast, failure to promote the self-determination of a client would amount to an ethical violation (S.1.02), but it would not amount to a criminal offense. Thus, social workers may be held accountable through the criminal justice system. However, given that criminal laws do not focus on professional standards of conduct, social workers are more likely to be held accountable for professional misconduct under other systems.

Civil Law—Accountability to Individuals

Civil law refers to the branch of law that regulates relations between individuals.[12] Civil wrongs (torts) include assault, defamation, nuisance, and unlawful confinement. Generally, civil lawsuits are initiated by the person harmed by the tort (exceptions include cases brought by parents on behalf of a child). Whereas the most common criminal law sentences are incarceration, fines, and probation (intended for punishment and deterrence), the most common legal remedy for torts is a court order for the wrongdoer (or tortfeasor) to compensate the victim of the tort for the harm caused (Saltzman & Furman, 1999). In some cases, courts may order other remedies, such as restitution or doing something that puts the person back in a position as if the tort was never committed (e.g., rebuilding a house that the tortfeasor burned down).[13]

A person may be charged in criminal court and sued in civil court for the same act. Thus, the State of California charged former football star O. J. Simpson in criminal court for murdering Nicole Brown Simpson and Ronald Goldman. Goldman's parents also sued Simpson for wrongful death.[14] The prosecutors in the criminal case were not able to prove the murder beyond a reasonable doubt, so the court found him not guilty. In the subsequent civil trial, the parents did not have to prove their case beyond a reasonable doubt, but to the lesser standard of "on the preponderance of the evidence" (or greater than a 50–50 chance). Although the criminal court found Simpson not guilty of murder, the civil court found Simpson liable, and he was ordered to pay damages to Goldman's parents for the wrongful death of their son (*Rufo et al. v. Simpson*, 1997).

The primary tort related to professional accountability is malpractice (sometimes called professional negligence). Malpractice refers to

[10] They must abide by the provisions of the state's mental health laws regarding how to manage dangerous clients. See Chapter 13 for a discussion of involuntary committal laws.

[11] Different offenses require different types of mental states. For a more detailed description of criminal law, see Madden (2003) or Saltzman and Furman (1999).

[12] Civil law has different meanings, including a codified system of law used by most continental European countries, the state of Louisiana, and the province of Quebec. The rest of the United States and Canada base their legal systems on English common law (in which law developed through cases and legal principles determined by judges, in contrast to the Roman civil code). For the purposes of this chapter, civil law will refer only to the branch of law that regulates relations between individuals (Madden, 2003).

[13] Another civil remedy is an "injunction," which is a court order stating that the perpetrator must desist from certain types of behavior (e.g., causing a specific type of harassment or nuisance).

[14] Nicole Brown Simpson's family sued for battery rather than wrongful death.

"bad practice" or providing services in a manner that conflicts with standards reasonably expected of a prudent professional (Reamer, 2003). Clients may sue workers for malpractice if they believe their workers have not acted in accordance with relevant professional standards of practice and this breach of standards results in damages experienced by the client (Madden, 2003). To win compensation for malpractice, a client must prove

- The worker owed the client a *duty of care.*
- The worker *breached* that duty.
- The breach of the duty *caused harm* to the client.
- The breach was the *proximate cause* of the harm.

To illustrate how these criteria are applied, consider the following vignette.

Smadar is a school-based social worker who is working with a 7-year-old student named Clyde. Clyde's teachers referred him for an assessment at the beginning of the school year because he was having difficulties in class. Smadar performs a biopsychosocial assessment. She concludes Clyde's problems are related to inappropriate discipline used by his parents. She engages them in family counseling to redress this problem. Clyde's school performance does not improve and he fails second grade. Clyde's parents, frustrated with lack of progress, take Clyde to another social worker for an assessment. This social worker discovers that Clyde has a learning disability. Clyde's parents sue Smadar for malpractice.

Duty of care: A duty of care refers to the acceptance of responsibility to act in a reasonable manner toward another person or class of persons. For social workers, a duty of care is established whenever they engage clients in services. When Smadar offers her services to Clyde's family, she implicitly agrees to provide services in a professional manner. According to this criterion, social workers do not owe a duty of care to nonclients; for instance, if you pass a person on the street who needs assistance finding a safe place to sleep that night, you are not legally obliged to provide such assistance (even if you believe, morally, you should help). If you offer your professional services to the person, however, you would owe a duty of care.

Breach of duty: A breach of duty refers to acting in a manner that is inconsistent with what would reasonably be expected of a similar professional. The specific duty of care that social workers assume depends on their background and the context of practice. A worker with a BSW who is providing community organization services would be expected to perform services at a level reasonably expected of a competent BSW practitioner who is providing community organization services. A worker with an MSW and specialized training in sexuality therapy would be expected to perform at a level reasonably expected of a competent MSW practitioner with specialized training in sexuality therapy. Smadar is a school social worker with a BSW, so she would be expected to maintain the standards reasonably expected of a competent social worker with such a background. Courts may refer to a variety of sources to establish the standards to which the practitioner should be held accountable. One of the primary sources is the NASW Code of Ethics, given that this code is comprehensive and nationally recognized. In addition to the general Code of Ethics, the NASW also has standards for specific fields of practice, including addictions, school social work, palliative care, long-term care, health, and mediation (see http://www.socialworkers.org/practice). Even if a social worker is not a member of the NASW, the court may use NASW standards to establish what types of behavior are appropriate. As a sexuality therapist, the MSW practitioner noted above could be judged according to standards and ethical guidelines established for sexuality therapists (American Association of Sexuality Educators, Counselors, and Therapists, 2004). Courts may also use standards of practice established through research, theory, and best practices (Barsky, 2009). In other words, social workers should base their assessments and information on the best evidence available in their field. Failure to do so may result in a breach of the duty of care. As a school social worker, Smadar would probably be expected to be able to make a proper assessment for learning disabilities. Even if she is not responsible for making a specific diagnosis, she should have screened for disabilities as part of her assessment and referred Clyde for a more specific diagnosis from a specialist. Arguably, her shoddy assessment resulted in offering Clyde's family an intervention that was inappropriate, not dealing with the primary cause of Clyde's school problems.[15] Malpractice law does not require social workers to be perfect, but rather to act in good faith and make professional judgments to the best of their ability (Kanani et al., 2002). If it is reasonable for a school social worker to miss the learning disability and offer family counseling, then Smadar has not breached her duty. If no reasonable school social worker would have missed the learning disability, then Smadar has breached her duty.

Caused harm: To establish malpractice, clients must also prove that the social worker's breach of duty resulted in specific harm to the client (whether that client is an individual, family, group, organization, or community). In other words, there must be a causal link between the worker's inappropriate actions (or inactions) and the damages suffered by the client. Damages to clients may include biological, psychological, social, and spiritual damages. As a practical matter, it is much easier to prove damages that are physical or financial in nature. It is harder to prove less concrete harm, such as anxiety and loss of friendship. Clyde's family could argue that by not properly assessing Clyde's learning disability, Smadar caused Clyde to fail second grade. They could also argue that her breach caused the family mental anguish and that ultimately, Clyde would be financially dependent on his family for an extra year as a result of being held back a grade. Proving that a breach of duty resulted in specific harms is one of the most difficult parts of establishing a malpractice claim against social workers. The specific impact of social work interventions may be difficult to prove because of many possible intervening variables: Did Clyde fail because he did not receive a proper assessment, or because of ineffective teaching, improper parenting, or other problems not associated with Smadar's breach? How could the parents prove that Smadar's breach caused them anguish, and how can the court place a value on this breach? Assume that the family is able to prove the breach caused them financial loss, specifically, the cost of maintaining Clyde at home one more year plus one year of lost income for Clyde.

Proximate cause: Clients must not only prove a factual causal link between the breach and the resulting harm; they must also prove that the harm was a reasonably direct or foreseeable consequence of the breach. Was it reasonably foreseeable that missing a learning disability could result in Clyde's failing second grade, being financially dependent on his parents for an extra year, and losing one year's income over the course of his life? In this situation, the link between the breach and the claimed damages seems relatively direct and foreseeable. Suppose Clyde's parents claimed that they suffered additional losses because Clyde's younger sister suffered because she received less parental attention and she might be at higher risk of developing a drug addiction. These additional losses would not be sufficiently direct or foreseeable to satisfy the criterion of proximate cause.

Some of the more common claims of malpractice against social workers include allegations involving incorrect treatment, improper referrals, and boundary violations, including sexual relations with clients. Other possible bases for malpractice lawsuits include failure to obtain informed consent, not explaining the risks of an intervention, failure to consult or refer to a specialist, false imprisonment, breach of confidentiality, failure to report suspected child abuse or elder abuse, violating parental rights, client abandonment, practicing beyond scope of competency, inadequate record keeping, and failure to control a dangerous client (Corey et al., 2007; Dolgoff et al., 2009;

---

[15] In court, Smadar could argue that parenting problems were the most important issue, so the court would have to judge whether her assessment and intervention were appropriate, given Clyde's overall situation and what a competent school social worker would reasonably be expected to do.

Kirkland, Kirkland, & Reaves, 2004). There has been little research on malpractice claims against social workers since the 1990s, in part because of difficulty in gaining access to data from malpractice insurance companies. The relatively low rates for malpractice insurance for social workers, however, suggest that malpractice lawsuits against social workers are not as prevalent as for higher risk professions, such as law and medicine.

The best way to avoid and defend against malpractice suits is to engage in competent, ethically conscientious, client-centered practice (Houston-Vega & Nuehring, 1997). Ensure that your practice conforms to agency policy, the NASW Code of Ethics, and professional standards appropriate to your field of practice. Listen carefully to clients and explain the basis of your planned interventions. When family members have an influence on the client's decision making, consider asking the client if it would be appropriate to discuss the intervention plan with family members (Hagihara & Tarumi, 2007). Ensure that you have current and appropriate education, training, and supervision. Do not accept work that goes beyond your level and areas of competence. If you are unable to competently serve the needs of a particular client, consult with an expert or refer the client to someone who can provide competent services. Do not simply give the client the name of a referral; ensure that the client has access and connects with the referral. Otherwise, the client may claim abandonment. Maintain clear records regarding assessments, professional recommendations, and client decisions, particularly for situations involving higher levels of risk (e.g., suicidal ideation, suspicions of child abuse, and clients who present with active hallucinations or impairment due to drug abuse) (Kanani et al., 2002). When clients raise concerns about malpractice, consult with your supervisor, an expert in the field, or an attorney. Also, maintain proper malpractice insurance. Generally, you should not rely solely on the agency's insurance. The agency interests in a lawsuit may differ significantly from your interests (e.g., if the agency sues you for not following agency policies and procedures, your own insurance can pay for your legal costs).

Clients sometimes sue because they are unhappy, stressed, or angry, whether or not you have actually committed malpractice. Even if you successfully defend a malpractice suit, defending may take its toll on you, emotionally and financially. Pre-empt escalation of disputes by using your best conflict resolution skills when working with clients who express concerns about your practice (Barsky, 2007a). If you can work through concerns on an informal basis, you can avoid having to defend an actual lawsuit. Consider consulting an attorney even before an actual lawsuit is initiated. Attorneys can help you strategize the best ways to respond to grievances. Attorneys may advise against providing apologies for improper care, as they could be used in court as admissions of malpractice. On the other hand, providing apologies could be the best way to avoid being sued (Robbennolt, 2003). In some cases, you may be able to listen to and validate client concerns without admitting guilt. You may also be able to offer corrective action that precludes going to court. Even if a client initiates a lawsuit against you, the lawsuit is more likely to be resolved through pretrial negotiations, mediation, or settlement processes than through a full trial of the issues.

Some fields of practice present higher risks of malpractice lawsuits than others. Child custody evaluators, parenting coordinators, and mediators working with couples going through high-conflict divorces, for instance, may become the target of malpractice lawsuits because one or both spouses are dissatisfied with the outcomes of the divorce processes (Kirkland & Kirkland, 2006). Social workers may also face higher risks of being sued for malpractice in situations in which they are expected to assess for risk of serious violence, including child abuse, suicidal ideation, and homicidal ideation (Kanani et al., 2002). Courts do not expect social workers to be perfect in predicting which clients might act out violently, but families stricken by the death of a loved one may sue out of shock, grief, or anger. Although social workers might be tempted to refrain from practicing in areas where the risk of being sued is higher, they also have an ethical obligation to ensure that all people have access to needed services (Houston-Vega & Nuehring, 1997).

Thus, social workers should not abandon clients to avoid risks of being sued.[16]

"Qualified immunity" refers to a law shielding certain professionals from civil liability provided they act in good faith (Rothschild & Pollack, 2008). Qualified immunity laws are most common for social workers in fields such as child protection, in which the worker assumes a quasi-judicial role, having to make judgments that balance potentially conflicting public and private interests (e.g., parents' rights versus protecting the welfare of children). People performing adjudicary functions should have the freedom and confidence to assess situations and make judicial decisions without having to fear that either party might try to manipulate their judgments by threatening an arbitrary lawsuit if they are not happy with the professional's determinations (*Butz v. Economou,* 1978; Kirkland & Kirkland, 2006). Qualified immunity laws try to strike a balance between holding professionals accountable for their actions and ensuring that professionals are not subjected to unreasonable expectations and risks of liability. Unrealistic expectations and undue risks may result in restriction of services because social workers will avoid practicing in those fields (Collins, Coleman, & Miller, 2002). Different jurisdictions have different immunity laws, so social workers should consult relevant legislation and case law in their states to determine whether they are covered by immunity laws and what types of immunity are provided.[17] Immunity laws do not protect social workers from intentionally inflicting harm on clients (e.g., physically assaulting a client).

Professional Regulation—Accountability to Clients and the Profession

Whereas criminal and civil laws create systems of accountability for all people, professional regulations are designed specifically to ensure accountability for social workers and other professionals. By definition, professionals hold themselves to a higher standard of conduct than the general public. Professionals have specialized knowledge, skills, education, and training. They also agree to practice according to their profession's values and ethics (Collins et al., 2002). This section describes different approaches to professional regulation: government-regulated professions, self-regulating professions, and unregulated professions.

1. *Government-regulated professions* are established by laws designed to promote public health and welfare and protect clients from unethical and substandard practice by creating specialized systems of accountability. The highest level of regulation is licensure. Licensure restricts which occupational groups can perform certain functions or services (Collins et al., 2002). By law, only licensed physicians may perform surgery. Only licensed attorneys may represent clients in court and draft legal contracts. If a social worker performs surgery (or drafts a legal contract), that worker may be incarcerated, fined, or otherwise punished for unauthorized practice of medicine (or law). Laws governing professional licensure vary from state to state (Association of Social Work Boards, n.d., b). Some states provide licensure for clinical social workers, meaning that social workers must be licensed in order to perform certain clinical functions, such as psychiatric diagnoses, psychotherapy, supervision of other clinical workers, and initiating proceedings to commit suicidal clients on an involuntary basis. These functions overlap with functions provided by other types of professionals. Thus, mental health counselors, family and marriage therapists, psychiatrists, and psychologists may also be licensed to perform these functions. In order to obtain licensure, social workers must comply with the

[16] When working with a client who threatens to sue you, you may disengage with the client, but you should ensure appropriate referral or transfer to another worker.

[17] For a federal qualified immunity statute, see Civil action for deprivation of rights (2007). 42 U.S.C. §1983.

requirements of the specific laws that establish licensure. Licensure laws require that social workers meet certain qualifications, for instance, an MSW degree, supervised practice experience, passing a licensure exam, maintaining professional liability insurance, and taking a certain number of hours of continuing education credits each year. Some states have a tiered system of licensure, granting different licenses to social workers with different levels of education. Each tier of licensure permits social workers to perform different types of functions (e.g., generalist practice versus specialized clinical practice) (Collins et al., 2002). Licensed social workers must adhere to the specific laws that regulate them. Failure to comply may result in fines, temporary suspensions or restrictions on practice (e.g., restricted from practicing with children), conditions on practice (e.g., must attend weekly supervision), or revocation of licensure. Revoking licensure is a powerful legal consequence, since it prevents the affected individual from practicing his or her profession.

Certification, the second highest level of regulation, refers to a regulatory system that establishes certain professional credentials and provides the public with information on who has met these credentials. Thus, certification and accreditation are synonymous terms. Unlike licensure, certification does not restrict who can perform certain functions. Still, employers, clients, and referral sources may use certification status to determine which social workers to hire or work with. Certification credentials may include the same types of credentials as licensing—advanced professional degrees, knowledge, skill, and acceptance of a particular code of ethics. Sometimes, certification requirements are less onerous than licensing requirements because licensing suggests a higher level of professional expertise and expectations.[18] When professionals fail to comply with the terms of certification, the regulatory body can suspend or revoke their certification. Unlike licensing bodies, however, they cannot completely stop a person from practicing. Thus, if a social worker has his accreditation revoked for breaching client confidentiality, the social worker could still offer services as a nonaccredited social worker. Informed employers, clients, and referral sources, however, may refuse to engage him given his loss of accreditation.

Control of title[19] refers to laws that restrict who can call themselves by a particular professional title. Historically, people were able to call themselves social workers, whether or not they had specific training, knowledge, skills, or accreditation as social workers. In many jurisdictions this is still true. Licensing laws automatically protect title. For instance, only licensed attorneys may represent themselves to the public as attorneys. In some jurisdictions, social workers have advocated for protection of title so that agencies, referral sources, and clients will know that they are working with a "real social worker" when the person calls himself or herself a social worker. The question remains as to who is a "real social worker." Typically, title is granted to those with a particular diploma or degree. Some jurisdictions grant social work title only to people with MSW degrees. Others use the BSW degree as the minimum requirement. Still others permit people with social work-related college diplomas to call themselves

---

[18] In addition, newly developing professions go through an evolutionary process (Kirkland & Kirkland, 2006). Typically, they start out as unregulated professions and then develop voluntary associations with standards of practice. If they are able to secure government support for legislative regulation, they often receive registration or accreditation systems, which are less onerous and less expensive to operate than licensing systems. Also, since licensing systems restrict practice, other professional groups are more likely to challenge licensure for a new profession.

[19] Sometimes called protection or ownership of title.

social workers (Collins et al., 2002). Control of title does not include mechanisms for holding social workers accountable to any professional standards. It merely prevents others from calling themselves social workers. The penalty for violating a control of title law is typically a fine. The person may be able to continue to offer services but use a title other than social work to describe her line of work.

Registration refers to a system in which a governmental or nongovernmental body provides a list of people who practice in a particular field of professional work, for instance, addictions counseling, gerontology, or crisis intervention. Some people use the term *registration* interchangeably with certification or accreditation. Technically, registration does not require the regulating body to attest to the registrant's having met any special criteria. Often, registration systems do require professionals to comply with certain credentials, resulting in the overlap between regulation and certification (and confusion about how each term is used by different laws and different practitioners). When registration does not require credentialing, registration is the weakest form of regulation. It merely lists those people who say they practice in a particular field. Clients who want to ensure that social workers have certain credentials should check whether workers must meet such credentials in order to be registered.

Grievances against government-regulated professionals should be directed toward the government body that has been assigned by statute to enforce the professional regulations and standards (e.g., the department of health or another department responsible for regulating health professionals). Although professionals and referral sources may initiate complaints, clients are often in the best position to initiate them. Clients are most likely to have firsthand knowledge of the concerns. If another professional or referral source initiates a claim and only possesses secondhand (hearsay) evidence, the regulatory body may not have sufficient evidence to prosecute the grievance.

2. *Self-regulating professions* are professional groups that establish their own standards and enforcement procedures. Some, like the NASW, are voluntary associations that offer various types of membership levels and credentialing.[20] When students and workers join the NASW, they are voluntarily agreeing to abide by its code of ethics. Schools of social work and agencies may require students and workers to be members of the NASW, but most jurisdictions do not actually require NASW membership for people to practice social work. Some jurisdictions adopt the NASW Code of Ethics in their licensing or accreditation legislation, making their licensed or accredited social workers legally accountable to the standards enunciated in the NASW Code. If state laws do not specifically adopt the NASW Code, then social workers may be held accountable by the NASW but not by the government-run regulatory accrediting bodies. If a state mandates NASW membership and adherence to NASW standards, then the state-run regulatory body is responsible for monitoring and enforcing compliance with these standards.

The NASW National Ethics Committee (NEC) is responsible for promoting ethical practice among NASW members. It develops ethics policies and procedures, helps members interpret them, oversees development of ethics education and training, and hears complaints against members alleged to have violated the NASW Code of Ethics (NASW, 2005b). When clients or others initiate a complaint against NASW members, the NEC reviews the written "Request for Professional Review" to determine whether

[20] See http://www.naswdc.org/credentials/default.asp for the various types of credentialing offered by the NASW, including certifications for generalists, clinical social workers, gerontology, school social work, health-care practice, and substance abuse counseling.

it alleges specific misconduct that violates the NASW Code. If the complaint meets the basic eligibility requirements for review, the NEC refers the case to the appropriate state chapter for mediation or an adjudication hearing.[21] When mediation is authorized, an NEC-appointed mediator brings the complainant and social worker together to try to work out an amicable solution for the grievance. When adjudication is authorized, a panel appointed by the state ethics committee hears the case, and each party has an opportunity to provide evidence in a trial-like process.[22] When a panel finds an NASW member has violated the Code of Ethics, it may order various corrective actions and sanctions: compensation for damages; participation in a prescribed number of hours of professional consultation, supervision or training; private or public censures; suspension of or expulsion from NASW membership; and notification to state regulatory boards or credentialing bodies (NASW, 2005a). In many cases, the impact of revoking NASW membership is not as strong as revoking a license to practice. Most social workers may continue to practice even without NASW membership. Still, revoking NASW membership may have serious impacts on a social worker's ability to practice because

- Some social agencies require NASW membership as a condition of employment.
- Some schools of social work require NASW membership.
- Some referral sources and clients may avoid social workers who have had their NASW membership revoked.
- Insurance companies may require NASW membership.

In these circumstances, revoking NASW membership severely restricts the worker's ability to practice. Although NASW ethics committees may impose punitive consequences, their primary foci are to prevent ethics violations and take corrective actions in response to violations that do arise. Thus, revocation of NASW membership is only used for serious violations or ongoing patterns of violations, when other corrective actions and sanctions are not sufficient.

3. *Unregulated professions* have no laws, regulations, or professionally enforced codes of ethics. Anyone can perform the functions of the profession without legal or professional restrictions. Although many social workers are members of professional associations or are accredited by governmental regulations, many functions performed by social workers do not require the service provider to be a social worker or to hold any form of accreditation—for instance, facilitating a task group, assisting with policy development, organizing community members to advocate on their own behalf, teaching basic life skills, facilitating clients through the generalist problem-solving model, and providing instrumental help (e.g., assisting clients with budgeting, making doctors' appointments, and helping them arrange transportation to job interviews). Unless state laws provide otherwise, social workers who graduate with BSWs or MSWs may also offer such services without being members of NASW and without obtaining any government-sponsored accreditation. Some social workers and others call themselves "personal coaches" or "life coaches" specifically to avoid the higher levels of scrutiny that accredited social workers or other mental health professionals endure (NASW, 2008). In states with social work licensing, social workers without licensure cannot perform the functions that the laws

---

[21] Adjudication is typically required for cases involving sexual relationships, sexual harassment, physical contact, violence, and safety concerns (NASW, 2005b). Mediation is generally preferred for other cases, because it is less expensive and may lead the parties to creative, collaborative, future-oriented solutions.

[22] In instances where the state ethics committee has a conflict of interest, the case will be heard by the NEC.

> restrict to licensed professionals. Although enforcement officials may consider the titles social workers use to describe their roles and work, the primary issue is whether the functions they perform fall within the purview of the restricted activities. The term *paraprofessional* is sometimes used to describe practitioners who perform certain social work functions but are not regulated by professional associations, licensure, or accreditation. Social service workers and case managers, for instance, are sometimes called paraprofessionals because they perform some of the same types of work as social workers, but they are not accountable to a professional code of ethics or regulatory body.

So, why should social workers bother with NASW membership or professional regulation? Career and financial opportunities may be the source of motivation for some workers. Certain agencies will not hire social workers unless they are NASW members or meet particular standards of professional regulation. Some agencies pay higher salaries for credentialed social workers. Some professionals will not refer clients to social workers unless they are licensed or accredited. Some clients will not accept services from social workers unless they are licensed or accredited. And health insurance companies typically require licensure in order for social workers to be eligible for insurance reimbursement for mental health services. Ideally, financial factors are not the only motivation for obtaining credentials. Social workers can further important social work values (e.g., competence, respect for clients, accountability, and integrity) by becoming NASW members and qualifying with the relevant professional regulatory bodies.[23]

Agency Policies—Accountability to Clients and the Employing Agency

When clients[24] have concerns about the conduct of social workers, the most accessible avenue of recourse is within the agency that employs the social worker. Most agency grievance processes are less formal and less costly than civil lawsuits and professional review processes. Typically, agency policies specify that aggrieved clients should first discuss their concerns with the practitioner. The practitioner may not have been aware of the concern and may be able to negotiate a solution directly with the client (e.g., acknowledging the problem and agreeing to act differently in the future).[25] If the client is unable to achieve a successful resolution at this stage, the client can pursue her concerns up the chain of command, for instance, with the practitioner's supervisor, the program director, and the agency's board of directors. The agency may have specific conflict resolution or grievance procedures, including mediation, arbitration, and appeals processes (Honeyman, 2003). The agency may also have its own ethics committee that reviews ethics complaints (Csikai, 2002). Agencies may use following corrective actions and sanctions: assigning a different social worker to the client, providing additional social work supervision or training, suspending the worker, reassigning the worker to different functions, putting the worker on agency probation, and dismissing the worker (if the agency has just cause to fire).

When an agency reviews the conduct of a social worker, it holds the worker accountable to the laws and policies that govern the particular agency. Laws that regulate health-care facilities, for instance, include special provisions for protecting patient confidentiality (Health Insurance Portability and Accountability Act, 1996). The

---

[23] The names of professional regulatory bodies vary from jurisdiction to jurisdiction. Some states have bodies specific to social work, but many regulatory bodies cover social work within general health or mental health regulatory bodies. See the Association of Social Work Boards website for specific information on professional regulation in your own state—http://www.aswb.org/members.shtml.

[24] Although nonclients may also initiate grievances within an agency, agencies may not be able to deal with such grievances if to do so would involve disclosure of confidential client information.

[25] If a client feels too threatened to approach the practitioner directly, agency policy may specify others with whom the client may consult (e.g., a client advocate, an ombudsperson, or the practitioner's supervisor).

agency may have policies that supplement these legal rules, such as requiring the use of encryption to protect all client data sent over the Internet. If a social worker does not comply with these laws and policies, the agency may take corrective action or impose sanctions.[26] Unless the agency adopts the NASW Code of Ethics as a source of ethical guidance for its social workers, the agency cannot hold its workers accountable to this Code. Some agencies require their social workers to be NASW members, which implies that the agency does expect its workers to abide by the NASW Code. Even if agencies do not compel their workers to abide by the NASW Code, agency policies may include many of the same ethical standards as the Code (e.g., informed consent, confidentiality, and respect for clients). In addition, social workers have a responsibility to ensure that their agency policies and practices are consistent with the NASW Code (S.3.09[d]; Reamer, 2001a).

In sum, social workers may be held accountable according to the laws and policies that govern the agency. In many instances, these laws and policies promote the same types of ethical behaviors as the NASW Code or other professional standards. Thus, clients may choose whether to pursue grievances with the agencies, with other relevant professional regulatory bodies, or with a combination of venues. If agency policies and laws do not cover the aggrieved behavior, the client should consider taking the grievance to a venue that does cover such behavior.[27]

Legally Enforceable Contracts—Accountability to the Contracting Parties

When two or more people or organizational entities exchange promises, they enter into a contract (Madden, 2003; Stein, 2004). Contracts are enforceable by civil courts, provided that the parties have appropriate mental capacity to enter contracts and both parties enter the contract voluntarily (without coercion). When agencies hire social workers, they are entering into contractual relationships. Terms of contracts may be written, oral, or implied. For legal purposes, written contracts offer the benefit of providing tangible evidence of the contract.[28] Social workers are accountable for performing their duties as provided in their contracts (Walker, 2002). Thus, if they breach the terms of the contract, they may be sued (similar to a malpractice lawsuit as described earlier). Some employment contracts include provisions regarding confidentiality and other ethical standards similar to those in the NASW Code. Employment contracts may impose additional duties, such as noncompetition clauses. Noncompetition clauses state that workers will not engage in any practice outside the agency that competes with services offered by the agency. If a social worker accepts a client in private practice rather than as an agency client, the agency can sue for damages.

Social workers also enter into contracts with clients. Confidentiality agreements are essentially contracts that say the social worker will maintain confidentiality of client information except as otherwise agreed. Service agreements are contracts stating which services the worker will provide, as well as the obligations of the worker and client in carrying out the assessment and intervention. Thus, if a social worker acts in a manner that is inconsistent with the contract, the client may sue for damages. Consider a service agreement that states that the worker will ensure 24-hour, 7-day-per-week access to crisis intervention counseling. If the worker fails to provide such services and the client sustains injuries as a result, the worker may be liable to compensate the client. Thus, social workers may be held accountable for provisions in their agreements with clients that go above and beyond the standards

---

[26] If the agency itself is not complying with applicable laws, then the governmental body that regulates the agency may impose its own corrective actions and sanctions.

[27] E.g., an agency may not have policies that prohibit social workers from having sex with former clients. Former clients may need to pursue such grievances with the NASW rather than with the agency.

[28] For oral or implied contracts, it may be difficult to prove who agreed to what.

expressed in the NASW Code.[29] Given the potential legal consequences for breach of contract, agencies and social workers should consider obtaining legal advice before entering into legally binding agreements with clients or others. Attorneys can assist with clarification of each party's contractual obligations, as well as specifying what happens if either party breaches the contract. Some contracts state that contract-related disputes must be handled in mediation or arbitration rather than court.

Community Norms and Personal Conscience—Accountability to Self and Community

The final areas of social work accountability are related to community norms and personal conscience. Although the term *professional accountability* suggests that social workers are accountable to professional bodies (e.g., the NASW and licensing boards), social workers should also consider accountability to their communities and personal belief systems. As professionals, social workers should ensure that their practice is consistent with laws, policies, codes of ethics, and standards of practice that relate to their profession and context of practice. Yet these are not the only systems that influence social workers' judgments and conduct. Social workers operate within a social context that also includes their neighbors, friends, family, cultural community, and faith community. Thus, social workers are, to varying extents, accountable to these additional systems. True, given the confidential nature of social work, these systems may never know whether social workers are acting ethically in their private dealings with clients. Still, some professional conduct is open to the public, and other conduct may become open to the public if a case proceeds to court or a client takes a grievance to the media.[30]

In some instances, accountability to nonprofessional sources is very powerful. Consider a social worker who knows that boarding school teachers are abusing children, but takes no action to protect the children. Because child abuse goes against community norms, friends and neighbors may reject or alienate the worker when news of his complicity in the abuse comes to light. The court of public opinion may be particularly harsh when professional misconduct is picked up by certain media that tend to sensationalize a malpractice case. Media often ignore the good work of competent social workers and other helping professionals. A worker with a glowing professional record of 25 years could become media fodder for a single breach (or alleged breach) of professional ethics. Even family members may turn on a social worker who has been tainted by accusations of unethical or illegal behavior.

Social workers who ascribe to various religions are accountable to their higher powers (Heyman et al., 2006). Thus, a secular, professional code of ethics may suggest that it is ethical for social workers to facilitate divorces, yet the social worker's religious beliefs may suggest that facilitating divorces contravenes the laws of God. Each religion has its own rules and belief systems, including beliefs about the consequences for disobeying the tenets of the religion (Hugen & Scales, 2008). Thus, social workers should be aware of how their religious beliefs may affect their professional judgments and behaviors. For some social workers, faith, religion, and community norms are very powerful sources of accountability.

---

[29] If a social worker wants to enter into an informal understanding with a client rather than a legally enforceable contract, the worker should use language that clarifies this. Workers should avoid use of the terms *agreement* and *contract* if a signed document is not intended to be a binding contract. The document could specify, "The terms of this document represent a general understanding between the social worker and client, and do not establish a legally binding contract."

[30] Professional disciplinary hearings and agency grievances are typically confidential to protect both client and practitioner. The results of such hearings and grievances could be made public if the decision makers determine that publicizing the results is in the best interests of clients and the public (e.g., publishing names of professionals who have lost licenses so the public knows not to engage with them).

CONCLUSION

Social workers incur a range of ethical responsibilities in relation to the communities they serve. Although social workers' primary commitments are directed toward their particular clients, they also have responsibilities to promote social justice, as well as other values and ethics of the social work profession. Many social work standards are aspirational, meaning that social workers should strive for the highest ideals of social work. In contrast, minimum standards act as baselines. When social work judgments and conduct fall below these baselines, social workers may be held accountable for their actions. Different systems of accountability enforce different types of laws, agency policies, codes of ethics, contractual obligations, community norms, and personal belief systems. Social workers may be held accountable for a single act of professional misconduct in more than one forum. Although social workers may fear being held accountable, they should recognize that these systems of accountability are intended to foster ethical practice. Clients have a right to be protected from unethical behavior, and to receive compensation when harm has been caused.

DISCUSSION QUESTIONS AND EXERCISES

Exercises 1 to 4 are designed to help you differentiate and apply various types of professional standards, including minimum versus aspirational standards, and standards that promote social justice through different means. Exercises 5 to 9 are designed to help you understand, apply, and critique different systems of professional accountability. Exercise 10 is designed to help you identify ethical issues that may arise when social workers are acting as community organizers.

1. *Minimal versus Aspirational*: Review each of the following standards from the NASW Code: 4.01, 5.01, and 6.01. Analyze whether each standard is minimal, aspirational, or a combination of both.
2. *Minimum Standards*: For each of the following vignettes, identify the minimum standard from the NASW Code that the worker has violated and explain how the worker's behavior violates this standard:
   a. Siler administers a food bank. He is very authoritarian and refuses to permit community members to have any say in the agency's policies.
   b. Sabia works for a clinic that is inaccessible to people who use a wheelchair. Sabia does not do anything to remedy this problem.
   c. Shannelle hires a social worker to perform psychometric testing even though she knows the worker does not have the required training or credentials to do such testing.
   d. By day, Sumatra is a community organizer. By night, she transforms herself into a superhero and fights crime. Unfortunately, her night job makes her so tired that she can hardly stay awake when she is working with her clients.
   e. Spike wants to go fishing. He calls his supervisor and says he has to take the day off because he is sick.
3. *Aspirational Standards*: In each of the following scenarios, the worker is adhering to minimum standards of practice under the NASW Code. Identify at least two aspirational standards to which the worker should be striving and give two specific examples of how the worker could aspire higher with respect to the social problem identified in each example.
   a. Sherry reads a newspaper article that refers to social workers as "petty bureaucrats."
   b. Serge helps homeless clients find temporary shelter. He works with clients on a one-to-one basis, believing that personal service is the best approach to social work.
   c. Sahar works in an area with high frequency of violent crime. She has developed a network of agencies to serve crime victims.
   d. Selina has discovered a new and highly effective way to engage involuntary elderly clients with depression. She decides not tell anyone else about the intervention.

4. *Public Participation*: A social worker named Sheri encourages a client to participate in a protest supporting affirmative action to enable more Latin Americans to receive higher education. Sheri believes her encouragement is ethical, in light of Standard 6.02. What other standards might her actions violate? Why might different people disagree about whether promoting affirmative action is promoting social justice?
5. *Contrasting Regulatory Approaches*: Compare and contrast two of the following approaches to regulating social workers: licensure, accreditation, registration, protection of title, self-regulated, or completely unregulated. What are their respective advantages and disadvantages? Given your assessment, what would you recommend as the preferred approach to regulating social workers in your state?
6. *Professional Accountability*: For each of the following scenarios, identify which forums clients may use to pursue their complaints: criminal justice system, civil court, voluntary professional association, government-mandated licensing or accrediting body, or agency. Which of these forums should the client try to use first? Provide your reasoning in terms of accessibility, costs, available remedies, and chances of success.
   a. Shayla is a Licensed Independent Social Worker who provides counseling as a private practitioner. Cora is a client with sleeping problems. Shayla uses dream analysis to help Cora. Cora believes Shayla's counseling has made her problems worse, as she now experiences horrible nightmares.
   b. Steffi has an MSW, but no licensure or accreditation. She works for a health maintenance organization that puts a lot of pressure on social workers to decrease their number of billable sessions with clients. Consuela believes that Steffi terminated too early, given this pressure, but Consuela cannot identify specific damages that she has suffered as a result.
   c. Simeon has a BSW and is an NASW member. He works in a nursing home, where he has sex with a client, Cindylou. Cindylou is an adult with full mental capacity. She believes Simeon manipulated her into having sex and she now feels very ashamed because of it.
   d. Herb is a human service provider at a social assistance office. He has no social work degrees, but he calls himself a social worker. The state does not have laws protecting social work title. A client named Cait finds out Herb has been depositing some of her social assistance checks into his own bank account.
   e. Svetlana is a BSW-level worker who works for an agency that provides groups for people intending to marry. Svetalana and Cahil (her client) sign a service agreement in which Svetlana agrees to maintain confidentiality. Svetlana accidentally sends a report to Cahil's fiancé, who has a similar email address. The fiancé reads the report, finds out Cahil has been dating other women, and calls off the engagement.
   f. Shahar is a state-accredited social worker with an MSW and NASW membership. He advises the Campbell family (former clients) to rearrange their retirement savings so they can take advantage of certain tax credits. Years later, the Campbells discover this was bad advice, costing them thousands of dollars. When they contact Shahar's agency, they learn he no longer works there. The agency claims it is not responsible for his misconduct because he was not authorized to provide tax or investment advice (functions regulated by other professions).
7. *State Regulation*: Identify which body(ies) regulate social workers in your state (http://www.aswb.org/members_reglinks.shtml). Locate the primary website for each of these bodies. What type(s) of regulation are available in your state: licensure, accreditation, registration, or protection of title? Describe what types of grievances clients may submit to each of the bodies that regulate social work in your state. What are the first steps a client should take when

submitting a grievance to each of these bodies?

8. *Regulation Debates*: Choose one of the following debate issues. Select a position, pro or con, and write an advocacy brief in support of your position.
   a. Some people argue that professional regulation is motivated by self-interest; it does not protect the public so much as create elitist groups and erect inequitable and discriminatory barriers against professional status for minority groups (Collins et al., 2002).
   b. In some states, the only type of social work licensure available is for clinical practice. Critics argue that too many social workers are attracted to financially lucrative private practice, providing psychotherapy to middle-class clients and neglecting their historic roles of promoting community empowerment and social justice (Specht & Courtney, 1994). Social workers should advocate for regulatory laws that promote generalist practice, inclusive of community practice, and resist being lumped together with psychologists and other mental health professionals.
   c. Some social workers believe that social work accreditation should be available for social workers with either a BSW or MSW degree (not just for those with MSWs). Including either degree will increase the pool of accredited social workers and the larger numbers will give social workers more political clout in comparison with other professions.
9. *Malpractice*: For each of the following scenarios, use the following questions to analyze whether the situation satisfies the criteria for a successful malpractice lawsuit: *(i)* Did the social worker owe the other person a duty of care? *(ii)* What professional standards, if any, did the social worker breach? *(iii)* Was there a causal connection between the breach and the harm experienced by the person? *(iv)* Was the damage the proximate cause of the breach? If you require further information to answer these questions, state what information you would need.
   a. Salwa (an NASW member) tells Charlton she is going to use hypnosis to help him retrieve childhood memories. Salwa does not tell him about the risks of this intervention. After paying for two sessions of hypnosis, Charlton decides it is not working and wants to know if he can sue Salwa for malpractice.
   b. An African American community hires Skip to help them advocate for better social services. Skip uses appropriate advocacy skills and strategies, but his efforts are unsuccessful. The community considers suing for return of its payments to Skip because he did not actually help them achieve anything.
   c. Selda receives a phone call from a boy asking for help. Selda says she does not work with children, so she gives him the name and phone number of another social worker. The boy is too distraught to call another worker and attempts suicide by jumping out a window. He breaks both legs. When his parents find out about the call to Selda, they wonder if they can sue her.
   d. Shadé told Chaïm that she is a trained psychoanalytic therapist. In fact, she has only generalist social work training. After four months of intensive therapy, Chaïm loses his job (including his $100,000 per year salary). He blames Shadé because her psychoanalysis surfaced abandonment issues from his childhood. He became so obsessed with these issues that he could not concentrate at work. He also became rude to customers who bore any resemblance to his mother. When he told his boss that he was undergoing psychoanalysis and he was not feeling very emotionally secure, his boss fired him.
10. *Community Organizers*: The NASW Code of Ethics provides similar ethical guidelines to social workers, regardless of whether their clients are individuals, families, groups, organizations, or communities. Unfortunately, some of the provisions

are written primarily for individual and family work, thus leading to challenges when social workers are involved in community organization (Hardina, 2004). For each of the following scenarios, identify the primary ethical issue, which of the standards in Section 1 of the NASW Code of Ethics apply, and what special concerns community organizers may have in trying to apply these standards to their work.

a. Shamus is a community organizer for his town of 15,000 people. He is helping the town develop recreational activities for youth. When Shamus hires his neighbor to help build the recreational center, others accuse Shamus of favoritism. Shamus does not believe he has violated any rules. The town is small and he hired the best builder available.
b. Mrs. Smith is working with a Vietnamese American community to help bring better resources for elders. Initially, Mrs. Smith had the support of key members from the community. Recently, the community has become disenchanted with Mrs. Smith, finding her tactics for advocacy are too aggressive, thus shaming the community.
c. Mr. Santana is organizing a group of citizens who do not want a toxic waste dump to be built in their community. Mr. Santana recommends that the group initiate a series of negative advertisements to try to embarrass the politicians who are currently in favor of building the dump. The proposed ads would include embellished facts and exaggerations about the politicians' motivations and integrity. Some citizens raise questions about the ethics of these negative ads, but Mr. Santana says that the means (stretching the truth a bit) is justified by the ends (protecting the community from exposure to toxic waste).

Chapter 10

Policy, Values, and Ethics

Policies are guidelines that regulate behavior. Agency policies regulate the behavior of workers and clients within the organization.[1] Social policies regulate the behavior of governments, communities, organizations, families, and individuals for the purposes of enhancing human welfare and satisfying human needs in areas such as child welfare, education, health care, housing, public safety, and social security (Kirst-Ashman & Hull, 2006a; Segal, 2007). Policies provide a plan of action, informing people how to conduct themselves and what types of conduct to avoid.[2] As you are learning in your policy and social welfare history courses, policy formation is determined by a confluence of factors, including

- The values and priorities of the population (e.g., within an agency, city, state, nation, or group of nations that is determining its policies).
- Who has the greatest decision-making power and influence.
- How well different people or groups can communicate, cooperate, problem solve, and resolve conflicts in a constructive manner.
- What resources are available for implementation of the policy (Jansson, 2008).

This chapter explores how social workers may use social work values and ethics to guide their involvement in policy formation processes.

Values and ethics play important roles in terms of both policy process and policy outcomes. The process of policy making refers to the methods used to determine policy. When an agency

[1] This chapter focuses on social policy. Chapter 12 will deal more specifically with agency policies, including how to draft policies.

[2] Policies may be enforced through various methods of accountability, depending on whether they are formalized as laws or agency policy. For further discussion of social worker accountability, see Chapter 9.

develops new policies, does one person simply write and impose the policies on the agency? Or does the agency consult with clients, practitioners, and other stakeholders? When Congress determines social policy, how does it gather information and opinions, and what methods does it use to make use of such input? Policy outcomes refer to the substance of the policies resulting from policy formation processes. For instance, an agency might adopt a policy requiring all workers to be tested for drug use. Congress might decide to link minimum wage increases to the consumer price index. Social workers are morally active professionals, regardless of their areas of practice (Hugman, 2003). When social workers participate in policy-making processes, they should be cognizant of how values and ethics may be applied to both process and outcome issues.

To illustrate how to apply values and ethics in a policy development situation, we will follow a case that involves the distribution of scarce resources. Although policy issues cover a broad range of subjects, the allocation of limited resources is often one of the key questions faced by policy makers and those advocates wanting to shape policy. Social justice, a core social work value, often requires the redistribution of resources to vulnerable or disadvantaged populations. Political and power struggles often arise over the right way to share resources. The following case deals with the distribution of healthcare resources:

> With the threat of an influenza pandemic looming, the State of Minnesota has decided to develop policies on how to respond, if and when an outbreak occurs. Stella has been hired to facilitate the process for developing a policy for an outbreak of a highly contagious lethal respiratory virus (flu). Minnesota has 5,200,000 residents of whom 1,500,000 will probably contract flu, 770,000 will require outpatient medical care, 170,000 will require hospitalization, 26,000 will require intensive care, and 33,000 will die (Vawter, Gervais, & Garrett, 2007).[3] The first vaccines for the particular flu strain will not be available until at least 6 months into the pandemic. Initially, Minnesota will receive only 420,000 doses of vaccine, meaning that one of Stella's primary tasks is to develop a clear and fair policy on how to ration vaccinations. Other people have been hired to develop policies on related issues, such as how to allocate hospital beds, whether to invest more money in flu prevention or flu treatments, whether to quarantine certain segments of the population, and what types of other restraints on civil liberties may be required to prevent transmission (reducing the number of illnesses and deaths from the pandemic) and ensure public order in terms of policing, utilities, food distribution, and other essential services (Infectious Diseases Society of America; 2007; Zoloth & Zoloth, 2006).

LEARNING OBJECTIVES

Upon successful completion of this chapter, students will be able to

- Design policy formation processes informed by core values and ethical principles, including accountability, inclusiveness, transparency, reasonableness, and responsiveness.
- Critique social policies in relation to social work values and ethics.
- Advocate for policies based on specific ethical theories, including libertarianism, egalitarianism, utilitarianism, and deontology.
- Identify five ethically flawed approaches to making policy decisions: the squeaky wheel, clandestine bribery, nepotism, coercion, and misplaced fiduciary relationships.

INFORMING POLICY FORMATION PROCESSES

This section provides a framework for ensuring that policy formation processes are informed by

[3] This case example is fictional, although these statistics have been derived from an actual study.

professional ethics. You may be wondering why we are focusing on the ethics of policy processes. After all, isn't the outcome of a policy process more important than the process itself? The NASW Code of Ethics (1999) says social workers should promote social justice—an outcome. The Code does not provide ethical standards that relate specifically to policy processes. Still, the ethics of policy processes are important, and there are general principles from the NASW Code that we may apply to policy processes, for instance, showing respect for the dignity and worth of all people. By ensuring that policy processes are respectful, fair, and equitable, we raise the likelihood that socially just outcomes will emerge. Policy issues are often difficult to resolve because different people have different information, opinions, interests, and positions. If we can engage people in ethically appropriate processes, then they are also more likely to view policy decisions as legitimate. Even if some people are not happy with the outcomes, they may be more willing to accept them because the process was reasonable and valid (Daniels & Sabin, 2002; Nuffield Council on Bioethics, 2007). If we do not engage people in fair, civic processes, we are more likely to experience disruptive behaviors, such as queue jumping, hoarding, black marketeering, and scapegoating vulnerable minority groups[4] (Gostin, 2006; Zoloth & Zoloth, 2006).

In the flu case, assume that Stella assembles a group of four friends who have expertise in allocating health-care resources. Upon consulting with them, she announces that should a pandemic erupt, the first people to receive vaccinations would be state legislators, law enforcement officials, and health-care workers. How do you think the public and specific stakeholder groups would react to this announcement? Even if the decision about whom to prioritize is ethically justifiable, how do you think different stakeholders would feel about the process? Why might they question the legitimacy of Stella's policy formation process?

To ensure ethical legitimacy, policy processes should be guided by the following five principles: *accountability, inclusiveness, transparency, reasonableness,* and *responsiveness* (Thompson, Faith, Gibson, & Upshur, 2006). The ensuing analysis defines each of these terms and demonstrates how they correspond with the core values of social work. Certainly, the nature of a specific policy process will depend on a range of issues, including the types of decisions to be made and the types of systems involved in decision making. Thus, social work values and ethics do not dictate a specific process to be used in all cases, but rather a general framework for designing a policy process consistent with key values and ethical principles.

Accountability

The principle of accountability suggests that the policy formation process should include specific mechanisms for holding people responsible for their actions in the process. Systems of accountability provide checks and balances to ensure that ethical decision making is sustained throughout the policy process (Thompson et al., 2006). These checks and balances promote confidence among those affected by policy decisions (Daniels & Sabin, 2002). Accountability reflects two core values of social work: integrity and competence. In terms of integrity, policy processes should be guided by the ideas of trust and honesty rather than exploitation, trickery, or corruption (Torda, 2006). People contributing to policy formation should be competent in their roles, for instance, as policy facilitators, experts, or analysts. Accountability provides a system for monitoring competence and making corrections, as needed. The principle of accountability does not dictate a specific method of accountability for all processes. Rather, accountability

[4] During the outbreak of bubonic plague in fourteenth-century Europe, Jews were unjustly blamed for spreading the disease. More Jews died from the resulting burnings and murder than from the plague itself (Zoloth & Zoloth, 2006). Examples of queue jumping, hoarding, and black marketeering are provided under the heading Flawed Ethical Reasoning in this chapter.

may be achieved through one or a combination of mechanisms:

- *Administrative supervision*: designating certain people to monitor the process, offer suggestions, and enforce process rules and procedures.
- *Appeals process*: providing stakeholders with an opportunity to challenge decisions that they believe were made due to a faulty process.
- *Election*: providing stakeholders with the opportunity to vote on who should be making policy, allowing them to elect different people should they be dissatisfied with policy processes used by current policy makers.
- *Audit*: engaging independent professionals to conduct a one-time or periodic review of the process to ensure compliance with particular process standards (Reamer, 2001a).

In the flu case, Stella asked four friends to help her develop policy. The vignette does not indicate any methods of accountability. She was hired by the government, but does she have a contract that says what she is supposed to do, how she is supposed to do it, and whom she is supposed to do it with? Without a system of accountability, will anybody even know that she has hired four friends and whether doing so constitutes a conflict of interest? How will government or any other stakeholder know whether the process of decision making was honest or whether Stella was even competent to lead this process?

To hold Stella and her colleagues to account, the government agency hiring Stella should have articulated clear standards or codes of conduct from the outset. Their contract should have responded to process questions such as

- Who should be involved in the policy process?
- What are each of their roles and what types of competence should each possess?
- What types of standards should they use to guide their policy-making process?
- What types of resources (financial and otherwise) may be used to conduct the process, and how will the cost-effectiveness of the process be measured?

The following sections—Inclusiveness, Transparency, Reasonableness, and Responsiveness—offer further guidelines that may be incorporated into the system of accountability. By articulating these expectations at the beginning of a policy process, leaders and other participants in the policy process are provided with clear notice regarding the standards to which they will be held accountable.

Inclusiveness

Inclusiveness refers to ensuring that policy decisions are made with stakeholder[5] views in mind (Levine et al., 2007). The principle of inclusiveness builds on the social work value of respect for dignity and worth of all people. By honoring the principle of inclusiveness, policy makers acknowledge that all stakeholders have valid and important views to consider. Further, they have a right to participate in decisions over matters that affect their lives (similar to an individual client's right to self-determination).

Often, policy processes provide stakeholders with opportunities to provide input directly. Sometimes, designated representatives speak on behalf of stakeholder groups. In other situations, decision makers do not consult with stakeholders or their representatives, but make conscious efforts to consider the views of various stakeholders in their deliberations (e.g., based on needs assessments, past experience, or mere speculation). Providing stakeholders with direct participation in policy-making processes tends to provide them with the greatest sense of legitimacy. People want to have their say and to be heard by those making decisions. When they are denied direct participation, they may question whether their perspectives have been considered. Inviting input from stakeholders may be costly, in terms of time and financial costs.

[5] Stakeholders are people affected by policy decisions. When an agency is establishing policies on confidentiality, for instance, its stakeholders include clients, family members, professional staff, and law enforcement.

Accordingly, costs should be considered in terms of how to implement the principle of inclusiveness. Policy makers should also allot sufficient time to allow for appropriate participation.

Those facilitating policy processes should consider what type of participation should be solicited from various stakeholder groups. For instance, will stakeholders simply provide input (presenting information, opinions, and suggestions) or will they have decision-making power? If they will have decision-making power, will decisions be made through majority vote, consensus, or some other means? The ethical principle of inclusiveness does not prescribe a specific type of participation. It merely highlights the general need for including the perspectives of various stakeholder groups. In terms of implementation, however, stakeholders may be more likely to support and follow through on policy recommendations if they believe they have had a valid form of input into the policy-making process.

Stella included four friends in her decision-making process. The vignette does not indicate whether these participants are representative of any or all stakeholders. The issue of how to allocate vaccinations during a flu pandemic involves many stakeholders: state legislators, health-care providers, law enforcement officials, and the general public (who may be divided into groups such as parents, children, elder adults, educators, business people, employees, and so on). One of the primary ways that Stella's process lacks ethical legitimacy is that the stakeholders have no way of knowing whether their perspectives were even considered during the decision making. In this scenario, the allocation of resources has life and death implications: those who do not receive vaccinations during early stages of the pandemic are more likely to die. By giving state legislators priority to receive vaccinations, other stakeholders may find the decision self-serving. If there were a more inclusive process, stakeholders could discuss whether government officials should receive priority, thus giving the process greater legitimacy. Arguably, a process for determining how to allocate vaccinations during a crisis should include direct consultation with a broad spectrum of stakeholders. The decision is a very important one. Also, it is important to have broad support for the decision, to promote cooperation and avoid chaos should a flu crisis erupt. If stakeholders feel angry or disenfranchised by an ethically questionable process, they could create civil disorder as a form of protest. Nurses, for instance, might refuse to comply with the policy on vaccination priorities.

Transparency

The principle of transparency suggests that people affected by the policy decisions should have access to information about the process and the basis on which decisions are made (Thompson et al., 2006). Whereas social workers value privacy and confidentiality with respect to work with individual clients, openness and disclosure are key principles in public policy processes. NASW Standard 3.07(b) recognizes the importance of transparency, suggesting that resource allocation procedures should be open and fair. Transparency is related to the principle of accountability in that transparency makes policy makers accountable to the public. Transparency fits with the social work value of integrity, as it ensures that policy decisions are made openly, honestly, and in good faith. Both transparency and integrity build trust and solidarity between policy makers and the population they serve. Transparency is particularly important in times of crisis when the public's cooperation may be crucial to successful implementation of policy decisions. Various constituencies may view policy makers as stewards of resources. Unless the decision-making processes are transparent and ethical, these constituencies may lose trust in their stewards and sabotage their efforts (Torda, 2006).

Transparency may be implemented in various ways:

- Permitting the public or particular stakeholders to view debates, oral hearings, discussion documents, or other communications that inform the policy process.
- Providing the public or particular stakeholders with reports that summarize the policy process, including who was involved, what information and opinions were discussed, what decisions were made, and what criteria were used to make the decisions.

- Requiring participants to declare (publicly) conflicts of interest, biases, or any other factors that may bring the legitimacy of their participation into question.
- Assigning an ethics oversight committee to monitor the process.[6]
- Providing the public or various stakeholders with a communication plan that informs them how to access particular information, for instance, through formal requests for information to an information officer or ombudsperson (Thompson et al., 2006).

Stella disclosed the outcomes of her policy process, but she did not permit public access into the decision-making process. Further, she did not publish reasons for the decisions. These failures render her process suspect. Stakeholders have no idea how the decisions were made and on what basis. Stakeholders do not know whether decisions were made on the basis of valid criteria. The principle of transparency does not tell Stella specifically how to ensure that stakeholders have access to information about the policy-making process. Because she is working for the government, she should consider the "open government" or "access to public information" laws in her state (see Open Government Laws, n.d. at http://www.rcfp.org/ogg). These laws require certain types of meetings to be open and certain types of documents to be accessible to the public. They also limit access to certain meetings and documents, to protect privacy and protect certain interests (e.g., national security).

The principle of transparency is linked to the next principle, reasonableness. When policy processes are open to stakeholders, stakeholders have an opportunity to assess the legitimacy of the rationale for the decisions. In other words, transparency offers stakeholders a chance to judge the reasonableness of the decisions.

Reasonableness

The principle of reasonableness suggests that policy decisions should be based on factors that stakeholders believe are relevant and valid (Thompson et al., 2006). Reasonableness coincides with the social work value of integrity. Reasonable people may disagree on how to resolve particular policy issues. Integrity, however, suggests that people should act honestly and in good faith when they are making policy decisions. Conversely, they should not base their decisions on false, unfair, deceitful, irrelevant, or otherwise unreasonable criteria.

When assessing the reasonableness of a policy process, one may consider whether the policy makers

- Gathered relevant information required to inform their decision making.
- Interpreted the information in a plausible or rational manner.
- Made choices based on legitimate criteria (i.e., criteria that fair-minded people would accept as sensible or acceptable).
- Applied decision-making criteria in a consistent manner.
- Used critical thinking skills, rather than relying on assumptions, biases, or faulty logic (Paul & Elder, 2006).

Assume that Stella articulated the reasons for her policy decisions as follows:

> "We concluded that state legislators will be given the highest priority for vaccinations because they are our elected officials. Health-care providers also have high priority because they will be at high risk of contracting flu from working with patients. Further, we do not want health-care providers transmitting flu from one patient to another..."

Stella's explanation for prioritizing legislators is a non sequitur—there is no logical connection between giving priority to legislators and their status as elected officials. Although there may be a reasonable explanation for giving legislators priority, Stella has not provided one. Stella's explanation for providing priority to health-care

[6] For matters of national security, for instance, some processes may require privacy; an oversight committee provides some reassurance that the process is conducted in an ethical manner.

workers does sound reasonable. Providing protection for people who are at the highest risk of contracting flu seems to be a good use of the limited resources. Further, providing vaccines to health-care workers provides an element of protection to other vulnerable people: patients. Reasonable people may disagree with Stella's specific assessment about prioritizing health-care workers, but her initial analysis seems reasonable.

The concept of "reasonableness" is challenging to apply because different people may have different concepts of what would be reasonable in a particular situation. Legislators, for instance, might view their receiving priority as reasonable. The concept of reasonableness, however, must be considered from an objective perspective. Legislators have a self-interest in receiving priority, so their personal perspectives may not be objective. Reasonableness requires the ability to look at policy choices from a range of perspectives, with a conscious attempt to apply objective, unbiased criteria (Paul & Elder, 2006).

Responsiveness

The principle of responsiveness suggests that policy processes should include mechanisms for receiving and reacting to new information and concerns. Whereas inclusiveness refers to involving stakeholders in policy processes, responsiveness highlights the importance of not just listening, but answering. Responsiveness does not require policy makers to provide answers that satisfy everyone, an impossible task. Responsiveness does, however, suggest that policy makers should receive input in good faith, using it to revisit and reconsider policy issues and decisions (Thompson et al., 2006). Responsiveness fits with the social work value of respect for the dignity and worth of all people. By acknowledging and responding to feedback from stakeholders, policy makers are showing respect for their views, interests, and positions.

Methods of implementing the principle of responsiveness include

- Holding public hearings in which policy leaders respond directly to questions from stakeholders.
- Inviting stakeholders to submit questions, information, and concerns in writing, and responding in writing (e.g., on an interactive website or in a paper report).
- Assigning people to monitor or evaluate implementation of policy, including feedback from stakeholders and responses from policy makers (e.g., an action research approach, as discussed in Chapter 4).

Stella's policy was based on the assumption that the state would initially receive 420,000 doses of vaccine. In the event of an actual pandemic, what if the state receives only 10,000 doses? Alternatively, what if health-care workers find that the vaccination is not effective at preventing flu? Stella and the other policy makers should have a specific plan for how to gather this new information and address such concerns as efficiently as possible (Infectious Diseases Society of America 2007; Thompson et al., 2006).

The principles of accountability, inclusiveness, transparency, reasonableness, and responsiveness provide general ethical guidelines for planning and conducting policy processes. We now turn to the ways in which values and ethics may be used to inform policy outcomes.

INFORMING POLICY OUTCOMES

Policy issues often involve questions about allocating resources; for instance, who do we think is deserving of certain benefits, and what do we think is a fair way to distribute the wealth of the society, community, or organization? How we allocate resources reflects our values and ethics. Accordingly, we should make our allocation choices deliberately, conscious of the relationship between these choices and our values and ethics (Nathoo, 2000; Yeskey, 2008). Given that social workers are advocates for social justice (NASW, 1999, S.6.01), we must be able to advance solid arguments in favor of allocating necessary resources for the benefit of our constituencies, particularly for disadvantaged and vulnerable groups. In this section, we explore four major theories that may be used to inform policy decisions regarding the allocation of resources: libertarianism, egalitarianism, utilitarianism, and deontology.[7] The ensuing analysis includes a critique of these theories in relation to social work's core values—service, social justice, dignity and worth of the person, importance of human relationships, integrity, and competence—and the ethical principles emanating from these values (NASW Code of Ethics, 1999). By learning how to analyze theories of allocating resources in relation to social work values and ethics, you will gain a better understanding of the strengths and limitations of each theory. You will also learn how to advance policy arguments based on values and ethical principles, responding to others who may be coming from different theoretical approaches.

Before delving into the issue of allocating resources, a word of caution: When faced with a policy decision that looks like an issue of how to divide limited resources, consider whether division is actually necessary. Dividing resources is necessary when resources are so scarce that the total resource pool is insufficient to meet the needs and interests of the relevant stakeholders. In the flu situation, it appears that there will not be enough doses of vaccine to protect everyone who is at risk of dying from a virulent flu strain. However, there may be different options to protect the population from severe illness or death. If a large segment the population quarantined itself for a period of time, for instance, they would not be exposed to the flu virus and would not need to be vaccinated. Although quarantines may present other problems (e.g., restrictions on civil liberties and ability to secure food and other essentials during the quarantine), this example shows that there may be creative ways to create value rather than simply distribute existing resources. Distributing resources is sometimes called a zero-sum game. It assumes a fixed quantity of resources that needs dividing. If one group gains resources, it does so at the expense of another group that loses equivalent resources. Creative conflict resolution strives for win-win solutions, in which the various stakeholders use problem-solving skills to find new resources, eliminate waste, or use resources more wisely (Barsky, 2007a; Fisher, Ury, & Patton, 1997). Rather than assume her state will receive only 420,000 doses of vaccine, for instance, Stella could explore whether the state could produce its own vaccine. For the purposes of the following discussion, we will assume that the issues are primarily distributive—there will be people who win (benefit) and people who lose (suffer), depending on which policy decisions are made. In other words, resources are scarce and the policy makers have already secured all the resources they can.

Libertarianism

Libertarianism is a social philosophy that emphasizes the importance of individual rights and freedoms.[8] Libertarians believe the state should not exercise control over an individual's life, but rather support the rights of each individual to exercise full control over his or her life (Locke, 1689; Nuffield Council on Bioethics, 2007). The U.S. Declaration of Independence (1776) invokes libertarian principles in its statement that all men [*sic*] have inalienable rights, including the rights to "Life, Liberty, and the Pursuit of Happiness." Likewise, the 14th Amendment to the U.S. Constitution (1868) suggests that government shall not "deprive any person of life, liberty, or property, without due process of the law." Libertarianism is the basis for capitalism, an economic system in which most goods and services are owned, produced, and distributed by private corporations and individuals (Beauchamp & Childress, 2009). Government has a limited role in this type of economy, that of supporting a free market economy in which private producers and

[7] Other theories that may inform allocation of resources include communitarianism, capitalism, teleology, and socialism. Given space limitations, the present analysis focuses on four theories, but also indicates links between these and related ones.

[8] Libertarianism is similar to classic liberalism, in that both emphasize the freedom from control of others. Current uses of the term *liberalism*, however, suggest that liberals support a larger government role, for instance, promoting equality, nondiscrimination, and justice.

consumers determine what types of goods and services will be produced, and at what cost.

In terms of social policy and the distribution of resources, libertarianism offers three essential principles:

1. *Autonomy:* Individuals should be permitted to behave as they wish (autonomously, rather than controlled by government or others).
2. *Ability to Pay:* The distribution of goods and access to services should be according to each individual's ability to pay.
3. *Social Merit:* Social merit is an acceptable criterion for allocating resources within a society, community, or organization.

If Stella were to apply libertarian principles to the flu scenario, autonomy suggests that the government should play a limited role in the production and distribution of flu vaccine. This would allow private companies and the free market to determine how much vaccine to produce, when, and at what cost. According to the ability to pay principle, those who could afford to purchase vaccine would be free to do so. Libertarianism posits that those who could not afford to pay would be motivated to work harder and save money for the possibility of future medical emergencies. In other words, government should not subsidize the cost of vaccines for the poor, generally, because that would create incentives toward dependence, sloth, and laziness. Libertarians believe people should be self-reliant. The principle of social merit, however, does permit government to allocate resources to individuals deemed to be deserving of social support. The government might make vaccines available to war veterans who are deemed worthy of support because of their status as defenders of the country. People who "chose" not to work or not to become educated (e.g., because they "chose" to use drugs and alcohol) would not be deemed to have social merit and would not be worthy of receiving subsidized vaccines.

On first look, the autonomy principle seems consistent the NASW Code of Ethics, specifically with reference to values such as the "dignity and worth of the person" and ethical standards such as "self-determination" (S.1.02). Social workers respect clients' rights to decide how to conduct their own lives out of respect for their dignity and self-worth. Allowing people to take responsibility for their own lives provides them with a sense of dignity and permits them to realize their own sense of fulfillment. If Stella applied the principles behind self-determination to the flu issue, she might resolve that people should be able to choose whether to be vaccinated. Her policy would not impose vaccination on unwilling recipients unless they lacked mental capacity to decide for themselves. Libertarianism might also suggest that government should not impose quarantines, but merely support quarantines among those who choose to participate. Libertarianism permits individuals to decide what is in their own best interests, rejecting a paternal or protective role for government. Both libertarianism and self-determination suggest that social policies should increase people's choices, not limit or ignore them (Levine et al., 2007; Trotter, 2007).

Although social workers support client rights to self-determination, they recognize the importance of human relationships and the importance of social environment (S.6.01). Social workers believe that there is a role for people to be supportive of one another, within families, communities, and society. Whereas libertarians believe that government should play a minimal role in helping people with their problems, social workers believe that communities should be supportive of individuals and families. Community support, however, does not have to come only from government. It could also come from the private, voluntary sector, including nongovernmental and charitable organizations. Thus, Stella could advance the social work value of human relationships and still support libertarian principles by embracing a policy that allows nongovernmental and charitable organizations to play a stronger role in ensuring access to vaccinations and helping communities respond to a flu crisis.

In terms of the ability to pay principle, the Code of Ethics seems to reject distribution of resources based solely on the ability to pay. Social workers value access to resources and have a positive ethical duty to promote equal access to resources needed to fulfill basic human needs and to allow people to develop fully (S.6.04[a]). Social workers tend to support a significant role for government in redistributing resources in support of the needy, including through further development of the welfare state (Weiss, Gal, Cnaan, & Majiaglic, 2002). Given that flu vaccine may the best protection against a fatal virus, Stella would need to consider how the government can make vaccine accessible to people regardless of their ability to pay. Leaving the production and distribution of vaccine to be decided solely by market forces would put many segments of society at risk (e.g., the elderly, the unemployed, and other families living in poverty) (Gostin, 2006; Yeskey, 2008).

The libertarian principle of social merit conflicts with the social work value of respect for the dignity and worth of all people. Social work rejects the idea that some people are more deserving of respect (and resources) than others. Rather, social workers advocate for social justice based on the principle of equal opportunity and access to resources, with special regard for vulnerable, disadvantaged, oppressed, and exploited individuals and groups (S.6.04[b]). Applying this principle, Stella would reject prioritizing war veterans for vaccinations simply because of their status as war veterans. Different people may have contributed to the country in different ways. Stella would advocate a policy that provided equal access, regardless of status as war veterans, elected officials, rock stars, or other positions that libertarians might deem worthy of social merit. Stella would also advocate equal access to services for people that some might deem to be unworthy, for instance, people who contracted flu because they took extreme risks (e.g., kissing strangers during a flu pandemic) (Levine et al., 2007). Social workers do not believe that people should be denied basic needs due to moral questions regarding past behaviors or associations. All people deserve to be treated with dignity and respect.

Given that social workers value equal opportunity and access to resources, social workers might reject libertarianism in favor of egalitarianism. As the next section suggests, however, egalitarianism may not be a panacea or perfect solution to the questions of resource allocation.

Egalitarianism

Egalitarianism is a social philosophy that emphasizes legal, social, and economic equality[9] *for all people.* The U.S. Declaration of Independence (1776) incorporates egalitarian thought in its statement that "all men [sic] are created equal." True legal, social, and economic equality have remained elusive goals, though legal equality for slaves and women has been fostered by the abolition of slavery in 1865 (U.S. Constitution, 14th Amendment), granting women the right to vote (U.S. Constitution, 19th Amendment), and enactment of the Civil Rights Act in 1964. Social work acknowledges that legal, social, and economic disparities continue to exist, as promoting social justice and access to resources remain core components of social work's values and mission (Ss.6.01 and 6.04).

Egalitarianism may be based on a range of other theories, including rights theory and virtue theory. Rights theory suggests that all people have certain entitlements (or rights). Rights theory takes an objective assessment to ethical issues and behavior. It suggests we must *treat people equally* in order to fulfill their rights. In contrast, virtue theory suggests that morality is about character; we must *be moral* rather than simply *act morally* (Osmo & Landau, 2006). A virtuous person acts with good motivations rather than simply acting in a way to fulfill legal or moral obligations (Beauchamp & Childress, 2009). Thus, egalitarianism is a human trait that people live, rather than something they do.

[9] Legal equality refers to having laws that treat people equally, forbidding discrimination on the basis of race, ethnicity, sex, gender, nationality, sexual orientation, religion, disability, and so on. Social equality refers to the ways in which government and people actually treat one another; for instance, regardless of what the laws say, what is happening in practice? Are some people denied housing, health care, employment, or other needs because of discrimination? Economic equality refers to a relatively equal distribution of resources, including income and wealth, among a community or nation.

When trying to put egalitarianism into practice, policy makers should consider

- Does egalitarianism require treating everyone the same way or treating people differently in order to take difference into account?
- What combination of legal, social, and economic reforms is needed to promote egalitarianism?

As suggested earlier, libertarians might argue that social work's value of "respecting the dignity and worth of all people" means that social work should support social policies on the basis of individual rights and responsibility. Egalitarians might argue, however, that respecting dignity and worth comes through promoting policies that treat everyone equally. Egalitarianism rejects the libertarian principles of allocating resources on the basis of social merit or the ability to pay. The social work value of "access" suggests that all people have a right to needed resources, not just people who can afford them or people who hold high standing in a community.

Applying egalitarianism to the vaccination conundrum, Stella might advocate policies that provide equal access to vaccinations; in other words, to respect the dignity and worth of all people, everyone should have the same opportunity to take preventive actions against the flu virus. Because resources are often in short supply, putting egalitarianism into practice can be challenging. If Stella's state had enough vaccine to cover the entire population, equal access would not be so difficult to attain. Given the expected shortage, however, Stella needs to consider what methods of allocation best fit with the principles of egalitarianism. Some egalitarian ethicists favor a random selection process as a means of supporting equality for all candidates. Thus, Stella could implement a policy that allocates resources on first-come-first-served basis, or a lottery in which everyone has an equal opportunity of being selected for vaccination. Random selection processes do not necessarily ensure ethically justifiable results. A first-come-first-served process, for instance, might be slanted toward people who have the ability to come first, for instance, people with cars, higher levels of English literacy, access to computers, or free time. Lotteries may also be rigged, or suspected of being rigged, because of the difficulty in proving that the selection process is truly random. Even if the selection process is truly random, the process might lead to inefficient use of resources: vaccinations might be provided to people at low risk of contracting flu while being withheld from people at higher risk. If health-care workers do not receive priority, more people may die because there will be fewer healthy and qualified workers to provide needed medical care (Furnham, Ariffin, & McClelland, 2007).

Treating everybody equally does not necessarily mean treating everybody in exactly the same way. Egalitarians not only consider equal treatment, but also equal opportunity and equality of results (Banks, 2006). Consider a policy that says anyone who becomes pregnant may be fired. Women might argue this policy is blatantly sexist. On its face, this policy treats men and women the same. If a woman becomes pregnant, she may be fired. Likewise, if a man becomes pregnant, he may be fired. The effect of this policy, however, is sexist. Men do not become pregnant, so the policy has a much different effect for men than for women (Beauchamp & Childress, 2009). Rather than talking about a principle of equality, some ethicists talk about a principle of "equality and inequality" (Dolgoff et al., 2009). When people are in like circumstances, they should be treated alike. When people are in different circumstances, then equity and fairness may require differential treatment (Rawls, 1971). If a person is blind, should society expect that person to function in exactly the same way as everyone else, or should society make accommodations, such as providing education in the use of Braille and access to computers with screen reading capacity? The principle of equality and inequality permits differential treatment to rectify disparities and remove disadvantages (Banks, 2006). Essentially, the principle of equality and inequality directs us to treat people equitably or fairly, rather than simply treating everybody in exactly the same manner.

Some people believe that differential treatment goes against the principles of equality and egalitarianism. They focus on how people are treated rather than the effects of such treatment. From this perspective, affirmative action is a form of discrimination because it does not treat everyone in the same manner. As advocates for people in vulnerable situations, the profession of social work (though not all social workers) tends to consider the impact of social policy, not just the intent or manner of treatment. Thus, Standard 6.04(b) of the NASW Code asks social workers to "expand choice and opportunity for all people, *with special regard for vulnerable, disadvantaged, oppressed, and exploited people and groups*" (emphasis added). Do you believe affirmative action is ethical? Consider a community with high rates of unemployment. Would government be supporting egalitarianism or discrimination if it allocated extra resources to that community to promote job creation at the expense of taking away resources from a community with low unemployment?

If Stella applied the principle of equality and inequality to the issue of vaccination distribution, she would consider personal and social disparities in the population. Some people—for instance, the elderly and young children—may be at higher risk of dying from the flu than other people (Gostin, 2006). On this basis, these groups might be afforded higher priority for vaccinations. Similarly, Stella might allocate additional resources to educate homeless people about the flu because they generally have less access to health information than the general population.

One way to promote egalitarianism is to use the principle of proportionality to guide policy decisions. Given limited resources, it may be impossible to provide every single person with the same treatment and resources. The principle of proportionality suggests that policy makers should strike a balance between the benefits, costs, and risks experienced by different groups (Torda, 2006). During a flu pandemic, Stella and her colleagues may need to limit hospital admissions so as to give priority to people at the highest risk of severe illness and fatality from the flu. Such a decision may have a disproportionate effect on certain segments of the population, such as elders with health-care concerns unrelated to the flu. To ensure that elders are not hurt disproportionately by the hospital restrictions, policy makers could allocate a certain number of hospital beds for use by this group.

Some proponents of egalitarianism believe that the capitalistic market economy should be replaced with a socialist economic system. Under socialism, government or another central body[10] is responsible for production and distribution of goods and services. Its roles are to promote equality and ensure that everyone's basic needs are satisfied.[11] Whereas capitalism distributes resources according to each person's ability to pay, socialism distributes resources according to the Karl Marx (1875) maxim, "From each according to his ability, to each according to his needs." Thus, under a Marxist definition of social justice, society should allocate resources on the basis of meeting people's needs. At a minimum, society should ensure that basic needs (food, shelter, medical care) are provided to all people. If production in society is able to provide for more than just basic needs, then everyone in society should benefit equally from these additional resources.

Other proponents of egalitarianism support a mixed economy rather than a socialist one. A mixed economy is based on social democratic theory, which recognizes the limitations of a purely free market economy. According to this theory, free markets are dynamic and creative, encouraging people to invest and work hard. However, they may also create social dislocation and suffering, such as when there are boom and bust cycles of employment, large companies that take advantage of their monopoly power, and unequal distribution of resources. In a mixed economy, much of the production of goods and resources remains in the hands of private companies and individuals, but government plays a stronger role in controlling the market economy (Walker, 2002). Egalitarianism may be promoted

---

[10] E.g., a committee appointed by a community or organization.

[11] Socialism should not be confused with totalitarianism or dictatorship, although some totalitarian regimes have called themselves socialist. True socialism may involve the people making decisions through democratic elections or other means.

through human rights laws, employee protection laws, publicly funded education, social security, government-regulated health care, and other types of social programs (Nuffield Council on Bioethics, 2007).

Although no society has been able to achieve absolute equality, egalitarianism (like libertarianism) does not have to be an all-or-nothing proposition. Social workers may promote policies that improve equality among different groups and individuals, even if 100% equality is elusive. Social workers may disagree with one another about the best way to promote equality. Still, social workers overwhelmingly agree that promoting social justice and combating inequality are key components of their professional mandate.

Utilitarianism

As noted earlier, libertarianism suggests allocating resources according to each person's ability to pay. Egalitarianism suggests allocating resources according to each person's needs. In contrast, *utilitarianism suggests allocating resources according to the greatest good for the greatest number; that is, how an organization, community, or society can allocate a limited pool of resources in a way that maximizes benefits (or utility) for the greatest good* (Homer & Kelly, 2007). The term *utility* refers to ability of any resource to produce the experiences of benefit, advantage, pleasure, good, or happiness,[12] or to prevent the experiences of mischief, pain, evil, or unhappiness (Bentham, 1823). Good is achieved when the sum of the benefits outweighs the sum of the costs. Utilitarianism is based on teleology, a theory suggesting that the ethical appropriateness of an action (including social policy decisions) should be determined by the consequences of the action.[13] In other words, which actions result in the greatest good? Utilitarianism supports the ethical principles of beneficence (acting in ways that cause good) and nonmaleficence (avoiding actions that cause harm). Arguably, this aspect of utilitarianism fits with the social work value of respecting the dignity and worth of all people. In order to respect people, social workers should promote actions that lead to health, growth, positive social functioning, need satisfaction, and social justice; they should also avoid actions that cause harm, particularly to the most needy in society (NASW, 1999, Preamble & S.6.04[a]).

The concept of the greatest good for the greatest number requires an objective, rational assessment of the consequences of different courses of action (Mill, 1863). Decision makers weigh the potential benefits of each policy option against the costs (and risks) of each option. They then select the options with the highest benefit-to-cost ratio.[14] Using utilitarianism to guide her decision making, Stella would need to assess the best way to maximize the benefits of her limited supply of vaccine. She should not prioritize family members and friends simply because their lives are most important to her. She should assess the utility of people's lives from an objective perspective to determine what distribution of vaccines would maximize utility for the entire state of Minnesota. Thus, a vaccination policy based on utilitarianism could include provisions such as

- High priority to health-care providers and others who are at highest risk of contracting flu and cannot isolate themselves from others because they are needed to help people who become sick.
- High priority to children who are at highest risk of dying from the flu.
- Low priority to people who can easily isolate themselves from others until the

[12] Utility may come from tangible goods such as houses, cars, and clothes, but also from intangibles such as friendship, good health, knowledge, and beauty.

[13] Deontology is sometimes called consequentialism because it looks at the effects (or consequences) of actions.

[14] One of the key hurdles in applying a utilitarian approach is securing valid and reliable information to inform decisions. Unfortunately, it is often difficult to predict the precise effects of different policy options. More rigorous policy research can help facilitate utilitarian choices, but social policy decisions are too complex to expect that future research will ever make policy predictions 100% accurate.

crisis is over or more vaccinations become available.
- Low priority to people who may have severe allergic reactions to the vaccination.

These provisions seek to allocate the limited resources in a manner that maximizes the benefits and minimizes the harm produced.

Utilitarianism may also involve the social utility principle, in which decision makers assess the relative worth of specific individuals or groups in terms of their capacity to benefit (or harm) society. Allocating scarce health-care resources on this basis is akin to looking for the best return on investing such resources (Furnham, Ariffin, & McClelland, 2007). Thus, if policy makers were determining who should receive kidneys, surgery, vaccinations, or any other health-care resources, they might consider each patient's family role, potential future contributions to society, past contributions to society, and life expectancy (Clarke, 2007; Furnham et al., 2007). Thus, a child may be given preference over an older person, a parent may be given preference over a childless person, a person with high job skills may be given preference over a person with limited job skills, and a person who devoted a life to public service may be given priority over a person convicted of armed robbery. Allocating resources based on the relative social value of people is fraught with ethical controversy. To say "We should not give vaccinations to people who we know will die from them" is a relatively safe statement. To say "We should prioritize vaccinations for doctors and rock stars because they are worth more to society than teachers and bricklayers" involves moral judgments that run contrary to social work's value for the dignity and worth of all people. As discussed earlier, social work rejects the notion of providing resources to people who are deserving and denying resources to those who are undeserving. Who can judge whether one person's life is worth more than another's? How can anyone make an objective assessment of social utility when the notion of evaluating the worth of a person necessarily involves making a moral judgment?

Making policy choices that promote the greatest good for the greatest number means that one person or minority could be sacrificed for the good of the rest of society (Trotter, 2007). This type of utilitarian argument could be used to justify slavery or oppression of some workers for the benefit of many others in society. Utilitarianism does not necessarily produce compassionate, fair, or just results; in fact, sometimes it produces the opposite (Markóczy, 2007; Vawter et al., 2007). As advocates for vulnerable and oppressed populations, social workers are not only concerned about the greatest good for the greatest number. They are concerned about promoting good and avoiding harm for every person and group. In other words, there is a tension between good stewardship of resources (using resources efficiently) and respecting the dignity and worth of all people (Galambos, 1999). If policy makers decide to prioritize the allocation of resources to the sickest and most vulnerable people in society, they may exhaust all the resources and leave the rest of society vulnerable. In fact, some resources will be used for futile or non-cost-effective cases, sacrificing the greater good without producing appreciable benefits. On the other hand, if policy makers use health-care resources to promote the greatest good for the greatest number, they are essentially sacrificing the most vulnerable people (Daniels & Sabin, 2002).

Although some aspects of utilitarianism run into conflict with social work values and ethics, Standard 3.09(b) of the NASW Code does suggest that social workers should promote efficiency and effectiveness of their services. Thus, social workers are expected to make the best use of resources, as utilitarianism suggests. Social workers cannot simply say that everyone should have access to resources without considering how to ensure that an organization, community, or society can sustain itself and how to allocate resources to ensure this (Levine et al., 2007). The challenge for social workers is how to promote efficient and effective use of resources while also ensuring access to needed resources and respect for the dignity and worth of all individuals. When looking at the totality of the values and ethical standards in the NASW Code, the Code does seem to emphasize advocating for the needs of vulnerable minorities over advocating for the efficient use of resources for the benefit of the greatest number of people.

Deontology

Deontology, sometimes called duty-based ethics, refers to *the study of what we ought to intend.* People should do something because it is intrinsically the right thing to do, not because it satisfies some self-interest or leads to a particular type of result. Whereas utilitarians and other teleologists focus on the consequences of one's behavior, deontologists focus on whether the behavior is consistent with the moral rules and obligations we owe to others (Beckett & Maynard, 2005; Healy, 2007). If we value the dignity and worth of all people and believe that liberty is a universal right, then the act of owning slaves is morally wrong. Slavery violates our moral duties concerning liberty. Deontologists contend that the question of whether *most people benefit from slavery* is irrelevant. Even if slavery serves the greater good of a society according to some utilitarian assessment, slavery is still morally wrong. It is our moral obligation to respect others' right to freedom (Duff, 2005).

Deontologists believe that the ethics of any behavior should be determined by whether one intends to act in a moral way; in other words, is the person intending to do good for others? Pacifists, for instance, value peace and nonviolence. They strongly believe that violence is intrinsically wrong because they have a duty to treat others peacefully. These convictions are so strong that they will not resort to violence to defend themselves against violence from others. Rather, they will try to use whatever nonviolent strategies are available.[15] If nonviolence is not effective, they will accept the consequences rather than use fear of being hurt to justify fighting back in a violent manner. The means (acting morally) is more important than the end. Behaving nonviolently is doing the right thing, regardless of the end result. The end does not justify the means, in the sense that pacifists would not justify initiating violence to promote peace. They do not believe in the concept of a just war[16] (Orend, 2004).

Kant, one of the foremost contributors to deontology, suggests that people should be guided by universal rules or natural laws (Wood, 2006). He believed that although people have *free will* (the ability to choose to act as they please), they should act out of *good will* (Kant 1964/orig.1785). Kant developed the categorical imperative test as a way to determine what types of behavior are moral: "Act only on the maxim through which you can at the same time will that it should become a universal law" (Kant 1964/orig.1785, p. 88). According to this test, people should act in a manner that they would wish as a guide for how everyone should act. This test is similar to the biblical maxims, "Do unto others as you would have them do unto you" (Matthew, 7: 120)[17] and "Love your neighbor as yourself" (Leviticus, 19: 34). According to Kant, examples of categorical imperatives include never steal, never lie, and never break a promise. The morality of behavior is defined by our duty to others (Kant 1964/orig.1785).

Deontology is not the same thing as absolutism, although both ethical theories emphasize the importance of rules or duties. Absolutism suggests that there are certain rules people should follow in all situations. Although some deontologists are absolutists, other deontologists believe that the same core duties or rules apply to everyone, but not necessarily in every situation (Gert, 2006). Thus, the duty to protect life is a universal rule in the sense that it should apply to all people. An absolutist might believe that killing is wrong regardless of the situation. Other deontologists would note that Kant's categorical

[15] For instance, nonviolent protests, hunger strikes, and civil disobedience.

[16] A just war refers to a war that can be ethically justified. For instance, some people believe that it is ethical for a nation to engage in war only if it is attacked first; others believe that it is ethical to initiate a war as a pre-emptive measure when the enemy poses a grave danger (e.g., possesses weapons of mass destruction and threatens to use them).

[17] This rule has some limitations in terms of universality. There are many times when "do unto others" would not lead a person to act morally. If you were a thief, for instance, would you want the other person to report you to police? No, therefore, the "do unto others" maxim would suggest you should not report other thieves to police (Gert, 2006).

imperative does not prohibit killing in all circumstances. There may be circumstances—such as self-defense—in which killing is ethically justified. The conceptual and practical distinctions between deontology and absolutism are complex and difficult to explain in a layperson's terms. Even distinguished ethicists disagree and debate over the meanings of deontology, absolutism, and Kant's categorical imperative (Homer & Kelly, 2007).

If Stella were to apply deontology to the vaccination issue, she would reject utilitarian arguments about allocating the vaccinations according to the type of distribution that would create the greatest good. That type of reasoning is based on an assessment of the consequences. She would need to identify universal duties, ones that apply not just to the vaccination issue but to other policy decisions. Three rules or duties that may satisfy Kant's categorical imperative test include the duty to care, the duty to do no harm, and the duty to preserve life:

1. *Care*: People may have a duty to care that stems from their social roles (Homer & Kelly, 2007).[18] Parents have a duty to care for their children and teachers have a duty to care for their students. Government officials and other social policy makers have a moral responsibility to care for all people (Torda, 2006). This means that any allocation of resources in society should show compassion and concern for everyone (Thompson et al., 2006). Denying people vaccinations simply because they are elderly, sick, or noncitizens would go against this duty to care.
2. *Do no harm:* Policy makers should promote good, and conversely, avoid harm. Thus, the policy should not allocate vaccinations to people whom we know it will hurt (e.g., because they are allergic). In practice, policy makers may not know precisely who will benefit from vaccinations and who may suffer. Assume, for instance, that research indicates that a person who is unvaccinated has a 20% chance of contracting flu and a 5% chance of dying from it. The research also shows that the same person who is vaccinated is protected from the flu, but has a 0.2% chance of dying from an adverse reaction to the vaccination. Research provides probabilities rather than individual predictions, so policy makers may not know specifically who will be harmed by vaccinations. Thus, policy makers must make choices within the confines of the available research and knowledge.
3. *Preserve life:* Society places a high value on human life. Thus, policy makers may use the duty to preserve life as a guide for making vaccination allocation decisions. This duty suggests giving priority to those most at risk from dying from flu, rather than priority to those who may become sick but are not expected to die from it. Unfortunately, this duty does not suggest how to allocate limited resources when preserving everyone's life is not possible.

Although deontology may be useful in presenting policy makers with broad principles to follow, it may have difficulty offering direction for setting specific priorities when scarce resources make it impossible to satisfy duties owed to everyone. One might argue, for instance, that we should prioritize vaccinations to young people because they deserve to live as long as elderly people. However, one could equally make a moral argument that elderly people have just as much right to vaccinations as younger people (Clarke, 2007). As noted above, one might also argue that preservation of life is a universal imperative. Unfortunately, scarce resources mean that it is impossible to preserve everyone's life. Thus, we are faced once again

[18] Ethics of care theory suggests that ethical analysis does not require detached, objective analysis of issues, but rather a contextualized assessment. This theory suggests social workers should take emotions and relationships into account, rather than trying to assess situations as if they are completely independent and unbiased by relationships. When we are in close relationships we feel compassion, sympathy, fidelity, and so on, so we should not ignore these feelings (Beauchamp & Childress, 2009).

with the challenge of how to decide whose lives to protect first. Ethicists call this challenge the *duty of reality* (Beckett & Maynard, 2005). Policy makers may quarrel about ethical duties on and on, but reality may eventually require them to make a difficult choice.

Whereas Kant and many other deontologists believe that duties are derived from rational thought, many people of faith believe their duties extend from religion and their higher power.[19] The Ten Commandments, for instance, advise people to honor their parents and keep the Sabbath holy. They also prohibit murdering, stealing, coveting one's neighbor's wife, and worshiping other gods. People who accept these commandments as the word of God may follow them out of a sense of duty (Hugen & Scales, 2008). They may reject utilitarian analysis that would lead to actions contravening the teachings of the Bible, as this would go against God's word. This does not mean that all people of faith are deontologists or that all deontologists are people of faith. Rather, it reminds social workers that they should consider the source of a person's morality or duties to others. If a person's ethical arguments are based on religious duties, then social workers should respond with sensitivity to the religious context. If a person's ethical arguments are based on rational thought and humanistic values, then social workers should respond with sensitivity to these contexts (e.g., neither disrespecting a person for coming from a religious basis nor disrespecting a person for coming from a nonreligious basis).

Social workers may derive a sense of duty from their historical mandate, core values, and ethical principles. Social workers (and indeed, other professionals) may think of themselves as a community with certain moral obligations to the rest of society (Thompson et al., 2006). The preamble to the NASW Code of Ethics suggests, "The primary mission of the social work profession is to enhance human well-being and help meet the basic human needs of all people, with particular attention to the needs and empowerment of people who are vulnerable, oppressed, and living in poverty." When social workers address social justice issues, they often work on behalf of those who are the most distressed and in greatest need. Thus, applying a deontological perspective, social workers may advocate for resources to vulnerable and oppressed populations, regardless of whether such an allocation would be for the greater good of society. Social workers advocate for the least well-off in society because it is inherently the right thing to do (Farland, 2007).

In the vaccination scenario, social workers might advocate on behalf of the disabled community, a group that is often subject to misunderstanding and discrimination. Using utilitarian arguments, some policy makers might argue that vaccinations should be allocated to able-bodied people because they can contribute the most to society. Regardless of whether this utilitarian analysis is true, social workers should advocate for the rights and interests of the disabled. Social work's mission or duty is to act on behalf of vulnerable and oppressed populations. Doing so is intrinsically good. If social work does not act on their behalf, which profession will?

Deontology reminds social workers that there may be some rules or duties that are so fundamental they should be followed because of their intrinsic worth. Although deontology may not have pat answers for all policy questions that may arise in practice, the same criticism could be made for the other ethical theories discussed in this chapter.

Which is the best theory to apply to policy issues–libertarianism, egalitarianism, utilitarianism, or deontology? Each social worker or individual may decide which is best for him or herself. Different ethicists may favor certain ethical theories, but there is no broad consensus over the best theory for all social workers or all people. For those who like moral clarity, the following section offers some. This section identifies ways of thinking about ethical issues that are clearly faulty.

---

19 Heteronomous ethics refers to ethical analysis based on morality derived from nonhuman sources, such as God or another deity. Autonomous ethics refers to ethical analysis based on morality derived from humans.

Flawed Ethical Reasoning

Well-intentioned people may express strong differences about the best way to assess policy issues from an ethics perspective. Many of these differences are ethically legitimate, meaning that there are reasonable ethical justifications supporting the application of different ethical analyses. In this section, we explore five types of ethical reasoning that lack ethical legitimacy: the squeaky wheel, clandestine bribery, nepotism, coercion, and misplaced fiduciary relationships.

According to an old maxim, "The *squeaky wheel* gets the grease." In terms of resource distribution issues, this means that those individuals or groups who make the most noise are the ones who will get the greatest attention and largest resource allocation. Although this maxim may reflect the pragmatic reality in some policy arenas, the squeaky wheel principle lacks ethical legitimacy. It violates egalitarian principles by giving favored treatment to people who raise their voices, complain, or agitate, rather than allocating resources according to egalitarian criteria such as need, fairness, universality, or equality. The squeaky wheel principle violates libertarian principles, since people are receiving resources from government rather than paying for them. It violates deontology because of the problems it would create if everyone acted by the same rule. Responding to the squeaky wheel creates a problematic incentive; it encourages people to raise their voices, louder and louder. Although each group has a right to advocate for itself, and policy makers should listen (as per the inclusiveness principle discussed earlier), the public policy process should promote principled advocacy, not simply loud advocacy. Thus, policy makers may rightly respond to squeaky wheels by listening to and validating their concerns. However, they should not allocate a disproportionate amount of resources to squeaky wheels. Finally, although I have used the "squeaky wheel" metaphor to make a point, I have done so at the risk of offending certain groups. In practice, policy makers should not refer to individuals or groups with negative labels such as squeaky wheels, but rather should validate their participation in open, responsive policy processes.

Bribery arises when an individual or group offers certain resources or favors on the understanding that they will receive certain favors or resources in return. Consider, for instance, a wealthy family that is originally placed low on the priority list for flu vaccines. The family privately offers $700,000 to certain government officials to ensure that the family will receive vaccinations. Essentially, the family uses bribery to jump the queue for vaccinations. This type of bribery offends ethical principles such as equality, fairness, honesty, and transparency. People should not be able to buy certain policy decisions through clandestine agreements with policy makers.[20] Suppose, however, the family publicly offers to build the state a specialized hospital facility that can accommodate 500 people infected by the flu. Utilitarians might argue that accepting this form of bribe is ethical because it produces the greatest good for the greatest number. Also, because the deal is has been announced publicly, it is transparent and honest. Some people may believe that accepting such a deal is unethical because it is still a form of bribery that offends principles of equality and fairness. Although clandestine bribes that benefit only a few policy makers are clearly unethical, public offers of resources for the good of the community present policy makers with a dilemma between equal treatment and the greatest good. There is no clear-cut answer concerning how to respond to such offers. The ethical decision-making framework in Part II, however, offers suggestions for how to work through such dilemmas.

Nepotism refers to providing preferential treatment, such as a disproportionate share of public resources, to relatives. In a strict sense, nepotism refers to providing privileged treatment to people related by blood or marriage. Favoritism, a more general term, refers to preferential treatment to family, friends, allies, business associates, or members of the same ethnocultural community group. Preferential or privileged treatment suggests there is no ethical

[20] Within some cultures, paying governments to facilitate certain types of treatment is not considered unethical but rather a normal part of doing business (Bailles, 2006).

justification for providing special treatment to the individual or group (Paul & Elder, 2006). An archetypal example of nepotism would be for Stella to hire her nephew to administer the vaccination program—not because he is the most qualified person, but because he is a relative. Nepotism and favoritism offend principles of equality and fairness. Whenever policy makers allocate resources, they should declare any potential conflicts of interest, such as when a friend or relative may benefit disproportionately from a particular decision. Although there may be legitimate reasons for allocating resources or making other policy decisions that benefit friends and family, policy makers should be wary of making any decisions that put their honesty and integrity in doubt. For social workers, nepotism and favoritism are prohibited by NASW Standard 1.06. Nepotism and favoritism may also be prohibited by agency policies or ethics laws governing public officials.

Coercion refers to the use of fear, intimidation, or illegitimate threats to influence the decisions of others. Ideally, policy makers should not give in to coercion, as it violates the principles of fairness, integrity, and respect for all individuals (DeMarco, 2001). Allocating disproportionate resources on the basis of coercion also violates the principle of libertarianism, which favors freedom and thus, the absence of coercion (Anderson, 2006). In practice, policy makers may give into coercion, not because they believe it is the right thing to do, but because they are truly afraid. Consider, for instance, an anonymous group that threatens the lives of Stella's children if she does not allocate vaccinations to their group; further, they threaten to kill the children immediately if she discloses the threat to the police or anyone else. She knows that coercion is wrong, but she feels compelled to protect her children's lives. The policy process principles discussed earlier in this chapter—including transparency, inclusiveness, and accountability—may help to reduce chances of coercion because they promote openness, public participation, and a system of checks and balances to protect against process problems. Policy makers also need training on how to respond effectively and ethically to attempts to coerce (e.g., how to create safety plans for family, and how to consult attorneys or law enforcement officers in a safe manner).

Fiduciary relationships refer to associations between two or more people in which the people with greater power invite the trust of others with less power. The more powerful people owe a special obligation to act with a high degree of honesty and in good faith, on behalf of the less powerful (Galambos, 1999; Manderscheid, 2007). Thus, social workers have a fiduciary relationship with clients, agency administrators have a fiduciary relationship with their staff, and social policy makers (including elected government officials) have a fiduciary relationship with their constituents. In policy situations, the problem of a *misplaced fiduciary relationship* arises when policy makers make an error in deciding on whose behalf they are acting. Stella was hired to develop a vaccination policy for the whole state of Minnesota. If she assumes she is acting on behalf of health-care providers or law enforcement officers, then her ethical analysis will be distorted. Although these may be important groups given her role and mandate, all Minnesotans are important. Even though Stella may be asked to make tough decisions about whom to prioritize, she should remember that she owes a fiduciary duty to the whole state.

CONCLUSION

Libertarianism, egalitarianism, utilitarianism, and deontology provide four different theories that may be used to analyze and debate various policy issues. The NASW Code of Ethics includes principles that may be derived from these theories. Self-determination, for instance, recognizes libertarian principles such as freedom and autonomy. Social justice recognizes egalitarian principles such as equality and fairness. The Code implies utilitarianism by suggesting that social workers consider the context of their decisions and actions, as well as by suggesting that social workers have a duty not only to their individual clients but to society as a whole. The Code also incorporates the deontological principle of duty, particularly with respect to social workers' duty to advocate on behalf of the most needy and vulnerable in society (Hugman, 2003; Weiss,

Gal, Cnaan, & Majiaglic, 2002). Critiques of the Code might suggest that the Code is internally inconsistent, as it should be based on a single, coherent theory. Alternatively, by incorporating different ethical theories, the code recognizes the tensions between them, but does not impose a particular theory or solution for resolving these tensions. In doing so, the Code gives social workers a combination of guidance and discretion in how to determine priorities in relation to the core values, ethical principles, and duties of the profession. This combination of guidance and discretion applies to policy work as well as other areas of social work practice.

Although social workers may debate the relative importance of libertarian, egalitarian, utilitarian, and deontological principles, the principles behind what constitutes an ethically legitimate policy process are much clearer. In order to promote ethically legitimate processes, social workers should advocate for accountability, inclusiveness, transparency, reasonableness, and responsiveness. Fair policy processes tend to lead to fair outcomes. Also, when people view policy processes as legitimate, they are more likely to accept the results of policy decision-making processes and cooperate with implementation (rather than being upset and motivated to sabotage the results). In addition, social workers should advocate against the use of ethically flawed reasoning such as the squeaky wheel, clandestine bribery, nepotism, coercion, and misplaced fiduciary relationships. These approaches to decision making violate the principles of fairness, respect, equality, freedom, and responsible, cost-effective stewardship of resources.

By understanding the strengths and limitations of various ethical theories, social workers can help educate others about different ways of resolving policy issues in an ethically appropriate manner. Educating people about different approaches can build understanding and respect, as well as promote collaboration and consensus (Barsky, 2007a). Consider the following scenarios:

- A group with strong libertarian values is advocating that health-care resources be distributed solely according to each person's ability to pay. Social workers may validate their libertarian values, but also help them appreciate how the ability-to-pay principle is unfair to certain individuals and groups (e.g., because their reason for unemployment and having no money to pay is related to illnesses or disabilities that are not their fault).
- A group with strong egalitarian values is advocating that additional resources be allocated for the sickest people in society, hoping to provide them with the same opportunities as everyone else. Social workers may validate their egalitarian values, but also help them understand the limits of allocating additional resources to certain groups. If society allocates too many resources to one group, then it may not have sufficient resources to meet the needs of other groups. Further, some of the sickest people in society cannot be cured of their illnesses. Providing resources to try to cure an illness that cannot be cured may not benefit society or the person who is sick. Eliminating costs that are not producing appreciable benefits should not be ethically controversial
- A group with strong utilitarian values suggests allocating health-care resources on the basis of the greatest good for the greatest number. A social worker advocating for a particular client may validate her concern for the greatest good, but also educate the group about the importance of respecting the dignity and worth of a person. The social worker has a duty to promote respect for each client, even when the client's needs may conflict with societal ones. Social workers may also educate people about the tension between the individual and the collective good, helping them understand that policies based on utilitarianism may not be compassionate or fair to everyone.
- A group with strong religious values, including the sanctity of life, is advocating for policies that require doctors to maintain life, at whatever cost. Social workers may validate their faith and sense of duty regarding preservation of life, but also educate the group about the potential costs of such a policy. Although the sanctity of life may be a very

high priority, putting it into practice may require heroic and financially untenable medical efforts (Zoloth & Zoloth, 2006). To protect the lives of many, society may need to make some choices based on utilitarian criteria. People of faith may believe that "who shall live and who shall die" are choices for God. Although it may seem distasteful, people still play a role in life or death issues because they must decide how to allocate resources when demand outstrips supply (e.g., in the flu vaccine example).

Ethical theories do not give pat answers to tough policy issues. They do provide substantial guidance on process issues. Ethical theories also provide different ways of thinking about policy issues, keeping core values and moral beliefs in mind. By understanding how to apply different ethical theories to policy formation concerns, social workers can advocate more effectively for their clients and society in general.

DISCUSSION QUESTIONS AND EXERCISES

The following questions and exercises are designed to help you apply ethical principles and theories to case scenarios involving policy processes and outcomes.

1. *Policy Process*: Critique each of the following vignettes in terms of whether the policy makers put the five process principles into practice: accountability, inclusiveness, transparency, reasonableness, and responsiveness. For any deficits, describe how the process could be improved.
   a. The Recovery Agency offers residential treatment for people with addictions. The agency is trying to decide whether to open its services to involuntary clients, a group that it has rejected in the past. Ed, the executive director, asks all employees to complete a survey as a way to provide input into his policy decision. Ed plans to have his daughter, not an employee, analyze the data and provide him with a recommendation. Ed will announce his decision about admitting involuntary clients at the next staff meeting. He will not take further questions and the policy decision will be final.
   b. City councillors are trying to determine how to deal with a neighborhood blighted with trafficking and violent crime. They set up a "blue ribbon panel" to assess the situation and make recommendations. Members of the panel include city leaders of the business, faith, and education communities. The panel is directed to provide reasons for its recommendations, so city councillors can debate the pros and cons of the plans.
   c. A state government decides to review its policy on providing vouchers for students from F-rated public schools, so they may go to private schools. A governmental committee solicits feedback from private schools, public schools, teachers, parents, and students, including people from a range of socioeconomic groups. The committee says that it will make its decision about the future of the voucher program based on the following criteria: cost-effectiveness, equity, and constitutionality of the program.
2. *Ethical Theories*: Complete each of the following sentences with the most accurate response:
   a. Utilitarians determine what is ethical by
      i. Assessing what duties people should abide by.
      ii. Assessing which course of action produces the greatest good for the greatest number.
      iii. Applying fixed rules, in all cases, regardless of the consequences.
      iv. Considering how to treat people equally or fairly.
      v. Assessing which course of action is the best at promoting individual freedoms.
   b. Libertarians determine what is ethical by
      i. Assessing what duties people should abide by.
      ii. Assessing which course of action produces the greatest good for the greatest number.

   iii. Applying fixed rules, in all cases, regardless of the consequences.
   iv. Considering how to treat people equally or fairly.
   v. Assessing which course of action is the best at promoting individual freedoms.

c. Absolutists determine what is ethical by
   i. Assessing what duties people should abide by.
   ii. Assessing which course of action produces the greatest good for the greatest number.
   iii. Applying fixed rules, in all cases, regardless of the consequences.
   iv. Considering how to treat people equally or fairly.
   v. Assessing which course of action is the best at promoting individual freedoms.

d. Egalitarians determine what is ethical by
   i. Assessing what duties people should abide by.
   ii. Assessing which course of action produces the greatest good for the greatest number.
   iii. Applying fixed rules, in all cases, regardless of the consequences.
   iv. Considering how to treat people equally or fairly.
   v. Assessing which course of action is the best at promoting individual freedoms.

e. Deontologists determine what is ethical by
   i. Assessing what duties people should abide by.
   ii. Assessing which course of action produces the greatest good for the greatest number.
   iii. Applying fixed rules, in all cases, regardless of the consequences.
   iv. Considering how to treat people equally or fairly.
   v. Assessing which course of action is the best at promoting individual freedoms.

3. *Applying Ethical Theories*: Review each of the following advocacy statements and explain whether it is based on egalitarianism, libertarianism, utilitarianism, or duty-based (deontological) arguments:
   a. Government should not subsidize the cost of treatment for prostitutes who have contracted sexually transmitted diseases because they have chosen to engage in an immoral lifestyle.
   b. Higher education should be accessible to all people, regardless of their ability to pay.
   c. Immigration policy should be determined according to which people can contribute the most if they move to this country.
   d. People should be free to decide how and when to end their lives because this is a personal issue, not a state decision.
   e. Society should ensure that every child has access to adequate health care because society has a moral obligation to take care of its most vulnerable people.
4. *Alternate Ethical Theory*: Select one of the advocacy statements in Question 3. Critique this advocacy statement according to one of the other ethical theories (egalitarianism, libertarianism, utilitarianism, or duty-based). Identify what alternative policy a social worker would advocate for, according to this theory.
5. *Critiquing Policy Decisions*: Critique each of the following social policies according to the following questions: What social work values and ethical principles should the policy makers consider? What are the strengths and limitations of these policies in relation to social work values and ethical principles? How could the policy decisions be improved to provide a better fit with social work values and ethical principles?
   a. Congress decides to move one billion dollars from social security to fight terrorism.
   b. A city has an extra $100,000 in its budget to prevent youth-gang violence. The city has 10 agencies that provide youth-gang prevention services. Wanting to be fair to each agency, city councillors decide to allocate $10,000 to each of 10 social agencies. Unfortunately, $10,000

per agency does not give any agency sufficient funds to do much good. One agency could accomplish much more good if it received the entire $100,000.

c. A school faced with budget cuts decides to cut its art classes. The school wants its students to do well on standardized education tests and the tests do not include any questions about art.
d. A public housing development creates a policy that prohibits child molesters from living in their development.
e. Government changes social assistance (welfare) policies so that people who are "disabled from engaging in high-risk activities" will receive lower benefits than people who are "not responsible for their disabilities." The policy defines high-risk activities to include smoking cigarettes, using illicit drugs, snowboarding, and riding motorcycles.
f. An agency that serves people with eating disorders has a long waiting list. The agency decides to refuse treatment services to those with limited motivation so it can prioritize people who are most likely to benefit from services.
g. A food bank decides to shut down operations. The program's directors believe that its existence enables poverty, rather than solves it. They believe the food bank makes the community take comfort in the fact that economically disadvantaged people do not go hungry. Unfortunately, the community does not take responsibility for job creation, affordable child care, and other programs that deal with the underlying causes of poverty. Although shutting down the food bank creates short-term pain and crisis, it will produce broader social change over the long term by motivating the community to act.

6. *Flawed Ethical Reasoning*: For each of the following scenarios, identify the flawed ethical reasoning and explain how it conflicts with social work ethics.
   a. Ms. Sharp administers a privately funded agency that helps people make a smooth and effective transition to retirement. She develops policies in a manner that encourages clients to work as long as possible so they do not take advantage of government programs designed for retirees until absolutely necessary. These policies will ultimately save money for taxpayers, although they may create hardships for some of her clients.
   b. A lobbyist for a drug company discovers that a congressman had an affair with a student intern. The lobbyist threatens to disclose the affair to the public unless the congressman supports a bill that would lead to increased profits for the drug company. The congressman fears what disclosure will do to his family and career, so he decides to support the bill.
   c. An agency that conducts child welfare research receives a call from a tobacco company executive. The executive offers to donate $5,000,000 for child welfare research provided that the agency agrees not to do any research related to children and tobacco. The agency agrees to accept this donation on an anonymous basis so that nobody knows about the agreement.
   d. A state senator suggests that the state should allocate additional resources for infrastructure (such as highways, schools, and water management) in districts that support the senator's party.
   e. Nursing home staff members are tired of hearing complaints from a small group of residents who are constantly protesting about the color of the cafeteria. The nursing home decides to take money away from the recreational activities budget to pay for painting the cafeteria a new color.

PART II

ADVANCED VALUES AND ETHICS

Professional behavior may be defined by a variety of different sources:

- *Ethical Standards*: The NASW Code of Ethics (1999) articulates the core values of social work as well as general ethical principles and more specific ethical standards that provide social workers with guidance on what constitutes professional behavior with respect to interactions with clients, agencies, coworkers, and society in general. Social workers specializing in certain areas of practice[1] may also be bound by other codes of ethics or standards of conduct. Psychologists, physicians, attorneys, and other professionals possess their own codes of ethics.[2]
- *Agency Policies*: Social workers and others working in agency contexts are required to follow agency policies and procedures. Agency policies provide direction on how to implement ethical principles such as informed consent, confidentiality, and respect in the circumstances of the agency's mandate, focus, philosophy, and client base.
- *Laws*: Federal, state, and municipal laws may also define how social workers and other professionals should conduct their practice. Some laws regulate specific professions (e.g., social work, nursing, or law). Other laws regulate specific types of agencies (e.g., foster homes, hospitals, or hospices). Still others regulate the conduct of the general public, which includes social workers and other professionals (e.g., laws prohibiting fraud, discrimination, or unlawful confinement).[3]

---

[1] For instance, groupwork specialists, clinical social workers, feminist therapists, addictions counselors, family mediators, and sexuality therapists.

[2] For detailed discussion of other codes of ethics, see Chapter 2.

[3] For detailed discussion of the relationship between law and ethics, see the introduction to Part I.

LEARNING OBJECTIVES

Upon successful completion of this introduction to Part II, you will be able to

- Explain and apply the six stages of the framework for managing ethical issues.
- Distinguish between cases that require determination of ethical breaches, responses to ethical breaches, or managing ethical dilemmas.
- Analyze ethical issues using five different strategies for critical thinking: reflecting, considering multiple perspectives, identifying goals, identifying and weighing obligations, and brainstorming options and assessing consequences.

In Part I of this textbook, we learned how standards, policies, and laws can be applied to various aspects of social work theory and practice.[4] We also learned how one's actual moral choices and ethical decision making may be affected by a variety of biological, psychological, social, and spiritual factors (e.g., basic needs, cognitive abilities, personality characteristics, emotional responses, social norms, and religious values and beliefs).[5] Thus, when social workers are making ethical decisions, they should be aware of various processes that may be affecting their choices and conduct. When social workers are engaging others in ethical decision making, they should also consider this broad range of factors.

The process of ethical decision making is not merely the application of fixed rules or standards to a case situation. Although rules and standards may form one basis for ethical decision making, it is important to understand the reasons behind particular rules and standards. In some situations, the rules and standards may not provide clear guidance on how to respond to a particular situation. In other cases, the rules and standards provide conflicting advice on how to proceed (Homer & Kelly, 2007). In yet other cases, certain rules and standards may conflict with our ethics and morals. Ideally, laws, policies, and codes of ethics are consistent with ethics and morals; in practice, there may be some conflicts (e.g., when slavery was permitted by U.S. law). Applying fixed rules or ethical standards may be sufficient when there are no gaps or conflicts between them; when gaps and conflicts arise, we need additional theories and strategies for managing ethical issues.

Part I introduced a range of ethical theories that could be used to analyze ethical issues and determine the most ethical courses of action. Utilitarianism suggests that we assess ethical issues by brainstorming a range of possible solutions and selecting the option that provides the greatest good for the greatest number. In other words, utilitarianism looks at the consequences of various choices, encouraging conduct that promotes good (happiness, health, economic gain, and so on) and avoids harm (physical injury, psychological despair illness, social dysfunction, and so on). Deontology suggests that we identify what duties we owe to others and determine how to act in accordance with these duties, regardless of the consequences of such actions. Ethics of care theory suggests that we should focus on our relationships with others, taking our emotional connections and responsiveness into account when we determine how to respond to ethical issues (Marcellus, 2005; Roberts, 2004). By recognizing compassion for and empathy with others, social workers are motivated to resolve ethical issues by the wish to help, rather than hurt others (Boatright, 2006; Cohen & Cohen, 1999). Virtue theory suggests that ethics is not about how we act, but who we are. In other words, we should live our lives according to desirable qualities (e.g., respect, integrity, and social justice).[6] For professionals, such as social workers, these desirable qualities may be defined by the profession, rather than by each individual practitioner (Banks, 2006; Roberts, 2004).

---

[4] For detailed discussion of how NASW standards apply to various aspects of practice, see Chapters 2 to 10.

[5] For detailed discussion of the influences of biopsychosocial-spiritual factors on moral and ethical decision making, see Chapter 3.

[6] For a more detailed discussion of utilitarianism and deontology see Chapter 10. For duty of care ethics and virtue ethics, see Chapter 15. For absolutism, consequentialism, and teleology, see Chapter 3.

Although some ethicists view ethics of care as a branch of virtue theory, others treat them as separate theories (Beauchamp & Childress, 2009). Part II builds on the foundational theories and information provided in Part I. Specifically, this introduction to Part II provides a comprehensive framework for analyzing and managing ethical issues. In Chapters 11 to 16, you will have an opportunity to apply this framework to specific contexts of practice: supervision, administration, psychopathology and mental health, child welfare, criminal justice, and social work with elders. Chapters 11 to 16 also delve into other aspects of advanced ethical practice, including how to critique agency policies and codes of ethics, and how to create or revise agency policies and codes of ethics.

Although some ethics textbooks emphasize the importance of learning and using a specific ethical decision-making framework, decision making is just one aspect of managing ethical issues. In addition to decision making, ethical management requires reflection, discussion, action, and review processes (Spano & Koenig, 2003; Thompson et al., 2006). As Figure II.1 illustrates, *the first stage of managing ethical issues is identifying that an ethical issue exists.* To complete this stage, social workers may employ a range of strategies to raise their awareness and recognize that ethical issues exist. In the process of identifying ethical issues, they also need to define what the issues are. Clearly articulating ethical issues will help workers focus on how to proceed with the next stages. *In the second stage, workers determine who they can approach for help in analyzing and managing the ethical issues,* for instance, supervisors, attorneys, ethics experts, and clients themselves. This stage recognizes that managing ethical issues is not an individual endeavor. In other words, although social workers may think through ethical issues on an individual basis, they should also consider whether and how to engage others in the process of assessing and resolving the ethical issues they have identified. *The third stage, think critically, provides social workers with a framework for analyzing the ethical issues in a strategic manner.* Workers may use this framework individually or work with others to deliberate over the issues to be resolved. In some cases, the process of critical thinking will lead everyone to a specific solution that they can implement without the need for further conflict resolution processes (in other words, they can skip the fourth stage and move directly into planning and implementation). In other situations, workers will need to engage clients, coworkers, or others in conflict resolution to determine how to proceed. *During the fourth stage, workers and others affected by the ethical issues make use of various conflict management strategies and skills to determine how to proceed.* Whenever possible, social workers should try to engage others in collaborative conflict resolution, as collaboration fits with ethical principles such as respecting the dignity and worth of all people and promoting positive human relationships (NASW Code, 1999). When social workers need to engage in adversarial methods of conflict resolution, they may make use of persuasion skills and advocacy strategies to promote the best interests of their clients, social justice, or other worthy causes. *During the fifth stage, social workers and the relevant parties plan how to implement their decisions, including who will be responsible for which tasks, when tasks should be completed, and other details of how to carry out their decisions.* This stage recognizes that determining the most ethical response to a presenting issue is not sufficient. Social workers should participate in planning and implementation to ensure that everyone actually responds to the ethical issues in the most appropriate manner. *The sixth stage, evaluate and follow up, suggests that social workers should monitor implementation, determine what parts of implementation are working well, what parts are not working so well, and what further actions are needed to address the original ethical concerns or any new ones that have arisen.* The sixth stage provides social workers and other relevant parties with feedback on the implementation stage. When implementation goes well, evaluation provides the parties with positive feedback and encourages continued ethical conduct. When evaluation discovers problems or new issues, it gives everyone an opportunity to take corrective action as soon as possible.

While the six stages are presented in a linear sequence, note that there may be loop-backs between later stages and earlier ones. This indicates that as social workers (and others) are

1. Identify Ethical Issues

- Learn relevant laws, agency policies, ethical standards, and professional values
- Recognize ethical questions or problems as early as possible
- Articulate the specific issues that require attention

2. Determine Appropriate Help *

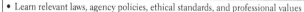

- Identify which types of help may be most useful (ethical or legal advice, clinical expertise, moral or financial support, conflict resolution, risk management, implementation)
- Determine which sources of support are appropriate (supervisor, attorney, ethics expert, professional association, insurer, colleague, client, friend, or others)

3. Think Critically *

- Reflect on one's own values, virtues, attitudes, beliefs, motivations, emotions, capacities, challenges, and social context
- Consider multiple perspectives
- Define goals for the ethical management process
- Identify and weigh obligations
- Brainstorm options and assess consequences

4. Manage Conflict *

- Analyze the nature of the conflict (rights, interests, power, miscommunication)
- Define goals for conflict resolution
- Determine appropriate strategies for engaging relevant parties in a constructive process (negotiation, mediation, advocacy, arbitration)

5. Plan and Implement Decisions *

- Determine who is responsible for performing which tasks, and when
- Develop strategies to avert problems and to raise the likelihood of success
- Monitor implementation to enable early response to problems that may arise

6. Evaluate and Follow Up *

- Evaluate the extent to which the goals were achieved and determine what types of follow-up (if any) are needed
- Evaluate the effectiveness of the ethical management process and determine recommendations for change

***Loop back to earlier stages as needed.**

FIGURE II.1 Framework for Managing Ethical Issues

working through a particular stage, they may determine that they need to return to an earlier stage rather than move forward. During the first stage, for instance, a social worker may determine that she has a confidentiality issue with a client who is living in a violent relationship. In the second stage, the social worker decides to engage her supervisor and the client in a discussion of this confidentiality issue. When they meet, the supervisor and client suggest that confidentiality is not the main issue. Thus, they should return to the first stage to identify and redefine the ethical issues. Similarly, a social worker may be implementing a decision, as per the fifth stage, but discover new problems that were not considered during the third and fourth stages (e.g., clients or coworkers are not cooperating with implementation because they do not agree with how goals were prioritized). The social worker would need to return to prior stages to assess and manage these new problems. Thus, although the framework in Figure II.1 suggests a general progression from stages 1 through 6, the order of stages should be used flexibly to accommodate the needs and context of the particular ethical issue.

To demonstrate the application of the Framework for Managing Ethical Issues (Figure II.1), we will use the following three scenarios.

Case 1: Sondra serves on a municipal committee that is reviewing proposals for a new day care center for senior citizens. During committee deliberations, Sondra indicates her support for the Oak Street proposal. She believes this is the strongest proposal overall. It also happens to be located close to the home of her elderly parents, so it would be convenient for them to attend. Sondra does not disclose that her parents live on Oak Street. She decides not to vote on the final decision about which proposal to accept so that nobody accuses her of having a conflict of interest on this decision.

Case 2: Shirley is a licensed clinical social worker who counsels students at a large university. She has been engaged in a sexual relationship with Chester for 2 months. During a discussion with Chester, she discovers that he participated in a group session conducted by Shirley on time management. This was a one-session group completed 18 months ago. Neither Shirley nor Chester recognized one another when they met at a party and started dating.

Case 3: Cadence is a 14-year-old student who was referred by her teacher to speak with Sherman, a school-based guidance counselor. Cadence discloses that her parents want to send her to India for an arranged marriage to a man from a village where they used to live. Cadence says she wants to honor her parents' wishes, but she does not want to marry a man she does not even know. She asks Sherman for advice.

1. IDENTIFY ETHICAL ISSUES

The first stage of managing ethical issues involves recognizing that an ethical issue exists and articulating the specific nature of the issue that requires attention (Manning, 2003). In some instances, the fact that an ethical issue exists may seem obvious: a client alleges that you have breached her confidentiality, your supervisor hands you a new agency policy that you know is inconsistent with state law, or you are having difficulty helping a particular client family because their values are so different from your own. When reading case scenarios in a textbook, however, ethical issues may appear to be more obvious than what you might experience in practice. As you are reading through the cases in this textbook, you know that we are focusing on ethical issues and you are particularly attuned to the possibility of conflicts between the ethics and values of social workers, clients, coworkers, and others. In practice, ethical issues may arise when they are least expected, or when you may be distracted by other issues. Thus, it is important to constantly be on the lookout for possible ethical issues (Mattison, 2000).

In Case 1, Sondra understands, at some level, that her voting on the placement of a seniors' center has ethical implications. However, she does not go through a strategic analysis of the ethical issues, assuming that she can simply avoid a conflict of interest by abstaining from voting. Had she analyzed the issues more thoroughly, she might have made a different decision. In Case 2, Shirley had no idea that she might have violated both legal and ethical prohibitions against having sex with clients when she first engaged in a sexual relationship with Chester. She knew about the prohibitions (e.g., NASW, 1999, S.1.09[c]). She was simply unaware that Chester was a prior client. Consider: Should Shirley have conducted a formal screening process to ensure that Chester was not a prior client before deciding to date him? Certainly, this would have preempted a potential problem, but is it reasonable to expect that Shirley should have known Chester was a one-time client? In Case 3, Cadence asks Sherman for advice on how to respond to her parents' plans for an arranged marriage. Given this request for advice, Sherman might simply offer his suggestions. Unless Sherman is aware that any suggestions could entail implicit biases, he may unwittingly impose his values and beliefs on Cadence. Although Sherman personally opposes the idea of an arranged marriage, he needs to respect the values, traditions, and beliefs of his clients. Thus, he should analyze the ethical issues before deciding how to respond to Cadence's request.

As these examples illustrate, social workers may first become aware that an ethical issue exists through a range of different processes. Ideally, social workers should identify ethical issues as early as possible—and certainly before a client issues a formal complaint or initiates a lawsuit. To identify issues at an organizational level, agencies could conduct periodic ethics audits; these are reviews of agency policies and practices to ensure they are in compliance with relevant laws, ethical principles, and standards of practice (Reamer, 2001a).[7] At a frontline practice level, social workers should maintain a high level of consciousness about the choices facing them and how they respond to issues raised by clients, coworkers, or other professional contacts. As Chapter 1 suggests, self-awareness may be enhanced through values clarification exercises, writing reflective journals, and engaging in supervision. I can think of many examples when I did not identify an ethical issue until I was debriefing with my supervisor. In my first field placement, I discovered that a client's infant daughter was playing with the client's bottle of methadone (a synthetic opiate used to treat heroin addiction). The child did not actually open the bottle and we discussed how the client would ensure that her methadone would be safely stored in the future. I thought this ended the issue until I met with my supervisor. My supervisor informed me that agency policy required me to report this incident to child protective services. Initially, I resisted making the report as it could diminish the trust that I was trying to build with my client. By working through the issues with my supervisor, I realized that the resistance was coming from me rather than from my client, as I wanted to avoid conflict. When I actually discussed my duty to report with the client, she understood my obligation to protect the welfare of her child and thanked me for being honest with her. With the help of my supervisor, I was able to identify and manage an ethical issue that reduced risks to the client, her daughter, the agency, and myself.

To identify ethical issues, social workers require knowledge of relevant laws, ethical standards, and agency policies. Thus, social workers require agency-specific training in addition to generalist training about legal and ethical issues. Because laws, standards, and policies may change, workers may require periodic training and reminders. Knowledge of laws, standards, and policies, however, is not enough. Social workers also require a high degree of moral sensitivity, that is, insight and awareness about human welfare, interests, and needs of various groups that may be affected by their work or professional behaviors (Cohen & Cohen, 1999). In particular, they need to be able to empathize with the conditions of others, for instance, how another person views abortion, capital punishment, sharing information about child abuse, and boundary violations with clients. Sondra may not think she has a conflict of interest; regardless, others may perceive that she has a conflict, so she should

[7] Chapter 12 describes the nature of an ethics audit.

recognize that an ethical issue exists and should be managed appropriately.

Once a worker recognizes that an ethical issue exists, the worker should articulate more specifically what that issue is. A vague or amorphous issue is difficult to manage because the worker and others do not have a clear sense of what problems they need to address. One way to clarify an ethical issue is to determine what type of issue it is. Some ethical issues relate to whether a law, ethical standard, or agency policy have been breached. In other cases, the parties know that a law, standard, or policy has been breached and the question relates to how to respond to such a breach or error in practice (Reamer, 2008b). In still other cases, the ethical issues relate to a dilemma rather than a specific breach. In a dilemma situation, no matter which course of action is taken, the welfare, interests, needs, or rights of one or more people will be put at risk. *Ethical dilemmas arise when a situation involves a conflict of values, ethical standards, agency policies, and or laws and there is no single, clear-cut answer about how to resolve such conflict* (Paul & Elder, 2006). When ethical dilemmas arise, workers may feel a certain level of angst as they search their hearts, minds, and souls for the best way to resolve the dilemma. In true dilemma situations, thoughtful, reasonable, and prudent social workers, when presented with the same facts, may disagree as to the most ethical course of action; although we may not be able to reach 100% consensus on how to resolve dilemmas, we still need to contemplate and discuss these cases because someone must make a decision on how to respond (Reamer, 2008a). The following sections describe how to identify whether an ethical issue concerns how to determine whether a breach has occurred, how to respond when a breach has occurred, or how to manage an ethical dilemma.

Determining Whether a Breach Has Occurred

Determining whether a breach has occurred is a retrospective question. The social worker asks, "Looking back on my conduct, have I violated any laws, policies, or ethical standards?" Alternatively, the social worker may be asking about the conduct of others, perhaps a client, coworker, supervisee, or professional in another agency. If you were Sondra's supervisor and she described how she advocated for the senior center, you might identify the question as, "Has Sondra violated any laws, policies, or ethical standards?" The question, as worded, is very broad. To make the question more specific, you could describe Sondra's behaviors and the context of her conduct. "Sondra serves as a member of a committee charged with reviewing proposals for a senior center. She advocated for the Oak Street proposal, but did not disclose that her parents live on Oak Street and would benefit from having the center located on Oak Street. Although Sondra abstained from voting on the proposals, did her advocacy constitute a violation of any laws, policies, or ethical standards?" This formulation of the question provides sufficient information to move onto the next stages of managing the ethical issue. Still, you could provide additional guidance by also identifying the specific laws, policies, or standards that Sondra might have breached. For instance, you might ask, "Did Sondra's advocacy violate the conflict of interest provisions in Standard 1.06(a) or (b) of the NASW Code of Ethics?" In some instances, you may know the specific laws, policies, or standards that need to be considered. In other instances, you may need to go onto the next stages, so that others may help you with identifying the specific laws, policies, or standards to consider. In Sondra's case, you might be familiar with Standard 1.06, but you may need the help of an attorney to determine which municipal or state laws may also apply to this situation. Thus, you could ask, "Did Sondra's advocacy violate Standard 1.06(a) or (b), or any other laws, policies, or standards?" This formulation ensures that you will explore a range of possible violations, rather than simply a breach of Standard 1.06.

In summary, to formulate a question concerning whether a breach has occurred, your statement of the issue should include

- The name(s) of the person or people whose conduct is in question.
- The specific behavior that is in question.
- The context of the behavior.

- What facts are known, and what assumptions or gaps in information need to be checked out.
- If possible, the specific laws, policies, or ethical standards that the person may have violated.

Once you have completed this stage you can move onto Stage 2, determining the appropriate forum(s) for the next stages of managing the ethical issue.

Responding to a Breach

Whereas determining whether a breach has occurred is a retrospective question, responding to the breach is future oriented. Responding to a breach asks, "Given that a breach has occurred, what should I (and/or others) do about it?" (Reamer, 2008a). Note how this question is open-ended and unbiased. The formulation of this question does not suggest a particular solution or course of action, but encourages consideration of a broad range of responses. This question applies whether a social worker is considering his or her own breach, or a breach by another person. In Case 2, Shirley knows she might have violated Standard 1.09(c) by having sex with a former client. Standard 1.09(c) does suggest that a social worker may be able to claim that "an exception to this prohibition is warranted because of extraordinary circumstances." As a licensed clinical social worker, however, she must also abide by the laws governing licensed clinical social workers. Assume that these laws prohibit workers from having sex with any client, without exception. Assume also that her agency policies are silent on this matter. Shirley's basic question is, "Given that I have acted in breach of state licensure laws [and may have acted in breach of Standard 1.09(c)], what should I do now?" To facilitate assessment of her ethical issue, she should also explain the context of the breach. "Chester participated in a time-management group that I ran 18 months ago. Neither of us remembered one another as this was a large, one-session group. I have recently engaged in an intimate relationship with Chester, which violates state licensure laws and the basic prohibitions in Standard 1.09(c) against having sex with former clients. What are my legal and ethical responsibilities at this point?" As much as possible, Shirley should state the facts as objectively as possible. If her formulation of the ethical issue includes misinformation or other biases, the subsequent analysis and management of the issues will also be skewed. In this case, she might be tempted to downplay or dismiss her violation. "Given that Chester was a one-time client in a large group and there is no risk of exploitation, can I continue to engage in an intimate relationship with him?" Although Chester was a one-time client, this close-ended question is biased because it assumes that Chester was not at risk of being exploited. The risk of exploitation in this case may indeed be low. Rather than make this assumption, however, Shirley should use the more open formulation of the question and leave the analysis of risk until later stages of the ethical issues management process.

The formulation of an ethical question related to how to respond to an ethical breach should include

- The names of the persons or people who breached the law, policy, or code.
- A description of the conduct that constituted a breach.
- Identification of the specific laws, policies, or ethical standards that the person breached.
- The context of the behavior that resulted in a breach.
- An open-ended, unbiased question about how to respond given the breach.

Questions related to breaches are relatively straightforward. Earlier, we discussed questions about whether a breach has occurred. Such questions are yes/no questions that lead to definitive answers: "Yes, the person's actions violated a particular law, policy, or standard," or "No, the person's actions did not constitute a violation." In this section, we explored questions related to how to respond to breaches. Although these questions are more open-ended, they still lead to relatively straightforward answers. In other words, there should be general consensus among social workers or other professionals about how to respond to particular violations. In the next section, we explore more complex ethical issues, specifically, questions that may not have a single, definitive answer.

Managing an Ethical Dilemma

An ethical dilemma arises when social workers or others are confronted by conflicting obligations and difficult choices. Regardless of which course of action they take, they risk violating some law, agency policy, or ethical standard. They may also risk hurting their clients, family members, their agencies, their coworkers, community members, or even themselves (Prilleltensky et al., 2002). Although the worker wants to promote good (beneficence), every possible course of action involves some risk of causing harm (maleficence). Questions pertaining to ethical dilemmas are future oriented. Basically, they ask, "Given my conflicting obligations, what course of action should I take?"

The formulation of a question for an ethical dilemma should include

- The name(s) and role(s) of the person or people who are faced with the dilemma.
- The relevant facts or context giving rise to the dilemma.
- The specific laws, policies, ethics, and/or values that are in conflict.
- Additional facts and information that need to be gathered.[8]
- An open-ended, unbiased question about how to manage the conflicting laws, policies, ethics, and/or values.

In Case 3, Sherman is a school-based guidance counselor who is faced with an ethical dilemma. By identifying his role as a guidance counselor, we know he should consider his obligations under school policy, as well as any laws that govern the relationship between staff and children. As a social worker, he should also consider his ethical obligations under the NASW Code of Ethics. Sherman faces a dilemma because his client, Cadence, has asked him for advice on how to respond to her parents' plans for an arranged marriage for her in India. He could provide advice, but he risks imposing his values and beliefs on Cadence. Under Standard 1.02, Sherman should respect his client's right to self-determination. If he withholds advice, however, Cadence may choose a risky course of action, for instance, running away from home to avoid being taken to India. Under Standard 1.02, Sherman also has a duty to protect clients from "serious, foreseeable, and imminent risk to themselves or others." Thus, Sherman could formulate the question for his ethical dilemma as follows:

> Cadence, 14 years old, may run away from home because her parents have said they are taking her to India for an arranged marriage. How should I manage my obligations to support client self-determination with my obligations to protect a client from serious, foreseeable, and imminent risks?

Given the limited facts in the case scenario, this may or may not be the primary ethical dilemma. Sherman needs to gather additional facts—for instance, what are the chances that Cadence will actually run away and what risks will arise if she does run away? If she has a safe plan for running away, then the obligation to protect Cadence from "serious" harm may not be the main issue.

Assume that Cadence told Sherman that she was not planning to run away, but that she was going to comply with her parents' plans for an arranged marriage. Under this scenario, Sherman knows that he should respect the values, traditions, and beliefs of his client and her family, but he is also aware that arranging a marriage in a foreign country for a 14-year-old goes

[8] When determining what additional information to gather, consider the following questions: What assumptions are we making? What information do we need to check out these assumptions? What other information do we need to make informed ethical decisions? What is the best way to obtain the missing information? How can we ensure against bias in ways that information is gathered or interpreted? If we are unable to gather all the information we need, we should acknowledge that the decision will need to be made based on incomplete information.

against his own values, traditions, and beliefs. Further, he is not sure whether the family would be violating any criminal laws or child protection laws (Chopra, 2006). Thus, he could initially formulate his ethical dilemma as follows:

> My 14-year-old client, Cadence, says she is going to go to India for a marriage that has been arranged by her parents. I understand that Cadence values respect for her parents and believes that it is appropriate for her to marry at 14. I am experiencing a values conflict. On the one hand, I would like to show respect for the values and traditions of Cadence's family. On the other hand, I personally believe that people should be at least 18 years old before they get married, and that people have a right to choose their own spouses. I need to find out what the U.S. and Indian laws say about arranged marriages for 14-year-old girls. My primary dilemma is, "How should I balance my ethical obligation to respect the choices of Cadence in her family with my ethical and legal obligations to protect the safety or interests of this potentially vulnerable minor?"

In this formulation, Sherman recognizes that he needs to gather additional information, but he provides sufficient information to begin the analysis and management of the ethical issue. By stating what information is missing (i.e., what laws may apply), Sherman ensures that this information can be picked up at a later stage.

Notice how Sherman states his dilemma question in an open-ended, unbiased manner, "How should I balance my ethical obligations . . . ?" Asking unbiased questions is one of the most difficult aspects of formulating questions for ethical dilemmas. Because Sherman believes that arranged marriages for minors are inappropriate he could have asked, "How should I prevent Cadence from entering into an arranged marriage?" This is a leading question because it presupposes that preventing the marriage is ethically necessary. By asking the more open-ended question, Sherman avoids this bias and allows for a full exploration of all the options, not just ones that include preventing Cadence from marrying. We must resist the temptation of asking an ethical question in a manner that suggests a solution that fits with our own biases and assumptions. Rather, we should ask questions in a manner that encourages us to explore from a variety of perspectives—the client's, the worker's, the agency's, the family's, and any others affected by the dilemma. If we want to engage others in a discussion of an ethical issue, we need to ask it in a manner that invites them to participate, regardless of their views or positions. If our questions indicate our preferred solutions, then others may be disinclined to participate in a discussion of the issues. The discussion has been biased from the start. If we begin with an unbiased question, we can voice our views and advocate for particular solutions at a later point in the process. By starting with an open, unbiased question, we promote full exploration of the issues. Whereas closed or leading questions restrict how we think about issues and what options are possible, open questions promote expansive thinking and creative solutions (Barsky, 2007a).

When developing an ethical question, you may find that there are many different foci or formulations you could follow. Initially, you may brainstorm a range of issues and then discard the ones that are irrelevant or trivial (Corey et al., 2007). Focus on the most important facts, laws, policies, standards, and conflicts. Provide sufficient detail so that you and others can identify which issues require your attention. Avoid providing too much detail so that you (and others helping you with the dilemma) may be distracted or overwhelmed by extraneous information. Sherman's statement might have included details on his religious background. If this was directly relevant to the ethical dilemma, then including this information would be appropriate. Otherwise, it should be excluded. Obviously, there is a fine balance between providing sufficient information and providing too much information. Remember that as you are analyzing and managing ethical issues, you can return to earlier stages. Do not fret if your initial formulation of the ethical question is not perfect. You can return to it and revise it—for instance, adding information or altering the form of the question as needed.

In Sherman's scenario, the primary conflict was between Sherman, his client, and his client's parents. Sherman could also have a conflict with his agency, for example, if agency policies conflicted with his own values, beliefs, or ethical standards. When formulating an ethical question, accurate identification of the parties involved in the conflict is important because it guides the worker on who is affected by the dilemma and whom to include in decisions about how to manage the dilemma. These decisions are particularly important in the next stage: determining who may help with analysis and management of the ethical issue(s).

2. DETERMINE APPROPRIATE HELP

In Stage 1, we determined that an ethical issue exists and formulated a question that articulates the crux of the question to be managed. In Stage 2, we determine who can help us analyze and manage the ethical issue. In this stage, we are basically asking who can provide us with the most valuable assistance at this time. Discussing ethical issues with others is a vital component of managing ethical issues because others can provide

- Additional facts or information needed to assess the ethical issues.
- Alternative perspectives for assessing ethical issues.
- Creative options for solution.
- A sounding board to test different lines of reasoning and reflect back their strengths and limitations (Strom-Gottfried, 2007).
- Moral support to help manage stress and to foster moral courage to do what is right even though it may entail certain risks.[9]
- Instrumental support, such as time, money, and other resources.
- Professional advice within the advisors' areas of expertise.

Ethical issues often entail conflict between two or more people. Thus, you may also need to engage others to work through such conflicts. The following sections examine the potential advantages and disadvantages of inviting various people into the process of managing the ethical issue. As the case examples will illustrate, we often begin by inviting a small circle of people to assist. These people can help decide whether or not to invite others into the process. It is generally easier to add people into the process than to ask them to leave.

Supervisor

Supervisors often play a key role in helping social workers manage difficult ethical issues. Supervisors are responsible for overseeing the work of their supervisees, which includes monitoring, consulting, guiding, and mentoring functions. Generally, supervisors are easily accessible, as they work in the same agency as their supervisees. They should be available for consultation on an as-needed basis, in addition to regularly scheduled supervisory meetings. Because supervisors and supervisees work in the same agency, supervisors are very familiar with agency policies and the client population that the agency serves. Further, social workers may disclose personal information about clients without concern about breaching confidentiality, as social workers advise clients that they may share information with their supervisors. Ideally, social workers have trusting relationships with their supervisors, making it easier to discuss potentially embarrassing situations with them. Supervisors should encourage supervisees to ask for help whenever challenging ethical questions arise. By encouraging social workers to discuss issues as early as possible, supervisors can help supervisees manage ethical issues and avoid exacerbating any problems. When Sondra received the Oak Street proposal for a seniors' center, she probably sensed that she might have a conflict of interest. Had she felt comfortable discussing this issue with her supervisor, her supervisor could have provided her with different options on how to handle this situation.

Although supervisors are among the first sources of help that social workers should consider, social workers may have various concerns that discourage them from accessing

[9] For instance, you may know that the right thing to do is to "blow the whistle" on your agency for illegal or shoddy activities, but doing so may put you at risk of losing your job. See Chapter 8 for further information on whistle blowing. Also, see the section on ethical courage, later in this chapter.

their supervisors (McAuliffe & Sudbery, 2005). Workers may fear negative consequences from disclosing ethical issues with supervisors. Sondra is not sure whether she breached any laws or standards regarding conflict of interest. She fears discussing this issue with her supervisor because she might be fired, suspended, or disciplined in some other manner. On the other hand, she could get into greater trouble if she does not ask for help. Some workers may resist asking for help so as to save face or protect their sense of pride. Within some cultures, asking for help may be difficult because it signifies weakness (Shiraev & Levy, 2004). If a supervisor overemphasizes the importance of workers taking responsibility and acting independently, workers may sense that asking for help is inappropriate. Shirley knows that she has breached the prohibition against having sex with clients, albeit unintentionally. She may feel embarrassed. She may also fear losing her job. Still, if she can muster sufficient moral courage, she can raise these concerns with her supervisor and begin the process of receiving help with her supervisor (Strom-Gottfried, 2007). When workers do not initially feel comfortable discussing ethical issues with their supervisors, they should consider others they can trust. After receiving support from others, they may reconsider approaching their supervisors.

Coworker or Coprofessional

Some social workers feel more comfortable discussing ethical issues with coworkers or other professionals in their field. If a supervisor does not come from a social work background, for instance, workers might be more inclined to ask a colleague with a social work background for help (Strom-Gottfried, 2007). Further, supervisors have the authority to fire or impose sanctions. Coworkers and coprofessionals do not, so they may be perceived as less threatening. Workers may also have stronger rapport, camaraderie, and trust with people who have similar positions and perspectives (McAuliffe & Sudbery, 2005). Sherman does not want to look foolish or ignorant to his supervisor. He consults a coworker for advice on how to respond to Cadence's concerns about an arranged marriage. The coworker does not provide direct advice, but helps him practice what to say when he asks for help with his supervisor.

Although coworkers and coprofessionals may be able to offer substantial assistance, consider the possible risks of asking them for help. First, sharing client information with them could constitute a breach of confidentiality, particularly if the other professional works for a different agency and the client has not provided permission to share information with this person. Second, the coworker or coprofessional may not have sufficient knowledge or skills to act as a consultant. Third, the agency may have strict policies about whom to consult, specifically, going up the organizational hierarchy for help rather than speaking with other work colleagues. A supervisor may feel slighted if a supervisee asks others for help rather than coming directly to the supervisor. Finally, a colleague may feel obliged to report misconduct or ethical issues to the agency, even if you ask the colleague to keep your information to him or herself (McAuliffe & Sudbery, 2005).

Ethics Committee

Some agencies have ethics committees[10] made up of people who are specifically designated to help with certain types of ethics issues (especially for research on human subjects or for end-of-life decisions). Ethics committees offer workers support *in house*, meaning that committee members are familiar with agency policies and can receive confidential client information. Often, ethics committee members are people with special expertise in ethics, law, and various aspects of practice. Workers may have some concerns about sharing potentially embarrassing information with an ethics committee (e.g., not wanting to look incompetent or unethical). It may be relatively easy for Sherman to ask an ethics committee for help, since he is asking about how to manage an ethical dilemma—a future-oriented question. Sondra and Shirley's questions relate to breaches, so they find it more embarrassing or difficult to ask for help. Often, ethics committees

[10] For further information on ethics committees, see Chapter 7.

do not have sanctioning power, though they may make recommendations to the agency about how to respond to a worker's violation of laws, policies, or ethical standards.

When seeking advice from an ethics committee, remember that the committee may be acting primarily on behalf of the agency rather than on behalf of you or your clients. Its recommendations may be designed to reduce risks for the agency, which may or may not be in the best interests of you or your clients. An ethics committee might advise Sherman to report Cadence's parents to child protective services for suspicions of child maltreatment. Reporting parents to protective services may be appropriate, but it may also be the committee's way of reducing the risk of liability for the agency should anything untoward happen to Cadence. Thus, social workers should consider the advice of the ethics committee, but evaluate its suggestions in light of the committee's role within the agency (Strom-Gottfried, 2007). This caution is not meant to demean the work of ethics committees. In practice, ethics committees take a broad range of perspectives into account, and their expertise may be very helpful to a worker in thinking through and resolving complex ethical issues.

Attorney

One of the primary advantages of consulting an attorney is that your communications will be confidential and privileged. In other words, you can admit breaking laws, violating agency policies, or breaching codes of ethics without fear that the attorney will turn you in or testify against you in a court of law or disciplinary proceeding. The only exception to attorney-client privilege is that an attorney may be required to take action to prevent serious harm to another person (e.g., if you threatened to kill your parents, the attorney would need to assess the situation and determine whether to report your threats to police, your parents, or some other authority). Generally, you should feel very safe discussing ethical breaches and ethical dilemmas with an attorney.

Attorneys are trained and licensed in law, so they can provide you with specific legal advice. A non-lawyer supervisor or consultant may provide you with legal information, but not legal advice. Sherman could ask his supervisor whether there are any state laws requiring social workers to take action to prevent a child from being taken to another country to be married. If there is a clear law on this matter, the supervisor may provide this information. If the law talks about protecting a child from mistreatment, but Cadence's situation may or may not fall within this definition, then Sherman could use legal advice. An attorney should be able to provide advice based not only with what child protection legislation says, but how courts might interpret this legislation, precedent cases, and legal principles that could be applied in this case.

When you receive help from an attorney, remember that the attorney may be focusing on legal issues rather than ethical ones. An attorney might advise Shirley that although she has violated laws prohibiting licensed social workers from having sex with clients, it is unlikely that she would be prosecuted because Chester is not complaining, nobody else knows he was a former client, and she did not know he was a client when they started dating. Still, Shirley should consider the ethical ramifications of her decisions—including her ethical obligation to be honest and forthright. Attorneys may have a different sense of professional ethics from that of social workers, particularly concerning professional boundaries. For instance, attorneys are not generally prohibited from having sex with clients.[11] Therefore, some attorneys may not appreciate the importance that social workers ascribe to maintaining professional boundaries with potentially vulnerable clients. One of the primary barriers to access to attorneys is cost (e.g., $200 to $600 per hour). If the worker has professional liability insurance, the insurance typically covers attorney fees. A worker could

[11] For instance, an attorney may draft a contract for her husband's company or provide tax advice to a sexual partner. Still, attorneys should not take advantage of vulnerable clients. For instance, it may not be prudent for a family law attorney to have sex with a client who is going through a difficult divorce process.

consult with the agency's attorney, but should remember that this attorney works primarily on behalf of the agency and the worker may need independent legal advice.

Liability Insurance Provider

Insurance companies[12] encourage professionals to contact them whenever significant legal or ethical issues arise—particularly, with concerns about legal violations or ethical breaches that may result in civil lawsuits. Insurers may not be willing to provide advice on ethical dilemmas when there is no immediate risk of a lawsuit. In Sherman's situation, an insurance company might provide him with some guidance on how to avoid a malpractice lawsuit, but Sherman's dilemma goes beyond that. He has to choose between a variety of courses of action based on clinical and ethical issues, not just legal ones.

Insurers have legally trained staff, so they are able to offer legal advice. Insurers often have an interest similar to that of the professional—wanting to encourage ethical, competent practice. Because insurers want to help professionals reduce risks of legal liability, their advice may tend to be conservative. In some cases, a social worker may want to take a risk that the insurer advises against. For instance, an insurer might advise Sondra to report her conflict of interest to prevent lawsuits arising in the future. Sondra may think she will lose her job if she reports her conflict of interest. Therefore, she might resist the advice of her insurance company.

Professional Association or Licensing Body

Professional associations (e.g., NASW) and licensing bodies[13] have ethics committees mandated to provide members with support regarding ethical violations and dilemmas. When complex legal issues are at stake, they may say they cannot provide legal advice and refer you to your own attorney. Still, they may be able to provide useful information and guidance. One of the advantages of consulting with social work associations and licensing bodies is that they specialize in social work ethics. Attorneys in private practice or working with insurance companies may not be as familiar with social work perspectives and concerns.

Professional associations and licensing bodies do not represent social workers per se. Their role includes promoting competent, ethical practice and safeguarding clients from harm. Thus, social workers should find it relatively easy to consult with them on ethical dilemmas. When dealing with ethical breaches, however, social workers may be more reticent. They may not want to admit breaching the NASW Code or other regulations, as they may face suspension or other discipline from the professional association or licensing body. Before admitting a violation, therefore, social workers may be wise to consult with an attorney. An attorney can provide advice on whether, when, and how to admit a potential breach. Shirley's attorney, for instance, might advise her to disclose her unintentional violation of Standard 1.09 through an attorney's letter. The letter can be used to provide a clear and comprehensive explanation of her actions rather than risk misinterpretation through a telephone call to her licensing body. The attorney might also advise Shirley to document the unintentional breach in her case records in order to explain the sequence of events, what she did when she became aware of the breach, whom she consulted, and what she has done to minimize the risks arising from the breach. Accurate documentation of errors in practice demonstrates professional integrity and accountability. Documentation of errors in practice should be stated in descriptive terms

---

[12] This section focuses on a social worker's insurance provider. Agencies may also have their own insurance providers. Although the agency and worker may have similar interests, they also conflict (e.g., an agency that blames a worker for disobeying agency policy and causing damage to a client). In such cases, social workers should consult their own attorneys rather than rely on one who works for the agency.

[13] For discussion on the mandates of professional associations, licensing bodies, and other forms of social work regulation, see Chapter 9.

(describing what happened), without ascribing blame or fault (Reamer, 2008b).

When discussing ethical concerns with a professional association or licensing body, protect your client's confidentiality as much as possible. If you are asking for help with an ethical dilemma, you may be able to discuss the issues without disclosing any identifying information about your client. If you are discussing an ethical or legal violation, then the professional association or licensing body may require identifying information in order to open up a case.

Client

Given the social work principle of showing respect for the dignity and worth of all people, social workers strive to empower clients to make self-determined decisions about important matters in their lives (S.1.02). When ethical issues arise, however, social workers may avoid engaging clients in discussions that may be of the utmost importance. Social workers may prefer to sort through ethical issues without consulting their clients for a variety of reasons.

- They may dislike conflict and try to avoid direct dialogue with clients.
- They may believe that it is better for professionals to work through the ethical issues and only speak with clients once they have reached a conclusion.
- They may believe clients have limited capacity to understand the ethical issues or are too vulnerable emotionally to put them through the stress of working through these issues.

Although there may be good reason to consult with supervisors or other professionals before speaking with clients, social workers should consider the benefits of engaging clients in discussions at some point in the process and perhaps early on. Consulting with clients not only shows respect for their views and interests—it assists with resolution of issues. Clients may be able to offer information, suggestions, or other forms of assistance that can help resolve the ethical issue in the most positive manner possible. Feminist social workers believe that power should be shared in the helping relationship, which suggests involving clients in all stages of ethical decision making (Corey et al., 2007). By including clients early in the process, you may foster trust and collaboration. Assume that Sherman and his supervisor discussed his dilemma with Cadence's family and came to the conclusion that the parents must be reported to child protective services. The parents may be particularly incensed with Sherman because he did not show the courtesy of discussing the situation with them prior to making this decision. If Sherman had met with them first, they might have been able to allay his concerns that Cadence was at risk of harm. Even if Sherman eventually concludes that he has to issue a child protection report, he might be able to develop a good working rapport with the family by involving them in discussions and validating their concerns.

In situations where social workers have breached ethical standards, attorneys or other consultants may advise against having direct discussions with clients. They may be concerned that the worker will admit fault, which subjects the worker and agency to legal liability. From an ethics perspective, admitting fault and taking responsibility may be the right thing to do (i.e., it fits with the principles of honesty and accountability). From a conflict resolution perspective, as discussed below, admitting fault and issuing an apology may contribute to a timely and amicable resolution of the issues (Porter, 2005; Robbennolt, 2003). Apology may lead to the healing of a troubled relationship. There are risks and benefits from admitting fault, just as there are risks and benefits from avoiding admissions. When faced with such a decision, consult with your attorney or supervisor to assess these risks and benefits to determine whether there are ways to maximize the benefits and limit the risks. In some jurisdictions, for instance, medical practitioners can provide apologies for certain acts without incurring additional legal liability.

Friend or Family Member

When faced with difficult ethical issues, social workers may turn to friends or family members for advice or support. Before doing so, they should consider the benefits and risks of their action. Perhaps the greatest advantage of turning to a friend or family member for help is that this is a person that you know and trust, someone who may offer you support even if you have engaged in unlawful or unethical behavior. Whereas discussing ethical concerns (particularly breaches) with a supervisor may put your job at risk, discussing them with a friend or family member may offer you a chance to vent, reflect, and ask for advice from someone who has distance from the agency and work situation (McAuliffe & Sudbery, 2005).

In some cases, friends or family members may have social work or ethics expertise, so they can provide guidance or suggestions from an informed perspective. Even if friends or family are not particularly knowledgeable about social work and ethics, they may still be a good source of moral support. Having moral support from friends and family can provide social workers with courage to face difficult situations and do the right thing. On the other hand, there is no guarantee that family or friends will provide positive support. They could pass negative judgments on the social worker, or encourage the social worker to something for expedience rather than because it is the right thing to do. If Shirley asked her sister whether she should report her violation to her licensing board, her sister might respond, "Why would you even consider doing that? You'll only get yourself into trouble." Although Shirley might eventually decide not to report herself, her sister's suggestion that she should not even consider this option is problematic. Shirley should consider the possibility of turning herself in, weighing the risks and benefits of this solution with those of other options. Reporting herself might entail some risks, but still be the right thing to do.

One of the most important limitations on engaging families and friends in discussions of ethical issues is the need to protect client confidentiality. Social workers should not disclose confidential client information to friends or family, even if they are asking friends or family for help that could be of assistance to the client (Standard 1.07). Social workers might be able to discuss a client situation without disclosing identifying information, but this still poses problems. First, the client has not provided consent to discuss the situation with friends or family. Second, friends or family may eventually discover who the client is (e.g., if the client says hello to you on the street as you and your spouse walk by). If Sherman discussed Cadence's situation with a friend, the friend could easily identify Cadence's family if the case were reported in the newspaper or went to a public court hearing. Third, friends or family members could be called into court or other hearings to testify against the social worker. In most jurisdictions, spouses have a "marital privilege" that essentially means that one spouse cannot be compelled in court to testify against the other spouse (*Wolfle v. United States*, 1934). This legal privilege only applies to married spouses, not to common law spouses or other family members. Further, there are numerous exceptions to this privilege. For instance, in some jurisdictions, the spouse can decide to testify, whether or not the accused social worker provides permission for the spouse to testify. Accordingly, social workers should be careful about discussing cases with family members, even if they do not disclose the client's identity.

Remember that not all social work communications are confidential. Sondra serves on a government board whose meetings and records are open to the public. Thus, Sondra could discuss her concerns about conflict of interest with family members or friends without concern about breaching client confidentiality. Still, she may be wise to discuss her concerns with her supervisor or attorney. These professionals have greater expertise on conflict of interest issues and are mandated to provide her with support on this type of concern.

3. THINK CRITICALLY

Critical thinking refers to assessing a situation or problem in a purposeful manner, taking relevant factors and sound arguments into account (Shiraev & Levy, 2004). During this stage of the ethical management process, social workers make use of a variety of strategies to help them work through the ethical issues. Successful resolution of this stage may or may not result in reaching a definitive decision. In some situations, critical thinking may lead workers to decide upon a particular course of action as the best way to resolve the ethical issues. In such cases, workers may implement their decisions (Stage 5) without needing to consult others. In other situations, critical thinking does not lead workers to a particular decision, but rather prepares them for Stage 4, conflict resolution. In such cases, workers cannot resolve the issues on their own. They need to engage others to determine how to proceed. Consider, for instance, an agency that is developing a policy on whether to use physical restraints for potentially violent clients. An individual social worker could use critical thinking to assess the relevant legal and ethical considerations, but the worker may not be able to determine agency policy without consulting and building agreement with other agency staff. By using critical thinking, the worker goes into the conflict resolution process with a better understanding of the issues and relevant considerations. Even if the worker has a sense of what she believes is the most ethical policy response, she can keep her decision tentative, ensuring that she is open to hearing the concerns, contentions, and arguments of others. None of us is infallible. Even if we have gone through the critical thinking process in a comprehensive manner, we can still learn from others.

In order to engage in critical thinking, social workers should strive to be kind, open-minded, impartial, honest, compassionate, and honorable.[14] They should guard against being spiteful, oppressive, egotistical, callous, deceitful, hypocritical, uncaring, or disingenuous (Paul & Elder, 2006). They should not rely on assumptions, stereotypes, intuition, or blind adherence to stated laws, agency rules, or ethical directives. Critical thinking not only helps social workers make better decisions; it also helps them provide well-reasoned arguments for the decisions they make. When ethical issues arise, there may not be one pat answer for the best way to respond. Thus, social workers should be able to explain why they took a particular course of action, particularly if harm to a client or others arises. Social workers are not expected to be perfect in their management of ethical risks and benefits; rather, they are expected to act honestly and prudently, based on critical thinking. Being able to provide a sound rationale for ethical decisions facilitates the social worker's accountability for actions taken in response to ethical issues (Osmo & Landau, 2006).

Some models of ethical problem solving instruct social workers to brainstorm a range of options and go through a rational decision-making process to determine which option is most likely to achieve the worker's primary goals. Although brainstorming options and rational thinking are useful strategies, thinking critically is not simply a cognitive or rational problem-solving approach. It also requires assessment of values, motivations, feelings, relationships, and sociocultural context (Corey et al., 2007). This section offers five strategies for thinking critically about ethical issues, as outlined in the third stage of Figure II.1.[15]

These strategies do not represent a sequence of steps but rather a checklist of approaches you may take in order to work through an ethical issue. Which combination of strategies works best, and in what order, may depend on the ethical issues being considered. In some cases, for instance, the most important strategies might be identifying goals and obligations. In other cases, the most useful strategies might be reflecting on values, brainstorming options, and assessing consequences. Although you might be tempted to make conclusions using just one or two strategies, I encourage you to consider all five strategies to ensure a comprehensive analysis of the issues. Even if you believe that a certain strategy is most important, you may benefit from going through the other strategies so that you will understand the perspectives of your supervisor, client, or others involved in the management of the ethical issues. As you read through the following analysis, it may seem messy. Thinking critically about ethical

---

[14] These character traits fit with virtue theory. Note, however, that the Framework for Managing Ethical Issues, blends virtue theory with other ethical theories such as deontology and teleology.

[15] For ease of reference, Figure II.1 is also presented on the inside of the front cover.

issues requires an appreciation for a complex set of factors. Do not expect a simple, linear process that leads you to a single, definitive conclusion.

Reflect

Reflection is an ongoing process of considering and questioning one's own values, attitudes, beliefs, motivations, emotions, capacities, challenges, and social context. Whereas rational ethical decision making asks the social worker to stand back and look at the issues as an objective or neutral third person, the process of reflecting recognizes that the social worker *is in the process*, not separate from it (Mattison, 2000). The ability to think through ethical problems may be hampered by a range of psychosocial challenges, for instance, fatigue, dogma, habits, and stress. By raising self-awareness, social workers can manage these challenges in a strategic manner. If I am aware that I am tired, I may put off decision making until I have had more rest. If I sense that I am applying my beliefs in a dogmatic fashion, I can ask myself, "What are some other ways that I could think about this issue?" If I feel that I am responding to ethical problems in a routine manner, I can try to put myself in someone else's shoes to get a fresh look at the issues. If I discern that am highly anxious, I can use stress management techniques to deal with the stress before determining how to manage the ethical problem. Reflection allows us to raise red flags[16] for ourselves, identifying feelings, beliefs, attitudes, and behaviors that may be hindering our ability to think through ethical situations (Quinn, 2005).

Reflecting fits with "ethics of care theory," which suggests social workers should acknowledge the importance of their relationships and the social context when assessing ethical issues (Beauchamp & Childress, 2009). A caring social worker is not someone who acts in a cool and detached manner, but someone who acknowledges feelings such as compassion, sympathy, fidelity, commitment, and concern. As social workers, we should care about all stakeholders affected by an ethical issue (Manning, 2003). When Shirley is trying to decide whether to end her sexual relationship with Chester (a former client), she should be aware of her feelings toward Chester and how they may be affecting her decision making. If she pretends that she does not love him, she cannot factor this emotion into her analysis of the issues. By acknowledging her love, Shirley is not deciding that her love is the most important factor to consider. It simply puts this factor on the table for consideration. She may eventually determine that her professional obligations are more important than her personal feelings for Chester, but at least she has made this a conscious decision.

In Chapter 1, we explored how reflection can be used to clarify our values. Reflection also helps social workers consider how emotions, attitudes, and so on may be affecting their decision making. In some situations, subconscious issues may be clouding one's thinking. As Chapter 3 described, a variety of factors may affect a person's moral decision making—biological, psychological, social, and spiritual. Assume, from a psychological perspective, that Sondra is a risk taker. In contrast to a person who is risk averse, she might be more willing to accept the risk of being fired for a conflict of interest. By being aware of her risk-taking style, she gains an appreciation for why her assessment of ethical issues may differ from those of her supervisor or others. Alternatively, assume Shirley tends to catastrophize. She may overreact to what may have been a relatively minor breach, unintentionally having sex with a former client (Cohen & Cohen, 1999). If Shirley's supervisor is aware of this tendency, she can help Shirley through reality-testing questions, helping Shirley see that her breach does not mean the end of the world.

Questions to ask yourself when reflecting on a particular ethical issue include these:

- What are my professional role(s) in this situation? (e.g., social worker, administrator,

---

16 Metaphoric warning signs. In one of my classes, students actually brought red flags which they raised every time they suspected a situation requiring special ethical attention.

psychotherapist, advocate, addictions counselor)

- Given my professional role(s), which of my professional values may be relevant to how this ethical issue is managed?
- How would I describe my social identity in terms of which group affiliations affect my values, attitudes, and belief systems? (e.g., specific religious, cultural, ethnic, political, gender, or other diversity-group affiliations)
- What identity-based values, attitudes, and belief systems may be affecting the way I am thinking about the ethical issues raised in this situation?
- What additional biological, psychological, social, or spiritual factors may be affecting my decision making?

In Case 3, Sherman identifies himself professionally as a social worker and a school guidance counselor. Given his school affiliation, he values education and protection of the welfare and interests of all students. Social work values relevant to his concerns about Cadence include respect for dignity and worth of all persons, human relationships, and integrity (NASW Code, 1999). These values suggest that Sherman is not only concerned about Cadence's safety and welfare; he is also concerned about respect for the parents and their culture, the relationship between Cadence and her parents, and his ability to serve Cadence and her family in an open and honest manner. Sherman also values social justice, which he may interpret as social justice for Cadence in particular, or for girls in general (i.e., that girls are provided equal opportunities and fair treatment).

In terms of social identities, Sherman identifies himself as White, Anglo-Saxon Protestant. Upon reflection, he detects the following values that stem from this social identity: egalitarianism and independence. He understands how these values tend to make him favor individual choice over obedience to parents. His personal values fit with his professional values in terms of supporting equal treatment for boys and girls. By raising consciousness of his social identity, Sherman can periodically check whether he may be imposing culture-based values on his clients (Appleby et al., 2007). Without such awareness, he would not be able to discern how his culture-based values are affecting his thinking.

As Sherman assesses his biopsychosocial-spiritual context, he realizes that feelings about his own childhood may be affecting his thinking. He describes his parents as authoritative. He still harbors resentment for times they tried to impose their will on him, particularly when they tried to dissuade him from going into social work. Sherman reminds himself that Cadence's relationship with her parents is a very different issue from his relationship with his parents. He may use consultation and feedback from his supervisor to make sure his thinking is not biased by his childhood experiences. If he wants to work through his feelings toward his parents in a therapeutic manner, he should seek the help of a psychotherapist from a different agency rather than rely on his supervisor for this type of assistance.

As noted earlier, virtue theory suggests that it is important to *be ethical* rather than simply *act in an ethical manner* (Cohen & Cohen, 1999). Virtues are not rules or choices, but enduring moral character traits by which people live (Boatright, 2006). Aristotle, Hursthouse, and other proponents of virtue ethics believe that virtues are personal character traits that people need to flourish or live well (Banks, 2006). Consider what virtues help define who you are and what character traits you need to live well. Although you (and every social worker) may make personal decisions about the most important virtues, the following list provides examples of virtues[17] that

[17] Aquinas identifies the four cardinal virtues as prudence, temperance, justice, and fortitude. Some people derive the virtues to which they aspire from religious or spiritual leaders (Sherwood, 2008a), such as Abraham, Isaac, Jacob, Sarah, Rebecca, Rachel, Leah, Jesus, Moses, Mohammed, Bhudda, Confucius, or Gandhi. Social workers may strive to model the virtues of Jane Addams, Mary Richmond, or other social work leaders.

may be particularly valuable when you are facing difficult ethical issues:

- *Ethical humility* suggests that people should be modest or unassuming concerning their knowledge, morals, and sense of what is right or wrong. They should be open to acknowledging their limitations, including the possibility that their thinking may be egocentric or biased. Remember to ask yourself, "What if I am wrong? Is there something [information, beliefs, or ethical obligations] I am overlooking?" (Pope & Vasquez, 2007, p. 14).
- *Ethical courage* suggests that people should be brave in the face of challenging situations. Often, doing the right thing is not easy. Acting ethically does not mean you will be the most popular person. In fact, you may face strong opposition, particularly when you are defending the rights of a minority. You may also face risks, such as losing your job, attracting negative media attention, or even receiving scorn from clients, coworkers, close friends, or relatives.
- *Ethical integrity* refers to being honest and forthright when assessing and managing ethical issues. Integrity includes being honest with yourself, as well as with others. You should not provide false information or arguments to justify your actions or positions. You should not deride others with personal (ad hominem) attacks to detract others from relevant ethical arguments. You should admit when you have caused harm or acted in a manner that conflicts with public laws, agency policies, or ethical standards.
- *Ethical perseverance* refers to being tenacious in pursuit of determining what is ethically correct and following through on doing what is right. When faced with challenges and frustrations (including opposition from others), perseverance provides the strength and motivation to continue to strive for what is right.
- *Fairmindedness* refers to the willingness to consider various ethical viewpoints, including those of clients, supervisors, coworkers, and different cultural groups. Fairmindedness requires you to suspend judgments and be open to the possibility that others have valuable insights and perspectives to contribute to the assessment and management of the ethical issues.
- *Ethical empathy* refers to placing yourself in the position of others in order to understand their values, beliefs, concerns, and perspectives (Paul & Elder, 2006).

The last two virtues, fairmindedness and ethical empathy, form the basis of the following section.

Consider Multiple Perspectives

When faced with ethical issues, some people become preoccupied with their own concerns and perspectives. Unfortunately, this blinds them to the concerns or views of others. Sherman might be thinking, "How can I protect Cadence from being forced into marriage?" Given the focus on his child protection role, he might disregard other perspectives, such as "What values and beliefs might be encouraging Cadence's family to plan an arranged marriage?" Considering multiple perspectives (sometimes called "perspective taking") demonstrates respect for the dignity and worth of all people. Considering multiple perspectives also enhances insight, critical thinking, and creative problem solving (Paul & Elder, 2006).

Both professionals and clients may be vulnerable to egocentricity and flawed thinking, including stereotyping, making assumptions, and interpreting the world in a manner that satisfies self-interests.[18] Considering multiple perspectives helps one see things as they are, or could be, rather than as one assumes or hopes they will be (Paul & Elder, 2006). The following examples illustrate how flawed thinking may arise and how considering other

[18] Other examples of flawed thinking include dichotomous thinking ("We are good. You are evil"), selective memory (recalling only the facts that support your own case), and artificial crisis (acting as if decisions must be made immediately, even though there is time to gather information, deliberate, and plan).

perspectives can be used to promote more effective thinking.

- Sherman might be acting on stereotypes about families of Indian origin, perhaps assuming that Cadence's parents are using an arranged marriage to suppress her. If Sherman meets the parents and remains open to hearing their views on arranged marriage, he may see their motivations in a more positive light.
- If Sondra has a sense of self-righteousness, she might assume that she acted ethically, not even considering the possibility that advocating for the Oak Street proposal raised a conflict of interest issue. If Sondra reflects on how the proponents of other proposals might view her advocacy, she might gain a better appreciation of why they believe her failure to disclose a conflict of interest was unfair.
- Shirley's assessment of the risks entailed by her relationship with Chester might be hindered by egocentric myopia or short-sightedness, as she is only considering the present, when her relationship with Chester is positive. If she looked into the future, she might also consider what could happen if the relationship sours and Chester decides to report her for violating state laws.

Flawed thinking is not necessarily conscious. People may oversimplify, generalize, rationalize, or make other errors in critical thinking without being aware that their thinking is self-biased. Thus, considering the perspectives of others is a critical component of ethical assessment and management (Paul & Elder, 2006).

Identify Goals

Identifying goals[19] refers to articulating what you hope to accomplish through the process of managing an ethical issue. Articulating clear and specific goals helps focus everyone on desired outcomes—in other words, what needs to be done in order to resolve or reduce problems raised by the ethical issue (Dolgoff et al., 2009). Thus in order to identify goals, begin by referring back to the ethical issue stated in Stage 1. The type of ethical issue that you defined will affect the types of goals you identify.

Determining a Breach

If the issue concerns the existence of a breach, then the goal is simply "To determine whether or not a particular person has violated a law, agency policy, or ethical standard." In Case 1, the primary goal is to determine whether Sondra violated conflict of interest laws.

Responding to a Breach

If the ethical issue concerns how to respond to a breach, then the goal is "To determine what action(s) should be taken to

- Mitigate[20] risks or damages from the breach.
- Hold the person accountable for the breach.
- Compensate anyone who may have been harmed by the breach.
- Prevent further breaches and protect people from harm.

In some cases, all four bulleted points apply. In other cases, perhaps one or two points apply. In any situation, different people may have different views on which goals are most important. In Case 2, Shirley knows she has violated laws prohibiting sex with clients. She needs to decide what to do about this violation. Her primary goal may be to mitigate risks arising from the breach—for instance, protecting Chester from harm

[19] In your research and practice courses, you may have discussed the differences between goals and objectives. Whereas goals are general statements of what you would like to achieve, objectives are more specific, measurable indicators of successful outcomes. At this stage of managing the ethical issues, identifying general goals is sufficient. If you identify specific objectives at this stage, you may be locking yourself into particular outcomes too soon, which will hinder creativity and collaborative problem solving.

[20] Reduce.

and protecting herself from having her license revoked or suspended. Her supervisor and the state licensing board might be concerned about holding Shirley accountable[21] for the breach and protecting Chester and future clients from harm. Given that nobody has been hurt by the breach, the question of compensation does not arise at this point in time. If Chester had experienced harm as a result of Shirley's dual relationship with him, then compensation would be a relevant goal.

Ethical Dilemmas

As defined earlier, an ethical dilemma refers to a situation in which a social worker has conflicting obligations or directives. Regardless of which course of action the worker chooses, the worker risks violating at least one of these obligations. The worker also risks hurting one or more persons (Dolgoff et al., 2009). When setting goals, consider each of the outcomes various parties affected by the ethical dilemma would like to achieve. The goals should reflect what each party would like to achieve, not just the outcomes preferred by the social worker or social agency. The parties do not need to agree to each of the goals; they just need to acknowledge that their own goals are accurately reflected somewhere in the list of goals. In Case 3, Sherman might identify the following goals:

- To respect the values, traditions, and autonomy of Cadence's family.
- To protect Cadence's physical safety and psychosocial welfare.
- To empower Cadence.
- To comply with child protection laws.

If Sherman could achieve all of these goals, he would have the perfect solution in terms of satisfying everyone's concerns. Note, however, that the goals conflict. Thus, a perfect solution may not be possible. Respecting the traditions of Cadence's family may suggest that Sherman should not interfere with their plans for an arranged marriage. Protecting Cadence's safety and welfare, however, may require him to intervene and prevent the family from taking Cadence to India. At this point, do not try to reconcile conflicting goals. Simply state them. You will be able to prioritize goals and resolve the conflicts during subsequent stages.

Identify and Weigh Obligations

Obligations refer to directives and duties that guide the conduct of social workers and others. Obligations may stem from a variety of sources including public laws, agency policies, professional codes of ethics, culture-based systems of morality, and religious convictions.[22] When analyzing an ethical issue, identify all the relevant obligations for each of the people affected by the issue. Although you may be able to identify such obligations on your own, consulting others may be beneficial. Consider consulting with

- An attorney to identify relevant laws.
- A supervisor to identify relevant agency policies.
- An ethics committee, supervisor, or professional association to identify relevant ethical standards.
- The client to identify relevant moral and religious obligations, from the client's perspective.

In Case 3, Sherman identifies the relevant state laws concerning child protection and when he may have a duty to report. He is not sure how they apply to the possibility of an arranged marriage in a foreign country so he and his supervisor consult one of the school board's attorneys. They also review school policy concerning confidentiality and safeguarding the welfare of children. In addition, Sherman identifies the following standards from the NASW Code of Ethics:

- S.1.01—Primary commitment to client.
- S.1.02—Self-determination of client, except when immediate foreseeable risk.

---

[21] Holding her accountable does not necessarily require suspension or other severe punishments. Given Shirley's innocent intentions, nonpunitive, corrective action could be sufficient.

[22] See the introduction to Part I for descriptions of each of these sources of obligations.

- S.1.05—Understanding and sensitivity regarding client's culture and religion, as well as oppression.
- S.1.07(c)—Exception to confidentiality in order to prevent "serious, foreseeable immediate harm" against client.
- S.1.07(f) and (g)—Confidentiality among family members.

When Sherman reflects on his personal morals and religious convictions, he notes that he believes people should be at least 18 before they can marry and that parents should not force children into marriage with a particular person, whether or not the child is an adult. He understands, however, that his professional obligations to respect client culture and self-determination take precedence over his personal morals and religious convictions.

Sherman decides to meet with Cadence and her parents, in part to discuss his obligations and to explore what obligations stem from their cultural and religious convictions. They discuss the importance of maintaining the honor of their family. They explain that as Hindus of Indian descent, they view marriage as the union of two bloodlines. Therefore, the reputation of the family that a child marries into is very important. Cadence's parents view an arranged marriage as a means of ensuring the honor of their family (Bradby, 1999). Cadence also discloses her moral obligation to honor the wishes of her parents. Sherman uses paraphrasing to demonstrate that he understands these convictions. He does not try to debate or challenge the correctness of their convictions.

Once you have identified all relevant obligations, consider whether there are any courses of action you can take to fulfill all of these obligations. Ethical dilemmas involve conflicting obligations, so you will need to decide which obligations to prioritize if there is no solution that permits you to satisfy all the identified obligations. The NASW Code of Ethics gives limited guidance about how to manage conflicting obligations, suggesting that the Code "does not specify which values, principles, or standards are most important and ought to outweigh others in instances when they conflict" (1999, Purpose section). The Code recognizes that different social workers may have reasonable differences of opinion on how to prioritize obligations, so it provides social workers with discretion to use their informed judgment. The Code goes on to state that social workers should make reasonable efforts to resolve conflicts between laws, agency policies, and ethical obligations. Although the Code provides guidance on how to resolve certain conflicts,[23] it is virtually silent on how to resolve others.

One example in which the Code does provide guidance concerns the conflicting obligations of maintaining client confidentiality and protecting the client or others against harm. Ordinarily, a social worker should honor a client's right to confidentiality. However, Standard 1.07(c) states that the expectation of maintaining confidentiality "does not apply when disclosure is necessary to prevent serious, foreseeable, and imminent harm to a client or other identifiable person." In other words, the Code suggests that safety takes precedence over confidentiality, at least in situations involving serious, foreseeable, and imminent harm. In situations where the Code provides guidance on how to resolve conflicting obligations, the conflict may be resolved relatively easily.

---

[23] When interpreting laws, ethical standards, and agency policies, remember to pay close attention to the wording of each rule or standard. Some rules or standards are mandatory whereas others provide general guidelines. Still others may provide permission to act in a particular way without imposing a legal or ethical specific obligation. Consider, for instance, the Health Insurance Portability and Accountability Act (1996). This legislation says that health-care agencies are not required to obtain specific consents from patients in order to release routine information to insurance companies for the purposes of reimbursement. HIPAA only requires the health-care agency to provide patients with notice of what types of routine information they may be releasing. Note that these requirements are minimum (floor) requirements. The NASW Code of Ethics or state laws may require that social workers ask clients for specific consents to release such information. Such standards or ethics do not conflict with the federal HIPAA laws. They supplement the HIPAA laws (Legal Defense Fund, 2005).

For situations in which the Code is silent on how to resolve conflicting obligations, different social work ethicists offer different hierarchies of ethical principles. Dolgoff, Loewenberg, and Harrington's (2009, p.66) Ethical Principles Screen, for instance, ranks seven ethical principles in descending order of priority:

- Protection of life
- Equality and inequality[24]
- Autonomy and freedom
- Least harm
- Quality of life
- Privacy and confidentiality
- Truthfulness and full disclosure

According to these ethicists, protection of life is the highest priority, equality and inequality is the second highest priority, and so on. To use this hierarchy, identify which principles apply to the decision to be made. Next, choose a course of action that gives precedence to the principle that is highest among those in conflict. Assume that Sherman was concerned that Cadence's parents might kill her if they found out that she disclosed their plans about the arranged marriage to Sherman. Given that truthfulness and full disclosure is a lower principle than protection of life, Sherman could use this hierarchy to ethically justify a decision to lie or withhold information in order to protect her life. Thus, if the parents asked Sherman what he discussed with Cadence, he could disclose some of the issues they had talked about[25] but avoid disclosing anything about the arranged marriage.

Although Dolgoff, Loewenberg, and Harrington's Ethical Principles Screen offers specific guidance on how to resolve conflicts, their ordering of principles may or may not fit with everyone else's prioritization, including your own. By prioritizing protection of life over autonomy and freedom, for instance, the Screen supports a pro-life stance on issues such as abortion and euthanasia. However, many people support a woman's right to choose abortion and a dying patient's right to determine the time and manner of ending his or her life. In other words, they may rank autonomy and freedom over life, at least in the context of abortion or euthanasia decisions.[26] Because different people may have a different sequence of priorities, it may be prudent to review the Ethical Principles Screen together before applying it. If people agree upon the ordering of the principles, then you may apply it. If people do not agree upon the ordering of the principles, then you may need to use conflict resolution strategies (as described below) to work through the issues.

Reamer (2006b) ranks ethical rules and principles through the following six guidelines:

- Rules against basic harm to an individual's survival take precedence over rules against harms such as lying or revealing confidential information or threats to additive goods.[27]
- An individual's right to basic well-being takes precedence over another individual's right to self determination.
- An individual's right to self-determination takes precedence over his or her right to basic well-being.
- The obligation to obey laws, rules and regulations to which one has voluntarily and freely consented ordinarily overrides one's right to engage voluntarily and freely in a manner that conflicts with these.

[24] See Chapter 10 for further discussion of this principle. In addition, the Glossary contains a definition of each of the principles in this hierarchy.

[25] Remember that Sherman would already have a general agreement with Cadence and her parents about what would and what would not be shared with the parents (S.1.07[f]). In order to obtain Cadence's permission about what information to share with her parents at this time, Sherman could discuss what specific details he intended to share and reassure Cadence about what information he would not share.

[26] Pro-choice arguments could be argued from another perspective, specifically, that an abortion is not the termination of a life but rather the termination of a potential life.

[27] Reamer defines "additive goods" as resources or qualities that enhance a person's capacity to fulfill goals (e.g., education, knowledge, material wealth). Additive goods do not include basic needs for survival such as food, water, and shelter.

- Individuals' rights to well-being may override laws, rules, regulations, and arrangements of voluntary associations in cases of conflict.
- The obligation to prevent basic harms and to promote public goods such as housing, education, and public assistance overrides the right to complete control over one's property.

To apply Reamer's guidelines, first identify which types of obligations are in conflict. Then identify which rule is most relevant to the situation. Thus, if Sherman were considering whether to withhold information from Cadence's parents to protect her life, the first guideline would apply. The result would be similar to that using the Ethical Principles Screen. The first five guidelines essentially cover the same principles as those in the Ethical Principles Screen. The sixth guideline prioritizes public good over an individual's right to complete control over his or her property; for instance, social workers could advocate for the government to purchase a parcel of land through eminent domain to build a highway, hospital, or other facility for the public good, even if the owner does not wish to sell. As with Dolgoff's Ethical Principles Screen, one cannot assume that everyone will agree with Reamer's ordering of rules and principles. Thus, it is still important to ask people (including yourself) how ethical principles and other standards should be ranked.

Another approach to resolving conflicting ethical obligations is to apply the principles of deontology. As discussed in Chapter 10, deontology suggests that there are certain duties or imperatives that people should follow, regardless of the consequences. These duties may be so vital that they supersede agency policies or public laws. For instance, some people believe that life is sacrosanct, not because it is ranked highest in a secular ethicist's ranking of principles, but because of their religious convictions. A social worker with absolute convictions concerning the sanctity of life would reject helping a client commit suicide, even if public laws and agency policies permitted assisted suicide. The worker would have to consider other options that did not conflict with his or her convictions about preserving life.

Social workers may also look to the core mandate of social work in order to determine which duties should be given highest priority: enhancing human well-being, promoting social justice, and helping people obtain basic needs, with particular attention to the needs of vulnerable and oppressed populations in society. Thus, social workers have a duty to give priority to advocating for the needs of the most vulnerable and oppressed populations, even though other people may have valid needs and interests. In Case 3, Cadence is particularly vulnerable as a minor girl who may be taken to another country to marry. This vulnerability suggests that Sherman should give priority to advocating for Cadence's interests, even if her parents are also Sherman's clients.

Whereas Sherman's case involved an ethical dilemma, Cases 1 and 2 involve breaches of obligations. The assessment of obligations is relatively simple in such cases (Paul & Elder, 2006). Identify the relevant obligations (especially which legal rules, agency policies, or ethical standards may have been breached). In breach situations, there are no conflicting obligations, so you do not need to go through the process of prioritizing them. Once you have identified the relevant obligations, you can use the other strategies in this framework to assess whether any obligations have been breached or what should be done in response to the breach.[28]

---

[28] Beauchamp and Childress (2009) offer another framework for managing conflicting obligations. They suggest that in order to justify overriding a primary obligation (such as respect for client autonomy), six conditions must be met: "(1) Good reasons must be offered to act on the overriding norm rather than on the infringed norm; (2) The moral objective justifying the infringement has a realistic prospect of achievement; (3) No morally preferable alternative actions are available; (4) The lowest level of infringement, commensurate with achieving the primary goal of the action, has been selected; (5) Any negative effects of the infringement have been minimized; and (6) All affected parties have been treated impartially" (p. 23).

Brainstorm Options and Assessing Consequences

Brainstorming options refers to generating a list of possible solutions. Brainstorming stimulates imagination, a vital aspect of assessing and managing difficult ethical issues (Lederach, 2005). Often, we see just one side of an ethical issue—our own side. We tend to see our own way of doing things as the right way. When others propose contradictory solutions, we may assume they are wrong. Such egocentricity locks us into seeing just one possible solution. Brainstorming opens our minds, permitting us to experiment by thinking through various courses of action to see what might happen. To help us remain open to the possibility of other solutions, we should remind ourselves, our clients, and our coworkers that "An act tried out in imagination is not final or fatal" (Dewey, 1922, cited in Casebeer, 2003, p. 30). In fact, experimenting with different decisions in our imagination permits us to consider new and creative ideas, increasing the chances that we will choose the best course of action.

Brainstorming and thinking through the ends of different courses of action fits with a teleological approach to ethical reasoning. Teleology, and utilitarianism in particular, suggests that ethical decisions should be guided by which course of action produces the greatest good for the greatest number (Bentham, 1823; Mill, 1863). In other words, what can we do in order to *(a)* maximize benefits such as health, safety, happiness, financial resources, and psychosocial well-being; and *(b)* minimize risks such as illness, physical harm, emotional despair, economic hardship, and psychosocial problems.[29]

In order to brainstorm, refer back to the central ethical issues or conflicts to be managed. When you are thinking of different options, write them down as each idea comes to mind. Do not assess or critique the options as you are generating them because this may lead you to discount options before fully considering them (Fisher et al., 1997). Even silly or bad options can be used to stimulate imagination and ideas for better solutions. Although you may brainstorm options on your own, consider brainstorming with others, as each person can build on the others' ideas.

In Case 3, Sherman is concerned about how he can safeguard Cadence from harm while also respecting the autonomy of the parents and family. Before meeting with the family, Sherman and his supervisor brainstorm over 20 options for managing these conflicting interests. For illustration purposes, we will consider the following four options:

- Do nothing (allowing the parents to take Cadence to India for an arranged marriage).
- Report Cadence's parents to child protection authorities.
- Counsel Cadence on how she may talk to her parents about their plans for the arranged marriage.
- Offer to escort Cadence and her family to India for the arranged marriage.

After brainstorming a list of options, the next step is to assess the consequences of each option. Consider a full range of possible consequences, including positive and negative effects, and short-term and long-term consequences. Consider possible impacts on everyone who may be affected by the decisions, including individuals, families, groups, organizations, specific communities, and society in general. Also, consider impacts on all realms of human welfare: biological, psychological, social, spiritual, legal, and economic. In practice, you will need to focus on the aspects most relevant to a particular decision in order to make the analysis more manageable. Thus, you may need to start by thinking broadly, but then narrow the focus by concentrating on the most significant consequences of each course of action.

Once you have identified the consequences of each option, select the option that is most likely to satisfy the goals that you have previously identified. If none of the options can satisfy all of the goals, then determine which goals are most

---

29 Note that according to utilitarianism, individuals may need to act against their own interests in order to benefit the greatest good for the greatest number.

important and select an option that is most likely to achieve those most important goals. Although a purely utilitarian approach suggests choosing an option that promotes the greatest good for the greatest number, remember that social workers owe their primary commitment to their clients (S.1.01). Further, social workers should also promote social justice and work on behalf of vulnerable and oppressed populations (Ss.6.01 and 6.04[b]). When assessing options, you should recognize the tensions between these goals and criteria for selecting options. You may need to prioritize some goals and criteria over others. When you describe why you chose a certain course of action, your analysis should acknowledge both the strengths and limitations of the option you choose.

In many cases, you cannot predict the precise benefits and risks of each option with certainty. Use the best information you have. Weighing benefits and risks is an important aspect of managing ethical issues. Select options that promote good and reduce the chances of harming clients or others. Determine who stands to benefit and who stands to lose from each option. Consider the risks and benefits to your clients, agency, and others affected by the decisions. Also, consider how you can reduce the risks of exposing yourself to malpractice lawsuits or professional complaints (Kirkland & Kirkland, 2006).

Sherman begins assessing options by considering "doing nothing." By permitting the family to take Cadence to India without any interference, Sherman respects the values, traditions, and autonomy of Cadence's family. Although this option supports Sherman's first goal, it does little to promote the other goals. In particular, he will have no way of knowing whether Cadence's welfare will be put at risk when she is taken to India. "Doing nothing" fails to address Cadence's request for help. It also fails to empower her to address her concerns with her parents. Finally, Sherman does not know whether he should report the family to child protection authorities. He may not have enough information to know whether there is a reasonable suspicion of abuse or neglect. Thus, he would need to gather more information from Cadence and her family to make such a determination.

As Sherman considers the second option, reporting the family to child protective services, he realizes that this would relieve him of responsibility for reporting suspected child neglect or abuse. As mentioned above, however, he should have more information before he reports any suspicions. Unless Cadence's welfare is in immediate danger, he should probably talk with Cadence and/or her family to discuss their plans and to determine whether there truly is a child protection issue. Reporting the family without gathering further information runs contrary to the goal of respecting the values, traditions, and autonomy of Cadence's family. This option also fails to empower Cadence. In fact, reporting them with such little information may be tantamount to acting on stereotypes and assumptions. Sherman might be protecting Cadence's physical safety and psychosocial welfare by reporting them—assuming that child protective services are able to conduct an effective assessment and intervention. Unfortunately, reporting the family prematurely makes it difficult for Sherman to maintain a working relationship with Cadence or her family. More broadly, premature reporting may foster mistrust of all social workers, as people may question their competence and respect for clients. If Sherman tries to engage the family first, he might be able to establish trust and work through some of the concerns on a voluntary, collaborative basis.

The option of counseling Cadence on how to speak with her parents supports the goal of empowering Cadence. Rather than taking responsibility for speaking to her parents, Sherman provides her with skills and practice so that she may advocate on her own behalf. This option may further the goal of respecting the family's values, traditions, and autonomy, depending on how it is implemented. Sherman would need to be sensitive to their traditions and values, perhaps asking Cadence for information about family roles, rules, and norms. For instance, it may be culturally inappropriate for Cadence to contradict her parents directly. Thus, rather than repudiate an arranged marriage outright, she might be able to discuss American laws and traditions. Alternatively, she might suggest that she wants to respect their plans for an arranged marriage, but ask them to consider delaying the actual marriage until she has finished school. Sherman could consult with a cultural interpreter in order to determine what strategies might be culturally appropriate (Appleby et al., 2007). Further, he should check with Cadence so they may jointly decide whether and how Cadence could approach her parents. In terms of protecting Cadence from harm, this option entails potential risks and benefits. If Cadence is able to engage her parents in a constructive conversation, they may come to a conclusion that ensures her physical safety and psychosocial welfare. If her parents react negatively, this option could put her at greater risk of harm (e.g., if one or both parents feels defensive and responds violently).

The primary advantage of the final option, offering to escort Cadence to India, is that it may allow Sherman to ensure that her safety and welfare are protected. Certainly, there is no assurance that offering to escort Cadence will have any positive impact: The parents may perceive this offer as a rude intrusion into their lives; it may be culturally inappropriate for Sherman to escort Cadence; and Sherman may not be able to safeguard Cadence in India even if he does go. Sherman realizes this option was not a serious option, as it goes beyond his role and mandate as a school social worker. Still, this option helps him think of other creative options: If Cadence does go to India with her parents, perhaps they could make some sort of culturally appropriate arrangements to ensure her welfare. Perhaps the family's original plans already take care of her welfare.

Sherman and his supervisor weigh the pros and cons of each option. They determine that Cadence is not at immediate risk of harm, so the goals of respecting the values, traditions, and autonomy of Cadence's family and empowering Cadence should be given priority, at least in the initial stages of intervention. They decide that Sherman should first meet with Cadence to conduct a further assessment of child protection risks, and to determine the appropriateness of counseling her to speak directly with her parents about the arranged marriage plans. Sherman can also discuss cultural concerns and the possibility of conducting a joint meeting with Cadence and her parents. Sherman and his supervisor acknowledge that although this plan fosters certain goals, it still entails some risks: If Sherman does not report child protection suspicions right away and something untoward happens to Cadence, he and the school may be held liable; if the parents find out that Cadence has been speaking with Sherman, they may try to remove her from the country before anyone else can intervene; and Cadence may not want Sherman to meet directly with her parents, even if Sherman thinks such a meeting would be beneficial. Still, *they view management of the ethical issues in this case as a process, rather than a single decision to be made at a particular point in time.* Their discussion of the pros and cons of various options has given them insight into the ethical issues. As Sherman proceeds to speak with Cadence and possibly her family, he will use conflict resolution skills (as described below). He will also continue to consult with his supervisor to determine further steps in managing the issues raised by this case.

In Case 1, Sondra's first question is whether she breached any conflict of interest laws, policies, or standards. To answer this question, she does not need to identify and weigh options. However, if she does determine that she has breached any conflict of interest directives, she should then consider what to do in light of this breach. At this point, her options could include reporting her conflict to the head of the municipal committee, her licensing board, or the police. Because she is still determining whether she violated any directives, we will not go through the analysis of her options.

In Case 2, Shirley has determined that she has violated state laws regarding having sex with former clients.[30] It may be useful for her to discuss her options with an attorney, particularly given the legal ramifications of her breach. An attorney might be able to explain why it could be advantageous to report her own violation to her licensing

[30] She may have also violated Standard 1.09(c), but given the nature of the prior relationship and the low levels of risk, her situation likely falls within the definition of "extraordinary circumstances" that would permit her to continue the intimate relationship.

board and to her employer (Reamer, 2008b). By being up front and honest about her violation, they may be more likely to agree that she has acted with integrity and respect for state laws and agency policies. She may also consider the risks of reporting herself: Will she lose her license, will she be asked to terminate her personal relationship with Chester, or will she be fired or disciplined by the agency? Once again, an attorney could provide advice on the legal issues raised by this case. For instance, although the law clearly prohibits sexual relations with prior clients, it is intended to ensure that workers to not take advantage of vulnerable clients (Abbott, 2003). Chester was not particularly vulnerable, given that he participated in a single time-management group and never had a close professional relationship with Shirley. Ultimately, Shirley still needs to decide which risks to accept and which course of action to choose. If Shirley decides to disclose her violation to her licensing board and agency, she should consider using conflict resolution strategies, as described below. Her decision to disclose does not solve all the issues. The licensing board and agency still need to decide how to respond. If Shirley can engage them effectively, they may be able to arrive at a mutually acceptable response to her unintentional breach.

4. MANAGE CONFLICT

The management of ethical issues is not merely an individual decision-making process. It often involves interactive conflict resolution processes such as negotiation, mediation, advocacy, and arbitration (Barsky, 2007a; Corey et al., 2007). Social workers need to know how to gain entrée and facilitate ethics discussions with clients, supervisors, coworkers, professional disciplinary committees, and others (Dodd & Jansson, 2004). By understanding the nature of conflict, they can assess ethical issues in relation to context, power, politics, and communication. By understanding different approaches to conflict resolution, they can determine which strategies and skills can be used to bring people together to discuss and resolve ethical issues more effectively.

When determining how to manage ethical conflicts, social workers should clarify which type of conflict resolution roles they will play. When an ethical issue directly affects the rights and interests of a social worker, then the social worker takes on the role of a negotiator, using conflict resolution skills and strategies to bargain on his or her own behalf. When an ethical issue does not directly affect the rights and interests of the social worker, then the social worker may assume the role of mediator, advocate, coach, or arbitrator. A mediator is an impartial third person who facilitates communication between people involved in a conflict for the purpose of helping them work through the ethical issues (Moore, 2003). A mediator does not impose decisions or take sides, but rather helps people listen to one another and work toward solutions by consensus or agreement. An advocate helps one person or group advance their rights, needs, or interests (Dodd & Jansson, 2004). Advocacy may include speaking on behalf of a client, acting as the client's mouthpiece or representative. Advocacy may also include helping clients advocate on their own behalf. A coach is an advocate who provides guidance, conflict resolution training, and support to an individual or group, helping them negotiate more effectively (Barsky, 2007a). An arbitrator is an impartial third person who receives information or evidence from people involved in a conflict and makes decisions for them. A public court judge is one form of arbitrator. People involved in conflicts may select private arbitrators (including social workers) to make decisions for them. The primary advantages of using private arbitrators are *(a)* The parties may select an arbitrator with particular types of expertise, and *(b)* the parties may agree to a process that suits their needs—for instance, a less formal and less expensive process than traditional court hearings (Barsky, in press; Galambos, 1999).

In Case 1, assume that someone complains to Sondra's municipal committee, claiming she had a conflict of interest. When Sondra speaks to the committee, defending her actions, she is acting as a negotiator. She uses her conflict resolution skills to try to persuade the committee that she did not violate any conflict of interest laws or policies.

In Case 2, Shirley's attorney advises Shirley to report herself to the state licensing board for breaching laws prohibiting sexual relations with clients. When the licensing board tries to determine the appropriate consequences, Shirley may negotiate on her own behalf or engage her attorney to act as her advocate. As a negotiator, Shirley tries to persuade the licensing board that her breach was unintentional and did not cause any harm to Chester, her former client. She also offers options to help reduce future risks to Chester or others (e.g., offering Chester a consultant to determine whether he perceives any risks related to his dual status as former client and current intimate partner with Shirley). If the licensing board believes that Shirley did not knowingly engage in an intimate relationship with a former client, then the conflict resolution process may be relatively simple. They would probably want to ensure that Chester was not being put at risk as a former client. Given the unintentional nature of the breach, they would probably not insist on other corrective or punitive actions.

Case 3 may require intensive conflict resolution processes, given the complex nature of the ethical dilemma. Sherman may assume different conflict resolution roles in relation to different parties. When Sherman meets with his supervisor to try to decide how he should respond to Cadence's request, he takes on the role of negotiator. Sherman and his supervisor may have different views on what is the most ethical response, so he may need to negotiate based on what course of action he believes is best. Sherman's supervisor may play the role of coach, preparing him for conflict resolution discussions with his clients. If Sherman decides to bring Cadence and her family together to help them work through the issues related to the arranged marriage, then Sherman assumes the role of mediator. He helps them communicate and try to resolve their differences about the proposed marriage. For discussion purposes, assume that Cadence tells Sherman she does not want to confront her parents about the arranged marriage because she fears how they will react. Sherman decides to meet with the parents to discuss their plans and assess the situation. If he believes their plans put Cadence's welfare at risk, he may need to report them to child protective services. Before he makes this determination, however, he assumes the role of an advocate for Cadence. They try to negotiate an agreement that respects the parents' values and traditions, but also ensures Cadence's welfare. If they are unable to resolve their concerns through negotiation, Sherman may be required to issue a report to protective services. The protection worker is mandated to negotiate a solution on a voluntary basis; however, if the worker and parents cannot resolve the protection issues through negotiation, the worker may need to take the case to court to be arbitrated.

Negotiations are generally preferable to arbitration, in court or otherwise. Negotiations are less formal and less costly. They also promote voluntary participation, collaboration, and mutually satisfactory agreements. Court tends to be adversarial and costly. Parties often feel disempowered because a judge is making decisions, rather than the parties themselves (Moore, 2003). When workers seek to resolve ethical issues with clients, negotiations demonstrate respect for client self-determination (S.1.02). Although arbitration or court trial may be required for some situations, other alternatives should be considered first (Honeyman, 2003).

Once you have identified the role you are assuming in the conflict resolution process, consider which approach to conflict resolution may be best suited to resolving the ethical issues. In Chapter 7, we studied five approaches: debate, the Socratic method of inquiry, dialogue, interest-based mediation, and transformative mediation. Note how each of these approaches may be useful for different situations:

Debate—In debates, each party takes a position on an ethical issue and tries to convince the other party of the correctness of that particular position. This approach fits with adversarial processes such as arbitration and court trials. Debates are generally most appropriate when the most important aspect of conflict resolution is determining whose position is right. Assume, for instance, that the conflict of interest grievance against Sondra is referred to an ethics committee that conducted a disciplinary hearing. During the hearing, Sondra argues that she did not breach conflict of interest laws and policies; the complainant argues that she did. Each side uses debating strategies, such as providing well-reasoned arguments, presenting sound evidence of supportive facts, clearly articulating relevant laws and policies, and raising doubts about the case brought forward by the other party (Barsky & Gould, 2002). Unfortunately, debates tend to polarize people into adversarial camps rather than bring them together. Thus, debates are not generally appropriate for informal counseling sessions between social workers and their clients.

Socratic method of inquiry—The Socratic method of inquiry is a learning discussion that may be used to help social workers enhance their understanding of ethical issues from a variety of perspectives. The Socratic method may be particularly useful for social workers who are assuming the role of coach—for instance, coaching a supervisee or a client. When Sherman's supervisor coaches him on how to discuss the ethical issues with Cadence's parents, she uses the Socratic method to help Sherman work through the ethical and legal issues raised by the case. By asking him a series of questions, she invites Sherman to explore the issues from different angles, preparing him for various issues and considerations that may arise in his meeting with the parents.

Dialogue—Dialogues are open discussions designed to promote understanding and increase insight among the parties. Dialogues offer parties an opportunity to explore one another's worldviews, beliefs, and moral perspectives about what is a right or wrong response to an ethical problem (Spano & Koenig, 2003). Dialogues are particularly useful during early stages of conflict resolution, before disputes have crystallized into court trials or disciplinary hearings. Social workers may facilitate dialogues as part of negotiation processes with coworkers, clients, or others. When Sherman meets with Cadence's parents, he engages them in an informal dialogue. He explores their plans for an arranged marriage. He asks questions to help them think about the impact of the marriage on Cadence, potential conflicts between the norms and traditions of American versus Indian cultures, and ways of respecting their culture while also ensuring the welfare of their daughter. He also remains open to learning from Cadence's parents, checking out assumptions and building trust so the parents are able to express their true thoughts and feelings. At the end of the dialogue, they may not agree about the most ethical course of action, but they have gained greater insight into one another's perspectives.

Interest-based mediation—The interest-based approach to mediation is a problem-solving process facilitated by an impartial third party. The mediator helps the parties identify underlying interests and work toward mutually agreeable win-win solutions. Assume that Sherman engages Cadence's parents in a dialogue, but they are unable to resolve the ethical issues. The parents plan to take Cadence to India to be married. Sherman believes that Cadence's welfare is at risk because she plans to run away rather than marry and stay with a man she does not even know. Sherman suggests that they ask a mediator to help them work through these issues. Initially, the parents' position is that they have a right to arrange a marriage for their daughter without interference from outsiders. Sherman's position is that an arranged marriage for a 14-year-old is not only inappropriate, but puts Cadence's life and welfare at risk. The mediator uses an interest-based approach. The parents identify their interests as finding a good husband for their daughter, ensuring her future, and maintaining family honor within their community (Bradley, 1983). Sherman identifies his professional interests as ensuring Cadence's welfare and respecting the family's autonomy, traditions, and culture. He discusses his ethical and legal obligations regarding protection of children, but remains open to different options for resolving their conflict. As they brainstorm a list of options, Sherman raises options that he generated during earlier stages of the ethical management process. The family adds their own suggestions. As they consider various options, one option emerges that seems to satisfy most of their interests: The parents will enter into a marriage contract with the man they identified for the arranged marriage, but the contract will not go into effect until Cadence is 18 years old. The solution is not perfect. Cadence's immediate welfare is assured, but she may still oppose the marriage when she turns 18. Cadence expresses approval of the proposed plan because it allows her to honor her parents, rather than showing disrespect and embarrassing the family by rejecting their marriage plans outright.

The mediator helps them work through various issues, asking "what if" questions to determine how they will respond to potential issues that may arise (Barsky, 2007a). They agree to help Cadence identify people she can talk to, now or in the future, including elders from the Indian American community. They acknowledge that postponing the marriage may allow Cadence and her family to reassess and renegotiate their roles within the family, their cultural community, and American society (Bradby, 1999). Interest-based mediation is particularly useful when achieving a mutually satisfactory solution to ethical issues is paramount.

Transformative mediation—In transformative mediation, the mediator brings conflicting parties together to foster more constructive patterns of interaction between them. Transformative mediators focus on building empathic relationships and empowering the parties to have greater choice, self-determination, and autonomy. Reaching agreements or solving ethical issues is of secondary importance (Bush & Folger, 2005). Transformative mediation may be particularly useful for intractable ethical conflicts, when deep chasms between the parties seem irresolvable. When dealing with hot-button issues such as abortion, capital punishment, same-sex marriage, or gun control, people on opposing sides of the issues may be so entrenched in their positions that a mutually satisfactory agreement does not seem possible. Transformative mediation offers a process designed to help them engage in meaningful discussions, promoting understanding and respectful ways of moving forward. Transformative mediation also fits with a narrative approach to resolving ethical issues, as the mediator may help the parties share their individual stories and jointly construct new narratives based on shared understandings and values (Barton, 2008). Assume that Sherman and Cadence's parents reach a deadlock in their discussions: The parents insist on proceeding with their plans for an immediate marriage and Sherman insists that he will report the family to protective services. Transformative mediation may help them reopen their discussion, providing them with a safe environment to sit, share views, and hear one another without the expectation that they need to reach agreement. Sherman may still report the family to protective services, but at least the family will understand that this was not an easy choice for him, that he wanted to do whatever was possible to respect the family's culture and autonomy. The mediator may empower the parents by guiding Sherman to share information about the child protection process so they will know what to expect after Sherman issues his report. When social workers and clients can agree upon how to resolve an ethical dilemma, both sides are more likely to be satisfied with the results and cooperate with implementation of the decisions. In some ethical dilemmas, however, social workers may need to impose decisions to protect children, disabled persons, or other vulnerable people from harm. In these situations, a transformative approach may be particularly beneficial. Both workers and clients gain insights, experience validation, and feel empowered through the conflict resolution process.

These five examples illustrate some of the more common approaches to conflict resolution, though there are many others: family group conferences, healing circles, narrative negotiation, and evaluative mediation, to name a few (Barsky, 2007a; Barton, 2008). When discussing ethical issues, people often become entrenched in certain positions, falling into patterns of debate and defense of their positions. By making deliberate choices about conflict resolution roles and approaches, you may be able to engage clients, coworkers, and others in more meaningful, collaborative, and productive discussions and interactions.

5. PLAN AND IMPLEMENT DECISIONS

In the earlier stages of managing ethical problems, we have identified the issues, assessed them, and determined solutions based on critical thinking and conflict resolution. During the planning and implementation stage, we take these solutions and determine the best way to put them into action. In some situations, the solutions are relatively straightforward and simple to execute. In Case 1, for instance, assume the municipal ethics committee finds that

Sondra breached its conflict of interest policies and decides to reprimand her as a consequence (e.g., through a statement placed in the record of the next municipal council meeting). Once the reprimand is issued, implementation of the decision has been completed. In other situations, planning and implementation may be more complicated. In Case 2, assume that Shirley and her licensing board agree that she may continue her relationship with Chester, but Chester will be offered supportive counseling to ensure that he is aware of the risks involved in dual relationships. They also agree to offer him support in case any future issues arise. During the planning and implementation stage, they need to decide who is responsible for linking Chester with a counselor, who pays for the counselor, and what type of information, if any, will be shared between the counselor and the licensing board. If the parties do not pay sufficient attention to planning and implementation, even a good solution can go awry.

The nature and extent of planning depends on the particular facts of the ethical problems and proposed solutions. The following questions offer a general guide for issues to be considered in the planning and implementation stage:

- What specific tasks (or actions) need to be performed in order to carry out the proposed solution?
- For each task, who will be responsible for ensuring that the task will be performed? How will the task be performed? What is the expected or required time-frame for completion of the task?
- What potential obstacles may arise during implementation? What can be done to preempt these obstacles or to overcome them if they do arise?

Careful planning and attention to detail can be used to avert problems and raise the likelihood of successful implementation (Kirst-Ashman & Hull, 2006b).

In Case 3, Sherman and Cadence's parents have agreed that the parents will arrange Cadence's marriage now, but the marriage will not take place until Cadence is at least 18 years old. As they plan for implementation of this decision, they identify the following tasks and timelines:

- Within the next 2 weeks, Sherman will meet with the family to discuss and agree upon a plan for connecting Cadence with support persons from the Indian American community.
- During April, the parents will travel to India to meet with the family of a prospective husband for Cadence in order to plan their marriage. Cadence will stay at home with her paternal grandparents and continue to go to school while her parents are away.
- Sherman will meet with Cadence and her parents within 1 week of their return from India to discuss the marriage plans and to explore any concerns that may have arisen.

As they develop this plan, they explore potential obstacles: What if they cannot find or agree upon a support person for Cadence? What if the prospective husband's family rejects the arranged marriage because they will have to wait until Cadence is 18 to finalize the marriage? What if Cadence eventually refuses to abide by the arranged marriage? They use their conflict resolution skills to work through these problems. They agree, for instance, that if the prospective husband's family insists that the marriage take place before Cadence turns 18, they will need to consider marriage into another family. Sherman and Cadence's parents acknowledge that their plans may not resolve the conflict, but rather put off the conflict until Cadence is 18. Still, they agree that this is the best way to manage the ethical issues at this time. The parents are satisfied, believing that Cadence will follow through on the arranged marriage once she is older and more mature. Cadence is satisfied that her parents will continue to provide appropriate care, and will not force her to marry before she becomes an adult. Sherman is satisfied that the plan offers appropriate safeguards for Cadence as a vulnerable minor, while respecting the family's traditions and values.

6. EVALUATE AND FOLLOW UP

In the final stage of managing ethical issues, we evaluate the implementation of decisions and action plans. Evaluation helps us determine the extent to which we have achieved our goals and objectives. Remember, when managing an ethical dilemma, we may have conflicting goals and objectives. Thus, it would not be unusual for an evaluation to find success in meeting some goals, but problems in achieving others. In a case involving suicidal ideation, for instance, we might find success in achieving the goal of saving a life, but problems in fulfilling the goal of honoring client self-determination. Evaluation gives us an opportunity to reassess an ethical situation and determine what additional steps, if any, should be taken to address outstanding issues. A review of the suicide situation, for instance, might lead us to offer the client alternate services as part of a follow-up effort to enhance client choice and self-determination.

In some instances, the evaluation process is formal, making use of specific instruments or data gathering techniques to assess the extent to which goals and objectives were met. When designing a formal evaluation process, consider the following questions:

- Who will be responsible for evaluating the outcomes?
- How will the outcomes be measured?[31]
- How will information from the evaluation be used to inform follow-up, in the specific case and also on a macro level (e.g., future training or policy changes to help workers deal more effectively with similar ethical issues in the future)?

In other instances, the evaluation process may be informal. For instance, the social worker may reflect back on the ethical management process, considering what aspects of the process were effective, what aspects were problematic, and what steps may be useful to address the problems that arose (Manning, 2003). The social worker may also consult with a supervisor, client, or other stakeholders for their input on these questions.

In Sherman's case, his supervisor agrees to take responsibility for evaluating the effectiveness of their plans for resolving the ethical issues with Cadence's family. The supervisor conducts individual follow-up interviews with Sherman, Cadence, and her parents in order to obtain feedback on how the ethical issues were resolved. During these interviews, the supervisor gathers qualitative information and measures success in relation to the previously identified goals: *(1)* to respect the values, traditions, and autonomy of Cadence's family; *(2)* to protect Cadence's physical safety and psychosocial welfare; *(3)* to empower Cadence; and *(4)* to comply with child protection laws. Because of the legal aspect of the fourth goal, the supervisor consults with agency attorneys to assess whether their course of action complied with child protection laws (especially the duty to report risk of maltreatment). The supervisor determines that all four goals have been satisfied, at least for the present time. Given the ongoing nature of the concerns, she institutes a plan for monitoring the situation until Cadence turns 18. Sherman will contact the family every 6 months for follow-up interviews, meeting personally with Cadence and contacting her parents by telephone. Should any further concerns arise, Sherman will discuss these immediately with his supervisor to determine how to respond.

At a macro (policy) level, Sherman's supervisor notes that child protection laws are not very clear about professionals' reporting responsibilities when they find out that parents are arranging a foreign marriage for a minor child. The supervisor follows up by contacting the state legislature's child welfare department, requesting that it study and develop administrative guidelines for this issue.

[31] Use information from your research and evaluation courses to help determine appropriate methods of measuring outcomes.

CONCLUSION

This chapter has provided a comprehensive framework for analyzing and managing ethical issues. The level of detail offered in this chapter illustrates the potential depth and complexity of ethics analysis. At the same time, it is important not to get lost in the details and lose sight of the basics: what issues are we trying to address; who can provide help; what are different ways that we can think about the issues; and how can we bring people together to work toward a collaborative solution?[32] If you just commit these fundamental questions to memory, you will have a ready resource that you can apply reflexively whenever you are faced with a difficult ethical issue (Strom-Gottfried, 2007).

This chapter is intended to provide an introduction to the framework managing ethical issues. If you feel somewhat uncertain or overwhelmed by the range of strategies presented above, such feelings would not be unusual for this stage of your learning. Chapters 11 to 16 will offer you further experience in applying these strategies. As you work through various exercises, refer back to the specific strategies listed in this chapter. These strategies offer a range of different approaches and factors to consider. Remember, different ethical issues may require different approaches to analysis. Although identifying relevant laws and policies may be the most helpful strategy in some cases, self-reflection or brainstorming options may be most helpful in others. Applying ethical theories such as deontology and virtue ethics is not easy, even for seasoned practitioners. As you practice applying them, however, you will gain confidence and competence in how they may be utilized. Do not discount certain approaches to ethical analysis just because they are difficult. Do ask for help—from supervisors, instructors, ethics experts, or others. Regardless of one's level of experience in social work practice and ethics education, consultation with others is a vital component of analyzing and managing ethical issues.

DISCUSSION QUESTIONS AND EXERCISES

The following questions and exercises are designed to provide you with practice applying various strategies from the framework for managing ethical issues, as described in this chapter. Each question focuses on applying one stage or strategy, so you can focus on learning one stage or strategy at a time. In subsequent chapters, you will be presented with additional case scenarios that you can use to work through all the stages.

1. *Identify Ethical Issues*: Select *one* of the following case scenarios and identify the primary ethical issue raised by the case. Formulate a clear and balanced question that can be used to guide your analysis and management of the ethical issue. Indicate whether the issue relates to determining whether a breach has occurred, determining how to respond to a breach, or determining how to respond to an ethical dilemma.
   a. Assume that you work for an agency that provides psychosocial support services for the elderly. Your supervisor often says that the cornerstone of social work is building a trusting relationship, and trust is based on respecting client confidentiality. One day, a man named Harvey telephones you. He says that his wife (Chlöe), your client, is suicidal and he does not know what to do. Chlöe has not given you permission to talk to Harvey. Harvey says that Chlöe is in a desperate situation and he needs your help right away.

[32] These four questions cover the first four stages of the framework illustrated in Figure II.1. The last two stages, "plan and implement decisions" and "evaluate and follow up," are also important, but you probably do not need an explicit reminder to consider them.

b. Professor Tardy arrives 50 minutes late to class. He says he was caught in traffic. Three students were scheduled to provide a 1-hour presentation of their social work ethics project. Even though they have only 40 minutes left in class, Professor Tardy insists that they present today. He grades them using the same criteria as if they had had the full hour. When they receive a "C" for their presentation, they are outraged. Professor Tardy insists he was just following school policies. He also says that these students were late for previous classes, so they have no right to complain. The students feel it is unfair for Professor Tardy to retaliate just because they were not on time for prior classes.

c. Francis (a field instructor) meets with Sabina (a social work student) to review her most recent session with Clovis, a client who recently lost his job. Sabina reports that Clovis was very angry and made racist comments toward her. She told Clovis that she would not tolerate racism and that she could no longer serve him. Francis advises Sabina that Standard 1.16(b) of the NASW Code says workers should not abandon clients who are in need of services. Sabina acknowledges her mistake.

2. *Determine Appropriate Help*: Refer to the case in exercise 1(a). Which of the following people, if any, should you turn to for help with the ethical issues: supervisor, coworker, ethics committee, attorney, family member, insurance company, NASW, your professional licensing body, Harvey, or Chlöe? Explain specifically why you would or would not turn to each of these people for help.

3. *Think Critically—Reflect*: Assume you are the student social worker in exercise 1(c). What is your professional role in this situation? As a professional, how should you respond when the client hurls racist insults toward you? In your personal life, how would you describe your racial and ethnic identities? How would you feel if one of your friends insulted you with a racist remark? If the friend refused to apologize, would you end your friendship? Given what you know about your personal reactions to racism, why might it be difficult for you to respond professionally to Clovis's insults? What does the virtue of "ethical integrity" tell you about how you should respond to this situation?

4. *Think Critically—Consider Multiple Perspectives*: Review the facts in exercise 1(a). Analyze the case from the perspectives of Harvey, Chlöe, your supervisor, and yourself. What values, beliefs, and interests do each of these people bring to the ethical issues raised by this case? What are the potential conflicts among their perspectives?

5. *Think Critically—Identify Goals*: If you were faced with the ethical issues in exercise 1(a), what goals would you establish? In other words, if you could achieve a perfect solution, what ethical consequences would your preferred outcome include?

6. *Think Critically—Identify and Weigh Obligations*: In exercise 1(b), what are Professor Tardy's obligations in relation to how he should have handled the students' presentations? Consider obligations that he may derive from state laws, accreditation policies, agency policies, professional ethics, and contracts with the students (assume that the situation arose in your own state and at your own social work program). Which specific obligations, if any, did Professor Tardy breach? If there are any conflicts between Professor Tardy's obligations, which obligations should he have prioritized, and why?

7. *Think Critically: Brainstorm Options and Assess Consequences*: Review exercise 1(a). Identify at least eight options for responding to Harvey's request for help. Be creative, including options that you may initially think are ludicrous or unfeasible. Identify the risks and potential benefits of each option. Referring back to your answers in exercise 5, analyze the options in relation to how well each one satisfies

your primary goals. Which option do you think will lead to the greatest good? Does your answer depend on whose perspective you are using to define what is the "greatest good" (e.g., from Harvey's, Chlöe's, your agency's, or society's perspective)?

8. *Manage Conflict*: In exercise 1(c), assume that Clovis calls Francis to complain that Sabina mistreated him by abandoning him in a time of need. Clovis threatens to report Sabina to the NASW. Francis agrees to facilitate a meeting with Clovis and Francis so they can try to work things out within the agency. Which conflict resolution roles will Francis and Sabina play in this meeting: negotiator, mediator, advocate, coach, or arbitrator? Explain which approach to conflict resolution Francis should use—debate, Socratic method, dialogue, interest-based mediation, or transformative mediation. Designate three people to role-play Clovis, Francis, and Sabina. Francis should prepare for the role-play by reflecting on her role and which approach to conflict resolution she will use.
9. *Plan and Implement*: Sunee is a social worker in a small, isolated town. One of her clients, Candace, has cancer. Sunee believes that Candace would benefit from home nursing care rather than being moved to a hospital in a large city, 120 miles away. Sunee searches for available nurses. The only one she can find is her sister, Nancy. Sunee and her supervisor discuss how referring Candace to Nancy would raise conflict of interest issues as per the NASW Code, Standard 1.06. They also note that Sunee's primary commitment is to her client (S.1.01) and that as her client, Candace has a right to self-determination (S.1.02). They decide to offer Candace a referral to Nancy, but note they should do so in a way that minimizes the risks discussed on Standard 1.06. Develop a plan of action for Sunee and her supervisor. Identify who will be responsible for doing what, and how they can manage the risks that arise out of the dual relationship and conflict of interests.
10. *Evaluate and Follow up*: Syera wants to use "paradoxical interventions" for families who are concerned about children with pyromania, a mental condition marked by strong impulses to set fires. Her agency, Family Empowerment Inc., is concerned about the ethical and legal issues (Cullin, 2005), given that Syera plans to encourage children to light fires as part of the intervention. Syera provides the agency with a plan that they believe will minimize the risks and maximize the potential benefits (e.g., having clients set fires under a controlled environment). Family Empowerment gives Syera permission to use the intervention with five families. They identify the following general goals for management of the ethical issues: (a) to make use of paradoxical intervention in a competent manner, (b) to ensure parental consent is voluntary and informed, (c) to minimize risks associated with setting fires, and (d) to discontinue the use of paradoxical interventions if they prove to be too risky or ineffective at treating pyromania. Your task is to develop a plan for evaluation and follow-up that specifies how each goal will be measured, who will take responsibility for gathering and assessing data, and how this information will be used by the agency to make further decisions about the use of paradoxical interventions.
11. *Additional Perspectives*: We have considered a range of ethical theories in this textbook, including deontology, teleology, virtue ethics, and ethics of care. Although these theories represent some of the more popular theories used to inform the assessment and management of ethical issues, there are many other ethical theories, philosophies, and concepts that we could consider—for instance, Aristotle's Nicomachean Ethics, Kant's Categorical Imperative, Hegel's Dialectics, Nietzche's Superman (Uebermensch), Horkheimer's Critical Theory, Dialectics, Stoicism, Rawl's Theory of Justice, Nozick's Libertarianism, Philippa Ruth Foot's Trolley Problem, Simone de Beauvoir's Feminist Ethics,

Buddhist Social Philosophy, Soleveitchik's Halakhic Man (Jewish), Confucian Ethics, Avicennian Philosophy (Islamic), Aquinas's Four Cardinal Virtues (Catholic), and Lao Tzu's Taoism. Select one of these theories, philosophies, or concepts and read a scholarly book or article on it. Describe what lessons the theory, philosophy, or concepts could teach social workers about the assessment and management of ethical issues.

Chapter 11

Supervision, Values, and Ethics

Supervisors play a vital role in promoting ethical social work practice (McAuliffe & Sudbery, 2005). Although frontline social workers typically have the most direct contact with clients, supervisors are responsible for providing frontline workers with education, oversight, feedback, guidance, and moral support (Kadushin & Harkness, 2002; Munson, 2002; Shulman, 1992). As teachers and mentors, supervisors provide frontline workers with a safe place to explore their interactions with clients, how they are using themselves, and how to manage ethical issues as they arise in practice (Meyers, 2007). As representatives of the agency, supervisors ensure compliance with agency policies, norms, and expectations. As professional social workers, supervisors advance the values of social work: service, social justice, dignity and worth of the person, importance of human relationships, integrity, and competence (NASW, 1999).

As noted above, supervisors play many vital roles in promoting the highest values and ideals of the profession. Supervisors should also be aware of the basic ethical standards for which they are responsible and the ways in which they may be held accountable if they do not live up to these standards. In Chapter 8, we explored Standard 3.01 of the NASW Code of Ethics. This standard establishes four fundamental obligations for supervisors: *(a)* to have the necessary knowledge and skill to supervise appropriately and to supervise only within their areas of knowledge and competence; *(b)* to set clear, appropriate, and culturally sensitive boundaries with supervisees; *(c)* to avoid dual or multiple relationships with supervisees if there is a risk of exploitation or harm to the supervisee; and *(d)* to evaluate the supervisee's performance in a manner that is fair and respectful.[1] Supervisors who breach these standards may be subject to professional review

[1] Standard 3.03 adds that evaluation should be based upon previously stated criteria. The NASW National Council on the Practice of Clinical Social Work (1994) provides guidelines specific to clinical social work

from the NASW. Supervisors may also be held accountable for misconduct through agency discipline, professional review from licensing or accrediting bodies, or civil lawsuit, as described in Chapter 9. Supervisors are not only responsible for their own misconduct through direct liability; they may also be responsible for the misconduct of those they supervise through indirect or vicarious liability (Buck, 2005; Falvey, 2002). In civil law, the doctrine of vicarious liability (or *respondeat superior*)[2] suggests that supervisors may be held legally liable for the negligent acts or omissions of their supervisees under the following circumstances:

- The supervisee has agreed to work under the direction and control of the supervisor in ways that benefit the supervisor, whether or not financial gain occurs.
- The supervisor has authority to control the supervisee.
- The supervisee's activities fall within the purview of the agreed-upon training or supervision objectives (Houston-Vega & Nuehring, 1997; *Nelson v. Gillette*, 1997).

Thus, if a supervisee breaches client confidentiality and the supervisor should have provided the supervisee with proper guidance about confidentiality, then the supervisor may be liable for the breach. Similarly, if a supervisee had sexual relations with a client and the supervisor should have detected sexual transference between the supervisee and client, the supervisor may be liable (Allen, 2003). The supervisee is not excused for the breach simply because a supervisor failed to provide proper supervision. Both the supervisor and supervisee may be held liable.

Whenever social workers act in a supervisory capacity, they incur the risk of vicarious liability. Regardless of how well supervisors perform their roles, they cannot guarantee that supervisees will always act in an ethical, competent manner, or that clients will never suffer harm caused by the acts or omissions of a supervisee (Robb, 2003).

LEARNING OBJECTIVES

In this chapter, we explore the roles of a supervisor in relation to the six stages of the Framework for Managing Ethical Issues (see Figure II.1 in Part II or inside the front cover). Upon successful completion of this chapter, you will be able to

- Identify ways in which supervisors can provide supervisees with support and guidance in each stage of the Framework for Managing Ethical Issues.
- Apply the principles of risk management to complex ethical problems.
- Establish appropriate supervisory boundaries with supervisees.

Supervisors can use a range of risk-management techniques to encourage ethical practice and reduce their exposure to vicarious liability. When hiring frontline workers, supervisors should ensure that supervisees have sufficient ability and professionalism to perform the work that will be expected of them. When orienting new workers, supervisors should provide them with sufficient information and training about the agency, its policies, the needs of the client population, and how to manage ethical issues that are likely to arise in practice. When establishing expectations, supervisors should model and promote high, exemplary standards rather than adherence to minimum expectations. When monitoring the work of supervisees, supervisors should institute regular meetings to review worker–client interactions and provide the supervisee with guidance on how to proceed with the client. Supervisors should also be on constant guard for risks such as supervisee impairment (e.g., drug abuse, mental health issues, or high levels of anxiety) so they may offer support and ensure that clients are receiving proper professional care and attention (NASW, 1999, S.2.09; Robb, 2003). Given the insidious nature of boundary violations, supervisors should pay particular attention

---

supervision, including professional conduct provisions related to learning plans, format and schedule of supervision, supervisor and supervisee responsibilities, accountability, evaluation measures, documentation and reporting, conflict resolution, client notification, and duration and termination of supervision.

[2] Meaning, "the supervisor shall answer" or be held to account.

to whether the supervisee is maintaining appropriate boundaries with their clients (Koenig & Spano, 2003). When evaluating supervisees, supervisors should provide feedback in a fair and respectful manner (NASW, 1999, S.2.09), fostering a trusting supervisor-supervisee relationship. When supervisees lack trust in supervisors, they are less likely to reach out for help, particularly when complex ethical dilemmas or embarrassing breaches arise (Phelan et al., 2003). Perhaps one of the most important messages that supervisors can provide to supervisees is that when difficult issues arise, *do not worry alone* (Gutheil & Brodsky, 2008). Supervisors should encourage supervisees to come to them with problems or concerns, rather than suffer through them without supervisory assistance.

SUPERVISORY ROLES IN THE SIX STAGES

1. Identify Ethical Issue(s)

In the first stage of the Framework for Managing Ethical Issues, workers must become aware that a potential ethical issue exists and then be able to specify the nature of that conflict. Supervisors play a vital role in helping supervisees to identify issues through two processes: orientation and ongoing supervision.

Orientation

Supervisors are responsible for orienting social work practicum students and other new workers as they enter the agency. Orientation provides workers with the information they need to practice in a professional, ethical manner, given the specific mandate of the agency and needs of its clients. Supervisors should ensure that supervisees are aware of the laws and agency policies that govern their work, and how these laws and policies fit with their obligations under the NASW Code of Ethics.[3] Understanding the applicable laws, policies, and ethical standards is crucial to being able to recognize that an ethical issue exists. Consider a simple request by a client to schedule a session after regular work hours. If the worker is unfamiliar with policies prohibiting after-hours sessions, the worker might think nothing of scheduling such a meeting. Some agencies require supervisees to sign statements acknowledging that the supervisee has read, understands, and agrees to abide by particular agency policies or codes of ethics (Falvey, 2002).

Supervisors should not only explain the agency's rules and guidelines, but also the reasons for these rules and guidelines. Supervisees are more likely to adhere to laws, policies, and ethical standards when they understand their rationale. When supervisees appreciate the underlying rationale, they are more likely to apply such rules and guidelines in a critical, purposeful manner. If supervisors simply demand compliance to rules (without explaining why they are important), supervisees may follow them by rote, in a rigid, ritualized manner (Kadushin & Harkness, 2002). This may discourage them from thinking through the consequences of following rules in a particular case, ignoring special needs and ethical concerns that may arise.

In many agencies, learning the relevant laws, policies, and standards of practice takes time. Policy manuals and orientation materials may consist of hundreds of pages. Further, reading these materials before having practice experience may make it difficult for new workers to understand the context and relevance of the rules and guidelines. Supervisors need to help supervisees prioritize what they need to learn and when. For instance, before a new worker meets her first client, it may be particularly important for her to know the agency's policies on informed consent, client confidentiality, and the management of professional boundaries with clients. Ideally, new workers should also understand policies such as how to manage clients with suicidal ideation. If suicidal ideation is a rare event at the agency, however, the supervisor might not

[3] Unless otherwise stated in this chapter, examples will assume the supervisee is a professional social worker. When supervisees are members of other professions, then supervisors should consider how the codes of conduct of those professions would apply.

prioritize this information as part of the worker's initial orientation.

One method of prioritizing what to include in the initial orientation to the agency is to conduct a needs assessment. The supervisor first identifies what information the supervisee needs to know, given the particular kinds of social work to be performed. The supervisor could develop a checklist of information based on the most pertinent information from the agency's policy book. The supervisor then uses the checklist to assess the supervisee's current knowledge and identify information that the supervisee needs to learn. For instance, the supervisee may be familiar with the general requirements of client confidentiality, but may not be familiar with the agency's specific forms for releasing confidential information. Mere understanding of information is not sufficient. The supervisor should also ensure that the supervisee possesses the skills to put the information into practice. Thus, with respect to confidentiality, the supervisor should assess whether the supervisee can properly explain confidentiality and engage a client in a discussion of the limits of confidentiality. Rather than simply ask the supervisee about confidentiality, the supervisor could engage the worker in role-plays to assess the supervisee's capacities and determine whether further training is required.

When developing plans for orienting a new supervisee, supervisors should take the supervisee's stage of professional development into account (Forehand, 2005). If working with an undergraduate student in her first field placement, for instance, the supervisor may need to focus on basic information. Helping the student understand agency policies comes before helping the student apply those policies in practice situations. Once the student becomes comfortable with understanding and applying basic policies, the supervisor may present the student with more complex ethical dilemmas. In contrast, it may be inappropriate to expect a new student to analyze complex ethical dilemmas that may arise in extraordinary circumstances before the student has had a chance to learn and integrate the more basic, black and white policies, and standards that govern everyday practice.[4]

One of the most important ethical standards to review with new supervisees is the concept of competence. Social workers should undertake particular roles or tasks only if they have the requisite knowledge and skills to perform those tasks in a capable manner (NASW, 1999, S.1.04[a]). Thus, supervisors should clarify which roles and tasks the supervisee is competent to perform, and which roles or tasks go beyond the supervisee's current level of knowledge and skills (Falvey, 2002).[5] A supervisee who is skilled in individual therapy, for instance, may not be competent to provide family therapy. By raising supervisees' awareness of the limits of their areas of competence, supervisors help supervisees recognize when ethical issues may arise before they actually get into trouble. When clients ask for help, helping professionals may feel a sense of obligation to provide help, not wanting to disappoint clients or admit they lack the skills or knowledge required to provide the requested help in a competent manner. Supervisors should reassure their supervisees that declining a request for services that goes beyond the supervisee's competence is not only ethical, but truly in the client's best interests. Supervisees should not feel ashamed about the limits of their competence. Rather, they should feel confident that they are helping their clients in the best way by restricting their practice to roles and tasks within their areas of competence. Supervisees may refer clients to other professionals for work that goes beyond their areas of competence or bring in their supervisors for consultation on how to proceed.

---

[4] This textbook illustrates how to use a developmental approach to teaching and learning ethics, providing more basic knowledge and skills in Part I and higher levels of knowledge and skills in Part II.

[5] Supervisors are also responsible for ensuring that supervisees have a caseload of a reasonable size. Further, supervisors should ensure supervisees do not have personal impairments that compromise their ability to work with certain types of client issues (e.g., a supervisee who has unresolved issues from growing up in an abusive home and has difficulty dealing with countertransference when working with parents who have abused their children).

Supervisors can help supervisees think about supervision for ethical issues as a normal part of practice by letting them know there will be times when they are unsure about what to do or when they feel a conflict between their personal beliefs and the expectations stated in agency policy, professional ethics, or applicable laws (DiFranks, 2008). Specifically, supervisors can encourage supervisees to access help by sharing stories of when the supervisor reached out for help with ethical issues.

Ongoing Supervision

The majority of social worker–client interactions are private encounters in which the supervisor does not directly observe what takes place (Falvey, 2002). Accordingly, supervisors rely upon the reports of supervisees (and to some extent, clients)[6] to monitor whether supervisees are acting in an ethical manner. Supervisors may use a variety of techniques to solicit information for monitoring purposes: engaging supervisees in face-to-face supervisory meetings, reviewing progress notes or process recordings, or soliciting written or verbal feedback from clients. Reports from supervisees may or may not exhibit accurate reflections of what actually transpired during the social work process, as supervisees report their perceptions of what transpired, or in some cases, their perceptions of what should have transpired (Kadushin & Harkness, 2002). Consider a worker who makes an inappropriate sexual comment to a client but is unaware of its inappropriateness. The worker may not even think to discuss this issue with the supervisor (Falvey, 2002). Reports from clients also depend on their personal perceptions and agendas. Consider, for instance, a client who has ethical concerns about a worker but provides only positive feedback due to fears of retribution if the client provides a negative report. In other words, supervisors should understand the potential limits on the accuracy of the reports they receive, regardless of the source of the information.

Supervisors can engage in direct observation of worker–client interaction through a variety of strategies: cocounseling with the supervisee, observing through a one-way mirror, or reviewing videotapes of sessions (Kadushin & Harkness, 2002; Munson, 2002). Although these strategies permit the supervisor to monitor sessions without the filters of worker and client perceptions, they are labor-intensive. Most supervision tends to be indirect, given the practicalities of time constraints, client sensitivities about having their sessions observed, and the interests of promoting worker autonomy. Still, supervisors should consider using direct observation in the following circumstances:

- When a new supervisee enters the agency and the supervisor wants to gain a sense of the supervisee's ability to practice in a competent, ethical manner.
- When a supervisee is engaging in a particularly risky intervention and the supervisor wants to ensure that the risks are managed appropriately (e.g., when a supervisee is experimenting with an untraditional, untested clinical intervention with clients; or when the clients are at high risk for suicide or other forms of violence).
- When a client, supervisor, or colleagues have raised questions about a worker's ability to practice ethically, and the supervisor wants to appraise the worker's abilities more closely.

Given that most client interactions occur without direct supervisory observation, the supervisor–supervisee relationship is predicated on trust. Supervisors who show trust in their supervisees encourage them to take responsibility, act in a professional manner, and know when to ask for support and guidance. Supervisors may unintentionally dissuade supervisees from asking for help if they come across as distrustful, intrusive, overbearing, or controlling. Supervisees are more likely to come to supervisors for help, particularly

[6] During the informed consent process, social workers should inform their clients that they will be sharing client information with their supervisors. They should also provide clients with information on how to contact their supervisors should the clients have any concerns to discuss (Falvey, 2002).

with regard to potentially embarrassing professional issues, when they feel that their supervisors are respectful, supportive, and empowering. In other words, supervisors should foster a relationship that encourages the supervisee to discuss difficult issues, which are often the issues that matter most (Stone, Patton, & Heen, 1999). Asking for help is not a sign of weakness, but rather a key element of ethical reasoning and decision making. Discussing potential ethical breaches or problems does not indicate incompetence, but rather a professional desire to do what is best and to be accountable for one's actions (Quinn, 2005). Supervisees are typically motivated to use supervision because of the expertise supervisors can provide (Kadushin & Harkness, 2002).

One of the most effective ways of encouraging supervisees to identify and discuss potential ethical issues is to use active listening. The supervisor acts as a sounding board for the supervisee, empowering the supervisee to reflect on recent interactions with clients. The supervisor does not need to interrogate the supervisee, asking pointed questions or insinuating ethical misconduct. As with therapist–client relationships, supervisors can facilitate trust by demonstrating core conditions of a positive working relationship: genuineness, unconditional positive regard, and empathic understanding (Rogers, 1957). When supervisees discuss client interactions that may raise ethical issues, supervisors should provide them with the time, space, and support to identify the issues themselves. A supervisor who is too quick to point out ethical issues may put the supervisee on the defensive and discourage the supervisee from opening up and identifying ethical issues in a more autonomous manner. Consider the following scenario between Sheena and her field instructor, Felice:

SHEENA: Last week, we discussed referring my client, Carter, to an Alcoholics Anonymous (AA) meeting. Well, he went. I know because he showed up at my meeting.

FELICE: So you were at an AA meeting and Carter came to the same one [paraphrasing to show empathy, in a matter-of-fact tone of voice, without making judgments].

SHEENA: Yes, I was so embarrassed. I wasn't sure what to do.

FELICE: Sounds like it felt awkward for you. So, what did you do? [reflecting feeling and asking an open-ended question to elicit more information]

SHEENA: I don't know if I handled it well. I sort of pretended I didn't know him, and then he came over and said "hello" to me. So I said "hi" back to him, but that was all I said for the whole meeting.

FELICE: Thanks for bringing this issue for us to discuss in supervision. Perhaps we can start by talking more about what happened, and what types of issues this raises for you as a professional social worker. [reinforcing bringing issues to supervision; inviting discussion of ethical issues]

SHEENA: When I asked Carter to think about going to an AA meeting, I never thought he'd come to mine. He lives on the other side of town. I know you're going to tell me about keeping professional boundaries, but it wasn't my fault.

FELICE: I understand.... You did not invite him to your meeting. You know that would have been an intentional boundary violation. Given that he showed up at the same meeting that you did, what issues does this raise? [paraphrasing to show understanding; identifying strengths to show unconditional positive regard; using an open-ended question to focus Sheena on issue identification]

SHEENA: It muddles our relationship. We're supposed to be social worker and client, but when we're at the AA meeting, we're both group members. How can I talk about my personal life with a client present? This is my home meeting. If I have to go somewhere else, I'll lose one of my main support systems. But I don't want to end my work with Carter, either. We were just starting to develop a good working relationship.

FELICE: Exactly. Even though you never intended to enter a dual relationship with Carter, it just happened. Sometimes, when ethical issues arise, it's nobody's fault. We could talk about whether this type of boundary crossing could be prevented in the future, but for now, let's talk about how to deal with Carter's situation. [summarizing to show understanding of Sheena's predicament; refocusing what to do now]

Notice how Felice encourages Sheena to share her story, offering encouragement, understanding, and openness to hear whatever Sheena has to say. Felice allows Sheena to describe the ethical conflict in her own words. Felice avoids making judgments. In this example, Felice helps conceptualize the issue as an unintentional dual relationship (Kaplan, 2006). Alternatively, she could have permitted Sheena to explore the issues further and deduce her own conceptualization of the ethical issues raised by this case. Regardless of whether the supervisee or supervisor initially articulates the primary ethical issues, the supervisor should try to articulate an ethical issue that both can agree upon. Having a single, agreed-upon statement of the issue provides a distinct focus for the next steps of managing the ethical issues. If the supervisor and supervisee cannot establish an agreed-upon statement of the issue, they might take both of their statements into the next stage, making use of help from others. Perhaps with the aid of an administrator, attorney, or other support person, they can determine the appropriate focus for managing the ethical issues.

2. Determine Appropriate Help

In the introduction to Part II, we identified several potential sources of help for ethical issues: supervisors, coworkers, ethics committees, attorneys, liability insurance providers, professional associations, licensing bodies, clients, friends, or family members. In most instances, a supervisee's first line of support should come from his or her supervisor. Thus, it is incumbent on supervisors to foster conditions that make it more likely that supervisees will come to them for support. As noted earlier, supervisees are more likely to seek help from supervisors for support if they feel the supervisors will be supportive and can offer expertise for resolving the issues. Accessibility is critical (McAuliffe & Sudbery, 2005). Note in Sheena's situation, she found herself face-to-face with her client at an evening AA meeting. Sheena tried to manage the boundary issues as well as she could, but on her own. Because her supervisor (Felice) was not immediately available, she could not seek help until the following day at work. In this situation, it may not have been reasonable to expect Felice to be available during the evening. If the situation were different and Sheena had planned to have an evening session with Carter, then Felice should have either been available for consultation or provided Sheena with alternate supervisors within the agency whom she could consult (e.g., the supervisor on call).

Although some ethical management models emphasize the importance for frontline workers to seek help, it is also important for supervisors to know when and how to access help. Some supervisors feel too proud or too embarrassed to admit to a supervisee that they do not know the answer to an ethical question. As with frontline workers, supervisors should understand that accessing help in appropriate circumstances is a sign of professionalism, not a lack thereof. In some instances, supervisors may desire specialized expertise or guidance. Felice, for instance, might want to consult an attorney to discuss the potential legal liability involved if Sheena continues to attend the same AA meeting as her client. In other situations, supervisors may simply need to consult someone as a sounding board or for a reality check. Sheena might strongly believe that her right to attend her AA meeting is superior to her client's right. Felice might strongly believe that Sheena should cede her rights for her client's best interests. Felice might bring in the agency's program director to bounce ideas with someone who has a bit more distance from the situation. Likewise, Felice might consult Sheena's faculty field liaison to solicit the perspective of her school of social work. Some agencies provide a protocol for which ethical issues require consultation with various officials within the agency. For instance, frontline workers may be required to consult with supervisors whenever there are concerns related to suicidal or homicidal ideation. Consultations with attorneys may be required whenever a client initiates a grievance. Consultation with and approval of the program director may be required for any forms of practice that deviate from the usual policies of the agency. Thus, supervisors are often the first source of help with ethical issues, but both frontline workers and supervisors should understand that accessing additional sources of help may be prudent practice.

3. Think Critically

Supervisors should not underestimate or demean the ability of supervisees to think for themselves. At the same time, supervisors should be aware of the ways in which they can enhance the critical thinking process: professional distance, professional expertise, reality testing, alternative methods of thinking, and risk management.

Professional Distance

Professional distance refers to the types of boundaries that professionals maintain with their clients. Very rigid boundaries suggest the professional is distant or emotionally detached from the client. Very diffuse boundaries suggest the professional is overly emotionally engaged with the client. The ideal is somewhere in between, though different social workers may argue over exactly where the ideal levels of emotional engagement should be (Worden, 2003). Often, frontline workers are more emotionally engaged with clients than their supervisors are. After all, the frontline workers strive to establish a positive working rapport and have more direct contact with clients than does the supervisor. When thinking through ethical issues, supervisors may be able to offer a more objective perspective of ethical issues, particularly when workers are closely aligned with the clients. Assume that Sheena strongly identifies with Carter, given that both are in recovery and both believe passionately in the philosophies of AA. Her identification with Carter is not necessarily a bad thing; in fact, acknowledging her empathic and caring feelings for Carter may help her tune into his concerns (Mattison, 2000). On the other hand, her identification may cloud her thinking (Kaplan, 2006). Sheena believes that the only choices for resolving the ethical dilemma are to stop going to her local AA meeting or asking Carter not to go to that particular AA meeting. She finds neither of these options satisfactory because one or the other of them will be sacrificing a very important support system. Because Felice has some professional distance, she might be able to help Sheena explore alternatives to AA. Although there may be just one AA group within a reasonable driving distance, there may be other self-help or facilitated groups that Sheena or Carter could consider.

A much more challenging issue arises when workers have difficulty separating their religious or personal worldviews from their professional obligations (Spano & Koenig, 2007). Assume you are supervising Sadie, a social worker who identifies as a Jehovah's Witness. Given her faith, Sadie believes that the role of Christians is "to make disciples of all the nations" by spreading the good news of the Bible, particularly to people who are unhappy with the current situation of the world (Watchtower, 2000). When you advise Sadie that it would be unethical for her to impose her religious beliefs on her clients, she says, "I would never do that. I simply want to help clients become aware of what the Bible has to offer." She suggests that offering a spiritual intervention to clients is no different from offering them cognitive or narrative therapy. How would you respond to Sadie? If you simply tell her to follow agency policy or the NASW Code, how might she respond? One method of helping supervisees understand the potential impact of their actions is through role-reversal. Sadie would play the role of a client. You could play the role of a social worker who tries to introduce the client to the teachings of a different (non-Christian) religion. Through the role-play and debriefing, Sadie may experience the issues that arise when workers cross religious boundaries with a client. You may also affirm Sadie's right to promote her religion in her personal life, while reinforcing the importance of maintaining appropriate boundaries with clients when she is acting in her professional social work capacity.

Professional Expertise

Supervisors can bring much needed knowledge and experience to discussions of ethical issues. In fact, supervisees may view their supervisors as educators, coaches, or mentors because of their greater professional expertise (Kadushin & Harkness, 2002; McAuliffe & Sudbery, 2005). When Sheena met Carter at the AA meeting, she was caught off guard and did not know what to say. Felice may have experienced similar situations in the past, so she might share her insights:

> Meeting a client in a public setting can be awkward, for the client and for the worker. Sometimes, I've found it useful to hang back and wait for cues from the client. If the client seems to be avoiding eye contact with me, I may take this as a sign that the client doesn't want me to acknowledge our prior relationship. If the client greets me, I'll respond politely, but I won't discuss any social work issues or disclose any confidences. If someone asks how we know each other, I might provide a very general response, "Oh, we met a few weeks ago..."

Supervisors also use their expertise by providing supervisees with direction on where to access relevant laws, policies, and ethical standards. Novice workers may know generally, for instance, that they have a duty to warn or protect others who may be at risk of serious harm, but do they know what the local laws say, what agency policies say, or how Standard 1.07(c) of the NASW Code applies? Accordingly, supervisors may serve an important role in helping supervisees ground their decisions in relevant laws, policies, and ethical standards.

Reality Testing

Reality testing involves the use of questioning to help people think through the veracity of their thoughts and beliefs (Spangler, 2003). Supervisees (and all people) may be susceptible to faulty thinking for a variety of reasons: ethnocentric bias, selective attention, stress, fatigue, and so on. According to the psychological phenomenon of "naturalistic fallacy," for instance, some people tend to equate their description of "*what is*" with their prescription for "*what ought to be*" (Paul & Elder, 2006; Shiraev & Levy, 2004). Consider a social worker from an agency that has historically restricted services to citizens, denying services to noncitizens. The worker might believe that, given the agency's past practices, it should continue to restrict services to citizens. A supervisor could help the worker challenge his own thinking through the use of analogy.

> I understand that you believe noncitizens should be denied services because that's always been the way things have been done at this agency. Now, assume that you are left-handed and this agency has never hired a left-handed person before. Would it be ethical for the agency to deny you a position because you are left-handed? [pause for response] Couldn't the agency argue that it's just doing things the way it's always done them? [pause for response] Then, should this agency deny services to noncitizens simply because that's been the history here?

The supervisor's questioning should be geared toward helping the supervisee see things in a different light. To avoid embarrassing or denigrating the supervisee, the supervisor should ask the questions in an inquisitive rather than an accusatorial tone of voice. The supervisor may also help the supervisee save face by letting him know that many people assume that *what is* reflects *what ought to be*.

Assume Sheena has a tendency to catastrophize, suggesting, "If I'm not able to go to my own AA meetings, I'll implode... that will be the end of my recovery." Felice could help Sheena work through the possible consequences of not going to AA meetings on a more rational basis. Yes, giving up her AA meetings would be challenging, but would they be as devastating as Sheena seems to believe? Felice could help Sheena verbalize her feelings of frustration or anger over the possibility of having to sacrifice going to her usual AA group, while also helping her consider other possible sources of support.

Alternative Methods of Thinking

Perhaps one of the most challenging aspects of resolving ethical issues is to try more than one approach for thinking through the issues. When people start thinking through ethical issues in a particular manner, they may become locked into that way of thinking and have difficulty approaching the same issues through different approaches (Quinn, 2005). Supervisors may be able to free supervisees from constrained thinking by inviting them to try out other methods of analyzing ethical issues. As long as the supervisor can provide a safe place for discussing issues (e.g., helping the supervisee save face), there is really no cost in exploring issues from different angles (Casebeer, 2003).

Assume that Sheena is absolutist in her thinking (Gert, 2006). She strongly believes that agency rules must be followed, regardless of the circumstances. Her agency has a policy that says, "Social workers should avoid dual relationships with clients." She takes this to mean that she cannot go to the same AA meetings as Carter, regardless of the circumstances. Felice validates this manner of thinking, pointing out that it shows respect for agency policy. Still, she also encourages Sheena to consider alternate approaches to thinking. Felice explains how her thinking may fit with absolutist or deontological approaches, and that it may be useful to consider consequentialist or teleological approaches. As Felice engages Sheena in a discussion of what might happen if Sheena and Carter continue to attend the same AA meetings, they identify both potential benefits and risks. On the positive side, both continue to be able to draw support from the only AA meeting in the area. They may even develop closer bonds and Sheena may find new ways of helping Carter with his recovery. On the negative side, their professional-personal boundaries may become blurred: Carter may start to see Sheena as a friend rather than a social worker; Sheena may have difficulty remembering what she must keep confidential during AA meetings; and if Carter becomes upset with Sheena (for whatever reason), Carter may initiate a grievance or lawsuit based on her infringement of agency policies and professional standards of practice. Although Sheena might come to similar conclusions even though she has used different approaches to thinking, the exercise of using different approaches to thinking is worthwhile. In some cases, alternate approaches to thinking will confirm solutions that have already been considered; in other cases, alternate approaches will suggest disparate results. When a supervisor asks a supervisee to try alternate ways of thinking, the supervisee may feel confused and wonder why they cannot simply rely on one straightforward approach to thinking. The supervisor may need to explain how complex ethical dilemmas may require complex methods of thinking. After all, for every complex human problem, there is a neat, simple solution...and it is wrong...at least from some people's perspectives (Mencken, 1920).

Supervisors may assess which types of thinking their supervisees are applying: for instance, libertarian, egalitarian, deontological, or utilitarian.[7] They may then engage their supervisees in alternative ways of thinking through the use of Socratic discussion, as described in Chapter 7.

Risk Management

Risk management refers to the processes of identifying, assessing, preventing, and reducing risks or potential harms within an organizational setting (Green, 2007). Whereas professional ethics tell us what we "should do" and the law tells us what we "have to do," risk management helps us decide what we "choose to do" (Vincler, 2008). Risk management includes reducing the risks of breaking laws or breaching ethical standards, though it could include any risk of harm to clients, social workers, other people, or property.[8]

---

[7] See Chapter 10 for further descriptions and examples of these approaches.

[8] This section highlights risk management strategies that may be used in the critical thinking stage of the ethical management process. Other risk management strategies may be used on an ongoing basis. For instance, one of the primary methods of reducing risks is to ensure competent practice. As mentioned earlier, supervisors play a vital role in assessing the competence of social workers and ensuring that they are assigned to do work within areas of their competence. Supervisees should know their limitations and when to refer clients to other professionals for work that goes beyond their competence. Consultation is another key area for risk management. Supervisors and supervisees should consult with lawyers, ethicists, or other experts to ensure that they are acting within the bounds of the law, agency policy, and professional standards of practice. Other general strategies for reducing risks include ensuring that staff have proper training and continuing education, ensuring that staff are properly licensed or accredited for the work they are doing, ensuring that the agency has proper liability insurance coverage, and ensuring that workers properly document the work they are doing in client records.

When discussing ethical issues, supervisors may employ the strategy of risk management by helping supervisees think through the risks (and benefits) of various courses of action. Sheena, for instance, might see no harm in attending the same AA meetings as her client, Carter. She contends that attending meetings with Carter is actually empowering to him, as they would be respecting his self-determined right to attend meetings with her. Although Felice believes in a client's right to self-determination, she helps Sheena identify and assess risks that may arise, particularly with respect to the blurring of professional boundaries (e.g., when Carter hears Sheena discuss her issues at AA meetings, he may feel compelled to offer her support).

One method of reducing risks that is particularly useful in the context of managing ethical dilemmas is documentation (Falvey, 2002; Reamer, 2008a).[9] Whenever social workers are faced with difficult ethical or legal decisions, they should document the following information:

- The nature of the ethical or legal issue and how it arose.
- What steps the social worker took in order to assess the situation, including who was consulted and which laws, policies, and ethical standards were considered.
- The courses of action considered, including the advantages and disadvantages of each.
- The course of action taken, including the rationale for selecting this course of action over the others considered.

By documenting this information, the social worker has made the process and rationale for his or her decision making completely transparent. Remember, under malpractice laws, social workers are not required to act perfectly, but rather to act in a prudent manner. By demonstrating that they have used prudent clinical judgment in determining how to manage an ethical or legal issue, they fulfill their duty of care (Reamer, 2008a).

Assume that Sheena and Felice decide that Sheena should be able to continue to go to her AA meeting and that they will try to link Carter with another (non-AA) support group.[10] They should document how they came to this conclusion, including which options they considered and how they determined that this option was the most ethical (Caudill, n.d). If Carter later raises complaints about how he was treated, this documentation can be used to demonstrate that they thought carefully, using relevant laws, policies, and ethical standards, to inform their decision.

Supervisors may tend to be more conservative about taking risks than frontline workers. In part, this may be due to a supervisor's responsibility in enforcing agency policy. In contrast, frontline workers may align more with clients and be willing to assume risks in ways that they perceive will benefit clients. In other words, supervisors may be more pragmatic about risk taking, whereas less experienced workers may be more idealistic.

Some advocates for social change question whether supervisors should be so tied to enforcing existing rules and policies. To promote social justice, for instance, social workers may need to take risks, including challenging the status quo.

---

[9] In terms of ongoing risk management, supervisors should document all their meetings with supervisees, including dates and durations of meetings, cases discussed, critical feedback offered by supervisor to supervisee, treatment plans (interventions by the supervisee and referrals to others), and rationale for treatment decisions (Falvey, 2002). Documentation provides supervisors with a clear record to demonstrate whether their supervision was timely and appropriate.

[10] In this scenario, the supervisor is helping the supervisee manage an ethical dilemma. When a case involves an alleged breach of ethical standards or agency policies, the supervisor should consider the following actions: investigating the alleged violation with the supervisee and client or other complainant; providing close monitoring of the supervisee's future client contact or work; consulting with the supervisor's superiors or other professional consultants about how to respond; reporting the alleged incident to a relevant state licensing board, professional association, or ethics committee; and documenting each of these actions and the rationale for taking them (Falvey, 2002).

By merely following agency policy or current laws, supervisors may be accepting things the way they are, rather than advocating for the way things should be (Meacham, 2007; Specht & Courtney, 1994). Consider a social worker who is assisting a group of tenants living in slum conditions. The worker wants to help the tenants make use of civil disobedience to raise awareness of their cause (e.g., blocking traffic at a major street intersection). The supervisor may dissuade the worker from participating in this action because it puts the worker and agency at risk, legally and financially. Rather than completely discounting the possibility of civil disobedience, however, the supervisor and social worker might assess whether and how supporting the clients in such efforts might fit within the agency's mandate and risk tolerance. Certainly, if there are less risky interventions that could lead to success, they should be considered first. If less risky interventions have been exhausted or are deemed to be ineffective, then they may be able to justify the use of riskier interventions. Risk management is not simply about avoiding all risks, but rather about making deliberate decisions concerning which risks to accept. If the supervisor and frontline worker decide to move ahead with plans for civil disobedience, they should still consider how they may be able to reduce risks. For instance, they may reduce risks by ascertaining support of others in the agency, by training clients in methods of nonviolence (Walz & Richie, 2000), and by working with police to ensure that the police understand the nature of the event.

Ideally, supervisors and supervisees agree upon which risks to accept and which risks to avoid, prevent, or reduce. When disagreements persist, they may be able to use conflict resolution strategies, as described in the following section.

4. Manage Conflict

Supervisors may assume a variety of conflict resolution roles, including enforcer, mediator, coach, and arbitrator. In their capacity as administrators of agency policy, they are often responsible for ensuring that their supervisees adhere to agency policy (Kadushin & Harkness, 2002). Thus, when supervising frontline workers, they encourage compliance with agency rules and guidelines through education, encouragement, and, when necessary, through sanctioning (e.g., threat of suspension or other discipline for failure to comply with agency policy). Ideally, supervisors and supervisees agree upon the most appropriate ways to respond to ethical issues without the use of threats or other coercive techniques (NASW National Council on the Practice of Clinical Social Work, 1994). Given the authority and expertise of supervisors, supervisees may acquiesce to the will of the supervisor even when the supervisor has not used coercive power. In fact, supervisors may not even know when supervisees disagree with their positions, given that supervisees may be motivated to avoid conflict with their supervisors (Phelan et al., 2003; Stone et al., 1999).

As noted earlier, supervisors may not be aware that ethical concerns have arisen unless and until their supervisees approach them for assistance. When supervisors come across as dictatorial, uncaring, or disrespectful, they dissuade supervisees from seeking supervisory help (McAuliffe & Sudbery, 2005). Thus, supervisors may encourage supervisees to seek assistance by modeling collaborative, thoughtful, and respectful conflict resolution skills and strategies (e.g., through active listening, Socratic discussion, and interest-based and transformative conflict resolution approaches, as described in Chapter 7). These approaches build trust, a prerequisite for being able to raise ethical issues with one's supervisor.

Perhaps the most critical function of a supervisor in helping supervisees manage ethical issues is the role of mediator. As mediators, supervisors may bring together the key parties who are involved in the ethical situation, helping them communicate more effectively, sort through their interests, build common ground, and develop solutions that address their primary ethical concerns (Barsky, 2007a). Consider a family counseling agency that is developing policies regarding spousal abuse. Some therapists want agency policy to take a zero-tolerance stance toward spousal abuse, requiring that any incidents be reported to the police. Others want agency policy to leave the issue of reporting up to the decision of the spouse who has been victimized. Given the mandate of the agency, this issue is critical to how they will operate. The supervisor decides to bring the clinical staff together to mediate a solution for this policy issue. As a mediator, the supervisor encourages open discussion of the issues, but also encourages the staff to focus on their professional obligations and values: respect for client autonomy, beneficence (doing good), and nonmaleficence (not causing harm) (Hunter, 2001). Through skilful facilitation, the supervisor helps staff members realize that they each have valid concerns and there is no simple solution that completely satisfies all of them. She helps them brainstorm a range of creative options, opening up the discussion to new ways of thinking about the problems. They eventually settle on a policy that includes some compromises, but seems to address each of the most important ethical concerns:

- All therapists will conduct individual sessions with spouses to screen for possible abuse issues and to afford therapists with an opportunity to discuss abuse issues in a private setting.
- When any client raises concerns about spousal abuse, the therapist will engage the client in a discussion of possible responses (including, but not limited to, the possibility of reporting the abuse to the police or seeking a court order for protection).
- Although therapists will discuss the possibility of reporting abuse incidents to the police, the therapist will respect the victimized client's decision about whether to make such a report. The therapists will promote client self-determination by providing the clients with information, support, options, and time necessary to make informed and voluntary decisions about reporting abuse or taking other steps to ensure their ongoing safety.

The above example demonstrates how supervisors can mediate ethical conflicts between staff or professionals. Supervisors may also mediate ethical conflicts between frontline workers and clients. Felicity, for instance, might conduct a joint meeting with Sheena and Carter to help them sort through the ethical issues that arose when Carter attended Sheena's AA meeting. Carter may initially have concerns that Felicity will side with Sheena, so Felicity needs to establish trust by demonstrating that she is truly committed to helping them find solutions that will satisfy the needs and interests of both (Moore, 2003). In the interests of honesty and full disclosure, Felicity should also disclose any agency policies or professional standards of practice that may apply to this situation (e.g., guidelines regarding dual relationships and maintaining professional boundaries with clients). These policies and standards identify the parameters in which the supervisor and other agency workers must operate. Assume Carter suggests that going to the same AA meetings is of no concern to the agency because it occurs outside the agency. Felicity may need to educate Carter about why dual relationships are of concern to the agency, perhaps asking questions that allow Sheena to discuss the importance of maintaining professional boundaries. Felicity continues to help Sheena and Carter work through the ethical issues, brainstorming options and then identifying the pros and cons of each option. Sheena notes that she is a field student whose affiliation with the agency will end in 3 weeks. She suggests that since she is leaving the agency anyhow, perhaps she could transfer Carter to another worker right away. Then she and Carter could both attend the same AA meeting without incurring many of the risks of a having an ongoing dual relationship. Felicity notes that dual relationships may be sequential. They discuss the risks that arise out of Sheena's and Carter's professional relationship, even after that relationship has been terminated. Eventually, Sheena and Carter agree that linking Carter with a non-AA support group is the most appropriate solution. They agree that Carter is not being barred from attending AA forever, but that he will refrain from attending Sheena's AA meeting for at least 2 years following termination of their professional relationship. They agree that if Carter does attend AA meetings with Sheena at that time, they will not disclose their prior professional relationship to other AA members, though they may acknowledge that they were acquaintances in the past.

In order to provide supervisees, clients, and others with a safe and productive forum for resolving ethical conflicts, supervisors may employ the following skills and strategies:

- Meeting parties individually before bringing them together, so as to provide them with an opportunity to vent strong feelings and to coach them on how to participate constructively in the joint meetings.

- Encouraging the parties to agree upon ground rules that promote respectful dialogue and permit people to express diverse opinions.
- Helping parties identify commonly shared ethical principles, as well as values or ethical standards where there may be disagreement.
- Facilitating active listening between the parties to ensure they understand one another's views and positions;
- Inviting parties to brainstorm options so they may consider the advantages and disadvantages of each.
- Identifying a process for problem solving and decision making that fosters consensus.
- Writing up any agreements, so that everyone is clear on what they have agreed upon (Barsky, 2007a).

5. Plan and Implement Decisions

Once the parties have decided how to resolve an ethical issue, the next stage includes planning and implementation. Supervisors may play a role in monitoring planning and implementation, as well as assuming specific roles in the implementation process. Without proper planning and implementation, good decisions may go awry. Someone needs to take charge of ensuring that people follow through on their commitments. In the spousal abuse policy case, for instance, someone needs to take the general agreement on policies and ensure that the agency's policy book is properly updated. The supervisor may take the general agreement to the agency attorney or program director to draft and insert the formal policies into the agency's policy book. The supervisor then needs to ensure that all clinical staff members are properly educated about the new policies. The supervisor may conduct an in-house training, helping staff understand the policy and conducting role-plays to ensure that staff know how to implement the policy in particular client situations.

In the AA case, someone needs to identify groups where Carter may be referred and ensure that Carter is satisfied with the referrals. Although Sheena may assume primary responsibility for these tasks, Felice should monitor the referral process and be ready to help out should Carter raise concerns. The supervisor's roles in planning and implementation obviously depend on the nature of the ethical issues. At a minimum, supervisors should provide monitoring and backup support for the supervisees who are responsible for carrying out particular tasks.

6. Evaluate and Follow Up

In the final stage of the ethical management process, someone needs to take responsibility for evaluating the effectiveness of the response to the ethical issues and deciding whether additional follow-up is required. While both supervisors and supervisees may assume responsibility for these roles, there are certain advantages in having a supervisor take primary responsibility. First, if the ethical issues involve significant risks to the physical or psychosocial welfare of clients or others, the agency will probably want a person with proper authority and expertise to oversee implementation, evaluation, and follow-up. Second, a supervisor may have greater objectivity in evaluating the effectiveness of the ethics response, particularly if the frontline worker is already feeling defensive about his or her involvement in an ethical crisis. Sheena, for instance, may feel anxious because she feels caught in an unavoidable dual relationship. She may be tempted to evaluate Carter's referral to a new agency favorably so she can terminate work with him as soon as possible. Because Felicity has greater professional distance with Carter, she may be more dispassionate in her evaluation of the referral.

Regardless of whether the supervisor or supervisee takes primary responsibility for evaluation and follow-up, documentation is vital. Whoever takes responsibility for evaluation and follow-up should keep a clear record of what the issues were, how they were managed, and whether there are any outstanding issues to be considered. Evaluation should not be a rubber-stamping of the validity of what was done, but a true assessment of whether the decisions were implemented as planned, what aspects of implementation led to positive consequences, and what aspects of implementation led to negative consequences. Difficulty in completely resolving an ethical issue in the first attempt is not necessarily a sign of failure. In fact, some ethical issues require a sequential approach for resolution. For instance, consider working with a client who has expressed suicidal ideation. The first step in trying to resolve this issue may be crisis-intervention counseling, to try to work through the issues on a voluntary basis. If this does not resolve the issues, the second step may be offering the client a safe place to stay, including monitoring on a voluntary basis. If various attempts at voluntary services are not effective, the supervisor and worker may need to initiate the process for an involuntary committal of the client to a mental health facility. By documenting their attempts at providing services on a voluntary basis, the supervisor and worker demonstrate that they tried to respect the client's right to self-determination, resorting to involuntary methods only when all other approaches were exhausted.

Frontline workers are often focused on ethical issues as they arise on a case-by-case basis. Supervisors should also consider how ethical issues that arose in one case may raise issues for other cases. In other words, an ethical issue that arises in one case may indicate the need for changes at an organizational level. Thus, follow-up to a particular ethical issue may include

- Changing agency policy to prevent recurrence of particular ethical issues or to provide staff with clearer guidance on how to manage them.
- Training staff so they may handle similar ethical issues more effectively.
- Dealing with underlying problems that may have contributed to the ethical issues (e.g., large caseloads, ineffective screening processes, or lack of support systems for frontline workers coping with stressful situations).

Finally, supervisors should consider seeking their own supervision. Ethical issues may take their toll on social workers, including supervisors. Supervision for supervisors provides them with an opportunity to reflect on what happened, how they managed the situation, and what they might do differently in the future. Supervision for supervisors may also provide them with moral support, encouragement, and relief from stress. The credo, *do not suffer ethical issues alone* (Gutheil & Brodsky, 2008), applies to both supervisors and supervisees.

SUPERVISOR–SUPERVISEE BOUNDARIES

In my consultations with various professional licensing bodies and professional review committees, boundary issues are cited as one of the most common factors implicated in the professional and ethical complaints that come their way (cf. Dolgoff et al., 2009; Reamer, 2008a; Strom-Gottfried, 2003). The primary case study described earlier in this chapter (Sheena and Carter's case) involves boundary issues between a frontline worker and her client. Boundaries issues also exist between frontline workers and their supervisors. In fact, supervisor–supervisee relationships may serve as models for how social workers should establish appropriate boundaries with their clients (Shulman, 2005). The concept of "parallel process" suggests that there are many similarities (or parallels) between the relationship that supervisors develop with their supervisees and the relationship that social workers establish with their clients: Both are professional helping relationships in which one person (the supervisor or the social worker) has more power than the other (the supervisee or the client). The person with greater power owes the other person a special fiduciary duty. This duty means the person with greater power has a professional obligation to look out for the best interests of the other person and not take advantage of the position of power. In particular, supervisors and social workers must be careful to respect the personal boundaries of their supervisees and clients, and avoid taking advantage of their vulnerabilities. Given their power, authority, and experience, the behavior of supervisors has significant influence on the ethical behavior of supervisees. By modeling appropriate professional boundaries, supervisors encourage supervisees to maintain appropriate boundaries with their clients (Stewart, 2004).

Some supervisors and supervisees view their working relationships as collegial and egalitarian, meaning that both people have equal or comparable power. After all, both are trained social workers who have been hired to perform certain professional responsibilities. Still, there may be a number of power differentials between them (Szymanski, 2003). Supervisors tend to have greater professional training and expertise. Further, they are mandated to monitor the performance of supervisees, taking corrective actions when necessary. Corrective actions may include providing the supervisee with education, information, or guidance, as well as dispensing sanctions, when needed (e.g., removing a worker from a particular case, suspending the worker, or imposing other agency-based discipline). Although sanctioning should be used sparingly, both supervisors and supervisees should acknowledge that supervisors possess such authority. In other words, it would be misleading for a supervisor to advise a supervisee that they are just like friends or are in an equal partnership, with the same roles and functions (Falvey, 2002).

Supervisors should discuss their supervisory role with supervisees, explaining how their role is similar to and different from the supervisee's relationships with clients. The role of a supervisor comprises a blending of the functions of an educator, coach, and manager. As an educator and coach, supervisors provide information, training, and support, preparing supervisees for their tasks, and helping them develop into increasingly competent practitioners. As managers, supervisors are responsible for monitoring the work of the supervisees and ensuring that their practice is consistent with relevant laws, agency policies, and professional standards of practice (Kadushin & Harkness, 2002). Although supervisors provide encouragement, moral support, and professional concern, supervisors should ensure that supervisees do not confuse these types of support with ones that are more appropriate for personal relationships. In particular, the role of a supervisor is different from that of a friend, parent, or family member. A supervisor helps supervisees with issues that are closely related to their work in the agency. Although supervisors may show empathy for personal issues that do not directly affect agency-related work, they should be careful to maintain professional boundaries. A supervisee who feels a strong level of support from a supervisor, for instance, may be tempted to ask the supervisor to provide advice on how to handle a personal, family situation (e.g., a conflict with the supervisee's spouse). Although it would be perfectly appropriate for a friend or family member to provide such advice, a supervisor should be careful about venturing into the supervisee's private life. To maintain appropriate boundaries, the supervisor should redirect the supervisee to other, more suitable forms of support (e.g., "Is there anyone in your family that you might talk to about this?" or "If you'd like to speak with a family therapist about this concern, I could provide you with some names to consider").

When a supervisor assumes the role of friend, family member, intimate partner, or therapist with the supervisee, the supervisor engages in a dual relationship. Standards 3.01(b) and (c) advise supervisors to maintain appropriate boundaries and to avoid dual relationships to protect supervisees from intentional exploitation or unintended harm. Some supervisors intentionally exploit their positions of power, for instance, by asking supervisees to provide sexual favors in return for positive supervisory treatment (e.g., raises, promotions, or positive performance evaluations). However, supervisees may experience harm even when the boundary violations are not intentional (Gutheil & Brodsky, 2008; Koenig & Spano, 2003). Consider the supervisor who provides advice to the supervisee who has asked for help with her beleaguered marriage. If the advice exacerbates the problems, the supervisee not only suffers in her spousal relationship, but also in her professional one. She may lose respect or trust in her supervisor and may find it difficult to continue working with the supervisor. The supervisor may also have difficulty separating her concerns with how the supervisee is handling her personal life from her concerns about how the supervisee is handling her professional obligations. In other words, by engaging in dual relationships, supervisors may compromise their ability to provide supervision in an objective manner.

To avoid the blurring of supervisory boundaries, supervisors should pay close attention to feelings of transference and countertransference that may arise in the supervisor–supervisee relationship. In this context, transference refers to an unconscious process whereby feelings the supervisee has for one person in his or her life are redirected toward the supervisor. The supervisee may have a tendency to recreate patterns of thinking, feeling, or behaving that were formed earlier in life, and apply them to his or her supervisor (Barsky, 2006). Sampson, for example, has difficulty taking directions from his supervisor. Sampson might be reacting this way due to transference of resentment toward a parent or other person who has exerted similar authority. Countertransference may also arise, whereby the supervisor redirects feelings for one person onto the supervisee. Fiona is a field instructor and also the mother of a 22-year-old. Unconsciously, she has formed a personal attachment with her supervisee, as if the supervisee were her own child. Transference and countertransference may lead to various forms of boundary violations (Schamess, 2006). Sampson might raise his voice and verbally attack his supervisor, breaching professional boundaries because he is treating the supervisor as if she were his parent. Alternatively, Fiona might ask her supervisee questions about his personal life, treating him as if he were her child. Both supervisors and supervisees need to be on guard for transference and countertransference, ensuring that such feelings do not lead them into boundary violations.

Unfortunately, many social workers fall into trouble with dual relationships and boundary issues even though they have good intentions (Reamer, 2008a). Consider Flora (a field supervisor) who takes Steve (a social work supervisee) out for lunch. Flora wants to acknowledge Steve's hard work and have an opportunity to become better acquainted. Unknown to Flora, Steve finds Flora sexually attractive. He interprets her lunch invitation as a sign that she is also attracted to him. During lunch, Steve wears special cologne, he holds Flora's chair for her, and he compliments her on her beautiful dress. Flora eventually notices these cues, but wonders how to address them. How does she re-establish professional boundaries with Steve without embarrassing or insulting him (Szymanski, 2003)? What if she identifies the possibility of erotic transference, but Steve denies this and refuses to discuss it further (Koenig & Spano, 2003; Stewart 2004)? Taking a supervisee out to lunch is not necessarily a boundary violation. Still, supervisors must be careful about how their behaviors are interpreted, not just what they intend.

Boundary issues that arise between supervisors and supervisees may be useful as educational opportunities, helping supervisees gain insights into their relationships with clients. Flora might discuss her relationship with Steve as a parallel to Steve's relationship with his clients (Schamess, 2006). She might ask him whether he would ever consider taking a client out for lunch, and under what circumstances. They could discuss how this situation would be similar to and different from Flora's asking Steve to lunch. In particular, they could discuss how supervisees and clients may be in vulnerable situations. Supervisees may feel vulnerable because their supervisors hold power in relation to their status in the agency (including performance evaluations, promotions, and dismissal decisions). In contrast, clients may feel vulnerable because they are disclosing personal problems and may be experiencing various levels of stress (physical, psychological, social, or spiritual). Both supervisory and counseling relationships are based on trust. Any violation of trust—including boundary violations—may cause significant harm to the ongoing working relationship (Reamer, 2008b). Accordingly, supervisors and social workers should be particularly cautious about maintaining appropriate boundaries.

In order to facilitate the supervisory process, supervisors strive to develop a high level of trust in their working relationships with supervisees. Trust encourages supervisees to come to them for help in times when they have transgressed agency policies or professional standards, as well as when they have questions about how to manage difficult ethical issues. While a trusting supervisory relationship provides supervisees with a safe context for discussing ethical issues, it also may also place supervisees in a vulnerable situation. Although supervisors may offer supervisees guidance, concern, and support as part of their professional role, they must also be careful to maintain appropriate professional boundaries so as not to misuse their positions of power or take advantage of the trust that supervisees have placed in them.

DISCUSSION QUESTIONS AND EXERCISES

Questions 1 to 5 are designed to help you explore the roles of a supervisor in the six stages of managing ethical issues (Figure II.1). Questions 6 and 7 provide you with an opportunity to apply the principles of risk management to case situations. Question 8 invites you to assess cases involving supervisor–supervisee boundary issues and determine the most ethical way to manage them.

1. *Suffering Alone*: Sharon is an MSW student who is doing her foundation-year field placement at the Fly-by-the-Seat-of-your-Pants Counseling Center (FSP). Sharon thought this agency would provide a great field opportunity because it emphasized concrete-experiential learning, which fit with Sharon's preferred learning style. Besides, after four years of university, how much more theory was there to learn? Sharon's field instructor, Francesca, takes a laissez-faire attitude toward supervision, believing that students who are trusted are more likely to take initiative and thrive in directions of their own interests. Besides, if Sharon ever had problems, Francesca's door was always open.

   During the third week of placement, Sharon begins working with a Cosmo, a 17-year-old youth who had been living on the street for 14 months. He says he left home because his parents sexually abused him. Cosmo came to FSP because he heard this agency could help him get off the streets and turn his life around. Toward the end of the first session with Sharon, Cosmo seems despondent. Sharon asks what is troubling him. Cosmo says he was thrown out of the hostel where he was staying and had nowhere safe to go that night. It is late Friday evening and it is brutally cold outside. Sharon's supervisor has already left the agency. Sharon does not know what else to do, so she says Cosmo can crash at her place for the weekend. Later that night, Sharon finds Cosmo crying in his bed. Cosmo says he was feeling alone and scared. He asks Sharon if he can sleep with her. Sharon consoles him and eventually offers to share a bed with him. They cuddle during the night but do not have sexual intercourse. Sharon believes that sleeping with Cosmo was appropriate, even empowering. Cosmo wanted to sleep with Sharon and Sharon believed in client self-determination. Also, she was able to model positive, consensual human contact and show him that he was worthy of being loved. This fit with the social work value of respect and the agency's policy about reducing the power gap between social workers and clients.

   First thing Monday morning, Sharon meets with Francesca to report what transpired over the weekend. Francesca is flabbergasted. With Sharon still in the office, Francesca calls Lucille (the university's faculty-field liaison) to ask her to terminate Sharon's placement. Lucille asks what happened. Francesca responds that their clients required ethical and competent social workers, but Sharon completely lacks appropriate knowledge, skills, and boundaries for this type of work. As Sharon listens to this discussion over the speakerphone, she feels distraught and unable to defend herself.

   a. Identify the standards of the NASW Code of Ethics that Sharon has breached, and describe how her behaviors violated these standards.
   b. Identify the standards of the NASW Code that Francesca has breached, and explain how she should have conducted herself in order to properly fulfill her ethical obligations as a supervisor.
   c. Identify ways in which Sharon and Francesca breached the policies of your school of social work (which may be found in your program's field education manual).
   d. What types of corrective actions do you think that the agency and the school should take with regard to the concerns Francesca has raised about Sharon? Provide your reasons, taking ethical

principles from the NASW Code and your field manual into account.

e. Assume that Sharon had an opportunity to meet with Francesca to discuss Cosmo's situation during the evening that he asked to come home with her. Describe how Francesca could have helped Sharon through the first three stages of the ethical management process: identifying issues; determining appropriate help, and critical thinking. For the purposes of this assignment, assume that there are no easy answers to Cosmo's predicament; in particular, there are no safe hostels or shelters where Cosmo can sleep tonight, and if he has to sleep on the streets, he could suffer from hypothermia, theft, or violence. To provide Cosmo with a safe place to sleep, Sharon and Francesca may need to take a risk and cross their usual professional boundaries, in some manner.

2. *E-Problems*: Sanjiv conducts online counseling with the Self-Actualization Web-Therapy Institute. Sanjiv has been providing services to a client who identifies himself as Cyrus Jung. After five sessions, Sanjiv checks Cyrus's payment record and discovers his account was billed to the credit card of someone called Howard Yewes. Sanjiv suspects the client has been fraudulently billing his services to someone else's account. However, Sanjiv is nervous about contacting the credit card company or Mr. Yewes because he does not want to breach Cyrus's confidentiality. Why might Sanjiv feel afraid to ask his supervisor for help? What could the supervisor do to encourage Sanjiv to seek help for this type of situation? Describe how Sanjiv's supervisor might be able to help him with the ethical issues raised by this case, focusing on the first four stages of the Framework for Managing Ethical Issues.
3. *Keeping Mum*: While conducting a group session for clients with grief issues, Susan invites clients to participate in a visualization exercise that takes them back to childhood. Susan had not told her supervisor that she was going to do a visualization exercise as she did not think it was a big issue. During the visualization, one of her clients, Carrie (42), begins to scream. Susan terminates the exercise and debriefs Carrie. Carrie discloses that the exercise triggered a traumatic memory of childhood sexual abuse by her mother. Susan's first instinct is to downplay the issue with the group and try to bury the issue. Describe how a supervisor might be able to help Susan with the ethical issues raised by this case, focusing on the first four stages of the Framework for Managing Ethical Issues. Why is it particularly important in this case for Susan to consult with her supervisor as soon as possible?
4. *Thoughts-Feelings-Behaviors*: Shyla tells her field instructor Faith, "I cannot do home visits in a Black neighborhood because I wouldn't feel safe walking down the street." Has Shyla breached the NASW Code of Ethics by expressing these thoughts and feelings, or is her statement ethically neutral until she acts upon them? How should Faith respond to Shyla's comments?
5. *Implement and Evaluate*: A daycare facility reports the Campbell family to child protective services because of suspicions of medical neglect. Celia Campbell (3 years old) has been having ear infections that may lead to significant hearing loss if she does not receive proper treatment. When Swati, a child protection worker, begins investigating the case, Mr. and Mrs. Campbell say they cannot afford medical care for Celia. Swati suggests free medical services may be available for their child, but they refuse to accept charity. Swati's supervisor, Fern, helps mediate the following solution: Mr. and Mrs. Campbell agree to take Celia for medical treatment at the Community Health Foundation and they will pay for services by working for the Foundation on weekends (helping to paint the facility). Everyone believes this solution will address their primary ethical goals: protecting Celia's health and welfare, honoring the family's right to self-determination, and respecting the family's

wish to pay for services rather than receive charity. They also acknowledge that bartering for medical services is unusual and they will need a detailed implementation plan to reduce any risks related to bartering. Describe how Fern could assist Celia with the last two stages of the ethical management process—planning and implementation, and evaluation and follow-up. In particular, what steps can Fern take to ensure successful implementation of the plan, and how can she evaluate the extent to which their goals are achieved?

6. *Criminal Record*: Assume that you are a field instructor working in an agency that provides vocational counseling services to people who have been laid off and cannot find jobs in their original career areas. A BSW student named Shay has been assigned to work with you for her field education. During the interview process, you find out that Shay has served time for a felony conviction related to possessing a dangerous weapon while holding up a convenience store. Shay says she had a drug problem at the time, but she is now in recovery and has had no further conflicts with the law. Neither the school of social work nor the agency prohibits people with felony convictions from practicing social work. In fact, they believe people should be given a second chance. What risk-management strategies could you use, as supervisor, to reduce specific risks associated with Shay's criminal offense history?
7. *Recovery in the Mountains*: Stavros is planning to take a group of recovering alcoholics to the mountains for a therapeutic retreat. The retreat will include group counseling, guided nature walks, team-building exercises, and wilderness-survival skills training. What risks should Stavros and his supervisor consider? What risk-management strategies could they use to manage these risks?
8. For each of the following situations, identify the potential boundary violations and dual relationships. Describe how a supervisor should respond to each situation. Provide reasons for your suggestions based on ethical principles and standards from the NASW Code of Ethics:
   a. Shane provides therapeutic counseling for victims of torture. Felix (Shane's supervisor) believes that Shane overidentifies with his clients and is at risk of burning out from vicarious trauma. Upon exploring Shane's affect, motivation, and energy level, Felix believes Shane is clinically depressed. Felix teaches Shane how to make use of meditation to help him cope more effectively with the stress that he is internalizing from work with his clients.
   b. Frieda has a pile of paperwork to review before tomorrow's audit of the agency's records. Her supervisee, Sigourney, offers to pick up Frieda's daughter from school and babysit her, allowing Frieda to stay at the office and finish her work. Frieda says she does not want to impose, but Sigourney insists, saying, "It's for the good of the agency."
   c. Serenity has just graduated with her MSW degree and works in a day center for seniors. She is working toward clinical social work licensure and needs a licensed social worker to provide her with supervision. Nobody in her agency has such licensure. She lives in an isolated rural area where the only other licensed social worker who has experience working with the elderly is her Aunt Farrah. Farrah offers to provide supervision. Farrah refuses payment for her services because Serenity is a family member (Falvey, 2002).

Chapter 12

Administration, Values, and Ethics

Social work administrators are responsible for leading their organizations. At one level, their functions comprise technical roles such as budgeting, staffing, organizing, facilitating communication, and managing the resources of an agency in an efficient manner (Manning, 2003). In these capacities, administrators are constantly making decisions. Even though some administrative decisions are mundane or monotonous, almost every decision made by an administrator has ethical implications. Consider, for instance, a decision about whether to purchase a new photocopier. An administrator could look at this decision as a simple matter of whether a new photocopier is needed and whether there is money in the budget for this expense. On the other hand, what are the ethical implications of spending money on a piece of office equipment when it could be spent on raising the salary of a poorly paid caseworker who has difficulty meeting the basic needs for himself and his family? Thus, this "simple" purchasing decision becomes a resource allocation issue requiring the administrator to consider both the administrative needs of the agency and social justice for the caseworker (Brody, 2005). This social justice issue exists whether or not the administrator actually considers the needs of the caseworker when deciding to purchase the photocopier. Inattention to an ethical issue does not mean the issue does not exist. Although many administrative decisions do not require complex ethical analysis, administrators should be aware that virtually all of their decisions have ethical implications, and they should make deliberate choices about when to engage in more intensive analyses of the ethical implications of specific decisions.

As we learned in Chapter 10, social workers may use a variety of social philosophies and ethical theories to inform their resource allocation decisions: egalitarianism, libertarianism, utilitarianism, deontology, and so on. We also learned that the processes used to make decisions have ethical implications. Social workers value human relationships, respect for the dignity and worth of all individuals, and integrity (NASW, 1999). In order to put these values into practice, administrators may engage their staff (and clients, when appropriate) in participatory decision making. Whereas administrators with autocratic management styles impose decisions with little or no consultation, participatory administrators focus on relationships, consult with their constituencies, and respond to their concerns in a meaningful way (Brody, 2005). In order to foster integrity, participatory administrators ensure that their decisions are transparent, ensuring that relevant constituencies know the basis of their decisions and can hold them accountable (Thompson et al., 2006).

As true leaders, administrators are not only responsible for making technical management decisions. They are also responsible for inspiring the organization toward higher values or ideals (Manning, 2003). In their planning functions, for instance, administrators help their agencies develop vision and mission statements. These statements may reflect the core values of social work[1] (service, social justice, dignity and worth of the person, importance of human relationships, integrity, and competence) as well as the agency's specific mandate (e.g., promoting mental health, preventing domestic violence, or serving the needs of a particular sociocultural population). Effective vision and mission statements provide agency staff with a clear sense of their priorities—what is the agency's raison d'être,[2] what pursuits does the agency consider to be good or desirable, and (by inference) what pursuits does the agency consider to be undesirable or harmful?

Given the service orientation of social agencies, it is particularly important for administrators to promote a value-based culture throughout the organization (Manning, 2003). In order to promote the biopsychosocial-spiritual well-being of particular clients, groups, or society in general, all members of the organization should be working toward the same moral vision and goals. Fostering a values-based climate in the agency also promotes worker satisfaction, acting as a buffer to workplace stress and burnout (Ulrich et al., 2007). Agency values may be reflected in the formal policies, implicit norms, rules, expectations, and work habits promoted by the agency (Brody, 2005). Formal policies may be used to operationalize the agency's vision, mission, and values. For instance, an agency that values the dignity and worth of its clients should have policies that provide staff with guidance on how to respect clients (e.g., honoring their rights to self-determination and confidentiality, and being nonjudgmental). Having good policies, however, is not sufficient. An agency may look highly ethical on paper, but the experience of staff and clients may tell a completely different story. Accordingly, the administrator's role in promoting a value-based culture does not end at putting appropriate policies into place.

One of the key strategies for inspiring an agency to act ethically is to model ethical behavior. An administrator who demonstrates respect for staff not only wins their trust and support, but also encourages them to show respect toward coworkers and clients. In contrast, an administrator who discriminates against certain employees not only harms those employees, but also teaches staff that discriminatory behavior may be condoned or encouraged throughout the agency's functions. Administrators who rely on a "do as I say, not as I do" approach may experience resistance from staff who experience the administrator's leadership methods as hypocritical or demeaning.

Administrators should ensure that organizational structures promote ethical conduct. In other words, do agency procedures and practices advance or inhibit the types of behavior that the

LEARNING OBJECTIVES

Upon successful completion of this chapter, students will be able to

- Administer an ethics audit in a social agency.
- Develop agency policies based upon a strategic assessment of relevant laws, values, ethics, and social context.

[1] When agency staffing includes doctors, attorneys, or other types of practitioners, their professional values should also be considered.

[2] Reason for being.

agency hopes to promote? Although this suggestion may seem obvious, organizational structures often promote forms of conduct that deviate from the agency's stated vision, mission, and policies. In many instances, the disconnect between policies and practices is unintentional. Still, these problems need to be redressed. Consider the following examples:

- Quality service—An agency's mission statement says the quality of services to clients is paramount. But what happens if the agency does not provide sufficient resources for staff to be able to provide high-quality services? Insufficient staffing, for instance, may result in high caseloads and make it difficult for staff to meet the needs of clients.
- Collegiality—An agency's policy states that staff should act in a collegial manner. If the agency evaluates staff members individually, however, the structure of the evaluation may foster competitiveness. Each employee may strive to look good in order to get a good evaluation (and perhaps a promotion), even if it is at the expense of coworkers. Alternatively, if the agency evaluated staff effectiveness from a team perspective, it could promote a stronger sense of collegiality.
- Integrity—An agency vision statement identifies integrity as a core value. In practice, the agency does not permit clients to view their own records and does not make its program evaluations available to the public. These forms of secrecy give people the perception that the agency has something to hide.

In each of these examples, administrators need to take steps to ensure that practice conforms to the agency's vision, mission, or policies.

The first half of this chapter provides a strategic framework that administrators can use for auditing an agency's policies and practices. The primary function of an ethics audit is to assess whether an agency's policies and procedures comply with relevant laws and ethical standards. An audit provides the agency with information on its strengths and needs for improvement. In other words, an audit helps administrators and other agency personnel identify ethical concerns needing remedial action (Reamer, 2001a). The second half of this chapter focuses on developing agency policies, including new policies and redrafts of existing ones. This material builds on Chapter 10, which explored how to critique agency policies. Whereas the cases in Chapter 10 involved situations in which there were relatively clear ethical and legal directives, the cases in this chapter involve ethical dilemmas (in other words, cases in which there are conflicting or ambiguous ethical or legal directives). To develop policies that address complex ethical issues, we will be using the Framework for Managing Ethical Issues presented in the introduction to Part II.

ETHICS AUDIT

Social agencies use a variety of tools to ensure the quality of their services: establishing policies and procedures, hiring staff with appropriate qualifications and competence, providing ongoing supervision and training, documenting services through case records and other data collection procedures, and conducting periodic reviews (or audits) of the agency's policies and practices. Quality assurance reviews may be required by the agency's funding body, board of directors, or enabling legislation (e.g., legal regulations governing hospitals, child protection services, and nursing homes). An ethics audit may be used as a specific component of an overall quality assurance review, or as a distinct review process aimed at ensuring the agency's compliance with relevant laws and ethical standards. The purposes of an ethics audit include

- Protecting client rights.
- Promoting high standards of practice.
- Reducing risks associated with faulty practice, including harm to clients or others.
- Reducing the risks of malpractice lawsuits, professional disciplinary hearings, or other grievance procedures (Kirkpatrick, Reamer, & Sykulski, 2006; McAuliffe, 2005b).

Ethics audits are proactive, taking steps to prevent ethical violations or malpractice, rather than waiting until actual harm is incurred. Audits provide administrators with a structured assessment tool that may help them verify policies and practices,[3] detect areas of risk, and respond to them before more serious problems become manifest (Reamer, 2001a). Although ethics audits may be used in a punitive fashion, they are best used as a tool for corrective action. In other words, rather than simply punishing staff for noncompliance with laws, policies, or ethical standards, administrators focus on what can be done to improve compliance and raise standards of practice. Further, ethics audits should not merely focus on adherence to basic standards (or minimum ethical standards, as described in Chapter 9). They should also be used to inspire staff to reach for high standards or ideals of practice, for instance, providing incentives to individual staff or groups whose practice reflects the highest aspirations of the agency (Kirkland & Kirkland, 2006). The following sections describe the process of the conducting an ethics audit and the specific topics that may be reviewed in an ethics audit.

Steps of an Ethics Audit

The process of conducting an ethics audit may vary, depending on the particular needs and resources of the agency conducting the audit. The basic steps of an ethics audit typically include

1. Determining who will conduct the audit.
2. Identifying the focal areas of the audit.
3. Gathering information for the audit.
4. Assessing specific risks or areas requiring corrective action.
5. Developing a detailed action plan for risks or areas requiring corrective action.
6. Monitoring, evaluating, and following up on implementation of the action plan (Kirkpatrick et al., 2006).[4]

In Step 1, administrators determine who will conduct the ethics audit. In making this decision, they should consider the expertise and credibility of potential auditors. In terms of expertise, auditors should be well versed in professional ethics (Reamer, 2001a). Agency staff may include attorneys, social workers, or other professionals who are familiar not only with general professional ethics, but also with the specific laws, policies, and standards of practice that apply to their particular agency. The downside of using agency staff to conduct an ethics audit is that they may be seen as lacking independence or neutrality. Hiring outside auditors may provide a greater sense of credibility to the audit because they may bring fresh, outside perspectives; they may also be less likely to be influenced by interpersonal politics and inappropriate pressures within the agency (Kirkpatrick et al., 2006). Consider, for instance, a social worker who conducts an audit of her own agency, but feels reluctant to cite the agency for problems because it might make her coworkers or superiors look bad. The worker may even fear retaliation if she raises certain concerns (Danis et al., 2008). On the other hand, auditors from within the agency have the advantage of knowing the internal workings of the agency. They may have a better sense of questions to ask, where to look for information, and how to engage staff members in a collaborative review process. Thus, the question of whether to hire external auditors or make use of current employees depends on needs and perceptions. If an agency is required by law to have an external auditor, then the choice has already been made for the agency. If the agency's integrity is under investigation (e.g., due to allegations of fraud or other gross misconduct), the agency might want to use an external auditor to help clear the agency of any suspicions. If the agency's primary

[3] Reamer (2001a) refers to "policies and procedures" rather than "policies and practices." I have used the latter phrase because some agencies use the term "procedures" to describe the steps that the agency prescribes to achieve certain goals or objectives. In other words, this use of the term *procedures* does not relate to the actual practices of the agency, just the practices that the agency asks its staff to follow. The term *practices* is less ambiguous, as it refers specifically to the actual conduct of agency staff, rather than the agency's policies or other guidelines for conduct.

[4] The ethics audit framework provided in this chapter draws primarily from Reamer's (2001a) risk-management tool. Although Reamer's tool is wonderfully comprehensive and strategic, I have altered some of the language and processes to demonstrate how audits may be conducted differently in different agency contexts.

purpose for the audit is to enhance its policies and practices, and the agency has staff members who have the trust of the agency, then an internal audit may be appropriate. When an audit is being used solely for internal purposes, administrators do not have to worry about whether people outside the agency will view the auditors as independent and unbiased.

The people selected to conduct an audit may be constituted as a formal audit committee or as a less formal group of people who have been assigned certain auditing tasks. An individual administrator, for instance, may decide to review agency policies on her own. Alternatively, a group of social workers may decide to review clinical practices pertaining to a particular area of risk (e.g., how to manage clients who come to the agency while intoxicated). Some agencies have ongoing ethics committees that may take responsibility for auditing tasks. Other agencies create audit committees from time to time, to respond to particular needs (e.g., reaccreditation requirements or responses to specific client grievances).

Regardless of how auditors are selected, they need to clarify the focus of their work as early as possible. In this second step of the auditing process, regulatory bodies or agency administrators often provide auditors with a specific list of topics to cover. In other instances, auditors must develop their own list of topics, which may then be submitted to agency administrators for approval. Rather than start from scratch and recreate the wheel, auditors may draw topics from a comprehensive tool, such as Reamer's (2001a) auditing instrument or the list of topics described later in this chapter. Even when auditors are tasked with providing a comprehensive review of agency policies and procedures, they should clarify which aspects of the audit are most important or require special attention. In an agency that serves vulnerable populations, for instance, it may be particularly vital to determine how the agency protects those populations from abuse or other forms of mistreatment (e.g., enlisting advocates to act on behalf of vulnerable minors, ensuring access to services for people with disabilities, or providing alternate forms of consent for people with mental illness). In an agency that receives referrals from court, it may be particularly important to ensure that practitioners are properly trained in the functions of record keeping and responding to requests from attorneys and the court (Barsky & Gould, 2002; Cumming et al., 2007).

In Step 3 of the auditing process, auditors identify what types of information to gather. Information gathering often begins with identifying relevant documents: laws, policies, ethical standards, consent forms, client records, program evaluations, and other paperwork that illustrates the policies and practices of the agency. If the focus of the audit is to review agency policy, then examining the policies, laws, and ethical standards may be sufficient. If the audit includes a review of actual practices, then the auditors will need additional sources of information. Reviewing case records and other documentation provides auditors with some sense of agency practices. Gathering information from practitioners and clients may provide additional insights. If the agency has been conducting periodic program evaluations, these evaluations may provide feedback from practitioners and clients. Unfortunately, many program evaluations focus on the outcomes of specific services or interventions, without documenting the actual practices that lead to these outcomes. For example, an agency servicing recent immigrants might report success in terms of how many clients found jobs or school placements, but may not report on how well the practitioners honored their clients' rights to self-determination and informed consent. In the absence of evaluations that include information on agency practices, auditors may decide to gather information directly from staff members, clients, or other constituencies—through individual interviews, focus groups, or written surveys (Kirkpatrick et al., 2006). Of course, such information gathering techniques require the consent of agency administrators, as well as those people being interviewed. Staff and clients may have concerns about confidentiality and how the information will be used. Accordingly, the auditors may need to institute procedures to ensure the confidentiality or anonymity of respondents. In small agencies, ensuring confidentiality or anonymity may be impossible. If an agency has only two social workers, for instance, then auditors may simply have to acknowledge that administrators will know which practitioners they are interviewing. Remember, if the auditors are able to present the auditing process as a collaborative method of improving services (as opposed to an inquisition designed to punish people for misconduct), they may be more successful in building trust with agency staff and gathering the information they need.

The scope of the audit, including data gathering, may depend on pragmatic issues, including the resources that the agency has designated for the auditing process. Reviewing the agency's policies is generally much less labor intensive than assessing the agency's practices. Although an agency might be interested in gathering information from practitioner and clients, it may not have the resources to conduct such an analysis. When auditors and administrators discuss their plans for an ethics audit, they need to address not only what types of data gathering are desirable, but also what types of data gathering fit within the agency's budget. By ensuring that administrators understand the strengths and limitations of various forms of information gathering, they can make informed decisions about which types of information gathering to use and which to dismiss, taking the agency's limited resources into account.

In Step 4, the auditors review the information gathered in Step 3 in order to assess for specific ethical risks or areas requiring corrective action. The auditors may use the list of topics identified in Step 2 as an inventory, ensuring that they review the key subject matters identified for the audit. For each topic area, the auditing process may assess the agency's policies and practices based on the following questions:

- Does the agency have policies that relate to the specific topic area?
- Do the agency's policies comply with relevant laws and professional standards of practice?
- Do agency staff members have an adequate understanding of the agency's policies?
- In practice, do staff members adequately adhere to the relevant laws, policies, and ethical standards that apply to this topic area?

If the answer to any of these questions is "no," then that topic should be flagged as an area of risk or one requiring corrective action. In order to prioritize the need for corrective action, auditors may also rate the level of risk as minimal, moderate, or high (Reamer, 2001a). Items rated as high risk indicate the agency should prioritize taking corrective action in a decisive and timely manner in these areas. Although the agency should address all deficiencies, the moderate and minimal risk areas are less urgent.

In addition to identifying risks and deficiencies, auditors could also help the agency identify areas for aspirational growth and development. Rather than focusing only on compliance with basic standards, the auditors could suggest ways in which the agency's policies and practices may be raised even higher. An agency may be providing its clients with ethical services, for instance, but it may not be serving potential clients who cannot afford their services. Even though the agency may not be legally required to offer services to people who cannot afford to pay, the auditors may highlight this concern as a possible area to address based on the aspirational ethical principles of access to resources and social justice (NASW, 1999).

In Step 5, the auditors develop plans for redressing areas of risk and other concerns requiring corrective action (McAuliffe, 2005b). Auditors should provide specific details in the action plan in terms of what tasks need to be completed, by whom, and over what period of time. Auditors could also explain the rationale for their recommendations so that agency staff will know why the recommended changes are important. If the agency lacks a policy statement pertaining to termination of services, for instance, the plan could indicate what policies are needed, why they are needed, who should assume responsibility for developing the policies, the timeframe for developing the policies, and what additional steps may be necessary for implementing the policies (e.g., review by attorneys, approval by the board of directors, and training for staff to help them put the policies into practice). If the auditors discover that various staff members have engaged in dual relationships with clients, for example, they might suggest the following corrective actions: providing in-house training on dual relationships, instituting probation periods with close supervision for social workers who have violated the agency's dual relationship policy, and ensuring newly hired workers are familiar with the agency's policy on dual relationships. The auditors could explain the rationale for these suggestions by giving case examples of how the agency, workers, and clients may each be put at risk when workers engage in dual relationships with clients.

Although auditors should recommend plans for all areas of risk, they should also help the agency prioritize which issues require the most immediate attention. Given that agencies have limited staff time, money, and other resources, they may not be able to respond to all the issues at once. By indicating which issues are most urgent, agency administrators can make informed decisions concerning which issues to resolve first (Reamer, 2001a).

Auditors may be asked to report the results of an audit—orally and in writing—to one or more of the following constituencies: agency administrators, frontline staff, clients, or an accrediting body that oversees the agency. Auditors should take their audiences into account when delivering their reports, making sure they use language that is appropriate to the nature and needs of each audience. Auditors should be particularly careful about avoiding judgmental language, focusing instead on factual findings about policies and practices, as well as specific action plans that are backed up by appropriate ethical justifications. Rather than reporting, "Record keeping is shoddy," for instance, auditors should report the specific nature of the shoddiness in nonjudgmental terms: "Current record-keeping practices violate state regulations in the following manners: client records are not being stored in locked filing rooms, some records are being destroyed prior to the 2-year holding requirement, and approximately 25% of case records are missing the client intake forms." By focusing on objective information and providing specific plans to redress ethical concerns, auditors may encourage compliance without judging or deriding agency staff and administration.

Step 6 entails monitoring implementation of the action plan, evaluating the extent to which corrective actions have been completed, and developing follow-up plans for areas of ongoing concern (Kirkpatrick et al., 2006). If the action plan calls for policy revisions in 2 months, the auditors could review the new policies at that time. Although the auditors may assume responsibility for monitoring and evaluation, they could also suggest that others in the agency assume these responsibilities. The program director or an internal ethics committee, for instance, might assume responsibility for evaluating the success of the in-house training on dual relationships. Regardless of who is responsible for monitoring, evaluation, and follow-up, these processes should be documented by those taking such responsibility. By creating a paper trail of steps taken to redress ethical risks, the auditors and agency are in a better position to monitor which corrective actions have been completed and which issues require further action. In addition, the paper trail may protect the agency from legal liability, as it provides evidence of steps taken to manage ethical risks in a competent manner (Reamer, 2001a).[5]

Focal Areas

An ethics audit may encompass a broad range of ethical issues or focus on a few specific areas, depending on the agency's needs. In either case, auditors should clarify which ethical issues to review during the auditing process. Given the vast differences in agency contexts, one auditing tool does not fit all situations. Government-accredited agencies may be required to follow a particular protocol for quality assurance, including ethics review, as part of their accreditation processes. If a particular auditing protocol is not required by law, auditors could take an existing auditing tool, such as Reamer's (2001a) instrument, and tailor it to the agency's particular needs and context. Alternatively, an agency and auditors could develop their own checklist of

[5] Remember that malpractice requires proof that professionals did not conduct themselves as would be expected of reasonable, prudent professionals of similar backgrounds. By documenting the auditing process, auditors and administrators can demonstrate how they have exercised this duty of care.

topics to cover. This section describes how to develop such a checklist.

The potential list of topics for an audit largely depends on the context of the agency: what is the mandate of the agency, what services does it provide, what ethical issues may arise in delivery of those services, what are the rights of the clients or others receiving services, what are the legal and ethical obligations of the agency and staff who provide services? Consider an agency that is mandated to assist female survivors of intimate partner abuse. The agency provides shelter and counseling services to women who are leaving abusive relationships. Given the nature of the work, protecting the safety of the clientele is likely to be an important ethical issue (Hunter, 2001). Likewise, the agency may need to balance the interests of protecting their clients' safety with each client's right to self-determination. Accordingly, auditors should review the agency's policies and practices on how it manages the issues of client safety and self-determination. Given the safety concerns, client confidentiality may also be particularly important for an ethics audit: if clients are seeking refuge from abusive partners, then the agency may need to be particularly careful about protecting the privacy of their clients. Agency context also includes client diversity. If the agency services a large Caribbean American population, for instance, then cultural competence in work with this group may be an important topic for the audit. By understanding the context of the agency, auditors can begin to identify ethical topics that may be of particular importance for the audit.

Auditors should consider legal context by reviewing laws that regulate the agency and professionals who operate within the agency. Medical settings, for instance, must comply with the Health Insurance Portability and Accountability Act (HIPAA, 1996). This legislation includes rules related to informed consent and confidentiality regarding medical records. It requires agencies to use specific forms for transmitting information to health insurance providers and obtaining a client's consent to release confidential information to other agencies. Thus, an audit of an agency governed by HIPAA could review the agency's policies, forms, and practices to ensure compliance with this legislation.

If agency staff includes professionals who are licensed or accredited, auditors should also consider whether to review their compliance with the relevant legislation. State laws, for instance, might provide privilege for confidential client communications with licensed clinical social workers (Falvey, 2002). Accordingly, agency policies should reflect the fact that there is privileged communication with licensed workers, but there may not be privilege for unlicensed workers.[6] Auditors could also consider reviewing the agency's policies and practices in terms of verifying the qualifications of licensed or accredited workers, and ensuring compliance with other legal requirements (e.g., respecting client confidentiality, not engaging in sexual relationships with clients, and reporting suspicions of child abuse or neglect).

Professional codes of ethics provide auditors with perhaps the most comprehensive source of ethical topics to consider. The NASW Code of Ethics, for instance, includes 51 standards, categorized into six types of ethical responsibilities: responsibilities to clients, responsibilities to coworkers, responsibilities in practice settings, responsibilities as professionals, responsibilities to the social work profession, and responsibilities to broader society. Although this textbook focuses on the NASW Code of Ethics, auditors should consider the ethics topics from the codes of ethics of each of the professions represented in the agency (e.g., physicians, nurses, psychologists, family counselors). Various mental health and helping professions have similar ethical obligations (e.g., regarding informed consent, confidentiality, and record keeping), but auditors should also take note of differences (e.g., the NASW's [1999] inclusion of topics such as social justice,

---

[6] The laws governing privilege are complex and may vary from jurisdiction to jurisdiction. Unlicensed workers working under the direct supervision of a licensed social worker may be covered by the licensed supervisor's statutory privilege; however, unlicensed workers who are supervised by unlicensed social workers will not be covered by privilege, even if they work in the same agency.

human relationships, and diversity issues versus the American Psychological Association's [2003] inclusion of topics related to research on animals and using psychological tests with clients).

When determining which ethics topics to include or exclude, auditors may ascribe priority to protection of client rights, for instance, informed consent, self-determination, confidentiality, and freedom from coercion, fraud, dishonesty, discrimination, sexual misconduct, or other boundary violations (McAuliffe, 2005b). Auditors may also prioritize topics that help agencies reduce risks: ensuring proper hiring, supervision, continuing education and professional development, documentation, and management of high-risk situations (e.g., policies and procedures for responding to clients with suicidal or homicidal ideation) (Reamer, 2008b). Auditors may give lower priority to aspirational ethics, such as promoting social justice and respecting diversity. Prioritization of topics, however, should be negotiated between the auditors and agency administrators. Some administrators may want their auditors to provide feedback on aspirational topics, particularly if they have a strong record of meeting basic ethical standards and would like their auditors to help the agency reach toward higher values and ideals.

The choice of topics to include in an audit clearly has a crucial impact on the entire auditing process. Auditors are much more likely to discover ethical risks in areas that they have targeted for the auditing process. Auditors may happen upon ethical concerns that go beyond the original scope of the audit. Even then, they may need to consult with agency administrators about whether and how to report those concerns. The agency may or may not be ready to deal with such concerns.

DEVELOPING AGENCY POLICIES

The need for administrators to develop policies may arise in a range of circumstances. In the previous section, we saw how ethics audits could be used to help an agency identify the need to develop policies to fill gaps or to correct existing policies. Administrators also need to develop policies when a new agency is created, when an agency is adding new services, or when the laws governing the agency change. Finally, agencies may identify the need to develop or redraft policies in response to specific problems. In the final stage of the ethical management process (Evaluation and Follow-Up, Figure II.1), for instance, social workers should consider whether policy changes could help prevent similar problems from arising in the future. In Chapter 10, we looked at how to develop or critique policies for relatively uncomplicated ethical situations. In this chapter, we explore the process of policy development in the face of complex ethical dilemmas.

When an agency is faced with the prospect of managing an ethical dilemma, the primary challenge is how to balance conflicting laws, policies, values, ethical standards, principles, or interests. Given that there is no single option that completely satisfies all of these factors, reasonable, prudent professionals could come to different conclusions about the best way to resolve the same dilemmas (Reamer, 2008b). Still, this does not mean that any decision is justifiable, or that decisions can be made without going through a rigorous deliberation process. The following intellectual standards may be used to ensure the integrity of ethical reasoning:

1. Accountability: Upon making their decisions, the decision makers should be willing and able to state the reasoning behind their decisions.[7]
2. Duties: The reasoning should include an examination of relevant laws, policies, ethical standards, and principles.
3. Consequences: The reasoning should include an examination of harms (being avoided, prevented, or caused) and of

[7] In some instances, particularly for public policy decisions, it may be appropriate for the decision makers to defend their reasons publicly. For agency policy, the decision makers may need to be able to defend their policies within the agency. For clinical ethical decisions, the decision makers generally need to respect client confidentiality, meaning that they may need to defend their decisions to the client, supervisor, or frontline worker, but not to the public.

benefits (being promoted or lost) of various courses of action.

4. Breadth: The reasoning should include an evenhanded examination of relevant points of view (e.g., those of social workers, clients, or other professionals, depending on which individual or groups are most directly affected by the decision). To avoid distorting alternative viewpoints, the decision makers should examine the reasoning for prejudice and inconsistencies in how logic is applied.
5. Relevance: The reasons should include relevant considerations and avoid nonrelevant concepts, facts, or arguments (e.g., ad hominem attacks, irrelevant arguments, or misinformation). The reasons should also focus on the most significant ethical dimensions and avoid overstating the significance of trivial ethical arguments.
6. Clarity: The ethical reasoning should be stated in understandable terms (with definitions, examples, or illustrations provided when necessary to clarify the reasoning). The language used should be appropriate to the audience who will be hearing or reading the reasoning. The levels of detail and depth should be sufficient to adequately address the ethical issues.
7. Accuracy: The information and arguments should be logical, true, and free from distortion or misrepresentation. Accuracy includes full disclosure, as hiding information may be just as misleading as providing misinformation.
8. Limits of Information: When the decision makers are relying on imperfect information, they should acknowledge the limits of this information (e.g., lack of empirical research evidence, missing data, or problems with the validity or reliability of the research methods).
9. Prioritizing: When the decision overrides certain laws, policies, ethical standards, the decision makers should acknowledge this fact and provide an explanation for why some laws, policies, or standards are given priority over others.
10. Mitigation: When the decision causes harm to certain groups or individuals, the decision makers should acknowledge this fact and determine whether there is an appropriate way to mitigate harm or provide reparations (Meyers, 2007; Paul & Elder, 2006).[8]

The following scenario will be used to demonstrate the use of ethical reasoning in the context of developing policies. As you read through the analysis, consider the extent to which the ethical reasoning fulfills the 10 intellectual standards described above:

> Humanitaria[9] is a newly formed nongovernmental organization whose mission is to provide humanitarian relief to people who are living in civil war zones. Humanitaria's founding directors include three social workers with international relief experience. They are concerned about whether Humanitaria should offer humanitarian aid to groups who may be considered terrorists. On the one hand, they believe that everyone is deserving of basic needs such as food, shelter, and medicine. On the other hand, if Humanitaria provides aid to terrorists, then it may become complicit in further violence, death, displacement, and other consequences of terrorism.

The first stage of the Framework for Managing Ethical Issues (Figure II.1) requires identification of the issue.[10] In this case, the board of Humanitaria is faced with an ethical dilemma

[8] Although these guidelines are derived from Paul and Elder, Meyers adds substantive guidelines related to setting goals and complying with the beliefs of the people being most directly affected.

[9] This agency is fictional, although the ethical issues are ones faced by many international aid agencies, such as the International Red Cross and Red Crescent.

[10] For the purposes of this chapter, we will focus on the third stage of the ethical issues management process: critical thinking.

concerning a policy issue: How should the agency manage its goal of "providing humanitarian aid to all who need it" with the potential problem of "providing aid to terrorist groups who may use the aid to inflict further violence on vulnerable populations"?

In the second stage, the board of directors identifies people who may be able to offer help, for instance, people with expertise on humanitarian aid, civil war conflicts, international law, U.S. law, and ethics. They may be able to draw from people who have knowledge and experience in connection with humanitarian relief efforts for past or current civil wars (e.g., in Lebanon, the former Yugoslavia, Darfur, and Iraq).

The third stage, critical thinking, invites decision makers to apply a range of strategies to help them reflect, assess, and problem solve. The directors of Humanitaria, for instance, may reflect upon their thoughts, feelings, values, and motivations about providing humanitarian aid. Some may have been motivated to work for this agency because of their value for the life and well-being of all people. Others may have been motivated by political reasons (e.g., promoting democracy), religious beliefs (e.g., doing God's work), or professional reasons (e.g., the mandate of social work to promote social justice).[11] Regardless of their motivations, they need to be aware of personal experiences or opinions that may unduly bias their thinking (e.g., a director who has unresolved feelings of anger toward a particular ethnic group because his daughter was killed by terrorists). By raising self-awareness regarding potential biases, the directors can guard against allowing irrelevant arguments affect their decision making.

When assessing the issue of providing aid to terrorist groups, the directors should consider the legal and ethical contexts. In terms of international law, the Geneva Conventions (1864, revised 1949, 1977, 2005), provide certain rights and protections for noncombatant military and civilian participants in an armed conflict. Such protection includes the right of impartial humanitarian organizations to have access to provide care. Although the United States is a signatory to the Geneva Conventions, the International Emergency Economic Powers Act (IEEPA, 2000) allows the president to restrict and prohibit the activities of humanitarian organizations' activities in armed conflicts in which the United States is a party. President George W. Bush has used these powers for the conflicts in Afghanistan and Iraq, thus suggesting an override to American commitments under the Geneva Conventions (White, 2006).[12] In addition, U.S. criminal law makes it illegal to aid or abet terrorist organizations. Thus, U.S. law may not only prevent Humanitaria from having to provide aid to certain groups it also deems providing aid to terrorist groups illegal.

The term *terrorism* suggests the illegitimate use of violence to further particular political causes. Terrorism is associated with repeated threats and acts against noncombatants in a manner that promotes fear in the targeted population. One of the difficulties in defining and applying the term is the subjective nature of what is a legitimate use of violence. What one group views as terrorists might be viewed by another group as freedom fighters (United Nations Office on Drugs and Crime, 2008). Thus, the U.S. government may deem a certain group to be a terrorist organization, even though others may view this group to be using force in a necessary and valid manner (e.g., to free a particular group from violence, oppression, or other social injustices). Thus, the directors of Humanitaria should recognize the subjective and political components of defining, "What is a terrorist organization?"

---

[11] Because this is an international scenario, social workers should also consider the Statement of Principles of the International Federation of Social Workers and International Association of Schools of Social Work, (2004). Principle 4.1 describes a social worker's responsibilities in relation to promotion of social justice. Interestingly, this principle suggests that resources should be distributed according to need. However, this code does not specifically deal with the issue of providing humanitarian aid to groups that have been deemed terrorists.

[12] At the time of writing, President Obama's administration was reviewing these issues and may reverse some of President Bush's policies.

Humanitaria strives for political neutrality in its endeavors, recognizing that if it takes sides in political conflicts or civil wars, then it loses its integrity as a humanitarian organization. Further, if Humanitaria takes sides, then its workers are more likely to be targeted for violence by groups that it has sided against. This highlights one of the ethical conundrums for Humanitaria: It wants to remain neutral and provide aid to all who need it, but U.S. law may prevent it from providing aid to members of groups that have been deemed to be terrorist organizations. If Humanitaria refuses aid to certain groups in order to comply with the law, then some groups may view Humanitaria as biased (an agent of the U.S. government) and target its workers for violence.

When deliberating about this dilemma, the directors should research how other organizations have managed these issues. Rather than recreate the wheel from scratch, the directors could consider the policies of nongovernmental humanitarian organizations. For instance, the charter for Médecins Sans Frontières[13] (n.d.) states:

> Médecins Sans Frontières observes neutrality and impartiality in the name of universal medical ethics and the right to humanitarian assistance and claims full and unhindered freedom in the exercise of its functions.

This organization places high value on neutrality and impartiality, and strictly guards its independence from any government or political organization. It understands that many people may criticize it for assisting members of groups deemed terrorist. However, it believes that it cannot fulfill its mission without maintaining its neutrality and impartiality. Similarly, the Code of Conduct of the International Red Cross (1996) emphasizes the importance of these values.

To sort through complex ethical issues and arguments in a strategic manner, it may be useful to create a table comparing the arguments for each alternative. To simplify the example for demonstration purposes, assume this dilemma has just two alternatives:[14] to remain neutral and provide aid to all (including members of terrorist organizations), and to withhold aid from members of terrorist organizations. Figure 12.1 summarizes the key arguments for each alternative.

Figure 12.1 identifies valid[15] arguments on both sides of this issue, so Humanitaria's policy

FIGURE 12.1 Comparing Ethical Arguments

For Providing Aid to All	For Withholding Aid to Members of "Terrorist Organizations"
1. Deontological argument: Providing aid to all is an imperative duty for humanitarians. All people have a right to basic needs such as water, food, shelter, and medicine (International Red Cross, 1996).	Deontological argument: Promoting social justice is an imperative duty (e.g., from a social work perspective in NASW, 1999, S.6.01). Providing aid to groups that promote violence and terror goes against this imperative.
2. Utilitarian argument: Humanitaria needs to remain impartial in order to do the greatest good for the greatest number (Walker, 2004). It cannot effectively provide relief to people affected by civil wars unless it is seen as impartial. If it refuses aid to groups deemed as terrorist, then it loses credibility and workers become targets for violence. Humanitarian workers will not work for an organization that puts its workers at such high risk.	Utilitarian argument: If Humanitaria provides aid to terrorists, then it is promoting further violence and terror. In order to promote the greatest good, humanitarian aid should be provided to people who promote good, not people who promote terror.

13 Doctors Without Borders.

14 To consider more than two alternatives, add extra columns to the table.

15 Used in this context, *valid* means that the arguments are worthy of merit, even though prudent, reasonable people might disagree about which arguments are most persuasive.

3. Definitional challenge: People who are regarded as terrorists by some may be regarded as freedom fighters and promoters of social justice by others. By remaining impartial, Humanitaria does not have to make political judgments about who is a terrorist.	3. Definitional challenge: Humanitaria does not have to define "terrorist organization" as it could rely on definitions provided by the U.S. government, the United Nations, or some other body.
4. Virtue ethics: Humanitarians live by the principles of humanity (access to basic needs), impartiality (nondiscrimination), neutrality (freedom from religious or political biases) and independence (freedom from control of government or other organizations) (Hilhorst, 2005; International Red Cross, 1996).	4. Virtue ethics: Good people live in a manner that promotes the welfare, safety, and security of all (Cohen & Cohen, 1999).* Good people do not aid and abet terrorists.
5. Support: In order to receive financial and moral support for its humanitarian relief projects, Humanitaria must live up to the principles of neutrality, impartiality, and independence.	5. Support: Humanitaria can raise more funds and solicit support if it abides by U.S. laws, refuses to aid terrorists, and uses its resources to ensure that the innocent victims of war are provided with basic needs.

*Aristotle, one of the earliest proponents of virtue ethics, believed that wise people can identify the right way to behave without having rules or someone else telling them what is legal or ethical (Knight, 2007).

decision is not easy. In terms of duties, it could look at this issue as whether its primary obligation is providing humanitarian aid or promoting social justice. If it truly sees itself as a social justice organization, then it may need to take a stance on political issues rather than remain as an impartial provider of aid. Although Humanitaria's board of directors includes social workers, assume they determine that the core ethical principles of humanitarianism (access to aid, impartiality, neutrality, and independence) take precedence for their agency. This determination does not mean that they devalue social justice, but recognizes that their agency's primary mission requires them to prioritize humanitarian values. They will leave political action and other methods of pursuing social justice to other organizations.

In terms of utilitarian arguments, one could make a case for both sides as the best way to promote the greatest good. Unfortunately, we do not have experimental research results to let us know unequivocally which approach better enables humanitarian organizations to promote the greatest good. We can look at the successes of humanitarian organizations such as the International Red Cross, Médecins Sans Frontières, Oxfam, and various United Nations relief agencies. Their proponents strongly advocate neutrality, impartiality, and independence as the safest and most effective means of being able to provide humanitarian aid to those in need. Still, various nations and governments decry aid to members of terrorist groups, not wanting to provide support to those who are apt to cause more harm (Hilhorst, 2005).

On balance, assume the board determines that it is first and foremost a humanitarian aid organization. Accordingly, it develops the following policies:

1. Humanitaria's primary mandate is to provide humanitarian aid to people affected by civil wars.
2. Humanitaria, its workers, and volunteers are guided by the ethical principles of neutrality and impartiality, and independence.
3. In order to remain neutral and impartial, Humanitaria provides aid to people on the basis of need alone, without discriminating on the basis of race, creed, color, nationality, ethnicity, religion, disability, sex, sexual orientation, gender identity and expression, or political affiliation.

The directors of Humanitaria decide to remain a U.S.-based agency so they can draw volunteers, hire workers, and raise funds from this country. To steer clear of violating U.S. law, the directors decide to focus their humanitarian work in areas where the U.S. has not deemed any of the combatants to be terrorist organizations. This decision means that they are forfeiting some of their independence because they will not be able to provide aid in a number of areas affected by civil war. Still, Humanitaria is a relatively small agency that would not be able to offer aid in all the conflicts. By selectively limiting the areas where they will offer aid, they can focus on providing aid and reduce their risk of running afoul of domestic laws. The directors acknowledge that this is not the perfect solution, but they have determined that it is the best of the imperfect options available. They also acknowledge that they are depending on other international aid organizations to provide services in areas that Humanitaria has decided it will not enter.

By understanding the strengths and limitations of their decisions, Humanitaria's directors can better defend the policies that they have enacted. When asked by their constituencies or critics to explain their policies, they may make use of the foregoing arguments and the table in Figure 12.1. In doing so, they can demonstrate that they have made their decisions based on a comprehensive and well-reasoned analysis of the relevant laws, policies, ethical standards, and principles, as well as the potential harms and benefits of each policy alternative. If the directors receive criticism for refusing to provide help in certain types of conflicts, they can validate this criticism but explain the reasons for their compromise. Further, they can commit to expanding their humanitarian services to different types of conflicts as their agency matures and their resources expand. Resolving policy dilemmas at this time does not mean the policies are written in stone. They may be revised based upon the agency's experiences, as well as changes in the legal and social context, at home and abroad.

CONCLUSION

In this chapter, we have focused upon two important roles for agency administrators: assessing an agency's policies and practices to ensure compliance with relevant laws, ethical principles, and standards of practice; and developing agency policies in situations involving complex ethical dilemmas. Although these roles are important, it is also important for agency administrators to model ethical behavior and to help others within the agency to aspire to the highest values and visions of their agency and profession. As with all social work roles, however, administrators should not feel as if they have to manage ethical dilemmas on their own. Administrators may use help from others for support, feedback, technical assistance, and specialized expertise. Leading by example includes demonstrating that the management of ethical issues often requires collaboration with others.

DISCUSSION QUESTIONS AND EXERCISES

The following questions and exercises are designed to provide you with a practical understanding of two important administrative roles—conducting an ethics audit and developing policies that deal with complex ethical issues.

1. *Auditing Practice*: Identify a social agency that will allow you to conduct an audit of some of its policies and practices (e.g., your field agency or an agency your professor has approved for this exercise). Use the following directions to gather information and prepare a report on how the agency ensures appropriate access to services for the population it is mandated to serve:
   a. Identify and obtain copies of the laws, policies, and ethical standards that govern the agency in relation to the mandate of the agency, criteria for accepting or rejecting clients for services, criteria for terminating services with clients, and obligations to ensure that clients receive appropriate services.
   b. Develop a written critique of the agency's policies in terms of the extent to which they satisfy the agency's legal and ethical obligations. In particular, identify the strengths and limitations of

the policies with respect to articulating clear and fair eligibility criteria (including guidelines for making referrals for other services) and providing appropriate safeguards when terminating services (e.g., giving clients proper notice, ensuring that clients are not abandoned in times of need, and documenting the rationale for terminating services).

c. Conduct an interview with an agency social worker, inquiring about the agency's actual practices in relation to how the agency ensures proper access to needed services. In particular, ask about the agency's practices in relation to applying its eligibility criteria, what happens to people who are denied services, how practitioners handle client needs that it cannot serve, and how the practitioners manage concerns related to termination of services. Develop a written critique of the agency's practices, based on your assessment of the social worker's feedback.[16]

d. Present your findings to your class, orally, as if you were making an audit report to the agency. Make sure you provide information in a clear, nonjudgmental manner, identifying both strengths and limitations of the agency's policies and practices. For areas in which the agency's policies and practices are deficient, provide concrete suggestions for how to bring them into compliance with relevant laws, ethical principles, and professional standards.

2. *Internal Auditor*: Assume your agency has asked you to conduct an ethics audit. While conducting the audit, you determine that the executive director of the program has been misusing agency funds, funneling them toward uses that serve her personal benefit. You are afraid to raise this concern for fear of losing your job. You talk to other agency supervisors who advise you to leave well enough alone, as the executive director is very powerful and the agency is doing well in spite of the possibility of financial fraud. What do professional ethics tell you about how you should respond to this situation? What types of strategies could you use to do what is right, but also to protect your interests? How would you know if and when it is appropriate to "blow the whistle" and go public with your information about the misused funds (Boatright, 2006)?

3. *Developing Policies*: For each of the following scenarios, identify and assess the primary ethical issue using the critical thinking strategies outlined in the introduction to Part II: reflecting, considering multiple perspectives, identifying goals, identifying and weighing obligations, and brainstorming options and assessing consequences. Develop a policy designed to manage the ethical issue. Ensure that the policy is drafted in a manner that is clear, concise, and consistent with relevant laws and ethical standards.[17] Provide your rationale for why this policy is the best of the options available. Ensure that your rationale reflects relevant considerations and acknowledges the limitations of the proposed policy (e.g., the possibility of compromising some ethical principles or values in order to satisfy others, or having certain winners and losers in relation to the risks and benefits of the policy).

a. The board of directors of Gendranium Hospital is exploring the issue of sex discrimination within the hiring practices of the hospital. The majority of physicians, nurses, social workers, and other professional employees in the hospital are women. Less than 10% of the hospital's managers are women. Some proponents of equality suggest that the hospital make use of affirmative action to raise the number of women in management positions. Others suggest that this would be reverse discrimination.

b. The current policy of a shelter for homeless men states, "To ensure the safety of

[16] As this is a practice audit, the directions ask you to interview only one worker. In practice, you should gather information about practices from more than one source.

[17] See Chapter 10 for suggestions on how to critique a policy.

all clients and staff, all clients may be subject to random drug testing. Any client who tests positive for alcohol or any illicit drug will be required to leave the shelter immediately." Last week, a client tested positive for cocaine and was asked to leave the agency. Shortly after leaving the agency, the client walked into traffic and was killed. The agency is now reconsidering its policy on drug testing.

c. Sebastian successfully sued his former employer, LOAF Family Services, for wrongful dismissal. He was fired for alleged lack of competence, but his annual performance evaluations for the past 5 years were consistently positive (Brody, 2005). His supervisor said he provided positive evaluations because he believed in the strengths perspective and did not want to put negative things in Sebastian's personnel file (as per the principle of nonjudgmentalism). Further, the supervisor felt Sebastian might respond violently if confronted by critical feedback. After the lawsuit, the LOAF's executive director decided that new agency policies would be needed to avoid similar problems from arising in the future.

d. Empowerment Education is a residential school designed for teenagers with emotional problems who have been expelled from other schools. Recently, a number of students contracted tuberculosis (TB) while staying at the school. Health authorities are unsure why the outbreak took place, although the school does have one risk factor: many students were born in developing countries. Teaching staff suggest implementing a policy requiring all students to be screened for TB and to have TB vaccinations (bacille Calmette-Guérinprior) prior to admission. The social work staff is concerned that some parents may not permit their children to be vaccinated because of the risks of adverse reactions, meaning that they would be barred from the school. The principal supports a policy of requiring TB vaccinations, arguing that this policy is for the greater good and the federal government has a program to compensate the minority of people who have adverse reactions to vaccinations.

e. Benita is a huge benefactor of Miles Mental Health Services (a private nonprofit organization). Benita also owns a construction company. Miles is planning a $100 million expansion of its facilities. Benita offers to provide Miles with a $10 million donation if Miles gives it the contract to build the new facilities without an open bidding competition. Miles' board of directors decides it needs to write a policy on contracting for services, donations with conditions attached, and potential conflict of interests. The directors agree that Benita's offer is a good deal financially and they trust her company implicitly. Still, they want to be careful about the precedent they set.

f. Cyberlife Coaching Services is an agency that provides online life skills training to people who want to enhance skills such as communication, assertiveness, time management, and parenting. Cyberlife uses videoconferencing, Twitter,[18] and password-protected chatrooms when working with individuals and groups. An ethics audit revealed the agency lacked policies related to maintaining records of online interactions. In particular, should clients be permitted to save files containing online interactions between themselves and Cyberlife's coaches? Some coaches are concerned that clients could save copies of their online conversations and use those copies for inappropriate purposes. For instance, if clients save copies of group sessions, they could divulge confidential information from the group to nonclients. If clients have a grievance with their coaches, they could use copies of their sessions as evidence in court (Banach & Bernat, 2000). Other coaches say that clients should have a right to copies of their records, so copies

[18] See http://twitter.com.

of online interactions should be no different from copies of records of in-office interactions. Further, once a session is provided online, how could the agency enforce a policy that prohibits saving copies of sessions? (cf. Finn & Banach, 2002; Heinlen, Welfel, Richmond, & Rak, 2003).

g. Holistic Assistance provides alternative health and social services to people with cancer. Some workers suggest the agency implement a policy that forbids the hiring of smokers. Because smoking is a major risk factor for cancer, they believe that having smokers on staff would provide poor role modeling. Also, if the agency hired smokers, it might incur higher costs for medical insurance, more missed days of work, and lost productivity from staff who are taking smoking breaks. Other workers argue such a ban is discriminatory, unfair, and an invasion of people's privacy. They suggest that smoking is legal and addictive, so the agency should be more accepting and respectful of smokers.

4. *Ethical Justification*: ElderSystems provides outreach and support to isolated elders. Most of its clients speak Spanish, but the agency has only one Spanish-speaking social worker. The agency decides on a policy of giving preference to Spanish-speaking workers for the next three workers it hires. Critics suggest this policy is discriminatory. Write an explanation explaining the rationale for ElderSystem's policy in a manner that addresses this criticism. In particular, how could the agency acknowledge the limitations of its policy, and how could the agency include a plan to reduce the harm to applicants who are not Spanish speaking?

5. *Intellectual Standards*: An agency that serves people with traumatic brain injuries adds a new condition in its service agreement, stating that clients agree not to subpoena their workers or case records for court purposes.[19] The directors explain the rationale for this policy as follows:

> In the past two years, the number of our social workers being subpoenaed to court has doubled. Most of these cases involve clients who are suing for compensation against people alleged to have caused the damage. On average, a social worker spends 12 hours preparing and 6 hours sitting in court for each case in which he or she is subpoenaed. These hours represent valuable time lost in relation to providing clients with the clinical services they need. If social workers need to be concerned about the possibility of court, the must spend extra hours documenting all their cases, not knowing whether they will be called into court. Given that social workers owe their primary obligation to clients (NASW, 1999, S.1.01), they should spend their time in direct provision of services, not just testifying in court. Further, our agency does not receive sufficient remuneration for the time that workers spend in court, putting our limited resources under further strain.
>
> Our social workers are trained to provide clinical counseling services, not to provide forensic evidence. In order for our workers to stay within their areas of competence (NASW, S.1.04), we must advise clients that our workers cannot be expected to conduct forensic evaluations or provide testimony in court. Further, by informing clients that they cannot subpoena our workers, we are honoring their right to self-determination (NASW, 1.07) and informed consent (NASW, 1.03).
>
> We apologize to those clients who would like our agency to provide forensic evaluations and testimony. However, we would be pleased to provide them with referrals to other agencies that may be able to assist them.

Identify the strengths and limitations of the forgoing ethical analysis in terms of how well it addresses the 10 intellectual standards for assessing the integrity of ethical reasoning: accountability, duties, consequences, breadth, relevance, clarity, accuracy, limits of information, prioritizing, mitigation.

---

[19] For the purposes of this assignment, you may assume that all the clients have sufficient mental capacity to be able to provide informed consent.

Chapter 13

Psychopathology, Mental Health, Values, and Ethics

Given the history of mistreatment of people with mental illness, values and ethics play a particularly important role in the field of mental health. People with mental illness have been warehoused in asylums and maintained under inhumane conditions. They have undergone harmful treatments such as blood-letting and lobotomies, absent any scientific basis for the effectiveness of such treatment (Freud-Loewenstein, 2004). They have been treated like animals or inanimate objects, as if they have no rights to privacy, dignity, or informed consent. And they have been prosecuted and punished for crimes even when they lacked the mental capacity to be held morally accountable (Szasz, 2003). In some cases, the mistreatment of people with mental illness has been brought about by professionals who have deliberately sought to discriminate or take advantage of this group (Quinn, 2005). In many cases, mistreatment has been unintentional, caused by well-meaning professionals applying the best information or scientific evidence they possessed (Porter, 2002; Scheyett, 2006). In any case, the ethical treatment of people with mental health issues needs to be fostered through professional education, laws, agency policies, ethical standards, and practices that ensure the rights and interests of this group are protected (American Psychological Association, 2007; *Lessard v. Schmidt*, 1972; National Association of Social Workers, 1999, Ss. 1.01, 1.05[c], 4.02, and 6.04[d]). Fortunately, many social workers and mental health professionals have learned from the mistakes of the past, ensuring that they provide services in a respectful, competent, and affirming manner. Still, social workers and mental health professionals must be vigilant in their work, maintaining awareness of their potential for causing harm, intentionally or not (Pope & Vasquez, 2007; Roberts, 2004). People with mental illness are not only worthy of the dignity and respect that we afford to all human beings; they are worthy of special protections because of their vulnerability (Beauchamp & Childress, 2009).

This chapter begins by exploring the ethics of diagnosis. Specifically, what are the ethical implications for social workers who include psychological diagnoses as part of their assessment and intervention process? In what ways might psychological diagnoses conflict with social work values and ethics, and how can social workers address these conflicts? The second section—Autonomy, Beneficence, Paternalism, and Social Control—focuses on ethical dilemmas arising when a patient[1] with mental illness poses a risk to the health or safety of self or others. In other words, how should social workers manage the principles of patient autonomy and self-determination when the health or safety of the patient or others is in peril? At what point might social workers become agents of social control rather than agents of social change and social justice? The third section—Mental Illness, Mental Capacity, and Mental Competence—delves into the legal and psychological criteria used to determine whether patients have or should have the ability to make decisions on their own behalf. The final section—Surrogate Decision Makers and Advance Directives—explains how patients may indicate their wishes for future health and mental health decisions, should they become mentally incapacitated. By informing patients about surrogates and advance directives, workers can promote patient self-determination in a manner that will continue even if their cognitive or mental condition declines.

LEARNING OBJECTIVES

Upon successful completion of this chapter, students will be able to

- Identify the ethical risks for social workers who incorporate psychological diagnosis in their assessment and intervention process.
- Implement strategies to reduce the ethical risks inherent in using psychological diagnoses.
- Critically assess ethical dilemmas in which the principles of patient autonomy, beneficence, and protection of others are in conflict.
- Distinguish the concepts of mental illness, mental capacity, and mental competence.
- Inform patients about the use of powers of attorney and psychiatric advance directives to make their wishes known in the event they become mentally incapacitated.

ETHICS OF DIAGNOSIS

Psychological diagnosis refers to the process of examining a patient's emotions, thoughts, behaviors, and other psychological processes to determine whether the patient has a clinical condition that fits within a particular category of psychopathology or mental disorders (Corey et al., 2007). The U.S. mental health system relies on the *Diagnostic and Statistical Manual of Mental Disorders* (*DSM*-IV-TR, American Psychiatric Association, 2000), which establishes the criteria for determining whether the person has a particular condition. In some jurisdictions, only psychiatrists are permitted to diagnose. In other jurisdictions, professional licensing laws permit certain classes of social workers, psychologists, and other mental health professionals to diagnose.[2] Social workers should be aware of the ethical risks inherent in making or using diagnoses: reductionism, disrespect, and malpractice. The following sections describe these risks and offer risk-management strategies.

Reductionism

The generalist model of social work suggests that social workers should assess clients using a broad, biopsychosocial-spiritual perspective (Kirst-Ashman & Hull, 2006b). Holistic assessments fit with the social work value for human relationships and ethical standards regarding

[1] This chapter uses the term *patient* rather than *client* to conform to the language most commonly used in the field of mental health. Although the NASW Code of Ethics uses the term *client*, mental health legislation, hospital policies, and the codes of ethics of mental health professions refer to patients. Some mental health facilities refer to service users as customers, clients, or residents because they believe it is more respectful or empowering than traditional medical terminology. Critics of the use of the term *patient* claim that it suggests the person must submit to medical authority (Roberts, 2004).

[2] For instance, licensed clinical social workers or licensed mental health professionals.

the promotion of social justice (NASW, 1999, S.6.04). Whereas generalist social work assessments are holistic, *DSM* diagnoses focus on mental disorders. In other words, a diagnostician explores whether the patient demonstrates the signs of particular mental disorders, such as schizophrenia, depression, or learning disorders (under Axis I of the *DSM*), or mental retardation or personality disorders (under Axis II). The *DSM*'s focus on psychopathology leads clinicians to focus on change processes within the individual. Interpersonal problems and interventions directed toward family or other social systems may be ignored or underemphasized. Although the *DSM* includes physical and social conditions under Axis III and Axis IV, these factors apply only if they are relevant to the primary mental disorders. In other words, if a patient is going through a divorce and this is related to the patient's diagnosis of depression, then the divorce would be considered within the diagnosis. On the other hand, if a patient's divorce was unrelated to any of the primary psychological diagnoses, then the divorce would be excluded from the diagnosis. Whereas generalist assessments encompass all realms of the patient's life, diagnoses reduce the focus to mental disorders and those factors directly linked with those disorders. From an ethics perspective, the narrow focus on mental disorders means that social work priorities such as human relationships, cultural diversity, social justice, and spiritual issues may be overlooked or discounted.

The *DSM*'s de-emphasis on social issues is marked by its relegation of cultural issues to the appendix at the back of the manual. Because cultural considerations are placed at the end of the *DSM*, clinicians may be less inclined to consider how cultural factors may be pertinent to their primary diagnoses. Consider, for instance, a 34-year-old woman who lives with her parents and relies very heavily on them for financial, emotional, and social support. A clinician might think these dynamics fit with a diagnosis of dependent personality disorder. If the clinician understands the patient's cultural context, for instance, he might consider that the patient comes from a communitarian culture, in which greater levels of reliance on other people is culturally appropriate rather than indicative of psychopathology. Mental illness is not an objective fact, but a socially constructed phenomenon (Roberts, 2004). What might be considered pathological or dysfunctional in one culture or during one period of history might be considered healthy and functional in another. Consider, for instance, how masturbation was once thought to be a sign of mental illness. It is now considered by mainstream American mental health professionals to be normal, healthy behavior (Szasz, 2003). This example illustrates how values cannot be excluded from diagnostic criteria and processes. Accordingly, social workers using the *DSM* must be cautious about the cultural biases built into its definitions of what is a disorder and the diagnostic criteria used to indicate whether a patient has a particular disorder (Karls & O'Keefe, 2008; Prichard, 2006).

Given the concerns regarding reductionism, one could argue that social workers should not rely on the *DSM*, but instead use assessment tools that are more holistic and culturally inclusive.[3] Further, one could argue, in the interests of social justice, that social workers should advocate for abolition of the entire *DSM* system (Carniol, 2005; Szasz, 2003). The question of whether to use the *DSM*, however, need not be a simple either/or debate. For social workers practicing in the field of mental health, the *DSM* is a fact of life. It is broadly accepted by professionals, agencies, insurance companies, and health maintenance organizations (HMOs). If a social worker wants to collaborate with other mental health professionals, wants to be hired by a mental health agency, or wants to claim financial reimbursement from a health insurance company or HMO, then the worker is expected to use the *DSM*. Although social workers could provide services outside the mainstream mental health system, it may also be helpful for workers to work within it, taking steps to redress the ethical challenges of the *DSM*. Thus, social workers could use the following strategies to curtail the ethical risks of reductionism:

[3] For instance, PIE, the person-in-environment assessment tool (Prichard, 2006).

- Integrate cultural considerations throughout the diagnostic process, rather than leaving them to be considered as an afterthought or neglected altogether.
- View a *DSM* diagnosis as just one part of holistic biospsychosocial-spiritual assessment, rather than relying solely on the diagnosis to determine the preferred treatment or intervention for the patient.
- Advocate for changes to the *DSM*[4] and mental health system, to ensure more holistic approaches to diagnosis and assessment, including multicultural and social justice perspectives.

Disrespect

Respect for the inherent dignity and worth of the person is a core social work value. This value is operationalized through several ethical standards—for instance, making client well-being the worker's primary interest (NASW, 1999, S.1.01), respecting client self-determination (S.1.02), and using respectful language with clients (S.1.12). Unfortunately, the process of diagnosis entails risks to each of these standards. With respect to promoting patient well-being, social workers should ask why they are providing diagnoses: Are diagnoses truly helpful for the patient, or are they being used to promote the interests of mental health professionals, agencies, insurance companies, or others? If a worker's motivation to diagnose is to receive third-party insurance reimbursement, for example, then one could question whether the worker is actually putting the patient's interests ahead of her own (Specht & Courtney, 1994). Yes, a worker may be using the diagnosis to ensure that the patient has access to necessary services. Still, the system creates financial incentives for clinicians to attribute mental disorders to patients whether or not their patients actually benefit from the diagnoses (Furman, 2003).

In terms of self-determination, social workers help patients identify their goals through a mutual assessment and planning process. In other words, social workers help patients explore their needs, wants, strengths, resources, and challenges in order to develop a joint understanding of the patient's situation and determine what interventions, if any, to pursue (Kirst-Ashman & Hull, 2006b). Diagnosis follows the medical model and evidence-based practice, in which the professional acts as an expert who identifies the patient's psychopathologies and prescribes the best treatment for the patient (especially medication and individual psychotherapy). Although the medical model permits patients to agree or disagree with the prescribed treatment, the patient plays a more passive role in a diagnostic process than in a mutual assessment process. The medical model encourages patients to trust the expert's diagnosis and prescribed treatments, potentially limiting the patient's ability to voice concerns and exercise self-determination (Scheyett, 2006).

One of the strongest social work indictments of the *DSM* is that diagnoses focus on illnesses or pathologies. Whereas the strengths perspective of social work encourages workers to identify and build on the positive attributes and resources of patients (Saleebey, 2009), much of the *DSM*'s focus is on patient problems. True, Axis V does include an assessment of global functioning, but this assessment often gets short shrift in comparison with the diagnoses of mental disorders under the first two axes. By focusing on negatives, social workers may be demonstrating disrespect to the individuality and worth of the patient (Hill & Lightfoot, 2009). Some criteria that mental health professionals use to diagnose psychopathology could be viewed as a patient's strengths. A person who is diagnosed with delusions of grandeur, for instance, could be considered to be poised and confident, particularly when social context is taken into account. Politicians, athletes, rock stars, and other prominent individuals may use their high sense of self-importance to energize and drive themselves to success, or to insulate themselves from the slings and arrows of competitors and naysayers.

The problems of focusing on patient deficits are compounded by the negative effects

[4] At the time of writing, the *DSM* was undergoing revision for the purposes of developing the fifth edition, expected to be finalized in May 2012. See http://www.psych.org/dsmv.asp.

of labeling. When patients are diagnosed with mental disorders, they may become stigmatized by family, friends, employers, neighbors, and even mental health professionals (Yip, 2006). Common stereotypes for people with mental disorders suggest they are crazy, dangerous, or self-destructive (Ganzini, Volicer, Nelson, Fox, & Derse, 2005; Szasz, 2003). Further, the name of each mental disorder is a label describing a general condition, whereas each patient is a unique individual (Roberts, 2004). When a person is diagnosed with a mental disorder, people may assume this person is just like every other person who has that disorder, devaluing the person's individuality. Phrases such as "He is bipolar" or "She is borderline" tend to objectify the person as a disorder. One could argue that such labeling contravenes Standard 1.12, which says social workers should not use derogatory language to describe patients. Mental health professionals might argue that diagnoses of mental disorders are no different from diagnoses of physical disorders, such as having congestive heart failure or appendicitis: in either case, these diagnoses describe a medical condition requiring treatment. Unfortunately, people often ascribe negative connotations to mental disorders. Historically, "imbecile" and "lunatic" were legally recognized terms used to describe people with cognitive disabilities and mental illness (Wright, 2000). Today, what social worker could describe patients as lunatics or imbeciles without drawing censure from other professionals for showing disrespect? Consider, given the negative connotations ascribed to labels such as bipolar or borderline, are they any better than referring to someone as an imbecile or lunatic? Does the *DSM* promote the attachment of negative labels to patients?

As noted earlier, there are many occasions when social workers need to use *DSM* diagnoses. Diagnoses may be beneficial for patients in a number of ways. They establish a baseline of information about the patient from which to evaluate progress or problems in treatment. The *DSM* narrows the scope of treatment options by focusing on treatments that have been shown to be effective for particular diagnoses (Scheyett, 2006). Diagnoses also provide mental health professionals with a common language with which to discuss patient problems and challenges (*DSM*, 2000). Finally, diagnoses provide patients with medically based explanations for problems being experienced. When patients who have been described as lazy drunks or weak-willed addicts are diagnosed with substance dependence, they may begin to see themselves as good people experiencing medical illnesses, rather than irresponsible people with moral deficits (Fisher & Harrison, 2005).

As the foregoing analysis demonstrates, psychological diagnoses may entail both benefits and risks. The following strategies may be used to resolve or lessen the ethical risks of disrespect associated with the use of such diagnoses:

- Avoid affixing *DSM* labels or diagnoses to patients unless ascribing a diagnosis is in the patient's best interests (e.g., does the patient need to have a diagnosis, or is the worker providing a diagnosis merely for the worker's financial gain?). Patient benefits from a diagnosis may include gaining access to services and fostering insight about the patient's situation. If there is no need for a *DSM* diagnosis, then refraining from providing a diagnosis may help the patient avoid stigma and discrimination from others, as well as avert self-defeating thoughts from internalized stigma and fears about mental illness or cognitive impairments.
- Include a thorough assessment of social and cultural factors, as contemplated by the *DSM*, rather than focusing only on the major psychiatric disorders, cognitive disabilities, and personality disorders in Axis I and Axis II.
- Offset the problem-based focus of diagnoses by providing strengths-based assessments, helping patients identify their positive qualities and resources, and using positive language to validate patients as unique individuals who are worthy of respect.
- Provide patients with a full explanation for any diagnosis, including the reasons for the diagnosis, how it may be used, and the implications of a particular assessment (e.g., how mental health professionals, health insurance providers, family members, and

others may react in response to learning of their diagnosis).

- Enhance self-determination by engaging patients in a discussion of all possible interventions (not just medication, individual psychotherapy, or other treatments directed toward the patient, but also interventions involving the family, workplace, cultural community, or other social systems).
- Provide patients with information and strategies to help them avoid and/or cope with the risks of diagnosis (e.g., explain their rights to confidentiality, equality, and nondiscrimination; role-play how patients might talk to others about their diagnoses in a manner that promotes respectful treatment; discuss methods of dealing with people who treat them with disrespect based on their diagnosis; or offer patients information about advocacy organizations that can assist them).
- Promote the use of respectful terminology in describing people with mental disorders (e.g., "the patient experiences delusions," rather than "the patient is delusional").
- Educate families, schools, workplaces, professionals, and other social systems about the nature of mental disorders, correcting misconceptions or stereotypes, and encouraging respectful, nondiscriminatory treatment of people with mental disorders.
- Advocate for patients who experience discrimination as a result of their diagnosis.[5]

Now that we have explored the first two ethical risks of diagnosis—reductionism and disrespect—we turn to a third risk, malpractice.

Malpractice

Malpractice (as defined in Chapter 9) refers to providing services in a manner that conflicts with standards reasonably expected of a prudent professional. Social workers may be held liable for compensation for any harm experienced by patients as a result of malpractice. For social workers in the mental health field, two of the more common types of malpractice are misdiagnosis and providing inappropriate treatment[6] (Caudill, n.d.; Kutchins & Kirk, 1987; Reamer, 2003). Misdiagnosis includes failure to identify a particular mental disorder that a patient is experiencing as well as incorrectly identifying a disorder that a patient does not have. Given that the *DSM* is broadly accepted among mental health professionals, courts may expect clinical social workers to adhere to the *DSM* as the basis for any diagnosis (Kutchins & Kirk, 1987). Accordingly, if a social worker does not apply the diagnostic criteria in the *DSM*, this could constitute grounds for malpractice. Courts may dismiss a worker's contention that he or she does not believe in the medical model, so he does not need to follow the *DSM* (Caudill, n.d.).[7] Grounds for malpractice also include not applying the diagnostic criteria correctly. One of the challenges of applying the *DSM* is inter-rater reliability. Ideally, if two different people diagnose the same patient, they should arrive at the same diagnosis. In practice, this is not always the case (Kutchins & Kirk, 1987). Remember, however, that malpractice law does not require professionals to be perfect, but reasonable (Stein, 2004). Accordingly, a court may ask, "Would it be reasonable for a prudent social worker applying the *DSM* to arrive at this particular diagnosis for this patient?"

When considering the appropriateness of treatment, the court may consider what the *DSM* says is appropriate for a particular diagnosis. If the *DSM* suggests psychotropic medication for a particular mental disorder, for instance, then the social worker making the diagnosis might be expected to refer the patient to a physician who could prescribe and monitor the effects of the medication. So, what if the social worker

---

[5] Advocacy could include advocating for changes in the *DSM*'s fifth edition, due for publication in 2012.

[6] Treatment may include interventions provided by the professional who performs the diagnosis or referrals to other professionals for treatment.

[7] Caudill suggests that this argument is analogous to a person saying she does not believe in the tax code, so she does not need to follow it. In social work, this question may depend on the context of practice: If reasonable, prudent social workers in a particular field of practice apply the *DSM*, then a social worker in this field may be expected to follow the *DSM*.

does not believe in psychotropic medicine? If the *DSM* suggests various alternatives, then a court would likely conclude that the worker could recommend any of these alternatives. If the *DSM* does not recommend the intervention proffered by the social worker (e.g., narrative therapy), then this could be used as evidence of malpractice. The worker would need to show that a prudent worker could reasonably conclude that narrative therapy was appropriate for this patient. The worker could draw upon research on narrative therapy, particularly if it shows that this intervention is effective for situations akin to that of the patient in question. Although courts may rely on the *DSM* to determine what constitutes an appropriate treatment, courts may also consider research on treatment effectiveness as well as evidence of what other mental health professionals consider to be appropriate forms of treatment.

Even though the *DSM* suggests particular treatments for each mental disorder, predicting the outcomes of treatment is difficult. Just because a patient experiences harm from a particular course of treatment does not mean that the patient will be able to make a valid claim for malpractice. The patient must be able to prove that the worker did not adhere to a reasonable standard of care (Houston-Vega & Nuehring, 1997), for instance, recommending a course of treatment that no prudent social worker with the same professional background would consider reasonable.

Given the risks of malpractice in relation to providing diagnoses, consider the following risk-management strategies:

- Do not provide *DSM* diagnoses unless you are competent to do so. Competence to diagnose may be achieved through relevant education, experience, licensing or accreditation, specialized *DSM* training, consultation, and supervision (S.1.04[a]). If you are not competent to conduct a diagnosis and one is needed, refer the patient to a properly accredited mental health professional who is competent to provide one (Kutchins & Kirk, 1987). Further, when conducting a diagnosis, you may need to refer the patient to certain specialists for areas requiring special expertise (e.g., referring the patient to a physician to provide medical information required for Axis III).
- Document your diagnostic processes, as well as the data and information you gather and use to substantiate a particular diagnosis (e.g., what did you observe about the patient that corresponded with the indicators of a particular mental disorder under the *DSM*?). Document both typical and atypical symptoms to demonstrate that you conducted a thorough analysis of all relevant information.
- When in doubt about which diagnosis to ascribe or which interventions to suggest, solicit help from other mental health professionals (e.g., consult with a supervisor or other clinician with specialized diagnostic training [S.2.05], or refer the patient to a mental health professional who can assess the patient and provide a second opinion about the appropriate diagnosis [S.2.06]).
- Provide a diagnosis that honestly and accurately reflects the client's situation (S.4.04). Do not provide a more severe diagnosis just to ensure that the client meets the eligibility requirements for health insurance reimbursement or other health-care supports (Pope & Vasquez, 2007). Do not provide a less severe diagnosis just to placate a client (e.g., stating a client has an adjustment disorder rather than borderline disorder in order to sidestep a defensive reaction from the client). Further, the law does not permit clinicians to provide one diagnosis for treatment purposes and another diagnosis for billing or insurance purposes (Caudill, n.d.). If you feel pressure from your agency or others to provide a more severe or less severe diagnosis than is properly indicated (Furman, 2003), consult with a supervisor, attorney, ombudsperson, or other support people about how to handle this pressure.
- If a patient rejects a diagnosis or a recommended treatment, document your discussions about the diagnosis and recommended treatment, including the patient's reasons for rejecting them (S.3.04[a]).

Consider referring the patient for a second opinion (S.1.16[e]).

- If your recommended treatment is inconsistent with the treatments recommended by the *DSM*, provide the patient with information about each of these options, including their risks and benefits, to ensure the patient is fully informed and consents on a voluntary basis (S.1.03[a]). Document the informed consent process, as well as the reasons that you recommended a course of treatment other than that prescribed by the *DSM* (S.4.01[c]).
- If your recommended treatment is not authorized by the patient's health maintenance organization or insurance provider, advocate for the patient to try to ensure the patient receives appropriate services (e.g., ask insurance company for an exception, link patient with a patient advocacy group, identify a charitable foundation that could pay for services, or offer services at a reduced cost [S.1.01]). If the patient is unable to receive recommended services, document your attempts to try to secure appropriate services for the patient.

AUTONOMY, BENEFICENCE, PATERNALISM, AND SOCIAL CONTROL

Social work's value for client autonomy is reflected in Standard 1.02, which defines a client's right to make self-determined choices. Social workers believe that respecting the inherent dignity and worth of clients means that clients should be able to decide which interventions, if any, are in their best interests (Dolgoff et al., 2009). Self-determination suggests that social workers should not impose their values or beliefs, or interfere with a patient's rights to choose, even if the worker disagrees with the patient's values, beliefs, or choices. Although social workers value patient autonomy, they also value beneficence, or doing good. Often, social workers can advance patient autonomy and beneficence at the same time. Unfortunately, patient autonomy and beneficence may conflict when

- A social worker has an obligation to report patients for suspicions of child abuse or neglect (S.1.01).
- A social worker's obligation to promote social justice supersedes the worker's obligation to promote the patient's interests (Ss.1.01 and 6.04).
- A social worker has an obligation to safeguard patients or others from serious, foreseeable, and imminent risks (S.1.02).

This section explores how social workers can manage the conflict that arises between autonomy and beneficence when patients with mental disorders pose a risk to self or others (especially suicidal or homicidal ideation).

In an ideal social worker–patient relationship, each patient has full decision-making autonomy and exercises it in his or her own best interest. In this ideal situation, social workers do not feel compelled to limit patient self-determination because patients are motivated, free from cognitive distortions, and able to exercise informed consent on a voluntary basis. Patients trust their workers but balance this trust with healthy skepticism. They listen to their worker's information and professional opinions but also ask questions, raise concerns, and assert their own interests and decisions. These conditions do exist in some social work relationships, but workers must also be prepared to work with other realities: patients whose decision making may be impaired by mental illness, cognitive disabilities, or distorted perceptions and beliefs; patients who lack motivation or are ambivalent about addressing serious problems in their lives; and patients who distrust helping professionals regardless of how well-meaning, knowledgeable, and skilful they are. Each of these conditions poses challenges for social work practice. The key question is how to manage such conditions in an ethical manner, honoring both patient autonomy and beneficence to the highest possible degree, and using critical thinking skills to determine how to respond when autonomy and beneficence come into conflict.

Beneficence conflicts with autonomy in two situations, paternalism and social control. *Paternalism refers to the policy or practice of having persons in positions of authority make decisions for patients, based on their assessment of what is in the patients' best interests* (Roberts, 2004). The root of the term *paternalism* refers to acting like a father in protecting and caring for his children (Beauchamp & Childress, 2009). Within the social work and the mental health professions, one of the primary justifications for paternalism is to protect patients from imminent, serious, and foreseeable harm. Thus, when patients are suicidal, acts of paternalism could include control and restraint, seclusion, locked wards, special observations, covert administration of medicines, compulsory admission (involuntary commitment), or treatment mandated by civil courts. To determine which paternalistic strategies are permitted and under what circumstances, social workers should consider their state mental health laws and agency policies. Whereas paternalism is based on protection of the patients' health and safety, *social control refers to policies or practices that limit a patient's rights in order to protect others.*[8] Social control includes the use of legal or social pressure to coerce patients or restrict their freedom for the perceived good of other people (Wild, 2006). When patients are homicidal, for instance, acts of social control may consist of the same strategies as described above for paternalism. Although social control strategies such as involuntary committal may be authorized by mental health laws, additional social control strategies may be authorized by state and federal criminal laws (*Lessard v. Schmidt*, 1972). Criminal courts may impose incarceration, fines, and probation for individuals who have committed crimes, in part to punish, but also to protect the public from future crimes (Madden, 2003). Once individuals have completed their criminal sentences, however, criminal courts may not keep them in prison just because they continue to pose a danger. If further restraints are necessary to protect others, the individual could be committed through civil court, according to mental health legislation. In general, criminal courts cannot impose restraints on an individual's rights and freedoms, except as punishment for committing a particular crime (*Smith v. Doe*, 2003).[9]

When considering whether to impose interventions on patients, social workers should be careful to distinguish between having a mental disorder and posing risks to self or others. Some people who have mental illnesses, substance dependencies, or cognitive impairments pose risks to self or others. For instance, a depressed person may be suicidal, a person addicted to cocaine may be homicidal, or a person with severe cognitive impairment may engage in high-risk behaviors without due concern for safety issues. However, many people with mental illnesses, substance dependence, or cognitive impairments do not pose serious risks to self or others. *Although a social worker might wish to commit a patient to a mental health facility for the patient's own good, legal and ethical standards require evidence of serious risk to the patient or others in order to commit the patient.* Further, involuntary committal to a mental health facility does not mean that the facility can impose medication or other treatments on the patient (Bentley, 1993). Committal typically means that the patient may be required to stay at the facility until the patient no longer poses a danger to self or others (i.e., the suicidal or homicidal ideation subsides). Unless a court specifically mandates medication or other treatment, the patient is not required to accept treatment.[10] Still, patients

[8] Involuntary committal or coerced treatment should not be imposed unless there is an immediate threat to someone's life. If a patient is merely damaging property or inconveniencing people, then the patient should be held accountable for such actions but should not be forced into accepting medication or other treatments. Further, mental health professionals should not use the threat of coerced treatment to force people to conform to the ways or will of the majority. Consider a woman with schizophrenia who says she wants to live on the streets, even though it is –30° F. Should a social worker help this woman survive on the streets, or try to commit her to a mental facility so she will be safe and receive proper treatment for her mental illness?

[9] In some circumstances, criminal and family courts may impose restraining orders and orders for protection to keep a potentially violent person away from specific intended victims (e.g., in spousal abuse situations).

[10] Under the Marchman Act in Florida, for instance, people with substance dependence can be involuntarily ordered to receive substance dependence treatment.

may feel pressure to accept treatment in order to be released from the facility. The facility's staff may be inclined to impose pressure to accept treatment, either out of an honest interest in the patient's well-being or wanting the patient to comply in order to make their jobs easier.

Social workers should identify and become familiar with the specific mental health laws, policies, procedures, and practices that apply to their states (Butler, 2004). In general, mental health legislation strives to balance the interests of autonomy and beneficence, ensuring that the rights of people with mental disorders are protected while also securing the physical safety of the patient and others (*Lessard v. Schmidt*, 1972). To protect the safety of a patient or others, specifically authorized mental health professionals[11] may initiate involuntarily examinations of a patient whom they believe may need involuntary committal or treatment in order to protect the safety of the patient or others.[12] The patient's rights are protected through a range of procedural guidelines and prerogatives. First, when a patient is taken to a mental health facility, that facility must evaluate whether the patient meets the statutory criteria for involuntary committal or treatment (e.g., the person has a mental illness and poses a serious risk of bodily injury to self or others). If the patient does not meet the requirements for involuntary committal or treatment, the patient must be discharged from the receiving facility. If the patient meets the requirements, then the facility must file a petition with the court. Patients have a right to be heard at the court hearing as well as the right to have an attorney to represent them. The court decides whether the patient may be kept in the mental health facility for a certain period (typically up to 6 months). If the facility believes the patient needs to be maintained in the facility beyond this initial period, it must file another motion with the court. Some states also permit courts to order involuntary outpatient services.

State mental health legislation enunciates a range of patient rights, typically including the right to be treated with dignity and respect, the right to privacy, the right to participation in treatment planning, the right to refuse medication or other interventions, and the right to be notified of rights. Social workers play a key role in protecting the rights of patients with mental illness, as this population is vulnerable to discrimination, misunderstanding, and disrespect. Patient rights are not absolute rights, meaning that mental health professionals should respect these rights as much as possible; they may limit certain rights, *but only to the extent necessary* to protect patients and others from serious bodily harm. Thus, staff at a mental health facility are permitted to physically restrain patients to prevent them from severely hurting themselves, even though this cuts into patients' rights to control over their own bodies. Even when physical restraint is justified, patients have a right to be free from harms caused by excessive force. Emergency interventions such as isolation or medication should not be used as punishment or for the convenience of staff. Staff should only use the least restrictive and least intrusive interventions necessary to protect the patient or others (Pope & Vasquez, 2007).

Respecting patient rights during crisis situations can be very challenging. To promote autonomy and self-determination for patients who might be posing serious risks to self or others, consider the following strategies.

- Ensure your decisions to initiate involuntary committal or treatment are based on actual risks to patients or others rather than on stereotypes, frustration with the patients, power struggles, or other inappropriate factors.[13] Do not assume patients

[11] Judges, police, and others may also be permitted to initiate examination or other proceedings leading to involuntary committal of people who may pose substantial risks to self or others.

[12] This may include patients who are suicidal or homicidal, as well as patients who refuse to care for themselves in a manner that creates a substantial harm to themselves.

[13] Paternalism may be ethically justified to protect people from harm and alleviate suffering. Paternalism is not justified by the desires to maintain the cultural status quo or to pursue certain political agendas (Roberts, 2004).

pose risks simply because they have mental disorders, deviate from social norms, or disagree with your suggestions for intervention. Employ evidence-based assessment tools to assess for suicidal or homicidal risks (Quinn, 2005).[14] Make use of supervision or consultation with other mental health professionals to reflect on the basis of your decisions and check for potential biases or emotional reactions.

- When patients do pose risks to self or others, make use of the least intrusive means to ensure the safety of those at risk.
  - o Engage patients in a discussion of the risks and various methods of dealing with the risks (e.g., crisis intervention counseling, contracting a safety plan, involvement of family to monitor the patient, medical and residential services with monitoring capabilities, or different types of medications). Do not focus only on the use of medication if other viable options are available. Discuss the benefits of accessing services and support on a collaborative, noncoercive, and informed basis (Rooney, 2002).
  - o Rather than simply imposing treatments or interventions, consider engaging patients on a voluntary basis through interventions that demonstrate respect, foster strengths, build trust, and promote patient self-determination (e.g., empathy-based, client-centered counseling [Rogers, 1957], the transtheoretical model of change [Prochaska & Norcross, 2007], solution-focused counseling [Guterman, 2006], and collaborative conflict resolution [Barsky, 2007a]).
  - o If medical professionals are recommending medication but the patient is resisting it, consider engaging the medical professionals and patient in a discussion of other options that could be tried first. Medication is not necessarily the best or only treatment for patients at risk. Patients may be more willing to accept medication if they have been permitted to try other options first.
  - o If it may be helpful to alert family members, friends, potential victims, police, or other authorities about the potential risks posed by the patient, engage the patient in a discussion of the benefits and risks of contacting them. If the patient provides permission to disclose certain information to particular people, then you may be able to honor the patient's self-determination and still protect the patient or others from harm.
  - o In situations in which you have an ethical or legal duty to contact the police or others to prevent harm[15] and the patient does not provide consent, advise the patient of your duty. Reassure the patient that you will strive to protect his or her autonomy and confidentiality as much as possible (e.g., by limiting whom you will contact and what information you will provide).
- When working with involuntary patients, utilize strategies designed to protect their interests and improve outcomes for them: for instance, identify treatments or interventions with proven effectiveness and minimal risks or side effects; involve patients in treatment planning; ask them to identify their own preferred outcomes; allow them to voice their concerns and narratives about taking medications, submitting to surveillance, or receiving other psychiatric treatments (Scheyett, 2006); explain what is required and what is not required of them;[16] allow patients to have choices; remove pressure; and support self-determination as much as is permissible (Rooney, 2002).

---

[14] For instance, factors associated with elevated risk of suicide include statement of intent to kill oneself, specific and feasible plan, clinical depression, substance abuse, sense of hopelessness, impulsivity, and rigidly thinking that suicide is the only alternative to one's problems (Quinn, 2005).

[15] Confidentiality and the duties to protect, warn, and report are introduced in Chapter 5.

[16] For instance, a court order may require a patient to be admitted to a mental health facility, but the specific choice of mental health facilities may be negotiable.

Social workers may experience professional dissonance or value conflicts when working with patients who pose serious risks to self or others. On the one hand, they value the autonomy and self-determination of their patients. On the other hand, they may need to act as agents of paternalism or social control to protect their patients or others (Taylor, 2007). Although social workers may feel anxiety over role conflicts and value tensions, such anxiety may actually be a good thing (Mattison, 2000). In fact, social workers who do not perceive dissonance in such situations are missing an essential part of the equation. Consider Stockton, a social worker who finds the ethical question of imposing treatment on clients to be very easy. "This client is suicidal, so it is obvious that we need to commit him." Stockton's use of the word "obvious" may indicate that he is making assumptions about the need to commit. He may not be open to exploring other options. Further, Stockton may not be sensitive to the client's need for autonomy and respect. Contrast Stockton's comments with those of Sabrina, a second worker. "I understand the patient is suicidal and requires inpatient care. Still, I am feeling a bit uneasy about the impact of involuntary treatment on this client." Although Sabrina agrees the patient needs to be committed, her statement of uneasiness suggests she appreciates the tension between protecting people from harm and preserving self-determination. Such appreciation may indicate she is more open to hearing information and arguments for all sides of the issue. She may also be able to convey a higher level of empathy with the patient because she is not assuming that involuntary committal is an easy choice. Thus, workers should understand that experiencing professional dissonance is not only normal when dealing with ethical dilemmas; it may be helpful. Workers who are aware of dissonance can reflect upon it, understanding that ethical and values conflicts are not easy but nevertheless require decisions to be made (Mattison, 2000; Taylor, 2007).

When a patient refuses medication or other prescribed treatments, mental health professionals may feel their primary role is to persuade the patient to accept this treatment, for his own good. Given social work's ethical obligation to serve vulnerable populations (S.6.04[b]), social workers should consider advocating for the patient's wishes, even when they do not believe these wishes reflect his best interests. Whether or not a social worker should advocate for the client's wishes or interests may depend on agency policies and the worker's role within the agency. If the worker cannot advocate for the patients' wishes, then the worker should ensure that the client has access to an advocate who may assume this role (e.g., an independent social worker, an attorney, a family member, a designated advocate, or another person whom the patient trusts).

A patient advocate may help by identifying legal rights and protections—for instance, rights to privacy and respect, and prohibitions against cruel and unusual punishment (Bentley, 1993). The advocate may also help by giving voice to the patient's concerns and demonstrating how refusing prescribed treatments may not be illogical or irrational. For instance, patients may experience a broad range of side effects from psychotropic medications (e.g., drooling, lethargy, sleep disturbances, rashes, and sexual dysfunctions). The advocate may also remind other professionals that a patient's right to self-determination includes the right to be wrong. As long as there is no immediate risk to the life of the patient or others, patients have a right to refuse medication or other treatments that could be helpful to them.

Consider a situation in which a psychiatrist presents a suicidal or homicidal patient the following ultimatum, "Accept medication or you will be admitted into a mental health facility." A patient advocate should ensure that the psychiatrist is not simply using the threat of committal as a way to manipulate the patient into compliance. Patients should not be involuntarily committed merely for refusing to consent to prescribed treatment. The psychiatrist may be correct that the patient may be able to avoid committal by accepting the medication, but the advocate could show greater respect for the client by reframing the way this information is presented:

> "The attending psychiatrist believes you need to be admitted to the hospital to ensure that you are safe. She also believes that if you take your antidepressants, you will start to feel

better and won't need hospitalization. What do you think will happen if you take the medication? (pauses for response and then paraphrases to demonstrate empathy) What do you think will happen if you do not take the medication?"

The patient advocate educates the patient to enhance his ability to make an informed decision (S.1.03). The client needs to know the possible consequences of his choices, but these consequences should be presented as information, not threats. The advocate also discusses different options to enhance the client's choice set and self-determination (S.1.02). The advocate understands that the patient's reasoning may be affected by irrational thoughts, hallucinations, delusions of grandiosity, paranoia, or other consequences of his mental illness. Still, the advocate's role is to ensure that the patient's wishes and perspectives are heard. Simply having irrational thoughts or hallucinations does not mean the patient should have no say in whether to receive a particular treatment.

Although social workers may have clear mandates from agency policy and their ethical standards to advocate for the rights and wishes of a mental health patient, they should be aware that such advocacy may draw scorn or disapproval from their professional colleagues and the patient's family:

"Why are you agreeing with this patient? If she doesn't take her medication, there's a strong chance she'll kill herself. Then how will you feel? The best thing you could do is to convince her to take her medication. Once she takes it, she'll feel better and she'll thank you."

When assuming the role of an advocate for a vulnerable mental health patient, workers need to be able to withstand external pressures in order to be able to do what is right and fulfill their roles (Prilleltensky et al., 2002). This may take personal fortitude, support from supervisors, and positive self-messaging:

"This patient needs someone to help her voice her views and wishes. I am that person. Other professionals may be mandated to assess risks, persuade the client to accept treatment, or initiate involuntary services, if necessary. Given our different roles, we may be in conflict. Conflict is not necessarily a bad thing. We can all benefit from having different professionals express different views. Discussing and assessing the issues from different perspectives helps us make better-informed decisions. I would like to work out a solution that everyone can agree with. Even if the patient is involuntarily committed or mandated into treatment, however, I will know that I did my best to ensure this patient's voice was heard."

By acknowledging the tension between autonomy and beneficence, social workers can ensure that they give appropriate consideration to both client self-determination and the safety of the client and others (Mattison, 2000). How social workers manage this tension depends on a variety of factors: the patient's capacities, the level and urgency of the risks, and the specific role and mandate of the worker. Ideally, social workers can promote solutions that satisfy both self-determination and safety. In situations when this is not completely possible, workers should remember that respect for self-determination and other client rights is not an either/or proposition. When workers need to initiate involuntary committals or other interventions (in the interests of safety), they should consider what steps they can take to respect a client's right to self-determination, privacy, and dignity as much as possible.

MENTAL ILLNESS, MENTAL CAPACITY, AND MENTAL COMPETENCE

The concepts of *mental illness, mental capacity,* and *mental competence* are related terms, but they have distinct meanings and connotations for professional practice. In spite of these important conceptual differences, many professionals and laypeople confuse these terms. You may even find certain agency policies and state mental health laws that misuse these terms. Thus, you should be aware that not everyone understands these terms in the same way (Beauchamp & Childress, 2009; Braun, Pietsch, & Blanchette,

2000) and it may be prudent to clarify how people are using each of these terms in their interactions with you. The following sections provide definitions to help you clarify the differences among these terms.

Mental Illness

Mental illness refers to a psychological condition "characterized by impairment of an individual's normal cognitive, emotional, or behavioral functioning, and caused by social, psychological, biochemical, genetic, or other factors, such as infection or head trauma" (Mental Illness, n.d.). Although some people equate mental illness with very severe impairments, the severity of mental illness may vary from person to person, and within the same person over a period of time. Mental illnesses (or disorders) may be diagnosed by mental health practitioners who have appropriate training and licensure for making diagnoses. One of the primary purposes of diagnosing mental illnesses is to determine whether psychiatric or psychosocial interventions are needed, and what those interventions should be (*DSM*, 2000).

Mental Capacity

Mental capacity refers to the ability of a person to think, understand, reason, and remember. Social workers and other helping professionals should assess clients' mental capacity to determine whether they have sufficient decision-making capacity[17] to provide informed consent (S.1.03[c]; Stein, 2007). When patients clearly have decision-making capacity, there is no need for a formal assessment process. When patients have cognitive impairments or their decision-making capacity is in doubt, professionals should conduct a formal assessment of four decision-making components: the ability to communicate a treatment choice, the ability to understand relevant considerations, the ability to understand the risks and benefits of various treatment choices, and the ability to think rationally about the choices (Rao & Blake, 2002; Quinn, 2005). A helping professional does not have to be licensed to conduct mental health diagnoses to be able to assess for mental capacity for the purposes of informed consent, though the professional should have training in how to assess the four areas of decision-making capacity.[18]

A practitioner who is uncertain about the mental capacity of a patient could refer the patient for a second-level assessment from a mental health professional with specialized expertise. However, assessment of mental capacity by the patient's primary practitioner is often preferable because the practitioner has an ongoing working relationship with the patient and is able to track the patient's decision-making abilities, goals, wishes, and reasoning over time (Ganzini et al., 2005).

If a patient does not have sufficient capacity to provide informed consent for services, the professional should seek consent for services from an appropriate third person (NASW, 1999, S.1.03[c]), such as a guardian, surrogate, or next of kin (Quinn, 2005).[19] A patient may lack decision-making capacity due to the consequences of mental illness, for instance, having hallucinations, delusions, anxiety, or impaired cognition (Roberts, 2004). However, mental illness should not be equated to lack of decision-making capacity. A person with mental illness may have sufficient decision-making capacity to provide informed consent because

- The mental illness does not have a severe impact on the person's ability to think, reason, understand, or remember.

---

[17] The terms *mental capacity* and *decision-making capacity* are synonymous.

[18] If there is a court case to determine mental capacity (e.g., in an adult guardianship case), then the court may require a formal assessment conducted by a specially trained mental health professional, as designated by state legislation. Elements of assessments in guardianship cases typically include an evaluation of the patient's alertness and attention, information processing, thought disorders, and ability to modulate mood and affect. Some states require the use of specific assessment tools (Quinn, 2005).

[19] When a client has a mental incapacity and a proxy decision maker provides consent, workers should still request the client's assent, demonstrating respect and affirmation (Guinn, 2002).

- The mental illness is under control from medication or other treatments.
- Even though the mental illness has an impact on the person's ability to think, reason, understand, or remember, the person is still able to understand the nature of the services offered and make a reasonable assessment of the risks and benefits of the services.

Thus, there are many situations in which people with mental illness have sufficient mental capacity to provide informed consent. On the other side of the equation, some people lack mental capacity even though they have no mental illness. Consider, for instance, a woman who is temporarily intoxicated from alcohol or who is under an extreme level of stress from her social environment. Although she does not have any mental illness, her decision-making capacity may be temporarily impaired. Consider, also, a young child. Although the child does not have a mental illness, the child may lack cognitive, verbal, or other abilities necessary to provide informed consent.

Mental Competence

Mental competence is a legal term referring to whether an individual has the legal status to make certain types of decision on his or her own behalf. Whereas social workers and other helping professionals may assess a patient's mental capacity, only a judge may determine and declare whether a person is mentally incompetent (Meyer & Weaver, 2005). Professionals, patients, or their families may go to court for a ruling on mental competence when there is a dispute about whether the patient has a permanent decision-making incapacity or when there is a dispute concerning which person should be appointed as a surrogate (or substitute) decision maker. Competency hearings may be time-consuming and expensive (Ganzini et al., 2005). If a judge rules that a patient is mentally incompetent, then social workers should consult the surrogate decision maker for informed consent (i.e., the guardian or person appointed by the court or other legal documentation, as described in the following section on psychiatric advance directives). Although judges determine whether a person is mentally incompetent, they may make use of testimony or other evidence from social workers or other mental health professionals. A decision to declare a person mentally incompetent does not depend on whether the person is experiencing mental illness but whether the person has a serious impairment in mental capacity (thinking, understanding, reasoning, and memory). If a judge has declared a person mentally incompetent, social workers and other professionals cannot override this decision simply by reassessing the person's mental capacity (Stein, 2007). A judge must hear evidence of the person's mental capacity and rule on whether to declare the person mentally competent.

Judges may make decisions about a person's general competence or specific competence. General competence relates to the person's legal status to handle all of her affairs—for instance, making financial or health-care decisions, writing a will, signing a contract, and standing trial for criminal charges. Specific competence relates to the person's legal status in relation to just one of these acts. When a judge determines specific competence, the judge considers the person's mental capacity in relation to the particular type of act. Thus, for a decision about whether a woman is legally competent to make a decision about having coronary bypass surgery, the judge would focus on whether the woman has the cognitive ability to understand the nature and consequences of the proposed surgery and other options. For a decision about general competence, the judge would consider a broader range of cognitive abilities and decisional contexts (Rao & Blake, 2002).

To determine mental competence with respect to health and mental health decisions, judges generally consider one or more of the following criteria:

- The ability to understand the treatment situation and choices: Does the person understand the nature of his condition and the various options for treatment?
- The ability to identify a treatment choice: Can the person communicate a choice beyond a yes or no, and maintain that choice long enough to act on it.

- The ability to make a reasonable choice: Does the person understand the facts relevant to the proposed treatment decision?
- The ability to appreciate the consequence of the proposed decision: Does the person understand the benefits and risks of the proposed treatment choice?
- The ability to provide rational reasons for the treatment choice: Can the person provide rational reasons for his decisions? (Rao & Blake, 2002).

These legal criteria for mental competence are similar to the criteria that social workers and other professionals may use to determine mental capacity to provide informed consent. As noted earlier, judges determine a person's mental competence, though they may use evidence from social workers or other mental health professionals who have worked with the person.

Myths about Mental Capacity

In a survey of medical and mental health professionals, Ganzini et al. (2005) identified a number of myths or false assumptions that practitioners hold with regard to assessing a patient's mental capacity.[20] The following points identify these myths and indicate how practitioners should be careful to avoid making assumptions.

1. *Myth*: Lack of mental capacity may be presumed when patients want to go against medical or professional advice. *Reality*: Although mental capacity includes the patient's ability to reason, the patient's reasoning and conclusions do not need to be identical to those of the professional service providers. Patients may have a variety of valid reasons for thinking differently or reaching different conclusions about treatment options, including different values and different assessments of risks and benefits. Patients may refuse antipsychotic medication, for instance, because they do not like the side effects. Professionals should be careful not to discount a patient's right to self-determination just because the patient does not agree with their opinions (Ganzini et al., 2005). As Aristotle suggests, respecting autonomy of the individual means each person has a right to define his or her own pleasure, fulfillment, and happiness (Knight, 2007). This right does not depend on whether patients have the same reasoning abilities and preferences as their helping professionals.

2. *Myth*: Professionals do not need to assess mental capacity unless patients go against medical advice. *Reality*: Professionals should assess decision-making capacity regardless of whether the patient agrees with medical advice. Assessing mental capacity is particularly important when a client has a mental illness and when the risks of the proposed intervention are significant. If a patient lacks the requisite cognitive functioning to make treatment decisions, the professionals should identify a surrogate decision maker who has authority to make decisions on the patient's behalf (S.1.03[c]). Even when a patient lacks mental capacity, practitioners should consider whether and how they can involve patients in the decision-making process (Ganzini et al., 2005). Although a surrogate may be responsible for the ultimate decision, respect for the dignity of the patient suggests the patient's wishes should be heard and considered (S.1.03[c]). When the surrogate and patient disagree, the practitioner may use conflict resolution strategies to seek a resolution that satisfies the wishes and interests of both parties.

3. *Myth*: Determining a patient's mental capacity is an "all or nothing" decision. *Reality*: Patients may have different levels of mental capacity for different types of situations or different decisions. Different decisions require different skills and abilities. A person who does not have the capacity to understand the implications of coronary surgery might have the capacity to make decisions about less complicated and less risky issues, for instance, making dietary choices while in the hospital (e.g., a Jewish client asks for Kosher meals). Accordingly, practitioners

[20] The following points deal with 7 of the 10 myths identified by Ganzini et al. The other myths have been explained earlier in this chapter, when the definitions of mental capacity and mental competence were explained.

should conduct a context-specific assessment when determining a patient's mental capacity. Practitioners should consult with supervisors, attorneys, or ethics committees when they are unsure about the parameters of a patient's mental capacity (Ganzini et al., 2005).

4. *Myth*: Cognitive impairment equals lack of mental capacity. *Reality*: Although cognitive impairments may affect mental capacity, the simple fact of having a cognitive impairment does not necessarily mean the patient lacks capacity to provide informed consent (Ganzini et al., 2005). Each patient should be assessed on a case-by-case basis. Consider a woman who has dementia. In the early stages of dementia, the woman may be able to make rational choices, in spite of her impairment. In later stages, her impairment may become so severe that she would lack mental capacity.

5. *Myth*: Lack of mental capacity is a permanent condition. *Reality*: Determining mental capacity is not a one-time event; it requires ongoing assessments. For some people, lack of mental capacity is permanent. For others, it may be temporary or intermittent (Ganzini et al., 2005). The woman with dementia, for instance, may have some good days and some not-so-good days. During the good days, she may have sufficient mental capacity to make decisions. On the other days, she may lack capacity. Capacity may even change over the course of a day. Consider a man whose cognitive functioning is related to when he takes his medication. The medication may make him drowsy for a period of time after taking it, diminishing his mental capacity. After that period, however, his capacity may improve. Some patients have complained that professionals use medication effects to manipulate their assessments of mental capacity—that is, they intentionally assess patients during periods when their mental functioning is diminished so they can impose decisions against the patient's wishes. Ethically, professionals should do whatever they can to enhance a patient's decision-making capacity before assessing the patient's capacity—for instance, putting the patient at ease, giving the client ample time to think and reason, providing the patient with treatments that alleviate the impairments, and meeting the client during a part of the day when the patient is functioning best. If a decision has to be made while the patient is temporarily incapacitated, the practitioners should treat the decision as a temporary decision and return to the patient for informed consent once capacity has returned. These strategies enhance the patients' right to self-determination and informed consent (Ss.1.02 and 1.03).

6. *Myth*: Patients who have not been given relevant and consistent information about their treatment lack mental capacity. *Reality*: As part of the informed consent process, professionals have a responsibility to ensure that patients have sufficient information about their treatment options (Ganzini et al., 2005). In some cases, patients may appear confused or irrational, not because of a problem with mental capacity but rather a problem with the information they have received. Consider a patient who does not understand complex medical or mental health explanations for proposed treatments. If the professionals provide their information in plain language, the patient may be able to make informed, rational decisions.

7. *Myth*: Patients who have been involuntarily committed lack mental capacity. *Reality*: The decision to commit a patient to a mental health facility is based on risk to the client or others, not whether the client has decision-making capacity. Thus, a patient who has been involuntarily committed due to suicidal ideation may still have the capacity to make decisions about the choices of treatment within the facility. Mental incapacity should not be assumed simply because the person has been committed involuntarily (Ganzini et al., 2005).

As this section has highlighted, the complexity of terms such as *mental illness*, *mental capacity*, and *mental competence* may lead to confusion and misunderstandings between professionals as well as between professionals and patients. Social workers may play an important role in clarifying the meanings of these terms. To protect the rights and interests of mental health patients, social workers should be careful about applying appropriate criteria for assessing each patient's mental capacity. They should also be on guard about making assumptions or relying on myths that may lead to inappropriate assessment decisions.

Remember, deciding that a patient lacks mental competence has serious consequences. It means the patient loses the right to make certain decisions on his or her own behalf. In order to empathize with your patients, imagine how you would feel if mental health professionals found you to be mentally incapacitated, or if a court declared you to be mentally incompetent. Would you feel safe and secure, or would you feel at least some elements of anger, frustration, and fear? Imagine also how your feelings might be amplified if you were also experiencing paranoia, hallucinations, forgetfulness, or high levels of anxiety as a result of a mental illness?

Now that we have explored the criteria for determining mental capacity and mental competence, we turn to who makes decisions when a patient is mentally incapacitated or declared mentally incompetent.

SURROGATE DECISION MAKERS AND ADVANCE DIRECTIVES

According Standard 1.03(a) of the NASW Code of Ethics, social workers should provide services to patients on the basis of informed consent (S.1.03[a]). Standard 1.03(c) adds that when clients lack mental capacity, workers should seek permission from an appropriate third party. Unfortunately, the NASW Code does not define what constitutes an "appropriate third party," in part because this is a complex issue and in part because the terminology and criteria may vary from jurisdiction to jurisdiction. This section provides guidance on determining who is an appropriate third party, though you will also need to consult your state laws and agency policies.

Terms such as surrogate, substitute, *or* proxy *are general terms used to describe people who have authority to make decisions on behalf of a person who lacks mental capacity or who has been declared legally incompetent* (Stein, 2004). In situations when there are no court orders or legal documents stating who is to make decisions on the patient's behalf, hospitals, social agencies, and mental health professionals typically rely on the patient's next of kin to act as a surrogate decision maker for the purposes of informed consent to services (Kim et al., 2008). Thus, if a man suffering from Alzheimer's is unable to provide informed consent, a worker might ask the man's wife to give permission on his behalf. If it is clear that the wife is the patient's next of kin and nobody is contesting her position as surrogate, then there is no need for a court order authorizing her status (*In re Quinlan*, 1976). If there is a dispute about who should have decision-making authority,[21] then it may be necessary to go to court for a ruling.[22]

Ideally, patients take precautionary steps to appoint surrogate decision makers in case they become mentally incapacitated. Remember, people cannot appoint surrogates after they have become incapacitated (Kim et al., 2008). Social workers who are working with patients at risk of becoming incapacitated should consider counseling patients about the possibility of appointing a surrogate. Prior to going for surgery, for instance, hospitals ask patients to sign a power of attorney to delegate decision-making authority if there are any emergencies while the person is under anesthetic or otherwise incapacitated. Social workers may provide information and help clients complete power-of-attorney forms (ABA Commission on Law and Aging, 2005). However, if a patient asks for or requires legal advice, the worker should refer the patient to an attorney (Stein, 2004).

A *power of attorney (POA) essentially authorizes one or more people (the attorneys) to act on behalf of the person granting the power of attorney (the grantor)*. A POA may be oral or written, though written POAs are generally preferred because they provide documentary evidence

[21] E.g., a widow who has two adult children contesting who has authority to make medical decisions on her behalf.

[22] The parties could also go to mediation or hire attorneys to help them negotiate a solution without having to go to court (Center for Social Gerontology, n.d.; Quinn, 2005).

of the POA and the specific powers granted to the attorney. Essentially, an attorney acts as an agent or surrogate decision maker for the grantor (Quinn, 2005). Most social agencies, hospitals, and financial institutions will not honor a POA unless it is in writing (Sabatino, n.d.). Different types of POAs provide the attorney with different types of decision-making authority. A financial POA provides the agent with authority to make financial decisions for the grantor (e.g., management of bank accounts, investments, household expenses, financial contracts, and other fiscal decisions). A health-care POA provides the agent with authority to make health-care decisions for the grantor (e.g., providing consent for medical assessments and treatments, hospitalization, surgery, dietary choices, or mental health services). A health-care POA is sometimes called a durable power of attorney because it endures after the person becomes mentally incapacitated (Stein, 2004).[23]

In addition to health-care POAs, people can state their health-care wishes in an advance directive. *An advance directive informs health-care providers about how they wish to be treated under certain circumstances, for instance, if they become mentally incapacitated or become unconscious* (Kim et al., 2008). Different jurisdictions have different laws, different names, and different forms for advance directives (Sabatino, n.d.). One of the more commonly used advance directives is a living will. A living will indicates what types of treatments a patient wants or does not want; for instance, use of artificial ventilation, feeding tubes, blood transfusions, dialysis, cardiopulmonary resuscitation, emergency trauma surgery, or intrusive or heroic measures to save or sustain life (Quinn, 2005).

Some jurisdictions allow for psychiatric advance directives that indicate the types of psychiatric treatment desired by a person in the event of being mentally incapacitated. For instance, the person may state preferences in terms of medication, psychotherapy, housing, and safety precautions. Proponents of psychiatric advance directives suggest that they extend the person's right to self-determination to situations when the person's mental capacity has been diminished. Advance directives may cover a very broad area of medical, psychological, social, and spiritual preferences (e.g., how they want to be treated in relation to religious traditions and rituals, personal grooming and bathing, palliative care, pain management, and having friends or family at their bedside) (Aging With Dignity, n.d.). Advance directives may also foster greater compliance with treatment: When patients indicate their treatment preferences in advance, the patient and family members may be more likely to follow their treatment plans (Kim et al., 2008).

One criticism of psychiatric advance directives is that people may not be able to predict exactly what will happen and what they would really like to happen to them in such events. Consider a woman who says she does not want to receive a particular psychotropic drug because of its side effects. When the time comes to actually make a decision about medication, there may be a new drug that counteracts the side effects of the first. Health-care professionals are not necessarily required to provide certain types of care just because a patient has requested it in an advanced directive (Kim et al., 2007). When a patient's stated wishes in an advanced directive conflict with the patient's interests, social workers and other professionals should consult with their supervisors, ethics committees, or legal counsel in order to review relevant state laws and agency policies, and determine how to proceed (Butler, 2004).

Two alternatives to financial POAs are trusts and co-ownership. *To create a trust, a person designates a trustee who will be responsible for management of the assets designated in the trust* (e.g., specifically identified bank accounts, stocks, land, or other property). The trustee manages the assets in accordance with the wishes expressed by the person in a trust document. *In co-ownership, property is placed in the names of two or more people* (e.g., a joint bank account or a house with joint title). If one of the people becomes incapacitated, the other person can manage the property

---

[23] If a POA does not say that it endures after the person becomes mentally incapacitated, then the POA terminates upon incapacitation or death of the grantor.

as per the co-ownership agreement. Once again, social workers may provide information about different options for financial management but should refer clients for legal or financial planning advice.

As mentioned earlier, courts may become involved in determining who has decision-making authority when a person becomes mentally incapacitated and there is a question or dispute over who has authority (Kim et al., 2008). *Whereas a person may appoint an "attorney" or "proxy" to make decisions, a court appoints a "guardian."*[24] The court may indicate specific roles and areas of decision-making authority for the guardian. *A guardian of the person is granted decision-making authority over health-care, religious, social, and other decisions. A guardian of the estate is granted authority over property and financial decisions. A guardian ad litem is granted authority to act on the person's behalf for the purposes of litigation* (e.g., a civil or family court trial). The courts may appoint a family member, a friend, a nonprofit agency, or a professional[25] to act as a guardian (Quinn, 2005). The advantages of a family member or friend include this individual's intimate knowledge of the person's situation, beliefs, and wishes. Further, family members or friends may be more willing to provide their services for free. The advantages of nonprofit agencies and professional guardians are that they have special training, skills, and expertise (e.g., in handling financial matters). Also, when there has been a high level of conflict among family members, a nonprofit or professional guardian may provide someone they can trust because of their training, objectivity, and lack of prior relationships with all family members (Kroch, 2009).

When conflicts over surrogate decision making or guardianship emerge among patients, family members, or significant others, social workers may refer them to a mediator who specializes in such matters (Center for Social Gerontology, n.d.). Mediation may help them resolve ethical and legal issues without having to incur the time, costs, and aggravation of going to court (Butler, 2004). Mediation may also help them develop creative, individualized solutions and foster more positive ongoing relationships (Abdool, 2007; Quinn, 2005). If the primary patient clearly lacks mental capacity, an attorney or other advocate may represent the patient during mediation. If the patient's mental capacity is in doubt, the patient may participate in mediation with the aid of an attorney or other advocate. The parties may be able to resolve the issue of mental capacity by themselves, or they may agree to refer the patient to a mental health professional for an independent assessment. Social workers may participate in mediation as an advocate for the patient or as a resource that the patient and family members may use for various types of psychosocial support (e.g., providing counseling to help the family adjust to the patient's diminishing mental or physical capacities). Also, when social workers are familiar with legal concepts such as powers of attorney, advance directives, living wills, and trusts, they can help patients and family members understand their options by explaining them in plain language.

CONCLUSION

This chapter has highlighted a range of ethical concerns when working with patients in the field of mental health. Although social workers may find it easy to say they respect the dignity and worth of people with mental health issues, putting respect into practice is not always as simple or trouble-free as one might expect. From the basic decision of whether to ascribe a label of mental illness to a patient, to the complexities of balancing the wishes, needs, and interests of patients and others, social workers should ensure that values and ethical concerns are considered in all their practice decisions. As advocates for people in vulnerable situations, social workers provide an important function by giving voice to the concerns of people with mental illness. Although social workers are important allies for

[24] Terminology for such roles may vary from state to state.

[25] E.g., a lawyer, financial advisor, or social worker, depending on the expertise needed for the particular type of guardianship being granted.

the wishes and needs of their patients, they also recognize that a patient's wishes may come into conflict with the values of safety, social welfare, and social justice. When such conflicts arise, social workers can play vital roles as educators, case managers, problem solvers, facilitators, mediators, and proponents of the highest ethical standards of professional practice.

DISCUSSION QUESTIONS AND EXERCISES

The following questions and exercises are designed to help you apply the information in this chapter to a variety of mental health scenarios.

1. *In Principle*: Select one of the following scenarios and analyze it from the perspectives of the social worker, the patient, and the public. Which ethical principles may be applied to help you decide how to respond?
   a. Assume you have just diagnosed Patricia with bipolar disorder. Patricia refuses help for this disorder. Given your role in the diagnosis, are you compelled to treat Patricia's condition?
   b. Assume your supervisor asks you to change Paul's case records, suggesting that he has a physical disability rather than the mental illness you originally indicated. Your supervisor's rationale for changing the record is that Paul comes from a culture with a strong social stigma toward mental illness, and Paul will likely refuse help unless you refrain from using the language of mental illness. Should you change the records as requested?
   c. Assume you are a psychiatric social worker who has been working with Penny, a patient who lacks mental capacity due to schizophrenia-related delusions. Penny's psychiatrist wants to put the patient on antipsychotic medication, but her closest relative (a son) opposes the use of medication. You believe that Penny will regain mental capacity if she receives the prescribed medication. Should you advocate for use of medication or should you support the son's decision to refuse medication?
   d. Assume you are a street outreach worker who meets Philip, who has been living on the street for 3 weeks. You have offered to help Philip find a safe shelter, but he rejects your help. You believe he refuses help because he is clinically depressed, though not suicidal. Given forecasts for extremely cold weather and a spate of violence against homeless people in the past few weeks, you are concerned about Philip's life if he remains on the street. Should you initiate an involuntary committal?
2. *Mitigating Risks*: For each of the following scenarios, identify the specific type of harm experienced by the patient. In retrospect, what could the social worker have done differently to reduce the risks of such harm?
   a. After conducting a thorough assessment, Sequoia advises Mandy that her son Peter has conduct disorder. Sequoia suggests that Mandy consider cognitive therapy and a special education program for Peter. Mandy does not understand what conduct disorder is, so she trusts Sequoia's judgment and goes along with her recommendations. Months later, Peter says he hates special education and wants to drop out. Mandy feels distraught because she did not ask enough questions before agreeing to Sequoia's advice.
   b. Peggy and Phineas are having marital problems but cannot afford therapy. They ask Sven (a social worker) if he can give one of them a diagnosis of depression so their health insurance will cover the costs of therapy. Sven says this is dishonest and refuses to do so. The couple's marriage deteriorates and they divorce (Hill & Lightfoot, 2009).
   c. For the past 3 years, Portia has been seeing Soledad for counseling. Curious to see what Soladad has been writing in her records, Portia files a request to see

them. Upon reading them, she discovers Soledad thinks she has narcissistic personality disorder. On the way home, Portia becomes so furious that she has a car accident. "It's all Soledad's fault."

3. *State Laws*: Identify and locate the state legislation that governs mental health issues such as involuntary committal of people with mental illnesses, mental health patient bill of rights, surrogate decision makers, and adult decision makers for people who lack capacity or competence to make decisions on their own behalf (see http://www.nasmhpd.org/mental_health_resources.cfm#Other to locate your state's mental health agency's website, which will include links to relevant mental health legislation and plain-language explanations designed for the public).
   a. What criteria does this legislation use to determine whether a person may be involuntarily committed to a mental health facility? What procedural safeguards does this legislation provide to balance patient autonomy (respect for the dignity of the individual) with beneficence (protection of the patient and others)?
   b. Does the legislation permit the individual to make advanced instructions or assign a mental health power of attorney? If yes, then what terminology does the legislation use to describe these advance directives? What does the legislation say about a medical health professional's ability to override such advance directives?
   c. What criteria does a court use to determine whether to appoint a guardian for a person who lacks mental capacity? How does a family member initiate legal proceedings in order to have a guardian appointed?
4. *Myths*: For each of the following scenarios, identify the myth(s) upon which the social worker is relying. Assume you are trying to refute the myth(s). What words would you use to help the worker correct her interpretation of the situation?
   a. Shuman provides psychotherapy to Paula, a patient who suffers panic disorder. During panic attacks, Paula loses her ability to think rationally. Given these panic attacks, Shuman assesses that Paula is mentally incompetent and needs to have a guardian appointed to act on her behalf.
   b. Priti has obsessive-compulsive personality disorder. Her social worker, Sandi recommends that she quit her job as a proofreader for a book publication company because her work is aggravating her disorder. Priti refuses. When writing her progress notes, Sandi states that Priti is "mentally incapacitated because she is unable to make rational decisions about her career."
   c. Patience is a 22-year-old woman recently diagnosed with a mild form of Asperger's syndrome. When Patience asks what Asperger's is, her social worker, Suzette, explains, "Asperger's is a disorder of uncertain nosological validity, characterized by the same kind of qualitative abnormalities of reciprocal social interaction that typify autism, together with a restricted, stereotyped, repetitive repertoire of interests and activities." Although this information (quoted directly from the *DSM*-IV) is correct, Patience does not understand Suzette's explanation. Suzette decides that Patience is mentally incapacitated because she does not understand what Asperger's is and therefore cannot make informed treatment decisions. For the next treatment planning meeting, Suzette invites Patience's parents, but says Patience is too incapacitated to participate.
5. *Application*: Select one of the following scenarios and analyze it by applying the first three stages of the Framework for Managing Ethical Issues, described in the introduction to Part II.
   a. Plato decided to enter a residential addiction program during a family intervention. At the family intervention, various family members told him that he had to go for treatment for his alcoholism or there would be consequences: for instance, his wife would divorce him, his sons would cut off

contact with him, and his best friend would stop lending him money and covering up for him at work. As Plato was detoxifying at the addiction program, he started to become violent. Sandrew, the social worker, tried to de-escalate the situation, but Plato started to yell and break furniture. Nester, a nurse, tried to physically restrain Plato. During the restraint, Plato broke an arm. Plato screamed, "I'll sue, you bastards. First, you drag me into this rat hole against my will. Then, you say I gave informed consent, but I can't. I have an addiction. Now, you jump all over me and break my arm. You'll pay for this!"

b. When Pandora turned 18, her father (an attorney), had her sign a living will, indicating that she did not want to be kept on artificial ventilation or feeding tubes if she was in a persistive vegetative state. Pandora appointed her parents to be her health-care powers of attorney, but she is now 30 and her parents have passed away. Pandora was recently in a car accident and now lies in a hospital, in a persistive vegetative state. Her husband, Hal, informs Sarafina (the social worker) about the living will, but says that the doctors must keep her alive. Pandora is 5 months pregnant. Hal argues that Pandora never considered the possibility that she would be pregnant when the living will was to take effect. Sarafina expresses concern that the hospital could be sued if they do not follow the living will. Also, the doctors do not believe the fetus will survive, even if they keep Pandora on the ventilators and feeding tubes. Hal asks the social worker not to tell the doctors that the living will exists, since it will only complicate matters. Sarafina is conflicted about what to do. In addition to the legal and ethical issues, she has a personal moral conflict. Her Christian religious beliefs tell her that life is sacrosanct. On the other hand, she is a pro-choice feminist who believes that women should be able to have control over decisions affecting their own bodies.

c. Pascale is a 37-year-old male-to-female transgender person who presents as a woman but has not had sex-reassignment surgery. Pascale has applied for admission to a residential program for female survivors of intimate partner abuse. Doris, the program director, suggests that Pascale is not eligible because "she is technically a man, and the female clients in the program would have difficulty feeling safe with a man in the residence and in their therapeutic groups." In addition, there are pragmatic concerns, such as where Pascale would sleep, bathe, and use the toilet because the facility has group dorms for sleeping and shared bathroom facilities for the women. Sonja, who conducted Pascale's intake interview, believes she has a right to service and should not be discriminated against just because of her mental disability, gender identity disorder. This agency is the only one of its kind within 750 miles.

d. The Lacihtenu Drug Company has developed a new medication for hyperactivity, called Calminex. Calminex has not been approved for use in the United States and Lacihtenu wants to test it in Algeria. They ask Sanju, a social worker with expertise in Algerian culture, to help them promote the use of Lacihtenu in Algeria. Traditionally, Algerians have low levels of medication use and Algerian physicians have been reluctant to prescribe psychotropic medications for mental conditions.

6. *Assessing Mental Capacity*: This role-play is designed to help you practice assessing mental capacity. Assign one person to play Sheba and another to play Paris. Sheba works in a facility that provides family planning services. She is concerned that one of her clients, Paris is mentally challenged (low IQ). During the role-play, Paris says she wants a tubal ligation in order to prevent pregnancies. Sheba will offer Paris other options for birth control, including

birth control pills and condoms. Sheba will explain the risks and benefits of each option. Sheba will then use the following questions as a guide to assess Paris's four areas of decision-making competence:[26]

a. ***Ability to choose***
   - Have you made a decision about the intervention options[27] we discussed?

b. ***Ability to understand relevant information***
   - Please tell me in your own words what I've told you about
     - o the nature of your condition
     - o the intervention recommended
     - o the possible risks (or discomforts) of the intervention
     - o other possible interventions that could be used, and their benefits or risks
     - o the possible risks and benefits of no intervention at all
   - We have talked about the chance that X might happen with this intervention. In your own words, can you tell me how likely you think it is that X will happen?
   - What do you think will happen if you choose not to have this intervention?

c. ***Ability to appreciate the situation and its consequences***
   - What is your main concern about your current situation (health issue, psychosocial problem)?
   - Do you believe it is possible that the proposed intervention could help you?
   - Do you believe it is possible that the proposed intervention could harm you?
   - We talked about other possible interventions. Can you tell me, in your own words, what they are?
   - What do you believe will happen if you decide you do not want to have this intervention?

d. ***Ability to reason***
   - Tell me how you reached your decision to have [or not have] this intervention?
   - What things were important to you in making the decision you did?
   - How would you balance those things?

[26] These questions were derived from Appelbaum & Grisso (unpublished), cited in Ganzini et al., 2005, at p. 102.

[27] In this case, the possible interventions are the different birth control options. In other cases, the interventions may include various types of psychotherapy, diagnostic tests, assessment procedures, or medication.

Chapter 14

Child Welfare, Values, and Ethics

The child welfare system comprises a group of governmental and nongovernmental services designed "to promote the well-being of children by ensuring safety, achieving permanency, and strengthening families to successfully care for their children" (Child Welfare Information Gateway, 2008). From a narrow perspective, child welfare includes services designed to protect children from abuse and neglect. More broadly, however, child welfare may include any policy or program designed to improve the opportunities and quality of life for children—from providing better water and sanitation, to safe neighborhoods and playgrounds, to availability of healthy foods, to access to health care, to income support for families who have difficulty meeting the basic needs of their children. Social workers believe children (and all people) have the right to social justice and access to resources to fulfill basic needs (NASW, 1999). Children should not be denied such rights simply because of the socioeconomic class or neighborhood that they were born into (Nuffield Council on Bioethics, 2007).

For social workers practicing in the field of child welfare, value conflicts and ethical issues are pervasive.[1] How to define the welfare of a particular child, for instance, raises issues of

[1] The NASW Code of Ethics makes only two references to children: the duty to report child abuse (S.1.01) and the social worker's obligation to clarify roles when acting as a child custody evaluator (S.1.06[d]). Most provisions in the Code are intended to apply across the life span, rather than having different standards for work with people at different life stages. The NASW has passed policy statements in relation to child abuse and neglect, family policy, family violence, foster care and adoption, physical punishment of children, public child welfare, and temporary assistance for needy families (NASW, 2006). Although some of the policy statements give guidance on ethical issues, they are not generally as well known or consistently applied as the standards in the NASW Code.

who decides and based on what criteria. To what extent should we honor the autonomy of parents and families to define how children should be raised, disciplined, and cared for? At what point is there a child protection concern that is so grave that state intervention is necessary to safeguard a vulnerable child? How can social workers determine what is in the best interests of a child without imposing cultural values and beliefs on families from diverse backgrounds? When parents or guardians disagree on important parenting decisions, who has the right to decide how the child will be raised? At what age do children have the right to make decisions for themselves? The list of issues could go on and on.

Although ethical issues are pervasive, this does not mean that all child welfare cases are fraught with uncertainty. In many cases, rights of children and the ethical obligations of social workers are relatively clear. If a social worker wants to initiate counseling services with a 5-year-old child, for instance, the worker should request consent from the parents. If a worker observes a parent physically abusing a child, the worker has a legal and ethical duty to take steps to protect the child (Strom-Gottfried, 2008). At the very least, the worker should call the police or child protective authorities. In Part I of this textbook, we have already explored how to apply informed consent, confidentiality, the duty to report, and other ethical standards in reasonably straightforward situations. In this chapter, we delve into more complex, less certain situations. What guidelines can we use when there are no clear-cut answers to the ethical issues? What processes can we use to bring people together, when tough choices need to be made and the parties have difficulty agreeing?

This chapter begins by exploring the sources of children's rights and the legal obligations that parents, social workers, and others have toward children. To advocate effectively for the rights of children, workers must understand the specific laws that reflect these rights. Understanding child welfare laws is also critical to ensuring that everyone, social workers included, knows how to comply with the laws. Following laws is not the only requirement for ethical practice; however, even if you believe that there may be ethical justifications for rejecting a particular law, it is important to understand the source of the law. The second section of this chapter delves into the concepts of informed consent and assent as they apply to work with children and adolescents. Although some practitioners believe that parental consent is required for any medical, mental health, or social services, the answer depends on a number of factors (e.g., state laws, mental capacity, and the specific context of the decision). The third section offers different strategies for engaging clients in discussions of ethical issues. In particular, it is helpful to recognize whether differences of opinion are caused by conflicting information or conflicting values and religious beliefs. Whereas informational conflicts can often be resolved through sharing information, workers should not necessarily expect to reach full agreement over conflicting values and religious beliefs. The final section focuses on making difficult decisions in child protection cases. Social workers know that they should prioritize the safety of the child when there is a clear and severe threat to the child's welfare. In cases where the laws or facts are not so clear, however, workers need to be able to make fine distinctions about where to draw the line. Specifically, when should workers impose interventions to protect the welfare of children,

LEARNING OBJECTIVES

Upon successful completion of this chapter, students will be able to

- Identify state, national, and international sources of children's rights and legal obligations toward them.
- Engage parents and children in informed consent and assent processes, taking the mental capacity and legal competence of the children into account.
- Differentiate between worker–client conflicts based on different information and worker–client conflicts based on different values and religious beliefs.
- Use critical thinking strategies to determine how to balance the ethical principles of child protection with respect for the autonomy, self-determination, and privacy of parents and family.

and when should workers stand back and respect the rights of parents and families to autonomy, self-determination, and privacy?

SOURCES OF CHILDREN'S RIGHTS AND LEGAL OBLIGATIONS TOWARD CHILDREN

Sources of children's rights and legal obligations toward them include state laws, federal laws, state and federal constitutions, and international laws.[2] Being able to identify and locate laws and policies that establish children's rights is an important aspect of the critical thinking stage of the Framework for Managing of Ethical Issues (as presented in the introduction to Part II). Although an investigation of relevant laws is just one aspect of ethical analysis, it often provides a useful starting point: that is, what do the laws tell us about how to respond to a particular situation? In many instances, following the law is consistent with ethical practice. However, even in situations when ethical principles and standards are at odds with legal rules, it is important to know and acknowledge the sources of those laws. Simply ignoring the law and having each person decide what is right in a particular circumstance may lead to anarchy (*Olmstead v. United States*, 1928).

States have primary authority for regulating child welfare. Accordingly, social workers should refer to state legislation for matters pertaining to family services, mandatory reporting of child abuse and neglect, foster care, adoption, education, and other child welfare matters. The Child Welfare Information Gateway (n.d.) provides a user-friendly website (http://www.childwelfare.gov/systemwide/laws_policies/state/index.cfm) for identifying state laws governing a broad range of child welfare issues.[3]

You may be asking, "Why do I need to reference a specific state law. Legislation is hard to access and it uses such cumbersome, technical language. Why can't I just reference my social work textbooks, which explain the laws in plain language?" Although your textbooks may include accurate information, they are secondary sources. They may be obsolete because of changes in the law, or they may address general rights and obligations without attending to the specifics. Assume that your textbook says doctors, psychologists, family counselors, social workers, and other professionals have a duty to report child abuse and neglect. This statement is true, but only to a certain point. One limitation of this statement is that it does not specifically define child abuse and neglect. In most states, for instance, child protection statutes explicitly state that emotional abuse is a reportable form of abuse. The statutes in Georgia and Washington, however, do not mention emotional abuse. Similarly, about 18 states include abandonment in their definition of child abuse and neglect. The others do not (Child Welfare Information Gateway, n.d.). These legislative differences could have significant impacts on what types of situations are reportable (Pollack, 2007). Another limitation of the textbook statement is that its list of professionals who are mandated to report is not complete. In some states, clergy are required to report child abuse and neglect. In other states, clergy are not mentioned. In still others, legislation provides clergy with privilege protections, which may limit their ability and obligation to report. Thus, simple statements about American child welfare laws may or may not be accurate for particular states. Rather than rely on secondary sources, identify and read the specific legislation for your state. If you need help identifying or understanding the legislation, ask for assistance from your agency attorney, from a legal librarian, or from another professional with legal training.

State laws are not the only source of children's rights and professional obligations. The federal government has passed many laws that relate to

---

[2] Rights and obligations may also be established by agency policy and professional codes of ethics, as described in Chapter 8. From a legal perspective, state and federal laws take precedence over agency policies. The Preamble to the NASW Code of Ethics, however, indicates that social workers may be placed in an ethical dilemma if their ethical obligations conflict with agency policy or the law.

[3] For another user-friendly gateway, see Smith (n.d.).

child welfare issues. The Child Abuse Prevention and Treatment Act (1974, as amended), for instance, strives to provide national leadership and consistency on how child abuse issues are handled across the country (Polowy & McLeod, 2004). This act provides federal funding for child welfare services and establishes minimum standards that states must incorporate into their child protection legislation. Thus, if a state's definition of abuse does not meet the baseline requirements of the federal law, then workers may advocate for the state to come into compliance with the federal law. States may provide protections above and beyond what is required federally. For instance, the federal law is silent on the issue of whether children observing abuse by one parent against the other is considered to be child abuse. Some states have specifically defined abuse to include observations of abuse between parents, while others have not.

Federal legislation also deals with children's rights in relation to education (No Child Left Behind Act, 2001), health care (Family and Medical Leave Act, 1993), divorce (Family Support Act, 1988), and many other areas. Even though states have primary jurisdiction for legislating in these areas, it is important to check whether there are also federal laws that may apply.

Constitutional laws are the basic or fundamental laws of the land. They establish the powers of government as well as relationships between the government and private individuals. The constitutional laws of each state take precedence over general laws passed by the state legislature (Madden, 2003). That is, state laws must comply with the state constitution or they may be declared unconstitutional and invalid. The U.S. Constitution (http://www.usconstitution.net) takes precedence over both federal and state laws. In child welfare cases, the most important area of constitutional law is likely to be the Citizenship Rights in the 14th Amendment, specifically:

> No State shall make or enforce any law which shall abridge the privileges or immunities of citizens of the United States; nor shall any State deprive any person of life, liberty, or property, without due process of law; nor deny to any person within its jurisdiction the equal protection of the laws.

The implications of this law for child welfare include the following:

- Children may not be deprived of their liberty or freedom without due process.
- Children have a right to equal protection, including freedom from discrimination.
- Children may not be removed from parents without due process (Andrews & Patterson, 1995).

For the most part, current state child welfare laws are consistent with these rights. However, if there are any conflicts, social workers may advocate for the rights of children based on the Constitution.

Children's rights are also established at an international level. The United Nations has developed a series of conventions on the rights of children, the most recent and comprehensive one being the U.N. Convention on the Rights of the Child (1989). This convention establishes a broad range of children's rights, including the rights to know and be cared for by one's parents, the right to freedom of thought and religion, and the right to express views and have them given due weight in decisions affecting the child, taking the child's age and maturity into account. The United States has not ratified this particular convention,[4] though it has ratified prior conventions that commit this country to respecting some the same rights and freedoms. The right to be heard and considered is new to the 1988 convention. It could have profound implications if this right was more broadly accepted in the United States, particularly in relation to health care, education, religion, and child rearing. Although the United States has not ratified the 1988 convention and it is not legally enforceable, social workers and other child advocates may use its principles and proclamations, as United Nations conventions may provide moral suasion (Woll, 2001).

[4] Somalia is the only other country that has not ratified this convention (Cook & Dickens, 2007).

Social workers are used to advocating on the basis of client needs and wishes. While these criteria are important, social workers also need to be able to identify and understand laws pertaining to children's rights and obligations toward them. In some situations, children, parents, social workers, and other parties are represented by attorneys. Attorneys are specifically trained to think and advocate on the basis of rights. By understanding the importance of needs, wishes, and rights, social workers can help to ensure that decisions on ethical issues take all these considerations into account.

INFORMED CONSENT AND ASSENT

Respect for the dignity and worth of all individuals includes respect for the dignity and worth of children. After all, children are thinking, feeling human beings who are deserving of moral status and protections (Beauchamp & Childress, 2009). Many policies and practices, however, treat children differently from adults.[5] Treating children differently is not necessarily morally wrong or unethical. However, it is important to understand and articulate ethical justifications when we do not afford children with the same rights and treatment as adults. In this section, we explore the rights to self-determination and informed consent, including ways in which children may be treated differently from adults.

Standard 1.02 of the NASW Code suggests that clients have a right to self-determination. This right is not limited to adults. As with adults, however, a child's right to self-determination is not an absolute right. There are exceptions, for instance, when the life of the client or others is in danger. Standard 1.03(a) suggests that clients have a right to informed consent. Once again, this right is not limited to adults. Standard 1.03(c) places a critical limitation on informed consent: when a client does not have sufficient decision-making capacity, social workers should obtain consent from an appropriate third party. For children lacking decision-making capacity, the appropriate third party is usually their parents or guardians. Thus, when someone other than the child makes a decision for the child, one of the primary ethical justifications is that the child lacks capacity to provide informed consent.[6] The ethical principle of beneficence suggests that we are justified in making decisions for the good of others, particularly when they are not able to make such decisions on their own behalf. Decision-making capacity (defined further in Chapter 13) basically refers to the person's ability to think, understand, reason, and remember. Although a child's capacity may be related to age, different children have different capacities at different ages (Drotar, 2008). Accordingly, each child's capacity should be assessed on a case-by-case basis: Does the child understand the nature of the problem or situation; does the child understand the treatment or intervention options (including the possibility of doing nothing); does the child understand the benefits and risk of these options; is the child able to make a reasonable assessment of the risks and benefits (Rao & Blake, 2002); and is the child able to make a decision independent from those of his parents, guardians or caretakers?

From a legal perspective, a child's right to self-determination is not solely dependent on the child's mental capacity. In many cases, it is also dependent on a legal definition of the age of majority. The age of majority refers to the age at which an individual is treated as an adult with competency to provide informed consent in all aspects of his or her life. Minors (children under

[5] For instance, children are required to go to school, they may be charged with criminal offenses that do not apply to adults, and they are not afforded the same rights to privacy as adults.

[6] Another justification for requiring parental consent is the notion that parents have a right to care and control over their children, derived in part from 14th Amendment of the U.S. Constitution (1868). Historically, the law treated children as the property of their parents. In the late 19th century, the laws started to recognize children's rights, though tension continues to exist between parental rights and children's rights (Keller-Micheli et al., 2007).

a legally defined age of majority) are deemed to be legally incompetent to provide informed consent, regardless of their mental capacity (Cook & Dickens, 2007). Laws defining age of majority are typically justified on the basis of the need to protect vulnerable children. Many people believe that the legal age of majority is 18 years. Actually, it depends. Although most states define the age of majority as 18, Alabama and Nebraska establish the age of majority as 19. Mississippi and Pennsylvania establish the age of majority at 21 (Keller-Micheli et al., 2007). State laws may also define the age of consent differently for different purposes. For voting, people need to be 18. For driving, different states have different age requirements for learner's permits, restricted (graduated) permits, and full driver's licenses (generally ranging from 15 to 18 years). For sexual intercourse, the ages of consent vary from 14 to 18, depending in part on the age of the partner. For medical, mental health, and social work services, the age of consent varies from state to state and for different types of services. In some situations, parental consent is not required, even for a very young child. Consider an 8-year-old student who falls off the monkey bars in a school playground and scrapes a knee. The child may give consent for the school nurse to provide noninvasive services, such as cleaning the wound and putting on a bandage. The risks of the intervention are low and it is more important for the child to receive immediate attention (to reduce risk of infection and to psychologically console the child) than to require parental consent. For riskier services, particularly in nonemergency situations, the legal age for consent tends to be higher. For consent to abortion, for instance, some jurisdictions require parental consent for children under 18. Other jurisdictions require parental notification, though not necessarily consent, for 16- and 17-year-olds. Some jurisdictions have provisions for going to court to waive parental notification and consent, for instance, if there are concerns that the parents would abuse the child upon notification (Cook & Dickens, 2007).[7]

Social workers should not assume that the question of who gives consent—child or parents—will be divisive or controversial. Ideally, social workers consult both the parents and the child for informed consent. If the parent is the ultimate decision maker, it is still important to seek the child's permission. Not only does seeking the child's permission demonstrate respect for the child (S.1.02) but it also makes the child's cooperation with services more likely. Many social work services require the child's cooperation in order to be effective. The term *assent* refers to permission from clients who lack mental capacity or legal competence to provide informed consent on their own. Thus, the social worker may seek *consent* from the parents, but *assent* from a child who lacks decision-making capacity or legal competence. As noted in Chapter 5, consent may be provided orally or in writing, though written consent is generally preferred for risky procedures (e.g., addiction treatment for a client with alcoholism who needs to go through withdrawal). Assent may also be provided orally or in writing. For a child who is unable to read or write, asking for assent orally may be sufficient. For a child with functional literacy skills, asking for written assent may be used to demonstrate that the child is being given the same respect as the parents. In many cases, both the child and parents agree to services, so there is no dispute or ethical dilemma.

For situations in which a child has mental capacity and legal competence to provide informed consent, social workers are legally permitted to provide services without consulting the parents or asking for their permission. As a practical matter, however, workers should consider the potential benefits and risks of consulting the parents. Once again, there may be no controversy. Even though the child is able to provide consent on her own, she may readily agree to involve her parents in the informed consent

[7] Children may also petition the court to be declared emancipated minors, thus being treated as an adult with the legal competence to provide informed consent. To be declared emancipated, children must prove they are able to be self-sufficient and manage their own affairs (e.g., because they are married, in the armed forces, or economically self-sufficient) (Keller-Micheli, Morgan, Polowy, & Bailey, 2007).

process. For situations in which the child is reluctant to notify the parents about the presenting problem or the request for services, the worker should explore the nature of the reluctance. The child may identify a range of concerns:

- The child may fear her parents will react in an angry or abusive manner (e.g., if they find out their child has been involved in activities that they deem immoral or bad).
- The child may simply be embarrassed and not know how to inform her parents in a constructive manner.
- The family may have cultural taboos about discussing family matters outside the family or speaking with a mental health professional.

The worker should validate the concerns, but also explore the veracity of these risks. The child's concerns may be real, but they may also be exaggerated or distorted. By counseling the child around the risks, a worker may be able to develop a plan that would enable parental notification and consent in a safe manner. The worker may also help the child explore the potential benefits of notifying and consulting the parents:

- By involving parents, the social worker or child may request their emotional, moral, financial, or other support to help the child deal with her concerns.
- By including parents in the social work process, the worker can manage problems from a family systems perspective rather than focusing only on changes that the child can pursue on her own.
- By notifying the parents now, the worker may pre-empt problems that could arise if the parents were initially excluded and later discover the presenting problem or the child's request for services (e.g., parents who become angry at the child or the service provider for not notifying them earlier).

The following scenario illustrates the management of ethical issues that may arise when a child initially refuses parental notification or involvement in services:

> Dawn is a 16-year-old who is seeking services from a reproductive health program. During intake, she tells Syesha (her social worker) that she thinks she has a sexually transmitted infection (STI). She also says she needs absolute privacy, because her parents would ***kill her*** if they found out she was having sex.

As the meeting progresses, Syesha thinks about issues of legal competence and capacity. She knows that state laws permit 16-year-olds to consent to treatment for STIs without parental notification or consent. Thus, Dawn is legally competent to provide consent. To assess for mental capacity, Syesha asks Dawn about her situation to see what she knows about STIs, how they may be diagnosed, and how they may be treated. Dawn is well informed, as she has obtained information over the Internet. They discuss the nature of an examination and testing. Dawn understands that the risks of examination and testing are minimal. She also understands that she will be able to decide upon treatment, if any, once a diagnosis has been confirmed. Syesha assesses that Dawn has sufficient knowledge, understanding, reasoning, and memory to provide consent. Syesha is concerned, however, about Dawn's statement that her parents would kill her if they found out she was having sex.

Rather than assume she knows what Dawn meant, Syesha asks openly, "What did you mean when you said your parents might kill you?" Dawn explains that they would probably yell at her, ground her, or even kick her out of the house. She did not mean that they would literally kill her, but she was afraid of their reactions. Upon exploring these fears further, Dawn expresses strong concerns that her parents might kick her out of the house. Syesha assesses for suspicions of child abuse and neglect and determines that given the current level of risks, the situation is not reportable to protective services. The parents have not abused her in the past and her concerns about abandonment pertain only to her parents finding out she has been having sex. Still, Syesha helps Dawn develop a safety plan, just in case her parents ever do kick her out of the house (e.g., going to certain friends or family who could provide safe shelter). Syesha also helps Dawn explore the possible benefits of informing her parents of her current situation and request for services. Ultimately, Syesha honors Dawn's privacy and self-determination by ensuring that she receives services without notifying the parents of her situation or request.

From an ethical perspective, Syesha is trying to balance the interests of Dawn's autonomy with the parents' concerns for her medical, emotional, moral, and spiritual well-being. Syesha recognizes that Dawn's parents might expect to be notified and involved in her request for services. However, Syesha's primary commitment is to her client, Dawn (S.1.01). Given that Dawn has legal competence and mental capacity, Syesha should respect Dawn's right to self-determination and privacy (S.1.02 and 1.07).

The ethical issues become more difficult if Dawn lives in a state that requires parental notification before providing a minor with treatment for an STI.[8] On the one hand, Dawn still has mental capacity to make an informed decision for herself. She has reflected on her situation and reasonably believes that informing her parents of her situation could have detrimental effects. On the other hand, the agency is not legally permitted to provide services without notifying Dawn's parents. With Dawn's permission, they bring in Syesha's supervisor to help them work through the ethical issues. Together, they identify common goals: to ensure Dawn's physical and emotional health, to respect her privacy, and to promote a positive relationship with her parents. The agency also has concerns about following the law, acting with integrity, and obtaining a solution in a timely manner (i.e., the sooner Dawn is tested and treated, the better). Syesha also notes that the parents have a moral concern that Dawn currently disagrees with: abstaining from sex until she marries.

Dawn, Syesha, and the supervisor brainstorm various options:

- Having Dawn notify her parents.
- Having the agency notify her parents.
- Providing services without parental notification (and risk consequences for violating the law, including criminal charges and a possible lawsuit from the parents).
- Referring Dawn to an attorney to help her initiate court proceedings to seek approval for services without parental notification.
- Reporting the situation to child protective services, given fears of abandonment and the need for urgent medical services.
- Sending Dawn to a different facility where she could lie about her age and receive services.
- Escorting Dawn to a jurisdiction that permits minors to obtain treatment for STIs without parental notification.

As they go through the options, none of them seems completely satisfactory. Each satisfies some goals but not others. The supervisor decides to use gentle persuasion to encourage Dawn to allow the agency to notify her parents. The supervisor justifies her use of persuasion because the law requires parental notification. At the same time, the supervisor engages Dawn in problem solving to try to minimize the concerns she has about notifying her parents. As they discuss options for notifying the parents, Dawn notes that she is more concerned about her father's reaction than her mother's. After further discussion, Dawn agrees that Syesha will call her mother and they will have a joint meeting to discuss Dawn's situation. At the meeting, they will gauge her mother's response before deciding upon the next steps. In the best-case scenario, Dawn's mother will be supportive and consent to services without raising concerns of abuse or abandonment. If abuse or abandonment concerns arise, they may need to make use of their safety plan and contact child protective services. Dawn admits she feels some pressure to agree to notify her mother. However, she says she feels satisfied with the plans and validated by her input into the decisions. Syesha acknowledges that the decision was not easy, but some decision had to be made.

When working with children, social workers should consider both the legal age of consent

---

[8] Most states permit any minor to consent to treatment for STIs. Although some states require parental notification, many of these states have provisions to waive notification in certain circumstances (Keller-Micheli et al., 2007).

and mental capacity, taking the context of the decision into account. In cases where children are not legally competent to provide consent, workers should still explain their proposed interventions and seek their assent. Ethical issues may arise when parents and children disagree about services, or when children request services but do not want the agency to notify the parents or ask for their consent (Strom-Gottfried, 2008). Social workers should explore various options and make use of conflict resolution processes to see whether a solution can be reached by consensus. When consensus cannot be reached, social workers should consult their supervisors, ethics committees, or attorneys to help them work through the legal and ethical considerations. Social workers should also consider whether the parents and children should have separate social workers or advocates to support them through the ethical decision-making process.

MANAGING CONFLICTING VIEWS: INFORMATION VERSUS VALUES AND RELIGIOUS BELIEFS

During work with families, social workers may encounter conflicting views at various levels: The social worker and the clients may disagree, the parents may disagree with the children, and the two parents may disagree with one another.[9] To resolve ethical conflicts based on conflicting views, it may be useful to identify the nature of the conflicting views. In some cases, the conflicts are based on differences in information. In other cases, the conflicts are based on differences in values or religious beliefs. As the following scenario illustrates, different conflict resolution strategies may be useful depending on the nature of the conflicting views.

> Mary and Felix bring their 11-year-old child, Dora, for counseling concerning gender issues. Dora describes herself as a boy who is trapped in a girl's body. Upon further assessment, Samantha (a licensed clinical social worker who specializes in gender issues) confirms that Dora is female-to-male transgender (Holman & Goldberg, 2006). Dora wants to start going to school dressed as a boy and be identified as "Denzel." Felix says he wants to support Dora, but he has strong reservations about supporting her desire to make changes to her gender expression. Mary completely rejects any plans that encourage Dora to identify as a boy. She says Dora is just confused and simply needs therapy to help accept herself as a girl.

As Samantha thinks about the ethical issues raised by this situation, she begins by reflecting on her own disposition. She notes that her values and beliefs ally with Dora's.[10] Both believe that a person should be allowed to express gender identity as he or she wishes. They also believe that transgenderism is not an issue that can be cured by therapy aimed at having the person accept the body he or she was born into (de Vries, Cohen-Kettenis, & Delemarre-Van De Waal, 2006). Although Samantha's values and beliefs ally with Dora's, Samantha reminds herself that she owes her ethical commitment to the whole family, as the entire family is her client (S.1.01). Accordingly, Samantha should not impose her values or beliefs on the parents, even if she thinks this is in Dora's best interests.

Giving clients access to information is not the same as imposing values or beliefs. In fact, providing clients with access to information may help them enhance their right to self-determination, as they will be able to make better-informed choices. Samantha offers to provide Mary and Felix with information about transgenderism, including research and articles on the types of interventions that are helpful or unhelpful for

---

[9] Conflicts between social workers, between social workers and their agencies, and between workers from different agencies are discussed in other chapters.

[10] This analysis refers to Dora rather than Denzel because the client is still deciding when she wants to make the transformation to a male identity. Social workers should respect a client's wishes about how to be identified.

transgendered clients (Holman & Goldberg, 2006; Israel, Gorcheva, Walther, Sulzner, & Cohen, 2008). She also provides them with information about groups for friends and family of transgendered or questioning people. Felix is pleased to receive this information. Although he questions what is the right way to respond to Dora's gender concerns, his questions are based primarily on his lack of knowledge: What causes transgenderism; is it the parents' fault; and does transgenderism mean that Dora needs surgery to add a penis (Holman & Goldberg, 2006)? He finds it difficult to accept that his child may have been born in the wrong body. However, discussing transgenderism with Samantha and other families going through similar concerns helps him see things from Dora's perspective.

Mary says she does not care what the research or other families say: Dora is a girl and that is all there is to know. She quotes Deuteronomy 22:5:

> A woman shall not wear anything that pertains to a man, nor shall a man put on a woman's garment; for whoever does these things is an abomination to the Lord your God.

When Samantha hears this quotation, her first inclination is to debate it. How could wearing different clothes be an abomination to God? And doesn't God want people to live a happy life, rather than one filled with secrecy, depression, and shame? Pausing to reflect, Samantha realizes that Mary's concerns about transgenderism are not related to misinformation or lack of information, but to her value for the authority of God and the Bible. She knows that debating Mary about the meaning of Deuteronomy or her other religious beliefs would be unethical and counterproductive. Samantha validates Mary's beliefs, acknowledging, "It must be very difficult to hear Dora say that she wants to dress as a man. It goes against some of your most basic beliefs." Samantha does not expect Mary to fully accept Dora's gender identity and desire to live her life as a man. Mary may change some of her values and beliefs over time, but it is important for Samantha to begin where the client is. By validating Mary's beliefs, Samantha builds trust with her.

Mary, Felix, and Dora still need to decide how to respond to Dora's gender concerns. There is no universally correct answer. For some families, the best course of action is to help the transgender child start making the transition to cross-living as soon as possible. For others, the best course is to delay making any decision or transition until the child is older, perhaps as an adult. Samantha engages the family in a discussion about the pros and cons of different courses of action. Dora says she is ready to start making the transition now because she wants to be honest and open about her gender. She says this is crucial to being able to accept herself. They discuss the pragmatics of coming out, including the teasing and discrimination she may face in school, church, and the broader community (Holman & Goldberg, 2006). Mary threatens to disown Dora if she ever came home dressed like a man. Samantha realizes that if the family feels forced to make decisions today, Dora might leave home or be kicked out. Samantha may even need to call child protective services. Samantha reminds the family that they do not have to make decisions right away. They can take more time. Sometimes, clients or workers feel a sense of urgency in resolving ethical conflicts when there is no real need for a quick decision. By slowing down the decision making, Samantha reduces tensions and avoids a crisis.

As Samantha continues to work with the family, she is careful about imposing values or beliefs. Samantha tries to help the family within their own religious belief systems. She offers to conduct a joint meeting with the family and their pastor.

Prior to the joint meeting, Samantha speaks with the pastor to ensure that they have a common understanding of the purpose of the meeting and what will make the meeting as constructive as possible. The pastor agrees to provide spiritual and religious guidance, as well as information about ways that other families have managed similar issues. For instance, some families have allowed their child to cross-dress in private, but not in public situations. This gives the family a chance to determine for itself if the child's gender concerns are just a passing stage or a more enduring condition. This also provides family members with time to get used to having a family member who is transgender before coming out of the closet (i.e., disclosing the child's gender identity to others).

In some cases, the main ethical issues may be resolved at a particular point in time. In this case, the ethical issues are ongoing. At one point, Mary insists that Dora needs reparative therapy, that is, therapy aimed at helping Dora accept herself as female. Samantha validates Mary's desire for a therapy that can resolve Dora's gender concerns. Samantha moves on to explain how reparative therapy can be detrimental to Dora (de Vries et al., 2006) and that it has been rejected by all of the national associations representing the mental health professions (National Association of Social Workers, 2006). Mary says that if Samantha will not help them with reparative therapy, then she will find someone else who can. Samantha reflects back Mary's frustration to demonstrate empathy. She offers to refer Mary and her family to other professionals if they would like a second opinion or help from a different practitioner (S.2.06[a]). She says she cannot refer them to a reparative therapist because, as a professional social worker, she cannot condone or support any therapy that is exploitative and harmful (S.6.04; Steigerwald & Janson, 2003). Mary walks out in anger. Samantha advises Dora and Felix that she can continue to work with them, or she can refer them for other forms of support should they so desire.

This case illustrates how ethical issues based on differences in values and religious beliefs can be particularly difficult to manage. Social workers may validate the values and beliefs of their clients to try to build trust and problem solve in a collaborative manner. Slowing the pace for decision making may be instrumental in bringing everyone to joint understandings and solutions. In some cases, however, solutions by consensus are not possible. Although social workers should strive to facilitate client self-determination, social workers may need to place limits on it in order to protect children from harm.

CHILD ABUSE AND NEGLECT—DRAWING THE LINE

Each state's child welfare laws require social workers and other mandated professionals to report suspicions of child abuse or neglect to the appropriate state authorities (i.e., child protective services and/or the police). The laws mandate child protection workers (CPWs) to investigate the reports within a certain time period. If the child is in need of protection, the CPW is mandated to ensure the child's welfare and safety (Pollack, 2007). In some respects, the ethical principles regarding child protection issues are relatively straightforward: *Although social workers respect the privacy and autonomy of families, the interests of protecting children from abuse and neglect take precedence.* Thus, client confidentiality may be abridged when it is necessary to report suspicions of child abuse or neglect (S.107[c]). Reporting child abuse and neglect not only protects the child suspected of being abused, but also other vulnerable children (Filinson, McCreadie, Askham, & Mathew, 2008). Further, CPWs may abridge self-determination for parents and families when it is necessary to protect children from abuse or neglect. For instance, CPWs may initiate legal proceedings to remove a child from parental care when it is necessary to protect the child from abuse or neglect (Caplan, 2006).

While the legal rules and ethical principles are relatively straightforward, putting them into practice may require social workers to draw lines and make fine distinctions. In some cases, the decisions are fairly easy. A social worker observes a client beating a child with an electric cord, causing bruises. This is clearly abuse, so the worker should not have difficulty deciding to report it. Likewise, a CPW has tried working with a family on a voluntary basis for 3 months, but the parents continue to leave a 6-year-old at home without supervision for extended periods of time. The worker is clearly justified in imposing conditions to ensure that the child has adequate supervision. In other cases, the decisions are not so clear-cut. A worker observes a client belittling her son, calling him stupid every time he does something wrong. The worker wonders whether the client's behavior is reportable as emotional abuse. Likewise, a CPW is working with a mother who is doing the best she can, but still has trouble caring for her children due to her depression. The children's welfare is at some risk, but separating them from their mother may be more harmful than helpful. This section offers guidance regarding how and where to draw the line when making difficult decisions about child protection concerns. In particular, workers should consider how to deal with decision-making challenges related to imprecise laws, personal and institutional attitudes, and predictive uncertainty.

Imprecise Laws

When determining how to respond to a child protection issue, referring to the relevant laws provides some guidance. As mentioned earlier, each state provides its own definition of what is reportable as a child protection issue. For instance, some jurisdictions define physical abuse as "the knowing use of force on a child that is likely to cause great harm or death" (Kalichman, 1999, p. 23). Others define physical abuse as "any nonaccidental physical injury to the child" (Child Welfare Information Gateway, 2007, p. 2). Clearly, this definition includes intentionally striking, kicking, burning, or biting the child and causing significant physical impairment or wounds. This definition would not include accidentally tripping a child, even though the child is hurt by the accident. Further, this definition would not include play-fighting with a child when the child is not put at any significant risk of injury. No state prohibits corporal punishment (hitting a child for the purposes of discipline), provided the force is reasonable or not excessive. But how do mandated reporters determine the difference between "reasonable" and "unreasonable" force, or between "excessive" and "nonexcessive" force? Regardless of how well the law defines what is reportable, there is bound to be some vagueness or ambiguity (Arad-Davidzon & Benbenishty, 2007; Polowy & McLeod, 2004). Laws are created to cover a broad range of circumstances, but it is impossible to cover every specific circumstance that may arise (Kalichman, 1999).

Consider, for instance, a child who has facial scars. When the worker asks the parents about the cause of the scars, they explain that they were part of a cultural rite of passage into adulthood (Hansen, 1998). The parents intentionally caused the scarring, so it seems to fit the legal definition of physical abuse. On the other hand, the scarring has a value within the culture and it is not threatening the life of the child. One of the questions left to the social worker is, "How serious must the harm be in order for it to be reportable as abuse?"

When in doubt, consult. You may discuss the case within your agency, particularly with your supervisor, agency attorney, or other persons designated for such purposes. You may also consult with child protective services without disclosing identifying information about the child or family. Protective services can help you determine where to draw the line between what is reportable and what is not. If the situation is reportable, you may then provide protective services with identifying information.

From a legal perspective, social workers may discharge their duties to report by contacting protection authorities whenever there is a reasonable suspicion[11] to report (Pollack, 2007). The worker does not need to prove that there was maltreatment or risk of future maltreatment. Protective services are responsible for determining whether the reported suspicions require further intervention. Social workers who want to ensure compliance with reporting laws may decide to err on the side of caution. In other words, to protect against liability for failure to report, workers may report situations that they do not think they are required to report, but which fall close enough to the line of reportability to

[11] Different states use different language in their legislation to describe when reporting is required. For instance, some states require "reason to believe" there has been child abuse or neglect, whereas others require "having reasonable cause to suspect." In spite of these legal standards for reporting, some social workers and other helping professionals refuse to report suspicions of child maltreatment unless they are reasonably sure that maltreatment is occurring. Although many helping professionals believe that reporting child maltreatment will hurt their working relationship with clients, research shows that reporting does not necessarily have a negative impact. In fact, the honesty and concern demonstrated through reporting could have a positive impact (Kalichman, 1999).

warrant a report, just in case. State and federal child welfare legislation provides immunity from civil or criminal liability for workers who report child maltreatment as long as their reports are made in good faith (Kanani, Regehr, & Bernstein, 2002; Kalichman, 1999).[12]

In some situations, the source of ambiguity is a conflict in the laws. Consider, for instance, a social worker who is hired by an attorney to conduct a forensic family evaluation for a client who is involved in a child custody lawsuit. During the evaluation, the worker determines that the client has neglected the child by failing to provide adequate health care when the child has been sick. The general child welfare laws suggest that the worker must report the client to protective services. However, laws pertaining to attorney–client privilege suggest that when attorneys hire other professionals to work on a case, their work is also covered by attorney–client privilege (Hall, 2006). So, is the social worker required to report child neglect as per the general child welfare laws, or is the worker bound to maintain the client's confidentiality as per the attorney–client work-product privilege rules? Ideally, the worker's contract with the attorney and client includes an exception for reporting child protection issues (Dixon & Dixon, 2006). If the attorney and client have agreed to this exception, then the worker clearly has authority to report the neglect. If not, the worker may need to consult an independent attorney for advice on how to handle such a case. Some jurisdictions have laws that specifically exempt reporting child protection concerns from the rules of attorney–client privilege. In other jurisdictions, the laws are not so clear. Ethically, the protection of vulnerable children should take precedence over confidentiality (Dixon & Dixon, 2006), although it may be worth exploring options that may satisfy both legal and ethical obligations (e.g., by seeking consent to report from the attorney and client).

Given the ambiguities and complexities of the law, it is no wonder that social workers know they are supposed to report child abuse and neglect, but may be confused about what this means in practice (Brown, 2006). Training, supervision, and consulting are key to helping social workers learn when the duty to report is triggered, and what legal considerations need to be taken into account.

Personal and Institutional Attitudes

Child maltreatment is a socially constructed concept. Different people have different understandings of what constitutes maltreatment, above and beyond what is defined by law (D'Cruz, 2004). Accordingly, assessments of maltreatment risks may be easily swayed by attitudes. *An attitude is a predisposition or way of thinking about a particular situation.*[13] Although we might like to think of ourselves as open-minded, critical decision makers, attitudes can affect our ability to evaluate ethical issues in an unbiased, rational manner. Attitudes may be specific to individual social workers or pervasive within a social agency. This section explores how attitudes may affect decision making in child protection cases. By raising awareness of such attitudes, you can help yourself and others make more deliberate choices about how to respond to ethical issues (Paul & Elder, 2006).

When faced with questions of how to respond to child protection concerns, CPWs and other social workers are called upon to use their discretion. Consider a CPW who is determining whether to remove a child from a home due to sexual abuse by the mother's boyfriend. The simple fact that abuse has occurred does not mean that the child should be withdrawn from the home. If the CPW determines that the mother

---

[12] Social workers may be civilly and criminally liable for failure to report child abuse or neglect (Kalichman, 1999). Also, CPWs may be held liable for failure to protect a child who has been reported to child protection services or is under their care (Alexander & Alexander, 1995). Liability for failure to report varies from state to state (Polowy & McLeod, 2004).

[13] The differences between attitudes, values, beliefs, feelings, and convictions are discussed further in the introduction to Part I.

can and will adequately protect the child from further abuse, then the CPW may decide the child can remain in the home. Unfortunately, different CPWs might make different decisions based on the same situation, in part, because they come into the process with different attitudes. A CPW who is predisposed to thinking that no good mother could allow her child to be sexually abused may be less inclined to work toward a solution that keeps the child living at home. A CPW who is predisposed to thinking that foster care is a lousy alternative may be more inclined to support a solution that keeps the mother and child together. In other words, the CPW's assessment of the right course of action is affected by pre-existing attitudes (Arad-Davidzon & Benbenishty, 2007).

Although social workers are legally required to report child maltreatment, surveys indicate that approximately one-third of social workers have had at least one instance of maltreatment which they decided not to report (Kalichman, 1999). Workers may decline to report maltreatment for a variety of reasons (Besharov & Laumann, 1996; Pollack, 2007). Some believe they need to protect client confidentiality to preserve the therapeutic relationship and that they can help the client more by not reporting the abuse (Gushwa & Chance, 2008). Others believe that reporting will serve no purpose because CPWs are already overburdened, ineffective, or unable to prioritize any cases but the most serious ones (Strozier, Brown, Fennell, Hardee, & Vogel, 2005). Ethically, however, workers should report abuse even when they have concerns about how helpful a response they will receive from the child protection system. If a worker has concerns that a CPW may not properly investigate a report, the worker should follow up with the CPW or a supervisor. If the problems are systemic, then the worker should advocate for better resources or other changes to correct the problems (Gushwa & Chance, 2008; NASW, 1999, S.6.04[c]).

Agency attitudes toward child maltreatment may be reflected formally in agency policies or informally through the agency's implicit culture (Fry, 1981). Consider, for instance, a child protection agency whose policy states, "We believe the best home for children is one with their biological parents and families." This policy encourages CPWs to do whatever they can to keep biological families together and to return children to their biological families as soon as possible. Its emphasis on keeping families together, however, may bias the CPWs' assessment of risks. CPWs may tend to underestimate the risks of returning a child to a family where maltreatment has occurred, given the agency's focus on family reunification. Thus, a policy that has an ethical purpose (respecting the family unit) could lead to harmful results (further child maltreatment). Agency policies and attitudes may change over time, sometimes emphasizing maintenance of the family unit and sometimes emphasizing protection of children from harm. Assessing risks of maltreatment and weighing them with the risks and benefits of removing the child from the home is an imprecise science. Accordingly, it would be unreasonable to expect perfect assessments all the time. We could ask, however, if there are going to be errors from time, is better to err on the side of *keeping families together* or *keeping children safe* from maltreatment by their parents? Once we have determined a priority of risks, we could then ask protection agencies to make use of more objective, evidence-based risk assessments, rather than relying on predispositions or other biases (Kindler, 2008).

The foregoing example illustrates agency attitudes that are formalized in policy. Agency attitudes may also be reflected in the implicit culture of an agency. Consider, for instance, an adoption agency that has a tradition of matching children with adoptive parents of the same race. Attitudes of racial matching may persist even if new state laws and agency policies prohibit race from being considered. Supervisors and frontline workers may collude to continue to match adoptive parents by race. CPWs who oppose the practice of racial matching may find it difficult to go against agency policy. They may also find it hard to blow the whistle on those who are flouting the nondiscrimination law (Greene & Latting, 2004). Whether racial matching is ethical is a dilemma that could be debated both ways. Still, adoption and other child protection decisions should be based on honest discussions with full disclosure of reasons. Such decisions should not be based on unspoken attitudes that percolate below the radar.

Acting on the basis of predispositions or attitudes may be risky, as attitudes do not necessarily reflect what is right or ethical in a particular situation. Accordingly, it is useful to identify and deconstruct the attitudes that may be affecting our responses to ethical issues. Discussing attitudes may be particularly useful in supervisory meetings, though discussing attitudes may also be appropriate in other meetings where ethical issues are under consideration. Strategies for discussing attitudes include

- Creating a safe environment by acknowledging that everyone has attitudes and it is useful to explore the basis of these attitudes.
- Obtaining consensus on ground rules, such as "All attitudes should be discussed, regardless of whether they are popular," and "Everyone will show respect for one another, regardless of whether they share similar attitudes."
- Identifying attitudes that may be affecting analysis of child protection issues.
- Deconstructing attitudes by exploring the life experiences, values, beliefs, convictions, and feelings that may underlie particular attitudes.
- Identifying which life experiences, values, beliefs, convictions, and feelings are relevant to the decisions to be made, and which are extraneous.

To illustrate the deconstruction of attitudes, consider a supervision meeting in which the field instructor, Fanya, is helping a social work student, Sue, assess the risks of returning a child home to parents who have a long history of alcoholism. The parents have just completed a 3-month treatment program. The program reports both parents have maintained their abstinence and are doing well with their recovery. Still, Sue suggests that the risks of returning the child home are too high. Fanya asks Sue if she would be open to discussing her general views of parents with alcoholism, noting that different people have different mind-sets about this issue. Sue wonders where Fanya is going with this conversation, but trusts Fanya from past supervisory experiences and agrees to discuss her views. Fanya asks about past experiences with alcoholism in families. Sue says her best friend in high school had an alcoholic father. Her friend's mother would kick him out when he became too abusive, but allow him back in every time he came home promising he would change. Sue recalls feeling disgust toward her friend's father for all the chaos and violence he had inflicted on the family. By exploring her experiences, Sue begins to see how she has developed a belief that parents with alcoholism cannot change and cannot be trusted when they say they have changed. Fanya helps Sue consider whether attitudes developed from past experiences are biasing her assessment of risk in the current clients' situation. Fanya acknowledges that it is important to consider the risks that the parents will relapse. Still, child protection risks are different for different families; they should be evaluated on a case-by-case basis. Fanya helps Sue identify criteria that she can use for a more objective, evidence-based risk assessment (D'Andrade, Austin, & Benton, 2008). The decision still depends on weighing the interests of family preservation and protecting the children from harm. By raising Sue's awareness of her experiences, feelings, and dispositions, however, Fanya and Sue are in a better position to assess these interests on the basis of critical thinking rather than pre-existing attitudes.

Predictive Uncertainty

Ethical decision making in child protection cases may be complicated by predictive uncertainty (Levenson & Morin, 2006). *Predictive uncertainty refers to the challenges of accurately predicting child protection risks.* If we do not know the precise likelihood of a child's being abused in the future, then how can we make informed decisions on how to manage the ethical principles of "safeguarding vulnerable children" while "respecting the dignity and worth of the parents and family"? Consider the following scenario:

> Marsha and Fez have recently separated. They have a 7-year-old daughter, Dani. Marsha asked Fez to leave because she thought he was having an affair. Their

interim[14] court order states that Dani's primary residence is with Marsha, and Dani will spend alternate weekends with Fez. Marsha calls child protective services to report suspicions of child sexual abuse. When the CPW, Shivaun, asks why she suspects abuse, Marsha claims she found pornographic images of men with young girls on Fez's old computer. Marsha says she cannot allow Dani to be alone with her father because she thinks he is a pedophile.

If Fez poses a significant risk of abusing Dani, then Shivaun's legal and ethical duties are clear: She is mandated to use the least intrusive means to ensure Dani's safety. Unfortunately, Shivaun has very limited information about the actual risks. She has heard allegations from a former spouse, who may have reported her suspicions in good faith or may be acting out of spite or other inappropriate motivations. Because of the serious nature of the allegations, Shivaun needs to gather further information to make a proper assessment. Assume she meets individually with each family member. Fez denies all of Shivaun's allegations. He sounds honest and sincere, but Shivaun is still not certain about his sexual proclivities. Marsha presents her allegations in an honest and sincere manner. Her only concrete evidence is the computer, which has pornographic images saved on its hard drive. Marsha cannot prove whether Fez, Marsha, or someone else downloaded the images. In an initial screening assessment, Dani shows no signs of sexual abuse, though Shivaun still needs to be concerned about future abuse. Ethically, Shivaun knows that she must balance the interests of Dani's safety with the interests of respecting Fez's autonomy, dignity, and worth. For Fez, the consequences of treating him as an abuser are high. Shivaun suggests supervised visitation until Fez completes a full psychological workup. Fez contends that supervised access is unnecessary and harmful. How will his daughter feel about being able to see her father only in the presence of a supervisor?[15] Further, validating Marsha's allegations will only encourage her to make more false allegations in the future. Fez also says his reputation will be tarnished when family, friends, and neighbors find out that he cannot see his daughter by himself. His employers may also find out or be suspicious when he has to take time off work to go for a psychological evaluation. Thus, even a decision to restrict visitation on a temporary basis can have significant impacts on Fez and Dani.

Child protection workers cannot predict child abuse with 100% certainty. Accordingly, they need to make decisions based upon imperfect information (Levenson & Morin, 2006). One method of managing predictive uncertainty is to weigh the risks in terms of severity and probability (U.S. Department of Health and Human Services, 2007). In other words, when determining whether the safety of a child should take precedence over autonomy, self-determination, privacy, or other parental interests,[16] CPWs should take both the severity and the probability of the harm into account.

- *Severity Principle*: CPWs should tend toward protecting safety when the severity of the possible harm is high. CPWs should tend toward protecting parental autonomy, when the severity of the possible harm is low. Thus, when CPWs are concerned that a parent might kill a child, limiting parental autonomy in favor of protecting a child is easily justified. If a CPW is concerned that the parents' use of corporal punishment embarrasses a child but does not

[14] Temporary, or pending further, more permanent orders of the court.

[15] The worker should also consider the potential long-term effects of forcing a father to make use of supervised access if the mother is making her allegations out of spite. The worker's actions may encourage the mother to continue to make false allegations in the future, hurting the father and children (Eddy, 2003).

[16] To simplify the discussion, the rest of the analysis will refer to principle of protecting the parent's autonomy, though the worker could be concerned with protecting additional parental interests, including privacy, dignity, and self-worth.

leave serious scars (emotional or physical), favoring parental autonomy over child protection may be ethically justified.

- *Probability Principle*: CPWs should tend toward protecting safety when the probability of harm is high. They should tend toward respecting parental autonomy when the probability of harm is low. Thus, if the probability of abuse is high (e.g., 70% to 100% chance), the CPW has better ethical justification for limiting parental autonomy than if the probability is low (e.g., 0% to 30% chance).

Probabilities of risk must be weighed in relation to severity of harm. When the severity and probability of harm are both high, then a decision to prioritize safety is relatively easy. Similarly, when the severity and probability of harm are both low, then a decision to prioritize autonomy is relatively easy. Determining priorities is ethically more difficult when severity and probability fall into the middle ground. Likewise, determining priorities is more difficult when severity is high, but risk is low, or vice versa. In some cases, ongoing monitoring leads to different assessments of risks and different needs for involuntary intervention at different points in time (Fry, 1981).

The severity and probability principles may seem intuitive or obvious. However, we should not assume that CPWs are automatically applying these principles. CPWs and their supervisors should articulate the severity and probability of harm in their deliberations over how to respond to child protection concerns. They may use actuarial assessment tools to help them determine risks (Levenson & Morin, 2006). Although risk-assessment tools have their limitations in terms of predictive ability, the ethical standards of competence and integrity suggest that CPWs should use the best assessment tools and processes that are available (Ss.1.04; 5.01[a]). It is difficult, if not impossible, for CPWs to make all risk-assessment decisions solely on the basis of objective measures. Still, CPWs should be able to articulate and document why they are assessing risks in a particular manner, as the basis for how they are balancing the interests of child protection and parental autonomy. Even if the risk is low, there is still a risk that the child may be harmed (Banks, 2006). In the event that a child is actually harmed, CPWs are in a better position to justify their decisions if they have documented their risk assessments.

As the foregoing analysis demonstrates, the principles of probability and severity are useful for determining which ethical principles to prioritize. A third factor comes into play when looking at protection issues from a legal perspective: evidence. CPWs should be able to substantiate maltreatment, or risks of maltreatment, within their agencies and possibly in court. The information that social workers might ordinarily gather and rely upon for clinical purposes may not stand up in court as reliable, credible evidence. In Shivaun's case, assume she assesses Fez and believes he has pedophilic tendencies. Given her assessment, it might be ethical for Shivaun to propose supervised visitation. However, if the case went to court, she might have difficulty proving supervised visitation is needed. Thus, Shivaun may need to back down on what she thinks is ethically appropriate if Fez challenges her position and she is unable to prove her case in court.

The foregoing sections illustrate how ambiguous laws, agency and institutional attitudes, and predictive uncertainty may raise challenges to the ethical decision-making processes of CPWs and other social workers. Although this chapter focuses on child protection issues, similar issues may arise in other contexts of practice. Consider, for instance, a probation officer who is trying to determine the risk of a client re-offending, or a social worker who is deciding whether to commit a suicidal patient to a mental health facility. The first step in dealing with challenges to effective ethical decision making is identifying the nature of the challenge. Once you identify the nature of the challenges to ethical decision making, you can work on strategies for managing them.

CONCLUSION

Given the vulnerability of children regarding exploitation and other forms of maltreatment, social workers have an ethical obligation to promote the welfare of children and protect them from harm (NASW Code of Ethics, 1999,

Preamble; S.6.04[b]). This obligation may come into conflict with other ethical obligations, including those regarding self-determination, informed consent, and privacy (Ss.1.02, 1.03, 1.07[c]). Although the NASW Code of Ethics and state child protection laws direct social workers to give priority to the protection of children, the issues and conflicts are not always so black and white. At what point, for instance, do children have sufficient mental capacity to provide informed consent? Even if they lack mental capacity, how can social workers respect client self-determination and the right to have a voice, as much as possible? How do social workers draw the line between parenting practices that are questionable but still within the parent's right to choose, and parenting practices that cross the line into abuse or neglect? How should social workers balance their obligations to parents and children when their goals or wishes are in conflict? Social workers may use ethical standards, agency policy, and laws as the starting point for making difficult decisions. However, they may also need to use supervision, consultation, evidence-based assessment tools, and sophisticated clinical judgments to assess risks, explore options, and determine the best courses of action.

While social workers aspire to the highest standards of practice, they should also remember that they are not expected to be perfect. As noted in Chapter 9, social workers may be held liable for malpractice (professional negligence) if they do not abide by the standards of practice reasonably expected of a prudent professional with a similar background. Assume that a social worker does not identify a child–client as having a learning disorder and the child fails a grade in school. If a reasonable social worker, acting prudently, would have diagnosed the disorder, then the worker may be liable to compensate the client for damages (e.g., loss of one year's wages due to falling behind in school). In child protection situations, social workers may have limited immunity from lawsuits (Alexander, 1993; Rothschild & Pollack, 2008). For instance, workers who report child abuse are protected from being sued, provided that they have made the reports in good faith. Also, CPWs who remove a child from home are protected from liability, provided once again that the removal was made in good faith. Laws that provide legal immunity are meant to encourage social workers to err on the side of protecting children from harm (Legal Defense Fund, 2007).[17] Still, social workers should use their best clinical and ethical judgments to maximize client autonomy, self-determination, informed consent, and confidentiality, while still protecting the safety and welfare of children.

DISCUSSION QUESTIONS AND EXERCISES

The first exercise asks you apply the doctrine of parmountcy, helping you understand which law, policy, or ethical obligation should be prioritized in cases where these rules and guidelines conflict. The second exercise is designed to provide you with an opportunity to apply the concepts of *consent* and *assent* when working with minors. Exercises 3 to 6 give you an opportunity to work through the various stages of the Framework for Managing Ethics Issues (Figure II.1) for cases involving children. Exercise 7 invites you to critique and redraft the confidentiality standards in the NASW Code of Ethics.

1. *Paramountcy:* In each of the following hypothetical situations, identify which law, policy, or ethical obligation is paramount in the event of a conflict between them. Explain why you believe that law, policy, or ethical obligation is paramount.
   a. State law says that the age of consent to have an abortion is 18. The policy of a clinic that provides abortions says they will not require parental consent for 16- or 17-year-olds.
   b. A family mediation code of ethics says mediators should remain neutral concerning the parents' wishes and plans for parenting after divorce. State laws say

[17] Social workers may be sued for failure to protect children from harm (Alexander, 1993).

that mediators should help parents make decisions based on the best interests of the children.

c. The U.S. Constitution says that people cannot be deprived of life, liberty, or property, without due process of law. Federal law (the Patriot Act) authorizes the FBI to conduct "sneak and peak" searches without obtaining a warrant. This law has been used to permit searches of school lockers, particularly for foreign-born students suspected of being terrorists.

d. The United Nations Convention on the Rights of the Child says children have a right to preserve their identity and family relations. State law permits closed adoption processes, in which adopted children will have no contact with their biological families.

2. *Consent and Assent*: For each of the following scenarios, identify how you would go about obtaining consent and/or assent to the proposed services or intervention plans. Provide your rationale, making reference to the NASW Code of Ethics and your state's laws.

   a. Simba is mediating a divorce between Misty and Fred. They agree that their daughter, Dorothy (aged 14), will live primarily with Misty. When Simba meets with Dorothy, she explains that she does not want to live with her mother. She says she will just run away to live with her father, regardless of what her parents agree. Dorothy's reasoning seems immature, as she is more concerned about punishing her mother for the divorce than deciding which parent can provide her with the better home environment.

   b. Salim provides outreach services for street youth. He encounters Damien (16 years old) who says he has been on the streets and involved in prostitution for the past 10 months, ever since his parents threw him out of the house. He says he's happy living on the streets and has no intention of ever seeing his parents again. He refuses to provide his last name or any other identifying information. When Salim offers to teach him harm reduction techniques that he can use to reduce risks when he is prostituting, Damien says, "I might be interested. You won't try to contact my parents, will you?"

   c. Daphne is 12. Her parents brought her to a therapeutic residential program for girls with weight and eating problems. Although Daphne has not formally been diagnosed with an eating disorder, her weight is in the 5th percentile for her age and her doctor considers her at high risk for anorexia. When Sofia explains the program in plain language, Daphne's parents provide consent. Daphne rejects services. Daphne seems to understand the nature of the services, but presents as sad and unmotivated.

   d. Drusilla is 13. After a science class on the reproductive systems of different animals, Drusilla confides in her teacher that she has never talked to her parents or any other adults about sex, menstruation, or dating. She says that her parents come from an ethnocultural background in which sex is simply not discussed. The school offers human sexuality education, but her parents have refused consent for Drusilla to attend the classes. The teacher refers Drusilla to the school social worker. School policy suggests that parental consent is required for any counseling pertaining to human sexuality. Drusilla tells the school social worker that she is too embarrassed to ask her parents for consent and she would rather forgo counseling than have to talk to her parents about sex.

3. *Managing Issues*: Use the first three stages of the Framework for Managing Ethical Issues (Figure II.1) to analyze the following cases. For Stage 3, use at least two different approaches to critical thinking (e.g., deontology, teleology, virtue ethics, ethics of caring, religious ethics, humanistic ethics). Identify whether any of the challenges to effective decision making relate to imprecise laws, personal and agency attitudes, or predictive uncertainty. If so, apply the

strategies (discussed earlier in this chapter) for dealing with such challenges.

a. Diego (14) has been having terrible nightmares, so his parents take him to see Sonia for psychotherapy. Sonia uses hypnotherapy, which helps Diego recover memories of sexual abuse by his parents. Sonia encourages Diego to report his parents to child protective services. After a thorough investigation, protective services say the allegations are unsubstantiated. The parents sue Sonia for malpractice, claiming she put the false memories into Diego's head. The parents claim damages for emotional distress, family discord, and public embarrassment. Without Sonia's knowledge, Diego met with the press and described how his parents abused him.
b. Manya and her 7-year old daughter, Dulcie are seeing Sarit for counseling to improve their relationship. During the fourth session, Sarit discovers that Manya does not have legal custody of Dulcie. Floyd (Manya's former husband) has custody. Sarit informs Manya that she needs to contact Floyd for his permission to counsel Dulcie. Manya asks Sarit not to contact Floyd, as he could use this confidential information against her in upcoming custody proceedings. Manya also asks Sarit to advise Dulcie not to tell her father anything about the counseling because it is a private, secret matter between her and her mother.
c. Mona, Fergus, and their 16-year-old son, Don, are seeing Seth (a social worker) to help them communicate more effectively. Don is not very verbal with his parents or with Seth. During counseling, Mona and Fergus say they allow Don and his friends to have parties and drink alcohol in their basement. They say they would rather have Don and his friends at home, where they can monitor them, rather than have the teens out on the streets, in bars, or other dangerous places where they could get into more trouble. By hosting the parties, they can ensure that Don and his friends do not overdo the alcohol or switch to illicit drugs. When Seth asks whether they are concerned about the reactions of the friends' parents, they say they have talked with the parents and have received their oral permission to allow them to drink—as long as nobody drives home. Seth's initial feeling is that these parents are crazy: How could they condone alcohol abuse in their children? Seth does not share his feelings with the parents, but says he has to consult his supervisor about whether this situation needs to be reported to child protective services.
d. Delilah is a 17-year-old who self-identifies as lesbian. She is in the process of being admitted into a group home for youth who have had conflicts with the law. She had trouble in her prior group home, as others harassed and picked fights with her for the ways she dressed and acted. Pablo, the group home's program director, suggests that Delilah should try to "pass" as heterosexual. The social worker, Stockard, responds, "Would you ask a fair-skinned African American youth to try to pass as a White person in order to avoid being beaten up?" Delilah's parents think she should try to pass as straight until she is independent and can live on her own, but the group home has temporary guardianship of Delilah.
e. The state's Safe Haven Act says that a mother who has a baby can voluntarily surrender the baby to the care of a hospital within 7 days of the child's birth. The hospital will take care of the baby, and hospital staff will not try to force or coerce the mother into answering any questions. The mother will not be subject to any negative consequences for surrendering her baby as long as the child has not been abused. The law requires all instances of abuse to be reported to child protective services. In one case, when Mildred drops off her baby (Dreyson), the social worker Sinead

immediately notices that the child has bruise marks, indicating possible abuse. Sinead meets her field instructor, Frank, to discuss whether to report Mildred for abuse. Sinead believes that Dreyson will quickly recover from the bruises and nobody needs to know about the possibility of abuse. Sinead believes this mother did the right thing by turning the baby over to the hospital and should not be punished. Besides, if they report this mother to child protective services, it will send the message to other mothers that this facility is not a safe haven where they can take a newborn who needs alternate care.

f. Dionne (5) was born with severe physical and cognitive disabilities. She cannot talk, walk, sit up, or use her hands. She is completely dependent on her parents, Melanie and Ferris, for feeding, bathing, moving, and all the necessities of life. Melanie and Ferris have consulted their doctors about growth attenuation strategies—medical and surgical processes to stop her growth and development, including use of growth-stunting medication and removal of her uterus and breast buds (Terry & Campbell, 2008).[18] These strategies can be used to make it easier for the parents to care for Dionne as she grows older. Also, by preventing her from going through puberty, they may be lessening the chances of sexual abuse should she need to be placed in an institution. The request for growth attenuation goes before a hospital ethics committee. Melanie's primary physician, Dr. Philips, supports the parents' right to make medical decisions on her behalf. Scarlett, a social worker, believes that removing Melanie's uterus and breast buds is an affront to women. On the other hand, she empathizes with the parents' challenges in taking care of Melanie. Nomi, a nurse, believes that people with disabilities need to be protected from procedures that disrespect their right to dignity and worth, just to make things more convenient for the parents or other caretakers. Lucia, a lawyer, fears legal liability, particularly if advocates for the rights of the disabled receive information about this case.

4. *Manage Conflict*: Select one of the scenarios in Exercise 3 as the basis for a role-play exercise. Assign members of your group to role-play each of the practitioners and clients involved in the case. Identify whether the primary conflicts are related to differences in information, values, or religious beliefs. The person role-playing the social worker should develop a strategy for conflict resolution based upon the type of conflict and the parties' goals for the meeting.[19]
5. *Plan and Implement*: The Department of Children and Families (DCF) is concerned about the incidence and severity of child obesity across the state. To determine how to balance the rights of families to autonomy and privacy with the state's obligation to protect children from harm, DCF conducted public ethics discussions with community members. The discussions led to consensus that the state should not try to prohibit families from allowing their children to eat candy, drink sugary sodas, or munch on starchy and greasy fast foods. Ordinarily, parents should be treated as best judges of their children's diets. However, obesity significantly affects both quality of life and life expectancy. Applying John Mills' ethical analysis of personal liberty versus protection of lives, they decided to develop a program that permits DCF to "advise, instruct, and persuade" parents to help their children make healthy eating choices, without

[18] This scenario is based on Ashley's case, a situation in which the hospital did comply with the parents' wishes. In spite of this result, the ethical issues raised by this case are very controversial and may be decided differently depending on who is involved in the decision making.

[19] Refer to Chapter 7 for additional information on conflict resolution.

trying to coerce them (Nuffield Council on Bioethics, 2007). Your task is to develop and recommend plans for a program that implements this decision. Identify specific strategies that fit with the decision to "advise, instruct, and persuade" but do not cross over into "coercing" parents and families. Consult the research on obesity prevention programs to ensure that your recommendations are ethically sound and evidence-based.

6. *Evaluate and Follow Up*: Dana (13) tells her social worker, Stewart, that she has joined the Demonlicans. Stewart believes this is a dangerous cult group and engages Dana in a discussion about advising her parents so they can help her separate from this group. Dana threatens to terminate services and commit suicide unless Stewart agrees not to inform her parents. Reluctantly, Stewart agrees, hoping that by continuing to work with Dana, he can ensure her safety. Stewart believes that by prioritizing Dana's right to self-determination and confidentiality now, he will be in a better position to safeguard her life and welfare in the longer term. He does not sense that she is at high risk for self-harm, as she has no plans for suicide or other dangerous activities. Before their next meeting, Dana kills herself as part of a suicide pact with the Demonlicans. Dana's parents sue Stewart and the agency for malpractice. The agency settles out of court, admitting liability and agreeing to a generous compensation package. The agency decides to evaluate what has happened and determine whether any additional follow-up plans are needed. Evaluate the ethical issues raised by this case and identify what types of follow-up by the agency may be useful.
7. *Confidentiality Critique*: Standard 1.07 of NASW Code of Ethics suggests that it is important to maintain confidentiality, but then lists many exceptions concerning the protection of vulnerable people and promotion of the public good. Some social workers believe that the ethic of confidentiality is based on an individualistic view of private versus public interests that does not adequately take communitarian interests into account (Clark, 2006). What are the advantages and disadvantages of the NASW Code's approach to defining confidentiality and its limits? Assume that you are developing an ethics code for an ethnocultural group such as a Native American community that values communitarianism over individualism. Re-draft Standard 1.07 from a communitarian perspective (Walker, 2002). In particular, how would issues of child maltreatment be handled from a communitarian perspective?

Chapter 15

Criminal Justice, Values, and Ethics

Ethical issues are endemic to the criminal justice system. From a policy perspective, legislators determine which types of activities should be considered right and lawful, and which types of activities should be considered wrong and unlawful (Roberts & Springer, 2007). When there is broad consensus on the morality of certain acts, then the ethical issues are relatively easy to resolve. The vast majority of society, for instance, would agree that murder and theft are immoral and should be deemed crimes. Society is more conflicted over other acts, such as whether euthanasia, possession of marijuana, or procuring an abortion are immoral and should be deemed crimes. In addition to determining which acts should be unlawful, legislators must also decide the appropriate consequences for people who break the law. Should the focus of the consequences be punishment, retribution, deterrence, compensation, restitution, rehabilitation, or restoration (Gelman & Pollack, 2007; Gumz, 2004)? If the focus is punishment and deterrence, on what basis do legislators determine whether to use incarceration, fines, probation, or some other means? How can the ethical principles of social justice, autonomy and freedom, beneficence (promoting good), and nonmaleficence (not causing harm) be factored into the analysis?

From an organizational perspective, courts, police, probation officers, and other components of the criminal justice system determine how to enforce the laws. For instance, should police be permitted to do ethnic profiling in order to focus their resources on communities where crime tends to be highest? Can ethnic profiling be justified on the basis of utilitarianism (using resources efficiently, for the greatest good), or does ethnic profiling offend ethical principles such as equality, respect, and social justice? Should social service agencies in the private sector accept clients who are mandated into treatment, or should they only admit clients based on voluntary informed consent? What types of professional backgrounds and training should corrections offices require when hiring new probation officers? Should they require a master's degree in social work, or can people without professional training perform the services of a probation officer in an ethical and competent manner (Scheurell, 1983)?

From a clinical perspective, social workers have to determine how to balance the interests of autonomy, respect, privacy, and public safety, given the unique contexts of each client they serve (Roberts & Springer, 2007; Scheurell, 1983). Consider a social worker who is asked to prepare a presentencing report for a client who has been convicted of armed robbery. The worker discovers that the client comes from a background marked by poverty, physical abuse, and discrimination. How does the worker manage her responsibilities to the court and society with her obligations to the client as a member of a vulnerable population? Consider also a client serving time for pimping. During counseling, the client tells his prison-based social worker about an international prostitution ring. He asks the worker not to say anything to law enforcement authorities or his life will be endangered "by the mob." How should the worker manage the interests of the client's privacy and personal safety versus the interests of the criminal justice system in prosecuting those responsible for the prostitution ring? The list of issues could go on and on.

Rather than try to cover the full spectrum of ethical issues within the criminal justice system, this chapter focuses on five topics: *(1)* how professional role affects the practitioner's ethical responsibilities; *(2)* how to manage ethical obligations to maintain confidentiality when served with a subpoena to testify in court; *(3)* how to maximize client rights to informed consent, self-determination, and confidentiality when working with involuntary clients; *(4)* how to determine whether and how to persuade a survivor of violent crime to press charges and cooperate with law enforcement officials; and *(5)* how to analyze the ethicality of using civil disobedience to pursue a social cause. One tension that cuts across all of these topics is the potential conflict between the social worker's roles as "an agent of social change" and "an agent of social control" (Burman, 2004; Specht & Courtney, 1994). As agents of social change, social workers promote the values of client autonomy, privacy, respect for the dignity and worth of all people, and social justice. As agents of social control, social workers promote the values of protection, accountability, retributive justice, and the rule of law. How social workers manage these tensions depends on a number of factors: the worker's role, the agency's mandate, the nature of the client, and the legal context governing the worker, agency, and client. Ideally, workers can find solutions that minimize the conflicts among their roles, promoting good for both the client and society. In situations when the conflicts cannot be fully resolved, social workers may need to make difficult decisions about whose interests to prioritize and how to minimize the risks to clients and society (Dolgoff et al., 2009).

LEARNING OBJECTIVES

Upon successful completion of this chapter, students will be able to

- Compare and contrast how helping professionals with different roles may apply the concepts of autonomy, privacy, safety, and justice when working with clients who may have violated criminal laws.
- Determine how to respond to subpoenas, taking into account the principles of confidentiality, privilege, informed consent, integrity, competence, and respect for the rule of law.
- Enhance the rights of involuntary clients to informed consent, self-determination, and confidentiality while taking into account agency mandates and professional roles.
- Determine the ethicality of encouraging survivors of violent crime to cooperate with law enforcement officials who are interested in charging and convicting the perpetrator.
- Evaluate the ethical implications of a decision to pursue a social cause through the use of civil disobedience.

PROFESSIONAL ROLES

If you asked helping professionals from various backgrounds whether their professions valued autonomy, safety, privacy, and justice, you would probably find broad consensus in support of these values. In other words, social work does not have sole ownership over values such as autonomy and the principles behind client self-determination, confidentiality, and informed consent. Likewise, criminal court judges and other law enforcement officials are not so focused on protection of the public that they ignore the rights to autonomy and privacy (International Association of Chiefs of Police, n.d.). Yet, in spite of shared values across the professions, there are significant differences in the priorities that different professionals give these values. There are also significant differences in the ethical obligations of these professionals. This section explores how different professionals may make different ethical judgments based on differences in their professional roles and codes of ethics. Social workers may be proud of their values and ethics. However, they should be careful not to judge other professions as having *deficient* values or ethics. Having different values and approaches to ethical situations may be justified by the different roles and responsibilities assumed by each profession.

To illustrate how various professionals might manage an ethical dilemma, consider the following case.

> Curt is a 22-year-old college student who was approached on the street one evening by Harold, a homeless person asking for money to buy something to eat. Without thinking, Curt pulled out a knife and stabbed Harold to death. Nobody saw them and Curt threw the knife into a river to get rid of the only evidence that could be linked to him. Curt is not sure what he should do next. He contemplates seeking help from an expert, but he is not sure from whom—his pastor,[1] a lawyer, a social worker, or a psychiatrist.[2]

Curt has some sense of the different roles played by a pastor, a lawyer, a social worker, and a psychiatrist, including why he might seek help from each. However, like most members of the general public, he does not fully appreciate the differences in their ethical obligations, particularly in terms of their obligations to maintain confidentiality and to protect others from harm. His fate, however, could be markedly affected by his choice of which professional he chooses to speak with first.

Assume that Curt decides to go to his pastor, the Reverend Goodly, to confess his sins[3] and ask for moral guidance. The Reverend Goodly does not define his role or explain confidentiality to Curt, as this is not the custom in their church.[4] Like most of the Reverend Goodly's parishioners, Curt has grown up in the church and feels he can trust the pastor with confessions or other potentially embarrassing information. He does not need the pastor to explain his role and responsibilities. The Reverend Goodly encourages Curt to share his concerns. Curt says he murdered a homeless person. The Reverend Goodly invites Curt to describe what happened in greater detail. Curt describes the events without any signs of emotion: no sadness, no excitement, no fear, and no remorse. The Reverend Goodly thanks Curt for coming to him and agrees to help Curt repent for his sins. He encourages Curt to go to the police and turn himself in, explaining that he needs to take responsibility for his actions (Annenberg Media, 1988). Curt refuses, saying

---

[1] This illustration will use the terms *pastor* and *clergy* interchangeably and could refer to a priest, minister, rabbi, imam, or other clergyperson. Different faith organizations may have different expectations and rules of conduct for their clergy, though the general tension between ethical principles will be similar for pastors of various faiths.

[2] The format of this case analysis is derived from a video by Annenberg Media (1988), though the case facts and parts of the ethical analysis have been changed.

[3] In this scenario, Curt is Protestant, so there is no formal, sacramental confession as in the Catholic Church. Still, parishioners of various faiths may confess their sins in order to receive religious guidance, if not forgiveness and absolution.

[4] Kane (2006) suggests that clergy should adopt ethical standards similar to those of social work and the mental health professions. By explaining the nature of confidentiality and its exceptions, for instance, clergy may be able to pre-empt ethical dilemmas and permit parishioners to make informed decisions about what information to share.

that he wants to clear his conscience, but he does not want to spend the rest of his life in jail. Curt asks if the pastor plans on turning him into the police. The Reverend Goodly explains that he will honor Curt's right to come to him in confidence, so he will not report Curt to the police or anyone else (Kane, 2006).[5] Curt thanks the pastor and says he needs to talk to others before deciding what to do.

Curt decides to meet with a criminal defense lawyer, Lana. When Curt begins to explain he might have murdered someone, Lana stops him so she can explain her professional role and ethical obligations. She notes that anything he tells her will be held in strict confidence: Under the legal doctrine of attorney–client privilege, she cannot be compelled in court to testify against her client (Bernstein & Hartsell, 2004). Curt seems pleased with this, as he wants to talk to someone he can trust. Lana explains that, should she agree to take his case, her role is to be a zealous advocate in his defense (American Bar Association, 2003). Lana cautions Curt, however, that she also has ethical obligations to the court and the system of justice. She cannot intentionally mislead the court or present false evidence (American Bar Association, 2006a, Rule 3.3). In other words, if Curt tells Lana that he committed a murder or some other crime, she could not put him on the stand and have him lie. Simlarlly, she could not knowingly put another person on the stand to lie on his behalf. Curt is much more dubious at this point, asking, "What good is it for me to tell you the truth if it means that you can't defend me, as you say, in a *zealous* fashion?" Lana advises Curt that he has a right to know what she can and cannot do so he can make informed decisions about what to tell her. Lana explains that she encourages her clients to provide her with full, truthful disclosure so that she can be as helpful an advocate as possible. If he does not share certain information or provides misinformation, she will have difficulty advising him. She notes that even if a client says he killed someone, this does not mean that there was a murder. She also notes that the prosecuting attorney must prove each element of the offense in order to convict a person—for murder, this includes the act of causing death and the intent to kill (American Bar Association, 2006a, Rule 3.1). Lana suggests that there are many ways she can advocate on his behalf, even if he tells her that he killed someone. After further discussion, Curt says he will have to think about what he wants to do and then get back to Lana. Lana suggests that thinking is good. Lana warns him against talking to others, particularly friends or the police, until he has had a chance to receive proper legal advice. Curt is too embarrassed to admit that he has already spoken with his pastor.

Curt ignores Lana's advice about talking to others and seeks the help of a social worker, Sipora. Before Curt begins to describe his situation, Sipora starts to explain confidentiality. Curt interrupts, saying his lawyer already explained confidentiality. Sipora explains that social workers and lawyers have different rules about confidentiality. Although both professions respect a client's right to confidentiality, they have different ethical obligations and legal protections. Sipora explains that she may need to report information to the authorities if there is a child protection concern or the life of the client or another person is threatened (NASW, Ss.1.01; 1.07[c]). Curt asks about a situation in which someone has already died. Sipora explains that this situation is a bit more complicated. She notes that social workers do not have a general obligation to report past crimes, though different agencies and different social workers have different policies about how to deal with such issues. She explains that her policy is not to report past crimes. She believes people need confidentiality in order to

[5] Historically, some clergy believed that their obligation to maintain the confidentiality of their parishioners was absolute. When Catholic priests received sacramental confession, for instance, they would not divulge confidences, even for child abuse or risks of serious bodily harm. Since the 1980s, the Catholic Church has been confronted for covering up child sexual abuse scandals. Given public and internal concerns about child abuse, there has been a movement for clergy to take a similar stance to that of mental health professionals concerning confidentiality and the duties to report child abuse and risks of future harm (Kane, 2006).

have a safe place to talk to helping professionals (S.1.07). She notes that it is not an easy choice because a crime may have been committed and the authorities will want to know about it. Curt asks, "So whatever I tell you will stay between you and me?" Sipora explains that she will try her best to honor his confidentiality, but there are exceptions, such as if she were subpoenaed. Even though she will not initiate contact with the police, it is possible that she could be ordered by the court to testify about information that Curt shares with her (Barsky & Gould, 2002). Sipora explains that state laws provide a special privilege to licensed clinical social workers and mental health professionals, but she is not licensed, so privilege cannot be guaranteed (*Jaffee v. Redmond*, 1996). Curt says he better find one of those licensed mental health professionals.

Curt meets Percy, a psychiatrist. Before Curt starts to tell his story, he asks Percy if he is licensed and if communications with him are privileged. Percy says he is licensed and yes, there is a state law that says he cannot be compelled as a witness to testify against his clients. Curt inquires, "Does that mean that a client could tell you that he committed a crime and you would not turn him into the police?" Percy explains that his response would depend on the situation, including the seriousness of the crime. Curt says he just talked to a social worker who said she would not call the police, so why would a psychiatrist? Percy notes that psychiatrists, social workers, and mental health professionals have similar ethical standards regarding confidentiality and the duty to report. They all have the duty to report or protect others when clients may cause serious harm to themselves or others (American Psychiatric Association, 2006, Section 4, Annotation 8; Quattrocchi & Schopp, 2005; *Tarasoff v. Regents*, 1976). In terms of past crimes, there is no general duty to report, but different mental health professionals and different agencies have different policies on this matter. Percy explains that he reserves the right to use his discretion to report past crimes. He describes how he tries to work with clients on a voluntary basis, but there may be rare instances when he has to report a client to the police without the client's consent. Curt is not sure whether to disclose any further information to Percy, so he says he needs to talk to his lawyer first. Percy validates Curt's decision to speak with a lawyer, noting that he can talk to the lawyer with full confidence. Once Curt receives legal advice about all his options, he can decide whether he wants to see Percy or any other helping professionals.

This abbreviated story begins to illustrate the differences and similarities between the roles and ethical obligations of four professions. All four value client privacy and protection of the public, though they balance these values in different ways. As a defense attorney, Lana prioritizes her client's right to privacy and confidentiality, even when she knows her clients have committed serious crimes. Lawyers believe clients have a right to legal representation to defend themselves in criminal court, and strict confidentiality is vital to encouraging clients to seek legal advice. Defense lawyers know that their role is to defend their clients as vigorously as possible (Saltzman & Furman, 1999). They trust judges and the prosecution to ensure that society is protected and justice is done. Although critics might charge that defense lawyers are amoral, they believe that their role needs to be understood in the whole context of the criminal justice system. If the system did not include others who focused upon protection of the public, defense lawyers could not justify their roles as zealous, unwavering advocates for their clients (Annenberg Media, 1988).

Although clergy, social workers, and psychiatrists also value confidentiality and protection of the public, they may give these ethical principles different priorities in different contexts. From a legal perspective, clergy, social workers, and other mental health professionals need to consider local laws regarding confidentiality and privilege. Whereas communications with lawyers have absolute privilege, the laws and how they have been interpreted vary from state to state.[6] If a particular type of practitioner (e.g., addictions

[6] Also, privilege depends on the particular venue for a hearing. Different laws may apply for state courts, federal courts, congressional hearings, or other legal processes.

counselors working in a licensed treatment center) has privilege, then those practitioners can advise clients that they cannot be compelled to testify in court. If the laws do not specifically grant privilege, then a court may decide not to compel a practitioner to testify in order to protect confidentiality (*Jaffee v. Redmond,* 1996); however, the practitioner cannot guarantee this. Unless the law specifically grants privilege, there is a chance that the practitioner could be compelled to testify (Rosenbaum, Warnken, & Grudzinskas, 2003).

Reporting past crimes to authorities is different from the issue of testifying. Practitioners and agencies should analyze how they plan to balance their obligations to the client (respect, confidentiality, and self-determination) with their obligations to the victim and society (justice, accountability, and protection of the public). Assume Sipora works in an agency that does outreach to clients who are underserved and do not ordinarily come to social workers on their own (e.g., because they are involved in illegal activities and are not sure whether they can trust social services to maintain confidentiality). Because of the agency's mandate and the nature of its clientele, it may have decided not to report past crimes in order to facilitate engagement of clients (Burman, 2004). If Sipora worked for an agency where most of the clients are law abiding and they initiate services on their own, the agency might have opted for a policy that permitted reporting past crimes. Because different practitioners and different agencies have different policies on whether to report past crimes (particularly serious crimes such as murder and sexual assault), practitioners should explain their particular policies when they are explaining confidentiality and its exceptions to their clients.

Note how tweaking the facts could lead to different responses by the various professionals. For instance, if Curt told Lori that he planned to commit a murder rather than reporting a past murder, Lori would have a duty to protect, for instance, by warning the potential victim or ensuring that Curt received immediate crisis intervention counseling in a mental health facility. Although attorney–client privilege prevents an attorney from testifying against a client, the principle of protection becomes paramount when there is the relatively certain risk of future harm, such as killing or substantial bodily injury (American Bar Association, 2006a, Rule 1.06[b]). Similarly, the obligations change if the past crime is considered treason. Whereas social workers and other professionals do not have a general obligation to report past crimes, all people have a legal duty to report acts of treason to law enforcement authorities (Misprision of Treason, 18 U.S.C. 2382). Thus, if Curt admitted he killed the president of the United States, Sipora would be legally obliged to report Curt for an act of treason. Given the complexities of the rules of confidentiality and privilege, consult with your supervisor and attorney whenever a difficult question arises. The legal and ethical issues may turn on the specific facts and context of the case.

RESPONDING TO SUBPOENAS

When explaining confidentiality to clients, social workers often explain that one of the exceptions to confidentiality is when they are "otherwise required by law" to disclose information. This catch-all phrase includes situations in which a social worker is subpoenaed. When a social worker receives a subpoena, the worker is required by law to appear before court[7] at a particular place and time to provide testimony.[8] The subpoena may also require the worker to bring relevant case records and documents to enter into evidence at the hearing (Polowy et al., 2005; Saltzman & Furman, 1999). This section explores various ways of trying to thwart disclosure of confidential client information at trials. Be warned: Many of these approaches are

[7] Or another form of legal hearing, such as a congressional hearing. For some hearings, a subpoena-like document may have a different name, for instance, a "notice to attend."

[8] The worker, agency, or client may challenge the legal basis for the subpoena, as described later (Polowy et al., 2005).

illegal and unethical. To illustrate, consider the following scenario.

> Sydnee counsels survivors of intimate partner abuse. One of her clients, Collette, left her abusive partner, Otis, and is staying with friends in an undisclosed location. Collette has brought charges against Otis for aggravated assault. Sydnee receives a call from Leroy, who says he is Otis's lawyer and that he wants to talk to Sydnee about Collette's situation. Sydnee responds politely, saying her agency has a strict policy about confidentiality and she cannot even confirm or deny whether a particular person is a client. Leroy issues a subpoena, requiring Sydnee to appear in court with regard to the criminal charges against Otis.

Sydnee fears that if she has to testify, she may be required to divulge embarrassing information about Collette. Collette has had problems with emotional instability, erratic behavior, and questionable life choices. Wanting to protect Collette's right to confidentiality, Sydnee considers various ways of thwarting disclosure. Fortunately, she decides to consult her supervisor and the agency's attorney for support and advice:

- Ignoring the subpoena—The attorney advises Sydnee that ignoring a subpoena is like an ostrich putting its head in the sand. Sydnee can pretend there is no problem, but the problem does not go away. If she does not appear in court, the judge may find her in contempt of court. Punishment for contempt could include incarceration.
- Altering or shredding client files—Ordinarily, social workers may change or destroy client files as long as they do so within the parameters of agency policy and standards of practice expected for their context of practice. In fact, some professionals working with survivors of intimate partner abuse intentionally keep limited records to help protect client confidentiality in the event of a subpoena. If, for instance, Sydnee's supervisor was reviewing Collette's case file before the subpoena, the supervisor could legally and ethically ask Sydnee to rewrite some of her progress notes to focus only on clinically necessary information and to remove extraneous information. However, once Sydnee receives the subpoena, it is illegal to alter or shred her records. She could be held liable for obstruction of justice (Barsky & Gould, 2002; Doyle, 2007).
- Separate official records from personal notes—Sydnee thinks that her private, handwritten notes about Collette do not need to be submitted to court because they do not form part of the client's official case records. This belief is inaccurate. All of Sydnee's private notes and official records are subject to subpoena. She could be subject to contempt of court charges for lying, for instance, by falsely telling the court that the official file contains all her notes (Doyle, 2007).
- Selective memory—Sydnee wonders whether she could testify regarding information that helps her client, but tell the court she does not remember if she is asked for information that could be embarrassing to Collette. Although Sydnee could get away with this strategy, she would be lying to the court. Once again, she could be subject to contempt of court charges (Doyle, 2007). Further, her competence and integrity as a professional social worker could be put into question, even if everyone believed that she could not remember significant information (NASW, S.1.04; 5.01).

Sydnee's supervisor and attorney inform her about legal and ethical approaches to protecting her client's right to confidentiality. First, she should inform her client about the subpoena (Polowy et al., 2005). Confidentiality is owned by the client, not the worker or the agency, so it is primarily the client's decision about whether to permit Sydnee to testify in court. Suppose Collette agrees to waive confidentiality and privilege, permitting Sydnee to testify. Perhaps she believes that Sydnee likes her, so she will only say good things. Sydnee should encourage Collette to seek independent legal advice to help explain the pros and cons of allowing her to testify. In order to exercise informed consent about whether to waive privilege (Ss.1.03[a]; 1.07[b]), Collette needs to know that Sydnee cannot simply provide favorable information. Sydnee has a duty to the court to be fully honest and open, which could include revealing potentially embarrassing information about Collette.

An attorney could help Collette file a motion to quash[9] the subpoena (Polowy et al., 2005). Just because Sydnee received a subpoena does not mean she has to testify. The court may agree to quash (or cancel) the subpoena on the grounds of social worker–client confidentiality and privilege (*Jaffee v. Redmond,* 1996).[10] In particular, if Sydnee is a licensed clinical social worker and state law grants privilege to such professionals, then the court should not require Sydnee to testify unless Collette waives her right to privilege. Assume, however, that Sydnee has a BSW and that client communications with her are not covered by any statutory privileges. The court could decide to quash the subpoena to protect client confidentiality, but the result of such a motion is not certain. Thus, legal advice is critical when determining whether and how to challenge a subpoena. If Collette cannot afford an attorney, Sydnee and the agency should try to facilitate access to one (e.g., finding an attorney who will act on a pro bono[11] basis). The agency could also hire an attorney to file a motion to quash on its own behalf. The agency has an interest, not only in protecting Sydnee's confidentiality, but in giving other clients assurance that their confidential information will not be subject to disclosure in court. If the client and the agency do not assist in blocking the subpoena, Sydnee may be wise to consult her own attorney for advice and to check whether her professional liability insurer will provide coverage for legal representation (Polowy et al., 2005).

In the event that the court rejects any motions to quash the subpoena, Sydnee still has other legal and ethical options for protecting her client's confidentiality. First, the agency attorney can help Sydnee prepare for court, giving her guidance on how to answer questions truthfully, but also limiting what personal client information she shares to what is needed. The attorney advises Sydnee, for instance, not to respond too quickly to any questions from Otis's attorney. Pausing permits the prosecuting attorney[12] a chance to challenge any inappropriate questions (Barsky & Gould, 2002). For instance, evidentiary laws may restrict defense attorneys from asking questions about the victim's sex life. Under Standard 1.07(j), social workers are instructed to ask a court to limit the scope of an order to disclose information. For instance, the court could permit the worker to conceal certain portions of case records on the grounds that this information is irrelevant to the proceeding, or too harmful to the client. The court could also limit public access or reporting by the media (Polowy et al., 2005), though courts may be reluctant to impose such restrictions given the value of transparency for court trials.

Assume the court orders Sydnee to testify, despite objections from Collette and herself. An agency attorney might help Sydnee explain

---

[9] An attorney may also help with additional legal devices such as a written objection, a protective order, or a motion to modify. A written objection informs the subpoenaing party that the recipient objects to the subpoena and identifies the basis for the objection (e.g., the information is privileged or the requested information is irrelevant for the court's purposes). The written objection provides the social worker and client with additional time to file motions to the court to quash or modify the subpoena. The social worker may also need to submit a request to the court for a protective order, which protects the worker from having to comply with a subpoena on a temporary or permanent basis. A motion to modify a subpoena may be used to limit the information that needs to be disclosed. Given the complexity of these legal devices, social workers should consult attorneys to determine whether any or all of them may be helpful in responding to a subpoena (Polowy et al., 2005).

[10] Note that in some situations, a social worker has a duty to report imminent danger to authorities. This duty to report does not waive privilege for court purposes (*People v. Bierenbaum,* 2002). In other words, a social worker may have to call police to protect a potential victim, but this does not mean that the prosecution can use the social worker's report or other information in a future criminal court case.

[11] Free, for charitable purposes.

[12] Typically, criminal cases involve attorneys for the prosecution and for the defense. The victim and other witnesses do not usually have separate legal representation involved in the court hearing.

her professional responsibilities to be read into the official court records (Barsky & Gould, 2002):

> As a professional social worker, I must abide by the National Association of Social Worker's Code of Ethics. Standard 1.07 guides me to maintain my client's right to confidentiality. Confidentiality is crucial to encouraging clients in need to seek services and trust the worker to keep their personal information private. Given my professional ethics, I am not in agreement with the court's decision to require me to share client information. However, I will reluctantly comply with the court's ruling on this matter.

Different attorneys may give different guidance on whether to make such a statement in court. The advantage of the statement is that it educates the court about the worker's responsibility and puts the worker's ethical stance on public record. The challenge is ensuring that the worker does not lose credibility, inadvertently suggesting that she is not going to provide full and frank information to the court. A worker who feels very strongly about protecting client confidentiality could refuse to provide certain testimony. If the worker refuses, she should be honest about her intentions rather than lie about forgetting information or making up false information. Although the worker might have sound ethical justification for refusing to testify, she should know the potential consequences of refusing to testify, including the possibility of incarceration for contempt of court.[13] Regardless of a worker's initial inclinations on how to respond to a subpoena, obtaining guidance and advice from supervisors and attorneys is vital.

WORKING WITH INVOLUNTARY CLIENTS

Clients may be mandated into social services by a judge, probation officer, parole officer, or another official of the criminal justice system. In some cases, clients are ordered into services without their consent. A judge may order a violent offender, for instance, to go for a psychiatric evaluation to assist the court with sentencing. In many cases, however, clients provide consent, albeit under some level of pressure or coercion. A person charged with a drug-related offense, for instance, might agree to be diverted to a drug court that provides treatment for substance abuse.[14] The person agrees to services, but under the strain of knowing that the alternative could include criminal conviction and incarceration (Rooney, 2002). Similarly, a convicted person might agree to participate in psychotherapy in order to gain early release (parole) from prison. In each of these cases, the person is subject to some level of coercion, which social workers should take into account. Social workers are supposed to promote client self-determination (S.1.02) and offer services on a voluntary basis (S.1.03). When clients are mandated or pressured, social workers should acknowledge that the clients are not receiving services on a purely self-determined, voluntary basis. Validating the circumstances that bring clients into services demonstrates that the worker understands their situation. The worker does not need to agree or disagree with the decisions made by criminal justice officials, but the worker should strive to prevent exploitation and protect client rights as much as possible (Burman, 2004; Scheurell, 1983). This section provides strategies for maximizing rights of involuntary clients to informed

---

[13] See "Civil Disobedience" below for additional factors to consider when determining whether to violate the law for a higher purpose.

[14] Note that the Fifth Amendment of the U.S. Constitution says that no person "shall be compelled in any criminal case to be a witness against himself." In many court diversion programs, alleged offenders may be referred for treatment services even though they have not been found guilty of any offense. During treatment, social workers may ask the person to admit committing the crime as part of the recovery process (e.g., a man accused of spousal violence who is asked to take responsibility for his actions). To protect the client's Fifth Amendment rights against self-incrimination, the worker should ensure that the client's admission cannot be used against the client in further criminal court processes (Kalichman, 1999).

consent, self-determination, and confidentiality, in light of agency mandates and other professional obligations.

Informed Consent

Standard 1.03(d) states that social workers should provide involuntary clients with "information about the nature and extent of services, and about the extent of clients' right to refuse services." Although involuntary clients, by definition, are not receiving services on a purely voluntary basis, workers should still explain the nature of the services, their benefits, and risks. Workers should invite clients to discuss any concerns about the services. By ensuring that clients understand the nature, risks, and benefits of services, workers maximize the "informed" component of informed consent. Consent ordinarily includes the freedom to accept or reject services. If an involuntary client rejects services, the worker can explain the consequences of rejecting services or refer the client to speak with the probation officer, parole officer, or other person responsible for the referral.

> I understand that you are here because of a court order requiring you to participate in addictions treatment. Now that you have a better understanding of our services, you can make a better informed decision about whether to accept them. From your earlier comments, I know you still have some reservations about accepting services. I'm not here to physically force or impose treatment upon you. You have a choice, but you also have a right to understand the legal consequences if you decide not to accept services.... Perhaps you'd like to speak with your attorney or probation officer before making a final decision.

The worker may provide general information about the possible consequences of refusal to accept services, but should not render legal opinions or advice. Judges, probation officers, and other criminal justice officials have discretion in terms of the consequences they impose for failure to comply with court orders, conditions of probation, and so on. Clients may receive legal opinions from their attorneys or contact the criminal justice official responsible for their case for more specific guidance on the consequences for failure to comply.

Self-Determination

When involuntary clients are mandated to receive services, they typically have some freedom of choice in terms of which specific service provider or treatment modality they are required to use. Social workers can enhance client self-determination (S.1.02) by discussing choices available to the client. Depending on the court order or other mandate, options may include choosing different practitioners from the same agency, choosing services from a different agency, choosing different methods of intervention (e.g., individual, family, group, inpatient, outpatient), and choosing different models of intervention (e.g., cognitive therapy, pharmacotherapy, 12-step programs). The worker can also foster self-determination by developing personalized goals with the client.

> I understand that coming to our addictions group was not initially a choice you would have made on your own. Now that you're here, let's talk about what we can do that meets the requirements of your probation, but also makes good use of your time. Perhaps we can begin by identifying goals that *you* want to pursue.

In some cases, workers may believe their clients do not truly need the services they were mandated to receive. Consider, for instance, a client who was charged with driving under the influence of alcohol and was mandated to go to an addictions treatment program. If the client does not have an addiction, then is an addictions treatment program really appropriate? If not, the worker may advocate on the client's behalf to change the mandate to a more appropriate referral (e.g., community service with survivors of car accidents, as a way to repay the community and also receive education about the consequences of drinking and driving).

When providing services to clients mandated by the criminal justice system, social workers need to balance their duties to their clients (as agents of help) with their duties to society and the criminal justice system (as agents of social control) (Burman, 2004). In trying to achieve this balance, workers should consider the effectiveness of mandated services for each client they receive. If research suggests involuntary clients have a reasonable chance of benefiting from a particular type of mandated services, then providing services for such clients can be ethically justified on the basis of beneficence (doing good for the client) and protection of the public (if successful intervention reduces risks of future harm). However, if research suggests that a particular type of mandated service is ineffective or very risky, then providing such a service cannot be justified on the basis of beneficence or protection of the public (Wild, 2006). Clients should not be mandated into social services for the purposes of punishment. When social services are mandated, social workers should ensure that they are offered on the basis of which services are most effective and least intrusive (Andrews & Patterson, 1995).

Although society often views people who have violated criminal laws as dangerous and in need of punishment, social workers should also consider how this population may be vulnerable and in need of advocacy (S.6.04[b] & [d]; Scheurell, 1983). Consider, for instance, an African American client who claims his criminal conviction was the result of discrimination, false evidence, and lack of appropriate legal representation at the trial. In legal terms, the client believes his constitutional rights to equal protection and due process were violated (Andrews & Patterson, 1995; U.S. Constitution, 14th Amendment). The worker's response may depend on the agency's policy and the worker's role within the agency. If the social worker practices in a probation office, probation policies may limit the worker's ability to question the practices of judges or other law enforcement officials. In spite of the worker's professional duty to promote self-determination, agency policy would not permit the worker to provide the client with direct help in challenging the criminal court decision. The worker may help the client access an attorney or other criminal justice advocates. If the worker does not work within a probation office but is merely receiving a referral, then the worker would have more leeway in helping the client seek redress for alleged abuses in the criminal justice system.

Confidentiality

As with other clients, the nature of confidentiality should be discussed with involuntary clients as early as possible in the helping relationship (S.1.07[e]). Explaining confidentiality is particularly important for clients mandated by the criminal justice system because the social worker may have split loyalties between the client and the system. The NASW Code permits social workers to make different types of arrangements for confidentiality, provided that the client knows about these arrangements from the outset of the helping process. Consider, for instance, a client who has been involved in trafficking heroin. The client may or may not divulge such information depending on whether the social worker has to report this to the client's probation officer, parole officer, or another law enforcement official. Providing clients with information on whether and how information will be shared with others demonstrates respect for client self-determination.

Possible confidentiality agreements include

- The worker will provide specific types of reports to the court, probation officer, or other corrections officials (e.g., when the court requires a psychosocial assessment for the sentencing process).
- The worker will provide designated corrections officials with information concerning the dates of sessions that the client attends and does not attend, but the worker will not disclose the content of the sessions.
- The worker will provide corrections officials with information about any breaches of conditions of probation or parole.
- The worker will provide corrections officials with periodic reports on the client's motivation, participation, and progress with services.[15]

[15] Probation officers and other corrections worker should advise clients that their communications are not privileged. These officers have an obligation to report new offenses or suspected offenses to law enforcement authorities, though they may exercise discretion for minor offenses (Scheurell, 1983).

Note that the worker needs to negotiate an agreement for confidentiality with both the client and the corrections agency. By securing agreement from the outset, the worker can avoid ethical conflicts, for instance, when clients share information that they do not expect to be disclosed to others or used against them in a criminal justice proceeding (Kalichman, 1999). When negotiating confidentiality with a corrections agency,[16] the worker may advocate for limiting disclosures and reports to the corrections agency. This not only enhances the client's right to privacy (S.1.07[a]) but may also improve the chances that the services will be successful. When clients are concerned that personal information may be used against them, they may be less likely to share information and develop a positive working relationship (Rosenbaum et al., 2003).

Although social workers may want to promote client privacy and confidentiality, they must also consider protection of the public. To protect the public from harm, sharing information with law enforcement officials may be necessary or desirable. Once again, workers should balance the conflicting interests of privacy and protection, taking the risk of harm into account (Freshwater & Westwood, 2006). When clients have been involved in serious crimes (e.g., murder, rape, armed robbery), there may be greater ethical justification for sharing information with law enforcement officials. When the risks to the public are high, protection of the public tends to take on greater importance than confidentiality. For criminal activities of a less serious nature (e.g., possession of small quantities of marijuana), social workers may be ethically justified in advocating for greater protections of client privacy. Social workers may educate law enforcement officials about levels of risk associated with different mental illnesses. Many people assume that all people with mental illness are dangerous. The actual danger depends on the type of mental illness and whether it is under control (Freshwater & Westwood, 2006). By negotiating the balance between client privacy and public safety up front, social workers can ensure that the client and all parties know how the social worker may or may not share particular types of information with the criminal justice system.

Now that we have explored ethical issues that may arise when working with offenders, we turn to ethical issues that may arise when working with victim–survivors of criminal offenses.

WORKING WITH VICTIM–SURVIVORS OF VIOLENT CRIMES

When someone commits a violent crime, the criminal justice system labels the person subjected to the violence as the victim.[17] Applying a strengths perspective, social workers often use the term *survivor* rather than *victim* (Saleebey, 2009). Whereas *victim* has connotations of weakness and passivity, *survivor* implies that the person has strengths, resilience, vitality, and coping abilities. This section uses the term *survivor*, though social workers should note that different terminology may be required to communicate in different contexts. In particular, this section explores one of the more challenging ethical issues when working with survivors—whether to encourage survivors of serious violent crimes to cooperate with law enforcement officials when involvement in the criminal justice system might be detrimental to the survivor's recovery process and overall psychosocial welfare. As the introduction to Part II suggests, there are many different approaches to ethical analysis and critical thinking. The ensuing discussion illustrates two approaches—the rational application of ethical principles and the ethics of care approach—using the following scenario.

Calla has been receiving psychotherapy from Sonya, a social worker specializing in work

[16] In some cases, the worker's agency has an ongoing contract with law enforcement and the contract provides the terms of confidentiality for all mandated clients.

[17] Note that the criminal justice system is based on the presumption of innocence. The prosecution must prove–beyond reasonable doubt—that the accused committed the crime. Prior to conviction, the accused is the alleged offender or perpetrator of the offense, and the victim is actually the alleged victim.

with survivors of sexual assaults. Calla says she was violently assaulted by Orville, who raped her in his car outside a nightclub. Calla initially contacted police to bring charges, but recently recanted. Police have asked Sonya to encourage Calla to cooperate with them. If she does not cooperate, then they cannot successfully prosecute the case against Orville, and a violent offender will still be at large in the community (Vonk, 2000).

Rational, Principled Approach

A rational, principled approach to ethics suggests that the decision makers should identify and apply ethical principles that are most relevant to a particular ethical situation (Banks, 2006). If more than one principle applies, then the decision maker determines which principle should take priority; for instance, protection of life generally takes precedence over client confidentiality (Dolgoff et al., 2009). Both deontology and utilitarianism[18] (as defined in Chapter 10) make use of a rational, principled approach. Deontologists focus on the rational application of ethical principles as fixed moral duties or imperatives. Utilitarians also apply ethical principles, but they determine the preferred course of action based upon an analysis of the consequences of various options for solution: in particular, they explore which course of action will create the greatest good for the greatest number (Beauchamp & Childress, 2009). The following analysis considers both deontological and utilitarian perspectives on Sonya's case.

Standard 1.01 of the NASW Code of Ethics advises social workers that their primary responsibility is to promote the well-being of their clients, yet they may also have commitments to broader society. This standard is based on the ethical principles of beneficence, nonmaleficence, autonomy, and justice. The principles of beneficence and nonmaleficence suggest that social workers should choose actions that do good and avoid actions that cause harm. If an action has potential risks and benefits, the worker should balance the benefits against the risks (Beauchamp & Childress, 2009). When Sonya analyzes how she should respond to the police request to encourage Calla to cooperate with police, she can look at beneficence and nonmaleficence from the perspectives of three constituencies: Calla, the police, and the community. From Calla's standpoint, Sonya wants to promote her psychosocial well-being. In some cases, participating in the criminal prosecution of an offender can be therapeutic for the survivor. Research suggests that involvement in the criminal justice system "potentially has a positive effect on the [survivor] with regard to expression of anger, emotional processing of the event, a sense of empowerment, and reduction in feelings of victimization" (Steketee & Austin, cited in Vonk, 2000, p. 52). In this case, however, Calla is highly fearful of what will happen if she cooperates: Will she have to testify against Orville face to face, will the police or court compel her to answer embarrassing questions, and will she be put at greater risk if she cooperates but Orville is found not guilty? Sonya assesses that Calla is in a fragile emotional state, still traumatized by the rape. Sonya's professional judgment is that cooperating with law enforcement at this time is not in Calla's best interests. In fact, it could cause her emotional harm. From the perspectives of the police and community, however, Calla's cooperation is required in order to convict Orville and protect society from a dangerous offender. If he is not held to account, then he is more likely to assault other women. Moreover, if Calla decides to cooperate, this not only helps protect the community from Orville, but it also sends a message to other survivors that they should help police hold offenders accountable and protect the community from harm. Utilitarians might argue that in spite of the risks to Calla, helping the police is for the greater good of society. On the other hand, deontologists might argue that all citizens have a moral duty to assist law enforcement officers, simply because it is the right thing to do.

[18] Utilitarianism is a form of teleology.

Sonya could encourage Calla to cooperate with police by suggesting, "If Orville raped another woman in your neighborhood, wouldn't you want her to cooperate with the police?"[19]

The principle of autonomy suggests that social workers should support client self-determination (S.1.02) and informed consent (S.1.03) rather than impose their own values and beliefs. From this perspective, Calla has a right to decide whether to cooperate with police and Sonya should respect this decision. Remember, however, that self-determination and informed consent depend on the client's having sufficient mental capacity and information to make a free and informed decision. Calla is 25 years old, so as an adult, she is presumed to have capacity unless she exhibits particular problems in her memory, reasoning, and other cognitive abilities. The laws pertaining to child abuse and elder abuse do not apply.[20] As Sonya assesses Calla's mental capacity, she notes that Calla may be suffering from post-traumatic stress disorder and her decision not to cooperate is based largely on fear. Arguably, how can Calla make a reasonable, informed decision when her levels of anxiety are making it difficult for her to think rationally? Sonya understands, however, that many of Calla's fears are valid concerns. Sonya knows she should not substitute her decision for Calla's simply because they have different views on the risks and benefits of cooperating with the police. Although Calla's thinking is affected by her emotional response, Calla does not lack the mental capacity to make an informed decision. Sonya decides she should not pressure Calla into making a quick decision. By providing Calla with information and attending to her anxiety over a period of time, Sonya can enhance Calla's right to self-determination and respect the principle of client autonomy.

The principle of justice suggests that social workers should promote a fair and equitable distribution of resources, opportunities, risks, and benefits (Beauchamp & Childress, 2009). In particular, Standard 6.04 suggests that social workers should take action to protect the rights of vulnerable populations and prevent exploitation. Encouraging Calla to cooperate with police could be viewed as a way to protect Calla and other women in the community from rape and other violent crime. In other words, both Calla and the community would benefit from holding Orville accountable for his actions. In order to convict Orville, however, Calla would be taking the majority of the risks. Thus, is it fair to force Calla to assume the emotional and social costs of participating in a criminal prosecution? Sonya thinks that if the community expects Calla to assume these risks, then the community should provide her with additional victim–witness support services and protections (Andrews, 2007). For instance, would taxpayers be willing to pay for Calla's relocation to another community if this would help make Calla feel safe?

Sonya carefully examines the various ethical principles and how they relate to Calla's predicament. Sonya applies Dolgoff, Loewenberg, and Harrington's (2009) Ethical Principles Screen,[21] which suggests giving priority to the principle of autonomy, specifically Calla's right to self-determination. Sonya acknowledges some anguish over the decision, as Calla's decision not to cooperate with police means that Orville remains free and dangerous. Arguably, having Calla cooperate would lead to the least harm, at least from a community perspective. Still, the Ethical Principles Screen says to prioritize autonomy over least harm. If Sonya knew that Orville was going to attack a particular person, she would prioritize that person's life and safety. In this case, however, there is no specific foreseeable and identifiable victim (*Tarasoff v. Regents*, 1976).

Sonya does not stop her analysis at this point. There are some steps she can take to reduce harm, even if Calla does decide not to cooperate

[19] This question is a simplified version of Kant's categorical imperative, as described in the introduction to Part II.

[20] For analysis of "autonomy versus beneficence or protection from harm" with vulnerable populations, see Chapters 13 (mental capacity), 14 (child abuse), and 16 (elder abuse).

[21] Described in the introduction to Part II.

with police. First, Sonya decides to initiate an educational campaign, raising awareness of date rape and strategies for preventing such violence. Although Orville is free in the community, Sonya can empower potential victims to take precautions. Second, Sonya continues to work with Calla, helping her work through her trauma and fears. With Sonya's assistance, Calla may decide at some point to press charges against Orville and cooperate with the prosecution. Survivors tend to feel empowered when workers validate their autonomy and decision-making ability (Buttell, Carney, & Miller, 2006; Linzer, 2004).

Virtue Ethics and the Ethics of Care

Ethics of care, a branch of virtue ethics, suggests that people should strive to be agents of care and compassion. Whereas principled ethics suggests that people should act in an ethical manner by following a set of ethical principles or rules, virtue ethics suggest that people act in an ethical manner because they are operating on good, internal motivations (Beauchamp & Childress, 2009). The virtue of care is particularly relevant to social work because social workers are inspired by the ideals of helping others and promoting social justice (NASW, 1999).[22] Assume that, rather than applying a principled approach, Sonya adopts ethics of care to guide her responses to Calla's situation. Rather than rationally analyzing the ethical principles that apply to the case, Sonya asks, "What would a caring social worker do in this situation?" To determine what a virtuous, caring worker would do, she reflects on her caring qualities, acknowledging her emotional responsiveness and interdependence with the client and others involved in this situation (Gilligan, 1982).[23] Caring social workers embrace six virtues or dispositions:

- Attentiveness—noticing others and seeking awareness of their needs and perspectives; alterness, active regard, and compassion for the welfare of others.
- Responsibility—accepting the role of a helper or caregiver as an implicit duty (rather than a rule or standard that one must follow); being conscientious or doing what is right because it is right.
- Competence—having the ability to provide the care or help that others need.
- Responsiveness—remaining alert and open to the needs of others, their reactions, and the possibility that the recipient of care might experience the care offered in a negative manner.
- Integrity of care—soundness, reliability, wholeness, and synthesis of moral character; viewing ethical situations from a holistic perspective; making decisions about conflicting needs and strategies by taking social context, power, and special needs into account; ethical principles may be considered to help think through the issues, but principles should not be used to distance oneself from the people and relationships.
- Discernment—sensitive insight, astute judgment, and the ability to apply wisdom by using an appropriate balance of reason, desire, and emotion

(Banks, 2006; Beauchamp & Childress, 2009; Vonk, 2000).

In terms of *attentiveness*, Sonya notices that she is in a caring relationship with her client, Calla. Calla's most immediate needs are emotional. She feels distressed and scared. She has expressed the need to take care of herself and has difficulty even thinking about Orville, never mind participating in a criminal justice process

[22] Different professions may aspire to different virtues, reflecting the roles and ideals of those professions. For instance, the fundamental virtues of medicine, nursing, and the healing professions are compassion, discernment, trustworthiness, and conscientiousness (Beauchamp & Childress, 2009). Additional social work virtues include loyalty, nonjudgmentalism, benevolence, and altruism.

[23] Gilligan suggests that a principled approach is based upon a male perspective, using an individualized, rational approach to ethical decision making and justice. In contrast, an ethics of care approach fits with a female sense of ethics, with moral responsibility stemming from relationships rather than rules.

to convict him. Calla wants to regain a sense of control and emotional stability as soon as possible (Vonk, 2000). Although Sonya feels that her primary allegiance is to her client, she is also aware that she cares for the police and the community. She would like to have a good relationship with the police and wants to assist them, not just out of civic duty but because she is concerned about what would happen to the community if members of the public did not cooperate with them. She feels some pressure from the police to enlist Calla's cooperation, but understands they are trying to do their job, not trying to take advantage of Sonya or her client. Sonya feels her strongest natural inclination for care is to her client, yet she also acknowledges her concern for the community at large. She believes the personal is political, meaning that what happens to her client on a personal basis also has implications for greater society. Thus, she accepts *responsibility* to help not only her client, but also the police and the community.

Regarding *competence*, Sonya possesses the essential knowledge and skills to help survivors work through trauma and related psychosocial issues. When reflecting on her ability to help Calla navigate the criminal justice system, she identifies some gaps in her knowledge and understanding. She consults with a forensic social worker who can offer guidance and build Sonya's competence.

Rather than making her own ethical decisions about whether to encourage Calla to cooperate with police, Sonya uses her relationship with Calla to explore the issues with her. In terms of *responsiveness*, Sonya strives to tune in and acknowledge Calla's feelings and perspectives. In prior discussions, Calla has already expressed reluctance to cooperate with police. Thus, Sonya begins her discussion by reflecting back Calla's concerns and checking to see that she understands them accurately. As she broaches the possibility of cooperating with the police, Sonya is conscious of the power relationship that exists between a social worker and client. Social workers are in a position of power and influence, given their expertise and status as professional helpers. In particular, survivors of sexual abuse may feel particularly vulnerable, given the stress, embarrassment, fear, and confusion that may arise from the experience of being assaulted (Vonk, 2000).

Given her disposition toward *integrity of care*, Sonya takes extra precautions to help Calla feel safe and empowered. Sonya asks Calla if it is all right to discuss the issue of collaborating with the police, rather than assuming Calla is ready to discuss it. Sonya also confirms that Calla is free to agree or disagree with any of the questions or information that Sonya provides. Sonya says she would like to discuss the risks and benefits of collaborating, and is particularly interested in hearing Calla's perspective.

Although Sonya has good intentions when she offers to discuss the situation, Calla may experience the discussion as coercive, manipulative, or demeaning. Thus, Sonya strives to discuss the issues in an open manner rather than trying to persuade or maneuver Calla into a particular course of action (Vonk, 2000). Accordingly, Sonya avoids the use of persuasion, debate, bribes, or guilt. Sonya raises the ethical principles of respecting Calla's autonomy, promoting good, and limiting harm. Unlike the earlier discussion of principles, however, Sonya allows Calla to define good and harm. This helps ensure that principles are not used to distance the actors from the situation: They consider the principles, but also the unique people and social context affected by the issues. Calla identifies good as reducing stress, maintaining her privacy, and moving on with her life. She wants to avoid exposure to the public, which she finds embarrassing and stressful. Sonya validates these concerns, which they use to establish goals. Sonya invites Calla to explore the situation from the perspectives of the police and the community. Calla agrees to discuss them, feeling safe in her working relationship with Sonya. Calla acknowledges that the police and public are interested in protecting the public and holding Orville responsible for his crime. Sonya validates the possible conflict between the goals of Calla's well-being and the community's well-being (Vonk, 2000).

Sonya senses Calla's anxiety rising as they discuss possible solutions. Sonya reassures Calla that they do not have to make any decisions today, or even over the next few weeks. Sonya also confirms that Calla may ultimately decide against cooperation, and Sonya will respect that decision. Calla agrees to discuss options, as long as she does not feel pressured into making any commitments. Sonya shares her knowledge of the criminal justice process, including safeguards that the criminal justice system can use to protect survivors who testify. For instance, evidentiary laws restrict defense attorneys from asking certain types of questions about the witness's morality and sexual history. Sonya notes that a victim services agency can provide her with emotional and informational support throughout the trial. Sonya presents information in a supportive manner but avoids the temptation to embellish or persuade. The types of protections that Sonya presents do not seem to be the primary concerns for Calla. Calla simply wants to get on with her life and try to forget what happened. In her own mind, Sonya questions whether trying to forget what happened is the best way for Calla to cope with and move beyond her traumatic experience. Sonya keeps these thoughts to herself and validates Calla as the person who is in the best situation to determine what is right for her.

As a social worker who embraces *discernment*, Sonya considers the ethical principles of autonomy and justice, but strives to apply them in a manner that respects Calla's beliefs and subjective reality. A rational application of the principle of justice might suggest that Orville should be held criminally responsible for assaulting Calla. To bring about this notion of justice, Sonya could persuade Calla to cooperate with police. As a social worker who has gained practice wisdom from work with other survivors, however, Sonya knows that participation in a criminal prosecution can be psychologically harmful for clients. Although there are good reasons to persuade Calla to participate, Sonya knows that, on balance, it is more important at this moment to respect Calla's autonomy, particularly her decision not to cooperate with the police.

Although Calla decides not to cooperate with police, Sonya still accepts responsibility for care toward the police and the community. Sonya helps establish a community advisory group, consisting of law enforcement officials, social workers, and other helping professionals who work with survivors of sexual abuse (Vonk, 2000). The purpose of the group is to foster policies and procedures that will allow more survivors to participate in criminal prosecutions in a manner that also promotes their psychosocial well-being, or at least minimizes the risks to their recovery processes.

Neither the principled approach nor ethics of care provides a simple, pat answer to this or any other ethical dilemma. Regardless of which approach is used, the social worker and other actors are faced with difficult choices, and reasonable people may come up with different, but equally valid decisions. Currently, the principled approach to ethics is more popular among social workers, though ethics of care may be more common among radical and feminist social workers (Banks, 2004). My own opinion is that neither approach is inherently superior to the other. Both approaches have merit (Beauchamp & Childress, 2009). Being able to work through ethical issues from both perspectives provides social workers with insights that they might not have if they restrict themselves to one approach. The Framework for Managing Ethical Issues (in the introduction to Part II) includes aspects of both approaches. This framework guides workers to consider laws, agency policies, ethical principles, and ethical standards. However, it also invites workers to self-reflect and to consider alternate approaches to critical thinking (e.g., deontology, utilitarianism, ethics of care, and virtue ethics).[24]

[24] Banks (2006) suggests that many ethicists and ethics educators focus on rational, principle-based approaches because they are easier to teach than virtue ethics and ethics of care. Yes, it is easy to articulate characteristics that make practitioners virtuous, but how do social workers actually learn or develop character? Reading textbooks and having rational case discussions are not sufficient. I might be very brave in a hypothetical situation, saying that I would blow the whistle on the chief executive officer of my company, even though it meant risking my job. Would I be so brave if the situation and stakes were real? Role-plays and discussions of hypothetical cases are helpful learning tools. To develop virtues, however, workers also need to experience

CIVIL DISOBEDIENCE

Civil disobedience refers to the use of "a public, nonviolent, conscientious yet political act contrary to law usually done with the aim of bringing about a change in the law or policies of the government" (Rawls, 1971, p. 354). Arguably, civil disobedience is implicitly authorized by Standard 6.04(a) of the NASW Code of Ethics. This standard advises social workers to "engage in social and political action" and "advocate for changes in policy and legislation to improve social conditions in order to meet basic human needs and promote social justice." Ordinarily, social workers should promote social change and law reform through legal means; for instance, lobbying government, mobilizing the community to advocate, and educating the public (Lens, 2004). However, the Code does envision situations when social workers might be ethically justified[25] in violating the law in order to pursue a higher ethical purpose. The Purpose statement in the Code suggests that when ethical standards conflict with legal obligations, social workers "must make a responsible effort to resolve the conflict in a manner that is consistent with the values, principles, and standards expressed in this Code. If a reasonable resolution of the conflict does not appear possible, social workers should seek proper consultation before making a decision." Other than suggesting that workers seek proper consultation, the Code does not provide much guidance on when, if ever, social workers are justified in disobeying the law in order to promote a higher value. Perhaps the Code remains vague on this issue due to lack of consensus in the profession. The issue of civil disobedience is controversial and the NASW may be hesitant to provide members with specific instructions on when violating the law may be ethical. The following discussion offers analysis of the ethical issues to be considered when determining whether and when social workers may participate in or promote civil disobedience. As with other ethical dilemmas, reasonable people may disagree about which responses are most ethical.

When considering whether a proposed act of civil disobedience is ethically justifiable, social workers and other decision makers should analyze three factors: the importance of the cause in relation to the seriousness of the legal violation, the willingness of the parties to openly admit they are breaking the law, and the willingness of the parties to accept the consequences of breaking the law.

Importance of the Cause

Although the NASW Code instructs social workers to promote social justice and take action against discrimination and oppression, each social worker makes individualized decisions about which causes to pursue and how to go about pursuing them. Given limited time, energy, and resources, workers need to prioritize where to put their efforts. The more important the cause, the more important it is for a worker to give the cause priority. As per utilitarianism, social workers might ask themselves, "If I have to choose between two causes, which cause will promote the greatest good, for the greatest number?"[26] Thus, based on Maslow's hierarchy of needs (Maslow et al., 1987), one could justify a decision to advocate for food for 100 starving clients rather than advocating for movie tickets

---

real ethical dilemmas. Supervised field placements provide excellent opportunities for experiential learning, enhancing emotional intelligence and virtue development. In the field, new social workers have the opportunity to model the virtues of their experienced field instructors. Further, field instructors facilitate development of professional personas by providing supervisees with ongoing feedback and moral support.

[25] Remember, ethically justified does not mean the same as ethically required. Although some workers might believe an act of civil disobedience is ethically justified, others may disagree, as they are not ethically required to participate in civil disobedience.

[26] Utilitarianism is provided as just one example of how to determine priorities. See Chapter 10 for other approaches to setting priorities and allocating resources (especially deontology, egalitarianism, and libertarianism).

for 100 mildly bored individuals. When considering the use of civil disobedience to pursue a cause, social workers should not only consider whether the cause is important in relation to other causes, but also whether it is so important that civil disobedience is justified.

Although civil disobedience may be useful in promoting social justice, civil disobedience also entails risks and costs. Professional social workers, and indeed all citizens, should ordinarily follow the rule of law. Following the law promotes order, decency, security, liberty, and respect for the rights of others. If people could justify breaking the law simply because they personally disagreed with it, society could fall into chaos and anarchy. Crime may be contagious. If one person is allowed to break the law with impunity, then everyone else may feel he also has a right to break the law (*Olmstead v. United States*, 1928). Thus, social workers should ensure they have strong justification before engaging in civil disobedience.

For some social workers, breaking the law is never justified. They may view following the law as an absolute duty. This duty does not prevent them from challenging the law and advocating for changes, but only through legal means. For other workers, breaking the law may be justified, depending on the consequences. In order to determine the ethicality of civil disobedience, such workers would ask, "Does the end justify the means?" Consider a group of African Americans who believe the state government has an unofficial policy restricting African American–owned businesses from obtaining an equal share of government contracts. They ask you (a community organizer) to help plan a protest and blockade that would involve circling the state capitol with vehicles to prevent legislators from entering or leaving the building. On its face, the cause appears ethical: challenging discrimination (S.6.04). But does this cause warrant the proposed form of civil disobedience? As a social worker, you should first help the group verify that discrimination is actually taking place. You could then help the group consider other means of promoting its cause: What forms of advocacy have they already tried, what alternative forms of advocacy are available, and which of these, if any, should be tried before resorting to the blockade? Civil disobedience should be viewed as a last resort, to be used only after the group has made good-faith attempts to change laws or social policies through legal means (Macauley, 2005). You should also help the group explore the risks involved in a blockade—for instance, will it help or hurt their public image, what is the likelihood that protesters or others may be injured, how will the protest affect the running of the government, and what other unintended harm may arise? How willing is the group to accept these risks? How willing is the group to impose risks on innocent bystanders?

In addition to having a good cause (or end that justifies the means), some ethicists argue that there must be a reasonable chance of success in order to justify civil disobedience (Rawls, 1971). If the cause is futile, then why incur the risks (Barsky, 2007a)? Others, from a deontological perspective, suggest that civil disobedience may be justified because challenging social injustice is the right thing to do, regardless of the consequences (Kant, 1979/Orig.1779). Thus, social workers must not only consider whether the cause is good, but whether and how to take the consequences of the actions into account.

Openly Admit Breaking the Law

The primary purpose of civil disobedience is not to *break* the law, but to *change* it. Given this purpose, social workers who plan to participate in civil disobedience should be willing to admit that they are going to break the existing law (Kalichman, 1999). Their intent is not to hurt others, seek vengeance, or surreptitiously violate laws for personal gain. Rather, their intent is to promote social justice (Goodin, 2005). In San Francisco, for instance, public officials of the City and County of San Francisco acted unlawfully by issuing marriage licenses to same-sex couples, even though the existing law restricted marriage as between a man and a woman (*In re Marriage Cases*, 2008). Organizers of this act of civil disobedience ensured that the act was open to the public, inviting media to cover the event. The purpose of the event was not to flout the law, but to provide a test case for the fairness and constitutionality of the existing law. In contrast, consider a social worker who refuses to report child abuse because she believes mandatory reporting laws are ineffective at protecting children and harmful to social worker–client relationships. If the worker does not go public with her refusal to report abuse, then her actions are unlawful, but they are not acts of civil disobedience (Kalichman, 1999).

In the blockade example, cutting off access to the state capitol is a public event. Proponents of the blockade are not simply acting out of anger or aggression toward authority. They are advocating for social justice (Stevanović, 2005). Thus, as their community organizer, you could help them present the blockade to the public in a positive manner. For instance, you could work with the media in advance of the blockade to provide them with background information on the blockade, you could prepare protestors for how to respond to law enforcement officials in a nonviolent manner,[27] and you could help the protesters present themselves as courageous advocates of social justice, rather than criminals or misfits. These strategies help reduce risks and increase the likelihood of successful social advocacy (National Lawyers Guild, n.d.).[28]

Accept the Consequences of Breaking the Law

The third standard for civil disobedience is that those participating in the civil disobedience should be willing to accept the consequences of breaking the law (Goodin, 2005; Rawls, 1971). The willingness to accept the consequences of engaging in illegal acts provides participants with the moral authority to commit those acts. They are not just paying lip service to support a cause; they are willing to make significant sacrifices for the cause.[29]

When social workers are helping others consider civil disobedience, they should ensure that participants know they may charged with and convicted of particular crimes. Many of the more common crimes associated with civil disobedience are misdemeanors: causing public nuisance, violating traffic control laws, trespass, unlawful assembly, failure to disperse, resisting arrest, and violating specific municipal codes (National Lawyers Guild, n.d.). The penalties for misdemeanors typically range from warnings to suspended sentences, probation, fines, and jail time of up to 1 year. More serious offenses, called felonies, may result from assaulting a police officer, seriously damaging property, or using weapons to cause injury (National Lawyers Guild, n.d.). Felony convictions may lead to harsher sentences, including incarceration in federal penitentiaries. In addition, people with felony convictions must cope with a criminal record for the rest of their lives (barring a pardon from the state governor or U.S. president). For social workers, the impact of a felony conviction may be severe, as many social agencies screen out workers with felony convictions. Further, many social work licensing laws prohibit licensure of social workers with felony convictions.

Social workers may be held criminally responsible for helping with civil disobedience, whether or not they actually participate in the primary activities that violated the law. Assume, for instance, you help organize the blockade of the capitol but you are not actually present for the blockade. As someone who helped plan the event, you could be charged with conspiracy. If you also assisted in the commission of the particular crimes (e.g., providing resources that the protesters used to commit the offense), you could be charged with aiding and abetting. If you helped protesters hide from the police after they committed the crime, you could be charged with obstructing justice or being an accessory to the offense (Saltzman & Furman, 1999). Thus,

---

[27] E.g., protesters could politely inform an arresting police officer that they would like to speak with an attorney before answering any questions.

[28] See Chapter 11 for additional examples of risk management (e.g., documenting the rationale for civil disobedience, building supportive coalitions, and obtaining legal advice).

[29] Consider, for instance, an activist who is arrested, but law enforcement officials agree to let the activist free if she promises not to re-offend. The activist might refuse this deal in order to maintain her moral authority and maintain pressure on the government. She might even engage in a hunger strike to demonstrate her moral commitment and put greater pressure on the government to change the unjust laws.

all planners, organizers, supporters, and other participants in civil disobedience should be apprised of the potential consequences of their roles.

Although people considering civil disobedience should be willing to accept the possibility of criminal charges and conviction, they should also note that criminal prosecution and conviction are not certainties. Police have discretion in whether to press charges. In some instances, the legal violations or harm done are not serious enough to warrant charges. In other cases, the police may be sensitive to public support for the protestors or the possibility of public backlash from pressing charges against a group that is standing up for a good moral cause. Similarly, the prosecuting attorneys may decide to drop charges or plea bargain to reduce charges in return for a guilty plea. In court, alleged offenders could raise the defense that they were challenging unjust and unconstitutional laws. However, good intent (breaking the law to change it) is not necessarily a legal justification for crimes committed during acts of civil disobedience—particularly if the court finds the laws challenged to be valid (Goodin, 2005; Lambek, 1987). Individuals or groups considering civil disobedience would be wise to consult attorneys who specialize in this area. Attorneys may be able to provide legal information as well as advice on how to manage the legal risks of civil disobedience (National Lawyers Guild, n.d.).

Some social workers and administrators of social agencies may be astonished to see an ethics textbook that provides guidance on how to break the law. Likewise, if you were to suggest civil disobedience to your colleagues or your social agency, you might be met with shock, resistance, or derision. Decisions to promote social justice by violating the law should not be taken lightly. However, it is useful to remember historical examples in which civil disobedience was instrumental in bringing about significant social change: for instance, Martin Luther King Jr.'s civil rights movement, which used nonviolence to challenge the racist Jim Crow Laws; Mahatma Gandhi's use of nonviolence to promote equality and challenge poverty in South Africa and India; Cesar Chavez's campaign of nonviolence to protest the treatment of farmsworkers in California; and the women's suffrage movement to advocate for women's right to vote (Goodin, 2005; Macauley, 2005; Starr, 1999). Note that the use of nonviolent strategies (including noncooperation with laws, passive resistance, work stoppages, and going limp at arrests) provides participants with moral justification for the means of their actions, not just their ends (Macauley, 2005). Note also, that many of the world's greatest civil rights advocates have served time in prison, even when they pursued social justice through nonviolence.

Because many social agencies are funded and regulated by the state, social workers who wish to participate in civil disobedience may not be able to count on support from their agencies. They may need to participate in civil disobedience as private citizens rather than in their professional capacities. Even then, they may be subjected to discipline or dismissal from their agencies.

Ethically, participating in civil disobedience may be justified as the right thing to do. Still, the principles of informed consent suggest that people should not be led into civil disobedience unless they are aware of the potential risks and benefits. Social workers must be particularly careful about taking advantage of vulnerable populations or putting them at risk by encouraging them to participate in civil disobedience (S.6.04).

CONCLUSION

This chapter has explored a range of ethical responsibilities and challenges that may arise for social workers practicing in the field of criminal justice. In some roles—probation officers, parole officers, and prison-based practitioners—social workers are working within the system and have specific mandates to protect the public. In other roles—providing community-based services to alleged offenders, convicted offenders and survivors—social workers are not working within the criminal justice system but still maintain ethical obligations regarding protection of the public. In yet other roles—as advocates of social justice—social workers may even support the breaking of a law in order to change the law. In all of these roles, social workers need to determine how to manage the potential conflicts between professional values, ethical standards, agency policies, and laws. These decisions may require a rational analysis of the worker's duties and options, as well as awareness of the worker's personal convictions, beliefs, emotional responses, and ethics of care.

DISCUSSION QUESTIONS AND EXERCISES

The following exercises are designed to help you put material from this chapter into practice. The first seven exercises invite you to analyze challenging ethical situations involving criminal justice issues. Try using the first three stages of the Framework for Managing Ethical Issues (in the introduction to Part II) to help you work through the issues: identify the ethical issues, determine appropriate help, and think critically. The role-play scenarios in Exercise 8 invite you to practice discussing ethical issues with clients and professional colleagues. In order to prepare, make use of the first three stages of the Framework. Also make use of the fourth stage, managing conflict, to help you work through the issues during the role-play (see Chapter 7 to refresh your memory about Socratic inquiry, debate, dialogue, and mediation).

1. *Comparative Ethics*: Assume Cordelia tells you that she robbed a convenience store. She claims she did it because she needed the money to pay her rent. Otherwise, her family would be living on the street. She used a gun in the robbery, but nobody was hurt. What are the ethical and legal obligations of a social worker who receives this admission? Compare and contrast these ethical obligations with those of a lawyer, a doctor, or a police officer who receives the same admission from Cordelia.[30]
2. *Mandated Autonomy*: Some ethicists argue that mandating people with addictions into treatment actually promotes autonomy rather than hinders it. According to this argument, people with addictions cannot make fully informed, voluntary choices while they are still addicted. If society mandates them into treatment for a period of time (e.g., 6 months), they will be able to make a more informed, voluntary choice (Caplan, 2006). What are the pros and cons of this argument from a social work perspective? What are the deontological and teleological perspectives on this issue? Should mandated treatment apply for all people with addictions, or only people who have committed drug- or alcohol-related offenses?
3. *Principles and Care*: Assume you are working with Claus, a 45-year-old man who wants you to help him overcome his fear of public places. His wife Ophelia is verbally and physically abusive toward him. She teases him about his facial deformity and speech impediment, she hits him with a broom handle, and she threatens to kick the cat if he does not obey her every command. Claus's life is not in immediate danger, though Ophelia's physical assaults have been severe enough to warrant police involvement. When you have talked to Claus about whether he wants to leave Ophelia, he says he wants to stay. She gives him financial security, friendship, and a sense of purpose. Claus has a low sense of self-esteem and tends to acquiesce to the demands of others. You are considering using your relationship with Claus to persuade him to leave Ophelia. Still, you are concerned about imposing your values and beliefs. Compare and contrast how you would deal with this situation from a principled approach and an ethics of care approach (Banks, 2006; Buttell et al., 2006; Linzer, 2004).
4. *Risky Records*: Luferac Counseling Services provides art and play therapy for clients

[30] Use the policies or code of ethics from your local police or from a larger law enforcement association, such as the International Association of Chiefs of Police (n.d.).

recovering from traumatic experiences. In a recent rape case, one of their workers was compelled to testify and bring her client records to court. Her client was the alleged victim. The records included the worker's interpretations of the client's drawings and dramatizations, which depicted a very disturbed psyche. The defense attorney used this information to question the client's credibility as a witness. The agency is revising its record-keeping policies to reduce the chances of embarrassing future clients. Some workers suggest keeping minimal client records, with just the basics of whether clients attend sessions and are benefiting from services. Others suggest they need to keep more complete records, not only to meet NASW standards but also to facilitate effective treatment. What are the advantages and disadvantages of each approach to record keeping, and are there any better approaches that Luferac should consider?

5. *Poppy Place*: Harmony Hills is a spiritual community of 550 families that cultivates opium poppies and uses the seeds for religious rituals. Although law enforcement officials generally ignore or tolerate the cultivation and use of small quantities of poppies, they have decided to press charges against the members of Harmony Hills because of the large quantities of poppy seeds they are using. In particular, law enforcement officials are concerned that the poppies could be used to produce heroin. Further, they believe that allowing Harmony Hills to cultivate poppies would place the state on a slippery slope toward legalization of all narcotics. From a social policy perspective, should Harmony Hills be permitted to cultivate and use poppies for religious purposes, or should they be subject to the same laws as everyone else? What ethical principles should be taken into account?
6. *Felon Social Workers*: A school of social work has recently had an incident in which a field student stole money from a client. The agency and client were particularly upset with the school when they found out the student had a felony conviction, for which he served a 2-year sentence. The school is reconsidering its policy on whether to admit students with felony convictions into its program. What ethical principles should the school consider in developing its policy? What policy would you recommend, and why? (Cowburn & Nelson, 2008)
7. *Unethical and Illegal*: A woman who is addicted to alcohol continues to drink during pregnancy, even after her physician and social worker warn her about the risks to her fetus. The baby is born with fetal alcohol syndrome. Should the woman be subject to criminal charges for drinking during her pregnancy? What goals would be achieved by pursuing criminal charges? What are the risks of pressing charges in such situations? What other approaches could be used to manage the legal, ethical, and clinical issues raised by this case? (Andrews & Patterson, 1995).
8. *Role-Plays*: For each of the following scenarios, select students in your group to play each role. To prepare for the role-play, identify the ethical issues and potential conflicts raised in each case. Also, identify strategies from this chapter that may help the social worker deal with these issues. Do not write full scripts for the role-play, though the person playing the social worker should jot down key points to remember.
   a. Chaisin has been convicted for assault in a hate crime targeting gay men. As a condition of probation, Chaisin has agreed to go for counseling with Suki. At the beginning of their first session, he tells Suki, "Those faggots deserved what they got. Wouldn't you agree?" Suki is lesbian and is particularly aghast at Chaisin's comments. She has not told him about her sexual orientation and does not want to make an issue of it, but her role is to help Chaisin with his homophobia.
   b. Santo provides anger management counseling for groups of men, including a client named Clay. One evening, two police (Sgt. Price and Sgt. Pointer)

come to the agency with a warrant for Clay's arrest. They want to charge Clay with public disturbance at an anti-war rally. Santo is the most senior staff member, so he agrees to speak with the police about the warrant. Clay has told Santo about the incident, claiming that he was acting in a peaceful manner until police started to harass the protesters.

c. Sylvester provides counseling for clients recovering from serious car accidents. His agency requires clients to sign forms stating that they agree not to subpoena workers to testify in any court proceedings. The agency does not want its staff to spend time in court, which would take away time from providing direct services. Also, the agency is concerned that clients might manipulate the way they present themselves to ensure that their workers provide positive testimony about them in court. One of his clients, Conan, has been charged with reckless driving and wants Sylvestor to testify on his behalf. Sylvester says that agency policy prohibits him from testifying about clients in court. He notes that Conan signed an agreement not to subpoena him. Conan asks Sylvester whether social workers are supposed to do *what their agency says* or *what is good for the client.*

d. Catarina has been charged with setting fire to a Hindu temple. Her lawyer is arguing that she is not criminally responsible because of her mental illness (dissociative personality disorder). The court orders Catarina to go for a mental status evaluation from Sharlee, a forensic social worker. During their first meeting, Catarina tells Sharlee that she is not insane and that she did not commit the offense. She asks Sharlee to advise her lawyer that they should drop the insanity defense and plead innocent at trial.

e. Christopher has been convicted of murder. The court is planning a hearing to determine whether he should receive the death penalty. The court has assigned Shaina, a forensic social worker, to evaluate Christopher and report back to the court on any mitigating circumstances (Schroeder, Guin, Pogue, & Bordelon, 2006). Shaina begins the session by explaining her role and the nature of confidentiality to Christopher.

f. Carla and Cyril arrange to meet with Salina, a social worker specializing in community empowerment and advocacy. They ask Salina to help them organize a sit-in at an upcoming city hall meeting. They are concerned about police brutality toward visible minorities in the community and want the city council to take action. City ordinances prohibit groups from holding organized demonstrations at city hall meetings. Carla and Cyril hope that their sit-in will provoke the police to attack members of their group, demonstrating that their concerns about police brutality are real. Salina asks if she can first help them assess the situation before deciding whether to engage in this form of civil disobedience. City hall meetings are broadcast on community cable television, although few people watch it. Cyril and Carla are willing to do whatever it takes to take on city hall. They are not so sure how many others will support them due to fears of encouraging further police brutality and recriminations.

g. Shanissy provides group counseling for inmates in a federal penitentiary. She has scheduled a meeting with the warden, Mrs. Wilcox, to discuss concerns about HIV transmission in the prison. Shanissy is concerned that inmates are having unprotected sex with each other and wants to make condoms available. Mrs. Wilcox responds that sex among inmates is prohibited, so the prison is not allowed to pass out condoms or condone sexual activities in any way. Shanissy wants Mrs. Wilcox to reconsider, as social workers are ethically obliged to advocate on behalf of vulnerable clients.

h. Chevy gave his pet snake live guinea pigs to eat. As a result, police charged him with feeding live prey. The court ordered probation, conditional upon his attending 8 hours of counseling. The order did not specify what the counseling was for, though the probation officer indicated Chevy needs to gain empathy for live animals and the suffering he has caused. Upon meeting his social worker Stewie, Chevy says, "I'm only here because I have to be here. I didn't do anything that doesn't already happen all the time in nature anyhow. I love my snake and I just want to take care of it as well as I can. So, could you please sign my form saying I've been here and let me go?" Stewie tries to engage Chevy by fostering his self-determination and confidentiality as much as possible.

i. Building on the scenario above, assume Chevy refused to open up because he was concerned Stewie would tell his probation officer anything that was discussed in their meeting. In this role-play, Stewie calls the probation officer, P. O. Patterson, to negotiate what types of information need to be shared and what types do not. P.O. Patterson wants full information because his role is to protect society—and in this case, animals—from harm. Stewie argues for very limited sharing of information so he has a better chance of engaging Chevy in a therapeutic process.

j. Sasha is a community mediator whose role is to act as an impartial third party, helping a client discuss conflicts and work toward mutually agreeable solutions. Police refer the leaders of two youth gangs to mediation, hoping to avoid further violence between the groups. Craig (17) is the leader of a youth gang called the Kantians. Clive (16) leads a group called the Benthamites. Sasha explains that mediation is a confidential process, so what they discuss in mediation stays within the room. During mediation, Sasha helps the groups work toward an agreement, basically dividing the turf where each group will operate. Although Clive and Craig seemed to support the agreement, Sasha overhears them talking when they are leaving the room. Clive asked if they were still on for tonight's action. Craig said, "Yes, but remember it's just knives. No guns." Sasha calls them back into the room to discuss her duty to report foreseeable, future danger to the authorities. Clive and Craig respond with anger, telling her that she promised confidentiality and "You know what happens when people don't keep their promises."

Chapter 16

Elders, Values, and Ethics

This chapter focuses on two substantive issues: end-of-life decision making and elder abuse. Although a myriad of other ethical issues arise in the context of social work with elders, these are two of the more challenging ones. Further, by concentrating on just two substantive issues, this chapter provides an in-depth exploration of how to manage these concerns in practice. In particular, this chapter focuses on the use of conflict resolution and communication strategies for managing ethical issues arising out of end-of-life (EOL) decision making[1] and elder abuse. Although social workers need to be able to analyze ethical issues to identify the best responses, rational analysis is not sufficient for the management of difficult ethical issues. Social workers also need to be able to bring people together to discuss issues, share perspectives, manage emotions, build consensus, and make difficult decisions even when consensus is not possible.

END-OF-LIFE DECISION MAKING

To say that end-of-life (EOL) decision making can lead to significant controversy and anguish is an understatement. As the notorious Terri Schiavo case in Florida illustrates, EOL situations may lead to considerable conflict, bitterness, and distress among family members, with the possible effects extending beyond family to religious communities, the media, the courts, state legislatures, Congress, and the White House (*Schindler ex. rel. Schiavo v. Schiavo*, 2005).[2] In spite of all

[1] The examples in this chapter will relate to EOL decision making for elderly clients; however, much of the information is also applicable for EOL decisions regarding clients of other ages.

[2] Terri Shiavo was a 41-year-old woman who went into a persistent vegetative state from 1990 to 2005, following a cardiac arrest due to a potassium imbalance. She had left no living will or other advanced directives, but her husband contended she would not want to be maintained on artificial life supports indefinitely. When he

the publicity of the heartache and hullabaloo surrounding the Schiavo case, however, we should remember that an overwhelming majority of individuals and families are able to make EOL decisions in a civil, friendly, private, and affirming manner, or at least without the involvement of court and the media (Bloche, 2005; Braun et al., 2000; Butler, 2004). This section provides social workers with information and strategies to help clients[3] manage EOL decisions compassionately and constructively. As the NASW (2004) Standards for Social Work Practice in Palliative and End of Life Care suggest, social workers require specialized knowledge and skills to be able to help clients assess, plan, and implement decisions for EOL care.

LEARNING OBJECTIVES

Upon successful completion of this chapter, students will be able to

- Describe the legal and ethical context for end-of-life decision making.
- Identify and apply relevant laws and ethical standards in elder abuse situations.
- Employ five constructive conflict resolution strategies for managing ethical issues: preparing for difficult conversations, establishing parameters for discussion, facilitating recognition, generating creative options, and apologizing.
- Describe the legal and ethical responsibilities of social workers in elder abuse situations.
- Apply the Transtheoretical Model of Change in situations in which clients refuse help for elder abuse and the worker needs to balance the interests of client autonomy and beneficence (protecting the client from harm).

Options

When people think of EOL decision making, they often focus on the issues of whether to provide, withhold, or remove treatments that can sustain life or bodily functions (especially breathing, hydration, nutrition, and renal function). In practice, EOL decision making is much broader, encompassing a broad range of decisions, many of which are noncontroversial but still very important. For instance, in the days, weeks, or months preceding death, individuals may make decisions concerning where they want to live (e.g., home, hospital, hospice), how they want to spend their time (e.g., relaxing, reflecting, engaging in certain activities, traveling), who they want to spend time with (e.g., family, friends, nobody), and how to bring spirituality or meaning into their final days (e.g., through prayer, meditation, connecting with others, or doing volunteer work) (Gott, Small, Barnes, Payne, & Seamark, 2008; Koenig, 2005). They may need to make health-care decisions ranging from the mundane (e.g., whether to take vitamins and brush their teeth) to the extraordinary (e.g., whether to try new cures or experimental treatments for acute conditions). For most of these decisions, social workers have little trouble with honoring client self-determination, abiding by the client's wishes rather than trying to impose their own preferences or those of the client's family (S.1.02). As long as the client has sufficient mental capacity to make a particular decision, then social workers should advocate for respecting the client's wishes (Ss. 1.01 & 1.03[a] & [c]; Rao & Blake, 2002).[4]

In some instances, individuals and families are faced with making a choice between curative treatment, life-sustaining treatment, and

---

instructed the medical care providers to remove the life supports (for hydration and nutrition) Terri's parents objected, taking their case to the media, Florida's legislature, the courts, and Congress in order to maintain Terri's life. Eventually, the courts determined that Terri's husband had authority to decide to remove life supports, as he was legally Terri's guardian and there was no other clear and convincing evidence of Terri's wishes.

[3] Medical facilities tend to use the word *patient*, whereas social service agencies tend to use the term *client*. EOL issues may arise in both medical and social service settings. For ease of reference, the terms *patient* and *client* will be used interchangeably in this chapter.

[4] For information on assessing mental capacity and identifying proxy decision makers, see Chapter 13.

palliative care. Social workers can help families make better informed choices by explaining these terms and how they can exercise these options:

1. *Curative treatment* refers to interventions aimed at alleviating medical problems and restoring the person to health. Some health-care professionals distinguish between ordinary and extraordinary curative treatments, with extraordinary treatments being those that are unusual, highly invasive, very risky, very expensive, or heroic in nature.[5]
2. *Life-sustaining treatment* refers to interventions aimed at maintaining the life or prolonging biological functioning[6] of the person, without reversing or curing the underlying disease or medical condition.
3. *Palliative care* refers to interventions and support designed to maximize quality of life for the client and family. Palliative care may include strategies to reduce pain or stress, helping clients function and perform the tasks of daily living, counseling clients and families to help them manage the biopsychosocial issues related to the client's condition or impending death, facilitating spiritual well-being, and affirming death as a normal process. Palliative care neither hastens nor postpones death[7] (Csikai & Chaitin, 2006; World Health Organization, 2004).

In general, a client's right to self-determination includes the right to accept or reject any and all of these forms of care (NASW, 2004; Patient Self-Determination Act, 1990). Thus, a cancer patient may refuse chemotherapy, whether or not physicians believe the cancer can be cured. Similarly, a patient may request chemotherapy, even though physicians believe the chances of cure are low. Although physicians are not required to participate in futile efforts to save the life of a patient, their code of ethics suggests they should respect the patient's right to self-determination (American Medical Association, 2001). Physicians have the authority to provide advice on how to manage medical conditions (Richter, Eisemann, & Zgonnikova, 2001), but ultimately the patient should have the final say. In contrast, social workers should avoid providing medical advice, but they may engage clients in discussions of options, helping them understand and explore possible courses of action (Leichtentritt & Rettig, 2001).

Many individuals and families have difficulty discussing issues pertaining to death and dying, so they delay talking about what will happen if particular family members lose their mental capacity and EOL decisions need to be made on their behalf. Unfortunately, if they do not discuss and plan for such events, the psychosocial and legal issues can become much more complicated when EOL decisions need to be made—particularly when quick decisions need to be made under urgent situations (e.g., when a patient has stopped breathing and the doctors need to know whether to resuscitate and put the patient on artificial respiration). Social workers can enhance client self-determination and help elders plan for EOL care

[5] Some health-care professionals believe there is an ethical obligation to provide ordinary treatments, but no obligation to provide extraordinary treatments. The distinction between what is ordinary and extraordinary, however, is open to interpretation. Beauchamp and Childress (2009) suggest that the distinction is not meaningful for the purposes of determining whether there are ethical obligations to provide certain forms of treatment.

[6] Note how the terminology is value laden: individuals who identify as pro-life may prefer terms such as *maintaining life*, whereas pro-choice individuals may prefer terms such as *prolonging biological functioning*. I have endeavored to give balance in this statement by using both terms, though I do not adhere to this standard throughout the chapter, as using both types of terminology becomes cumbersome. As a social worker, consider how you can use the terminology strategically, for instance, mirroring a client's language in order to build trust, demonstrate empathy, and engage the client; or using language that supports a particular cause when acting in an advocacy role.

[7] Note that some forms of pain medication may hasten death. Many health-care professionals believe that it is ethical to administer pain medication to terminal patients knowing that it may hasten their death, provided the primary purpose of administering the medication is to manage pain.

by encouraging them to consider what types of legal arrangements can be made to ensure that their EOL wishes are respected should they lose mental capacity (McInnis-Dittrich, 2005). State laws differ in terms of the language and legal instruments they use,[8] but all jurisdictions authorize two basic options for advance health-care planning: advance health-care directives and health-care proxies. *When using advance health-care directives (sometimes called living wills), individuals designate which types of treatments and care they want and do not want, should various circumstances arise.* For instance, one individual may want to receive cardiopulmonary resuscitation or other life-saving treatments in the event of a major heart attack, whereas another individual may not. Individuals may change their health-care directives as their medical and psychosocial situation changes, as long as they have sufficient mental capacity. *When using a proxy (such as a medical power of attorney), the individual designates one or more people to have decision-making authority over health-care issues, if and when the individual becomes mentally incapacitated.* The designated proxy (sometimes called a guardian, health-care attorney, conservator, or legally authorized caregiver) is empowered to make decisions over curative treatment, life-sustaining treatment, and palliative care (Butler, 2004). The individual may give the proxy broad discretion, or may limit the discretion by indicating his or her wishes for how to respond in various situations (for instance, instructing the proxy to reject certain curative treatment measures that are particularly intrusive or painful, or violate the individual's religious beliefs).

Social workers should not force elderly clients into signing advance directives, such as living wills or health-care proxies. Rather, workers may help clients consider the benefits and risks of these options in order to make better informed decisions (NASW, 2004). The usual benefits of advance directives and proxies include helping the family and doctors know how to honor the client's wishes, ensuring that desired forms of care are provided as soon as possible, and minimizing stress and conflict during periods of emergency and grief. Two risks of advance directives are subjecting the individual and family to stress and conflict as they are considering what types of plans to make for EOL decisions, and not being able to predict the exact circumstances over which an advance directive or proxy may be put into operation (Bloche, 2005). Consider, for instance, a client with an incurable, terminal illness who signs a proxy[9] giving his daughters authority over his health care. At the time the proxy is signed, all three seem to agree that the client should not be maintained indefinitely on life supports. When the time comes to make a decision, however, one of the daughters refuses consent, claiming (irrationally) that he can still be cured.[10] On balance, most social workers and health-care providers agree that advance directives and proxies are beneficial. Still, social workers should help the clients make their own choices, taking both the risks and benefits of such options into account (Medvene, Base, Patrick, & Wescott, 2007). Workers should also refer clients to attorneys if they need or desire legal advice.

Clients may have questions about the legality of certain types of EOL decisions, particularly ones in which medical treatment is refused or withdrawn, hastening death—or as others would say, selecting a time and manner of death so the individual may die with dignity. Although different clients, family members, and professionals have different values, morals, and religious beliefs concerning such EOL issues, the laws are relatively clear regarding many aspects of EOL decision making and advance directives. First, the laws typically distinguish between active euthanasia (taking proactive steps to cause death) and passive euthanasia (refusing or withdrawing medical

---

[8] To locate advance directive forms that may be used in your state, see http://www.uslivingwillregistry.com/forms.shtm. The ABA Commission on Law and Aging (2005) provides a toolkit on advance directives at http://www.abanet.org/aging/publications/docs/consumer_tool_kit_bk.pdf.

[9] Sometimes called a durable power of attorney for health care.

[10] As Florence Nightingale (1969, cited in Wainwright & Gallagher, 2007, p. 49) said, "I really believe there is scarcely a greater worry which invalids have to endure than the incurable hopes of their friends."

care) (Braun et al., 2000). The law allows individuals to refuse life-saving treatment or to ask for life-sustaining treatment to be withdrawn (Braddock, 2008). Health-care professionals should honor the directions of client with respect to refusing treatment. If the client does not have sufficient mental capacity, then the professionals should follow the client's advance directive or the decision of the health-care proxy.[11] Health-care professionals may also withdraw life-sustaining treatment according to the directions of the patient, the patient's living will, or the patient's health-care proxy[12] (Sabatino, n.d.). Participating in passive euthanasia (allowing a terminally ill person to die) is not illegal (*Cruzan v. Director, Missouri Department of Health*, 1990). Taking active steps to kill a person, however, constitutes a criminal offense (Bloche, 2005). Thus, a physician, social worker, or other person who administers lethal medication to a terminally ill patient may be convicted of murder or manslaughter (*Vaco v. Quill*, 1997).

Physician-assisted suicide differs from active euthanasia, in that the physician prescribes lethal medication to a terminally ill patient, but the patient administers it. Physician-assisted suicide (PAS) is illegal in the United States, with the possible exceptions of the states of Oregon and Washington (Government of Oregon, 2007; Smith, 2003).[13] In 1997, Oregon was the first state to enact a Death With Dignity Act, allowing terminally ill residents of Oregon to end their lives through the voluntary self-administration of lethal medications, expressly prescribed by a physician for that purpose (Government of Oregon, 2007). The federal government (through the offices of the attorney general) has challenged the Oregon legislation, arguing that assisting suicide is not a "legitimate medical purpose" within the federal Controlled Substances Act. The government of Oregon currently considers its law to be constitutional, including its immunity provisions for physicians who prescribe lethal medications (Government of Oregon, 2007). Further legal challenges could be pending.

Although PAS is not legal in other states, some physicians and other helping professionals believe that supporting client self-determination includes helping terminally ill clients choose the time and manner of death. Accordingly, some medical professionals may decide to assist suicide surreptitiously (e.g., providing terminally ill individuals with barbiturates, ostensibly for pain relief, but knowing they may use the drugs for suicide). Anyone who assists a client commit suicide, however, should know the possibility of legal consequences should the person be caught and convicted.[14]

Although the laws regarding the legality of passive and active euthanasia are relatively clear, these issues still raise considerable controversy for professionals and clients alike. The following list illustrates a range of ethical viewpoints on euthanasia, including possible justifications for these viewpoints.

- *All forms of euthanasia are unethical*—According to this perspective, life is sacrosanct (Smith, 2003). Protection of life takes precedence over autonomy, quality of life, and all other ethical principles. There is no

[11] If there is no advance directive or proxy, then the next of kin may make decisions. In an emergency situation, if there is no advance directive, proxy, or identifiable next of kin, then the physicians can make decisions on the patient's behalf (*In re Quinlan*, 1976). Physicians should make use of hospital ethics committees and other protocols to make such decisions. In nonemergency situations, health-care providers may initiate court proceedings to have a public guardian appointed.

[12] Some states do not recognize a health-care proxy's authority to decide to withdraw life-sustaining treatment unless there is clear and convincing evidence of the patient's wishes to do so (Braun et al., 2000; *Cruzan v. Director, Missouri Department of Health*, 1990). Accordingly, it is important to review the state's legislation, not only in relation to who can act as a proxy, but also whether they can make decisions to withdraw or refuse life-sustaining treatment without evidence of the patient's wishes.

[13] Other states have been considering similar legislation. Other countries, notably the Netherlands, also have provisions that permit physician-assisted suicide under prescribed circumstances.

[14] See Chapter 15 for civil disobedience strategies that may be used to challenge existing laws and promote social justice.

distinction between taking positive acts to kill and withdrawing life supports, as both lead to death (Wainwright & Gallagher, 2007). This deontological perspective may be based on religious convictions or professional duties. For instance, some people of faith believe that people are not fully autonomous because they have duties to God or their higher power, including the absolute duty to respect the sanctity of life (Annenberg Media, 2007). The absolute duty to protect life may also be derived from professional ethics. According to the Hippocratic Oath (circa 400 BCE), for instance, physicians pledge to preserve life, not to administer noxious substances, and "above all, to do no harm."[15] People who adhere to this perspective may also be concerned about maintaining a firm boundary around protecting life: If exceptions are made for some circumstances, then others may argue that more and more exceptions should be made (Smith, 2003).[16] Further, proponents may be concerned about possible abuses, such as coercion from family members, health-care providers, or insurance providers. In particular, individuals with limited resources and access to health care may feel pressured into prematurely terminating life. Finally, medical professionals may be fallible: They may misdiagnose a patient or not be aware of a possible cure. The state has an interest in protecting life, giving individuals every possibility of being cured (Braddock, 2008).

- *Passive euthanasia is ethically justifiable, but active euthanasia is not*—Terminally ill clients with no prospect of recovery should be allowed to refuse treatment or ask for treatment to be withdrawn, but taking positive steps to assist with suicide is unethical. This perspective balances the protection of life with the principles of client autonomy. Although life is still a high value, individuals with this perspective acknowledge that there are situations when the individual's quality of life and right to autonomy should take precedence (Wainwright & Gallagher, 2007). Proponents of this perspective may be applying the least harm principle. Given that the individual is going to die within a few months, why not let the individual have some choice in terms of EOL treatment and the timing of death? This perspective may also be based on the principle of compassion, offering individuals a humane alternative to unrelenting physical, psychological, or social suffering (Braddock, 2008).[17] Proponents of this perspective oppose active euthanasia, believing that the state has an interest in protecting life and ensuring that medical professionals do not take active steps to promote or facilitate suicide.
- *Active euthanasia (including assisted suicide) is ethically justifiable*—Terminally ill clients with no prospect of recovery should not only be allowed to refuse treatment or ask for treatment to be withdrawn; they should also be permitted to receive lethal medication or other assistance with

[15] Beauchamp and Childress (2009) suggest that the phrase, "above all, do no harm," is a strained translation of the Hippocratic oath, though the oath does express an obligation of nonmaleficence by stating that physicians will not use treatment to injure or wrong patients.

[16] This line of reasoning is sometimes called the "slippery slope" or "thin edge of the wedge" argument. For instance, if we allow euthanasia for terminally ill patients, then why not allow medical professionals to euthanize anyone with a poor quality of life? Slippery slope arguments should be taken seriously. However, the fact that a jurisdiction permits euthanasia for terminally ill cases does not mean that such a law would open up the floodgates for using euthanasia in inappropriate situations. One would need to research the potential and actual effects of such a policy (Beauchamp & Childress, 2009).

[17] This position could also be justified from certain religious perspectives. According to Catholic teachings, for instance, death is God's decision. If medical treatments do not provide a reasonable chance of improvement or recovery, then there are no obligations from Catholicism to continue medical treatment. Rather than killing, passive euthanasia may be seen as allowing the person to die, as God might have it (Annenberg Media, 2007).

the timing and manner of their death. Proponents of active euthanasia place high value on individual autonomy and dying with dignity. Although they value life, they do not believe that prolonging life (or biological functioning) is the most important principle. Some proponents may be applying a utilitarian perspective, basing their decisions on the greater good for society. Why should resources be wasted on futile attempts to save or prolong a terminally ill person's life (Beauchamp & Childress, 2009)? Other proponents may be applying a deontological perspective, giving priority to the principle of autonomy rather than the principle of protecting life. Proponents may argue that any distinction between passive and active euthanasia is artificial, as the primary purposes of either form of euthanasia are to honor client autonomy and to alleviate pain and suffering. The concept of justice, treating like cases alike, may suggest that if society allows withdrawal of life supports, then it should also allow assisted suicide. For some terminally ill patients, there are no life supports to withdraw; assisted suicide is the only option for helping them choose the time and manner of their death. Finally, proponents may believe that assisted suicide is already taking place, surreptitiously. By providing a legal means for managing requests for euthanasia, the state is promoting honesty and open discussions of important EOL issues (Braddock, 2008). Physician-assisted suicide may actually discourage premature suicide, as terminally ill patients will know their physicians will honor their wishes when the time is right. Physician-assisted suicide can also prevent patients from using more gruesome and painful approaches to suicide, such as hanging or jumping out of a window (Rogatz, 2003). To prevent abuses (such as coercion to suicide by insurance companies or family members), proponents suggest regulations of PAS could include strict documentation of the client's terminal condition and mental capacity, assessments by more than one mental health professional, and a requirement to offer palliative care to anyone requesting PAS (Rogatz, 2003).[18]

- *The ethicality of euthanasia depends on family input or consent*—Whereas the principle of autonomy is often used to validate an individual's control over his or her own destiny, this perspective considers the rights and responsibilities of family members. Proponents of this perspective believe that EOL decisions may affect the family, so the family should have a say in whether or not to accept treatments, withdraw treatments, or take active steps to help the individual choose the timing and manner of death (Wainwright & Gallagher, 2007). Proponents of this approach place communitarianism over individualism (Leichtentritt & Rettig, 2001).

What is your view on euthanasia? What values, religious beliefs, morals, or convictions inform or justify your view on euthanasia? Given your view, how would you feel if a professional colleague or client was advocating for one of the other views listed above? Would you feel disgust, anger, frustration, or helplessness (Weissman, 2001)? To remain nonjudgmental, social workers should be aware of their values and feelings so they can manage them effectively. Workers should also be able to understand, respect, and validate perspectives that may differ profoundly from their own (Adler, 2006). If a client asks for assistance with suicide, for instance, the worker is not ethically obliged

[18] Beauchamp and Childress (2009) identify nine conditions that should be satisfied to justify physician-assisted suicide: *(1)* The patient has decision-making capacity and voluntarily requests assisted suicide. *(2)* The physician has an ongoing relationship with the patient. *(3)* The physician engages the patient in a mutual, informed decision-making process. *(4)* The physician provides a supportive, yet critical and probing environment for the decision making. *(5)* The patient considers EOL care alternatives and rejects them. *(6)* The patient consults with other medical professionals. *(7)* The patient's expressed desire for assisted suicide is durable. *(8)* The patient is experiencing an unacceptable level of suffering. (9) The means of assisted suicide is as painless and comfortable as possible. Consider what role, if any, social workers should play in assisted suicide.

to provide such assistance (Braddock, 2008). Regardless of whether the worker agrees with the client's choice, the worker should be able to demonstrate empathy and unconditional positive regard for the client. Workers should also recognize that it may be futile to try to persuade others by offering rational arguments and trying to educate them about the facts. If the difference of opinion on EOL care is based on conflicting values and deeply held beliefs, logic-based arguments are unlikely to have an impact on what others believe is moral or immoral (Weissman, 2001).

The following section offers strategies and suggestions for engaging individuals, families, physicians, and other professionals in discussions over EOL concerns.

Engaging Clients and Professionals in EOL Discussions

When ethicists discuss EOL issues, they often become absorbed in rational analyses of ethical principles (autonomy, privacy, protection of life, quality of life, quality of death, dignity), options, and potential consequences of those options. Ethicists may also engage in thoughtful debates concerning what is life, what is death, and what are the state's interests in preserving life or delaying death. In practice, logic and rational analysis of ethical issues are not sufficient for managing EOL issues (Bloche, 2005). Although some conflicts over EOL care arise because of different values, ethics, and beliefs, conflicts may also arise because of miscommunication, fear, uncertainty, anger, regrets, and mistrust (Lask, 2003; Weissman, 2001). For social workers to help clients and co-professionals manage EOL issues more effectively, they need to attend to both rational and nonrational factors affecting the conflict. To demonstrate skills and strategies for engaging clients and professionals in constructive EOL discussions, consider the following scenario:

> Chelsie is a 76-year-old Navajo woman who was rushed to the city hospital when she accidentally fell and fractured her hip. An emergency room physician, Dr. Price, informs Chelsie that she will need surgery. He also provides her with information about her rights regarding health-care decisions and asks whether she has a living will or power of attorney. Throughout the discussion, Chelsie does not say anything. Dr. Price explains that the Patient Self-Determination Act (1990) requires the hospital to ask these questions so that patients can make informed choices about what should happen if they were to become mentally incapacitated or require life-sustaining treatment (Adler, 2006). Chelsie looks out the window and remains silent. Shortly after, Dr. Price asks Saba, the hospital social worker, to meet with Chelsie to see if she can engage Chelsie more effectively.

Preparing for Potentially Difficult Conversations

A difficult conversation arises when one or more participants dread participating in it. They may engage in the conversation reluctantly, postpone it, or try to avoid it altogether (Stone et al., 1999). Although some people are quite comfortable discussing EOL issues, others experience levels of discomfort ranging from mild to high. For clients, the anxiety may stem from a number of sources, for instance, cultural taboos about discussing death, past experiences with death and dying, and difficulty coping with the recent diagnosis of a terminal condition. Social workers and other professionals may experience anxiety for similar reasons. In addition, they may fear the reactions of their clients (Weissman, 2001), such as tears, denial, anger, or frustration. Given the potential for anxiety, social workers should conduct a preparatory assessment before engaging others in discussions of EOL issues (or indeed, any other difficult topic).

Questions to consider during a preparatory assessment include these:

- How do I feel about the upcoming discussion of EOL issues? If I feel anxious, what is the source of this anxiety? How can I manage the anxiety so it does not interfere with my interactions with others?
- What do I know about the other person's feelings toward discussing EOL issues? (If you know the person well, you may rely on

experience and discussions. If you do not know the person well, you may want to consider the client's cultural, religious, or ethnic background: What does the literature say about this group's values and beliefs in relation to EOL issues; should I consult with a cultural expert?)

Saba has been working with elderly clients for over 10 years and is relatively comfortable discussing EOL issues. As she reflects on her feelings toward the EOL issues in this case, she acknowledges her bias toward signing living wills. She has seen many families experience conflict and hostility when they have had to make challenging EOL decisions without the benefit of clear directions from the individual with a terminal condition. In one case, the family ended up in a terrible court battle. Saba reminds herself that, in spite of her own feelings, she should allow her client the freedom to sign or not sign a living will. She reminds herself to be open-minded, empathic, flexible, and curious when speaking with Chelsie (Lachman, 1999).

Saba does not know Chelsie personally or professionally, though she has worked with others from the Navajo community. Saba realizes that Native Americans are less likely than other Americans to have advance directives. In part, this may be due to mistrust, given a history of discrimination, lack of access to medical care, and broken treaties or promises by European Americans (Tilden, Tolle, Drarch, & Perrin, 2004). Saba knows that some Navajos believe that speaking about terminal illness will hasten death (Ellerby, McKenzie, McKay, Gariepy, & Kaufert, 2000; Van Winkle, 2000). She considers the possibility that Chelsie's reluctance to discuss advance directives with Dr. Price may be due to a cultural belief that discussing the future may be tempting fate (Beauchamp & Childress, 2009). To check this hypothesis, she notes that it will be important to allow Chelsie to determine the level and explicitness of information that she is ready to discuss (Ellerby et al., 2000). Saba also tries to tune into Chelsie's feelings when Dr. Price initiated the discussion about surgery and the need for advance planning. Some patients believe Dr. Price is callous and aloof, as he presents in a direct, concise, and business-like manner. Chelsie knows that Dr. Price cares deeply about his patients, though he shows this through his surgical skill and attention to detail, rather than through a warm bedside manner (Bloche, 2005; Weissman, 2001). Saba hypothesizes that Chelsie, as a Navajo, may have found Dr. Price's directness to be rude and abrupt. Saba plans to take more time up front, cultivating a relationship before engaging Chelsie in a discussion about advance directives. She knows she might need to talk about advance planning indirectly, perhaps inviting Chelsie to discuss how EOL decisions were made for family or friends who have already passed away (Van Winkle, 2000).

To develop rapport with Chelsie, Saba asks the nurses if she can bring Chelsie her lunch. This gives Saba an opportunity to spend time with Chelsie, letting them get to know one another before Saba broaches difficult topics. As Saba sits with Chelsie during lunch, neither speaks very much. Eventually, Saba notes there is a Navajo Yeii Spirit on Saba's bedside table. This shows Chelsie that Saba knows something about Navajo spirituality and gives an opening for Chelsie to talk about it (Kuczewski, 2007). Chelsie says it was a gift from her father and she always keeps it close to her. Saba refrains from asking what it means to Chelsie, not wanting to be too intrusive. After Chelsie finishes eating, Saba says she heard Dr. Price had come to talk about the surgery and her health-care options. Saba tries to use positive language. She does not directly mention the possibility of death or mental incapacity. Saba offers to answer any questions Chelsie may have, but also advises Chelsie that she has the right to decide what they will talk about. Saba notes that while many of her clients want to talk about advance planning, others find this goes against their traditional values and beliefs (Carrese & Rhodes, 1995). Saba offers to come back later, perhaps with an elder or family members present. In many Native American cultures,[19] elders and extended family are important

[19] For information on the ways in which other cultures view EOL decision making, see Braun et al. (2000).

sources of support, particularly for health and EOL issues (Ellerby et al., 2000). Chelsie says her son is coming later that afternoon, so perhaps Saba could return then. Although Chelsie has not been very verbal, Saba notes that her body language (especially subtle head nods) suggests she is starting to feel more comfortable with Saba.

Saba meets with her supervisor to discuss her meeting with Chelsie, as well as the plans to get together with Chelsie and her son. Saba expresses concern over Chelsie's reluctance to discuss EOL issues, noting that her cultural beliefs may be making it difficult for her to consider advance health-care planning. The supervisor asks Saba whether she considered other possible explanations for Chelsie's response. Saba knows that some elderly clients are uncomfortable with conflict (Weitzman & Weitzman, 2003), so she reassured Chelsie that she would respect any decisions Chelsie made, including a decision not to discuss health-care planning. Saba notes that she also screened for incapacity issues. Elderly clients, particularly ones who have suffered a serious fall, may be disoriented when brought into the unfamiliar surroundings of a hospital (Weitzman & Weitzman, 2003). Saba says that when they discussed other issues, Chelsie was lucid. There were no signs of confusion, memory loss, or dementia. The supervisor encourages Saba to keep her hypotheses about Chelsie's reluctance to speak as tentative, as other explanations could arise in upcoming meetings.

Establishing Parameters for Discussion

When broaching difficult topics, workers can pre-empt problems and foster positive norms by establishing parameters for discussion early in the process: What is the purpose of the meeting, what topics will be discussed, what topics will not be discussed, and what guidelines for communication should they use to ensure that everyone feels safe in the discussion? For high-conflict situations, setting specific ground rules may be desirable (e.g., treating others with respect, validating each other's right to different opinions, speaking on one's own behalf, and checking out assumptions with others). For low-conflict situations, less formal guidelines may be sufficient. By giving all the participants input into the parameters for discussion, they may take greater ownership of the process (Bush & Folger, 2005).

When Saba returns to Chelsie's room, Chelsie introduces her son, David. Saba does not delve into business right away, wanting to establish rapport and observe David's interactions with Chelsie when discussing noncontroversial issues. Saba asks if Chelsie has ever been in a hospital before. Chelsie says this is her first time. David explains that her mother has always gone to traditional healers from the community. Saba demonstrates empathy, noting how the hospital environment might seem strange and cold compared to being at home. Saba inquires whether she or the hospital can do anything to make them feel more comfortable. David jokes, "Just get my mother well and out of here as soon as possible." Saba validates, "I understand that it's important to be with your family and community."

In due course, Saba asks if it would be acceptable to talk about the surgery. Chelsie says, "My son can do that for me. I'll just listen." Ordinarily, Saba might want to empower a client to speak for herself, but she respects Chelsie's right to exercise autonomy by delegating decision-making responsibility to her son (Ellerby et al., 2000). Saba recognizes that whereas the NASW Code of Ethics envisions consent by the individual client, Navajo culture tends to be more communitarian, with family members involved in decision making. Saba explains that she is not a surgeon and she is not there to provide medical advice. She says Dr. Price has asked her to speak with the family about who is responsible for Chelsie's health-care decisions once surgery starts and whether Chelsie or the family would like to look at the hospital's health-care forms. Saba notes that some clients provide the hospital with very clear directions about what they want or don't want, whereas others simply indicate who is responsible for the client. Saba intentionally avoids talking about the risks of surgery unless David and Chelsea indicate they want such information. Saba asks how much information and detail they would like to have about the options. David explains that that they do not need to make plans because the Creator will decide what will happen. Saba understands that in traditional Navajo culture, language shapes reality, so discussing risks may lead to their fruition. Some Navajos believe that health is maintained and restored through positive ritual language (Carrese & Rhodes, 2000). Saba confirms, "I know that discussing health issues may be a difficult topic. I do not want to cause any harm, so we do not need to discuss anything that you do not want to discuss." David says his mother is going to be returned to full health and harmony. Saba validates David's positive thinking and engages him in further discussion of Chelsie's strengths, including her spirit, her compassion, and her ability to deal with difficult situations in the past. All of these are safe issues that the clients are willing to discuss, as positive thoughts and feelings foster restoration of good health. In spite of Saba's professional preference for encouraging clients to sign advance health-care directives, David and Chelsie have made it very clear that they do not want to discuss advance health planning or potential problems. These issues go to the root of their social identities, so Saba knows that it is particularly vital to respect their wishes (Stone et al., 1999).

Facilitating Recognition

When people become embroiled in conflict, they tend to focus on their own feelings and beliefs, sometimes blinding themselves to the feelings and beliefs of others. To help people manage conflict more effectively, social workers can facilitate recognition between them. Recognition refers to the process of listening actively to one another, demonstrating empathy and understanding (Bush & Folger, 2005). Social workers can model recognition by reflecting feelings and paraphrasing beliefs expressed by others. Workers can also teach clients and others how to paraphrase and reflect. When an individual feels his view on an ethical issue is right, validating the beliefs of others may be particularly difficult. For some people, acknowledging the validity of another's beliefs feels tantamount to admitting they are wrong. Workers can explain that ethical dilemmas are dilemmas because different people may have different opinions about how to resolve them. Workers can also explain that validating another's beliefs does not mean admitting one is wrong. Rather, it demonstrates that there is more than one way to think about a particular issue. Validating another person's beliefs demonstrates understanding, not agreement (Barsky, 2007a). When people validate one another's beliefs and feelings, they tend to open up and connect with each other in a more meaningful way.

Assume that Chelsie experiences a massive brain seizure during surgery. The physicians provide blood transfusions and put Chelsie on artificial respiration and feeding tubes, as she is now paralyzed. When Dr. Price meets with David following surgery, he is shocked to learn that David does not want his mother on artificial respiration and feeding tubes. David also tells Saba that he wants the life supports to be withdrawn as soon as possible. He does not want to see her suffer. He wants his mother to be treated with dignity, not disrespect. Saba advises David that she and Dr. Price will meet with the hospital ethics committee to review what has happened and decide how to proceed. Saba believes it is important to seek help and resolve problems before they escalate into court battles or other adversarial processes. An ethics committee offers a private, collaborative venue to resolve issues (Butler, 2004)

The ethics committee includes another physician, a nurse, and an attorney.[20] They also invite an elder from the Navajo community who acts as a cultural interpreter (Adler, 2006). Saba acts as facilitator, explaining the purpose of the meeting and noting the serious nature of the discussions. Initially, Dr. Price presents the case background. The attorney explains that, as next of kin, David has the right to determine whether his mother should remain on life supports. The attorney explains that the health-care providers could encourage David to consider his mother's wishes, as well as what is in her best interests (Beauchamp & Childress, 2009). Dr. Price tells the committee that it would be ridiculous to

[20] Ordinarily, a hospital ethics meeting includes more participants. This example uses a small number in order to streamline the discussion.

remove the life supports because it is too soon to tell whether Chelsie will recover. He questions David's ability to make decisions, given that he discouraged Chelsie to sign a living will or power of attorney. Saba starts to explain why David did not want to discuss advance planning. Dr. Price cuts her off, noting that the hospital's responsibility is to preserve life whenever possible, and this is not a futile or impossible situation. His voice gets louder and louder as he questions why David and Chelsie refused to provide a "do not resuscitate" order if they did not want her to live. Saba reminds herself not to debate Dr. Price but to validate his feelings and beliefs. "I understand how frustrating this is. You've gone to extraordinary lengths to save Chelsie's life and it seems premature to even consider withdrawing life supports." As Saba continues to demonstrate understanding, Dr. Price seems to cool down.

Saba invites Benny (the elder) to discuss Navajo belief systems about life and health care. Benny explains how people from his culture embrace life, though they also accept death as a natural part of the circle of life (Van Winkle, 2000). Death may even be valued as a process in which individuals join with ancestors who have gone before. Traditional Navajos have a preference for natural medicines and remedies, and the concepts of feeding tubes and respiration devices may be seen as artificial and against the will of the Creator (Hendrix, n.d.). The nurse notes, "Feeding patients and giving them oxygen to breath is not artificial. What could be more natural that letting people have the air and food they need to live?" Saba encourages the nurse to summarize what she heard Benny say, to ensure she heard him correctly. The nurse responds, "Benny, are you saying that Navajos have a problem with advanced medical technology?" Benny reframes the so-called *problem* as a preference for nature-based medicine—for instance, using herbs that are provided by the Creator or healing rituals by Navajo medicine people (Ellerby et al., 2000). Saba notes, "So David's request to remove life supports is not that he wants his mother to die, but that he wants her to receive more natural methods of health care." Dr. Price chimes in, "I understand that David believes in natural healing methods. Still, if we remove the life supports, Chelsea will die." The elder responds, "Yes, she may die. We should also consider whether she will die with dignity, or live without it." As other members of the ethics committee express their concerns about client autonomy versus protection of life, family versus hospital responsibility, the values of modern versus traditional medicine, and the right to life versus the right to die with dignity, Saba continues to facilitate active listening and mutual understanding within the group.

Generating Creative Options

Social workers can enhance the ability of clients to make informed EOL decisions by engaging them in option generation. Option generation refers to identifying and developing a broad range of options to resolve the ethical dilemma. Once people express a position or opinion on how they think a dilemma should be resolved, they may become attached or locked into that position. To stimulate openness and creative thinking, participants should be encouraged to brainstorm many different options before evaluating or stating which ones are best. One technique for spurring creativity is hat-switching: asking people to wear the hat (or assume the position) of someone else when they are brainstorming options (Menkel-Meadow, Love, Schneider, & Sternlight, 2005). Participants could assume each other's roles, or even the roles of famous people who are not directly affected by the conflict (e.g., "If you were Emmanuel Kant [or Mother Teresa, or Barack Obama, or Lucille Ball], what options for solution would you suggest?"). Participants should feel free to suggest silly or even unethical options, suspending judgment until they have generated a comprehensive list of options to consider (Fisher et al., 1997). Broadening the choice set helps to free people from their original positions, fostering collaborative rather than adversarial conflict resolution. Ideally, the parties identify an elegant solution, an option that resolves all the issues to everyone's satisfaction (Barsky, 2007a). If an elegant solution is not possible, the parties will need to choose between less than ideal solutions, using strategies presented earlier in this textbook (e.g., prioritizing laws and ethical principles, or selecting the option with the least harmful consequences).

In Chelsie's case, the attorney suggests that David, as next of kin, has the right to decide whether to withdraw Chelsie's life supports. Absent clear and convincing evidence that Chelsie wanted to be maintained on life supports, David should be able to make the decision (Stein, 2007). Dr. Price suggests the hospital could go to court to have another guardian appointed. The attorney starts to question this option, both in terms of cost and the harm that a lawsuit could create in the relationship between the hospital and the Navajo community. Saba invites everyone to brainstorm additional options and suspend evaluating options until they build a broader list of choices. Initially, participants tend to provide options that fit with their original positions: Benny suggests bringing in a traditional medicine person, Dr. Price suggests transferring Chelsie to a palliative care facility, the other physician suggests obtaining a second opinion on Chelsie's prognosis from an independent doctor (Braddock, 2008), and the nurse suggests continuing life supports until a court orders them to do otherwise. Saba encourages participants to think creatively by putting themselves into other positions. "If you were David, what other options might you suggest?" The attorney says that David might like to bring his mother home, perhaps with life supports (Gott et al., 2008). The nurse suggests making use of a combination of traditional and modern medicine, trying to bridge cultures. Saba builds on the nurse's point by suggesting that they could ask David what he means by treating his mother with dignity. Dr. Price asks whether David might be amenable to the use of life supports if elders from the community provided permission. Benny says inviting elders into the process of decision making could be useful, but the medical professionals should not try to tell the elders what to say or not say. They should respect the wisdom and knowledge that the elders bring to the table. Brainstorming leads parties to recognize that the ethical issues are much broader than merely a decision about whether to withdraw life supports.

As the ethics committee develops options, they realize that they need to decide how to bring David back into the decision-making process. Rather than presenting David with their preferred options, they decide to discuss a broad range of options. In principle, they agree that they should respect David's opinions regarding what type of medical care his mother receives, including the decision to remove life supports. They also agree that David's initial request to remove life supports may not be a fully informed decision. They agree to set up a meeting to discuss additional options with David to ensure that he is making a truly informed decision. They agree that the information should be provided in a culturally appropriate manner and that they should not rush David into making decisions (Medvene et al., 2007). In fact, they may encourage him to take his time to make decisions to see how his mother responds to medical care—modern or traditional—over the next few weeks. Dr. Price, Saba, and Benny agree to meet with David. They will also ask David if he wants to have any other family members or elders present.

Apologizing

Apologizing refers to accepting and declaring responsibility for acts or omissions that caused harm to another person (Porter, 2005). Apology can have a profound effect on both the provider and the recipient of the apology. People who have suffered harm may feel angry, vengeful, hurt, sad, or afraid toward the person who caused the harm. Receiving an apology validates the person's dignity and self-worth, helping the person move on. By accepting responsibility, the apologizer may benefit by alleviating feelings of guilt or self-reproach. Apology also offers both parties a chance to repair their relationship, start anew, and focus on solving future problems rather than remaining stuck in the past (Barsky, 2007a).

Apologizing by merely saying, "I'm sorry," is incomplete and may do little to repair the relationship between the parties. To maximize the effectiveness of an apology, a full and sincere apology should include the following components:

- Admitting that one's actions or omissions caused harm.
- Accepting responsibility for causing harm.
- Expressing sincere remorse for one's actions.

- Showing empathic understanding toward the victim's situation.
- Demonstrating a willingness to remedy the situation (going beyond words; taking active steps such as compensating the person, ensuring the harmful actions will be stopped, or repairing the relationship with the victim) (Porter, 2005; Robbennolt, 2003).

Social workers and other professionals should note that apologies may have legal ramifications. From a legal perspective, providing an apology may be tantamount to admitting guilt or responsibility. In certain circumstances, statements of apology may be used as evidence in criminal or civil court proceedings. In other circumstances, apology statements may be privileged or otherwise protected by laws. Because of the variations in laws in different jurisdictions and different circumstances, it may be wisest to consult an attorney before issuing an apology. Even when an apology is admissible in court, offering an apology may be desirable because it could lead to amicable resolution of issues without having to go to court (Robbennolt, 2003).

When Saba contacts David to arrange for a meeting, she asks him whether he would like to bring family members or anyone else. David says he does not want to bring anyone, but he is glad Benny will be there. At the meeting, Saba notes that the purpose of the meeting is to discuss Chelsie's health care. With David's permission, Benny offers a prayer for wisdom and guidance from the Creator (Kuczewski, 2007). Bringing spirituality into the discussion of EOL issues may provide clients with comfort and inspiration (Heyman et al., 2006; Koenig, 2005). Dr. Price offers an apology to signify regret for his part in past problems and to offer suggestions for avoiding similar problems in the future:

> David, when we had our ethics committee meeting, I had a chance to reflect on my earlier discussion with you. I want to apologize for the ways in which I did not show you the respect that you deserved. When I was in the operating room, my focus was doing everything I could to keep your mother alive. My job as a physician is to promote health and preserve life. When I met with you after the surgery, I was surprised to hear that you did not want your mother to be maintained on life supports. I panicked and I raised my voice in an unprofessional manner. Regardless of my surprise, I should have focused more on what you had to say. I think if I had listened to you... *really listened*... I could have eased your pain rather than adding to it. I know that I cannot erase what happened that day, but I do want to assure you that, today, I truly want to listen and hear what you have to say. Please, help me understand your concerns about keeping your mother on life supports.

David was not expecting an apology, and he is moved to tears by it. David describes his emotional turmoil on the day of his mother's surgery and how he was feeling overwhelmed. Saba asks David to discuss his current thoughts about his mother being maintained on life supports. David talks about how unnatural his mother looks, as if she's already dead but they are still keeping her hooked up to all these tubes and machines. Saba validates his feelings. Dr. Price and Benny discuss various views of what is natural and what is unnatural, noting that what one person thinks is unnatural may be thought of as natural by another (Hendrix, n.d.). When they mention *treating people with dignity*, David agrees this is the key. He wants his mother treated with dignity. Saba engages them in a discussion of options for treating Chelsie with dignity. They begin with some of the options generated in the ethics committee meeting but quickly welcome David's suggestions. David asks about whether his mother could "wear her ordinary clothes or have her hair fixed to look like normal." Although these concerns might seem trivial, the others treat his suggestions with the respect they deserve. When David expresses concern that his mother may be suffering needlessly, Dr. Price explains how they can use medication to ensure against pain. Toward the end of the meeting, David continues to say his mother should be allowed to rest in peace. Yet he is not as adamant that the feeding tubes be removed immediately. He agrees that it would be helpful to bring in a traditional healer from his community. Perhaps his mother will respond to natural medicine. Dr. Price and Saba agree to work with David and Benny to make such arrangements. Although Dr. Price and Saba have personal reservations about the effectiveness of folk medicine, they do not express these reservations. They know that this is an area where David has the right to make self-determined choices and they should be supportive. Even when medical treatment offers no reasonable chance of cure or improvement, there is no need for the professionals to hurry the family into making life and death decisions (Annenberg Media, 2007).

As the foregoing example illustrates, managing ethical dilemmas can be an ongoing process rather than a decision to be made at a particular point in time. Critics might argue that the solution of bringing in a traditional healer is no solution at all: Chelsie will remain in a paralyzed state and David will still insist on withdrawing life supports. Perhaps, but perhaps not. Chelsie's situation may change, perhaps improving as a result of the traditional healing process, or perhaps deteriorating. By providing time for traditional healing to be conducted, David has more time to think and process information. Extending the process may allow David to work through his shock, anger, or other feelings that arose when he first learned about his mother's terminal condition (Kübler-Ross, 1997). Bringing in the traditional healer also provides Dr. Price and other professionals with more time to think through and process the issues. Yes, they may still have to make difficult decisions about Chelsie's EOL care. By viewing management of the ethical issues as an ongoing process, however, they are building trust and fostering conditions that may allow them to ultimately reach their decisions by consensus. If the issues cannot be resolved through informal discussions and the work of the ethics committee, the parties may also consider bringing in a mediator, ombudsman, or other conflict resolution professional (Barsky, 2007a; Skelley-Walley, 1995; Skjørshammer, 2001).

When EOL issues arise, conflict resolution skills and strategies may be useful for managing conflicts between clients, family members, health-care professionals, and others (Stein, 2007). Rather than focusing solely on the ethics of EOL decision making, social workers can help the parties manage communication and emotions. The goal of managing EOL issues is not merely to reach the right decision, but to promote inclusionary dialogue, with respect for all parties affected and the fostering of positive relationships among them. Although discussion of EOL issues may lead to anger, strife, or permanent rifts (Bloche, 2005), viewed positively, such discussions may also lead to understanding, acceptance, and consensus. Even when the parties do not reach agreement, they may be able to transcend their differences by demonstrating respect for the dignity and worth for everyone involved and by applying their own notions of spirituality to construct meaning for the primary client's life and death (Kuczewski, 2007).

ELDER ABUSE

All states have elder abuse reporting laws designed to protect elders from maltreatment; however, each state has its own definition of what is reportable, by whom, and to whom (Bergeron & Gray, 2003). The National Center on Elder Abuse (n.d.) provides a comprehensive listing of each state's laws and government protection agencies (http://www.ncea.aoa.gov/NCEAroot/Main_Site/Find_Help/State_Resources.aspx). The National Committee for the Prevention of Elder Abuse (n.d.) provides access to research and other resources for preventing and responding to elder abuse (http://www.preventelderabuse.org). Typically, protection legislation defines elders as people over 60 years of age. Abuse refers to any form of maltreatment, including

- Physical abuse (hitting, burning, unjustified use of physical confinement or chemical restraints, abduction).
- Psychological abuse (intimidation, verbal denigration, humiliation, isolation).
- Sexual abuse (rape, nonconsensual sexual contact, sex with a person who lacks mental capacity).
- Financial abuse (fraud, telemarketing scams, stealing money or property).
- Neglect (intentional deprivation of needs such as food, bathing, medication, and

daily care; isolation; abandonment; inability to adequately provide care) (Brownell & Giblin, 2009; Nerenberg, 2006).[21]

People who mistreat elders are not necessarily bad or immoral. Although abuse and neglect may be intentional, there are also many cases of unintentional abuse and neglect. Consider, for instance, a person who lacks the financial resources or knowledge to obtain necessary medical care for an elder parent, or a person who is so stressed out at work that he becomes emotionally abusive to a demanding elder parent at home. In some cases, the caregiver may be mistreating the elder because of a history in which the elder abused the caregiver (Koenig, Rinfrette, & Lutz, 2006). Lack of resources, stress, or revenge for past abuse does not justify elder abuse. Elder abuse and neglect require intervention. Still, social workers need to understand the social context of the mistreatment rather than merely blaming the caregiver or other person who is mistreating the elder (Johnson, 2000).

Some states have special reporting laws for elder abuse that occurs within institutional settings (e.g., nursing homes). Most states have general elder abuse reporting requirements, including abuse by institutional care providers, family care providers, health-care professionals, friends, and strangers. Neglect may also include self-neglect, meaning that there may be a duty to report situations in which an elder is unable or unwilling to provide for his or her own basic needs (Bergeron, 2006). In some states, reporting suspicions of elder abuse is mandatory, though in others, reporting is voluntary (Bergeron & Gray, 2003). Most states designate a particular agency to provide adult protective services (APS). That agency may be responsible for protection issues involving elders as well as other vulnerable populations, including adults with mental and physical disabilities. This chapter focuses on elder abuse, though many of the same principles apply to work with other vulnerable adult populations.

From an ethical perspective, the issue of elder abuse often involves a balancing of client autonomy (including the elder's right to self-determination, privacy, and informed consent) with beneficence (including the interest in protecting the elder's life, welfare, and dignity) (Beauchamp & Childress, 2009). The NASW Code of Ethics (1999) does not specifically mention elder abuse, though workers are guided to promote the well-being of clients (S.1.01) and honor clients' right to self-determination (S.1.02), informed consent (S.1.03), and privacy (S.1.07). In some situations, elders welcome professional help for elder abuse, and there is no ethical conflict. In other situations, the elder does not want anyone to know about the abuse and may reject services. Some elders may feel too scared, ashamed, or embarrassed to admit elder abuse. Others may believe they are better off accepting the abuse than trying to challenge it. Elders who feel depressed, inadequate, frail, or hopeless may lack the energy to confront the abuse or actively participate with protective services (Bergeron, 2006). They may not want to make trouble for a family caregiver they love, or they may not trust that APS involvement will help. In some cases, the perpetrator is so endearing that the elder is not aware of being manipulated or controlled (Nerenberg, 2006). Some state laws are restricted to abuse cases in which the elder is vulnerable or incapacitated. Some state laws also require the APS worker to obtain the consent of the elder in all stages of the protection process; that is, the APS worker may not investigate a case or intervene on the elder's behalf unless the elder provides consent. The elder's consent is not required if the elder is deemed mentally incompetent. In other states, APS workers can investigate and intervene on the elder's behalf without the elder's permission (Bergeron & Gray, 2003). Thus, different states weigh the ethical principles of autonomy and

[21] Possible indicators of abuse include cuts, lacerations, poor skin, unexplained injuries, weight loss, sleep disturbances, soiled clothing or bed linen, unattended injury, dehydration, burns, absence of hair, withdrawal, helplessness, anger, denial, hesitation to speak openly, disorientation, fear, depression, and agitation (Brownell & Giblin, 2009; Kalichman, 1999). Workers need to assess whether there may be other explanations for these conditions, though their duty to report only requires suspicions of abuse, not documented proof.

beneficence in different manners, creating different legally defined roles and obligations for APS workers, social workers, and other professionals.

Although the ethical issues surrounding elder protection have some similarities to child protection (Chapter 14), there are also significant differences. Child protection laws are based on the premise that all children are vulnerable and need the protection from abusive or neglectful adults, particularly from abusive or neglectful parents, teachers, or other caregivers who are responsible for ensuring their safety and welfare. Child protection laws are also based on the premise that children do not have sufficient mental capacity to determine whether they should accept or reject protective services. The situation for elders is substantially different, first, because of the variance in their vulnerability, and second, because of their variance in mental capacity. In terms of vulnerability, some elders are dependent on family members, friends, or professional caregivers for provision of basic needs. Other elders are much less vulnerable, as they can take care of their own physical, psychological, social, financial, and spiritual needs. In terms of mental capacity, elders also run a broad gamut from complete lack of mental capacity (e.g., due to dementia) to limited mental capacity (e.g., due to depression or the side effects of medication) to full mental capacity (Filinson et al., 2008). Thus, assessing vulnerability and capacity on a case-by-case basis is crucial.[22]

When an elder is being subjected to abuse and the elder lacks mental capacity, then the need to prioritize beneficence over autonomy is clear. Regardless of whether state law mandates reporting, social workers should take appropriate steps to ensure the safety and welfare of the elder (S.1.01). The ethical issues become more complex when the elder is being subjected to abuse, but the elder does not lack capacity and refuses help from the worker or protective services. The NASW Code of Ethics provisions on informed consent (S.1.03) seem to suggest that, barring mental incapacity, an elder has the right to refuse help, even when the elder has been subjected to abuse or is suffering from self-imposed neglect. Self-determination and informed consent include the right to make bad decisions (Bergeron, 2006). Further, clients rather than social workers, should be able to define for themselves what are good or bad decisions.

Although social workers should not coerce or pressure elder clients into accepting help for abuse, social workers do not need to simply accept the client's initial rejection of help (Linzer, 2004). If the client's initial rejection of services is based on mistrust, fear, or misinformation, then is the client truly exercising self-determination? Social workers may be able to enhance client self-determination by helping elders manage some of the barriers to fully informed, voluntary decision making.

The Transtheoretical Model (TTM)[23] offers social workers a useful framework for engaging elders who initially refuse help for elder abuse. TTM is based on the premise that change can be a difficult process. Even if an elder is living in an abusive situation, the changes required to get out of that situation can be complicated and even scary (Levesque, Driskell, Prochaska, & Prochaska, 2008). Barriers to extricating oneself from an abusive relationship may include lack of money, family and social pressure, personal values and beliefs about relationships, isolation, and fear of retribution by the perpetrator of the abuse (Burkitt & Larkin, 2008). TTM suggests that, when faced with challenging situations, clients go through a series of stages, both before and after they are ready to make changes: precontemplation, contemplation, decision, preparation, action, and maintenance (Prochaska & Norcross, 2007). *During the precontemplation stage, clients are not aware that a problem exists or they are simply not thinking that the problem exists.* (For example, an elder refuses to believe

[22] Mental capacity should be assessed multiple times because it may fluctuate over the course of a day due to stress, fatigue, reactions to medication, feelings of intimidation, and other factors (Nerenberg, 2006). For further discussion of mental capacity, see Chapter 13.

[23] TTM (sometimes called the Stages of Change Model) has also been used to help people decide to sign advance directives (Medvene et al., 2007).

that her homecare nurse is not giving her proper medical attention.) *During the contemplation stage, clients are aware and begin thinking about the problem, but they are not yet ready to make changes.* (The elder realizes the homecare nurse is neglectful, but has not decided whether she should do anything about it. The elder may be concerned that she cannot afford a better nurse or that her family will be angry with her if she complains.) *At the decision stage, clients have considered the risks and benefits of making a change and decide to make a change.* (The elder decides that she needs to get a new nurse.) *During the preparation stage, clients plan and get ready to make change.* (The elder contacts a social worker to help her explore other options, such as the possibility of subsidized nursing.) *During the action stage, clients make the desired change.* (The elder terminates the contract with the original nurse and hires a new one.) *During the maintenance stage, clients continue to work on their goal, taking steps to preserve the gains they have made and avoiding a return to the original problem.* (The elder plans to have the social worker check in with her periodically to ensure that the new nurse is providing adequate care.) On their own, clients may or may not progress through each of these stages (Prochaska, Redding, & Evers, 2002). Also, progression is not necessarily linear, as clients may revert to earlier stages before moving ahead once again. TTM suggests that the social worker's role is to facilitate the client's progress from one stage to the next (Levesque et al., 2008). The Transtheoretical Model offers specific empirically based strategies or interventions that may be used for each stage of the change process (Medvene et al., 2007). If a client is in the precontemplation stage, for instance, the worker should not rush the client to make behavioral changes. Rather, the worker should help the client move from the precontemplation stage to the contemplation stage. TTM was originally developed for clients who were addicted to alcohol and other drugs, but it has also been used successfully to help clients extricate themselves from abusive situations (Burkitt & Larkin, 2008; Murphy & Maiuro, 2008).[24] In particular, TTM may be used to help clients overcome potential barriers that may be keeping them in abusive situations. TTM fits well with social work values and ethics, as it honors client self-determination while also promoting client well-being in situations when clients initially refuse help. The following two sections illustrate how social workers can engage clients in the precontemplation and contemplation stages of change, helping them work through barriers to accepting help and empowering them to make self-determined choices to remove themselves from abusive situations.

Precontemplation

When elder clients refuse help for abuse situations, they may be in the precontemplation or contemplation stage of change. Indicators that clients are in the precontemplation stage include denials that that they have been experiencing abuse, refusals to discuss the possibility of abuse, or difficulties even thinking about the possibility of a need for change. According to the Transtheoretical Model, elders do not need to admit they are being abused; they only need to start thinking about the possibility of change and how change can lead to positive differences in their life. Thus, the worker's role with a precontemplative client is not to pierce the client's denial about abuse or persuade the client to change, but to help the client start thinking about the possibility of doing something about the abuse.

The Transtheoretical Method suggests that the intervention processes most appropriate for precontemplaters include consciousness raising, dramatic relief, and environmental evaluation. To demonstrate each of these processes, consider the following scenario.

> Shelly is a social worker who has been helping Clarence (82) for the past 2 years, ever since he was discharged from the hospital after a bout of depression. Clarence's daughter, Dottie (63), recently separated

[24] Most of the published research on the use of TTM in abuse situations is related to intimate partner abuse with adult populations (not specifically with elders).

from her husband and moved in with him. During a regular home visit, Shelly notices a number of problems: Clarence's room is in disarray, he is behind in paying his rent, and he seems afraid to discuss anything about his relationship with Dottie. Shelly suspects financial and emotional abuse, but Clarence says he is fine and refuses any offers of help. Because Clarence has sufficient mental capacity, adult protective services will not intervene unless he provides consent.

Given that Clarence refuses to discuss the problems in his relationship with Dottie, Shelly assesses that he is in the precontemplative stage of change. If she tries to persuade him to deal with the abuse, he will resist her efforts and perhaps disengage with her altogether. Instead of telling Clarence what to do and why he needs to do it, she focuses on listening to him (Schirch, 2004). She needs to build trust and gather information from his perspective. By starting with the client, Shelly demonstrates respect for Clarence's situation and the issues he wants to work on. Clarence feels socially isolated, so Shelly has been helping him develop new social connections. By working on his goal, she is able to maintain contact with him and monitor for further abuse (Linzer, 2004). She hopes that she can help him before the abuse gets worse. If Clarence's mental capacity deteriorates or a life-threatening situation arises, she will also be in a position to assess and intervene as early as possible.

Consciousness raising is particularly useful for clients who do not perceive abuse as a problem or acknowledge that change may be helpful. The process of consciousness raising suggests that Shelly can help Clarence move from precontemplation to contemplation by fostering awareness of the abuse and its impact on him (Prochaska et al., 2002). Rather than telling Clarence he is being mistreated, Shelly gently asks questions to enhance his awareness of the mistreatment. Shelly avoids labels such as abuser and victim, as Clarence has difficulty viewing his daughter as an abuser or himself as a victim. Rather, Shelly focuses on nonjudgmental facts, behaviors, and concrete information that support a change in Clarence's situation. "Clarence, I notice that you are a bit behind on some bill payments. Have finances become a concern for you?" Shelly may also use questions to help Clarence link his identified concern (social isolation) with issues related to the abuse. "I've noticed that you haven't gone out to the movies since Dottie moved in.... I'm wondering what has changed." Shelly should be careful about the pacing of her consciousness-raising interventions, as she wants to help Clarence feel comfortable opening up. Pressuring or moving too quickly could make him feel defensive and close down.

Dramatic relief refers to the use of experiential interventions designed to have the client feel the discomfort of the current situation and recognize the relief that would come from making changes (Prochaska et al., 2002). Shelly could use psychodrama or gestalt interventions to help put Clarence in touch with his feelings regarding the way Dottie has been treating him. For instance, she might invite him to re-enact a situation in which he and Dottie were getting along well, and then role-play a situation in which he and Dottie were experiencing difficulties. By reflecting on the two situations, Clarence may realize how problematic the current situation is, but there may also be hope for returning to a more functional relationship with his daughter.

Self-evaluation refers to the process of reflecting on one's life, social identity, and strengths. Self-reflection offers clients an opportunity to think about their life goals and situation in relation to the problems they are facing. By reflecting back on various parts of their lives, clients may come to recognize that change is possible (Prochaska et al., 2002). Because Clarence feels his life is worthless and he should not be a burden to Dottie, he has little motivation or strength to confront the abuse. Shelly empowers Clarence by helping him build his self-esteem and confidence. Shelly invites Clarence to ponder his roles as father, grandfather, and retired teacher. She asks him questions to facilitate insight about the skills, knowledge, and wisdom he brings to each of these roles. Shelly provides Clarence with homework tasks that help him feel a stronger sense of self-efficacy. By successfully completing small tasks, Clarence builds confidence in his ability to make bigger changes. Over time, the concept of confronting his daughter's abuse becomes less threatening, as Clarence has a stronger sense of his abilities, including his ability to cope with stress.

Social workers can use consciousness raising, dramatic relief, and self-evaluation to help clients move from precontemplation to contemplation. At this point, the clients have not decided to accept help for the abuse situation. However, they are at least ready to discuss the possibility of accepting help.

Contemplation

When clients reach the contemplation stage, workers can engage them in more direct discussions about the abuse and the possibility of accepting help. Still, workers should not rush clients into making decisions. When abuse is at issue, workers may feel pressure to rescue the elder as soon as possible, not wanting the elder to suffer and not wanting to be liable for malpractice should the abuse take a turn for the worse. As long as the elder has mental capacity and the abuse is not life threatening, however, the elder still has the right to accept or reject help.

TTM suggests engaging contemplative clients in a discussion of the pros and cons of making change (Prochaska et al., 2002). This technique, called decisional balance, helps clients weigh the advantages and disadvantages of maintaining their current situation versus the advantages and disadvantages of accepting help for the abuse. Shelly starts by asking Clarence about the advantages of maintaining the status quo. Rather than simply focusing on the benefits of confronting the abuse, Shelly wants to show Clarence that she understands he has valid reasons for not confronting Dottie. Clarence says, "Things are not so bad. Dottie does help me with cooking and cleaning. I may not need her so much right now, but I'm going to be very dependent on her in a couple of years. I need to be careful so she doesn't get mad or abandon me." Shelly does not debate Clarence's beliefs. Instead, she demonstrates empathy through reflection and paraphrase.

After going through the various reasons for maintaining the status quo, Shelly asks Clarence what he thinks change would look like, particularly if he were willing to accept help for the way Dottie was treating him. Clarence thinks that if he accepts help, adult protective services will come in and tell Dottie that she has to leave. They might even call the police and press charges against her. Clarence discloses instances of theft, as Dottie has been using his credit cards and bank account without his permission. Clarence says he does not want his daughter to leave and he certainly does not want her to go to jail. Shelly asks Clarence if there are any other ways that abuse could be confronted. As they explore options, Clarence says that he could move in with his younger brother. He could tell Dottie that she could stay in his apartment without confronting her directly about the mistreatment. If Clarence stays with his brother, Dottie would have less access to his financial resources. Shelly does not jump on this option and encourage Clarence to move in with his brother. She continues to honor his right to self-determination by exploring the risks and benefits of each option, allowing Clarence to make the final decision. Shelly may or may not be completely satisfied with Clarence's decision; for instance, she may think that Clarence should press charges. Still, by empowering Clarence to make his own decisions, she is more likely to resolve the ethical issues of autonomy versus beneficence in an effective manner.

The foregoing case illustrates just some of the strategies that TTM has to offer. The Transtheoretical Method may be particularly useful for helping clients who reject services for abuse because it provides social workers with change-oriented strategies that fit with the client's current level of readiness for change. Although TTM does not magically turn tough ethical dilemmas into easy solutions, it does offer social workers and clients a range of processes to help them resolve abuse issues in a consensual, affirming manner.

CONCLUSION

Working with elders can be very rewarding, uplifting, and spiritually meaningful. At times, however, issues such as elder abuse and end-of-life decision making can pose significant challenges for social workers. As this chapter illustrates, the resolution of ethical dilemmas requires more than a rational analysis of conflicting laws, policies, and ethical obligations. Social workers must be able to reflect on their own feelings, values, and beliefs, as well as tune into the feelings, values, and beliefs of the elders, family members, and other professionals with whom they are working. Social workers may also need to draw on a range of conflict resolution, communication, and engagement strategies to help everyone discuss the issues in a constructive manner, listen to one another, and work toward successful resolution of the ethical issues (Johnson, 2000).[25]

Social workers often think of ethics as a search for the *right answers* to manage ethical issues. In practice, ethics often entails a search for the *right processes.*

DISCUSSION QUESTIONS AND EXERCISES

The following exercises are designed to provide you with practice implementing the Framework for Managing Ethical Issues in situations involving social work with elders. The cases in Exercise 1 are designed to help you analyze ethical issues relating to work with elders (using Stages 1 to 3 of the Framework presented in the introduction to Part II). The role-plays in Exercise 2 are designed to provide you with practice engaging clients and coprofessionals in ethics discussions pertaining to end-of-life decision making and elder abuse (focusing on Stage 4). The questions in Exercise 3 focus on planning and implementation (Stage 5). The questions in Exercise 4 focus on evaluation and follow-up (Stage 6).

1. *Analyze Elder Issues*: Select one of the following scenarios and analyze the ethical issues using the first three stages of the Framework for Managing Ethical Issues: identify the ethical issues, determine appropriate help, and think critically (Figure II.1). When considering the legal context, identify and apply the relevant laws for your state:
   a. The state government is planning to cut funding for Golden Times, a social agency that provides services to individuals and families affected by Alzheimer's disease. Some social workers at Golden Times want to take a group of elder clients to the state capitol (540 miles away) to help them advocate for reinstatement of funding. They believe that this is an opportunity to engage elder clients in civic processes and empower them to advocate for themselves (Hinterlong & Williamson, 2006). Other social workers believe that it would be inappropriate to use vulnerable clients to advocate for funding, even though they believe that legislators will listen more to clients than professional staff.
   b. Solomon is an adult guardianship mediator[26] who is working with Eloise (73) and her nephew, Nathan. Nathan does not believe Eloise can take care of herself any more and wants to put her in a nursing home. Eloise says, "Over my dead body! I'm staying home." Eloise cannot afford to pay for her own rent, and Nathan is threatening to cut off his financial support. As a mediator, Solomon's Code of Ethics says he is supposed to be neutral and impartial as he strives to help Nathan and Eloise resolve their conflict. As a social worker, his code of ethics says he is supposed to protect vulnerable populations. In this situation, Solomon views Eloise as a vulnerable elder and is concerned that Nathan is coercing Eloise into going to a nursing home.
   c. Salima works in a residential facility for elders from the Pakistani American community. Although the care provided in the facility is very good, Salima has discovered that the executive director of the program has been using agency funds to support political causes that are not directly related to the functioning of the program. When Salima brings this concern to her supervisor and the program

[25] Johnson refers to this approach as communicative ethics.
[26] For a description of adult guardianship mediation, see Center for Social Gerontology (n.d.).

director, they tell her to leave well enough alone. When she persists in telling them that this is a misuse of agency funding, they threaten to accuse her of mistreating elder clients. They also tell her that any bad news about the agency could cause ill will toward the Pakistani American community, which has already been targeted with false allegations about how it uses charitable donations.

d. Enid (68) was admitted to the hospital for heart surgery. When the social worker Sharleen asks if she can be of any assistance, Enid says she does not want any Hispanic nurses to take care of her. Sharleen explains that the hospital has a policy of nondiscrimination and many of the nurses are Hispanic. Initially, Enid says she cannot understand Spanish accents. Later, she confides that she was mugged by some Hispanic youths and she is still traumatized whenever she is face to face with someone who looks or sounds Hispanic.

e. Carina (60) is in a persistent vegetative state following a car accident that resulted in severe brain injury. Before the accident, Carina had signed an organ donor card that gives the hospital permission to use her organs to help save the lives of others. Carina's husband and health-care proxy, Fritz, says he wants to maintain Carina on life supports. Fritz believes that only God should decide when life should end. The health-care proxy does not specifically indicate Carina's wishes in terms of whether she would want to remain on life supports indefinitely. Carina's doctor and social worker believe Carina would want to permit the hospital to use her organs as soon as possible to maximize the chances of saving others. The longer Carina remains on life supports, the less viable her organs become for the purposes of transplantation.

2. *Role-Play Elder Issues*: Select one of the following scenarios and prepare for a role-play by reviewing the relevant materials in this chapter on discussing end-of-life issues or elder abuse issues. The student playing social worker should identify at least two or three specific strategies for engaging the others in an effective discussion of the ethical issues raised by the case.

   a. Edward (63) suffers from cancer of the esophagus, a terminal condition. His hospital file includes a copy of a living will stating that he does not want chemotherapy. He has told his social worker, Suzanne, and his physician, Dr. Prescott, that he wants to live out his days in comfort and does not want aggressive treatments that have no chance of success. Dr. Prescott tells Edward that there is a new form of chemotherapy that can cure him. Dr. Prescott does not tell Edward that the new treatment is experimental and there is no research to indicate its chances of helping. Suzanne is concerned that Dr. Prescott is pressuring Edward to receive a treatment he does not want. She calls for a meeting with Dr. Prescott and the head of the hospital's ethics committee, Dr. Rawls.[27] Dr. Rawls is a strong proponent of social justice. The role-play will include Suzanne, Dr. Prescott, and Dr. Rawls discussing their concerns.

   b. Maria (79) has late-stage dementia. She lives in a nursing home where she is being maintained on life supports. When she still had sufficient mental capacity, she signed a health-care power of attorney granting decision-making power to her two children, Carmelo and Catalina. Carmelo believes that Maria's quality of life has deteriorated to the point that life supports should be removed and Maria should be allowed to die in peace. Catalina believes that,

[27] Ordinarily, an ethics committee meeting would have more participants. For learning purposes, however, a meeting with three participants is easier to manage.

as Catholics, they should respect life and allow God to decide when their mother should pass on. Maria left no indication about what she wanted to happen, other than that her children should decide when the time is right. For the role-play, their social worker, Sherwin will meet with Catalina and Carmelo to discuss their options for EOL care and mediate a solution.

c. Sevita is working with a 61-year-old client, Constance, who refuses to accept her diagnosis of a malignant brain tumor that will likely lead to her death within 5 months. For this role-play, Sevita will meet with Constance to discuss the possibility of making EOL plans, including the option of signing an advance directive. Constance knows nothing about advance directives and initially says she does not want to talk about them.

d. Cato (67) was in a car accident 6 months ago. He has remained in a coma ever since. He is maintained on life supports at a public hospital. All the physicians agree that Cato has no chance of recovery. Cato was living on the streets and has no known relatives. For this role-play, Dr. Petty, Dr. Reamer, and Ms. Smits (the social worker) are meeting to discuss Cato's situation. The hospital has a shortage of beds. Accordingly, hospital administration would like to free up Cato's bed as soon as possible so it can serve more patients. Dr. Reamer suggests transferring Cato to a long-term care facility. Dr. Reamer believes Cato has a right to be treated with dignity, regardless of his social status in life. Dr. Petty suggests surreptitiously increasing Cato's pain medication so he can end his life without pain and they can use his bed sooner. Dr. Petty contends that waiting for a long-term facility to take Cato could take months, as all the publicly funded facilities have long waiting lists. Ms. Smits suggests going to court to appoint a public guardian. Dr. Petty argues against going to court, as it will eat up their limited time and resources—time and resources that could be used to save lives.

e. Essie (73) is an African American woman whose role in life was to take care of everyone else: her husband, her children, her grandchildren, and even kids from the street. Ever since she had a stroke and became nonambulatory, she has had to relinquish this role. She is very dependent on her children for her care. Unfortunately, her children have been neglecting many of her needs. One son recently moved out of the country and her two daughters (Dana and Denise) are working double shifts just to try to make ends meet. As a result, Essie is left alone for long periods of time, unable to feed herself or go to the bathroom. Siena, her social worker, offers help—perhaps a referral to a nursing home or support from the local adult protective services. Essie refuses help, saying she has managed her whole life living at home and she plans on continuing there until she dies. Siena believes Essie has sufficient mental capacity to make her own decisions. However, she is concerned that Essie's quality of life is severely compromised because she refuses help. For this role-play, Siena will conduct a follow-up meeting with Essie to assess her stage of change and make use of intervention strategies from the Transtheoretical Model.

f. Eun Mi (64) is a Korean American woman who lives with her son, Du-Ho, and daughter-in-law, Ae Cha. A neighbor called adult protective services to report abuse, after witnessing Ae Cha yelling at Eun Mi and pushing her down the stairs. The APS worker, Sitara, meets with Eun Mi to investigate the charges. She notes that Eun Mi has a cut across her face and bruises on her forearms. Eun Mi tells Sitara that her family loves her very much and she does not want to do anything to hurt them. She explains that she fell down the stairs accidentally, though she does not sound very convincing. Eun Mi admits that she and Ae Cha do not always see eye to eye, but she also knows that she can be hard to live with. Ae Cha has three children to care for, so she is dealing with a lot of stress. For this role-play, Sitara will assess whether Eun Mi is in the precontemplation or contemplation stage. Then, Sitara will use strategies that the Transtheoretical Model suggests are appropriate for Eun Mi's current stage of change.

3. *Plan and Implement*: In Exercise 2(f), assume that Eun Mi makes a decision to accept help for the physical and emotional abuse she has been experiencing with Ae Cha. According to the Transtheoretical Model, Eun Mi is now in the preparation stage of change. Develop a plan for implementing this decision. The plan should ensure Eu Mi's safety and well-being, but also respect her dignity, values, beliefs, and wishes. What cultural factors should Sitara take into account when helping Eun Mi develop this plan?
4. *Evaluate and Follow Up*: Shady Hills Hospital is an inner-city hospital that serves a diverse population, including a large Haitian American community. In a recent case, the family of Chanté, an elderly Haitian woman, sued the hospital for intentional infliction of emotional stress and malpractice. The family claimed the hospital staff kept insisting on telling Chanté she had cancer and was going to die. The family believed that Chanté become ill and died because the hospital told her she had cancer and was going to die. The hospital claimed it was only providing Chanté and the family with information so they could make informed decisions about what type of care she should receive. The court decided in favor of the hospital, finding that Chanté died of cancer, not because of what the hospital staff told her. The court also noted that the physicians could be liable for malpractice if they did not provide her with an accurate diagnosis and prognosis. After the court renders its decision, the hospital decides to evaluate how it handled Chanté's case. What sort of information should the hospital gather to determine how well they managed the ethical and legal issues raised by this case? In spite of winning the court case, what suggestions for follow-up should the hospital consider?

Glossary

absolutism an approach to ethical analysis based on applying fixed rules to all cases, regardless of the circumstances (cf. relativism)

autonomy and freedom the ethical principle of promoting liberty, choice, self-determination, or independence; uninhibited by restriction or control from the state or others

beneficence ethical principle of doing good (related to principle of doing no harm); may conflict with the principle of self-determination when doing good on behalf of a client means going against the client's wishes

boundary crossing an act of a professional that departs from the usual norms or expectations of the professional–client relationship, whether or not the client is harmed by the deviation from standard practice (e.g., offering a client money in an emergency situation to pay for food)

boundary violation an act of a professional that deviates from the usual or normal expectations of the professional–client relationship, and harms the client or puts the client at significant risk of harm (e.g., pressuring a client to lend money)

case law the body of legal principles that develop over time through the decisions of judges in individual cases (also called "common law")

certification a form of accrediting professionals by officially stating that the professional has met certain standards of education, training, or competence

communitarianism a philosophy emphasizing the social rights and responsibilities that people owe one another within a community, family, culture, or other group, recognizing that individual rights and interests need to be balanced with those of the larger group

confidentiality the ethical principle of protecting a client's privacy

conflict of interest situation in which a social worker or other person in a position of trust is perceived to have contradictory or competing obligations, often as a result of dual or multiple relationships (e.g., conflicting professional and personal interests)

conflict resolution any process aimed at helping two or more parties manage differences between them (e.g., negotiation, mediation, or advocacy)

damages harm experienced; in civil lawsuits, damages also refers to compensation for harm suffered

deontology an approach to analyzing ethical issues by applying fixed duties (moral rules), as opposed to looking at specific situation and the consequences of various alternatives (cf. teleology, virtue ethics)

dual (multiple) roles having two (or more) types of relationships with a client (e.g., a social worker who is also a friend or customer of the client)

duty an obligation to act in a particular manner (e.g., to follow particular laws, ethical obligations, agency policies, social norms, or family customs)

egalitarianism a social philosophy by which people are treated equally, without discriminating on the basis of age, gender, socioeconomic status, or other factors

equality and inequality the principle of treating people equally or the same if they come from similar situations, and also allowing for differential treatment when people come from different situations, to ensure fairness or equal opportunity for all (e.g., affirmative action programs at universities for applicants from certain groups that have been deprived of a good primary education)

equity the principle of treating everyone in a fair or socially just manner

ethical breach contravention or infringement of an ethical standard

ethical decision making a problem-solving process in which one or more decision makers identify ethical issues and work through a strategic process of analyzing the issues in order to reach a decision concerning the best way to respond (may be based on an analysis of laws, rules, principles, ethics, duties, values, beliefs, virtues, or other factors)

ethical dilemma a situation marked by a difficult choice in how to respond, given that there are conflicting ethical rules, no completely satisfactory option for resolving the ethical concerns, or lack of clear direction about what is ethically appropriate.

ethical problem a situation in which a professional must make a decision concerning how to resolve an issue related to conflicting values or ethics (may include dealing with an ethical breach or an ethical dilemma)

ethic a principle, guideline, or standard that indicates whether certain types of behaviors are right or wrong

ethics a system of principles and standards that guide judgments and behavior based upon a set of morals and values (cf. values, morals); the study of the right conduct, moral duties, good character, and the good life

ethics of care an approach to ethics based on the virtue of caring, emphasizing the importance of relationships and emotional responses in how professionals or others make moral and ethical decisions

fiduciary a relationship based on trust in which a professional with power or control over another person has special ethical obligations or higher standards of care in order to respect his or her position of trust

gray area a situation in which there is no single, clear, and right way of responding to an ethical issue; a matter in which there is ethical uncertainty or ambiguity

honesty the quality of being forthright, truthful, and law abiding

illegal or illicit unlawful, against the law, in contravention of criminal law

immunity legal protection against being sued. Social workers who report suspicions of child abuse, for instance, are protected from litigation as long as their decisions to report were made in good faith

integrity the quality of being honest, responsible, reliable, true, transparent, and consistent in relation to one's primary values and ethics

jurisdiction a legally defined geographic area such as a city, county, state, or country within which a government is empowered to pass laws over certain types of issues (e.g., states have primary authority to pass laws related to regulation of health and mental health professions)

justice the quality of fair treatment of individuals; an equitable sharing of rights, responsibility, resources, costs, benefits, and risks; conforming to legal rules or moral standards (cf. social justice)

justifiable an act that may be accepted as right or ethical based upon sound reasoning and judgments

law a system of rules that is passed by the state and enforced by the state (cf. ethics, morals, values)

least harm the ethical principle of choosing a course of action that poses the least damage or injury, particularly when there is no choice that eliminates the risk of harm altogether

legislation statutes, laws, or acts developed and enacted by state or national governments (cf. case law)

liable responsible; subject to criminal charges or civil lawsuits to recover damages for harm caused

libertarianism a social philosophy that emphasizes individual liberty and seeks to diminish or abolish control by the state or other social forces (cf. egalitarianism, communitarianism)

licensure a method of regulating professionals by limiting the right to practice to people who have completed certain courses and tests, or who have demonstrated certain types of competence

malpractice poor or shoddy practice; professional negligence; failure of a professional to exercise a reasonable standard of care or perform services in a manner reasonably expected of a prudent professional of similar background in similar circumstances, resulting in harm to the client

mandatory compulsory (e.g., required by law or agency policy)

mental capacity the ability of a person to think, reason, and remember; used by professionals to assess the ability of clients to provide informed consent (cf. mental competence)

mental competence a legal status, determined by the judge, that a person is able to enter into contracts or provide informed consent (antonym: mental incompetence)

morals a system of rules and principles that defines appropriate and inappropriate behavior for an individual, family, community, or other social unit (cf. ethics, values)

nonmaleficence the ethical principle of not causing harm; avoiding actions that may hurt others

principle a general guide for conduct, such as a professional's ethical principles or an individual's moral principles (cf. rule of law; standard)

privacy and confidentiality the ethical principle of respecting a client's personal information and situation from being shared with others, unless the client consents to disclosure

privilege a legal principle suggesting that information gathered within a confidential relationship should not be compellable in court (to determine when privilege arises, refer to applicable case law and legislation)

professional an individual who, through education and training, possesses specialized knowledge and skills, and agrees to abide by a code of ethics and standards of practice established by the profession

proportionality an ethical principle used to promote egalitarianism by ensuring that policy makers strike a balance between the benefits, costs, and risks experienced by different groups in an organization, community, or society

protection of life an ethical principle that promotes preservation of all human beings, shielding people from acts or conditions that may cause death or put their lives at risk; preserving and prolonging life, regardless of the economic cost or resulting quality of life (cf. quality of life)

protection of title a method of regulating professions by mandating that only people with certain educational backgrounds may use a specific professional name (e.g., in some jurisdictions, only people with an MSW or BSW may call themselves social workers)

quality of life the ethical principle of promoting the general welfare of people, including physical and mental health, happiness, spiritual fulfillment, family and social support, job satisfaction, clean environment, and so on (cf. protection of life)

relativism an approach to ethical analysis that explores the consequences of actions in particular circumstances, rather than applying fixed duties (or moral rules) that apply to all situations (cf. absolutism)

records progress notes, psychosocial assessments, psychosocial test results, videos, drawings, or any other documentation of the practitioner's work or professional interactions with a client

responsible having a legal, moral, or ethical obligation; accountable for one's actions or the consequences of one's actions

risk management using strategic decisions and plans to pre-empt harm, to reduce harm, or to reduce the negative consequences of a harmful event

rule of law legally defined mandates, requirements, or prohibitions that regulate behavior in a nation or society

self-awareness consciousness of one's own thoughts, feelings, attitudes, beliefs, morals, motivations, and behaviors; internal reflection

social justice equity and fair treatment in society, including equitable division of resources, access to the necessities of life, freedom from discrimination, and maximizing opportunities for people to fulfill themselves

standard a guideline for appropriate behavior, general expectations of behavior for professionals (as in a Code of Ethics)

standard of care the expected behavior of a particular practitioner based upon what would usually be expected of a similar professional acting prudently, under similar circumstances

subpoena a written mandate requiring a person to testify in court and/or to turn over records and other documents to be used as evidence in court

teleology an approach to analyzing ethical issues by looking at the situation and consequences of various alternatives, rather than simply applying fixed rules or moral duties to all situations (cf. deontology, virtue ethics)

transparency the principle of openness, for instance, by providing clients or the public with access to relevant information about decisions made, including the decision-maker's reasoning

truthfulness and full disclosure an ethical principle that promotes an honest and open sharing of information; candor (e.g., providing a client with complete, accurate information about the client's condition and intervention choices)

utilitarianism an approach to ethical analysis based upon a comparison of benefits and costs of different courses of action (cf. deontology, absolutism)

values core preferences or ideals about what is good or important (cf. ethics, morals)

virtue ethics an approach to ethics that emphasizes character traits for leading the good life, for instance, honesty, moderation, and generosity (cf. deontology, teleology, ethics of care)

voluntary decisions or choices made without undue influence from friends, family, or other sources, and without coercion by the law or legal systems

warrant a court order authorizing a police officer to make a search, seizure, or arrest (cf. subpoena)

Bibliography

REFERENCES CITED

Abbott, A. A. (2003). Understanding transference and countertransference: Risk management strategies for preventing sexual misconduct and other boundary violations in social work practice. *Psychoanalytic Social Work, 10*(2), 21–41.

Abdool, S. (2007). The unfortunate case of Mr. X...The Resolution. *Conflict Resolution Today, 20*(3/4), 13–14.

Adler, G. (2006). Applying NASW standards to end-of-life care for a culturally diverse, aging population. *Journal of Social Work Values and Ethics,* 3(2). Retrieved March 19, 2009, from http://www.socialworker.com/jswve/content/view/38/46.

Agard, A. (2005). Informed consent: Theory versus practice. *Nature Clinical Practice Cardiovascular Medicine* 2, 270–271. Retrieved March 19, 2009, from http://www.nature.com/ncpcardio/journal/v2/n6/full/ncpcardi00220.html.

Aging with Dignity. (n.d.). Retrieved March 19, 2009, from http://www.agingwithdignity.org.

Akers, R. L., & Sellers, C. S. (2004). *Criminological theories: Introduction, evaluation, and application* (4th ed.). Los Angeles: Roxbury.

Alexander, R. (1993). The legal liability of social workers after DeShaney. *Social Work, 38,* 64–68.

Alexander, R., & Alexander, C. R. (1995). Criminal prosecution of child protection workers. *Social Work, 40*(6), 809–814.

Allen, T. E. (2003). The foreseeability of transference: Extending employer liability under Washington law for therapist sexual exploitation of patients. *Washington Law Review, 78,* 525 (accessed through Lexus-Nexus).

Alzheimer's Association of Los Angeles. (n.d.). *Guidelines for Alzheimer's Disease management.* Retrieved March 19, 2009, from http://www.athealth.com/Practitioner/particles/alzguidelines.html#.

American Association for Marriage and Family Therapy. (2001). *Code of ethics.* Alexandria, VA: Author. Retrieved March 19, 2009, from http://www.aamft.org/index_nm.asp.

American Association of Sexuality Educators, Counselors, and Therapists. (2004). *Code of ethics*. Retrieved March 19, 2009, from http://www.aasect.org/codeofethics.asp.

American Bar Association. (2003). Guidelines for the appointment and performance of defense counsel in death penalty cases. Retrieved March 19, 2009, from http://www.abanet.org/deathpenalty/resources/docs/2003Guidelines.pdf.

American Bar Association. (2006a). *Model rules of professional conduct*. Chicago: Author. Retrieved March 21, 2009, from http://www.abanet.org/cpr/mrpc/mrpc_toc.html.

American Bar Association. (2006b). Commission on Law and Aging. Retrieved March 19, 2009 from http://www.aba.com/aging.

American Bar Association Commission on Law and Aging. (2005). Consumer's toolkit for health care advance planning. Retrieved March 19, 2009, from http://www.abanet.org/aging/publications/docs/consumer_tool_kit_bk.pdf.

American Bar Association Commission on Law and Aging, & American Psychological Association. (2005). Assessment of older adults with diminished capacity: A manual for lawyers. Retrieved March 19, 2009, from http://www.apa.org/pi/aging/diminished_capacity.pdf.

American Evaluation Association. (2004). Guiding principles for evaluators. Retrieved March 21, 2009, from http://www.eval.org/Publications/GuidingPrinciples.asp.

American Group Psychotherapy Association (AGPA). (2002). Guidelines for ethics. Retrieved March 21, 2009, from http://www.agpa.org/group/ethicalguide.html.

American Medical Association. (2001). *Code of ethics*. Washington, DC: Author. Retrieved March 21, 2009, from http://www.ama-assn.org/ama/pub/category/2512.html.

American Nurses Association. (2001). *Code of ethics*. Silver Spring, MD: Author. Retrieved March 21, 2009, from http://www.nursingworld.org/MainMenuCategories/ThePracticeofProfessionalNursing/EthicsStandards/CodeofEthics.aspx.

American Psychiatric Association (APA). (2000). *Diagnostic and statistical manual of mental disorders (DSM-IV-TR)*. Washington, DC: Author. Available (fee based) at http://www.psychiatryonline.com/resourceTOC.aspx?resourceID=1.

American Psychiatric Association. (2006). *The principles of medical ethics with annotations especially applicable to psychiatry*. Arlington, VA: Author. Retrieved March 21, 2009, from http://www.psych.org/MainMenu/PsychiatricPractice/Ethics.aspx.

American Psychological Association. (2002). *Ethical principles of psychologists and code of conduct*. Washington, DC: Author. Retrieved March 5, 2009 from http://www.apa.org/ethics/code2002.html

American Psychological Association. (2007). Mental health bill of rights. Retrieved March 21, 2009, from http://www.apa.org/topics/rights/#review. (NASW participated in the development of this bill of rights).

Amodio, D. M., Jost, J. T., Master, S. L., & Yee, C. M. (2007). Neurocognitive correlates of conservatism and liberalism. *Nature Neuroscience*. Retrieved March 21, 2009, from http:// www.psych.nyu.edu/amodiolab/Amodio%20et%20al.%20(2007)%20Nature%20Neuro.pdf..

Anderson, S. (2006). Coercion. In E. N. Zalta (ed.), *The Stanford encyclopedia of philosophy*. Retrieved March 21, 2009, from http://plato.stanford.edu/archives/spr2006/entries/coercion.

Andrews, A. B. (2007). Social work and survivor assistance. In A. R. Roberts & D. W. Springer (Eds.), *Social work in juvenile and criminal justice settings* (pp. 247–268). Springfield, IL: Charles C Thomas.

Andrews, A. B., & Patterson, E. G. (1995). Searching for solutions to alcohol and other drug abuse during pregnancy: Ethics, values and constitutional principles. *Social Work*, *40*(1), 55–64.

Appleby, G. A., Colon, E., & Hamilton, J. (2007). *Diversity, oppression, and social functioning: Person-In-Environment assessment and intervention*. Boston: Allyn & Bacon.

Arad-Davidzon, B., & Benbenishty, R. (2007). The role of workers' attitudes and parent and child wishes in child protection workers' assessments and recommendation regarding removal and reunification. *Children & Youth Services Review*, *30*(1), 107–121.

Ascension Health. (2007). Assessment tools: Evaluating your ethics committee. Retrieved March 21, 2009, from http://www.ascensionhealth.org/ethics/public/assessment_tools/evaluate_committee.asp.

Ashton, V. (2007). The impact of organizational environment on the likelihood that social workers will report child maltreatment. *Journal of Aggression, Maltreatment & Trauma*, *15*(1), 1–18.

Association for the Advancement of Social Work Practice with Groups (AASWG). (2006). Retrieved March 21, 2009, from http://www.aaswg.org/webfm_send/4.

Association of Family and Conciliation Courts. (2006). Model standards of practice for child custody evaluation. Retrieved March 21, 2009, from http://www.afccnet.org/resources/standards_practice.asp.

Association for Specialists in Group Work. (2007). Best practices. Retrieved March 21, 2009, from http://www.asgw.org/PDF/Best_Practices.pdf.

Association of Social Work Boards. (n.d., a). *Guide to social work ethics course development.* Retrieved March 21, 2009, from http://www.aswb.org/pdfs/ASWBEthicsCourseGuide.pdf.

Association of Social Work Boards. (n.d., b). Social work laws and regulations—Comparison database. Retrieved March 21, 2009, from http://www.aswb.org/members.shtml.

Bailles, R. (2006). Facilitation payments: Culturally acceptable or unacceptably corrupt? *Business Ethics: A European Review, 15*(3), 293–298.

Bailey, H. (n.d.). Values clarification. Retrieved March 21, 2009, from http://www.tntech.edu/honors/FacultyStaffandOfficial/handbook/8_values_clarification.pdf.

Banach, M., & Bernat, F. (2000). Liability and the internet: Risks and recommendations for social work practice. *Journal of Technology in Human Services, 1*(1), 153–171.

Bandura, A. (1977). *Social learning theory.* Upper Saddle River, NJ: Prentice Hall.

Banks, S. (1999). *Ethical issues in youth work.* New York: Routledge.

Banks, S. (2004). *Ethics, accountability, and the social professions.* New York: Palgrave Macmillan.

Banks, S. (2006). *Ethics and values in social work* (3rd ed.). New York: Palgrave Macmillan.

Barker, R. L. (2003). *The social work dictionary* (5th ed.). Washington, DC: NASW Press.

Barsky, A. E. (2006). *Successful social work education: A student's guide.* Belmont, CA: Brooks/Cole.

Barsky, A. E. (2007a). *Conflict resolution for the helping professions* (2nd ed.). Belmont, CA: Brooks/Cole.

Barsky. A. E. (2007b). Mediative evaluations—The pros and perils of blending roles. *Family Court Review, 45*(4), 560–572.

Barsky, A. E. (2008). A conflict resolution approach to teaching ethical decision making: Bridging conflicting values. *Journal of Jewish Communal Service*, 82(2/3), 164–169.

Barsky, A. E. (2009). Social work research and the law: How LGBT research can be structured and used to affect judicial decisions. In W. Meezan & J. I. Martin. (Eds.). *Research methods with gay, lesbian, bisexual, and transgender populations* (pp. 372–401). New York: Routledge.

Barsky, A. E. (in press). The legal and ethical context for knowing and using the latest child welfare research. *Child Welfare*, 88(2).

Barsky, A. E., & Gould, J. (2002). *Clinicians in court: A guide to subpoenas, depositions, testifying, and everything else you need to know.* New York: Guilford Press.

Barton, A. (2008). A narrative approach to bioethical decision making: The missing link between bioethics and conflict management. *Conflict Resolution Quarterly, 25*(4), 497–509.

Bashe, A., Anderson, S. K., Handelsman, M. M., & Klevansky, R. (2007). An acculturation model for ethics training: The ethics autobiography and beyond. *Professional Psychology: Research and Practice*, 38, 60–67.

Beauchamp, T. L., & Childress, J. F. (2009). *Principles of biomedical ethics* (6th ed.). New York: Oxford University Press.

Beckett, C., & Maynard, A. (2005). *Values and ethics in social work: An introduction.* Thousand Oaks, CA: Sage.

Bein, A. (2003). The ethnographic perspective: A new look. In J. Anderson & R. W. Carter (Eds.), *Diversity perspectives for social work practice* (pp. 133–145). Boston: Allyn & Bacon.

Bentham, J. (1823). *An introduction to the principles of morals and legislation.* Retrieved March 21, 2009, from http://www.laits.utexas.edu/poltheory/bentham/ipml/ipml.c01.html.

Bentley, K. J. (1993). The right of psychiatric patients to refuse medication: Where should social workers stand? *Social Work*, 38(1), 101–106.

Bergeron, L. R. (2006). Self-determination and elder abuse: Do we know enough? *Journal of Gerontological Social Work, 46*(3/4), 81–102.

Bergeron, L. R., & Gray, B. (2003). Ethical dilemmas of reporting suspected elder abuse. *Social Work, 48*(1), 96–105.

Bernstein, B. E., & Hartsell, T. L. (2004). *The portable lawyer for mental health professionals: An A to Z guide to protecting your clients, your practice, and yourself* (2nd ed.). San Francisco: Jossey-Bass (Wiley).

Besharov, D. J. (1984). Child welfare malpractice: Suing agencies and caseworkers for harmful practices. *Trial, 20*(3), 57–64.

Besharov, D. J. (1985). *The vulnerable social worker: Liability for serving children and families.* Washington, DC: NASW Press.

Besharov, D. J., & Laumann, L. A. (1996). Child abuse reporting. *Society,* 33(4), 40–46.

Black, P., Congress, E., & Strom-Gottfried, K. (2002). *Teaching social work values and ethics: A curriculum resource.* Alexandria, VA: Council on Social Work Education.

Bloche, M. G. (2005). Managing conflict at the end of life. *New England Journal of Medicine,* 352(23), 2371–2373.

Bloom, M., Fischer, J., & Orme, J. G. (2005). *Evaluating practice: Guidelines for the accountable professional* (5th ed.). Boston: Allyn & Bacon.

Boatright, J. R. (2006). *Ethics and the conduct of business* (5th ed.). Upper Saddle River, NJ: Pearson.

Bobek, B. L., & Gore, P. A. (2004). Inventory of work-relevant values. ACT Research Report Series. Retrieved March 21, 2009, from http://www.act.org/research/reports/pdf/ACT_RR2004-3.pdf.

Bosk, C. L., & De Vries, R. G. (2004). Bureaucracies of mass deception: Institutional Review Boards and the ethics of ethnographic research. *Annals of the American Academy of Political & Social Science,* 595, 249–263.

Boynton v. Burglass. (1991). 590 S0.2d 446 (Fla. Dist. Ct. App.).

Bradby, H. (1999). Negotiating marriage: Young Punjabi women's assessment of their individual & family interests. In R. Barot, H. Bradley, & S. Fenton, *Gender, ethnicity and social change* (pp. 152–166). London: Macmillan.

Bradley, D. (1983). Duress and arranged marriages. *Modern Law Review, 46*(4), 499–504.

Braddock, C. H. (2008). Physician-assisted suicide. Retrieved March 21, 2009, from http://depts.washington.edu/bioethx/topics/pas.html.

Bramstedt, K. A., Chalfant, A., & Wright, C. (2007). Emergency consults in the setting of transplant medicine: Dilemmas for social workers and bioethicists. *Progress in Transplantation, 17*(1), 36–39.

Brannen, S. J., Boling, C., & White, R. (2006, October). Bridge building into the future: Integrating the TTM with Bloom's Taxonomy in the classroom (Unpublished handout information and session). Baccalaureate Program Directors Conference, Council on Social Work Education, Los Angeles.

Braun, K. L., Pietsch, J., & Blanchette, P. L. (Eds.). (2000). *American Indian and Alaska Native cultures. Cultural issues in end-of-life decision making.* Newbury Park, CA: Sage.

Brody, R. (2005). *Effectively managing human service organizations.* Thousand Oaks, CA: Sage.

Brown, A. (2006). "In my agency it's very clear—but I can't tell you what it is": Work settings and ethical challenges. *Counselling & Psychotherapy Research,* 6(2), 100–107.

Brownell, P., & Giblin, C. T. (2009). Elder abuse. In A. R. Roberts & G. J. Green (Eds.), *Social workers' desk reference* (2nd ed., pp. 1106–1111). New York: Oxford University Press.

Buck, S. J. (2005). Church liability for clergy sexual abuse: Have time and events overthrown *Swanson v. Roman Catholic Bishop of Portland? Maine Law Review,* 57, 259–283.

Burkitt, K. H., & Larkin, G. L. (2008). The transtheoretical model in intimate partner violence victimization: Stage changes over time. *Violence & Victims, 23*(4), 411–431.

Burman, S. (2004). Revisiting the agent of social control role: Implications for substance abuse treatment. *Journal of Social Work Practice, 18*(2), 197–210.

Burson, I. (2007). Social work and female genital cutting: An ethical dilemma. *Journal of Social Work Values and Ethics, 4*(1). Retrieved March 21, 2009, from http://www.socialworker.com/jswve/content/blogcategory/14/50.

Bush, R. A. B., & Folger, J. P. (2005). *The promise of mediation: The transformative approach to conflict* (2nd ed.). San Francisco: Jossey-Bass.

Bush, S. S., Connell, M. A., & Denney, R. L. (2006). *Ethical practice in forensic psychology: A systematic model for decision-making.* Washington, DC: American Psychological Association.

Butler, K. A. (2004). Ethics paramount when patient lacks capacity. *Nursing Management,* 35(11), 18–52.

Buttell, F. P., Carney, M. M., & Miller, M. (2006). Empowering battered women by validating their decision-making skills: The role of moral development. *Journal of Social Service Research,* 32(4), 157–170.

Butz v. Economou. (1978). 438 U.S. 478, 512–13 (United States Supreme Court).

Caplan, A. L. (2006). Ethical issues surrounding forced, mandated, or coerced treatment. *Journal of Substance Abuse Treatment, 31,* 117–120.

Carniol, B. (2005). *Case critical: Social services and social justice in Canada* (5th ed.). Toronto: Between the Lines.

Carrese, J. A., & Rhodes, L. A. (1995). Western bioethics on the Navajo reservation: Benefit or harm? *Journal of the American Medical Association, 274*(10), 826–829.

Carrese J. 'A., & Rhodes L. A. (2000). Bridging cultural differences in medical practice: The case of discussing negative information with Navajo patients. *Journal of General Internal Medicine, 15*(2), 92–96.

Carson, T. (2006). The definition of lying. *Nous, 40*(2), 284–306.

Casebeer, W. D. (2003). *Natural ethical facts: Evolution, connectionism, and moral cognition.* Cambridge, MA: MIT Press.

Caudill, B. (n.d.). Malpractice & licensing pitfalls for therapists: A defense attorney's list. Retrieved March 21, 2009, from http://www.kspope.com/ethics/malpractice.php.

Center for Social Gerontology. (n.d.). Elder mediation. Retrieved March 21, 2009, from http://www.tcsg.org [includes access to Adult Guardianship Mediation Manual and Video].

Chasin, R., Herzig, M., Roth, S., Chasin, L., Becker, C., & Stains, R. R. (1996). From diatribe to dialogue on divisive public issues: Approaches drawn from family therapy. *Mediation Quarterly, 13*, 323–344.

Child Abuse Prevention and Treatment Act. (1974, as amended). 42 USC 5101 et seq; 42 USC 5116 et seq. Retrieved March 21, 2009, from http://www.acf.hhs.gov/programs/cb/laws_policies/cblaws/capta/index.htm.

Child Welfare Information Gateway. (2007). Definitions of child abuse and neglect: Summary of state laws. Retrieved March 21, 2009, from http://www.childwelfare.gov/systemwide/laws_policies/statutes/defineall.pdf.

Child Welfare Information Gateway. (2008). How the child welfare system works. Retrieved March 21, 2009, from http://www.childwelfare.gov/pubs/factsheets/cpswork.cfm.

Child Welfare Information Gateway. (n.d.). Retrieved March 21, 2009, from http://www.childwelfare.gov/systemwide/laws_policies/state/index.cfm.

Chopra, A. (2006). India tackles child marriages. *Christian Science Monitor*, 98, 125.

Citro, C. F., Ilgen, D. R., & Marrett, C. B. (2003). *Protecting participants and facilitating social and behavioral sciences research.* Washington, DC: National Academies Press—National Research Council.

Civil action for deprivation of rights (2007). 42 United States Code. §1983, Retrieved March 13, 2009 from http://www4.law.cornell.edu/uscode/42/1983.html.

Civil Rights Act. (1964). Public Law 88–352, 78 Statutes 241. Retrieved March 21, 2009, from http://www.historicaldocuments.com/CivilRightsAct1964.htm.

Civil Rights Act. (1996). United States Code, Title 42, §1983. Civil action for deprivation of rights.

Clark, C. (2006). Against confidentiality? Privacy, safety and the public good in professional communication. *Journal of Social Work, 6*(2), 117–136.

Clarke, C. M. (2007). Rationing scarce life-sustaining resources on the basis of age. *Journal of Advanced Nursing*, 35(5), 799–804.

Clinical Social Work Association. (1997). *Code of ethics.* Retrieved March 21, 2009, from http://associationsites.com/CSWA/collection//Ethcs%20Code%20Locked%2006%2Epdf.

Cohen, C. (1990). Ethical issues in mandatory drug testing. In R. Rosner & R. Weinstock (Eds.), *Ethical practice in psychiatry and law* (pp. 313–323). New York: Plenum Press.

Cohen, E. (2006). Conservative bioethics and the search for wisdom. *Hastings Center Report,* 36(1), 44–56.

Cohen, E. D., & Cohen, G. S. (1999). *The virtuous therapist: Ethical practice of counseling and psychotherapy.* Belmont, CA: Brooks/Cole.

Collins, D., Coleman, H., & Miller, P. (2002). Regulation of social workers: A confusing landscape. *Canadian Social Work Review,* 19(2), 205–225.

Common Rule. (1991). United States Code of Federal Regulations, Title 45, §46 (Authority: National Research Act [1974]. 5 U.S.C. 301; 42 U.S.C. 289[a]). Retrieved August 29, 2007, from http://ohsr.od.nih.gov/guidelines/45cfr46.html.

Congress, E. P. (1999). *Social work values and ethics.* Belmont, CA: Wadsworth.

Cook, R., & Dickens, B. M. (2007). Recognizing adolescents' "evolving capacities" to exercise choice in reproductive healthcare. *International Journal of Gynecology & Obstetrics,* 98(2), 182–187.

Cordain L., Eaton, S. B., Sebastian A., Mann, N., Lindeberg, S., Watkins, B. A., O'Keefe J. H., & Brand Miller, J. (2005). Origins and evolution of the western diet: Health implications for the 21st century. *American Journal of Clinical Nutrition, 81,* 341–354.

Corey, M. S., & Corey, G. (2006). *Groups: Process and practice* (7th ed.). Belmont, CA: Brooks/Cole.

Corey, G., Corey, M. S., & Callanan, P. (2007). *Issues and ethics in the helping professions* (7th ed.). Belmont, CA: Brooks/Cole-Wadsworth.

Council on Social Work Education. (2008). Educational policy and accreditation standards. Alexandria, VA: Author. Retrieved March 21, 2009, from http://www.cswe.org.

Cowburn, M., & Nelson, P. (2008). Safe recruitment, social justice, and ethical practice: Should people who have criminal convictions be allowed to train as social workers? *Social Work Education, 27*(3), 293–306.

Crisp, B. R., & Gillingham, P. (2008). Some of my students are prisoners: Issues and dilemmas for social work educators. *Social Work Education, 27*(3), 307–317.

Cruzan v. Director, Missouri Department of Health. (1990). 497 U.S. 261 (U.S. S.C). Retrieved August 25, 2008, from http://www.law.cornell.edu/supct/html/88–1503.ZO.html.

Csikai, E. L. (2002). The state of hospice ethics committees and the social work role. *Omega: An international journal for the study of dying, death, bereavement, suicide, and other lethal behaviors, 45*(3), 261–276.

Csikai, E. L., & Chaitin, E. (2006). *Ethics in end-of-life decisions in social work practice.* Chicago: Lyceum.

Csikai, E. L., & Jones, B. (2006). *Teaching resources for end-of-life and palliative care courses.* New York: Lyceum.

Cullin, J. (2005). The ethics of paradox: Cybernetic and postmodern perspectives on non-direct interventions in therapy. *Australian & New Zealand Journal of Family Therapy, 26*(3), 138–146.

Cumming, S., Fitzpatrick, E., McAuliffe, D., McKain, S., Martin, C., & Tonge, A. (2007). Raising the Titanic: Rescuing social work documentation from the sea of ethical risk. *Australian Social Work, 60*(2), 239–257.

Cummings, S., Adler, G., & DeCoster, V. (2005). Factors influencing graduate-social-work students' interest in working with elders. *Educational Gerontology, 31,* 643–655.

Curtis, K. A. (1994). Attributional analysis of role conflict. *Social Science and Medicine, 39*(2), 255–263.

Daley, M. R., & Doughty, M. O. (2006). Ethics complaints in social work practice: A rural-urban comparison. *Journal of Social Work Values and Ethics,* 3(2). Retrieved March 21, 2009, from http://www.socialworker.com/jswve/content/blogcategory/12/44.

D'Andrade, A., Austin, M. J., & Benton, A. (2008). Risk and safety assessment in child welfare: Instrument comparisons. *Journal of Evidence-Based Social Work, 5*(1/2), 31–56.

Daniels, N., & Sabin, J. (2002). *Setting limits fairly: Can we learn to share medical resources?* New York: Oxford University Press.

Danis, M., Farrar, A., Grady, C., Taylor, C., O'Donnell, P., Soeken, K., & Ulrich, C. (2008). Does fear of retaliation deter requests for ethics consultation? *Medical Health Care Philosophy.* Retrieved March 21, 2009, from http://www.springerlink.com/content/e705j318051pm653/fulltext.pdf.

Davydova, I., & Sharrock, W. (2003). The rise and fall of the fact/value distinction. *Sociological Review, 51*(3), 357–376.

D'Cruz, H. (2004). The social construction of child maltreatment: The role of medical practitioners. *Journal of Social Work.* 4(1), 99–123.

DeLamater, J. D., & Myers, D. J. (2007). *Social psychology* (6th ed.). Belmont, CA: Brooks/Cole.

DeMarco, J. P. (2001). Substantive equality: A basic value. *Journal of Social Philosophy,* 32(2), 197–206.

de Vries, A. L. C., Cohen-Kettenis, P. T., & Delemarre-Van De Waal, H. (2006). Clinical management of gender dysphoria in adolescents. *International Journal of Transgenderism,* 9(3/4), 83–94.

Dewees, M. (2005). *Contemporary social work practice.* New York: McGraw-Hill.

DiFranks, N. N. (2008). Social workers and the NASW *Code of Ethics*: Belief, behavior, and disjuncture. *Social Work, 53*(2), 167–176.

Dixon, J. W., & Dixon, K. (2006). Attorney-client privilege versus mandatory reporting by psychologists: Dilemma, conflict, and solution. *Journal of Forensic Psychology Practice,* 6(4), 69–78.

Dobrin, A. (1989). Ethical judgments of male and female social workers. *Social Work,* 34(5), 451–455.

Dodd, S., & Jansson, B. (2004). Expanding the boundaries of ethics education: Preparing social workers for ethical advocacy in an organizational setting. *Journal of Social Work Education, 40,* 455–465.

Dolgoff, R., Loewenberg, F. M., & Harrington, D. (2009). *Ethical issues for social work practice* (8th ed.). Belmont, CA: Brooks/Cole—Cengage.

Donaldson, T., & Werhane, P. H. (1996). *Ethical issues in business: A philosophical approach* (5th ed.). Upper Saddle River, NJ: Prentice Hall.

Donohoe, M. (2007). Parental notification and consent laws for teen abortions: Overview and 2006 ballot measures. *Medscape*, American College of Physicians. Retrieved March 21, 2009, from http://www.medscape.com/viewarticle/549316.

Dowd, D. (2002). *Understanding capitalism.* London: Pluto Press.

Doyle, C. (2007). Obstruction of justice: An abridged overview of related federal criminal laws. Washington, DC: Congressional Research Service. Retrieved March 21, 2009, from http://www.fas.org/sgp/crs/misc/RS22783.pdf.

Drewry, S. (2004). The ethics of human subjects protection in research. *Journal of Baccalaureate Social Work, 10*(1), 105–117.

Drotar, D. (2008). Ethics of treatment and intervention research with children and adolescents with behavioral and mental disorders: Recommendations for a future research agenda. *Ethics & Behavior, 18*(2–3), 307–313.

Duff, A. (2005). Social engineering in the information age. *Information Society, 21*(1), 67–71.

Eckhardt, E., & Anastas, J. (2007). Research methods with disabled populations. *Journal of Social Work in Disability & Rehabilitation, 6*(1/2), 233–249.

Eddy, W. A. (2003). *High conflict personalities: Understanding and resolving their costly disputes.* San Diego, CA: William A. Eddy.

Ehrenreich, J. H. (1985). *The altruistic imagination: A history of social work and social* policy in the United States. Ithaca, NY: Cornell University Press.

Ellerby, J. H., McKenzie, J., McKay, S, Gariepy, G. J., & Kaufert, J. M. (2000). Bioethics for clinicians: Aboriginal cultures. *Canadian Medical Association Journal, 163*(7), 845–850.

Ethics Resource Center. (n.d.). Glossary of terms. Retrieved March 21, 2009, from http://www.ethics.org/resources/ethics-glossary.asp.

Falvey, J. E. (2002). *Managing clinical supervision: Ethical practice and legal risk management.* Belmont, CA: Brooks/Cole.

Family and Medical Leave Act. (1993). Public Law 103–3. Retrieved March 21, 2009, from http://www4.law.cornell.edu/uscode/29/usc_sup_01_29_10_28.html.

Family Support Act. (1988). Public Law 100–485. Retrieved July 2, 2008, from http://thomas.loc.gov/cgi-bin/bdquery/z?d100:HR01720:|TOM:/bss/d100query.html|.

Farland, D. (2007). Principles, the methodological challenge and our obligations to the worst-off. *South African Journal of Philosophy, 26*(2), 133–142.

Ferraro, F. R., & Orvedal, L. (1998). Institutional review board issues related to special populations. *Journal of General Psychology, 125*(2), 156–164.

Filinson, R., McCreadie, C., Askham, J., & Mathew, D. (2008). Why should they be abused any more than children? Child abuse protection and the implementation of No Secrets. *Journal of Adult Protection, 10*(2), 18–28.

Finn, J., & Banach, M. (2002). Risk management in online human services practice. *Journal of Technology in Human Services, 20*(1/2), 133–154.

Fisher, G. L., & Harrison, T. C. (2005). *Substance abuse: Information for school counselors, social workers, therapists, and counselors* (3rd ed.). Boston: Allyn & Bacon.

Fisher, R., & Brown, S. (1988). *Getting together: Building relationships as we negotiate.* New York: Penguin.

Fisher, R., Ury, W., & Patton, B. (1997). *Getting to yes: Negotiating agreement without giving in* (3rd ed.). New York: Penguin.

Forehand, M. (2005). Bloom's taxonomy: Original and revised. Retrieved March 21, 2009, from http://www.coe.uga.edu/epltt/bloom.htm.

Fontes, L. A. (2004). Ethics in violence against women research: The sensitive, the dangerous, and the overlooked. *Ethics & Behavior, 14*(2), 141–174.

Forte, J. A. (2007). *Human behavior and the social environment: Models, metaphors, and maps for applying theoretical perspectives to practice.* Belmont, CA: Brooks/Cole.

Frankl, V. E. (2006/ orig.1946). *Man's search for meaning.* Boston: Beacon.

Freshwater, D., & Westwood, T. (2006). Risk, detention and evidence: Humanizing mental health reform. *Journal of Psychiatric and Mental Health Nursing, 13*(3), 257–259.

Freud-Loewenstein, A. (2004). In search of madness. *American Journal of Psychotherapy, 58*(1), 116–130.

Fry, A. W. M. (1981). Assessment in child abuse. *Child Abuse & Neglect, 5*(2), 159–165.

Furman, R. (2003). Frameworks for understanding value discrepancies and ethical dilemmas in managed mental health for social work in the United States. *International Social Work, 46*(1), 37–52.

Furman, R., Langer, C. L., Sanchez, T. W., & Negi, N. J. (2007). A qualitative study of immigration policy and practice dilemmas for social work students. *Journal of Social Work Education, 43*(1), 133–146.

Furnham, A., Ariffin, A., & McClelland, A. (2007). Factors affecting allocation of scarce medical resources across life-threatening medical conditions. *Journal of Applied Social Psychology, 37*, 2903–2921.

Galambos, C. (1999). Resolving ethical conflicts in a managed health care environment. *Health & Social Work, 24*(3), 191–197.

Gandhi, M. K. (1959). *The moral basis of vegetarianism.* Ahmedabad, India: Navajivan Publishing.

Gantt, A. B., & Levine, J. (1990). The roles of social work in psycho-biological research. *Social Work in Health Care, 15*(2), 63–75.

Ganzini, L., Volicer, L., Nelson, W., Fox, E., & Derse, A. R. (2005). Ten myths about decision-making capacity. *Journal of the American Medical Directors Association, 6*(3), S100-S104.

Gazzaniga, M. S. (2005). *The ethical brain.* Chicago: University of Chicago Press.

Gelman, S. R., & Pollack, D. (2007). Correctional policies: Evolving trends. Social work and survivor assistance. In A. R. Roberts & D. W. Springer (Ed.), *Social work in juvenile and criminal justice settings* (pp. 32–43). Springfield, IL: Charles C Thomas.

Gellerman, D. M., & Suddath, R. (2005). Violent fantasy, dangerousness, and the duty to warn and protect. *Journal of American Academy of Psychiatry and the Law, 33*, 484–495. Retrieved March 7, 2009 from http://www.jaapl.org/cgi/content/full/33/4/484

Geneva Conventions. (1864, revised 1949, 1977, 2005). Retrieved March 21, 2009, from http://www.icrc.org/Web/Eng/siteeng0.nsf/htmlall/genevaconventions.

Gert, B. (2006). Morality versus slogans. Dartmouth College Department of Philosophy (manuscript). Hanover, NH.

Geva, E., Barsky, A. E., & Westernoff, F. (2000). *Interprofessional practice with diverse populations: Cases in point.* Westport, CN: Greenwood.

Gibb, J. C. (2003). *Moral development and reality: Beyond the theories of Kohlberg and Hoffman.* Thousand Oaks, CA: Sage.

Gibbs, L. (2003). *Evidence-based practice for the helping professions: A practical guide.* Belmont, CA: Brooks/Cole.

Gibelman, M., & Gelman, S. R. (2005). Scientific misconduct in social welfare research: Preventive lessons from other fields. *Social Work Education, 24*(3), 275–295.

Gilligan, C. (1982). *In a different voice: Psychological theory and women's development.* Cambridge, MA: Harvard University Press.

Goodin, R. (2005). Toward an international rule of law: Distinguishing international law-breakers from would-be law-makers. *Journal of Ethics, 9*(1/2), 225–246.

Gorsuch, R. L., & Ortberg, J. (1983). Moral obligation and attitudes: Their relation to behavioral intentions. *Journal of Personality and Social Psychology, 44*(5), 1025–1028.

Gostin, L. O. (2006). Medical countermeasures for pandemic influenza: Ethics and the law. *Journal of the American Medical Association, 295*(5), 554–556.

Gostin, L. O., Lazzarini, Z., & Flaherty, K. M. (n.d.). Legislative survey of state confidentiality laws, with specific emphasis on HIV and immunization. Retrieved March 21, 2009, from http://www.epic.org/privacy/medical/cdc_survey.html.

Gott, M., Small, N., Barnes. S., Payne, S., & Seamark, D. (2008). Older people's views of a good death in heart failure: Implications for palliative care provision. *Social Science & Medicine.* DOI:10.1016/j.socscimed.2008.05.024.

Government Accountability Project. (n.d.). Retrieved March 21, 2009, from http://www.whistleblower.org.

Government of Oregon. (2007). FAQs about the Death with Dignity Act. Retrieved March 21, 2009, from http://www.oregon.gov/DHS/ph/pas/faqs.shtml#can.

Green, D. (2007). Risk and social work practice. *Australian Social Work, 60*(4), 395–409.

Greene, A. D., & Latting, J. K. (2004). Whistle-blowing as a form of advocacy: Guidelines for the practitioner and organization. *Social Work, 49*(2), 219–230.

Green, R. G., Kiernan-Stern, M., & Baskind, F. R. (2005). White social workers' attitudes about people of color. *Journal of Ethnic & Cultural Diversity in Social Work, 14*(1/2), 47–68.

Grinnell, R. M. (2007). *Social work research and evaluation: Foundations of evidence-based practice* (8th ed.). New York: Oxford University Press.

Guinn, D. E. (2002). Mental competence, caregivers, and the process of consent: Research involving Alzheimer's patients or others with decreasing mental capacity. *Cambridge Quarterly of Healthcare Ethics, 11*, 230–245.

Gumpert, J., & Black, P. N. (2006). Ethical issues in group work: What are they? How are they managed? *Social Work with Groups, 29*(4), 61–74.

Gumz, E. J. (2004). American social work, corrections and restorative justice: An appraisal. *International Journal of Offender Therapy & Comparative Criminology, 48*(4), 449–460.

Gushwa, M., & Chance, T. (2008). Ethical dilemmas for mental health practitioners: Navigating mandated child maltreatment reporting decisions. *Families in Society, 89*(1), 78–83.

Guterman, J. T. (2006). Mastering the art of solution-focused counseling. Alexandria, VA: American Counseling Association.

Gutheil, T. G., & Brodsky, A. (2008). *Preventing boundary violations in clinical practice.* New York: Guilford.

Hadley, M. (2001). *The spiritual roots of restorative justice.* Albany: State University of New York Press.

Hagihara, A., & Tarumi, K. (2007). Association between physicians' communicative behaviors and judges' decisions in lawsuits on negligent care. *Health Policy, 83*(1/2), 213–222.

Hall, S. R. (2006). Child abuse reporting laws and attorney-client privilege: Ethical dilemmas and practical suggestions for the forensic psychologist. *Journal of Forensic Psychology Practice, 6*(4), 55–68.

Handelsman, M. M., Gottlieb, M. C., & Knapp, S. (2005). Training ethical psychologists: An acculturation model. *Professional Psychology: Research and Practice, 36*, 59–65.

Hansen, K. K. (1998). Folk remedies and child abuse: A review with emphasis on caida de mollera and its relationship to shaken baby syndrome. *Child Abuse and Neglect, 22*(2), 117–127.

Hardina, D. (2004). Guidelines for ethical practice in community organization. *Social Work, 49*(4), 595–604.

Harrington, A. (2004). *Modern social theory: An introduction.* New York: Oxford University Press.

Haynes, S. R. (2002). *Noah's curse: The biblical justification of American slavery.* New York: Oxford University Press.

Health Insurance Portability and Accountability Act (HIPAA). (1996). Pub. L. 104–191, 110 Stat. 1936.

Healy, L. M. (2007). Universalism and cultural relativism in social work ethics. *International Social Work, 50*(1) 11–26.

Heinlen, K. T., Welfel, E. R., Richmond, E. N., & Rak, C. F. (2003). The scope of web counseling: A survey of services and compliance with NBCC standards for the ethical practice of web counseling. *Journal of Counseling & Development, 81*(1), 61–70.

Hendrix, L. R. (n.d.). Health and health care of American Indian and Alaska Native elders. Retrieved March 21, 2009, from http://www.stanford.edu/group/ethnoger/americanindian.html.

Hester, D. M. (2007). *Ethics by committee: A textbook on consultation, organization, and education for hospital ethics committees.* Blue Ridge Summit, PA: Rowman & Littlefield.

Heyman, J. C., Buchanan, R., Marlowe, D., & Sealy, Y. (2006). Social workers' attitudes toward the role of religion and spirituality in social work practice. *Journal of Pastoral Counseling, 41*, 3–19.

Hilhorst, D. (2005). Dead letter or living document? Ten years of the Code of Conduct for disaster relief. *Disasters, 29*(4), 351–369.

Hill, G., & Hill, K. (2006). *The people's law dictionary.* Retrieved March 21, 2009, from http://dictionary.law.com/default2.asp?typed=malpractice&type=1&submit1.x=28&submit1.y=10.

Hill, K., & Lightfoot, E. (2009). The dilemma between easing service access through a clear diagnosis of disability and unease in assigning labels to people with disabilities: A case study. *Journal of Social Work Ethics and Values, 5*(3). Retrieved March 16, 2009 from http://www.socialworker.com/jswve/content/view/104/66.

Hinman, L. M. (n.d.). Glossary. Retrieved March 21, 2009, from http://ethics.sandiego.edu/LMH/E2/Glossary.asp.

Hinterlong, J. E., & Williamson, A. (2006). The effects of civic engagement of current and future cohorts of older adults. *Generations, 30*(4), 10–17.

Hoeffer, R. (2006). *Advocacy practice for social justice.* Chicago: Lyceum.

Holman, C. W., & Goldberg, J. M. (2006). Ethical, legal, and psychosocial issues in care of transgender adolescents. *International Journal of Transgenderism, 9*(3/4), 95–110.

Homer, R., & Kelly, T. B. (2007). Ethical decision-making in the helping professions: A contextual and caring approach. *Journal of Religion & Spirituality in Social Work, 26*(1), 71–88.

Honeyman, C. (2003). Grievance procedures. Conflict Research Consortium, University of Colorado, Boulder. Retrieved March 21, 2009, from http://www.beyondintractability.org/essay/grievance_procedures.

Houston-Vega, M. K., & Nuehring, E. M. (1997). *Prudent practice: A guide for managing malpractice risk.* Washington, DC: NASW Press.

Hugen, B., & Scales, T. L. (Eds.). (2008). *Christianity and social work: Readings on the integration of Christian faith and social work practice* (3rd ed.). Botsford, CT: North American Association of Christians in Social Work.

Hugman, R. (2003). Professional ethics in social work: Living with the legacy. *Australian Social Work*, 56(1), 5–15.

Hugman, R., & Smith, D. (1995). *Ethical issues in social work.* New York: Routledge.

Hugo, V. (1987/orig. 1862). *Les miserables.* New York: Penguin.

Hunter, S. (2001). Working with domestic violence: Ethical dilemmas in five theoretical approaches. *Australian & New Zealand Journal of Family Therapy*, 22(2), 80–89.

Hursthouse, R. (2007). Virtue ethics. *Stanford encyclopedia of philosophy.* Retrieved March 21, 2009, from http://plato.stanford.edu/entries/ethics-virtue.

Infectious Diseases Society of America. (2007). Pandemic influenza. Retrieved March 21, 2009, from http://www.cidrap.umn.edu/idsa/influenza/panflu/biofacts/panflu.html.

In re Marriage Cases. (2008). Ct.App. Nos. A110449, A110450, A110451, A110463, A110651, A110652 (Supreme Court of California). Retrieved March 21, 2009, from http://www.courtinfo.ca.gov/opinions/archive/S147999.pdf.

In re Quinlan. (1976). 70 N.J. 10; A.2d 647.

Institute for the Study of Conflict Transformation. (n.d.). The transformative framework. Retrieved March 21, 2009, from http://transformativemediation.org/transformative.php.

International Association of Chiefs of Police. (n.d.) Model policy on standards of conduct. Retrieved March 21, 2009, from http://www.theiacp.org/PoliceServices/ExecutiveServices/ProfessionalAssistance/Ethics/ModelPolicyonStandardsofConduct/tabid/196/Default.aspx.

International Emergency Economic Powers Act (IEEPA). (2000). 50 U.S.C. 1701–1707.

International Federation of Social Workers. (2000). Definition of social work. Retrieved March 21, 2009, from http://www.ifsw.org/en/p38000208.html.

International Federation of Social Workers and International Association of Schools of Social Work. (2004). *Ethics in social work: Statements of principles.* Retrieved March 21, 2009, from http://www.ifsw.org/en/p38000324.html.

International Humanist and Ethical Union. (n.d.). About IHEU. Retrieved March 21, 2009, from. http://www.iheu.org/about.

International Red Cross. (1996). Code of conduct for the International Red Cross and Red Crescent movement and non-governmental organizations (NGOs) in disaster relief. Retrieved March 21, 2009, from http://www.icrc.org/web/eng/siteeng0.nsf/htmlall/code-of-conduct-290296.

Israel, T., Gorcheva, R., Walther, W. A., Sulzner, J., & Cohen, J. (2008). Therapists' helpful and unhelpful situations with LGBT clients: An exploratory study. *Professional Psychology: Research and Practice*, 39(3), 361–368.

Jaffee v. Redmond. (1996). 518 U.S. 1 (US SC).

Jane Adams Hull House Association. (n.d.). Center for Civil Society. Retrieved March 22, 2009, from http://www.hullhouse.org/policyandresearch/centerforcivilsociety.html.

Janis, I. L. (1972). *Victims of groupthink.* Boston: Houghton Mifflin.

Jansson, B. S. (2008). Becoming an effective policy advocate: From policy practice to social justice (5th ed.). Belmont, CA: Brooks/Cole.

Johnson, D. W., Johnson, R. T., & Smith, K. A. (1997). Academic controversy: Enriching college instruction through intellectual conflict. *ASHE-ERIC Higher Education Report*, 25(1), 1–157.

Johnson, T. F. (2000). Ethics in addressing mistreatment of elders: Can we have ethics for all? *Generations*, 24(2), 81–86.

Jones, J. W., & McCullough, L. B. (2008). The shifting sands of senility: Canceled consent. *Journal of Vascular Surgery*, 47(1), 237–238.

Jung, C. G. (1921). *Psychological types.* Princeton, NJ: Princeton University Press.

Kadushin, A., & Harkness, D. (2002). *Supervision in social work* (4th ed.). New York: Columbia University Press.

Kalichman, S. C. (1999). Mandated reporting of suspected child abuse: Ethics, law, and policy (2nd ed.). Washington, DC: American Psychological Association.

Kanani, K., Regehr, C., & Bernstein, M. (2002). Liability considerations in child welfare:

Lessons from Canada. *Child Abuse & Neglect, 26*(10), 1029–1043.
Kane, M. N. (2006). Risk management for Catholic priests in the United States: A new demand from the Code of Pastoral Conduct. *Journal of Religion & Spirituality in Social Work, 25*(1), 47–67.
Kant, I. (1964/Orig.1785). *Groundwork of the metaphysic of morals.* New York: Harper-Collins.
Kant, I. (1979/Orig.1779). *Lectures on ethics.* Translated by L. Infield. London: Methuen.
Kaplan, L. E. (2006). Dual relationships: The challenges for social workers in recovery. *Journal of Social Work Practice in the Addictions, 5*(3), 73–90.
Kaplan, L. E. (2006). Moral reasoning of MSW social workers and the influence of education. *Journal of Social Work Education, 42*(3), 507–522.
Karger, H. J., Midgley, J., & Brown, C. (Eds.). (2003). *Controversial issues in social policy* (2nd ed.). Boston: Allyn & Bacon.
Karls, J. M., & O'Keefe, M. (2008). *Person-in-environment system manual* (2nd ed.). Washington, DC: NASW Press.
Kass, L. R. (2003). The human life span should not be extended. *Death and dying: Opposing viewpoints* (pp. 132–141). San Diego, CA: Thomson.
Kaufman, C., & Ramarao, S. (2005). Community confidentiality, consent, and the individual research process: Implications for demographic research. *Population Research & Policy Review, 24*(2), 149–173.
Keller-Micheli, A., Morgan, S., Polowy, C. I., & Bailey, W. D. (2007). *Social workers and the legal rights of children.* Washington, DC: NASW Legal Defense Fund. Retrieved March 18, 2009 from http://www.socialworkers.org/ldf/lawnotes/children.asp.
Kharicha K., Illife, S., Levin E., Davey, B., & Fleming, C. (2005). Tearing down Berlin wall: Social workers' perspectives on joint working with general practitioners. *Family Practice, 22*, 399–405.
Killick, S., & Allen, D. (2005). Training staff in adolescent inpatient psychiatric unit in positive approaches to managing aggressive and harmful behaviour: Does it improve confidence and knowledge? *Child Care in Practice, 11*(3), 323–339.
Kim, M. M., Scheyett, A. M., Elbogen, E. B., Van Dorn, R. A., McDaniel, L. A., Swartz, M. S., Swanson, J. W., & Ferron, J. (2008). Front line workers' attitudes towards psychiatric advance directives. *Community Mental Health Journal, 44*(1), 28–46.
Kindler, H. (2008). Developing evidence-based child protection practice: A view from Germany. *Research on Social Work Practice, 18*(4), 319–324.
Kirkland, K., Kirkland, K. L., & Reaves, R. P. (2004). On the professional use of disciplinary data. *Professional Psychology: Research and Practice*, 359(2), 179–184.
Kirkland, K., & Kirkland, K. E. (2006). Risk management and aspirational ethics for parenting coordinators. *Journal of Child Custody*, 3(2), 23–43.
Kirkpatrick, W. J., Reamer, F. G., & Sykulski, M. (2006). Social work ethics audits in health care settings: A case study. *Health & Social Work, 31*(3), 225–228.
Kirst-Ashman, K. K., & Hull, G. H. (2006a). *Generalist practice with organizations and communities.* Belmont, CA: Brooks/Cole.
Kirst-Ashman, K. K., & Hull, G. H. (2006b). *Understanding generalist practice* (4th ed.). Belmont, CA: Brooks/Cole.
Knapp, S., Gottlieb, M., Berman, J., & Handelsman, M. M. (2007). When laws and ethics collide: What should psychologists do? *Professional Psychology: Research and Practice*, 38, 54–59.
Knight, K. (2007). *Aristotelian philosophy: Ethics and politics from Aristotle to MacIntyre.* Williston, VT: Polity Press.
Knights Party. (n.d.). Retrieved March 21, 2009, from http://www.kkk.bz.
Koenig, T. L. (2005). Caregivers' use of spirituality in ethical decision-making. *Journal of Gerontological Social Work*, 45(1/2), 155–172.
Koenig, T., Rinfrette, E., & Lutz, W. (2006). Female caregivers' reflections on ethical decision-making: The intersection of domestic violence and elder care. *Clinical Social Work Journal*, 34(3), 361–372.
Koenig, T. L., & Spano, R. N. (2003). Sex, supervision, and boundary violations: Pressing challenges and possible solutions. *Clinical Supervisor*, 22(1), 3–20.
Kohlberg, L., Levine, C., & Hewer, A. (1983). *Moral stages: A current formulation and a response to critics.* New York: Karger.
Konopka, G. (2005). The significance of social group work based on ethical values. *Social Work with Groups*, 28(3/4), 17–28.
Koocher, G. P. (n.d.). Ethical issues in supervision. Retrieved March 21, 2009, from http://www.us.oup.com/us/ppt/pdr/Supervision.ppt.

Krebs, D. L., & Denton, K. (2005). Toward a more pragmatic approach to morality: A critical evaluation of Kohlberg's model. *Psychological Review, 112*, 629–649.

Kristjánsson, K. (2006). Emulation and the use of role models in moral education. *Journal of Moral Education*, 35(1), 37–49.

Kroch, U. (2009). The experience of beign a dependent adult (ward) – A hermeneutic phenomenological study (Unpublished Ph.D. dissertation), University of Calgary, School of Social Work, Calgary, AB, Canada.

Kübler-Ross, E. (1997). *On death and dying.* New York: Macmillan.

Kuczewski, M. G. (2007). Talking about spirituality in the clinical setting: Can being professional require being personal? *American Journal of Bioethics*, 7(7), 4–11.

Kuschner, W. G., Pollard, J. B., & Ezeji-Okoye, S. C. (2007). Ethical triage and scarce resource allocation during public health emergencies: Tenets and procedures. *Hospital Topics*, 85(3), 16–25.

Kutchins, H., & Kirk, S. A. (1987). *DSM-III* and social work malpractice. *Social Work*, 32(3), 205–211.

Lachman V. D. (1999). Breaking the quality barrier: Critical thinking and conflict resolution. *Nursing Case Management*, 4, 224–227.

Lambek, B. D. (1987). Necessity and international law: Arguments for the legality of civil disobedience. *Yale Law & Policy Review*, 5(2), 472–402.

Lask, B. (2003). Patient–clinician conflict: Causes and compromises. *Journal of Cystic Fibrosis*, 2(1), 42–45.

Lederach, J. P. (2005). *The moral imagination.* New York: Oxford University Press.

Legal Defense Fund (NASW). (2005). *HIPAA desk reference.* Washington, DC: National Association of Social Workers.

Legal Defense Fund (NASW). (2007). Amicus brief filed in the case of *Franet v. County of Alameda California* (U.S. Court of Appeals in Ninth District, CA). Retrieved March 21, 2009, from https://www.socialworkers.org/assets/secured/documents/ldf/briefDocuments/Franet%20v.%20Alameda%20County.PDF.

Legal Information Institute. (n.d.). State statutes on the internet—Criminal law. Retrieved March 21, 2009, from http://www.law.cornell.edu/topics/state_statutes2.html#criminal_code.

Leichtentritt, R. D., & Rettig, K. D. (2001). Values underlying end-of-life decisions: A qualitative approach. *Health & Social Work*, 26(3), 150–160.

Lens, V. (2004). Social work and the Supreme Court: A clash of values; a time for action. *Social Work*, 49(2), 327–330.

Lessard v. Schmidt. (1972). 349 F. Supp. 1078; 1972 U.S. Dist. LEXIS 11526.

Levenson, J. S., & Morin, J. W. (2006). Risk assessment in child sexual abuse cases. *Child Welfare*, 85(1), 59–82.

Levesque, D. A., Driskell, M., Prochaska, J. M., & Prochaska, J. O. (2008). Acceptability of a stage-matched expert system intervention for domestic violence offenders. *Violence & Victims*, 23(4), 432–445.

Levine, M. A., Wynia, M. K., Schyve, P. M., Teagarden, J. R., Fleming, D. A., Donohue, S. K., Anderson, R. J., Sabin, J., & Emanuel, E. J. (2007). Improving access to health care: A consensus ethical framework to guide proposals for reform. *Hastings Center Report*, 37(5), 14–19.

Levy, C. (1993). *Social work ethics on the line.* Binghampton, NY: Haworth Press.

Liddle, H. A., Jackson-Gilfort, A., & Marvel, F. A. (2006). An empirically supported and culturally specific engagement and intervention strategy for African American adolescent males. *American Journal of Orthopsychiatry*, *76*, 215–225.

Lightman, D. (2007). AFCC 758: There's no such thing as difficult people (CD-ROM—audio). AFCC Digital Conference Providers (https://www.dcporder.com/afcc/?form_id=AFCC4).

Linzer, N. (1999). *Resolving ethical dilemmas in social work practice.* Boston: Allyn & Bacon.

Linzer, N. (2004). An ethical dilemma in elder abuse. *Journal of Gerontological Social Work*, 43(2/3), 165–173.

Locke, J. (1689). Two treatises of government. Retrieved March 21, 2009, from http://www.gutenberg.org/catalog/world/readfile?fk_files=28217.

Lum, D. (2004). *Social work practice and people of color: A process stage approach.* Belmont, CA: Brooks/Cole.

Lyons, H. D. (2007). Genital cutting: The past and present of a polythetic category. *Africa Today*, 53(4), 3–17.

Macauley, R. (2005). The Hippocratic underground. *Hastings Center Report*, 35(1), 38–45.

Madden, R. G. (2003). *Essential law for social workers.* New York: Columbia University Press.

Madden, S., Martin, D. K., Downey, S., & Singer, P. A. (2005). Hospital priority setting with an appeals process: A qualitative case study and evaluation. *Health Policy*, 73(1), 10–20.

Maiese, M. (2003a). What is moral conflict? Retrieved March 21, 2009, from http://www.beyondintractability.org/essay/intolerable_moral_differences/?nid=1036.

Maiese, M. (2003b). The need for dialogue. Retrieved March 21, 2009, from http://www.beyondintractability.org/essay/dialogue/?nid=1218.

Malone, R. E., Verger, V. B., McGruder, C., & Froelicher, E. (2006). It's like Tuskegee in reverse: A case study of ethical tensions in institutional review board review of community-based participatory research. *American Journal of Public Health*, 96, 1914–1919.

Manderscheid, D. J. (2007). First Nations and self-government: A matter of trust. *Canadian Journal of Law & Society*, 22(1), 109–121.

Manifold v. Ragaglia. (2004). 272 Conn. 410 (Connecticut Supreme Court).

Manning, S. S. (2003). *Ethical leadership in human services: A multi-dimensional approach*. Boston: Allyn & Bacon.

Mansbach, A., & Bachner, Y. G. (2008). On the readiness of social work students to blow the whistle to protect the client's interests. *Journal of Social Work Values and Ethics*, 5(2). Retrieved March 21, 2009, from http://www.socialworker.com/jswve/content/blogcategory/18/65.

Marcellus, L. (2005). The ethics of relation: Public health nurses and child protection clients. *Journal of Advanced Nursing*, 51(4), 414–420.

Markóczy, M. (2007). Utilitarians are not always fair and the fair are not always utilitarian: Distinct motives for cooperation. *Journal of Applied Social Psychology*, 37(9), 1931–1955.

Marson, S. M., & MacLeod, E. (1996). The first social worker. *New Social Worker*, 3(1), 11.

Marx, K. (1875). Critique of the Gotha program. *Marx/Engels Selected Works*, 3, 13–30. Retrieved March 21, 2009, from http://www.marxists.org/archive/marx/works/sw/index.htm.

Marx, K., & Engels, F. (1848). *The communist manifesto*. Retrieved March 21, 2009, from http://www.mdx.ac.uk/www/study/xmar1848.htm.

Maslow, A., Frager, R., & Fadiman, J. (1987). *Motivation and personality* (3rd ed.). Boston: Addison-Wesley.

Mattison, M. (2000). Ethical decision making: The person in process. *Social Work*, 45(3), 201–212.

Maxwell, K. J. (2007). The Socratic method. Retrieved March 21, 2009, from http://www.socraticmethod.net.

McAuliffe, D. (2005a). I'm still standing: Impacts and consequences of ethical dilemmas for social workers in direct practice. *Journal of Social Work Values and Ethics*, 2(1), Retrieved March 21, 2009, from http://www.socialworker.com/jswve/content/view/17/34.

McAuliffe, D. (2005b). Putting ethics on the organisational agenda: The social work ethics audit on trial. *Australian Social Work*, 58(4), 357–369.

McAuliffe, D., & Sudbery, J. (2005). "Who do I tell?" Support and consultation in cases of ethical conflict. *Journal of Social Work*, 5(1), 21–43.

McGee, G., Spanogle, J. P., Caplan, A. L., & Asch, D. A. (2001). A national study of ethics committees. *American Journal of Bioethics*, 1(4), 60–64.

McInnis-Dittrich, K. (2005). *Social work with elders: A biopsychosocial approach to assessment and intervention* (2nd ed.). Boston: Allyn & Bacon.

Meacham, M. G. (2007). Ethics and decision making for social workers. *Journal of Social Work Values and Ethics*, 4(3). Retrieved March 21, 2009, from http://www.socialworker.com/jswve/content/view/70/54.

Meals on Wheels (n.d.). Retrieved March 21, 2009, from http://www.meals-on-wheels.org.

Médecins Sans Frontières (n.d.). The MSF Charter. Retrieved March 21, 2009, from http://www.doctorswithoutborders.org/aboutus/charter.cfm.

Medvene, L. J., Base, M., Patrick, R., & Wescott, J. (2007). Advance directives: Assessing stage of change and decisional balance in a community-based educational program. *Journal of Applied Social Psychology*, 37(10), 2298–2318.

Melville, R. (2005). Human research ethics committees and ethical review: The changing research culture for social workers. *Australian Social Work*, 58(4), 370–383.

Mencken, H. L. (1920). *Prejudices: Second series*. New York: A. A. Knopf.

Menkel-Meadow, C., Love, L. P., Schneider, A. K., & Sternlight, J. R. (2005). *Dispute resolution: Beyond the adversarial model*. New York: Aspen.

Mental Illness. (n.d.). *The American heritage dictionary of the English language* (4th ed.). Retrieved March 21, 2009, from http://dictionary.reference.com/browse/mental illness.

Meyer, R. G., & Weaver, C. M. (2005). *Law and mental health: A case-based approach.* New York: Guilford.

Meyers, C. (2007). *A practical guide to clinical ethics consulting: Expertise, ethos and power.* Blue Ridge Summit, PA: Rowman & Littlefield.

Miley, K., & DuBois, B. (2007). Ethical preferences for the clinical practice of empowerment social work. *Social Work in Health Care, 44*(1–2), 29–44.

Mill, J. S. (1863). *Utilitarianism.* Retrieved March 21, 2009, from http://utilitarianism.com/mill1.htm.

Minow, M. (2007). Living up to rules: Holding soldiers responsible for abusive conduct and the dilemma of the superior orders defense. *McGill Law Journal,* 52(1), 1–55. Retrieved March 12, 2009 from http://lawjournal.mcgill.ca/documents/1219617374_Minow.pdf.

Misprision of Treason (n.d.). 18 U.S.C. §2382. Retrieved March 21, 2009, from http://www4.law.cornell.edu/uscode/18/usc_sec_18_00002382——000-.html.

Monin, B., Pizarro, D. A., & Beer, J. S. (2007). Deciding versus reacting: Conceptions of moral judgment and the reason-affect debate. *Review of General Psychology, 11*(2), 99–111.

Moore, C. W. (2003). *The mediation process: Practical strategies for resolving conflict* (3rd ed.). San Francisco: Jossey-Bass.

Mullen, E., & Skitka, L. J. (2006). Exploring the psychological underpinnings of the moral mandate effect: Motivated reasoning, group differentiation, or anger? *Journal of Personality and Social Psychology,* 90(4), 629–643.

Munson, C. (2002). *Clinical social work supervision* (3rd ed.). Binghamton, NY: Haworth.

Murphy, C. M., & Maiuro, R. D. (2008). Understanding and facilitating the change process in perpetrators and victims of intimate partner violence: Summary and commentary. *Violence & Victims,* 23(4), 525–536.

Myers, J. E., Madathil, J., & Tingle, L. R. (2005). Marriage satisfaction and wellness in India and the United States: A preliminary comparison of arranged marriages and marriages of choice. *Journal of Counseling & Development,* 83(2), 183–190.

Myers, J. E. B. (2002). Invited commentary. *Child Abuse & Neglect,* 26, 1007–1009.

Naglee v. Ingersoll. (1847). 7 Pa. 185 (Supreme Court of Pennsylvania).

Nathoo, A. (2000). The ethics of allocating healthcare (PowerPoint Presentation). Provincial Health Ethics Network, Calgary, AB, Canada.

National Association of Black Social Workers. (n.d.). Code of Ethics. Retrieved March 21, 2009, from. http://www.nabsw.org/mserver/CodeofEthics.aspx?menuContext=720.

National Association of Social Workers (NASW). (1999). *Code of ethics.* Washington, DC: Author. Retrieved March 21, 2009, from http://www.socialworkers.org/pubs/code/code.asp.

National Association of Social Workers (NASW). (2004). Standards for social work practice in palliative and end of life care. Washington, DC: Author. Retrieved March 21, 2009, from http://www.socialworkers.org/practice/bereavement/standards/default.asp.

National Association of Social Workers (NASW). (2005a). *NASW procedures for professional review* (4th ed.). Washington, DC: Author.

National Association of Social Workers (NASW). (2005b). National Ethics Committee. Retrieved March 21, 2009, from http://www.socialworkers.org/governance/cmtes/ncoi.asp.

National Association of Social Workers. (2006). Social work speaks: NASW policy statements, 2006–2009. Washington, DC: Author.

National Association of Social Workers. (2008). Social workers and coaching. Retrieved March 21, 2009, from https://www.socialworkers.org/ldf/legal_issue/2008/200805.asp?back=yes.

National Association of Social Workers (NASW). (n.d.). NASW Standards (for substance abuse, health, school social work and other fields of practice). Retrieved March 21, 2009, from http://www.socialworkers.org/practice.

National Association of State Mental Health Directors. (n.d.). State mental health agencies. Retrieved March 21, 2009, from http://www.nasmhpd.org/mental_health_resources.cfm#Other.

National Center on Elder Abuse. (n.d.). Retrieved March 21, 2009, from http://www.ncea.aoa.gov/NCEAroot/Main_Site/Find_Help/State_Resources.aspx.

National Committee for the Prevention of Elder Abuse. (n.d.). Retrieved March 21, 2009 from http://www.preventelderabuse.org.

National Council on the Practice of Clinical Social Work (NASW). (1994). *Guidelines for clinical social work supervisors.* Washington, DC: National Association of Social Workers.

National Lawyers Guild. (n.d.). Questions and answers about civil disobedience and the legal process. Retrieved March 21, 2009, from http://www.nlg-la.org/cd_questions.pdf.

Nelson v. Gillette. (1997). N.D. 205; 571 N.W.2d 332; 1997 N.D. LEXIS 263. Retrieved

March 21, 2009, from http://www.court.state.nd.us/court/opinions/960371.htm.

Nerenberg, L. (2006). Communities respond to elder abuse. *Journal of Gerontological Social Work, 46*(3/4), 5–33.

No Child Left Behind Act. (2001). Public Law 107–110. Retrieved March 21, 2009, from http://www.ed.gov/policy/elsec/leg/esea02/index.html.

North American Association for Christians in Social Work. (n.d.). Retrieved March 21, 2009, from http://www.nacsw.org/index.shtml.

Nuffield Council on Bioethics. (2007). Public health: Ethical issues. London: Author. Retrieved March 21, 2009, from http://www.nuffieldbioethics.org/fileLibrary/pdf/Public_health_-_ethical_issues.pdf.

Oakley, B. (2007). *Evil genes: Why Rome fell, Hitler rose, Enron failed, and my sister stole my mother's boyfriend.* Amherst, NY: Prometheus Books.

O'Brien, T. (2004). *Child welfare in the legal setting: A critical and interpretive perspective.* Binghamton, NY: Haworth.

Olmstead v. United States. (1928). 277 U.S. 438 (United States Supreme Court).

Open Government Guide. (n.d.). Retrieved March 21, 2009, from http://www.rcfp.org/ogg.

Orend, B. (2004). Kant's ethics of war and peace. *Journal of Military Ethics,* 3(2), 161–177.

Osmo, R., & Landau, R. (2006). The role of ethical theories in decision making by social workers. *Social Work Education, 25*(8), 863–876.

Oxford Dictionary of Proverbs. (2004). New York: Oxford University Press. Retrieved November 5, 2007, from http://www.answers.com.

Parrott, L. (2006). *Values and ethics in social work practice.* Exeter, UK: Learning Matters Press.

Parsons, R. D. (2000). *The ethics of professional practice.* Boston: Allyn & Bacon.

Patient Self Determination Act. (1990). 42 U.S.C. 1395. Retrieved March 21, 2009, from http://www.fha.org/acrobat/Patient%20Self%20Determination%20Act%201990.pdf.

Patriot Act. (2001). United States Code 50 U.S.C.A. §§ 1861, 1862.

Paul, R., & Elder, L. (2006). *The thinker's guide to understanding the foundations of ethical reasoning* (2nd ed.). Dillon Beach, CA: Foundations of Critical Thinking (http://www.criticalthinking.org).

Payne, B. K., & Gray, C. (2001). Fraud by home health care workers and the criminal justice system. *Criminal Justice Review, 26*(2), 209–232.

People v. Bierenbaum. (2002). 301 A.D.2d 119–141 (New York, Appellate Division).

Pettifor, J. (2004). Professional ethics across national boundaries. *European Psychologist,* 9, 264–272.

Phelan, A., Barlow, C., Myrick, F., Rogers, G., & Sawa, R. (2003). Discourses of conflict: A multidisciplinary study of professional education. *Alberta Journal of Educational Research,* 59(2), 201–203.

Piaget, J. (1999/orig.1932). *The moral judgment of the child.* New York: Routledge.

Pinderbughes, E. (1983). Empowerment for our clients and ourselves. *Social Casework, 64,* 331–338.

Pipes, R. B., Holstein, A. G., & Aguire, M. G. (2005). Examining the personal-professional distinction: Ethics codes and the problem of drawing a boundary. *American Psychiatrist, 60*(4), 325–334.

Policy concerning homosexuality in the armed forces. (1994). Title 10 U.S.C, Subtitle A, Part II, Chapter 37, § 654, Retrieved March 21, 2009, from http://www.law.cornell.edu/uscode/10/654.html.

Pollack, D. P. (2003). *Social work and the courts: A casebook* (2nd ed.). New York: Brunner-Routledge.

Pollack, D. P. (2007). Should social workers be mandated to report child maltreatment? An international perspective. *International Social Work, 50*(5), 699–705.

Polowy, C. I., & Gorenberg, C. (2004). *Client confidentiality and privileged communication.* Washington, DC: NASW Legal Defense Fund.

Polowy, C. I., & McLeod, P. (2004). *Social workers and child abuse reporting.* Washington, DC: NASW Legal Defense Fund.

Polowy, C. I., & Morgan, S. (2004). *Social workers and clinical notes.* Washington, DC: NASW Legal Defense Fund.

Polowy, C. I., Morgan, S., & Gilbertson, J. (2005). *Social workers and subpoenas.* Washington, DC: NASW Legal Defense Fund.

Polowy, C. I., Williams, N. H., Pelas, C., & Pryor, S. M. (2005). *Social workers and work issues.* Washington, DC: NASW Legal Defense Fund.

Pope, K. S., & Vasquez, M. J. T. (2007). *Ethics in psychotherapy and counseling: A practical guide* (3rd ed.). San Francisco: Jossey-Bass.

Porter, R. (2002). *Madness: A brief history.* New York: Oxford University Press.

Porter, S. E. (2005). Apologizing: Trying to get it right. *Journal of Psychosocial Nursing & Mental Health Services, 43*(5), 8–9.

Prichard, D. (2006). Deconstructing psychopathology: Contextualizing mental disorders in teaching psychosocial assessment. *Journal of Progressive Human Services, 17*(2), 5–26.

Prilleltensky, I., Valdes, L. S., Rossiter, A., Z., & Walsh-Bowers, R. (2002). Applied ethics in mental health in Cuba: Part II—Power differentials, dilemmas, resources, and limitations. *Ethics & Behavior, 12*(3), 243–260.

Prochaska, J. O., & Norcross, J. C. (2007). *Systems of psychotherapy: A transtheoretical analysis* (6th ed.). Belmont, CA: Brooks/Cole.

Prochaska, J. O., Redding, C.A., & Evers, K. E. (2002). The transtheoretical model and stages of change. In K. Glanz, B. K. Rimer & F. M. Lewis (Eds.). *Health behavior and health education: Theory, research, and practice* (pp. 99–120). San Francisco: Jossey-Bass.

Providing material support or resources to designated foreign terrorist organizations. (2007). 18 U.S.C. 2339 B. Retrieved March 21, 2009, from http://www4.law.cornell.edu/uscode/uscode18/usc_sec_18_00002339---B000-.html.

Quattrocchi, M. R., & Schopp, R. F. (2005). Tarasaurus rex: A standard of care that could not adapt. *Psychology, Public Policy, and Law, 11*, 109–137.

Quinn, M. J. (2005). *Guardianships of adults: Achieving justice, autonomy, and safety.* New York: Springer.

Rao, G. S., & Blake, L. (2002). Decision-making capacity in the elderly. *Primary Care Update for OB/GYNS*, 9(2), 71–75.

Rapley, M., McCarthy, D., & McHoul, A. (2003). Mentality or morality? Membership categorization, multiple meanings and mass murder. *British Journal of Social Psychology, 42*(3), 427–444.

Rapp, C. A., & Goscha, R. J. (2006). *The strengths model: Case management with people with psychiatric disabilities* (2nd ed.). New York: Oxford University Press.

Rawls, J. (1971). *A theory of justice.* Cambridge, MA: Harvard University Press.

Reamer, F. G. (1987). Ethics committees in social work. *Social Work*, 32(3), 188–192.

Reamer, F. G. (2001a). *The social work ethics audit.* Washington, DC: NASW Press.

Reamer, F. G. (2001b). *Ethics education in social work.* Washington, DC: CSWE Publications.

Reamer, F. G. (2001c). *Tangled relationships: Managing boundary issues in the human services.* New York: Columbia University Press.

Reamer, F. G. (2003). *Social work malpractice and liability* (2nd ed.). New York: Columbia University Press.

Reamer, F. G. (2006a). *Ethical standards in social work: A review of the NASW Code of Ethics* (2nd ed.). Washington, DC: NASW Press.

Reamer, F. G. (2006b). *Social work values and ethics* (3rd ed.). New York: Columbia University Press.

Reamer, F. G. (2008a, March 20). Boundary and dual relationship issues in social work: Ethical and risk-management considerations (NASW Teleconference Transcript and Continuing Education Test). Retrieved March 21, 2009, from http://www.socialworkers.org/sections/teleconferences/tcourses/Default.aspx?courseID=11c88e42-f693-43af-adfa-d4ca4394ca2c&header=OFF.

Reamer, F. G. (2008b). Social workers' management of error: Ethical and risk management issues. *Families in Society, 89*(1), 61–68.

Red Cross. (n.d.). Preparing professional rescuers. Retrieved March 21, 2009, from https://americanredcross.com/services/hss/courses/professional.html.

Reed, A., & Aquino, K. F. (2003). Moral identity and the expanding circle of moral regard toward out-groups. *Journal of Personality and Social Psychology, 84*, 1270–1286.

Restorative Justice Online. (n.d.). Introduction. Retrieved March 21, 2009, from http://www.restorativejustice.org/intro.

Richmond, M. (1917). *Social diagnosis.* New York: Russell Sage Foundation.

Richter, J., Eisemann, M., & Zgonnikova, E. (2001). Doctors' authoritarianism in end-of-life treatment decisions: A comparison between Russia, Sweden and Germany. *Journal of Medical Ethics*, 27(3), 186–192.

Robb, M. (2003). Supervisor beware: Reducing your exposure to vicarious liability. Washington, DC: NASW Insurance Trust.

Robbennolt, J. K. (2003). Apologies and legal settlement: An empirical examination. *Michigan Law Review, 102*, 460–517.

Roberts, A. R., & Greene, G. J. (Eds.). (2009). *Social workers' desk reference.* New York: Oxford University Press.

Roberts, A. R., & Jennings, T. (2005). Hanging by a thread: How failure to conduct an adequate lethality assessment resulted in suicide. *Brief Treatment and Crisis Intervention,* 5(3), 251–261.

Roberts, A. R., & Springer, D. W. (Eds.). (2007). *Social work in juvenile and criminal justice settings.* Springfield, IL: Charles C Thomas.

Roberts, M. (2004). Psychiatric ethics: A critical introduction for mental health nurses. *Journal of Psychiatric and Mental Health Nursing, 11*(5), 583–588.

Rogatz, P. (2003). Physician assisted suicide should be legalized. *Death and dying: Opposing viewpoints* (pp. 39–48). San Diego, CA: Thomson.

Rogers, C. (1957). The necessary and sufficient conditions of therapeutic personality change. *Journal of Counseling Psychology, 21*, 95–103.

Rooney, R. (2002). Working with involuntary clients. In A. R. Roberts & G. J. Green (Eds.). *Social workers' desk reference* (pp. 709–713). New York: Oxford University Press.

Rosenbaum, A., Warnken, W. J., & Grudzinskas, A. J. (2003). Legal and ethical issues in the court-mandated treatment of batterers. *Journal of Aggression, Maltreatment & Trauma*, 7(1/2), 279–303.

Rosenman, S. (1998). Psychiatrists and compulsion: A map of ethics. *Australian & New Zealand Journal of Psychiatry*, 32(6), 785–794.

Rosoff, A. J. (2001). Evidence-based medicine and the law: The courts confront clinical practice guidelines. *Journal of Health Politics, Policy, and Law, 26*, 327–355.

Rossi, P. H., Lipsey, M. W., & Freeman, H. E. (2004). *Evaluation: A systematic approach* (7th ed.). Newbury Park, CA: Sage.

Rothman, J. C. (1999). *The self-awareness workbook for social workers.* Boston: Allyn & Bacon.

Rothman, J. C. (2005). *From the front lines: Student cases in social work ethics.* Boston: Pearson.

Rothschild, K, & Pollack, D. (2008). When qualified immunity protects social workers from 42 U.S.C. 1983 lawsuits. *APSAC Advisor, 20*(3/4), 7–10.

Royse, D., Thyer, B. A., Padgett, D. K., & Logan, T. K. (2006). *Program evaluation: An introduction* (4th ed.) Belmont, CA: Brooks/Cole.

Rubin, A., & Babbie, E. (2008). *Research methods for social work* (6th ed.) Belmont, CA: Brooks/Cole.

Rufo et al. v. Simpson. (2001). Superior Court Numbers SC031947, SC035340, and SC036876 (California Court of Appeal). Retrieved March 21, 2009, from http://caselaw.lp.findlaw.com/data2/californiastatecases/b112612.pdf.

Sabatino, C. P. (n.d.). 10 legal myths about advance medical directives. ABA Commission on Legal Problems of the Elderly. Retrieved March 21, 2009, from http://www.abanet.org/aging/publications/docs/10legalmythsarticle.pdf.

Saleebey, D. (2009). *The strengths perspective in social work practice* (5th ed.). Boston: Allyn & Bacon.

Saltzman, A., & Furman, D. M. (1999). *Law in social work practice* (2nd ed.). Belmont, CA: Brooks/Cole—Cengage.

Scales, T. L., & Wolfer, T. A. (2006). *Decision cases for generalist social work practice: Thinking like a social worker.* Belmont, CA: Brooks/Cole.

Schamess, G. (2006). Transference enactments in clinical supervision. *Clinical Social Work Journal*, 34(4), 407–425.

Scheurell, R. (1983). Social work ethics in probation and parole. In A. R. Roberts (Ed.), *Social work in criminal justice* (pp. 241–251). Springfield, IL: Charles C Thomas.

Scheyett, A. (2006). Silence and surveillance: Mental illness, evidence-based practice, and a Foucaultian lens. *Journal of Progressive Human Services*, 17(1), 71–92.

Schindler Schiavo v. Schiavo. (2005). Case 05-11628 (U.S. Court of Appeals, 11th Circuit), Retrieved March 21, 2009, from http://f11.findlaw.com/news.findlaw.com/hdocs/docs/schiavo/33005ca11rhrng2.pdf.

Schirch, L. (2004). *The little book of strategic peacebuilding.* Intercourse, PA: Good Books.

Schmid, H. (2004). Organizational and structural dilemmas in nonprofit organizations providing social services. *Administration in Social Work*, 28(3/4), 1–22.

Schneewind, J. B. (2006). Autonomy, obligation, and virtue. *Cambridge companion to Kant* (pp. 309–341). New York: Cambridge University Press.

Schroeder, J., Guin, C. C., Pogue, R., & Bordelon, D. (2006). Mitigating circumstances in death penalty decisions: Using evidence-based research to inform social work practice in capital trials. *Social Work, 51*(4), 355–364.

Schultz, N. (2003). Distinguishing factors from values. Retrieved September 28, 2007, from http://www.beyondintractability.org/essay/facts_values/?nid=1233.

Schwartz, C. (2004). The attitudes of social work students and practicing psychiatric social workers toward the inclusion in the community of people with mental illness. *Social Work in Mental Health*, 2(1), 33–45.

Segal, E. A. (2007). *Social welfare policy and social programs: A values perspective* (1st ed.). Belmont, CA: Brooks/Cole.

Sherwood, D. A. (2008a). Doing the right thing: A Christian perspective on ethical decision making in social work practice. In B. Hugen, & T. L. Scales, T. L. (Eds.), *Christianity and social work: Readings on the integration of Christian faith and social work practice*

(3rd ed., pp. 333–350). Botsford, CT: North American Association of Christians in Social Work.

Sherwood, D. A. (2008b). Ethical integration of faith and social work practice: Evangelism. In B. Hugen & T. L. Scales (Eds.), *Christianity and social work: Readings on the integration of Christian faith and social work practice* (3rd ed., pp. 409–417). Botsford, CT: North American Association of Christians in Social Work.

Shiraev, E., & Levy, D. (2004). *Cross-cultural psychology: Critical thinking and contemporary applications* (2nd ed.). Boston: Allyn & Bacon.

Shulman, L. (1992). *Interactional supervision*. Washington, DC: NASW Press.

Shulman, L. (2005). The clinical supervisor-practitioner working alliance: A parallel process. *Clinical Supervisor, 24*(1/2), 23–47.

Siegel, L. (2006). *Criminology: Theories, patterns, and typologies* (9th ed.). Belmont, CA: Brooks/Cole.

Skelley-Walley, J. E. (1995). An ombudsman perspective. *Journal of Elder Abuse & Neglect*; 7 (2–3), 89–113.

Skitka, L. J., Bauman, C. W., & Sargis, E. G. (2005). Moral conviction: Another contributor to attitude strength or something more? *Journal of Personality and Social Psychology*, 88(6), 895–917.

Skjørshammer, M. (2001). Conflict management in a hospital: Designing processing structures and intervention methods. *Journal of Management in Medicine, 15*(2), 156–166.

Small, M. A., Lyons, P. M., & Guy, L. S. (2002). Liability issues in child abuse and neglect reporting statutes. *Professional Psychology: Research and Practice*, 33, (1), 13–18.

Smith, S. K. (n.d.). Mandatory reporting of child abuse and neglect, Retrieved March 21, 2009, from http://www.smith-lawfirm.com/mandatory_reporting.htm.

Smith v. Doe. (2003). 538 U.S. 84; 259 F.3d 979 (01–729) (U.S. S.C.). Retrieved March 21, 2009, from http://supct.law.cornell.edu/supct/html/01–729.ZS.html.

Smith, W. J. (2003). Physician-assisted suicide should not be legalized. *Death and dying: Opposing viewpoints* (pp. 49–57). San Diego, CA: Thomson.

Society for Social Work and Research. (n.d.). About SSWR. Retrieved March 21, 2009, from http://www.sswr.org/aboutus.php.

Solomon, B. (1976). *Black empowerment: Social work in oppressed communities*. New York: Columbia University Press.

Spangler, B. (2003). Reality testing. *Beyond intractability*. Conflict Research Consortium, University of Colorado, Boulder. Retrieved March 21, 2009, from http://www.beyondintractability.org/essay/reality_testing.

Spano, R. N., & Koenig, T. L. (2003). Moral dialogue: An interactional approach to ethical decision making. *Social Thought*, 22(1), 91–103.

Spano, R., & Koenig, T. (2007). What is sacred when personal and professional values collide. *Journal of Social Work Values and Ethics*, 4(3). Retrieved March 21, 2009, from http://www.socialworker.com/jswve/content/blogcategory/16/54.

Specht, H., & Courtney, M. E. (1994). *Unfaithful angels: How social work has abandoned its mission*. New York: Free Press.

Starr, K. (1999). The role of civil disobedience in democracy. Retrieved March 21, 2009, from http://www.civilliberties.org/sum98role.html.

Steigerwald, F., & Janson, G. R. (2003). Conversion therapy: Ethical considerations in family counseling. *Family Journal, 11*(1), 55–59.

Stein, G. L. (2007). Advance directives and advance care planning for people with intellectual and physical disabilities. Washington, DC: U.S. Department of Health and Human Services. Retrieved March 21, 2009, from http://aspe.hhs.gov/daltcp/reports/2007/adacp.htm.

Stein, T. J. (2004). *The role of law in social work practice*. New York: Columbia University Press.

Steinbock, B., Arras, J. D., & London, A. J. (2003). *Ethical issues in modern medicine*. New York: McGraw-Hill.

Stevanovié, B. (2005). Theoretical and valuable foundations of the right to civil disobedience. *Facta Universitatis: Series Philosophy, Sociology & Psychology*, 4(1), 1–10.

Stewart, N. (2004). Supervising the primary care counsellor within the psychodynamic frame. *Psychodynamic Practice, 10*(3), 354–372.

Stocking, C., Hougham, G. W., Baron, A. R., & Sachs, G. A. (2004). Ethics, public policy, and medical economics: Ethics reporting in publications about research with Alzheimer's disease patients. *Journal of the American Geriatrics Society*, 52(2), 305–310.

Stone, D., Patton, B., & Heen, S. (1999). *Difficult conversations: How to discuss what matters most*. New York: Penguin.

Strom-Gottfried, K. (2003). Understanding adjudication: Origins, targets, and outcomes of ethics complaints, *Social Work*, 48(1), 85–94.

Strom-Gottfried, K. (2007). *Straight talk about professional ethics*. Chicago: Lyceum.

Strom-Gottfried, K. (2008). *The ethics of practice with minors: High stakes, hard choices*. Chicago: Lyceum.

Strom-Gottfried, K., & D'Aprix, A. (2006). Ethics for academics. *Social Work Education*, 25(3), 225–244.

Strozier, M., Brown, R., Fennell, M., Hardee, J., & Vogel, R. (2005). Experiences of mandated reporting among family therapists. *Contemporary Family Therapy*, 2(2), 177–191.

Substance Abuse and Mental Health Services Administration. (2004). *The confidentiality of alcohol and drug abuse patient records regulation and the HIPAA privacy rule: Implications for alcohol and substance abuse programs*. Washington, DC: Author (also available at http://www.hipaa.samhsa.gov/Part2ComparisonCleared.htm).

Sweet, S. (1999). Using a mock institutional review board to teach ethics in sociological research. *Teaching Sociology*, 27(1), 55–59.

Swindell, M. L., & Watson, J. (2006). Teaching ethics through self-reflective journaling. *Journal of Social Work Values and Ethics*, 3(2). Retrieved March 21, 2009, from http://www.socialworker.com/jswve/content/view/37/46.

Swindell, M. L., & Watson, J. (2007). Ethical delegates in the social work classroom: A creative pedagogical approach. *Journal of Social Work Values and Ethics*, 4(1), Retrieved March 21, 2009, from http://www.socialworker.com/jswve/content/view/47/50.

Szasz, T. (2003). Psychiatry and the control of dangerousness: On the apotropaic function of the term "mental illness." *Journal of Social Work Education*, 39(3), 375–381.

Szymanski, D. M. (2003). The feminist supervision scale: A rational/theoretical approach. *Psychology of Women Quarterly*, 27(3), 221–233.

Tajfel, H., & Turner, J. C. (1986). The social identity theory of inter-group behavior. In S. Worchel & W. G. Austin (Eds.), *Psychology of Intergroup Relations*. Chicago: Nelson-Hall.

Tansey, M. (2006). How decision-making fails under the sunshine laws: An agency-based model. *Journal of Economics*, 32(1), 41–55.

Tarasoff v. Regents. (1976). 17 Cal. 3d 425 (Supreme Court CA).

Taylor, J. M., Gilligan, C., & Sullivan, A. M. (1995). *Between voice and silence: Women and girls, race and relationship*. Cambridge, MA: Harvard University Press.

Taylor, M. F. (2007). Professional dissonance: A promising concept for clinical social work. *Smith College Studies in Social Work*, 77(1), 89–99.

Taylor, M. F., & Bentley, K. J. (2005). Professional dissonance: Colliding values and job tasks in mental health practice. *Community Mental Health Journal*, 41(4), 469–481.

Terry, L., & Campbell, A. (2008). Forever a child: Analysis of the Ashley case. *Paediatric Nursing*, 20(2), 21–25.

Thompson, A. K., Faith, K., Gibson, J. L, & Upshur, R. E. G. (2006). Pandemic influenza preparedness: An ethical framework to guide decision-making. *BMC Medical Ethics*. Retrieved December 4, 2007, from http://www.pubmedcentral.nih.gov.ezproxy.fau.edu/articlerender.fcgi?tool=pubmed&pubmedid=17144926.

Tilden, S. J. (2005). Ethical and legal aspects of using an identical twin as a skin transplant donor for a severely burned minor. *American Journal of Law & Medicine*, 31(1), 87–116.

Tilden, V. P., Tolle, S. W., Drarch, L. L., & Perrin, N. A. (2004). Out-of-hospital death: Advance care planning, decedent symptoms, and caregiver burden. *Journal of the American Geriatrics Society*, 52(4), 532–539.

Tjeltveit, A. C. (2004). The good, the bad, the obligatory, and the virtuous: The ethical contexts of psychotherapy. *Journal of Psychotherapy Integration*, 14(2), 149–167.

Torda, A. (2006). Ethical issues in pandemic planning. *Medical Journal of Australia*, 185(10), 73–76.

Toseland, R. W., & Rivas, R. F. (2009). *An introduction to group work practice* (6th ed.). Boston: Allyn & Bacon.

Townsend, F. L. (2007). Tackling the graduate admissions process with a graduate education action plan. *New Social Worker*, 14(1), 16–17.

Trotter, G. (2007). *The ethics of coercion in mass casualty medicine*. Baltimore, MD: Johns Hopkins University Press.

Ulrich, C., O'Donnell, P., Taylor, C., Farrar, A., Danis, M., & Grady, C. (2007). Ethical climate, ethics stress, and the job satisfaction of nurses and social workers in the United States. *Social Science & Medicine*, 65(8), 1708–1719.

Umbreit, M. S., Coates, R. B., & Voss, B. (2005). Victim offender mediation: Evidence-based practice over three decades. In M. L. Moffitt & R. C. Bordone (Eds.), *The handbook of dispute resolution* (pp. 455–470). San Francisco: Jossey-Bass.

United Nations. (1948). Universal declaration of human rights. Retrieved March 21, 2009, from http://www.un.org/Overview/rights.html.

United Nations. (1989). Convention on the rights of the child. Retrieved March 21, 2009, from http://www.unhchr.ch/html/menu3/b/k2crc.htm.

United Nations Office on Drugs and Crime. (2008). Definitions of terrorism. Retrieved March 21, 2009, from http://web.archive.org/web/20070129121539/http://www.unodc.org/unodc/terrorism_definitions.html.

U.S. Army. (2007). PTSD/MTBI Chain teaching program (family readiness version). Retrieved March 21, 2009, from http://www.army.mil/-news/2007/07/18/4066-the-armys-post-traumatic-stress-disorder-and-mild-traumatic-brain-injury-ptsdmtbi-chain-teaching-program.

U.S. Code, Title 18, Crimes and Criminal Procedure. Retrieved March 21, 2009, from http://www4.law.cornell.edu/uscode/18.

U.S. Constitution.. (11th Amendment (1795); 14th Amendment (1868). Retrieved March 21, 2009, from http://www.usconstitution.net/const.html.

U.S. Declaration of Independence (1776). Retrieved March 21, 2009, from http://www.ushistory.org/declaration/document.

U.S. Department of Health and Human Services (2007). *National survey of child and adolescent well-being, no. 6: How do caseworker judgments predict substantiation of child maltreatment?* Washington, DC: Author.

U.S. Equal Employment Opportunity Commission. (2002). Sexual harassment. Retrieved March 21, 2009, from http://www.eeoc.gov/facts/fs-sex.html.

Vaco v. Quill. (1997). 521 U.S. 793. Retrieved March 21, 2009, from http://caselaw.lp.findlaw.com/scripts/getcase.pl?court= US&vol=000&invol=95–1858.

Van Den Bergh, N. (1995). *Feminist practice in the 21st century.* Washington, DC: NASW Press.

Vander Zanden, J. W., Crandelle, T. L., & Crandell, C. H. (2003). *Human development* (7th ed.). Boston: McGraw-Hill.

Van Winkle, N. W. (2000). *American Indian and Alaska Native cultures.* In K. L. Braun, J. Pietsch, & P. L. Blanchette (Eds.), *Cultural issues in end-of-life decision making* (pp. 127–144). Newbury Park, CA: Sage.

Van Wormer, K. (2004). *Confronting oppression, restoring justice: From policy analysis to social action.* Alexandria, VA: Council on Social Work Education.

Vawter, D. E., Gervais, K. G. & Garrett, J. E. (2007). Allocating pandemic influenza vaccines in Minnesota: Recommendations of the Pandemic Influenza Ethics Work Group. *Vaccine, 25*(35), 6522–6536.

Vincler, L. A. (2008). Law and medical ethics. Retrieved March 21, 2009, from http://depts.washington.edu/bioethx/topics/law.html.

Viner, R. M., Brain, C., Carmichael, P., & Di Ceglie, D. (2005). Sex on the brain: Dilemmas in the endocrine management of children and adolescents with gender identity disorder. *Archives of Disease in Childhood,* 90(Supplement II), A78.

Vonk, M. E. (2000). An ethic of care: A framework for ethical decision making with survivors of sexual assault. *Social Thought, 19*(1), 49–62.

Wainwright P., & Gallagher, A. (2007). Ethical aspects of withdrawing and withholding treatment. *Nursing Standard, 21*(33), 46–50.

Wakefield, J. C. (1998). Psychotherapy, distributive justice, and social work revisited. *Smith College Studies in Social Work, 69*(1), 25–57.

Walker, P. (2002). Understanding accountability: Theoretical models and their implications for social service organizations. *Social Policy and Administration,* 36(1), 62–75.

Walker, P. (2004). What does it mean to be a professional humanitarian? *Journal of Humanitarian Assistance* (online). March 21, 2009, from http://www.jha.ac/articles/a127.htm.

Walz, T., & Ritchie, H. (2000). Gandhian principles in social work practice: Ethics revisited. *Social Work, 45*(3), 213–222.

Wandersman, A. (2001). Program development, evaluation, and accountability. In L. H. Ginsberg (Ed.), *Social work evaluation: Principles and methods* (pp. 178–210). Boston: Allyn & Bacon.

Watchtower. (2000). Jehovah's Witnesses—Who are they? What do they believe? Retrieved March 21, 2009, from http://www.watchtower.org/e/jt/index.htm?article=article_03.htm.

Weinbach , R. W. (2005). *Evaluating social work services and programs.* Boston: Pearson.

Weiss, I., Gal, J., Cnaan, R., & Majiaglic, R. (2002). *International Social Work, 45*(1), 59–81.

Weissman, D. E. (2001). Managing conflicts at the end of life. *Journal of Palliative Medicine, 4*(1), 1–3.

Weitzman P. F., & Weitzman E. A. (2003). Promoting communication with older adults: Protocols for resolving interpersonal conflicts and for enhancing interactions with doctors. *Clinical Psychology Review, 23*, 523–535.

Welfel, E. R. (2002). *Ethics in counseling and psychotherapy: Standards, research and emerging issues* (2nd ed.). Belmont, CA: Brooks/Cole.

Wharton, T. C. (2008). Compassion fatigue: Being an ethical social worker. *New Social Worker, 15*(1), 4–6.

White, J. R. (2006). IEEPA's override authority: Potential for violation of the Geneva Conventions' right to access for humanitarian organizations. *Michigan Law Review 104*, 2019–2055.

Whistleblower Protection Act. (1989, as amended 2007). 5 U.S.C. §2302.

Whitaker, P. (2007). The Whistleblower Protection Act: An overview. Retrieved March 18, 2009 from http://www.fas.org/sgp/crs/natsec/RL33918.pdf.

Wild, T. C. (2006). Social control and coercion in addiction treatment: Towards evidence-based policy and practice. *Addiction, 101*(1), 40–49.

Wolfle v. United States. (1934). 291 U.S. 7, 54 S. Ct. 279, 78 L. Ed. 617 (U.S. Supreme Court).

Woll, L. (2001). Organizational responses to the Convention on the Rights of the Child: International lessons for child welfare organizations. *Child Welfare, 80*(5), 668–679.

Wood, A. W. (2006). Rational theology, moral faith, and religion. *Cambridge companion to Kant* (pp. 394–416). New York: Cambridge University Press.

Worden, M. (2003). *Family therapy basics* (3rd ed.). Belmont, CA: Brooks/Cole.

World Health Organization. (2004). Better palliative care for older people. Retrieved March 21, 2009, from http://www.euro.who.int/document/E82933.pdf.

Worthington, R. L., Dillon, F. R., & Becker, A. M. (2005). Development, reliability, and validity of the lesbian, gay, and bisexual knowledge and attitudes scale for heterosexuals. *Journal of Counseling Psychology, 52*(1), 104–118.

Wright, D. (2000). Learning disability and the new poor law in England, 1834–1867. *Disability & Society, 15*(5), 731–745.

Yassour-Borochowitz, D. (2004). Reflections on the researcher-participant relationship and the ethics of dialogue. *Ethics & Behavior, 14*(2), 175–186.

Yeskey, K. (2008). *Chest*, 3(4), Retrieved March 18, 2009 from http://www.chestnet.org/about/publications/chestPhysician.php.

Yip, K. (2006). A strengths perspective in working with an adolescent with self-cutting behaviors. *Child & Adolescent Social Work Journal, 23*(2), 134–146.

Zastrow, C., & Kirst-Ashman, K. K. (2007). *Understanding human behavior and the social environment* (7th ed.). Belmont, CA: Brooks/Cole.

Zehr, H., & Toews, B. (2004). *Critical issues in restorative justice*. Monsey, NY: Criminal Justice Press and Willan Publishing.

Zoloth, L. & Zoloth, S. (2006). Don't be chicken: Bioethics and avian flu. *American Journal of Bioethics, 6*(1): 5–8.

ADDITIONAL RESOURCES AND WEBSITES

Alden March Bioethics Institute: http://www.bioethics.net

American Society for Bioethics and Humanities: http://www.asbh.org

Association of Family and Conciliation Courts (Standards of practice for family mediators, parenting coordinators, and custody evaluators): http://www.afccnet.org/resources/standards_practice.asp

Association for Practical and Professional Ethics: http://www.indiana.edu/~appe.

Association of Social Work Boards: http://www.aswb.org

Association for Specialists in Group Work (Group Work Standards): http://www.asgw.org

Canadian Association of Social Workers: http://www.casw-acts.ca

Canadian Association of Schools of Social Work: http://cassw-acess.ca

Center for the Study of Ethics in the Professions: http://ethics.iit.edu/codes/coe.html

Council on Social Work Education (CSWE) (accreditation for social work schools in USA): http://www.cswe.org

Ethics and Malpractice: http://www.kspope.com/ethics/malpractice.php

Feminist Therapy Code of Ethics: http://feminist-therapy-institute.org/ethics.htm

Foundations of Critical Thinking: http://www.criticalthinking.org

Institute for Global Ethics: http://www.globalethics.org

Journal of Law, Medicine, and Ethics: http://www.jlme.org

Journal of Moral Education: http://www.tandf.co.uk/journals/archive/cjme-con.asp

Journal of Social Work Values and Ethics: http://www.socialworker.com/jswve

National Association of Social Workers: http://www.naswdc.org

National Institutes of Health—Human Subjects Review Training: http://ohsr.od.nih.gov/cbt/index.html

Tukegee University, National Center for Bioethics in Research and Health Care (including concerns specific to African Americans and other underserved people): http://www.tuskegee.edu/bioethics

VIDEOS

Annenberg Media. (1988). *Ethics in America: To defend a killer* (VHS). Washington, DC: Author. (VHS may be ordered from http://www.learner.org).

Annenberg Media. (2007). *Ethics in America II: A video series for middle school, high school, and adult learners* (DVD). Washington, DC: Author. (DVD may be ordered from http://www.learner.org).

Informed consent: Legal liability issues (DVD). (2004). New York: Insight Media.

Moyers, W. (2005). *On our own terms: Moyers on dying* (DVDs). Princeton, NJ: Films for the Humanities. (DVDs may be ordered from http://www.films.com).

Nichols, M. (2001). *Wit* (DVD with Emma Thomson playing a patient with cancer: Ethical issues include respect for client, informed consent, and end-of-life decision making). New York: Time Warner Entertainment.

Rochat, T. L. (2004). *Review of ethical principles and situations* (DVD). New York: Insight Media.

Rochat, T. L. (2004). *Ethics and the difficult client* (DVD). New York: Insight Media.

Social constructionist conversation on ethics (DVD). (2004). New York: Insight Media.

Index